PRACTICE AND PROCEDURE OF
THE INTERNATIONAL CRIMINAL TRIBUNAL
FOR THE FORMER YUGOSLAVIA

Practice and Procedure of the International Criminal Tribunal for the Former Yugoslavia

With Selected Materials from the International Criminal Tribunal for Rwanda

by

John E. Ackerman

and

Eugene O'Sullivan

Kluwer Law International

The Hague / London / Boston

Library of Congress Cataloging-in-Publication Data

ISBN 90-411-1478-5

Published by Kluwer Law International,
P.O. Box 85889, 2508 CN The Hague, The Netherlands.

Sold and distributed in North, Central and South America
by Kluwer Law International,
675 Massachusetts Avenue, Cambridge, MA 02139, U.S.A.

In all other countries, sold and distributed
by Kluwer Law International, Distribution Centre,
P.O. Box 322, 3300 AH Dordrecht, The Netherlands.

Printed on acid-free paper

02-1202-200 ts

PREFACE

This book project was begun in 1997, early in the Čelebići trial as the authors began compiling the materials that had been generated by the Tribunal. It was written gradually – over these many months as time would allow – awaiting, in many respects, the further development of Tribunal jurisprudence.

The book is designed to provide a quick yet comprehensive reference to the jurisprudence of both the ICTY and to some extent, the ICTR. It goes significantly beyond the Judgements of the Tribunal into the Orders and Decisions of the Trial and Appeals Chambers.

The book is organized by sections, according to each Article of the Statute and Rule of procedure and evidence. Following the text of the Article or Rule, there is a Commentary section, where appropriate and a digest of Judgements, Decisions and Orders of the Appeals Chamber and the Trial Chambers.

Materials will be found in the book from the beginning of the operation of the ICTY through the Furundžija Appeals Judgement and the amendments to the Rules in July 2000.

Thanks to Michael Greaves for his contribution of much of the material contained under Rule 47. Thanks to Dr. Nina Helene Borlase Jørgensen, University of Leiden, for the material from the ICTR regarding Genocide and Crimes Against Humanity.

Finally thanks are due to Barbara Baruch Ackerman for putting up with the many nights and weekends her husband spent at the computer working on this book instead of paying attention to her and for her constant encouragement and support.

TABLE OF CONTENTS

STATUTE OF THE INTERNATIONAL TRIBUNAL

(ADOPTED 25 MAY 1993)
(AS AMENDED 13 MAY 1998)

HAVING BEEN ESTABLISHED BY THE SECURITY COUNCIL ACTING UNDER CHAPTER VII OF THE CHARTER OF THE UNITED NATIONS, THE INTERNATIONAL TRIBUNAL FOR THE PROSECUTION OF PERSONS RESPONSIBLE FOR SERIOUS VIOLATIONS OF INTERNATIONAL HUMANITARIAN LAW COMMITTED IN THE TERRITORY OF THE FORMER YUGOSLAVIA SINCE 1991 (HEREINAFTER REFERRED TO AS "THE INTERNATIONAL TRIBUNAL") SHALL FUNCTION IN ACCORDANCE WITH THE PROVISIONS OF THE PRESENT STATUTE.

I.   COMMENTARY

The Tribunal was established pursuant to Security Council Resolution 827 (25 May 1993)[1]. By relying on the provisions of Chapter VII of the Charter of the United Nations, the Security Council determined that violation of the offences listed in the Statute were a "threat to peace and security."[2] The decision to establish the Tribunal and the adoption of its Statute was thus binding on all Members of the United Nations. The Secretary-General recommended that the Tribunal should not be established by the treaty process that requires State parties to sign and ratify a treaty.[3] Rather, because of the urgency of the situation and the considerable time needed to draft a treaty and have it enter into force, the Secretary-General stated that the legal basis for the Tribunal could be found in Chapter VII of the Charter of the United Nations:

> ... the Secretary-General believes that the International Tribunal should be established by a decision of the Security Council on the basis of Chapter VII of the Charter of the United Nations. Such a decision would constitute a measure to maintain or restore international peace and security, following the requisite determination of the existence of a threat to the peace, breach of the peace or act of aggression.

---

[1] S/Res/827 (1993).

[2] *See*, Charter of the United Nations, Chapter VII ("Actions with Respect to Threats to the Peace, Breaches of the Peace and Acts of Aggression", Articles 39-51). See, also, Cedric E. Evans, "The Concept of 'Threat to Peace' and Humanitarian Concerns: Probing the Limits of Chapter VII of the U.N. Charter", *Transnational Law & Contemporary Problems*, Vol 5, Spring 1995, No 1, pgs. 213-236; T. D. Gill, "Legal and Some Political Limitations on the Powers of the UN Security Council to Exercise its Enforcement Powers under Chapter VII of the Charter", *Netherlands Yearbook of International Law*, Vol 26, 1995, pgs. 33-138; Inger Osterdahl, "By All Means, Intervene! The Security Council and the Use of Force under Chapter VII of the UN Charter in Iraq (to protect the Kurds), in Bosnia, Somalia, Rwanda and Haiti", *Nordic Journal of International Law*, Vol 66, 1997, pgs. 241-271.

[3] Report of the Secretary-General, (S/25704), 1993, paras. 19-20.

In the particular case of the former Yugoslavia, the Secretary-General believes that the establishment of the International Tribunal by means of a Chapter VII decision would be legally justified, both in terms of the object and purpose of the decision ... and of past Security Council practice.[4]

By Resolution 827, the Security Council formally approved the Report of the Secretary-General and established the Tribunal, a subsidiary organ (of a judicial nature) of the Security Council within the terms of Article 29 of the Charter, as an enforcement measure under Chapter VII.[5] Thus, the Report of the Secretary-General, incorporating a draft statute and commentary was adopted by the Security Council, acting under Chapter VII, and became binding upon all member states of the United Nations.

The Report of the Secretary-General limited the jurisdiction of the Tribunal to international criminal law that is "*beyond doubt . . .* part of international customary law." (emphasis added).[6] The Secretary-General then found that this limitation would permit four conventional sources that had without doubt become part of international customary law, *to wit*: the Geneva Conventions of 12 August 1949 for the Protection of War Victims; the Hague Convention (IV) Respecting the Laws and Customs of War on Land and the Regulations annexed thereto of 18 October 1907; the Convention on the Prevention and Punishment of the Crime of Genocide of 9 December 1948; and the Charter of the International Military Tribunal of 8 August 1945[7]

It was important that jurisdiction of the Tribunal be limited to rules of international humanitarian law "which are beyond doubt part of customary law," because of the principle of *nullum crimen sine lege.*[8] In addition, the Statute did not come into force until after the date of commission of many of the alleged offences in the former Yugoslavia that have become the basis of Tribunal indictments. The rule against the *ex post facto* application of the law precluded the Security Council from attempting to create a statute which would apply to events which occurred prior to its enactment.

The rules regarding international criminal offences and international customary law are well established. International crimes can only be created by international law. The sources of international law are universally understood to be those set out in Article 38(1) of the Statute of the International Court of Justice. These are:

1. International conventions;

2. International custom as evidence of a general practice accepted as law;

3. General principles of law recognized by civilized nations; and

4. Judicial decisions and the teachings of the most highly qualified publicists, as subsidiary means for the determination of rules of law.[9]

---

[4] *Ibid.*, paras. 22-24.
[5] *Ibid.*, para. 28.
[6] *Ibid.*, para. 34
[7] *Ibid.*, para. 35.
[8] *Ibid.*, para. 34. (emphasis supplied).
[9] See, Macolm N. Shaw, *International Law*, 4th Ed., Cambridge University Press, 1997, pg. 55 and I. Brownlie,

As Article 38(1) indicates, customary international law is constituted through "evidence of a general practice accepted as law." It is universally understood that there are two basic elements in the make-up of customary international law. First is the material fact or the general patterns of practice or behaviour. Second is the general acceptance of the particular norm or evidence that a certain behaviour occurred out of a legal obligation to do so, which is often referred to as *opinio juris*.

In referring to its earlier, well-established case law, the International Court of Justice in the *Nicaragua* case described these two components of customary law in the following manner:

> ... for a new customary rule to be formed, not only must the acts concerned 'amount to a settled practice', but they must be accompanied by the *opinio juris sive necessitatis*. Either the States taking such action or other States in a position to react to it, must have behaved so that their conduct is 'evidence of a belief that this practice is rendered obligatory by the existence of a rule of law requiring it. The need for such a belief, *i.e.*, the existence of a subjective element, is implicit in the very notion of the *opinio juris sive necessitatis*.'[10]

Both the material and psychological elements must exist and coincide in order to find that a rule of customary international law has been established. Further, in the *Asylum* case, the International Court of Justice has found that the party relying on custom has the burden to prove its existence.[11]

Special Rapporteur Hudson, for the International Law Commission, has suggested that the following criteria should be applied in considering the establishment of a customary rule:

> (a) Concordant practice by a number of States with reference to a type of situation falling within the domain of international relations; (b) continuation or repetition of the practice over a considerable period of time; (c) conception that the practice is required by, or consistent with, prevailing international law; and (d) general acquiescence in the practice by other States.[12]

It is well established that to determine the existence of international custom, actual state practice must be examined, by asking the following questions: what is the duration and consistency of that practice? has it been repeated? can it be deemed a general practice? In speaking of duration and consistency as indispensable elements of customary law, the International Court of Justice, in the *North Sea Continental Shelf* cases determined that state practice must be "both extensive and virtually uniform in the sense of the provision invoked."[13]

Principles of Public International Law, 4th Ed., Oxford, 1990, pg. 3.

[10] *Case of Nicaragua v. United States (Merits)*, ICJ Reports (1986), 44, para. 77.

[11] *Asylum* case, ICJ Reports (1950), pgs. 276-77:
> The party which relies on custom . . . must prove that this custom is established in such a manner that it has become binding on the other party . . . that the rule invoked . . . is in accordance with a constant and uniform usage practised by the states in question (. . .).

[12] Villiger, *Customary International Law and Treaties*, Kluwer Law International, 2nd Ed. 1997, p. 15.

[13] ICJ Reports, 1969, pg. 3; 41 ILR, pg. 29.

Professor Mark E. Villiger, in referring to the first element, state practice, writes as follows:

> The condition of "general" practice refers to the number of States which have to contribute, actively or passively, towards the customary rule, and hence, introduces a quantitative dimension into the ascertainment of customary law. The term "general" would indicate that *common and widespread practice among many States* is required. While universal practice is not necessary, practice should be "representative",[14] at least of all major political and socio-economic systems. Beyond this formulation, the criterion of "general" practice becomes highly relative and depends on a number of considerations.[15]

In searching for evidence of both the material fact and the *opinio juris*, a common and valuable source is the work of jurists and commentators in the field of international law. Yet, one must be careful not to place emphasis upon what these jurists and commentators believe the law ought to be (*lex ferenda*), but only on what they believe the law actually is (*lex lata*). When a jurist or commentator makes a proposal as to what the law should be it is a very clear indication that that particular matter is not now the law.

It was inevitable that one of the first challenges to the Tribunal would be the legality of its creation. Never before had the Security Council used its Chapter VII powers to create a court. It was also inevitable that no matter the nature or substance of the challenge, the Tribunal would reject it. The Security Council having decided that it had the power to create the Tribunal, it could hardly be expected that the Tribunal, once created, would then determine that the Security Council did not have the power to create it in the first place.

The Preamble to the Statute provides that the Tribunal "shall function in accordance with the provisions of the present Statute." The Tribunal has come under criticism since it began functioning. Mostly this criticism has been leveled at the lack of arrests and the slowness with which trials proceed. Neither of these criticisms is justified. The Tribunal has no control over the arrest process, for it depends solely on the will of states with the power to make arrests. The nature of trials is such that it simply takes significant time to try the cases. The cases are mostly very complex. There are new and thorny legal issues that need to be litigated. Witnesses are hard to secure. Their testimony is extended due to the simultaneous interpretation of their testimony in court. At the beginning, the Tribunal had to function with just a single courtroom. Thus, when two trials were ongoing the courtroom had to be shared. When a second and third courtroom were built, the number of arrests increased and the case load grew, which meant that case conduct was still subject to delays.

There is a permanent Appeals Chamber at the Tribunal, but its composition sometimes changes as matters are brought before it. Often, a Judge who has participated in some meaningful way in a case at the pre-trial stage has become a member of the Appeals Chamber by the time the case reaches the appeal phase. This Judge must be replaced as a member of the Appeals Chamber for that particular case. The substitute

---

[14] *Referencing,* ICJ Reports 1969 43, para. 74.
[15] Villiger, *Customary International Law and Treaties*, Kluwer Law International, 2nd Ed. 1997, pg. 29.

judges come from one of the Trial Chambers which then handicaps that Trial Chamber in its efforts to move through its docket in a speedy and efficient manner. Suggestions have been made that the composition of the Appeals Chamber be made permanent and perhaps even separated from the Trial Chambers geographically. Appeals Judges would remain appeals Judges and trial Judges would not sit in the Appeals Chamber. Whatever the solution, one must be found. There is at least an "appearance of impropriety" when on Monday a Judge sits in a Trial Chamber and on Friday the same Judge sits on an Appeals Chamber.

The Tribunal has been criticized for failing to "function in accordance with the provisions of the present Statute". Primarily these criticisms revolve around the denial of statutorily guaranteed rights to the accused. Although Equality of Arms is statutorily mandated it does not seem to be uniformly enforced. Although the right to cross-examine witnesses is statutorily mandated it is sometimes denied or severely curtailed. Finally, the Tribunal has been criticized for creatively expanding its jurisdiction without regard to customary international law. Although the Security Council, in effect, mandated that the Tribunal should only apply that law which was beyond doubt part of customary international law, that directive has not always been honoured.

However, in spite of the criticisms that can justifiably be leveled at the Tribunal, it also comes in for high praise. For a completely new judicial system it has done a remarkable job of carrying out its mandate in the very short time it has been in existence. The jurisprudence of the Tribunal is very broad-based and comprehensive, as will be seen below. Many important legal issues have been visited and resolved. The Judges deserve enormous credit for performing at a very high level. Although the problems described above are real and troublesome, they can be remedied and the Tribunal can ultimately be seen as an experiment that succeeded and thereby establish a firm foundation for a permanent international criminal court.

II.   TRIBUNAL CASES

A.   APPEALS CHAMBER

PROSECUTOR V. TADIĆ, *Judgement*, IT-94-1-A, 15 July 1999, Shahabuddeen, Cassese, Tieya, Nieto-Navia & Mumba, JJ.

The Appeals Chamber discussed its view of the powers of the Security Council in drafting penal statutes, by stating that "it is open to the Security Council - subject to respect for preemptory norms of international law (*jus cogens*) - to adopt definitions of crimes in the Statute which deviate from customary international law."[16] The Chamber provided the example from Article 5 of the requirement of an armed conflict, thus *narrowing* the Statute from what customary international law would allow. The Chamber takes the position, then, that the Security Council might narrow customary international law, but not legislated beyond it.

---

[16] Para. 296,

In interpreting whether Article 5 of the Statute required a discriminatory intent, the Appeals Chamber noted that three representatives on the Security Council had made statements that appeared to impose such a requirement. The Chamber, however, took the position that discriminatory intent was not a required element of the offence. Since the representatives' statements were contrary to the Chamber's interpretation of the Statute, the Chamber made the following observation:

> The Appeals Chamber, first of all, rejected the notion that these three statements - at least as regards the issue of discriminatory intent - may be considered as part of the "context" of the Statute, to be taken into account for the purpose of interpretation of the Statute pursuant to the general rule of construction laid down in Article 31 of the Vienna Convention on the Law of the Treaties. In particular, those statements were not regarded as an "agreement" relating to the Statute, made between all the parties in connection with the adoption of the Statute.[17]

PROSECUTOR. V. TADIĆ, *Decision on the Defence Motion for Interlocutory Appeal on Jurisdiction,* IT-94-1-AR72, 2 October 1995, Cassese, Li, Deschênes, Abi-Saab & Sidhwa, JJ.

In this, the first Tribunal case, fundamental questions were raised regarding the jurisdiction of the Tribunal. Among these were issues regarding the very legality of the formation of the Tribunal. The Appeals Chamber adopted the Trial Chamber's formulation of these issues, as follows:

> It is said that, to be duly established by law, the International Tribunal should have been created either by treaty, the consensual act of nations, or by amendment of the Charter of the United Nations, not by resolution of the Security Council. Called in aid of this general proposition are a number of considerations: that before the creation of the International Tribunal in 1993 it was never envisaged that such an ad hoc criminal tribunal might be set up; that the General Assembly, whose participation would at least have guaranteed full representation of the international community, was not involved in its creation; that it was never intended by the Charter that the Security Council should, under Chapter VII, establish a judicial body, let alone a criminal tribunal; that the Security Council had been inconsistent in creating this Tribunal while not taking a similar step in the case of other areas of conflict in which violations of international humanitarian law may have occurred; that the establishment of the International Tribunal had neither promoted, nor was capable of promoting, international peace, as the current situation in the former Yugoslavia demonstrates; that the Security Council could not, in any event, create criminal liability on the part of individuals and that this is what its creation of the International Tribunal did; that there existed and exists no such international

---

[17] Para. 300.

emergency as would justify the action of the Security Council; that no political organ such as the Security Council is capable of establishing an independent and impartial tribunal; that there is an inherent defect in the creation, after the event, of ad hoc tribunals to try particular types of offences and, finally, that to give the International Tribunal primacy over national courts is, in any event and in itself, inherently wrong. (Decision at Trial, at para. 2.)[18]

The Appeals Chamber disagreed with the contention that the Security Council did not possess the power under Chapter VII of the United Nations Charter to establish a judicial organ, such as the ICTY. The Chamber found that power to reside in Article 41 of the Charter, which reads as follows:

The Security Council may decide what measures not involving the use of armed force are to be employed to give effect to its decisions, and it may call upon the Members of the United Nations to apply such measures. These may include complete or partial interruption of economic relations and of rail, sea, air, postal, telegraphic, radio, and other means of communication, and the severance of diplomatic relations. (United Nations Charter, art. 41.)[19]

As to whether the Security Council has the power to establish an Organ with judicial powers, the Chamber found that it could do so "as an instrument for the exercise of its own principal function of maintenance of peace and security, *i.e.* as a measure contributing to the restoration and maintenance of peace in the former Yugoslavia."[20]

The Chamber ruled that the question of the effectiveness of creating a Tribunal to restore peace and security to former Yugoslavia was a matter that fell within the wide discretion of the Security Council in choosing an appropriate remedy in dealing with the conflicts in the former Yugoslavia.[21]

The Defence contended that the Tribunal was not "established by law" in violation of Article 14 of the International Covenant on Civil and Political Rights which provides, in part, that:

In the determination of any criminal charge against him, or of his rights and obligations in a suit at law, everyone shall be entitled to a fair and public hearing by a competent, independent and impartial tribunal *established by law*.[22]

In addressing this issue, the Chamber first discussed the nature of democratic national systems as compared with the nature of the United Nations. National systems are most often created with a separation of powers between the executive, legislative and judicial. The Chamber interpreted the words "established by law" to refer to a national-type system where a court is created by a legislative body to be independent of both the executive and legislative branches of government. The United Nations is simply not structured in this way and the separations of powers analysis simply does not apply in an

---

[18] Para. 27.
[19] Para. 35.
[20] Para. 38.
[21] Para. 39.
[22] International Covenant on Civil and Political Rights, Article 14, Paragraph 1.

international setting. The obligation that a tribunal must be "established by law" is an obligation that only applies to states and their national systems.[23]

The Chamber held that the phrase "*established by law*" could be interpreted to mean that a court must be established in accordance with *the rule of law*. To be legitimate such a court "must provide guarantees of fairness, justice and even-handedness, in full conformity with internationally recognized human rights instruments."[24] The Chamber stated that the Rules of Procedure and Evidence created pursuant to Article 15 had certainly been established in accordance with the rule of law. The Chamber added:

> The fair trial guarantees in Article 14 of the International Covenant on Civil and Political Rights have been adopted almost verbatim in Article 21 of the Statute. Other fair trial guarantees appear in the Statute and Rules of Procedure and Evidence. For example, Article 13, paragraph 1, of the Statute ensures the high moral character, impartiality, integrity and competence of the Judges of the International Tribunal, while various other provisions in the Rules ensure equality of arms and fair trial.[25]

---

[23] Para. 43.
[24] Para. 45.
[25] Para. 46.

ARTICLE 1

COMPETENCE OF THE INTERNATIONAL TRIBUNAL

THE INTERNATIONAL TRIBUNAL SHALL HAVE THE POWER TO PROSECUTE PERSONS RESPONSIBLE FOR SERIOUS VIOLATIONS OF INTERNATIONAL HUMANITARIAN LAW COMMITTED IN THE TERRITORY OF THE FORMER YUGOSLAVIA SINCE 1991 IN ACCORDANCE WITH THE PROVISIONS OF THE PRESENT STATUTE.

I. COMMENTARY

The cases reported herein discuss the impact of Article 1. The *Delalić* case sets a limitation on the Tribunal's jurisdiction in light of the words "serious violations." All violations of international humanitarian law are not within the jurisdiction of the Tribunal. Only "serious violations" may be prosecuted. The taking of minimal money and jewelry from detainees in the Čelebići camp was found not to amount to "serious violations."

The *Tadić* Decision indicates that all Tribunal activity must be conducted in accordance with the Statute.

The language of the *Tadić* and *Delalić* cases indicates that the Tribunal's jurisdiction must not be expanded beyond that contemplated by the Statute and the intentions of the Security Council when adopting it. All violations of international humanitarian law are not "serious" as that word is used in this Article. Clearly, the only power conferred on the Tribunal by the Security Counsel is that specifically conferred by the Statute.

II. TRIBUNAL CASES

A. TRIAL CHAMBERS

PROSECUTOR V. DELALIĆ et. al., *Judgement,* IT-96-21-T, 16 November 1998, Karibi-Whyte, Odio-Benito & Jan, JJ.

1. SERIOUS VIOLATIONS

The Trial Chamber dismissed charges of plunder on the basis that the offences, as alleged, could not be considered to constitute such serious violations of international humanitarian law that brings them within the subject matter jurisdiction of the International Tribunal pursuant to Article 1. The Chamber observed that, even when considered in the light most favourable to the Prosecution, the evidence before the Chamber failed to demonstrate that any property taken from the detainees in the Čelebići prison camp was of sufficient monetary value for its unlawful appropriation to involve grave consequences for the victims.[26]

---

[26] Para. 1154.

The Chamber noted that in order for a violation of international humanitarian law to be "serious" within the meaning of the Statute, two elements must be fulfilled. First, the alleged offence must be one that constitutes a breach of a rule protecting important values. Secondly, it must also be one that involves grave consequences for the victim.[27]

PROSECUTOR V. TADIĆ, *Decision on the Defence Motion on Jurisdiction,* IT-94-1-T, 10 August 1995, McDonald, Stephen & Vorah, JJ.

The Trial Chamber held that Article 1 does no more than confer power to prosecute for serious violations of international humanitarian law and confines that power, spatially, to breaches committed in the territory of the former Yugoslavia and, temporally, to the period since 1991. It further requires that the power thus conferred be exercised in accordance with the provisions of the Statute.[28]

---

[27] Para. 1154.
[28] Para. 47.

ARTICLE 2

GRAVE BREACHES OF THE GENEVA CONVENTIONS OF 1949

THE INTERNATIONAL TRIBUNAL SHALL HAVE THE POWER TO PROSECUTE PERSONS COMMITTING OR ORDERING TO BE COMMITTED GRAVE BREACHES OF THE GENEVA CONVENTIONS OF 12 AUGUST 1949, NAMELY THE FOLLOWING ACTS AGAINST PERSONS OR PROPERTY PROTECTED UNDER THE PROVISIONS OF THE RELEVANT GENEVA CONVENTION:

(A)   WILFUL KILLING;

(B)   TORTURE OR INHUMAN TREATMENT, INCLUDING BIOLOGICAL EXPERIMENTS;

(C)   WILFULLY CAUSING GREAT SUFFERING OR SERIOUS INJURY TO BODY OR HEALTH;

(D)   EXTENSIVE DESTRUCTION AND APPROPRIATION OF PROPERTY, NOT JUSTIFIED BY MILITARY NECESSITY AND CARRIED OUT UNLAWFULLY AND WANTONLY;

(E)   COMPELLING A PRISONER OF WAR OR A CIVILIAN TO SERVE IN THE FORCES OF A HOSTILE POWER;

(F)   WILFULLY DEPRIVING A PRISONER OF WAR OR A CIVILIAN OF THE RIGHTS OF FAIR AND REGULAR TRIAL;

(G)   UNLAWFUL DEPORTATION OR TRANSFER OR UNLAWFUL CONFINEMENT OF A CIVILIAN;

(H)   TAKING CIVILIANS AS HOSTAGES.

I.   COMMENTARY

A.   GENERAL

Articles 2 through 5 of the Statute set out the offences that can be prosecuted by the Tribunal. In effect, these articles comprise, along with Article 7, the Penal Code of the Tribunal. It is clear upon first glance that these sections do read more like general pronouncements of policy than like normal penal statutes. As a result, the Tribunal has been required to supplement by providing the additional elements found in most penal statutes, such as the mental state that must be proved along with the acts and the specific elements of the offences.

B.   PROTECTED PERSONS

Since 1949 when the Geneva Conventions were adopted, much has changed. In recent times there have been a number of internal conflicts that seem to blur the line between the classic dichotomy of international and non-international armed conflicts. This has created serious questions regarding the nature of those conflicts and the status of persons detained by parties to those conflicts. The break-up of the former Yugoslavia provided a host of such problems.

In the *Delalić* case, detainees were Bosnian Serbs who were in the hands of Bosnian Croats and Muslims and confined in a prison facility. All parties were nationals of Bosnia and Herzegovina. The detained Serbs were civilians who, at least in some cases, had engaged in rebellious acts against the government of Bosnia and Herzegovina. The question before the *Delalić* Trial Chamber was their status as protected persons under the Geneva Conventions.

In the *Tadić* case, the detainees were non-Serb nationals of Bosnia and Herzegovina, being detained by the Army of Republika Srpska. Again all parties were nationals of Bosnia and Herzegovina and the question before the Trial and Appeals Chambers was whether the detainees were protected persons.

The *Tadić* Decision on Protected Persons

In the *Tadić* Appeals Chamber Judgement, the Chamber determined that the conflict was of an international character, and that the VRS (the Army of Republika Srpska) was a *de facto* organ of the FRY (The Federal Republic of Yugoslavia - Serbia and Montenegro). In addition the Chamber found that the detainees had a different nationality from the members of the VRS who were detaining them despite the fact that members of the VRS and the detainees were nationals of Bosnia and Herzegovina. However, if one accepts the Chamber's conclusion that the VRS was a *de facto* organ of a foreign power - Serbia and Montenegro - then all the conditions for an Occupation were seemingly fulfilled which would have rendered the detainees protected persons under the clear and specific language of the Convention. Instead the Chamber relied on the "preparatory works" which "suggest an intent on the part of the drafters to extend its application . . ."[29] The official commentary to the Conventions, however, is very clear on what was intended by its drafters: "The Convention thus remains faithful to a recognized principle of international law; it does not interfere in a State's relations with its own nationals."[30]

It appears that the Chamber did not consider the issue of protected persons in regard to changes, if any, in its application since 1949, as a matter of customary international law nor in regard to the principle of *nullum crimen sine lege*. It seems that state practice reflected the principle of state sovereignty in a manner consistent with the official commentaries to the Convention, particularly through the early 1990's the period relevant to the alleged offences in the *Tadić* case.

---

[29] Prosecutor v. Tadić, *Judgement*, IT-94-1-A, 15 July 1999, Para. 164, fn. 204.
[30] Jean S. Pictet Ed, *Commentary, IV Geneva Convention Relative to the Protection of Civilian Persons in Time of War*, International Committee of the Red Cross, 1958, p. 46.

B.   ARMED CONFLICTS

Early in the history of the Tribunal it was contended that there was no armed conflict associated with the charges brought against the defendant Duško Tadić. That prompted a Trial Chamber decision followed by a decision arising from an interlocutory appeal. The Appeals Chamber defined an armed conflict, as follows:

> [W]e find that an armed conflict exists whenever there is a resort to armed force between States or protracted armed violence between governmental authorities and organized armed groups or between such groups within a State. International humanitarian law applies from the initiation of such armed conflicts and extends beyond the cessation of hostilities until a general conclusion of peace is reached; or, in the case of internal conflicts, a peaceful settlement is achieved. Until that moment, international humanitarian law continues to apply in the whole territory of the warring States or, in the case of internal conflicts, the whole territory under the control of a party, whether or not actual combat takes place there.[31]

C.   INHUMANE CONDITIONS

In the *Delalić* Trial Chamber Judgement the Chamber was called upon to determine the issue of what constitutes "inhumane conditions." Defence counsel had presented evidence, and argued that the conditions prevailing in the Čelebići Camp were not dissimilar to those prevailing in the Konjic municipality where the Camp was located. Due to the war conditions and the influx of thousands of refugees, there was a shortage of food and medical supplies, and necessities such as warm clothing and blankets. There was evidence that the Čelebići detainees were provided with food of a quantity and quality very similar to that supplied to the personnel who were charged with guarding them. The issue in this case was whether a detaining power should not be obligated to provide conditions of detention any greater than those prevailing in the area at the time. The Chamber, took the position that there is a threshold below which conditions must not be allowed to fall. This threshold exists regardless of prevailing conditions in the area. If the threshold cannot be met then persons simply should not be detained.

Clearly there are times in war situations where persons must be detained. Consider, for instance, members of insurgent groups seeking to overthrow the government. International law recognizes that such persons may be detained, at least until the appropriate judicial findings have been made regarding their culpability. The minimum threshold of conditions which the Chamber made a part of its findings in relation to inhumane conditions should not be applied in the abstract to all situations. It seems that a Chamber must determine whether conditions existed as a result of prevailing circumstances brought about by the conflict or by a deliberate attempt to deprive people of the necessities of life.

---

[31] Prosecutor v. Dusko Tadić, *Decision on the Defence Motion for Interlocutory Appeal on Jurisdiction*, IT-94-1-AR72, 2 October 1995, Para. 70.

II.　TRIBUNAL CASES

A.　APPEALS CHAMBER

1. INTERNATIONAL/INTERNAL ARMED CONFLICTS

PROSECUTOR V. ALEKSOVSKI, *Judgement*, IT-95-14/1-A, 24 March 2000, May, Mumba, Hunt, Tieya & Robinson, JJ.

In this decision, the Appeals Chamber held that the "overall control" test for determining whether an international armed conflict existed at the time relevant to the indictment was incorrectly applied by the Trial Chamber. The Appeals Chamber cited with approval the formulation of the "overall control" test that the Chamber had articulated for the first time in the *Tadić Judgement*, as follows:

> As the Appeals Chamber has already pointed out, international law does not require that the particular acts in question should be the subject of specific instructions or directives by a foreign State to certain armed forces in order for these armed forces to be held to be acting as *de facto* organs of that State. It follows that in the circumstances of the case it was not necessary to show that those specific operations carried out by the Bosnian Serb forces which were the object of the trial (the attacks on Kozarac and more generally within opstina Prijedor) had been specifically ordered or planned by the Yugoslav Army. It is sufficient to show that this Army exercised overall control over the Bosnian Serb Forces. This showing has been made by the Prosecution before the Trial Chamber. Such control manifested itself not only in financial, logistical and other assistance and support, but also, and more importantly, in terms of participation in the general direction, coordination and supervision of the activities and operations of the VRS. This sort of control is sufficient for the purposes of the legal criteria required by international law.[32]

In analysing the "overall control" test, the Chamber observed that the responsibility of a State is engaged once it is established that a group is acting under its overall control, irrespective of whether specific instructions were given by the State to members of the group.[33] The Chamber held that the "overall control" test does not require proof of "specific instructions" or "direct involvement" of a State in order to find that a conflict is international in character. The "overall control" test calls for an assessment of all the elements of control taken as a whole, and a determination to be made on that basis as to

---

[32] Para. 137.
[33] Paras. 132-133.

whether there was the required degree of control. Finally, the Chamber considered that to the extent that it provides for greater protection of civilian victims of armed conflicts, this standard is wholly consistent with the fundamental purpose of Geneva Convention IV, which is to ensure "protection of civilians to the maximum extent possible."[34]

PROSECUTOR V. TADIĆ, *Judgement*, IT-94-1-A, 15 July 1999, Shahabuddeen, Cassese, Tieya, Nieto-Navia & Mumba, JJ.

The Appeals Chamber found that Article 2 does not apply, unless the conflict in question is international in scope. In setting out the rules for determination of the nature of a conflict, the Chamber held that the test set out in *Nicaragua v. United States*,[35] was incorrect. The Chamber ruled that the question turned on the degree of control exercised by FRY over the VRS:

> ... international rules do not always require the same degree of control over armed groups or private individuals for the purpose of determining whether an individual not having the status of a State official under internal legislation can be regarded as a *de facto* organ of the State. The extent of the requisite State control varies. Where the question at issue is whether a *single* private individual or a *group that is not militarily organised* has acted as a *de facto* State organ when performing a specific act, it is necessary to ascertain whether specific instructions concerning the commission of that particular act had been issued by that State to the individual or group in question; alternatively, it must be established whether the unlawful act had been publicly endorsed or approved *ex post facto* by the State at issue. By contrast, control by a State over subordinate *armed forces or militias or paramilitary units* may be of an overall character (and must comprise more than the mere provision of financial assistance or military equipment or training). This requirement, however, does not go so far as to include the issuing of specific orders by the State, or its direction of each individual operation. Under international law it is by no means necessary that the controlling authorities should plan all the operations of the units dependent on them, choose their targets, or give specific instructions concerning the conduct of military operations and any alleged violations of international humanitarian law. The control required by international law may be deemed to exist when a State (or, in the context of an armed conflict, the Party to the conflict) *has a role in organizing, coordinating or planning the military actions* of the military group, in addition to financing, training and equipping or providing operational support to that group. Acts performed by the group or members thereof may be regarded as acts of *de facto* State organs regardless of

---

[34] Para. 146.
[35] *Military and Paramilitary Activities in and Against Nicaragua (Nicaragua v. United States of America)* (Merits) Judgment, ICJ Reports (1986).

any specific instruction by the controlling State concerning the commission of those acts. (Chamber's italics).[36]

PROSECUTOR V. TADIĆ, *Decision on the Defence Motion for Interlocutory Appeal on Jurisdiction*, IT-94-1-AR72, 2 October 1995, Cassese, Li, Deschênes, Abi-Saab & Sidhwa, JJ.

Following a protracted discussion about the history of the adoption of the ICTY Statute and the context within which it was adopted, the Chamber arrived at the following conclusion:

> ... we conclude that the conflicts in the former Yugoslavia have both internal and international aspects, that the members of the Security Council clearly had both aspects of the conflicts in mind when they adopted the Statute of the International Tribunal, and that they intended to empower the International Tribunal to adjudicate violations of humanitarian law that occurred in either context. To the extent possible under existing international law, the Statute should therefore be construed to give effect to that purpose.[37]

Following an analysis of Article 2 of the Statute and its source, the Geneva Conventions of 1949, the Chamber concluded that it could only have application in international armed conflicts.

2. PROTECTED PERSONS

PROSECUTOR V. ALEKSOVSKI, *Judgement*, IT-95-14/1-A, 24 March 2000, May, Mumba, Hunt, Tieya & Robinson, JJ.

The Appeals Chamber held that the conflict was international by reason of Croatia's participation in the war in Bosnia and Herzegovina. This meant that Bosnian Muslim victims were in the hands of a party to the conflict, Croatia, of which they were not nationals and that, therefore, Article 4 of Geneva Convention IV is applicable.[38] Furthermore, the Chamber held that in certain circumstances a person might be accorded protected status even though he is of the same nationality as his captors. This interpretation of the concept of Protected Persons looks to the allegiance of the individual to a Party to the conflict and the latter's control over persons in a given territory. The Chamber observed that this approach examines the substance of the relations between the individual and a Party to a conflict, rather than the legal characterisation, based on nationality. This expansive interpretation of the concept of protected persons was found to meet the object and purpose of Geneva Convention IV, particularly in the context of present-day, inter-ethnic conflicts.[39]

---

[36] Para. 137.
[37] Para. 77.
[38] Paras. 149-150.
[39] Para. 152.

PROSECUTOR V. TADIĆ, *Judgement*, IT-94-1-A, 15 JULY 1999, Shahabuddeen, Cassese, Tieya, Nieto-Navia & Mumba, JJ.

The Appeals Chamber determined that detainees are only protected under Article 2 of the Statute of the Tribunal if two conditions are met. First, the conflict must be international in character. Second, the alleged victims must be protected persons as defined by the appropriate Geneva Convention. The Chamber found that both criteria were satisfied. In regard to the issue of protected persons, the Chamber reasoned that since the VRS was a *de facto* organ of the FRY, the victims found themselves in the hands of a State of which they were not nationals, the FRY. The Chamber stated:

> Hence, even if in the circumstances of the case the perpetrators and the victims were to be regarded as possessing the same nationality, Article 4 would still be applicable. Indeed the victims did not owe allegiance to (and did not receive the diplomatic protection of) the State (the FRY) on whose behalf the Bosnian Serb armed forces had been fighting.[40]

B.   TRIAL CHAMBERS

1. GENERAL

PROSECUTOR V BLAŠKIĆ, *Judgement,* IT-95-14-T, 3 March 2000, Jorda, Rodrigues & Shahabuddeen, JJ.

Extensive Destruction of Property

The Trial Chamber ruled:

> An occupying Power is prohibited from destroying movable and non-movable property except where such destruction is made absolutely necessary by military operations. To constitute a grave breach, the destruction unjustified by military necessity must be extensive, unlawful and wanton. The notion of "extensive" is evaluated according to the facts of the case - a single act, such as the destruction of a hospital, may suffice to characterise an offense under this count.[41]

Taking Civilians as Hostages

The Chamber defined the elements of this offense as follows:

> Within the meaning of Article 2 of the Statute, civilian hostages are persons unlawfully deprived of their freedom, often arbitrarily and sometimes under threat of death. However, as asserted by the Defence, detention may be lawful in some circumstances, *inter alia* to protect civilians or when security reasons so impel. The Prosecution must establish that, at the time of the supposed

---

[40] Para. 169.
[41] Para. 157.

detention, the allegedly censurable act was perpetrated in order to obtain a concession or gain an advantage.[42]

PROSECUTOR V. DELALIĆ *et. al.*, *Judgement*, IT-96-21-T, 16 November 1998, Karibi-Whyte, Odio-Benito & Jan, JJ.

Mistreatment not Resulting in Death

The Trial Chamber considered the regime set out in Article 2 and Article 3 for offences dealing with mistreatment that does not result in death. The Chamber observed that torture, a grave breach of the Geneva Conventions is punishable under Article 2(b) of the Statute, and as a violation of the laws or customs of war punishable under Article 3 of the Statute, as recognised by Article 3(1)(a) of the Geneva Conventions. Rape, as torture, a grave breach of the Geneva Conventions, is punishable under Article 2(b) of the Statute, and as a violation of the laws or customs of war punishable under Article 3 of the Statute, as recognised by Article 3(1)(a) of the Geneva Conventions. Wilfully causing great suffering or serious injury, a grave breach of the Geneva Conventions, is punishable under Article 2(c) of the Statute. Inhumane treatment, a grave breach of the Geneva Conventions, is punishable under Article 2(b) of the Statute. Cruel treatment, a violation of the laws or customs of war is punishable under Article 3 of the Statute and is recognised by Article 3(1)(a) of the Geneva Conventions.[43]

The Chamber made the following observations regarding the interrelationship of the mistreatment offences contained in Article 2. Torture is the most specific of those offences of mistreatment constituting "grave breaches" and entails acts or omissions, by or at the instigation of, or with the consent or acquiescence of an official, which are committed for a particular prohibited purpose and cause a severe level of mental or physical pain or suffering.[44]

The Chamber distinguished the offence of wilfully causing great suffering or serious injury to body or health from torture primarily on the basis that the alleged acts or omissions need not be committed for a prohibited purpose such as is required for the offence of torture.[45]

Inhuman treatment involves acts or omissions that cause serious mental or physical suffering or injury or constitute a serious attack on human dignity.[46]

As between the three offences, the Chamber observed that all acts or omissions found to constitute torture or wilfully causing great suffering or serious injury to body or health would also constitute inhuman treatment. However, this third category of offence is not limited to those acts already incorporated in the two others, and extends further to acts which violate the basic principle of humane treatment, particularly the respect for human dignity.

---

[42] Para. 158.
[43] Para. 440.
[44] Para. 442.
[45] Para. 442.
[46] Para. 442.

In regard to Article 3, the Chamber found that the offences of torture and cruel treatment, proscribed under common article 3, are also interrelated. The characteristics of the offence of torture under common article 3 and under the "grave breaches" provisions of the Geneva Conventions do not differ. The offence of cruel treatment under common article 3 carries the same meaning as inhuman treatment in the context of the "grave breaches" provisions. For the purposes of Article 3, the Chamber concluded that all torture is encapsulated in the offence of cruel treatment. However, this latter offence extends to all acts or omissions that cause serious mental or physical suffering or injury or constitute a serious attack on human dignity.[47]

The Chamber stated that in this framework of offences, all acts found to constitute torture or wilfully causing great suffering or serious injury to body or health would also constitute inhumane treatment. However, this third category of offence is not limited to those acts already incorporated into the other two and extends further to other acts which violate the basic principle of humane treatment, particularly the respect for human dignity. Ultimately, the question of whether any particular act which does not fall within the categories of the core group is inconsistent with the principle of humane treatment, and thus constitutes inhumane treatment, is a question of fact to be judged in all the circumstances of the particular case.[48]

Definition of Torture

The Chamber found that the elements of torture, for the purposes of applying Articles 2 and 3 of the Statute, are as follows:

(i)   There must be an act or omission that causes severe pain or suffering, whether mental or physical,

(ii)   which is inflicted intentionally,

(iii)   and for such purposes as obtaining information or a confession from the victim, or a third person, punishing the victim for an act he or she or a third person has committed or is suspected of having committed, intimidating or coercing the victim or a third person, or for any reason based on discrimination of any kind,

(iv)   and such act or omission being committed by, or at the instigation of, or with the consent or acquiescence of, an official or other person acting in an official capacity.[49]

---

[47] Para. 443.
[48] Para. 544.
[49] Para. 494.

Rape as Torture

The Chamber held that whenever rape and other forms of sexual violence meet the definition of Torture, then they should constitute torture, in the same manner as any other acts that meet these criteria.[50] The Chamber considered the rape of any person to be a despicable act that strikes at the very core of human dignity and physical integrity. The Chamber added that the condemnation and punishment of rape becomes all the more urgent where it is committed by, or at the instigation of a public official or with the consent or acquiescence of such an official. Rape causes severe pain and suffering, both physical and psychological. The psychological suffering of persons upon whom rape is inflicted may be exacerbated by social and cultural conditions and can be particularly acute and long lasting. The Chamber concluded by saying that it is difficult to envisage circumstances in which rape by or at the instigation of a public official, or with the consent or acquiescence of an official, could be considered as occurring for a purpose that does not, in some way, involve punishment, coercion, discrimination or intimidation.[51]

Definition of Wilfully Causing Great Suffering or Serious Injury to Body or Health

The Chamber found that the offence of wilfully causing great suffering or serious injury to body or health constitutes an act or omission that is intentional, being an act which, judged objectively, is deliberate and not accidental, which causes serious mental or physical suffering or injury. It covers those acts that do not meet the purposive requirements for the offence of torture, although clearly all acts constituting torture could also fall within the ambit of this offence.[52]

Definition of Inhumane Treatment

The Chamber found that inhumane treatment is an intentional act or omission, that is an act which, judged objectively, is deliberate and not accidental, which causes serious mental or physical suffering or injury or constitutes a serious attack on human dignity. The plain, ordinary meaning of the term inhumane treatment in the context of the Geneva Conventions confirms this approach and clarifies the meaning of the offence. The Chamber observed that inhumane treatment is intentional treatment that does not conform to the fundamental principle of humanity, and forms the umbrella under which the remainder of the listed "grave breaches" in the Conventions fall. Acts characterised in the Conventions and Commentaries as inhumane, or which are inconsistent with the principle of humanity, constitute examples of actions that can be characterised as inhumane treatment.[53]

---

[50] Para. 496.
[51] Para. 495.
[52] Para. 511.
[53] Para. 543.

Definition of Cruel Treatment

The offences charged as cruel treatment may be brought under Article 3 of the Statute, either in the alternative to charges of torture, or additional to charges of wilfully causing great suffering or serious injury or inhuman treatment, brought under Article 2 of the Statute.[54]

The Chamber found that cruel treatment constitutes an intentional act or omission, that is an act which, judged objectively, is deliberate and not accidental, which causes serious mental or physical suffering or injury or constitutes a serious attack on human dignity. The Chamber observed that it carries an equivalent meaning and therefore the same residual function for the purposes of common article 3 of the Statute, as inhumane treatment does in relation to grave breaches of the Geneva Conventions. Accordingly, the offence of torture under common article 3 of the Geneva Conventions is also included within the concept of cruel treatment. Treatment that does not meet the purposive requirement for the offence of torture in common article 3, constitutes cruel treatment.[55]

Definition Inhumane Conditions

Inhumane conditions was alleged in the indictment as wilfully causing great suffering and cruel treatment.[56] The Chamber observed that the phrase "inhumane conditions" is a factual description relating to the nature of the general environment in which detained persons are kept and the treatment that they receive. The Chamber applied the legal standards found for the offences of wilfully causing great suffering or serious injury to body or health and cruel treatment to this factual category.[57]

The Chamber ruled that the legal standards regarding inhumane conditions are absolute and not relative. The Chamber observed that when considering the factual allegation of inhumane conditions with respect to these legal offences, no reference should be made to the conditions prevailing in the area of detention in order to determine what the standard of treatment should have been. The legal standard in mistreatment offences delineates a minimum standard of treatment that also applies to conditions of detention. During an armed conflict, persons should not be detained in conditions where this minimum standard cannot be met and maintained.[58]

The Chamber concluded by stating that, in the context of Article 3 of the Statute, cruel treatment carries the same meaning as inhumane treatment in the context of Article 2, and thus an allegation of inhumane conditions is appropriately charged as cruel treatment. The Chamber was of the view that, while it is possible to categorise inhumane conditions within the offence of wilfully causing great suffering or serious injury to body

---

[54] Para. 545.
[55] Para. 552.
[56] Para. 553.
[57] Para. 556.
[58] Para. 557.

or health under Article 2, it is more appropriately placed within the offence of inhumane treatment.[59]

2. PROTECTED PERSONS

PROSECUTOR V BLAŠKIĆ, *Judgement,* IT-95-14-T, 3 March 2000, Jorda, Rodrigues & Shahabuddeen, JJ.

After discussing this issue at length and reviewing the Tribunal jurisprudence to date, the Chamber said:

> In an inter-ethnic armed conflict, a person's ethnic background may be regarded as a decisive factor in determining to which nation he owes his allegiance and may thus serve to establish the status of the victims as protected persons.[60]

Co-Belligerence

The Defence contended that the victims were not protected persons since the HVO and Bosnia and Herzegovina were co-belligerents. Article 4(2) of the Fourth Geneva Convention provides that nationals of co-belligerent states cannot be protected persons during any time when the state of which they are nationals has normal diplomatic relations with the state in whose hands they find themselves. Diplomatic relations were established between Croatia and Bosnia and Herzegovina on 25 July 1992.

The Chamber said that even though diplomatic relations existed, the parties did not act toward each other as co-belligerent states in the Central Bosnia Operative Zone and held that the conflict in this zone was not carried on between co-belligerent states.[61]

The Chamber found that the reasoning behind the rule regarding co-belligerent states and protected persons is that civilians will be protected and benefit from normal diplomatic relations. In those situations where civilians do not enjoy the normal diplomatic protection of their State, they should be accorded the status of protected person.[62]

3. PROTECTED PROPERTY

PROSECUTOR V BLAŠKIĆ, *Judgement,* IT-95-14-T, 3 March 2000, Jorda, Rodrigues & Shahabuddeen, JJ.

Although no issue in this regard was raised by the Defence, the Chamber made the determination that the Fourth Geneva Convention, Article 53, applied. This Article only applies where the property is located in occupied territory. Since the HVO, in effect, occupied the territory in question in this case, and since the Chamber found that the HVO

---

[59] Para. 558.
[60] Para. 127.
[61] Paras. 134-143.
[62] Para. 145.

was under the effective control of Croatia, the territory involved was deemed occupied territory for purposes of the application of the Convention.[63]

4. ARMED CONFLICTS

PROSECUTOR V. FURUNDŽIJA, *Judgement,* IT-95-17/1-T, 10 December 1998, Cassese, May & Mumba, JJ.

The Trial Chamber applied the test for determining the existence of an armed conflict that was set out by the Appeals Chamber in the *Tadić Jurisdiction Decision*[64], which states:

> [A]n armed conflict exists whenever there is a resort to armed force between States or protracted armed violence between governmental authorities and organised armed groups or between such groups within a State.

The Chamber found, on the clear evidence in the case that, at the material time, being mid-May 1993, a state of armed conflict existed between the HVO and the ABiH.[65]

PROSECUTOR V. DELALIĆ, *et. al. Judgement,* IT-96-21-T, 16 November 1998, Karibi-Whyte, Jan & Odio-Benito, JJ.

The Trial Chamber held that to apply the body of law termed "international humanitarian law" to a particular situation it must first be determined that there was, in fact, an "armed conflict," whether of an internal or international nature. The Chamber stated that without a finding that there was such an armed conflict it is not possible for a Trial Chamber to progress further to its discussion of the nature of this conflict and how this impacts upon the applicability of Articles 2 and 3.[66]

The Chamber adopted the test formulated by the Appeals Chamber in the *Tadić Jurisdiction Decision*, according to which:

> [A]n armed conflict exists whenever there is a resort to armed force between States or protracted armed violence between governmental authorities and organized armed groups or between such groups within a State.[67]

Furthermore, the Chamber adopted the following passage from that Decision:

> [I]nternational humanitarian law applies from the initiation of such armed conflicts and extends beyond the cessation of hostilities until a general conclusion of peace is reached; or, in the case of internal conflicts, a peaceful settlement is achieved. Until that moment, international humanitarian law continues to apply in the whole territory of the warring States or, in the case of

---

[63] Paras. 148-150.
[64] Prosecutor v. Tadić, *Decision on the Defence Motion for Interlocutory Appeal on Jurisdiction*, IT-94-1-AR72, 2 October 1995, para. 70.
[65] Para. 59.
[66] Para. 182.
[67] Para. 70.

internal conflicts, the whole territory under the control of a party, whether or not actual combat takes place there.[68]

The Chamber held that this test applies both to conflicts which are regarded as international in nature and to those which are regarded as internal to a State. In the former situation, the existence of armed force between States is sufficient of itself to trigger the application of international humanitarian law. In the latter situation, in order to distinguish from cases of civil unrest or terrorist activities, the emphasis is on the protracted extent of the armed violence and the extent of organisation of the parties involved.[69]

In addition the Chamber found that whether or not the conflict is deemed to be international or internal, there does not have to be actual combat activities in a particular location for the norms of international humanitarian law to be applicable. A Trial Chamber is not required to find that there existed an "armed conflict" in the particular municipality where alleged events occurred but rather in the larger territory of which it forms part.[70]

The Chamber held that there was an "armed conflict" in Bosnia and Herzegovina in the period relevant to the Indictment and regardless of whether or not this conflict is considered internal or international, it incorporated the municipality of Konjic. where events were alleged to have occurred.[71]

5. LINK BETWEEN ARMED CONFLICT AND ACTS

PROSECUTOR V. ALEKSOVSKI, *Judgement,* IT-95-14/1-T, 25 June 1999, Rodriguez, Vohrah & Nieto-Navia, JJ.

The Trial Chamber adopted the definition of an armed conflict that was enunciated in the *Tadić Jurisdiction Decision*, and found that an armed conflict existed in the present case.[72]

The Chamber observed that only those acts that are sufficiently connected with the armed conflict are subject to the application of international humanitarian law.[73]

PROSECUTOR V. FURUNDŽIJA, *Judgement,* IT-95-17/1-T, 10 December 1998, Cassese, May & Mumba, JJ.

The Trial Chamber accepted the evidence of Witness A about the nature of her interrogation by the accused. She was a civilian in the hands of the Jokers being questioned by the accused, who was a commander of that unit. He was an active combatant and participated in expelling Moslems from their homes. He also participated

---

[68] Para. 183.
[69] Para. 184.
[70] Para. 185.
[71] Para. 192.
[72] Paras. 43-44.
[73] Para. 45.

in arrests such as those of Witnesses D and E. The Chamber held that these circumstances are sufficient to link the alleged offences committed by the accused to the armed conflict.[74]

PROSECUTOR V. DELALIĆ, *et. al.*, *Judgement*, IT-96-21-T, 16 November 1998, Karibi-Whyte, Jan & Odio-Benito, JJ.

The Trial Chamber found that for the Tribunal to have jurisdiction over alleged offences there must be an obvious link between the criminal act and the armed conflict. If a crime were committed in the course of fighting or the take-over of a town during an armed conflict, for example, this would be sufficient to render the offence a violation of international humanitarian law. Such a direct connection to actual hostilities is not, however, required in every situation. In this regard, the Chamber referred to the *Tadic Jurisdiction Decision* on the nexus between the acts of the accused and the armed conflict:

> [I]t is sufficient that the alleged crimes were closely related to the hostilities occurring in other parts of the territories controlled by the parties to the conflict.[75]

The Chamber emphasised that there need not have been actual armed hostilities in the municipality where alleged events occurred in order for the norms of international humanitarian law to have been applicable. Nor is it required that fighting was taking place in the exact time-period when the acts alleged in the indictment occurred.[76]

---

[74] Para. 65.
[75] Para. 193.
[76] Para. 194.

ARTICLE 3

VIOLATIONS OF THE LAWS OR CUSTOMS OF WAR

THE INTERNATIONAL TRIBUNAL SHALL HAVE THE POWER TO PROSECUTE PERSONS VIOLATING THE LAWS OR CUSTOMS OF WAR. SUCH VIOLATIONS SHALL INCLUDE, BUT NOT BE LIMITED TO:

(A)   EMPLOYMENT OF POISONOUS WEAPONS OR OTHER WEAPONS CALCULATED TO CAUSE UNNECESSARY SUFFERING;

(B)   WANTON DESTRUCTION OF CITIES, TOWNS OR VILLAGES, OR DEVASTATION NOT JUSTIFIED BY MILITARY NECESSITY;

(C)   ATTACK, OR BOMBARDMENT, BY WHATEVER MEANS, OF UNDEFENDED TOWNS, VILLAGES, DWELLINGS, OR BUILDINGS;

(D)   SEIZURE OF, DESTRUCTION OR WILFUL DAMAGE DONE TO INSTITUTIONS DEDICATED TO RELIGION, CHARITY AND EDUCATION, THE ARTS AND SCIENCES, HISTORIC MONUMENTS AND WORKS OF ART AND SCIENCE;

(E)   PLUNDER OF PUBLIC OR PRIVATE PROPERTY.

I.   COMMENTARY

Although it seems from reading the Secretary-General's Report and the specific language of Article 3 that it is restricted to offenses arising out of the Hague Convention of 1907, the Tribunal has given it a much broader interpretation. The Tribunal has found that Article 3 provides jurisdiction for all violations of international humanitarian law that are either treaty-based or have become customary international law. Thus, the Tribunal has concluded that Article 3 common to the 1949 Geneva Conventions is incorporated into this Article through its residual clause, in the particular phrase "shall include but not be limited to." Although there is nothing in the Secretary-General's report that would lead one to this conclusion it has become relatively settled law at the Tribunal.[77] At no time in the process of incorporating Common Article 3 into Article 3 of the Statute did any Chamber perform the kind of rigorous analysis that is required to establish that Common Article 3 had become customary international law.[78] It seem to be contrary to generally accepted canons of statutory interpretation, *e.g. ejusdem generis,* to suggest that Common Article 3 could be included within the jurisdiction of the Tribunal on the basis of the words "shall include, but not be limited to" in Article 3. Murder and Torture are simply unlike any other prohibition contained in this Article 3. Finally, it seems that had the Security Council intended that Common Article 3 be within the jurisdiction of the

---

[77] The issue of whether Common Article 3 is within the jurisdiction of the Tribunal has been raised and argued in the *Čelebići* Appeal which is currently pending a decision.

[78] See the Preamble hereto for a detailed discussion of the sources of international law and how customary law is to be derived.

Tribunal it would have specifically incorporated it into the Statute as was done with the Rwanda statute.

Several of the cases below, and those reported under Article 1 have discussed the question of what constitutes a "serious breach" of international humanitarian law so as to vest jurisdiction in the Tribunal. It is generally agreed that a serious breach is one that constitutes a breach of a rule protecting important values and this breach must involve grave consequences for the victim.

II.   TRIBUNAL CASES

A.   APPEALS CHAMBER

PROSECUTOR V. ALEKSOVSKI, *Judgement*, IT-95-14/1-A, 24 March 2000, May, Mumba, Hunt, Tieya & Robinson, JJ.

Mens rea: No Proof of Discriminatory Required by Article 3

The Appeals Chamber found that it is not an element of offences under Article 3 that the perpetrator had a discriminatory intent or motive. In the instant case, the Chamber found that under Article 3, it was not necessary for the Trial Chamber to find that the accused had a discriminatory intent to conclude that he was guilty of the offence of outrages upon personal dignity.[79]

The Chamber added that evidence that an accused who had responsibility for detention conditions and discriminated between detainees in the conditions and facilities provided might be relevant. Proof of deliberate discrimination between detainees, poor conditions of detention that affect only one group or class of detainees, while other detainees enjoy adequate detention conditions, may contribute to a finding that the *mens rea* of the offence of outrages upon personal dignity is satisfied.[80]

The Chamber found that the general requirements that must be met for prosecution of offences under Article 3 have already been clearly identified in the *Tadić Jurisdiction Decision* and they do not include a requirement of proof of a discriminatory intent or motivation. The Chamber reiterated that the relevant violation of international humanitarian law must be "serious" in the sense that it must constitute a breach of a rule protecting important values and the breach must involve grave consequences for the victim. There is no requirement that the violation must be committed with discriminatory intent.[81]

Mens Rea: Discriminatory Intent Required for Persecution and Genocide

The Chamber considered that the specific discriminatory intent required for the international crimes of persecution and genocide distinguish these offences from other violations of the laws and customs of war.

---

[79] Para. 28.
[80] Para. 28, footnote 73.
[81] Para. 20.

PROSECUTOR V. TADIĆ, *Decision on the Defence Motion for Interlocutory Appeal on Jurisdiction,* IT-94-1-AR72, 2 October 1995, Cassese, Li, Deschênes, Abi-Saab & Sidhwa, JJ.

The Scope of Article 3

Tadić contended that Article 3 was derived from the 1907 Hague Convention (IV) which was restricted to international armed conflicts and that as a result this article is similarly restricted. The Chamber disagreed. The Chamber interpreted the phrase, "such violations shall include, but not be limited to" to broaden the reach of Article 3 well beyond the Hague Convention and to include all international humanitarian law. The Chamber concluded:

> . . that this list may be construed to include other infringements of international humanitarian law. The only limitation is that such infringements must not be already covered by Article 2 (lest this latter provision should become superfluous). Article 3 may be taken to cover *all violations* of international humanitarian law other than the "grave breaches" of the four Geneva Conventions falling under Article 2 (or, for that matter, the violations covered by Articles 4 and 5, to the extent that Articles 3, 4 and 5 overlap).[82] (Chamber's emphasis)

Specifically, the Chamber held:

> . . . that Article 3 is a general clause covering all violations of humanitarian law not falling under Article 2 or covered by Articles 4 or 5, more specifically: (i) violations of the Hague law on international conflicts; (ii) infringements of provisions of the Geneva Conventions other than those classified as "grave breaches" by those Conventions; (iii) violations of common Article 3 and other customary rules on internal conflicts; (iv) violations of agreements binding upon the parties to the conflict, considered qua treaty law, *i.e.,* agreements which have not turned into customary international law.[83] . . . Article 3 functions as a residual clause designed to ensure that no serious violation of international humanitarian law is taken away from the jurisdiction of the International Tribunal. Article 3 aims to make such jurisdiction watertight and inescapable.[84]

Having reached these conclusions, the Chamber then set out the conditions that must be met for an international humanitarian law violation to be subject to prosecution under Article 3. First, the violation must infringe some rule of international humanitarian law. Second, the rule must either be customary international law or treaty law. Third, the violation must be serious. The Chamber gave an example of someone appropriating a loaf of bread in an occupied village as being a violation that would not be seen as serious. Fourth, the violation must involve the individual criminal responsibility of the violator.

---

[82] Para. 87.
[83] Para. 89.
[84] Para. 91.

The Judges then stated that "it follows that it does not matter whether the 'serious violation' has occurred within the context of an international or an internal armed conflict, as long as the requirements set out above are met."[85]

Finally the Chamber determined that Common Article 3 of the Geneva Conventions of 1949 was clearly included within the residual clause of Article 3 of the Statute.[86]

B.   TRIAL CHAMBERS

1. INTERNATIONAL/INTERNAL ARMED CONFLICTS

PROSECUTOR V. TADIĆ, *Decision on the Defence Motion on Jurisdiction,* IT-94-1-T, 10 August 1995, McDonald, Stephen & Vohrah, JJ.

The Trial Chamber found that the character of the conflict, whether international or internal, does not affect the subject-matter jurisdiction of the International Tribunal under Article 3 to try persons who are charged with violations of the laws or customs of war."[87]

The Chamber concluded that Article 3 of the Statute provides a non-exhaustive list of acts that fit within the rubric of "laws or customs of war." The offences that it may consider are not limited to those contained in the Hague Convention and may arise during an armed conflict regardless of whether it is international or internal."[88]

The Chamber held that the customary international law doctrine of recognition of belligerency allows for the application to internal conflicts of the laws applicable to international armed conflict, thus ensuring that even in a non-international conflict an individual can be held criminally responsible for violations of the laws and customs of war.[89]

2. COMMON ARTICLE 3 OF THE GENEVA CONVENTIONS OF 1949

PROSECUTOR V. TADIĆ, *Decision on the Defence Motion on Jurisdiction,* IT-94-1-T, 10 August 1995, McDonald, Stephen & Vohrah, JJ.

The Trial Chamber found that common Article 3 imposes obligations that are within the subject-matter jurisdiction of Article 3 of the Statute because those obligations are a part of customary international law. Further, the Chamber found that violations of these prohibitions could be enforced against individuals. Imposing criminal responsibility upon individuals for these violations does not violate the principle of *nullum crimen sine lege.*[90]

---

[85] Para. 94.
[86] Para. 134.
[87] Para. 58.
[88] Para. 64.
[89] Para. 69.
[90] Para. 65.

The Judges stated that "the minimum standards of common Article 3 apply to the conflict in the former Yugoslavia and the accused's prosecution for those offences does not violate the principle of *nullum crimen sine lege.*"[91]

3. THE SCOPE OF ARTICLE 3

PROSECUTOR V. FURUNDŽIJA, *Judgement,* IT-95-17/1-T, 10 December 1998, Mumba, Cassese & May, JJ.

Applying the interpretation of Article 3 enunciated by the Appeals Chamber in the *Tadić Jurisdiction Decision*, the Trial Chamber found that it has very broad scope. It covers any serious violation of a rule of customary international humanitarian law entailing, under international customary or conventional law, the individual criminal responsibility of the person breaching the rule. The Chamber ruled that it is immaterial whether the breach occurs within the context of an international or internal armed conflict.[92]

Furthermore, based on the *Tadić Jurisdictional Decision*, the Chamber held that the list of offences contained in Article 3 is merely illustrative and that this provision also covers serious violations of international rules of humanitarian law not included in that list. The Chamber reasserted that more than the other substantive provisions of the Statute, Article 3 constitutes an "umbrella rule." Article 3 makes an open-ended reference to all international rules of humanitarian law. The Chamber concluded that pursuant to Article 3 serious violations of any international rule of humanitarian law might be regarded as crimes falling under this provision of the Statute, if the requisite conditions are met.[93]

As for the applicability of Article 3, the Chamber noted that it is well established that for international humanitarian law to apply there must first be an armed conflict, the nature of which is irrelevant. Citing the Appeals Chamber in the *Tadić Jurisdiction Decision* as binding authority, the Chamber held that it does not matter whether the serious violation occurred in the context of an international or internal armed conflict, provided the following requirements are met:

(i) the violation must constitute an infringement of a rule of international humanitarian law;

(ii) the rule must be customary in nature or, if it belongs to treaty law, the required conditions must be met;

(iii) the violation must be "serious", that is to say, it must constitute a breach of a rule protecting important values, and the breach must involve grave consequences for the victim;

---

[91] Para. 74.
[92] Para. 132.
[93] Para. 133.

(iv) the violation of the rule must entail, under customary or conventional law, the individual criminal responsibility of the person breaching the rule.[94]

PROSECUTOR V. FURUNDŽIJA, *Decision on the Defendant's Motion to Dismiss Counts 13 and 14 of the Indictment (Lack of Subject Matter Jurisdiction)*, IT-95-17/1-T, 29 May 1998, Mumba, Cassese & May, JJ.

Based on the *Tadić Jurisdictional Decision*, the Trial Chamber found that the relationship between Articles 2 and 3 could be described as one of concentric circles. Grave breaches are a species of violation of the laws or customs of war. When an act meets the criteria of a grave breach under Article 2 and therefore also Article 3, it falls within the subject matter jurisdiction of the more specific clause, namely Article 2.[95]

The Chamber reasoned that all grave breaches are violations of the laws and customs of war and can be charged under Articles 2 and 3, if the criteria for both provisions are satisfied. However, according to the doctrine of speciality, *lex specialis derogat generali*, in a choice between two provisions where one has a broader scope and completely encompasses the other, the more specific charge should be chosen.[96]

In the instant case, the Prosecution had withdrawn the specific charge alleging grave breaches of the Geneva Conventions, pursuant to Article 2 of the Statute. The Chamber found that the Prosecution was justified in relying on Article 3 of the Statute - the residual clause - to ensure that no serious violation of international humanitarian law escapes the jurisdiction of the International Tribunal.[97]

Nature of the Armed Conflict

The Chamber reiterated the findings in the Decision of the Appeals Chamber by agreeing that the nature of the armed conflict is irrelevant when acts are committed in violation of the minimum rules in Common Article 3 and that Article 3 of the Statute implicitly refers, *inter alia,* to the customary rules arising from Common Article 3. Common Article 3 specifically prohibits, *inter alia*, violence to life and person, in particular murder of all kinds, mutilation, cruel treatment and torture, and also prohibits outrages upon personal dignity, in particular humiliating and degrading treatment.[98]

The Judges noted that Common Article 3 is expressed in the Geneva Conventions as being applicable in the case of "armed conflict not of an international character," that is, internal armed conflicts. However, it accepted that the rules contained in Common Article 3 reflected "elementary considerations of humanity" applicable under customary international law to any armed conflict, whether it is of internal or international character.

---

[94] Para. 258.
[95] Para. 11.
[96] Para. 12.
[97] Para. 12.
[98] Para. 14.

The indictment in the *Furundžija* case alleged that the conflict was international and the Trial Chamber held that the Prosecution could rely on the rules of customary international law emerging from Common Article 3 and therefore Furundžija could be charged with violating Article 3 of the Statute.[99]

4. DEFINITION OF ARTICLE 3 OFFENSES

A. RAPE

PROSECUTOR V. FURUNDŽIJA, *Judgement,* IT-95-17/1-T, 10 December 1998, Mumba, Cassese & May, JJ.

The Trial Chamber found that the Tribunal has temporal, territorial and subject matter jurisdiction over torture and outrages upon personal dignity including rape under Article 3 of its Statute.[100]

PROSECUTOR V. FURUNDŽIJA, *Decision on the Defendant's Motion to Dismiss Counts 13 and 14 of the Indictment (Lack of Subject Matter Jurisdiction),* IT-95-17/1-T, 29 May 1998, Mumba, Cassese & May, JJ.

The Trial Chamber held that torture and outrages upon personal dignity including rape are covered by Article 3 of the Statute, as acts prohibited under customary international law at all times. In times of armed conflict, they also amount to violations of the laws or customs of war, which include the prohibitions in The Hague Conventions of 1907 and Common Article 3.[101]

PROSECUTOR V. DELALIĆ, *et. al., Judgement,* Case No. IT-96-21-T, 16 November 1998, Karibi-Whyte, Odio-Benito & Jan, JJ.

See a full report on Article 3 issues in this Judgement under Article 2.

---

[99] Para. 14.

[100] Para. 259. At paragraph 158, the Trial Chamber refers to its Decision of 29 May 1998 (Decision on the Defendant's Motion to Dismiss Counts 13 and 14 of the Indictment) wherein the Trial Chamber held that Article 3 covers torture and outrages upon personal dignity, including rape.

[101] Para. 13.

B.   UNLAWFUL ATTACK AGAINST CIVILIANS AND ATTACK UPON CIVILIAN PROPERTY

PROSECUTOR V BLAŠKIĆ, *Judgement,* IT-95-14-T, 3 March 2000, Jorda, Rodrigues & Shahabuddeen, JJ.

The Chamber wrote, as follows:

> The Trial Chamber deems that the attack must have caused deaths and/or serious bodily injury within the civilian population or damage to civilian property. The parties to the conflict are obliged to attempt to distinguish between military targets and civilian persons or property. Targeting civilians or civilian property is an offence when not justified by military necessity. Civilians within the meaning of Article 3 are persons who are not, or no longer, members of the armed forces. Civilian property covers any property that could not be legitimately considered a military objective. Such an attack must have been conducted intentionally in the knowledge, or when it was impossible not to know, that civilians or civilian property were being targeted not through military necessity.[102]

C.   VIOLENCE TO LIFE AND PERSON

PROSECUTOR V BLAŠKIĆ, *Judgement,* IT-95-14-T, 3 March 2000, Jorda, Rodrigues & Shahabuddeen, JJ.

As to the term "violence to life and person," the Chamber said:

> This offence appears in Article 3(1)(a) common to the Geneva Conventions. It is a broad offence which, at first glance, encompasses murder, mutilation, cruel treatment and torture and which is accordingly defined by the cumulation of the elements of these specific offences. The offence is to be linked to those of Article 2(a) (wilful killing), Article 2(b) (inhuman treatment) and Article 2(c) (causing serious injury to body) of the Statute. The Defence contended that the specific intent to commit violence to life and person must be demonstrated. The Trial Chamber considers that the *mens rea* is characterised once it has been established that the accused intended to commit violence to the life or person of the victims deliberately or through recklessness.[103]

---

[102] Para. 180.
[103] Para. 182.

D.   DEVASTATION OF PROPERTY

PROSECUTOR V BLAŠKIĆ, *Judgement,* IT-95-14-T, 3 March 2000, Jorda, Rodrigues & Shahabuddeen, JJ.

In defining the term "devastation of property," the Chamber said:

> Similar to the grave breach constituting part of Article 2(d) of the Statute, the devastation of property is prohibited except where it may be justified by military necessity. So as to be punishable, the devastation must have been perpetrated intentionally or have been the foreseeable consequence of the acts of the accused.[104]

E.   PLUNDER OF PUBLIC OR PRIVATE PROPERTY

PROSECUTOR V BLAŠKIĆ, *Judgement,* IT-95-14-T, 3 March 2000, Jorda, Rodrigues & Shahabuddeen, JJ.

The Chamber defined the elements of "plunder of public or private property," as follows:

> The prohibition on the wanton appropriation of enemy public or private property extends to both isolated acts of plunder for private interest and to the "organized seizure of property undertaken within the framework of a systematic economic exploitation of occupied territory. Plunder "should be understood to embrace all forms of unlawful appropriation of property in armed conflict for which individual criminal responsibility attaches under international law, including those acts traditionally described as 'pillage".[105]

F.   DESTRUCTION OR WILFUL DAMAGE TO INSTITUTIONS DEDICATED TO RELIGION OR EDUCATION

PROSECUTOR V BLAŠKIĆ, *Judgement,* IT-95-14-T, 3 March 2000, Jorda, Rodrigues & Shahabuddeen, JJ.

The Trial Chamber provided the following analysis:

> The damage or destruction must have been committed intentionally to institutions which may clearly be identified as dedicated to religion or education and which were not being used for military purposes at the time of the acts. In addition, the institutions must not have been in the immediate vicinity of military objectives.[106]

---

[104] Para. 183.

[105] Para. 184, quoting from the *Čelebići* Judgement at paras. 590-591. It must be noted that the *Čelebići* Trial Chamber refused to find plunder since the acts described in the evidence were *de minimis* and, therefore, did not rise to the level of "serious" violations.

[106] Para. 185.

G.   CRUEL TREATMENT

PROSECUTOR V BLAŠKIĆ, *Judgement,* IT-95-14-T, 3 March 2000, Jorda, Rodrigues & Shahabuddeen, JJ.

Amoung the forms of "cruel treatment," the Chamber found the following:

> The Defence asserted *inter alia* that using human shields and trench digging constituted cruel treatment only if the victims were foreigners in enemy territory, inhabitants of an occupied territory or detainees. The Trial Chamber is of the view that treatment may be cruel whatever the status of the person concerned.

The Trial Chamber adopted the *Čelebići* definition of this offence.[107]

H.   TAKING OF HOSTAGES

PROSECUTOR V BLAŠKIĆ, *Judgement,* IT-95-14-T, 3 March 2000, Jorda, Rodrigues & Shahabuddeen, JJ.

The Chamber delivered the following explanation of the law regarding the taking of hostages:

> The taking of hostages is prohibited by Article 3(b) common to the Geneva Conventions which is covered by Article 3 of the Statute. The commentary defines hostages as follows:
>
> > . . . hostages are nationals of a belligerent State who of their own free will or through compulsion are in the hands of the enemy and are answerable with their freedom or their life for the execution of his orders and the security of his armed forces.[108]
>
> Consonant with the spirit of the Fourth Convention, the Commentáry sets out that the term "hostage" must be understood in the broadest sense. The definition of hostages must be understood as being similar to that of civilians taken as hostages within the meaning of grave breaches under Article 2 of the Statute, that is - persons unlawfully deprived of their freedom, often wantonly and sometimes under threat of death. The parties did not contest that to be characterised as hostages the detainees must have been used to obtain some advantage or to ensure that a belligerent, or other person or other group of persons enter into some undertaking.[109]

---

[107] Para. 186.
[108] Quoting from the Commentary to the Geneva Convention of 1949.
[109] Para. 187.

I.   OUTRAGES UPON PERSONAL DIGNITY

PROSECUTOR V. ALEKSOVSKI, *Judgement*, IT-95-14/1-T, 25 June 1999, Rodriguez, Vohrah & Nieto-Navia, JJ.

Aleksovski was charged with "outrages upon personal dignity" under Articles 3, 7(1) and 7(3). Relying on the *Tadić Jurisdictional Decision*, the Trial Chamber held that Article 3 of the Statute incorporates Common Article 3 of the four Geneva Conventions, namely Article 3(1)(c) which prohibits outrages upon personal dignity, and, in particular humiliating and degrading treatment.[110]

Actus reus

The Chamber found that the act constituting an outrage upon personal dignity must cause serious humiliation or degradation to the victim. The act need not directly harm the physical or mental well-being of the victim. However, the act must cause real and lasting suffering to the individual arising from humiliation or ridicule. The Chamber found that the *actus reus* of the offense requires an objective element, namely, the humiliation of the victim must be so intense that a reasonable person would be outraged. This objective ingredient is intended to ensure that the accused is safeguarded against the unfairness of a subjective test that would depend not on the gravity of the act wholly but on the sensitivities of the victim.[111]

Mens Rea

The Chamber held that the accused must have committed the act with the intent to humiliate or ridicule the victim. The perpetrator must have acted deliberately or have deliberately omitted to act and need not have the specific intent to humiliate or degrade the victim. He must be able to perceive such results to be the foreseeable consequences of his actions.[112]

General Observations

The Chamber observed that the seriousness of an act or its consequences may arise either from the nature of the act *per se* or from the repetition of an act or from a combination of different acts which, taken individually, would not constitute a crime within the meaning of Article 3. In other words, the Trial Chamber stated that factors such as the form, severity and duration of violence, or the intensity and duration of physical or mental suffering would be determinative.[113]

---

[110] Para. 48.
[111] Para. 56.
[112] Para. 56.
[113] Para. 57.

36

ARTICLE 4

GENOCIDE

1.   THE INTERNATIONAL TRIBUNAL SHALL HAVE THE POWER TO PROSECUTE PERSONS COMMITTING GENOCIDE AS DEFINED IN PARAGRAPH 2 OF THIS ARTICLE OR OF COMMITTING ANY OF THE OTHER ACTS ENUMERATED IN PARAGRAPH 3 OF THIS ARTICLE.

2.   GENOCIDE MEANS ANY OF THE FOLLOWING ACTS COMMITTED WITH INTENT TO DESTROY, IN WHOLE OR IN PART, A NATIONAL, ETHNICAL, RACIAL OR RELIGIOUS GROUP, AS SUCH:

    (A)   KILLING MEMBERS OF THE GROUP;

    (B)   CAUSING SERIOUS BODILY OR MENTAL HARM TO MEMBERS OF THE GROUP;

    (C)   DELIBERATELY INFLICTING ON THE GROUP CONDITIONS OF LIFE CALCULATED TO BRING ABOUT ITS PHYSICAL DESTRUCTION IN WHOLE OR IN PART;

    (D)   IMPOSING MEASURES INTENDED TO PREVENT BIRTHS WITHIN THE GROUP;

    (E)   FORCIBLY TRANSFERRING CHILDREN OF THE GROUP TO ANOTHER GROUP.

3. THE FOLLOWING ACTS SHALL BE PUNISHABLE:

    (A)   GENOCIDE;

    (B)   CONSPIRACY TO COMMIT GENOCIDE;

    (C)   DIRECT AND PUBLIC INCITEMENT TO COMMIT GENOCIDE;

    (D)   ATTEMPT TO COMMIT GENOCIDE;

    (E)   COMPLICITY IN GENOCIDE.

I.   COMMENTARY

Case law from both the Tribunal for the former Yugoslavia and for Rwanda is presented below. Article 5 of the ICTY Statute is identical to Article 2 of the ICTR Statute.

II.   TRIBUNAL CASES

B.   Trial Chambers

PROSECUTOR V. JELISIĆ, *Judgement*, IT-95-10-T, 14 December 1999, Jorda, Riad & Rodriguez, JJ.

Actus Reus

Killing Members of the Group

The Chamber ruled that the material element of the offence of genocide is constituted by one or more of the acts enumerated in Article 4(2) of the Statute.[114]

In the instant case, the accused was charge with murder pursuant to Article 4(2)(a). Relying on the *Akayesu* Judgement, the Chamber ruled that the term "meurtre" in the French text was a more exact and favourable 8.term for the accused than "killing" used in the English text of the Statute. The Chamber applied general principles of criminal law by which the interpretation that most benefits the accused must be chosen. Thus, the term "meurtre" or murder was used by the Trial Chamber.

Mens Rea

Intent to Destroy, In Whole or In Part, a National, Ethnical, Racial or Religious Group

The Chamber ruled that the specific *mens rea* of genocide distinguishes it from ordinary crime and other crimes of international humanitarian law. Genocide is committed when the underlying act is perpetrated with the intent to destroy, in whole or in part, a national, ethnical, racial or religious group. It is an act committed against an individual because of his or her membership in a particular group as an incremental step in the overall objective of destroying the group.[115]

The Discriminatory Nature of the Acts

The Chamber determined that the victim of genocide is chosen because he or she is part of a group that the perpetrator is seeking to destroy. It is the membership of the individual in a particular group rather than the identity of the individual that is the decisive criterion in determining the immediate victims of the crime of genocide.[116]

The Chamber ruled that genocide is closely related to the crime of persecution, one of the forms of crimes against humanity. The perpetrator of a crime of persecution chooses his victims because they belong to a specific group. A crime characterised as genocide constitutes a crime against humanity within the meaning of persecution.[117]

---

[114] Para. 62.
[115] Para. 66.
[116] Para. 67.
[117] Para. 68.

Groups Protected by Article 4 of the Statute

Article 4 protects individuals belonging to a national, ethnical, racial or religious group and excludes members of political groups.[118] The Chamber found that members of a religious group could be determined using objective criteria. However, in the case of national, ethnical and racial groups objective criteria are not always easily applied in determining the national, ethnic or racial identity of an individual. The status of a national, ethnical or racial group must be analysed from the point of view of those who wish to single that group out from the rest of the community. The Chamber concluded that the victimized group may either consider itself a separate group because of a common language or culture, or it may be identified as a distinct group by others, including the perpetrators of the crimes, for those same reasons.[119]

The Chamber ruled that a group might be identified and stigmatized according to positive or negative criteria. A positive approach consists of identifying victims by their inclusion in a group. The perpetrators distinguish a group according to national, ethnical, racial or religious makeup, *i.e.*, a particular group is targeted by the perpetrators. A negative approach consists of identifying victims by exclusion. Individuals, from one or more groups, are not considered to be part of the group to which the perpetrator belongs, *i.e.* all groups other than the perpetrators.[120]

Proof of Discriminatory Intent

The factors that may be taken into account when determining the discriminatory intent of the accused are the general context in which the acts occurred, the statements and deeds of the accused and that the acts of the accused occurred against the backdrop of the widespread and systematic violence being committed against only one specific group. This combination of factors would show that the accused chose his victims discriminatorily.[121]

The Intent to Destroy the Group, in Whole or in Part

Genocide requires proof of a "special" form of criminal intent: discriminatory intent coupled with the intention to carry out a wider plan to destroy the discriminated group in whole or in part, as such.[122]

Definition

The Chamber held that an act of genocide requires proof that it is committed with an ulterior motive, which is to destroy, in whole or in part, the group of which the individual

---

[118] Para. 69.
[119] Para. 70.
[120] Para. 71.
[121] Para. 73.
[122] Para. 78.

is just one element. Genocide thus differs from the crime of persecution in which the perpetrator chooses his victims because they belong to a specific community but does not necessarily seek to destroy the community as such.[123]

The Chamber addressed two aspects of the issue of genocidal intent: (i) the proportion of the group which is marked for destruction and beyond what threshold could the crime be qualified as genocide and (ii) whether genocide may be committed within a restricted geographical zone.

Proportion of the Group and the Threshold to Qualify the Acts as Genocide

The Chamber found that genocidal intent might manifest itself in two forms.[124] First, it may consist of desiring the extermination of a very large number of the members of the group, in which case it would constitute an intention to destroy a group *en masse*. Second, it may also consist of the desired destruction of a more limited number of persons selected for the impact that their disappearance would have upon the survival of the group as such. This would then constitute an intention to destroy the group "selectively."

Genocide requires a showing that acts are committed with the intent of destroying a group "in whole or in part." On the one hand, it is not necessary to demonstrate that it was intended to achieve the complete annihilation of a group from every corner of the globe. On the other hand, the intent to destroy a group "in part" means that a "substantial" number of individuals are targeted either because the intent sought is to harm a large majority of the group or the most representative members of the group, such as civic, religious, academic and intellectual and business leaders. The selective targeting of the leaders in a group may amount to genocide if the remaining members of the group are deported or forced to flee.[125]

Genocide in a Restricted Geographical Zone

The Chamber held that under international custom acts might be characterized as genocide even when the exterminatory intent only extends to a limited geographic zone.

The Chamber accepted that although genocide may occur within a region of a country it expressed reservations that genocide could occur in restricted areas in the course of isolated events.[126]

The Degree of Intention Required

Before examining whether the accused had the intention to commit genocide, the Chamber made a finding that the Prosecution had failed to prove beyond reasonable doubt that there existed a plan to destroy the Muslim group in Brčko or elsewhere within which the accused committed murder.[127] Based on the evidence, the Chamber was unable to conclude that the choice of victims arose from a precise logic to destroy the most

---

[123] Para. 79.
[124] Para. 82.
[125] Para. 82.
[126] Para. 83.
[127] Para. 98.

representative figures of the Muslim community in Brčko to the point of threatening the survival of that community.[128]

As for the intention of the accused to commit genocide, the Chamber held that he singled out Muslims and killed arbitrarily rather than with the clear intention to destroy a group. The Chamber found that it was not proved beyond reasonable doubt that the accused was motivated by the *dolus specialis* of the crime of genocide.[129]

C.   ICTR TRIAL CHAMBERS

PROSECUTOR V. MUSEMA, *Judgement*, ICTR-96-13-T, 27 January 2000, Aspegren, Kama, Pillay, JJ.

Musema was convicted of genocide and crimes against humanity. He received a life sentence.

Conspiracy to Commit Genocide

The Chamber determined that such a conspiracy requires an agreement between two or more persons to commit the crime of genocide. The same intent is required as that required for genocide itself. It is the process of the conspiracy that is punishable, not the result. An accused can only be convicted of conspiracy if the substantive offence has not been realized or if the accused is part of a conspiracy that has been perpetrated by his co-conspirators, without his direct participation.

The Chamber recognized that under the common law an accused could, in principle, be convicted of both conspiracy and the substantive offense. The Chamber however adopted the definition most favourable to Musema, whereby the accused cannot be convicted of both genocide and conspiracy to commit genocide on the basis of the same acts. The Chamber determined that this reflects the intention of the drafters of the Genocide Convention.[130]

PROSECUTOR V. KAYISHEMA & RUZINDANA, *Judgement*, ICTR-95-5-T, 21 May 1999, Sekule, Ostrovsky & Khan, JJ.

Both defendants in this case were convicted of genocide. Kayishema had served as the Prefect of Kibuye and Ruzindana had been a commercial trader in Kigali.

The Chamber determined that the definition of genocide is based on the definition of Crimes Against Humanity. The major difference is that genocide requires proof of specific intent.

Mens Rea

The Trial Chamber determined that for the crime of genocide to occur, *mens rea* must be formed prior to commission of the genocidal acts. The individual acts do not require

---

[128] Para. 93.
[129] Para. 108.
[130] Paras. 185, 192, 193 & 196.

premeditation; the only consideration is that the act should be done in furtherance of genocidal intent.[131]

Proof of the Requisite Intent

Intent can be inferred either from words or deeds and may be demonstrated by a pattern of purposeful action. The Chamber considered evidence such as the physical targeting of the group or their property; use of derogatory language toward members of the targeted group; weapons employed and the extent of bodily injury; the methodical way of planning and the systematic manner of killing. The number of victims from the group is also important.

Although a specific plan to destroy does not constitute an element of genocide, it is not easy to carry out genocide without such a plan, or organization. The Chamber concurred with the view of Morris and Scharf that "it is virtually impossible for the crime of genocide to be committed without some direct involvement on the part of the state given the magnitude of this crime ...it is unnecessary for an individual to have knowledge of all details of the genocidal plan or policy."[132]

Destruction of a Group

This may include sexual violence and "it is not necessary to intend to achieve the complete annihilation of a group from every corner of the globe" (ILC).[133]

Whole or in Part

The Chamber suggested that both proportionate scale and total number are relevant. The Chamber determined that "in part" requires an intention to destroy a considerable number of individuals who are part of the group.[134]

National, Ethnical, Racial, Religious Group

Ethnic Group: Members share a common language and culture; or a group that distinguishes itself as such; or a group identified as such by others, including perpetrators of the crimes.

Racial Group: Based on hereditary physical traits often identified with geography.

Religious Group: Denomination, mode of worship, sharing common beliefs.[135]

---

[131] Para. 91
[132] Paras. 93,94.
[133] Para. 95.
[134] Para. 96.
[135] Para. 98

Actus Reus

Killing Members of the Group

The Chamber found virtually no difference between "killing" in the English version and "meurtre" in the French version and the word should be considered along with the specific intent of genocide.

Causing Serious Bodily or Mental Harm

This issue was the subject of contention during closing submissions of parties. The Chamber concluded the following.

Serious bodily harm: This is to be determined on a case-by-case basis using a common-sense approach, *e.g.* harm that seriously injures the health, causes disfigurement or causes any serious injury to the external or internal organs or senses.

Serious mental harm: Should also be determined on a case-by-case basis.[136]

Deliberately Inflicting on the Group Conditions of Life Calculated to Bring About its Physical Destruction in Whole or in Part

The Judges determined that this includes circumstances that will lead to a slow death, *e.g.*, lack of proper housing, clothing, hygiene, medical care or excessive work or exertion. It also includes methods of destruction which do not immediately lead to the death of members of the group, *e.g.* rape, starving, reducing medical services below a minimum, withholding sufficient living accommodation, provided this would lead to destruction of the group in whole or in part. The Chamber concurs with *Akayesu* on measures intended to prevent births and forcibly transferring children.[137]

PROSECUTOR V. AKAYESU, *Judgement*, ICTR-96-4-T, 2 September 1998, Kama, Aspegren & Pillay, JJ.

Killing Members of the Group, Article 2(2)(a)

In the French version of the Statute the word "muertre" is used. "Killing," as used in the English version is too general, since it could include both intentional and unintentional homicides. "Meurtre" is more precise.

Given the presumption of innocence and pursuant to general principles of criminal law, the Chamber held that the version of the Statute more favourable to the accused should be upheld and found that this Article must be interpreted in accordance with the definition of murder given in the Penal Code of Rwanda, according to which "muertre" is homicide committed with intent to cause death.[138]

---

[136] Paras. 108-110.
[137] Paras. 115-118.
[138] Para. 500-501.

Causing Serious Bodily or Mental Harm, Article 2(2)(b)

It is not necessary that the harm caused be permanent and irremediable. The Chamber took this section to cover acts of torture, whether bodily or mental, inhumane or degrading treatment or persecution. The Chamber specifically did not limit itself to this definition, however.[139]

Deliberately Inflicting on the Group Conditions of Life Calculated to Bring About its Physical Destruction in Whole or in Part, Article 2(2)(c)

The Judges determined that this section should be construed as the methods of destruction by which the perpetrator does not immediately kill the members of the group, but which, ultimately, seeks their physical destruction. This includes, *inter alia,* subjecting a group to a subsistence diet, systematic expulsion from homes, or reduction of essential medical services below the minimum requirement.

Imposing Measures Intended to Prevent Births Within the Group, Article 2(2)(d)

Such measures should be construed as sexual mutilation, sterilization, forced birth control, separation of sexes, prohibition of marriages and (in patriarchal societies) deliberate impregnation by a man of another group. These measures may be physical or mental. Groups can be lead through trauma not to procreate.[140]

Forcibly Transferring Children of the Group to Another Group, Article 2(2)(e)

The objective of this section is to sanction not only direct acts of this nature, but also acts of threat or trauma.[141]

Definition of Group: National, Ethnical, Racial, Religious

The *travaux préparatoires* of the Genocide Convention considered "groups" to be stable groups, constituted in a permanent fashion, membership of which is determined by birth. Mobile groups that are joined by a voluntary commitment are excluded. Membership in any of the four groups, national, ethnical, racial or religious, is not normally challengeable by its members, who belong to the group automatically, by birth, in a continuous and often irremediable manner.

A National Group is a collection of people who are perceived to share a legal bond based on common citizenship, coupled with reciprocity of rights and duties.

An Ethnic Group is a group whose members share a common language or culture.

A Racial Group is a grouping based on heredity and physical traits often identified with a geographical region, irrespective of linguistic, cultural, national or religious factors.

---

[139] Para. 502, 504.
[140] Paras. 507, 508.
[141] Para. 509.

A Religious Group is one in which the members share the same religion, denomination or mode of worship.

The Chamber determined that the intent of the drafters of the Genocide Convention was to ensure protection of any stable and permanent group and implied that groups should not be limited to those expressly protected.[142]

Intent

Special intent is the key element of an intentional offence. Such an offence is characterized by a psychological relationship between the physical result and the mental state of the perpetrator. To be genocide the act charged, such as murder, extends beyond its actual commission to the ulterior motive of destroying, in whole or in part, the group to which the individual belongs.

Specific intent of an offender is a mental factor that is difficult or even impossible to determine. In the absence of a confession from the accused, intent can be inferred from a certain number of presumptions of fact. The Chamber considered that it was possible to deduce the genocidal intent inherent in a particular charged act from the general context of the perpetration of other culpable acts systematically directed against that same group, whether these acts were committed by the accused or others. Other factors, such as the scale of the atrocities committed, their general nature, or the fact of deliberately and systematically targeting victims on account of their membership in a particular group, while excluding the members of other groups, could enable the Chamber to infer the genocidal intent of a particular act.[143]

Complicity in Genocide

Complicity necessarily implies the commission of Genocide as a principle offense. Complicity is sometimes described as "borrowed criminality." The conduct of the accomplice emerges as a crime when the crime has been consummated by the principle perpetrator(s). The accomplice has not committed an autonomous crime but merely facilitated the criminal enterprise carried out by others. It must be proven beyond a reasonable doubt that genocide was actually carried out before an accused may be convicted of complicity in genocide.

The Chamber determined that one could be tried for complicity even when the actual perpetrator of the genocide is neither tried nor convicted.[144]

An individual cannot be both the principle perpetrator of an act and the accomplice thereto. An act with which the accused is charged cannot be characterised both as an act of genocide and an act of complicity in genocide. The two are mutually exclusive.[145]

---

[142] Paras. 511-516.
[143] Paras 518-524.
[144] But, can one be convicted of Complicity if the actual perpetrator is acquitted. A Chamber could find that genocide was proved in the complicity case and not proved in the actual perpetrator's case. What then?
[145] Paras. 527-532.

Actus Reus of Complicity

The *actus reus* involves instigation, aiding and abetting or procuring the means by which the offense is committed. These include incitement through speeches, dissemination of written material or harbouring or aiding a criminal. Complicity by aiding and abetting implies a positive action that excludes, in principle, complicity by failure to act or by omission. The Chamber arrived at its definition of complicity by reference to the Penal Code of Rwanda.

Complicity - Intent

An accomplice must have acted knowingly, however willingness to participate in the principle offense need not be established. The intent of the accomplice is to knowingly aid or abet one or more persons to commit the crime of genocide. An accomplice to genocide need not necessarily possess the *dolus specialis* of genocide.

The *mens rea* required for complicity in genocide is knowledge of the genocidal plan, coupled with the *actus reus* of participation in the execution of such plan.

An accused is liable as an accomplice to genocide if he knowingly aided and abetted or instigated one or more persons in the commission of genocide while knowing that such persons were committing genocide, even though the accused himself did not have the specific intent to destroy, in whole or in part, a defined group.[146]

Statute and Complicity

Where a person is accused of aiding and abetting, planning, preparing or executing genocide, specific genocidal intent must be proven. Complicity requires a positive act, whereas aiding and abetting that is not complicity may consist in failing to act or refraining from action.[147]

---

[146] Paras. 538-545.
[147] Paras. 547, 548.

ARTICLE 5

CRIMES AGAINST HUMANITY

THE INTERNATIONAL TRIBUNAL SHALL HAVE THE POWER TO PROSECUTE PERSONS RESPONSIBLE FOR THE FOLLOWING CRIMES WHEN COMMITTED IN ARMED CONFLICT, WHETHER INTERNATIONAL OR INTERNAL IN CHARACTER, AND DIRECTED AGAINST ANY CIVILIAN POPULATION:

(A)   MURDER;

(B)   EXTERMINATION;

(C)   ENSLAVEMENT;

(D)   DEPORTATION;

(E)   IMPRISONMENT;

(F)   TORTURE;

(G)   RAPE;

(H)   PERSECUTIONS ON POLITICAL, RACIAL AND RELIGIOUS GROUNDS;

(I)   OTHER INHUMANE ACTS.

I.   COMMENTARY

In the *Kupreskić Judgement*, the Trial Chamber stated that the Security Council defined crimes against humanity more narrowly than is necessary under customary international law.[148] In the *Tadić Jurisdictional Decision*, the Appeals Chamber ruled that it is a settled rule of customary international law that crimes against humanity do not require a connection to any conflict at all.[149]

However, since the Statute governs, an armed conflict is a required element under Article 5.

---

[148] Para. 545.

[149] Prosecutor v. Tadić, *Decision on the Defence Motion for Interlocutory Appeal on Jurisdiction*, IT-94-1-AR72, 2 October 1995, para. 141.

II.   TRIBUNAL CASES

A.   APPEALS CHAMBER

1. SCOPE OF ARTICLE 5

PROSECUTOR V. TADIĆ, *Decision on the Defence Motion for Interlocutory Appeal on Jurisdiction*, IT-94-1-AR72, 2 October 1995, Cassese, Li, Deschênes, Abi-Saab & Sidhwa, JJ.

At trial, Tadić contended that Article 5 derived from the Nuremberg Charter and its coverage was limited to international armed conflicts, notwithstanding its specific language that provides that it applies to both international and internal armed conflicts. It was argued that the language seeking to apply it to internal armed conflicts violated the principle of *nullum crimen sine lege.*

    The Appeals Chamber determined that is was settled international customary law that crimes against humanity apply in the context of both international and internal armed conflicts and that there is, thus, no violation of the principle of *nullum crimen sine lege.*[150]

2. COMMITTED FOR A PURELY PERSONAL MOTIVE

PROSECUTOR V. TADIĆ, *Judgement*, IT-94-1-A, 15 JULY 1999, Shahabuddeen, Cassese, Tieya, Nieto-Navia & Mumba, JJ.

The Trial Chamber found that a crime against humanity could not be committed if the perpetrator's motive was purely personal. Both parties to the appeal conceded that this finding had no impact on the verdict. The Appeals Chamber, however, decided to resolve the issue since it was a matter of some importance to the Tribunal's jurisprudence. After reviewing a number of World War II cases, the Chamber reached the following conclusions:

> The Trial Chamber correctly recognised that crimes which are unrelated to widespread or systematic attacks on a civilian population should not be prosecuted as crimes against humanity. Crimes against humanity are crimes of a special nature to which a greater degree of moral turpitude attaches than to an ordinary crime. Thus to convict an accused of crimes against humanity, it must be proved that the crimes were *related* to the attack on a civilian population (occurring during an armed conflict) and that the accused *knew* that his crimes were so related.[151] (Chamber's emphasis)

---

[150] Paras. 141, 142.
[151] Para. 271.

For the above reasons, however, the Appeals Chamber does not consider it necessary to further require, as a substantive element of *mens rea,* a nexus between the specific acts allegedly committed by the accused and the armed conflict, or to require proof of the accused's motives. Consequently, in the opinion of the Appeals Chamber, the requirement that an act must not have been carried out for the purely personal motives of the perpetrator does not form part of the prerequisites necessary for conduct to fall within the definition of a crime against humanity under Article 5 of the Tribunal's Statute.[152]

3. DISCRIMINATORY INTENT

PROSECUTOR V. TADIĆ, *Judgement,* IT-94-1-A, 15 JULY 1999, Shahabuddeen, Cassese, Tieya, Nieto-Navia & Mumba, JJ.

The Trial Chamber had determined that all crimes against humanity require the showing of a discriminatory intent. The Prosecutor challenged this finding in its Cross-Appeal. The Appeals Chamber agreed with the Prosecutor.

The Appeals Chamber first interpreted Article 5 in light of the standard rules for interpreting treaties as announced by the International Court of Justice. That requires that the language be given its "natural and ordinary meaning in the context in which they occur."[153] In this light the Chamber found as follows:

> The ordinary meaning of Article 5 makes it clear that this provision does not require all crimes against humanity to have been perpetrated with a discriminatory intent. Such intent is only made necessary for one sub-category of those crimes, namely "persecutions" provided for in Article 5(h).[154]

> The aim of those drafting the Statute was to make all crimes against humanity punishable, including those which, while fulfilling all the conditions required by the notion of such crimes, may not have been perpetrated on political, racial or religious grounds as specified in paragraph (h) of Article 5. In light of the humanitarian goals of the framers of the Statute, one fails to see why they should have seriously restricted the class of offences coming within the purview of "crimes against humanity", thus leaving outside this class all the possible instances of serious and widespread or systematic crimes against civilians on account only of their lacking a discriminatory intent.[155]

Next, the Chamber interpreted Article 5 in relation to customary international law. The Chamber presumed that the Security Council in drafting the Statute intended to remain within the confines of such rules. The Chamber looked at the Nuremberg and Tokyo

---

[152] Para. 272.
[153] Para. 282.
[154] Para. 283.
[155] Para. 285.

definitions of crimes against humanity and determined that they supported its conclusion as regards discriminatory intent.[156]

The Chamber then considered the effect of the Report of the Secretary-General in relation to the Statute. The Chamber conceded that its interpretation of the Statute did not conform to the Report. The Report stated that crimes against humanity are "those committed as part of a widespread or systematic attack against any civilian population on national, political, ethnic, racial or religious grounds."[157] The Chamber held that the Report of the Secretary-General does not have the same binding authority as does the Statute, but it must be viewed as "an authoritative interpretation of the Statute." Since there appears to be a conflict between the Report and the language of the Statute, the Judges ruled that the Statute must prevail:

> Furthermore, it may be argued that, in his Report, the Secretary-General was merely *describing* the notion of crimes against humanity in a general way, as opposed to stipulating a technical, legal definition intended to be binding on the Tribunal. In other words, the statement that crimes against humanity are crimes "committed as part of a widespread or systematic attack against any civilian population on national, political, ethnic, racial or religious grounds" amounts to the observation that crimes against humanity as *a matter of fact usually are* committed on such discriminatory grounds. It is not, however, a legal *requirement* that such discriminatory grounds be present. That is, at least, another possible interpretation. It is true that in most cases, crimes against humanity are waged against civilian populations which have been specifically targeted for national, political, ethnic, racial or religious reasons.[158] (Chamber's emphasis)

Finally, the Chamber looked at statements made by some members of the Security Council at the time of the adoption of the Statute. These statements were also in conflict with the position taken by the Chamber with regard to the interpretation of the Statute. The statement of the U.S. representative for instance tracked the language of the Secretary-General set out above. With regard to these statements of understanding, the Chamber found:

> The Appeals Chamber, first of all, rejects the notion that these three statements - at least as regards the issue of discriminatory intent - may be considered as part of the "context" of the Statute, to be taken into account for the purpose of interpretation of the Statute pursuant to the general rule of construction laid down in Article 31 of the Vienna Convention on the Law of the Treaties. In particular, those statements cannot be regarded as an "agreement" relating to the Statute, made between all the parties in connection with the adoption of the Statute. True, the United States representative pointed out that it was her understanding that the other members of the Security Council shared her views

---

[156] Para. 290.
[157] Report of the Secretary General, para. 48.
[158] Para. 297

regarding the "clarifications" she put forward. However, in light of the wording of the other two statements on the specific point at issue, and taking into account the lack of any comment by the other twelve members of the Security Council, it would seem difficult to conclude that there emerged an agreement in the Security Council designed to qualify the scope of Article 5 with respect to discriminatory intent. In particular, it must be stressed that the United States representative, in enumerating the discriminatory grounds required, in her view, for crimes against humanity, included one ground ("gender") that was not mentioned in the Secretary-General's Report and which was, more importantly, referred to neither by the French nor the Russian representatives in their declarations on Article 5. This, it may be contended, is further evidence that no agreement emerged within the Security Council as to the qualification concerning discriminatory intent.[159]

4. Crimes Against Humanity are More Serious than War Crimes

PROSECUTOR V. ERDEMOVIĆ, *Judgement,* IT-96-22-A, 7 October 1997, Cassese, McDonald, Li, Stephen & Vohrah, JJ.

The *Erdemović* case was remanded to a Trial Chamber to allow the defendant to enter a new plea since his initial plea had not been properly informed. Judges Cassese and Stephen joined the opinion of Judges McDonald and Vohrah. The basis upon which the Chamber determined that the Defendant had not been properly informed was the fact that he had pleaded guilty to a crime against humanity rather than a war crime when he had a choice between the two. The Chamber found that he should have been informed of the difference between the two offenses, a crime against humanity being more serious and ordinarily entailing a more severe sentence.[160]

B. Trial Chambers

PROSECUTOR V. BLAŠKIĆ, *Judgement,* IT-95-14-T, 3 March 2000, Jorda, Rodrigues & Shahabuddeen, JJ.

As a preamble to its discussion of crimes against humanity, the Chamber made the following comment:

> . . . for the "underlying crimes," each with its own characteristics, to be characterised as a crime against humanity, they must be part of a single category – that of widespread or systematic attack against a civilian population – which gives this offence its specificity and distinguishes it fundamentally from other

---

[159] Para. 300.

[160] Paras. 20 and 27. See Rule 101 for significant sentencing materials as to the relative seriousness of Article 2-5 offences.

violations of humanitarian law defined by the Statute.[161]

Systematic Attack

The Chamber determined that there are four elements that make up a systematic attack:

- The existence of a political objective, a plan pursuant to which the attack is perpetrated or an ideology, in the broad sense of the word, that is, to destroy, persecute or weaken a community;

- The perpetration of a criminal act on a very large scale against a group of civilians or the repeated and continuous commission of inhumane acts linked to one another;

- The preparation and use of significant public or private resources, whether military or other;

- The implication of high-level political and/or military authorities in the definition and establishment of the methodical plan.[162]

Civilian Population

With regard to what constitutes a civilian population, the Chamber wrote:

> Crimes against humanity therefore do not mean only acts committed against civilians in the strict sense of the term but include also crimes against two categories of people: those who were members of a resistance movement and former combatants - regardless of whether they wore wear (sic) uniform or not - but who were no longer taking part in hostilities when the crimes were perpetrated because they had either left the army or were no longer bearing arms or, ultimately, had been placed *hors de combat,* in particular, due to their wounds or their being detained. It also follows that the specific situation of the victim at the moment the crimes were committed, rather than his status, must be taken into account in determining his standing as a civilian. Finally, it can be concluded that the presence of soldiers within an intentionally targeted civilian population does not alter the civilian nature of that population.[163]

PROSECUTOR V. KUPREŠKIĆ *et.al., Judgement,* IT-95-16-T, 14 January 2000, Cassese, May & Mumba, JJ.

The Trial Chamber held that under Article 5 of the Statute, the essence of a crime against humanity is a systematic policy of a certain scale and gravity directed against a civilian population.[164]

---

[161] Para. 198
[162] Para. 203.
[163] Para. 214
[164] Para. 543.

The Trial Chamber cited the *Nikolić* Rule 61 decision for the proposition that crimes against humanity comprise the following distinct elements:

- The crimes must be directed at the civilian population, specifically identified as a group by the perpetrators of those acts.

- The crimes must, to a certain extent, be organised and systematic. Although they need not be related to a policy established at State level, in the conventional sense of the term, they cannot be the work of isolated individuals alone.

- The crimes, considered as a whole, must be of a certain scale and gravity.[165]

The Trial Chamber then ruled that there are three core elements of crimes against humanity:

- The requirement of an armed conflict

- Acts directed against a civilian population

- Knowledge of the wider context in which the acts occurred.

The Requirement of an Armed Conflict

The Chamber ruled that the characterization of the armed conflict as international or internal is immaterial to the application of Article 5 of the Statute, since the wording of this provision is that the Tribunal has jurisdiction over crimes against humanity committed in armed conflict, whether international or internal.

The Chamber determined the threshold question on the existence of an armed conflict by relying on the generally accepted test in the jurisprudence of the Tribunal which was first pronounced in the *Tadić Jurisdictional Decision*:[166] "an armed conflict can be said to exist whenever there is a resort to armed force between States or protracted armed violence between governmental authorities and organized armed groups or between such groups within a State."[167] The alleged acts must be linked geographically and temporally with the armed conflict.[168]

Acts Directed Against a Civilian Population

The Trial Chamber divided its analysis of the question of acts directed against a civilian population into three parts.

---

[165] Para. 543.
[166] Prosecutor v. Tadić, *Decision on the Defence Motion for Interlocutory Appeal on Jurisdiction*, IT-94-1-AR72, 2 October 1995
[167] Para. 545. Prosecutor v. Tadić, *Decision on the Defence Motion for Interlocutory Appeal on Jurisdiction*, IT-94-1-AR72, 2 October 1995, para. 70.
[168] Para. 546.

Directed Against a Civilian Population

The Chamber ruled that the words "civilian" and "population" are intended to have a wide definition. In particular, the term "civilian" includes not only those who were never involved in the conflict but also those who at one time bore arms during the conflict or who were actively involved in the conflict or who were actively involved in a resistance movement.[169] The Chamber relied on the language of the *Barbie* case for this broad interpretation of the term "civilian".[170] In that decision, the French Court of Cassation ruled that a crime against humanity could be committed against individuals on the basis of race or religion or because of their opposition to a policy directed against them, whatever form their opposition may take.[171] Underpinning this broad interpretation of the term "civilian" is the policy consideration of prohibiting crimes against humanity, no matter who are the victims of such acts.[172]

Crimes Against Humanity and an Isolated Act

In keeping with the decision of the Appeals Chamber in the *Tadić Judgement*, the Chamber ruled that crimes against humanity are generally speaking committed against the civilian population as a matter of policy of certain scale and gravity, and not as an isolated, random act. The relevant portion of the *Tadić Judgement* reads, as follows:

> [C]learly, a single act by a perpetrator taken within the context of a widespread or systematic attack against a civilian population entails individual criminal responsibility and an individual perpetrator need not commit numerous offences to be held liable. Although, it is correct that isolated, random acts should not be included in the definition of crimes against humanity, that is the purpose of requiring that the acts be directed against a civilian population and thus "[e]ven an isolate act can constitute a crime against humanity if it is the product of a political system based on terror or persecution".[173]

The Chamber accepts the distinction between an act that occurs as a part of a widespread campaign of illegal activity – which is a crime against humanity – and an isolated act that does not take place in such a context – which is not a crime against humanity.[174] Furthermore, the requirement that the occurrence of crimes be widespread or systematic is disjunctive. The Trial Chamber found support for this proposition in the *Tadić Judgement*:

> it is now well established that the requirement that the acts be directed against a civilian "population" can be fulfilled if the acts occur on either a widespread basis or in a systematic manner.[175]

---

[169] Para. 547-548.
[170] *The Barbie Case*, French Court of Cassation (Criminal Chamber), 20 Dec. 1985, 78 ILR 125.
[171] Para. 548.
[172] Para. 547.
[173] Para. 550, fn. 809. Prosecutor v. Tadić, *Judgement*, IT-94-1-A, 15 JULY 1999, para. 649.
[174] Para. 550.
[175] Para. 544.

The Policy Element

The Chamber found that the policy element that directs the acts that constitute crimes against humanity need not necessarily be explicitly formulated or be the policy of a state. The Chamber cited two decisions of the International Tribunal in support of this proposition[176]:

> *Tadić Judgement* (para. 653): "[t]he reason that crimes against humanity so shock the conscience of mankind and warrant intervention by the international community is because they are not isolated, random acts of individuals but rather result from a deliberate attempt to target a civilian population". (See, also para. 654)

> *Nikolić*, Rule 61: (para. 26): "Although they [crimes against humanity] need not be related to a policy established at State level, in the conventional sense, they cannot be the work of isolated individuals alone".

The Chamber held that crimes against humanity must be sponsored by a State, Government or entity holding *de facto* authority over a territory, be a part of the policy of such an authority, or, at least, be tolerated by such an authority.[177]

Furthermore, although the Chamber recognized that national case-law requires a showing of a link between an offence and a large-scale or systematic practice to characterize the offence as a crime against humanity, it ruled that there may be cases where the authors of such crimes are individuals having neither official status nor acting on behalf of a government authority. There must be a showing of explicit or implicit approval or endorsement by State or government authorities that there is a policy to encourage the commission of the offences or that such offences fit into such a policy.[178]

Knowledge of the Wider Context in which the Act Occurred: the *Mens Rea* requirement

The Chamber found that the requisite *mens rea* for crimes against humanity are twofold. There must be proof of the *intent* to commit the underlying offence, combined with *knowledge* of the broader context in which the offence occurs.[179] The Chamber adopted the following language from the *Kayishama* case on the issue of knowledge:

> [T]he perpetrator must knowingly commit crimes against humanity in the sense that he must understand the overall context of his act. [...] Part of what transforms an individual's act(s) into a crime against humanity is the inclusion of the act within a greater dimension of criminal conduct; therefore an accused should be aware of this greater dimension in order to be culpable thereof. Accordingly, actual or constructive knowledge of the broader context of the attack, meaning that the accused must know that his act(s) is part of a widespread or systematic attack on a civilian population and pursuant to some

---

[176] Para. 551, fn. 811.
[177] Para. 552.
[178] Paras. 554-555.
[179] Para. 556.

sort of policy or plan, is necessary to satisfy the requisite *mens rea* element of the accused.[180]

Moreover, the Chamber held that two aspects of the subjective requirement of crimes against humanity are now settled law. First, among the prohibited conduct as a crime against humanity pursuant to Article 5 of the Statute, discriminatory intent is not an essential ingredient of the *mens rea* of crimes against humanity, except for the offence of persecution where discrimination constitutes an integral element of the prohibited conduct. Second, the motives of the accused – as distinct from his intent – are not pertinent.[181]

1. ARTICLE 5(A): MURDER

PROSECUTOR V. BLAŠKIĆ, *Judgement,* **IT-95-14-T, 3 March 2000, Jorda, Rodrigues & Shahabuddeen, JJ.**

The Trial Chamber first contrasted the word "assassinat", used in the French version of the Statute with the word "murder" as used in the English version. The Chamber observed that these words have a different meaning, the French term describing pre-meditated murder. The Chamber determined that the English version must prevail. The elements of murder were then defined as:

- The death of the victim;

- The death must have resulted from an act of the accused or his subordinate;

- The accused or his subordinate must have been motivated by the intent to kill the victim or to cause grievous bodily harm in the reasonable knowledge that the attack was likely to result in death.[182]

PROSECUTOR V. KUPREŠKIĆ *et. al., Judgement,* **IT-95-16-T, 14 January 2000, Cassese, May & Mumba, JJ.**

Relying on the *Akayesu Judgement* from the Rwanda Tribunal, the Trial Chamber ruled that the constituent elements or *actus reus* for murder under Article 5(a) of the Statute are the following. The death of the victim is the result of the acts or omissions of the accused, where the conduct of the accused was a substantial cause of the death of the victim. The accused is guilty of murder, if he or she, engaging in unlawful conduct, intended to kill another person or to cause this person grievous bodily harm and has caused the death of that person.[183]

---

[180] Para. 557. Prosecutor v. Kayishema and Ruzindana, *Judgement*, ICTR-95-1-T, 21 May 1999, paras. 133-134.
[181] Para. 558.
[182] Para. 217.
[183] Para. 560.

Relying on both the *Akayesu* and *Kayishama Judgements*, the Chamber held that the *mens rea* for murder under Article 5(a) of the Statute is the intent to kill or the intent to inflict serious injury in reckless disregard of human life. The killing must be both premeditated and intentional. It is premeditated when the actor formulated his or her intent to kill after a cool moment of reflection. It is intentional when it is the actor's purpose, or the actor is aware that it will occur in the ordinary course of events.[184]

2. ARTICLE 5(H): PERSECUTION

PROSECUTOR V. BLAŠKIĆ, *Judgement,* IT-95-14-T, 3 March 2000, Jorda, Rodrigues & Shahabuddeen, JJ.

The Chamber observed that Nuremberg and the two ad-hoc Tribunals all sanction the offense of persecution as a crime against humanity. None, however, define its subcategories and the forms such sanctions may take. The Chamber thus felt it necessary to examine customary international law in an effort to define these sub-categories.

Serious Bodily and Mental Harm, Infringements upon Freedom and Attacks Against Property as Forms of Persecution

After a detailed analysis of the Nuremberg and Control Council 10 cases, the Chamber formulated definitions of the sub-categories relevant to the *Blaškić* case.

The Destruction and Plunder of Property

In the context of the crime of persecution, the destruction of property must be construed to mean the destruction of towns, villages and other public or private property belonging to a given civilian population or extensive devastation not justified by military necessity and carried out unlawfully, wantonly and discriminatorily. In the same context, the plunder of property is defined as the unlawful, extensive and wanton appropriation of property belonging to a particular population, whether it be the property of private individuals or of state or "quasi-state" public collectives.[185]

The Unlawful Detention of Civilians

The unlawful detention of civilians, as a form of the crime of persecution, means unlawfully depriving a group of discriminated civilians of their freedom.[186]

---

[184] Para. 561.
[185] Para. 234
[186] *Ibid.*

The Deportation or Forcible Transfer of Civilians

The deportation or forcible transfer of civilians means "forced displacement of the persons concerned by expulsion or other coercive acts from the area in which they are lawfully present, without grounds permitted under international law."[187]

PROSECUTOR V. KUPREŠKIĆ et. al., Judgement, IT-95-16-T, 14 January 2000, Cassese, May & Mumba, JJ.

Persecution, as a crime against humanity, has never been defined in international treaty law and international and national judicial decisions do not provide a common definition of this offence.

The Chamber made the following preliminary observations concerning persecution, which it considered settled matters of law and fact[188]:

- It can take diverse forms and need not require a physical element provided the element of discrimination is proved.[189]

- Under customary international law, from which Article 5 derogates, victims of crimes against humanity, including persecution, may be civilians and military personnel. The Trial Chamber relied on two decisions of the French Court of Cassation in *Barbie* and *Touvier* for the proposition that a crime against humanity may be committed against both civilian and military personnel.

- The prohibited conduct must be motivated by a discriminatory animus, which according to Article 5(h) is persecution on political, racial and religious grounds.

Furthermore, the Chamber found that:[190]

- Persecution consists of the occurrence of a persecutory act or omission; and

- A discriminatory basis is required for the act or omission on one of the listed grounds.

Specifically, in relation to persecution under Article 5 of the Statute, the Chamber found that a finding that a crime against humanity has been committed requires proof of widespread and systematic commission of the prohibited conduct and that "discriminatory purpose" applies to discrimination only under Article 5(h).[191] There is a possible overlap between some of the offences listed in Article 5, namely "extermination" involves "murder," "torture" may involve "rape" and "enslavement" and may involve "imprisonment." As for "persecution", the Chamber held that it might include offences covered by other subheadings of Article 5.[192]

---

[187] *Ibid.* Quoting from the Statute of the International Criminal Court, Article 7(2)(d).
[188] Para. 568.
[189] Citing Prosecutor v. Tadić, *Judgement*, IT-94-1-T, 7 May 1997, Para. 707.
[190] Para. 572.
[191] Para. 570, citing Prosecutor v. Tadić, *Judgement*, IT-94-1-A, 15 July 1999, Para. 305.
[192] Para. 571

The Chamber ruled that persecution can be charged and prosecuted as a separate offence and that it need not be linked to any other offence found elsewhere in the Statute. Despite the wording of Article 7(1)(h) of the Rome Statute, 1998, which provides a broad definition of persecution and restricts it to acts perpetrated "in connection" with other crimes within the jurisdiction of the Court and therefore is indicative of *opinio juris* of States, the Chamber found that this provision in the Rome Statute was not consonant with customary international law. Furthermore, the Chamber held that Article 5 requires no connection between the crime of persecution and any other crime over which the Tribunal has jurisdiction.

Both Article 7(1)(h) of the Rome Statute and Article 6(c) of the Charter of the International Military Tribunal contain similar language in their respective provisions regarding persecution and the need for this crime to be linked to another crime within the jurisdiction of the court. Article 6(c) of the Charter reads as follows:

> Crimes against humanity: namely, murder, extermination, enslavement, deportation, and other inhumane acts committed against any civilian population, before or during the war, or persecutions on political, racial, or religious grounds in execution of or in connection with any crime within the jurisdiction of the Tribunal, whether or not in violation of the domestic law of the country where perpetrated.

Article 7(1)(h) of the Rome Statute states:

> Persecution, against any identifiable group or collectivity on political, racial, national, ethnic, cultural, religious, gender as defined in paragraph 3, or other grounds that are universally recognized as impermissible under international law, in connection with any act referred to in this paragraph or any crime within the jurisdiction of the Court.

The Chamber found that Article 7(1)(h) is reflective of customary law by abolishing the nexus between crimes against humanity and armed conflict. However, the Chamber ruled that *lex lata* as regards the definition of war crimes, crimes against humanity and genocide are well established, and, regardless of the formulation of crimes against humanity in the Rome Statute, crimes against humanity is an offence which can be prosecuted without connecting it with another crime within the jurisdiction of the Tribunal.[193]

The *Actus Reus* of Persecution

The Chamber rejected the definitions of persecution found in refugee law and human rights law and in the deliberations of the International Law Commission, as not being reflective of customary international law.

---

[193] Para. 580.

In regard to refugee law and human rights law, the Chamber found that it does not offer a definition of persecution. The test of whether a person is entitled to obtain refugee status is determined primarily on the state of mind of the person claiming to have been persecuted rather than on a factual finding of actual persecution. The Chamber ruled that refugee law or human rights law approaches the issue of persecution in a manner that is much wider than what is legally justified under the principle of legality which must be applied when imposing *criminal* responsibility.[194]

Similarly, the Chamber found that the work of the International Law Commission was not dispositive of the issue of the definition of persecution.[195] For this reason, the Chamber held that where the Statute and the Report of the Secretary-General do not assist in interpreting the Statute, the Tribunal must turn to other sources. The Chamber stated:

> Indeed, any time the Statute does not regulate a specific matter, and the *Report of the Secretary-General* does not prove to be of any assistance in the interpretation of the Statute, it falls to the International Tribunal to draw upon (i) rules of customary international law or (ii) general principles of international criminal law; or, lacking such principles, (iii) general principles of criminal law common to the major legal systems of the world; or, lacking such principles, (iv) general principles of law consonant with the basic requirements of international justice. It must be assumed that the draftspersons intended the Statute to be based on international law, with the consequence that any possible *lacunae* must be filled by having recourse to that body of law.[196]

The Chamber concluded that, as a matter of customary international law, the acts enumerated in sub-clauses, other than sub-clause (h) of Article 5, can constitute persecution. In other words, the Chamber rejected the proposition that persecution under Article 5 is limited to subheading (h), thus excluding the crimes enumerated in the other subheadings of that provision from the notion of persecution. The acts enumerated in sub-clauses (a) to (g) and (i) may either be prosecuted as acts of persecution if the requisite elements of a crime against humanity are proved, including discriminatory intent or as crimes against humanity, if committed without discriminatory intent.

In discussing the rationale behind its decision to include the other enumerated acts in Article 5 within the notion of persecution, the Chamber stated that to exclude those acts from persecution would cause a *lacuna* in the Statute as between the concepts of crimes against humanity and genocide[197]. The Chamber stated:

> It should be added that if persecution was given a narrow interpretation, so as not to include the crimes found in the remaining sub-headings of Article 5, a *lacuna* would exist in the Statute of the Tribunal. There would be no means of conceptualising those crimes against humanity which are committed on

---

[194] Paras. 588-589.
[195] Para. 590.
[196] Para. 591.
[197] See, also Para. 636. The Trial Chamber appears to confuse *actus reus* with *mens rea* in this portion of its decision.

discriminatory grounds, but which, for example, fall short of genocide, which requires a specific intent "to destroy, in whole or in part, a national, ethnical, racial, or religious group". An example of such a crime against humanity would be the so-called "ethnic cleansing", a notion which, although it is not a term of art, is particularly germane to the work of this Tribunal.[198]

Finally, the Trial Chamber ruled that "persecution" under Article 5(h) may be prosecuted as an offence in and of itself by accepting that persecution which amounts to ethnic cleansing on discriminatory grounds may be censured above and apart from non-discriminatory killings envisaged by Article 5.[199]

In arriving at the conclusion that under customary law prosecution may include acts enumerated in the other sub-clauses of Article 5, when committed with discriminatory intent, the Chamber reviewed international and national judicial decisions handed down following the Second World War. The Trial Chamber relied upon the following international judicial decisions:

International Military Tribunal (Nuremberg)

Mass murder, extermination, beatings, torture, killings which were widespread in the concentration camps;[200]

Persecution against Jews was consistent and systematic:

Discriminatory laws;
Restrictions on families and rights of citizens;
Excluded from German life;
Pogroms: burning and demolishing synagogues;
Businesses looted;
Prominent Jewish businessmen arrested;
Collective fine 1 billion marks;
Jewish assets seized;
Movement restricted;
Ghettos;
Wearing yellow star;[201]
Deportation, slave labour, extermination, discriminatory economic acts;
Frick: "drafted, signed and administered many laws designed to eliminate Jews from German life and the economy".[202]

Control Council 10

Murder, extermination, enslavement, deportation, imprisonment, torture;[203]

Deprivation of rights of citizenship, right to work and education, economic and property rights, arrest and confinement, beatings, mutilation, torture, deportation, slave labour.[204]

---

[198] Para. 606.
[199] Para. 607.
[200] Para. 594
[201] Para. 595.
[202] Para. 596.
[203] Para. 594.
[204] Para. 599.

The Chamber concluded that these courts understood persecution to include severe attacks on the person such as murder, extermination, and torture, which potentially constitute crimes against humanity under the other subheadings of Article 5.[205]

Furthermore, after citing decisions from national courts (Poland, Netherlands, Israel, France, Croatia) and *Tadić*, the Chamber found that these findings emphasize the conclusion that the crime of persecution did not consist only of those acts not covered by the other types of crimes against humanity. On the contrary, crimes such as murder, extermination and deportation were included in persecution.[206]

The Chamber identified acts which have been considered acts of persecution and which are not provided for expressly in Article 5:

> International Military Tribunal: Judgement[207]
>
> > Passing discriminatory laws;
> >
> > Exclusion of members of an ethnic or religious group from certain aspects of social, political, and economic life;
> >
> > Imposition and collection of fines;
> >
> > Restriction of movement and ghettos;
> >
> > Mark, *i.e.* yellow star.
>
> Josef Alstotter (Justice Trial)
>
> > Former judges, prosecutors, officials of the Reich Ministry of Justice
> >
> > Use of the legal system to implement a discriminatory policy
> >
> > Lesser forms of persecution – a part of universally practiced policy
> >
> > > Exclusion from legal profession
> > > Intermarriage prohibition
> > > Prohibition re: sexual intercourse
> > > Expelled from public service, schools, businesses
> > > Confiscation of property
> > > More severe punishment
> > > No due process
> > > Arbitrary punishment
> > > Punishment without trial

The Chamber concluded as follows on the *actus reus* of persecution:

> a.   A narrow definition of persecution is not supported in customary international law. Persecution has been described by courts as a wide and particularly serious genus of crimes committed against the Jewish people and other groups by the Nazi regime.

---

[205] Para. 600.
[206] Para. 604.
[207] Para. 610

b.   In their interpretation of persecution courts have included acts such as murder, extermination, torture, and other serious acts on the person such as those presently enumerated in Article 5.

c.   Persecution can also involve a variety of other discriminatory acts, involving attacks on political, social, and economic rights.

d.   Persecution is commonly used to describe a series of acts rather than a single act. Acts of persecution will usually form part of a policy or at least of a patterned practice, and must be regarded in their context. In reality, persecutory acts are often committed pursuant to a discriminatory policy or a widespread discriminatory practice.

e.   As a corollary to (d), discriminatory acts charged as persecution must not be considered in isolation. Some of the acts mentioned above may not, in and of themselves, be so serious as to constitute a crime against humanity. For example, restrictions placed on a particular group to curtail their rights to participate in particular aspects of social life (such as visits to public parks, theatres or libraries) constitute discrimination, which is in itself a reprehensible act; however, they may not in and of themselves amount to persecution. These acts must not be considered in isolation but examined in their context and weighed for their cumulative effect.[208]

In addition, the Chamber found that a persecutory act need not be prohibited explicitly in Article 5 or elsewhere in the Statute and that whether or not such acts are legal under national laws is irrelevant. Discriminatory laws are contrary to international legal standards.[209]

Actus Reus of Persecution

The Chamber quoted with approval the *Tadić Judgement* observations in relation to persecution:[210]

- Persecution is a form of discrimination on grounds of race, religion or political opinion that is intended to be, and results in, an infringement of an individual's fundamental rights.

- It is not necessary to have a separate act of an inhumane nature to constitute persecution, but rather, the discrimination itself makes the act inhumane.

- The crime of persecution encompasses a wide variety of acts, including, *inter alia*, those of a physical, economic, or judicial nature that violate an individual's basic or fundamental rights.

---

[208] Para. 615.
[209] Para. 614.
[210] Para. 616.

The Chamber held that for persecution to amount to a crime against humanity, the legal test must define more than a core assortment of acts and leave peripheral acts in a state of uncertainty. The Chamber made a distinction between the level of seriousness of the act and the types of acts that may constitute persecution.

As for the level of seriousness, the Chamber ruled that, at a minimum, acts of persecution must be of an equal gravity or severity to the other acts enumerated in Article 5. The Chamber defined persecution as the gross or blatant denial, on discriminatory grounds, of a fundamental right, laid down in international customary or treaty law, reaching the same level of gravity as the other acts prohibited in Article 5.[211]

This definition of persecution is closely tied to a campaign intended to deny fundamental human rights and to deny an individual's membership or participation in society on discriminatory grounds. In this regard, the Chamber stated that it is "possible to identify a set of fundamental rights appertaining to any human being, the gross infringement of which may amount, depending on the surrounding circumstances, to a crime against humanity. Persecution consists of a severe attack on those rights, and aims to exclude a person from society on discriminatory grounds."[212]

As a general proposition, the Chamber ruled that acts of persecution must be evaluated in context, looking at their cumulative effect, not in isolation. Thus individual acts, although not inhumane, may have an overall consequence of offending against humanity to such an extent that they can be characterized as inhumane. The Chamber did not identify which rights constitute fundamental rights for the purposes of defining persecution, nor did it enumerate the acts that constitute persecution. Instead, the Chamber opted for a similar approach to the one it took with regard to "other inhumane acts" under Article 5(h) of the Statute and held that courts should have the flexibility to determine cases on their merits, depending on the forms which attacks on humanity may take, forms which are ever-changing and carried out with particular ingenuity.[213]

The Chamber did not, however, exclude the possibility that a single act may constitute persecution, where there is clear evidence of discriminatory intent. Thus, if an individual participates in the single murder of a person and the intent to kill that person was based on political, racial, and religious grounds and this killing occurred as part of a widespread or systematic persecutory attack against the civilian population, this single murder may constitute persecution.[214]

Finally, the author of an act of persecution need not have taken part in the formulation of a discriminatory policy or practice by a government authority.[215]

Mens Rea of Persecution

The Chamber stated that the mental element of persecution consists of discriminatory intent on the grounds of political, racial and religious grounds.[216]

---

[211] Para. 621.
[212] Para. 621.
[213] Paras. 622-623.
[214] Para. 625.
[215] Para. 626.
[216] Para. 633.

Common Element of Acts of Persecution

The Chamber identified a common element of all acts of persecution that connects the criminal intent to the nature and gravity of the acts:

> [T]hose acts were all aimed at singling out and attacking certain individuals on discriminatory grounds, by depriving them of the political, social, or economic rights enjoyed by members of the wider society. The deprivation of these rights can be said to have as its aim the removal of those persons from the society in which they live alongside the perpetrators, or eventually even from humanity itself.[217]

3.　OTHER INHUMANE ACTS

PROSECUTOR V. KUPREŠKIĆ *et. al.*, *Judgement*, IT-95-16-T, 14 January 2000, Cassese, May & Mumba, JJ.

The Trial Chamber ruled that the inclusion of the phrase "other inhumane acts" as a crime against humanity in Article 5(i) of the Statute lacks precision and is contrary to the principle of the "specificity" of criminal law.[218]

The Chamber attempted to identify the conduct that could be included in the words "other inhumane acts" in the context of crimes against humanity. By way of reference to various international human rights instruments,[219] the Chamber decided that serious forms of cruel or degrading treatment of persons belonging to a particular ethnic, religious, political or racial group, or serious widespread manifestations of cruel or humiliating or degrading treatment with a discriminatory or persecutory intent amount to crimes against humanity. Along with the generality of the foregoing, the Chamber identified the forcible transfer of groups of civilians, enforced prostitution, and enforced disappearance of persons as specific examples of inhumane acts which may amount to crimes against humanity when carried out in a systematic manner and on a large scale and when it can be shown that these acts are as serious as the other classes of crimes contained in Article 5 of the Statute.[220]

---

[217] Para. 634.

[218] Para. 563. It is interesting to compare this Chamber's discussion of this dilemma in paragraphs 563-566 of the Judgement with the Appeals Chamber decision in Prosecutor v. Tadić, *Decisionon the Defence Motion for Interlocutory Appeal on Jurisdiction*, IT-94-1-AR72, 2 October 1995 regarding similar language (include but not be limited to) in Article 3.

[219] Universal Declaration of Human Rights 1948, United Nations Covenant on Civil and Political Rights 1966, European Convention on Human Rights 1950, Inter-American Convention on Human Rights, Convention against Torture 1984.

[220] Para. 566.

PROSECUTOR V. TADIĆ, *Decision on the Defence Motion on Jurisdiction*, IT-94-1-T, 10 August 1995, McDonald, Stephen & Vohrah, JJ.

The Trial Chamber emphasized that the definition of Article 5 is in fact more restrictive than the general definition of crimes against humanity recognised by customary international law. The inclusion of the nexus with armed conflict in the article imposes a limitation on the jurisdiction of the International Tribunal and certainly can in no way offend the *nullum crimen* principle so as to bar the International Tribunal from trying the crimes enumerated therein.[221]

4. DISCRIMINATION

PROSECUTOR V. BLAŠKIĆ, *Judgement,* IT-95-14-T, 3 March 2000, Jorda, Rodrigues & Shahabuddeen, JJ.

In discussing the requirement of discrimination, the Chamber pointed out that:

> The underlying offence of persecution requires the existence of a *mens rea* from which it obtains its specificity. As set down in Article 5 of the Statute, it must be committed for specific reasons whether these be linked to political views, racial background or religious convictions. It is the specific intent to cause injury to a human being because he belongs to a particular community or group, rather than the means employed to achieve it, that bestows on it its individual nature and gravity and which justifies its being able to constitute criminal acts which might appear in themselves not to infringe directly upon the most elementary rights of a human being, for example, attacks on property. In other words, the perpetrator of the acts of persecution does not initially target the individual but rather membership in a specific racial, religious or political group.[222]

5. *MENS REA*

PROSECUTOR V. BLAŠKIĆ, *Judgement,* IT-95-14-T, 3 March 2000, Jorda, Rodrigues & Shahabuddeen, JJ.

The Chamber determined that three aspects of *Mens Rea* needed to be considered in the specific context of the *Blaškić* case.

---

[221] Para. 83.
[222] Para. 235.

Knowledge of the Context

It must be shown by the evidence that the accused had knowledge of the general context in which his acts occurred and the nexus between those acts and that general context. The Chamber adopted the following definition from the Rwanda Tribunal in the *Kayishema-Ruzindna* Judgement:[223]

> Part of what transforms an individual's act into a crime against humanity is the inclusion of the act within a greater dimension of criminal conduct; therefore an accused should be aware of this greater dimension in order to be culpable thereof. Accordingly, actual or constructive knowledge of the broader context of the attack, meaning that the accused must know that his act is part of a widespread or systematic attack on a civilian population and pursuant to some kind of policy or plan, is necessary to satisfy the requisite *mens rea* element of the accused.

Knowing Participation in the Context

Following a review of the ICTY, ICTR and the French *Cour de Cassation* the Chamber concluded:

> . . . the *mens rea* specific to a crime against humanity does not require that the agent be identified with the ideology, policy or plan in whose name mass crimes were perpetrated nor even that he supported it. It suffices that he knowingly took the risk of participating in the implementation of the ideology, policy or plan. This specifically means that it must, for example, be proved that:
>
> - The accused willingly agreed to carry out the functions he was performing;
>
> - That these functions resulted in his collaboration with the political, military or civilian authorities defining the ideology, policy or plan at the root of the crimes;
>
> - That he received orders relating to the ideology, policy or plan; and lastly
>
> - That he contributed to its commission through intentional acts or by simply refusing of his own accord to take the measures necessary to prevent their perpetration.[224]

---

[223] Prosecutor v. Kayishema & Ruzindana, *Judgement*, ICTR-95-5-T, 21 May 1999, Para. 133.
[224] Para. 257.

Evidence: Knowledge Requirement

Finally, the Chamber concluded that evidence of the knowledge requirement may be "surmised from the concurrence of a number of concrete facts." These were listed as:

- The historical and political circumstances in which the acts of violence occurred;

- The functions of the accused when the crimes were committed;

- His responsibilities within the political or military hierarchy;

- The direct and indirect relationship between the political and military hierarchy;

- The scope and gravity of the acts perpetrated;

- The nature of the crimes committed and the degree to which they are common knowledge.[225]

Exclusion of Discriminatory Intent

In conclusion, the Chamber made it clear what is not required for proof of a crime against humanity:

> It ensues from the Tadić Appeal Judgement that for a widespread or systematic attack and the resultant crimes - murder, extermination, enslavement, deportation, imprisonment, torture, rape or other inhumane acts with the exception of persecution - to be characterised as crimes against humanity they need not have been perpetrated with the deliberate intent to cause injury to a civilian population on the basis of specific characteristics. In other words, to be found guilty of such an offence, those responsible for the attack need not necessarily have acted with a particular racial, national, religious or political intent in mind.[226]

C.   ICTR TRIAL CHAMBERS

The ICTR and ICTY Statutes with respect to Crimes Against Humanity differ in only one respect. The ICTY Statute requires the existence of an internal or international armed conflict. The ICTR Statute requires that the offense be part of a widespread or systematic attack. The ICTY Statute has been interpreted to require the "widespread or systematic attack" set out specifically in the ICTR Statute, however.

---

[225] Para. 259.
[226] Para. 260

PROSECUTOR V. AKAYESU, *Judgement,* ICTR-96-4-T, 2 September 1998, Kama, Aspegren & Pillay, JJ.

Elements of the Offense

The Chamber set out the elements of the offense as follows:

- The act must be inhumane in nature and character, causing great suffering, or serious injury to body or to mental or physical health;

- The act must be committed as part of a widespread or systematic attack;

- The act must be committed against members of the civilian population;

- The act must be committed on one or more discriminatory grounds, namely, national, political, ethnic, racial or religious.

A "widespread attack" is one that is massive, frequent, involving a large-scale action and carried out collectively with considerable seriousness and directed against a multiplicity of victims.

A "systematic attack" is one that is thoroughly organized and follows a regular pattern on the basis of a common policy involving substantial public or private resources. There is no requirement that the policy be formally adopted as the policy of the state, but there must be some kind of preconceived plan or policy.

The attack may be non-violent as in apartheid.

Members of the civilian population are those not taking any active part in the hostilities, including members of the armed forces who have laid down their arms and persons placed *hors de combat.* Where there are certain individuals within the civilian population who do not come within the definition of civilians, the population in general is not deprived of its civilian character.

Inhumane acts perpetrated against persons not falling within any one of the discriminatory categories could constitute Crimes Against Humanity if the perpetrator's intention was to further his attacks on the group discriminated against on one of the grounds mentioned in Article 3 of the Statute, provided that the perpetrator has the requisite intent for commission of a Crime Against Humanity.[227]

Enumerated Acts: Murder

Murder is the unlawful, intentional killing of a human being. The elements are that (1) the victim is dead; (2) death resulted from an unlawful act or omission of the accused or his subordinate; (3) at the time of the killing the accused or his subordinate had the intention to kill or inflict great bodily harm on the deceased knowing that such bodily

---

[227] Paras. 578-584.

harm was likely to cause the victim's death or that the act was carried out in reckless disregard as to whether death ensued.[228]

Enumerated Acts: Extermination

Extermination is an element of mass destruction. The elements are that (1) the accused or his subordinate participated in killing of certain named or described persons; (2) the act or omission was unlawful and intentional; (3) the unlawful act or omission was part of a widespread or systematic attack; (4) the attack was against a civilian population; and (5) the attack was on discriminatory grounds, namely, national, political, ethnic, racial or religious.[229]

Enumerated Acts: Torture

The essential elements of Torture are that (1) the perpetrator must intentionally inflict severe physical or mental pain or suffering upon the victim for one or more of the following purposes: (a) to obtain information or a confession from the victim or a third person; (b) to punish the victim or a third person for an act committed or suspected of having been committed by either of them; (c) for the purpose of intimidating or coercing the victim or a third person; (d) for any reason based on discrimination of any kind; (2) the perpetrator was himself an official, or acted at the instigation of, or with the consent or acquiescence of an official or of a person acting in an official capacity.

Torture becomes Crime Against Humanity if the torture is perpetrated as (1) part of a widespread or systematic attack; (2) against a civilian population; (3) on discriminatory grounds.[230]

Enumerated Acts: Rape

Rape is a physical invasion of a sexual nature committed on a person under circumstances that are coercive. It is a Crime Against Humanity when those elements which make Torture a Crime Against Humanity are present. (see above) It may include acts that involve the insertion of objects and/or use of bodily orifices not considered to be intrinsically sexual. Rape is torture when inflicted by or at the instigation of or with the consent or acquiescence of a public official or other person acting in an official capacity.[231]

---

[228] Para. 589.
[229] Para. 591.
[230] Paras. 593, 5.
[231] Paras. 596, 686, 7.

ARTICLE 6

PERSONAL JURISDICTION

THE INTERNATIONAL TRIBUNAL SHALL HAVE JURISDICTION OVER NATURAL PERSONS PURSUANT TO THE PROVISIONS OF THE PRESENT STATUTE.

I.   COMMENTARY

Unlike the Nuremberg Tribunal, this Tribunal only has jurisdiction over individuals. A group cannot be declared to be a "criminal organisation," nor may an individual be indicted and tried for being a member of any such group.[232]

---

[232] See Articles 9 and 10 of the Charter of the International Military Tribunal which does provide for such offences.

ARTICLE 7

INDIVIDUAL CRIMINAL RESPONSIBILITY

1.   A PERSON WHO PLANNED, INSTIGATED, ORDERED, COMMITTED OR OTHERWISE AIDED AND ABETTED IN THE PLANNING, PREPARATION OR EXECUTION OF A CRIME REFERRED TO IN ARTICLES 2 TO 5 OF THE PRESENT STATUTE, SHALL BE INDIVIDUALLY RESPONSIBLE FOR THE CRIME.

2.   THE OFFICIAL POSITION OF ANY ACCUSED PERSON, WHETHER AS HEAD OF STATE OR GOVERNMENT OR AS A RESPONSIBLE GOVERNMENT OFFICIAL, SHALL NOT RELIEVE SUCH PERSON OF CRIMINAL RESPONSIBILITY NOR MITIGATE PUNISHMENT.

3.   THE FACT THAT ANY OF THE ACTS REFERRED TO IN ARTICLES 2 TO 5 OF THE PRESENT STATUTE WAS COMMITTED BY A SUBORDINATE DOES NOT RELIEVE HIS SUPERIOR OF CRIMINAL RESPONSIBILITY IF HE KNEW OR HAD REASON TO KNOW THAT THE SUBORDINATE WAS ABOUT TO COMMIT SUCH ACTS OR HAD DONE SO AND THE SUPERIOR FAILED TO TAKE THE NECESSARY AND REASONABLE MEASURES TO PREVENT SUCH ACTS OR TO PUNISH THE PERPETRATORS THEREOF.

4.   THE FACT THAT AN ACCUSED PERSON ACTED PURSUANT TO AN ORDER OF A GOVERNMENT OR OF A SUPERIOR SHALL NOT RELIEVE HIM OF CRIMINAL RESPONSIBILITY, BUT MAY BE CONSIDERED IN MITIGATION OF PUNISHMENT IF THE INTERNATIONAL TRIBUNAL DETERMINES THAT JUSTICE SO REQUIRES.

I.   COMMENTARY

The *Blaškić* and *Delalić* Trial Chambers have disagreed over the question of the nature of the information a superior must possess before he can be held responsible under the "knew or had reason to know" test.[233]

    Although the *Tadić* view differs from that in *Delalić*, it may not change the rule in the latter case. The *Blaškić* analysis was in the context of a military commander and the requirements placed on military commanders. The Chamber relied upon Article 87 of Protocol I that reads:

> The High Contracting Parties and the Parties to the conflict shall require military commanders, with respect to members of the armed forces under their command and other persons under their control, to prevent and, where necessary, to suppress and to report to competent authorities breaches of the Conventions and of this Protocol.[234]

The Commentary to Protocol I, with regard to military commanders provides that:

---

[233] Both cases are in the Appeals process. The *Delalić* case has been argued and a decision is expected in the fall of 2000. The *Delalić* appeal may settle this issue.

[234] Para. 329

. . . their role obliges them to be constantly informed of the way in which their subordinates carry out the tasks entrusted to them, and to take the necessary measures of this purpose.[235]

The *Delalić* case, on the other hand, dealt largely with someone who, for at least part of the time involved was alleged to be a civilian superior in his role as Coordinator. It may be that separate rules are necessary for civilian superiors and military commanders due to the nature of the typical military organization as compared with civilian organizations.

In the *Akayesu* case reported below, the Rwanda Trial Chamber dealt with the problem of civilian superiors and the difference between military and civilian organizations.

II.   TRIBUNAL CASES

A.   APPEALS CHAMBER

1. COMMON PURPOSE

PROSECUTOR V. TADIĆ, *Judgement*, IT-94-1-A, 15 July 1999, Shahabuddeen, Cassese, Wang Tieya, Nieto-Navia & Mumba, JJ.

The Trial Chamber acquitted Tadić of the killing of five men from Jaskići. The Prosecutor appealed this acquittal and the Appeals Chamber reversed and convicted Tadić of the killings. The question was whether Tadić could be held criminally liable for the killings even though there was no evidence that he had personally committed any of them. The Chamber identified the two central issues as follows:

(i)   whether the acts of one person can give rise to the criminal culpability of another where both participate in the execution of a common criminal plan; and

(ii)   what degree of *mens rea* is required in such a case.[236]

The Chamber ruled that the Statute provides jurisdiction over "those persons who plan, instigate, order, physically perpetrate a crime or otherwise aid and abet in its planning, preparation or execution."[237] Furthermore, the Tribunal has jurisdiction over the instance when " several persons having a common purpose embark on criminal activity that is then carried out either jointly or by some members of this plurality of persons. Whoever contributes to the commission of crimes by the group of persons or some members of the group, in execution of a common criminal purpose, may be criminally liable "[238]

The concept of culpability through the common purpose doctrine includes three categories of collective criminality:

---

[235] *Ibid.*
[236] Para. 185.
[237] Para. 190.
[238] *Ibid.*

The first such category is represented by cases where all co-defendants, acting pursuant to a common design, possess the same criminal intention; for instance, the formulation of a plan among the co-perpetrators to kill, where, in effecting this common design (and even if each co-perpetrator carries out a different role within it), they nevertheless all possess the intent to kill. The objective and subjective prerequisites for imputing criminal responsibility to a participant who did not, or cannot be proven to have, effected the killing are as follows: (i) the accused must voluntarily participate in one aspect of the common design (for instance, by inflicting non-fatal violence upon the victim, or by providing material assistance to or facilitating the activities of his co-perpetrators); and (ii) the accused, even if not personally effecting the killing, must nevertheless intend this result.[239]

The second distinct category of cases is in many respects similar to that set forth above, and embraces the so-called "concentration camp" cases. The notion of common purpose was applied to instances where the offences charged were alleged to have been committed by members of military or administrative units such as those running concentration camps; *i.e.*, by groups of persons acting pursuant to a concerted plan. Cases illustrative of this category are *Dachau Concentration Camp*, decided by a United States court sitting in Germany and *Belsen*, decided by a British military court sitting in Germany. In these cases the accused held some position of authority within the hierarchy of the concentration camps. Generally speaking, the charges against them were that they had acted in pursuance of a common design to kill or mistreat prisoners and hence to commit war crimes. In his summing up in the *Belsen* case, the Judge Advocate adopted the three requirements identified by the Prosecution as necessary to establish guilt in each case: (i) the existence of an organised system to ill-treat the detainees and commit the various crimes alleged; (ii) the accused's awareness of the nature of the system; and (iii) the fact that the accused in some way actively participated in enforcing the system, *i.e.*, encouraged, aided and abetted or in any case participated in the realisation of the common criminal design. The convictions of several of the accused appear to have been explicitly based upon these criteria.[240]

The third category concerns cases involving a common design to pursue one course of conduct where one of the perpetrators commits an act that, while outside the common design, was nevertheless a natural and foreseeable consequence of the effecting of that common purpose. An example of this would be a common, shared intention on the part of a group to forcibly remove members of one ethnicity from their town, village or region (to effect "ethnic cleansing") with the consequence that, in the course of doing so, one or more of the victims is shot and killed. While murder may not have been explicitly

---

[239] Para. 196.
[240] Para. 202.

acknowledged to be part of the common design, it was nevertheless foreseeable that the forcible removal of civilians at gunpoint might well result in the deaths of one or more of those civilians. Criminal responsibility may be imputed to all participants within the common enterprise where the risk of death occurring was both a predictable consequence of the execution of the common design and the accused was either reckless or indifferent to that risk. Another example is that of a common plan to forcibly evict civilians belonging to a particular ethnic group by burning their houses; if some of the participants in the plan, in the process of carrying it out, kill civilians by setting their houses on fire, all the other participants in the plan are criminally responsible for the killing if these deaths were predictable.[241]

The Chamber summarised its findings as follows:

> In sum, the Appeals Chamber holds the view that the notion of common design as a form of accomplice liability is firmly established in customary international law and in addition is upheld, albeit implicitly, in the Statute of the International Tribunal. As for the objective and subjective elements of the crime, the case law shows that the notion has been applied to three distinct categories of cases. First, in cases of co-perpetration, where all participants in the common design possess the same criminal intent to commit a crime (and one or more of them actually perpetrate the crime, with intent). Secondly, in the so-called "concentration camp" cases, where the requisite *mens rea* comprises knowledge of the nature of the system of ill-treatment and intent to further the common design of ill-treatment. Such intent may be proved either directly or as a matter of inference from the nature of the accused's authority within the camp or organisational hierarchy. With regard to the third category of cases, it is appropriate to apply the notion of "common purpose" only where the following requirements concerning *mens rea* are fulfilled: (i) the intention to take part in a joint criminal enterprise and to further - individually and jointly - the criminal purposes of that enterprise; and (ii) the foreseeability of the possible commission by other members of the group of offences that do not constitute the object of the common criminal purpose. Hence, the participants must have had in mind the intent, for instance, to ill-treat prisoners of war (even if such a plan arose extemporaneously) and one or some members of the group must have actually killed them. In order for responsibility for the deaths to be imputable to the others, however, everyone in the group must have been able to predict this result. It should be noted that more than negligence is required. What is required is a state of mind in which a person, although he did not intend to bring about a certain result, was aware that the actions of the group were most likely to lead to that result but nevertheless willingly took that risk. In other words, the so-called

---

[241] Para. 204.

dolus eventualis is required (also called "advertent recklessness" in some national legal systems).[242]

2. AIDING AND ABETTING

PROSECUTOR V. ALEKSOVSKI, *Judgement*, IT-95-14/1-A, 24 March 2000, May, Mumba, Hunt, Tieya & Robinson, JJ.

This is the second decision of the Appeals Chamber that has dealt with the liability of a person charged with aiding and abetting. Previously, in the *Tadić* Judgement, the Appeals Chamber had discussed briefly the liability of one person for the acts of another, where the first person is charged with aiding and abetting another person in the commission of a crime. The *Tadić* Judgement contrasted the charge of aiding and abetting with the doctrine of common purpose.

The Chamber reviewed Tribunal jurisprudence on the question of aiding and abetting that is contained in the Judgements of Trial Chamber II in the *Furundžija* case and the Appeals Chamber the *Tadić* case. The Chamber held that the following propositions are found in the *Furundžija* Judgement:

(i)   It must be shown that the aider and abettor carried out acts which consisted of practical assistance, encouragement or moral support which had a substantial effect upon the commission by the principal of the crime for which the aider and abettor is sought to be made responsible.

(ii)   It must be shown that the aider and abettor knew (in the sense of was aware) that his own acts assisted in the commission of that crime by the principal.

(iii)   It must be shown that the aider and abettor was aware of the essential elements of the crime which was ultimately committed by the principal. In other words, it is not necessary to show that the aider and abettor shared the *mens rea* of the principal, but it must be shown that the aider and abettor was aware of the relevant *mens rea* on the part of the principal.[243]

From the *Tadić* Judgement, the Chamber gleaned the following points in relation to aiding and abetting:

(i)   The aider and abettor is always an accessory to the crime committed by the other person, the principal.

---

[242] Para. 220.
[243] Para. 162.

(ii)   It must be shown that the aider and abettor carried out acts specifically directed to assist, encourage or lend moral support to the specific crime committed by the principal, and that this support has a substantial effect upon the commission of the crime.

(iii)   It must be shown that the aider and abettor knew that his own acts assisted the commission of that specific crime by the principal.

(iv)   It is not necessary to show the existence of a common concerted plan between the principal and the accessory.

At trial, Aleksovski, as commander of the Koanik prison, was found to be individually responsible pursuant to Article 7(1) for aiding and abetting in the forced labour and the use of the prisoners as human shields outside the prison. He was found guilty as an aider and abettor by virtue of the fact that he was aware of how the HVO soldiers were using the prisoners. He was present occasionally when the prisoners were selected for that purpose, and, almost always, when the prisoners returned to the prison. The Trial Chamber found that as commander, he was responsible for the welfare of the prisoners and he failed to take measures open to him to stop them from going out to work in dangerous circumstances. The Trial Chamber had acquitted Aleksovski as an aider and abettor for any mistreatment of the prisoners by the HVO soldiers outside the prison, stating that the Prosecution had not claimed that the accused was individually responsible for that mistreatment.[244]

In finding Alesovski individually responsible for the mistreatment by the HVO soldiers outside the prison by way of having aided and abetted, the Appeals Chamber reviewed considerable evidence given by prisoners of mistreatment when digging trenches. The Chamber concluded that the Trial Chamber should have proceeded to make findings in relation to this mistreatment and it concluded that the only reasonable finding could have been that Aleksovski was individually liable as an aider and abettor for the mistreatment of the prisoners by the HVO outside the prison.[245]

PROSECUTOR V. TADIĆ, *Judgement,* IT-94-1-A, 15 July 1999, Shahabuddeen, Cassese, Wang Tieya, Nieto-Navia & Mumba, JJ.

In this case the Chamber took the opportunity to explain how aiding and abetting differs from the common purpose doctrine. In that connection the Chamber set out four criteria that may assist in making the distinction:

(i)   The aider and abettor is always an accessory to a crime perpetrated by another person, the principal.

---

[244] Para. 157.
[245] Paras. 165-172.

(ii)   In the case of aiding and abetting no proof is required of the existence of a common concerted plan, let alone of the pre-existence of such a plan. No plan or agreement is required: indeed, the principal may not even know about the accomplice's contribution.

(iii)   The aider and abettor carries out acts specifically directed to assist, encourage or lend moral support to the perpetration of a certain specific crime (murder, extermination, rape, torture, wanton destruction of civilian property, etc.), and this support has a substantial effect upon the perpetration of the crime. By contrast, in the case of acting in pursuance of a common purpose or design, it is sufficient for the participant to perform acts that in some way are directed to the furthering of the common plan or purpose.

(iv)   In the case of aiding and abetting, the requisite mental element is knowledge that the acts performed by the aider and abettor assist the commission of a specific crime by the principal. By contrast, in the case of common purpose or design more is required (i.e., either intent to perpetrate the crime or intent to pursue the common criminal design plus foresight that those crimes outside the criminal common purpose were likely to be committed), as stated above.[246]

3. CO-PERPETRATION

PROSECUTOR V. FURUNDŽIJA, *Judgement,* IT-95-17/1-A, 21 July 2000, Shahabuddeen, Vohrah, Nieto-Navia, Robinson & Pocar, JJ.

Furundžija contended that to establish his liability as a co-perpetrator that a "direct connection" needed to be established by the evidence between his questioning of Witness A and the infliction upon her of severe pain or suffering, whether physical or mental. He contended that there was neither allegation nor proof that he *intentionally* acted in concert with Accused B whom the evidence described as having been engaged in raping and beating Witness A whilst Furundžija was engaged in questioning her.

    The Chamber found that the Trial Chamber's use of the definition of co-perpetrator from the Rome Statue was appropriate. That section of the Rome Statute reads, in part, as follows:

3. In accordance with this Statute, a person shall be criminally responsible and liable for punishment for a crime within the jurisdiction of the Court if that person:

---

[246] Para. 229

(d) In any other way contributes to the commission or attempted commission of such a crime by a group of persons acting with a common purpose. Such contribution shall be intentional and shall either:

> (i) Be made with the aim of furthering the criminal activity or criminal purpose of the group, where such activity or purpose involves the commission of a crime within the jurisdiction of the Court; or

> (ii) Be made in the knowledge of the intention of the group to commit the crime;[247]

As to a definition of the legal elements of co-perpetration the Chamber relied on an earlier judgement of the Appeals Chamber in the *Tadić* case and adopted those findings. The elements are described as follows:

> There is no necessity for this plan, design or purpose to have been previously arranged or formulated. The common plan or purpose may materialise extemporaneously and be inferred from the fact that a plurality of persons acts in unison to put into effect a joint criminal enterprise.[248]

Applying these principles to the specific facts in the *Furundžija* case, the Chamber reasoned that "where the act of one accused contributes to the purpose of the other, and both acted simultaneously, in the same place and within full view of each other, over a prolonged period of time, the argument that there was no common purpose if plainly unsustainable."[249]

4. SUPERIOR RESPONSIBILITY

PROSECUTOR V. ALEKSOVSKI, *Judgement*, IT-95-14/1-A, 24 March 2000, May, Mumba, Hunt, Tieya & Robinson, JJ.

The issue on appeal regarding Article 7(3) was factual in nature, to wit: whether the accused was a commander of the guards, who were military police. The Trial Chamber found that the accused was not a member of the military police. He was found guilty under Article 7(3), however, because he had effective authority over the perpetrators of the crimes. The accused was found to have had the ability to give orders to the perpetrators of crimes and to punish them in the event of violations. In particular, the Trial Chamber found that the accused failed to report to superiors the situation in the prison, including incidents of mistreatment of prisoners.[250]

---

[247] Para. 117.
[248] Prosecutor v. *Tadić, Judgement*, IT-94-1-A, 15 July 1999, Shahabuddeen, Cassese, Wang Tieya, Nieto-Navia & Mumba, JJ, para. 227.
[249] Para. 120.
[250] Para. 70.

The Appeals Chamber ruled that Article 7(3) provides the legal criteria for command responsibility, thus giving the word "commander" a juridical meaning. The Chamber found that the provision becomes applicable only where a superior with the required mental element failed to exercise his powers to prevent subordinates from committing offences or to punish them afterwards. This necessarily implies that a superior must have such powers prior to his failure to exercise them.[251]

B.   TRIAL CHAMBERS

1. COMMON PURPOSE

PROSECUTOR V. FURUNDŽIJA, *Judgement,* IT-95-17/1-T, 10 December 1998, Mumba, Cassese & May JJ.

Actus Reus

The Trial Chamber held that the *actus reus* of aiding and abetting in international criminal law requires practical assistance, encouragement, or moral support which has a substantial effect on the perpetration of the crime. The nature of the assistance given by the accomplice need not have a causal effect on the perpetration of the crime or be a *conditio sine qua non* to the commission of the act. The Chamber elaborated on the point by saying that while any spectator can be said to be encouraging a spectacle - an audience being a necessary element of a spectacle - the spectator can only be found to be complicit if his status is such that his presence had a significant legitimising or encouraging effect on the principals. The Chamber added that the relationship between the acts of the accomplice and of the principal must be such that the acts of the accomplice make a significant difference to the commission of the criminal act by the principal. Having a role in a system without influence is not enough to attract criminal responsibility.[252]

The Chamber cited with approval the finding of the Rwanda Trial Chamber in the *Akayesu* judgement that the supporter must be of a certain status for his presence to be sufficient for criminal responsibility. The Chamber wrote:

> *Jean-Paul Akayesu* was the *bourgmestre*, or mayor, of the Commune in which atrocities, including rape and sexual violence, occurred. That Trial Chamber considered this position of authority highly significant for his criminal liability for aiding and abetting: "The Tribunal finds, under Article 6(1) of its Statute, that the Accused, having had reason to know that sexual violence was occurring, aided and abetted the following acts of sexual violence, by allowing them to take place on or near the premises of the bureau communal and by facilitating the commission of such sexual violence through his words of encouragement in other acts of sexual violence which, by virtue of his authority, sent a clear signal

---

[251] Para. 76.
[252] Paras. 232-235.

of official tolerance for sexual violence, without which these acts would not have taken place: . . .".[253]

The Chamber contrasted the accomplice liability of Akayesu as mayor of the Commune to the acquittal of Ruehl and Graf in the *Trial of Otto Ohlendorf and Others*, two low ranking individuals whose lack of objection did not contribute to the success of any executive operation. Knowledge of the criminal activities of the organisation combined with a role in that organisation was not sufficient for complicity. The acts of the defendants in carrying out their duties must have a substantial effect on the commission of the offence for responsibility to ensue.[254]

Similarly, in the *Zyklon B* case, the first gassing technician was acquitted on the basis that there was no evidence that he was in a position either to influence the transfer of gas to Auschwitz or to prevent it. The Chamber wrote that the act of the accomplice must have at least a substantial effect on the principal act - the use of the gas to murder internees at Auschwitz - in order to constitute the *actus reus*. The functions performed by the accused, Drosihn, in his employment as a gassing technician were an integral part of the supply and use of the poison gas, but this alone could not render him liable for its criminal use even if he was aware that his functions played such an important role in the transfer of the gas. Without influence over this supply, he was not guilty. In other words, *mens rea* alone is insufficient to ground a criminal conviction.[255]

Mens Rea

The Chamber found that the *mens rea* requirement for a charge of aiding and abetting is the knowledge that the acts in question assist the commission of the offence.[256]

The Chamber held that it is not necessary for the accomplice to share the *mens rea* of the perpetrator, in the sense of positive intention to commit the crime. Instead, it must be shown that the accomplice has knowledge that his actions will assist the perpetrator in the commission of the crime. The Chamber illustrated this by referring to cases from World War II in which persons were convicted for having driven victims and perpetrators to the site of an execution. In those cases the prosecution did not prove that the driver drove for the purpose of assisting in the killing, that is, with an intention to kill. It was the knowledge of the criminal purpose of the executioners that rendered the driver liable as an aider and abettor. The Chamber concluded that if it were not proven that a driver would reasonably have known that the purpose of the trip was an unlawful execution, he would be acquitted.[257]

---

[253] Para. 231.
[254] Paras. 219-221.
[255] Para. 223.
[256] Para. 249.
[257] Para. 245.

Furthermore, the Chamber ruled that it is not necessary that the aider and abettor should know the precise crime that was intended and which in the event was committed. If he is aware that one of a number of crimes will probably be committed, and one of those crimes is in fact committed, he has intended to facilitate the commission of that crime, and is guilty as an aider and abettor.[258]

Distinguishing between Perpetration of Torture and Aiding and Abetting Torture

To determine liability for alleged torture, the Chamber analysed the ways in which torture may be perpetrated and the role an individual may play in the commission of torture.

The Chamber concluded that the distinction between perpetration or co-perpetration and aiding and abetting of torture could be summarized as follows:

> (i)   to be guilty of torture as a perpetrator (or co- perpetrator), the accused must participate in an integral part of the torture and partake of the purpose behind the torture, that is the intent to obtain information or a confession, to punish or intimidate, humiliate, coerce or discriminate against the victim or a third person.

> (ii)   to be guilty of torture as an aider or abettor, the accused must assist in some way which has a substantial effect on the perpetration of the crime and with knowledge that torture is taking place.[259]

2. PLANNING, INSTIGATION AND ORDERING

PROSECUTOR V. BLAŠKIĆ, *Judgement,* IT-95-14-T, 3 March 2000, Jorda, Rodrigues & Shahabuddeen, JJ.

The Chamber wrote, as follows:

> The Trial Chamber holds that proof is required that whoever planned, instigated or ordered the commission of a crime possessed the criminal intent, that is, that he directly or indirectly intended that the crime in question be committed. However, in general, a person other than the person who planned, instigated or ordered is the one who perpetrated the *actus reus* of the offence. In so doing he must have acted in furtherance of a plan or order. In the case of instigating . . . proof is required of a causal connection between the instigation and the fulfilment of the *actus reus* of the crime.[260]

> Accordingly, planning implies that "one or several persons contemplate designing the commission of a crime at both the preparatory and execution phases." The Trial Chamber is of the view that circumstantial evidence may provide sufficient proof of the existence of a plan.[261]

---

[258] Para. 246.
[259] Para. 257.
[260] Para. 278.
[261] Para. 279, Quoting from Prosecutor v. Akayesu, *Judgement*, ICTR-96-4-T, 2 September 1998, Para. 480.

Instigating entails "prompting another to commit an offence." The wording is sufficiently broad to allow for the inference that both acts and omissions may constitute instigating and that this notion covers both express and implied conduct. The ordinary meaning of instigating, namely, "bring about" the commission of an act by someone, corroborates the opinion that a causal relationship between the instigation and the physical perpetration of the crime is an element requiring proof.[262]

It is not necessary that an order be given in writing or in any particular form. It can be explicit or implicit. The fact that an order was given can be proved through circumstantial evidence.[263]

The Trial Chamber agrees that an order does not need to be given by the superior directly to the person(s) who perform(s) the *actus reus* of the offence. Furthermore, what is important is the commander's *mens rea*, not that of the subordinate executing the order. Therefore, it is irrelevant whether the illegality of the order was apparent on its face.[264]

3. AIDING AND ABETTING

PROSECUTOR V. BLAŠKIĆ, *Judgement,* IT-95-14-T, 3 March 2000, Jorda, Rodrigues & Shahabuddeen, JJ.

The Chamber began its analysis of this issue by adopting the elements of aiding and abetting set out in the *Furundžija* case. The Chamber then expanded on its analysis, as follows:

The Trial Chamber holds that the *actus reus* of aiding and abetting may be perpetrated through an omission, provided this failure to act had a decisive effect on the commission of the crime and that it was coupled with the requisite *mens rea*. In this respect, the mere presence at the crime scene of a person with superior authority, such as a military commander, is a probative indication for determining whether that person encouraged or supported the perpetrators of the crime.[265]

Proof that the conduct of the aider and abettor had a causal effect on the act of the principal perpetrator is not required. Furthermore, participation may occur before, during or after the act is committed and be geographically separated therefrom.[266]

---

[262] Para. 280, Quoting from Prosecutor v. Akayesu, *Judgement*, ICTR-96-4-T, 2 September 1998, Para. 482 and the Concise Oxford Dictionary, 10th Ed. (1999), p. 734.

[263] Para. 281.

[264] Para. 282.

[265] Para. 284

[266] Para. 285.

As to the *mens rea* requirement for aiding and abetting, a distinction is to be made between "knowledge" and "intent." As held earlier in this Judgement, the *mens rea* required for establishing the responsibility of an accused for one of the crimes in Articles 2, 3 and 5 of the Statute is "willingness", comprising both direct and indirect intent. In the case of aiding and abetting, the Prosecution relies on *inter alia* the *Furundžija* Judgement and argues that the applicable *mens rea* applicable (sic) to the aider and abettor is "knowledge" that his acts assist the commission of the offence. In the submission of the Defence, however, Article 7(1) of the Statute requires proof of the specific intent on the part of the accused to commit the deliberate act to facilitate the commission of a crime. The Trial Chamber is of the view that in addition to knowledge that his acts assist the commission of the crime, the aider and abettor needs to have intended to provide assistance, or as a minimum, accepted that such assistance would be a possible and foreseeable consequence of his conduct.[267]

The Trial Chamber deems it appropriate to point out that a distinction is to be made between aiding and abetting and participation in pursuance of a common purpose or common design to commit a crime. In the case in point, it notes that the only question raised is the question of aiding and abetting.[268]

PROSECUTOR V. FURUNDŽIJA, *Judgement,* IT-95-17/1-T, 10 December 1998, Mumba, Cassese & May, JJ.

Common Design to Commit Crimes

The Trial Chamber distinguished the notion of aiding and abetting from the notion of common design. The Chamber held the legal ingredients of aiding and abetting in international criminal law to be the following: the *actus reus* consists of practical assistance, encouragement, or moral support which has a substantial effect on the perpetration of the crime. The *mens rea* required is the knowledge that these acts assist the commission of the offence. On the other hand, for the notion of common design, the *actus reus* consists of participation in a joint criminal enterprise and the *mens rea* required is intent to participate.[269]

Under the notion of common design to commit crimes, the organised and official nature of the system to commit war crimes adds a specific element to the "complicity" of the accused. The Chamber cited the elements identified by the United Nations War Crimes Commission that are necessary to establish guilt:

1. The existence of a system to ill-treat the prisoners and commit the various crimes alleged;

2. The accused's knowledge of the nature of this system; and

---

[267] Para. 286.
[268] Para. 288.
[269] Para. 249.

3.   The accused "encouraged, aided and abetted or participated" in enforcing the system.[270]

The Chamber observed that in the World War II cases, once the existence of the system had been established, a given accused was potentially liable for his participation in this system. The roles of the accused ranged from camp commanders to guards and prisoner functionaries and all were found guilty, with the difference in the levels of participation reflected in the sentences. The Chamber noted that holding any role in the administration of the camps was sufficient to constitute encouraging, aiding and abetting or participating in the enforcement of the system.[271]

In reviewing the *Dachau Concentration Camp* case the Chamber observed that regardless of whether the accused themselves had beaten or murdered the concentration camp inmates, the assistance they afforded to those who did, or the system, formed the basis of their guilt. The level of assistance required was low: any participation in the enterprise was sufficient, although as the accused were all members of staff of the camps, their contribution to the commission of the crimes was tangible - the carrying out of their respective duties - so that none were convicted on the basis of having lent moral support or encouragement alone.[272]

Finally, the Chamber found that the distinction made in Article 25 of the Rome Statute between liability for criminal participation as co-perpetrators who participate in a joint criminal enterprise or as aiders and abettors has crystallized these two notions in international law.[273]

4. MISCELLANEOUS

PROSECUTOR V. DELALIĆ *et. al., Judgement*, IT-95-21-T, 16 November 1998, Karibi-Whyte, Odio-Benito & Jan, JJ.

The Trial Chamber adopted the standard for imposition of individual criminal responsibility under Article 7(1) that was enunciated by Trial Chamber II in the *Tadić Judgement*.[274]

For there to be individual criminal responsibility for degrees of involvement in a crime under the Tribunal's jurisdiction which does not constitute a direct performance of the acts which make up the offence, a showing must be made of both a physical and a mental element.

---

[270] Para. 212.
[271] Para. 212.
[272] Para. 213.
[273] Para. 216.
[274] Para. 325.

Actus reus

The requisite *actus reus* for such responsibility is constituted by an act of participation which in fact contributes to, or has an effect on, the commission of the crime. Hence, this participation must have "a direct and substantial effect on the commission of the illegal act".[275]

Mens rea

The corresponding intent, or *mens rea*, is defined by the requirement that the act of participation be performed with knowledge that it will assist the principal in the commission of the criminal act. Thus, there must be "awareness of the act of participation coupled with a conscious decision to participate by planning, instigating, ordering, committing, or otherwise aiding and abetting in the commission of a crime".[276]

Aiding and abetting includes all acts of assistance that lend encouragement or support to the perpetration of an offence and which are accompanied by the requisite *mens rea*. Subject to the caveat that it be found to have contributed to, or have had an effect on, the commission of the crime, the relevant act of assistance may be removed both in time and place from the actual commission of the offence. Furthermore, such assistance may consist not only of physical acts, but may also manifest itself in the form of psychological support given to the commission of an illegal act through words or by physical presence at the scene of the perpetration of the offence.[277]

As regards the mental element of such participation, it is necessary that the act of participation be undertaken with knowledge that it will contribute to the criminal act of the principal. The existence of this *mens rea* need not have been explicitly expressed; it may be inferred from all relevant circumstances. Nor is it required to find that there was a pre-existing plan to engage in the criminal conduct in question. However, where such a plan exists, or where there otherwise is evidence that members of a group are acting with a common criminal purpose, all those who knowingly participate in, and directly and substantially contribute to, the realisation of this purpose may be held criminally responsible under Article 7(1) for the resulting criminal conduct. Depending upon the facts of any given situation, the culpable individual may, under such circumstances, be held criminally responsible either as a direct perpetrator of, or as an aider and abettor to, the crime in question.[278]

In conclusion, the following concise statement from the *Tadić Judgment* accurately reflects the view of the Trial Chamber on the scope of individual criminal responsibility under Article 7(1):

> the accused will be found criminally culpable for any conduct where it is determined that he knowingly participated in the commission of an offence that violates international humanitarian law and his participation directly and

---

[275] Para. 326.
[276] Para. 326.
[277] Para. 327.
[278] Para. 328.

substantially affected the commission of that offence through supporting the actual commission before, during, or after the incident. He will also be responsible for all that naturally results from the commission of the act in question.[279]

5. SUPERIOR RESPONSIBILITY

PROSECUTOR V. BLAŠKIĆ, *Judgement,* IT-95-14-T, 3 March 2000, Jorda, Rodrigues & Shahabuddeen, JJ.

Definition of a Superior

The Chamber made the following observations:

> The Trial Chamber has already characterised a "superior" as a person exercising "effective control" over his subordinates. In other words, the Trial Chamber holds that where a person has the material ability to prevent or punish crimes committed by others, that person must be considered a superior. Accordingly, it is a commander's degree of effective control, his material ability, which will guide the Trial Chamber in determining whether he reasonably took the measures required either to prevent the crime or to punish the perpetrator. . . . this implies that, under some circumstances, a commander may discharge his obligation to prevent or punish by reporting the matter to the competent authorities.[280]

> The Trial Chamber stresses that the obligation to "prevent or punish" does not provide the accused with two alternative and equally satisfying options. Obviously, where the accused knew or had reason to know that subordinates were about to commit crimes and failed to prevent them, he cannot make up for the failure to act by punishing the subordinates afterwards.[281]

Had Reason to Know

In its analysis of Article 7(3), the Trial Chamber was in basic agreement with the analysis of the Trial Chamber in the *Delalić* case, reported below. The Chamber departed, however, from the *Delalić* analysis with regard to the issue of "had reason to know." The *Delalić* analysis relied on the language of Article 86 of Protocol I to the Geneva Conventions. That Protocol, according to *Delalić* requires that to establish that a superior "had reason to know" the Prosecutor must provide evidence that "some specific information was in fact available to him which would provide notice of offences committed by his subordinates." The *Delalić* Chamber came to this conclusion following an exhaustive analysis of the post-World War II cases.

---

[279] Para. 329.
[280] Para. 335.
[281] Para. 336

The *Blaskić* Chamber performed a similar analysis of the post-World War II cases. The Chamber then analysed Article 86 of Protocol I and concluded that it does not require any specific information as held by the *Delalić* Chamber.[282]

PROSECUTOR V. DELALIĆ *et. al.*, *Judgement,* IT-95-21-T, 16 November 1998, Karibi-Whyte, Odio-Benito & Jan, JJ.

The Trial Chamber found that there are two types of superior responsibility. First, the criminal liability of a superior for positive acts, which follows from general principles of accomplice liability pursuant to Article 7(1). Second, the criminal responsibility of superiors for failing to take measures to prevent or repress the unlawful conduct of their subordinates, which is best understood when seen against the principle that criminal responsibility for omissions is incurred only where there exists a legal obligation to act. Citing the example of military commanders in the context of Article 87 of Additional Protocol I, the Chamber stated that international law imposes an affirmative duty on superiors to prevent persons under their control from committing violations of international humanitarian law. The Chamber held that it is ultimately this duty that provides the basis for, and defines the contours of, the imputed criminal responsibility under Article 7(3) of the Statute.[283]

Failure to Act

The Chamber ruled that the principle of individual criminal responsibility of superiors for failure to prevent or repress the crimes committed by subordinates forms part of customary international law.[284] The Chamber considered that there can be no doubt that the concept of the individual criminal responsibility of superiors for failure to act is today firmly placed within the corpus of international humanitarian law. Through the adoption of Additional Protocol I, the principle has now been codified and given a clear expression in international conventional law. Thus, Article 87 of the Protocol gives expression to the duty of commanders to control the acts of their subordinates and to prevent or, where necessary, to repress violations of the Geneva Conventions or the Protocol. The concomitant principle under which a superior may be held criminally responsible for the crimes committed by his subordinates where the superior has failed to properly exercise this duty is formulated in Article 86 of the Protocol.[285]

Three Constitutive Elements of Article 7(3)

The Chamber found that while it is evident that the commission of one or more of the crimes under Articles 2 to 5 of the Statute is a necessary prerequisite for the application

---

[282] Both of these cases are currently in the appeals stage. The *Delalić* case has been argued and a decision is expected in the fall of 2000. That decision my resolve this dispute.

[283] Para. 334.

[284] Para. 343.

[285] Para. 340.

of Article 7(3), the principle of superior responsibility properly is analysed as containing three constitutive parts. From the text of Article 7(3), the essential elements of command responsibility for failure to act are as follows:

(i)   the existence of a superior-subordinate relationship;

(ii)   the superior knew or had reason to know that the criminal act was about to be or had been committed; and

(iii)   the superior failed to take the necessary and reasonable measures to prevent the criminal act or punish the perpetrator thereof.[286]

Superior-Subordinate Relationship

The Chamber determined that the requirement of the existence of a "superior-subordinate" relationship which, in the words of the Commentary to Additional Protocol I, should be seen "in terms of a hierarchy encompassing the concept of control," is particularly problematic in situations such as that of the former Yugoslavia during the period relevant to the present case - situations where previously existing formal structures have broken down and where, during an interim period, the new, possibly improvised, control and command structures, may be ambiguous and ill-defined. Persons effectively in command of such more informal structures, with power to prevent and punish the crimes of persons who are in fact under their control, may under certain circumstances be held responsible for their failure to do so. The Chamber found that individuals in positions of authority, whether civilian or within military structures, may incur criminal responsibility under the doctrine of command responsibility on the basis of their *de facto* as well as *de jure* positions as superiors. The mere absence of formal legal authority to control the actions of subordinates should therefore not be understood to preclude the imposition of such responsibility.[287]

In addition, the Chamber ruled that the principle of superior responsibility in Article 7(3) extends to both military commanders and individuals in non-military positions of superior authority. The use of the generic term "superior" in Article 7(3), together with its juxtaposition to the affirmation of the individual criminal responsibility of "Head[s] of State or Government" or "responsible Government official[s]" in Article 7(2), clearly indicates that its applicability extends beyond the responsibility of military commanders to also encompass political leaders and other civilian superiors in positions of authority. The Chamber observed that this interpretation is supported by the uncontested explanation of the vote made by the representative of the United States following the adoption of Security Council resolution 827 on the establishment of the International Tribunal, who stated that Article 3 includes "the failure of a superior – whether political or military – to take reasonable steps to prevent or punish such crimes by persons under his or her authority." Furthermore, Trial Chamber I in its review of the Indictment pursuant to Rule 61 in *Prosecutor v. Milan Martić*, held that the Tribunal has jurisdiction over persons who, through their position of political or military authority, are

---

[286] Para. 346.
[287] Para. 354.

able to order the commission of crimes or who knowingly refrain from preventing or punishing the perpetrators of such crimes.[288]

Finally, the Chamber referred to certain trials following the Second World War, where military and paramilitary commanders as well as political leaders and public officials were held liable under the doctrine of command responsibility. The International Military Tribunal for the Far East (the "Tokyo Tribunal") found not only high ranking military leaders responsible for the commission of war crimes but also the Japanese Prime Minister Hideki Tojo, Foreign Ministers Koki Hirota and Mamoru Shigemitsu.[289] In the cases *United States v. Friedrich Flick and others,* and the *Roechling* case, leading civilian leaders and industrialists were convicted of the commission of war crimes and crimes against humanity based on an application of the responsibility of a superior for the acts of his inferiors which he has a duty to prevent.[290]

The Concept of Superior

The Chamber held that a superior, whether military or civilian, may be held liable under the principle of superior responsibility on the basis of his *de facto* position of authority. The doctrine of command responsibility is ultimately predicated upon the power of the superior to control the acts of his subordinates. A duty is placed upon the superior to exercise this power so as to prevent and repress the crimes committed by his subordinates, and a failure by him to do so in a diligent manner is sanctioned by the imposition of individual criminal responsibility in accordance with the doctrine. It follows that there is a threshold at which persons cease to possess the necessary powers of control over the actual perpetrators of offences and, accordingly, cannot properly be considered their "superiors" within the meaning of Article 7(3) of the Statute. The Chamber emphasized that while the fact finder must at all times be alive to the realities of any given situation and be prepared to pierce such veils of formalism that may shield those individuals carrying the greatest responsibility for heinous acts, great care must be taken lest an injustice be committed in holding individuals responsible for the acts of others in situations where the link of control is absent or too remote.[291]

For the principle of superior responsibility to be applicable, it is necessary that the superior have effective control over the persons committing the underlying violations of international humanitarian law, in the sense of having the material ability to prevent and punish the commission of these offences. With the caveat that such authority can have a *de facto* as well as a *de jure* character, the Chamber accordingly shared the view expressed by the International Law Commission that the doctrine of superior responsibility extends to civilian superiors only to the extent that they exercise a degree of control over their subordinates which is similar to that of military commanders.[292]

---

[288] Para. 356.
[289] Paras. 357-358.
[290] Paras. 359-361.
[291] Para. 377.
[292] Para. 378.

The Chamber found that the doctrine of superior responsibility does not establish a standard of strict liability for superiors for failing to prevent or punish the crimes committed by their subordinates. Under Article 7(3) a superior may be held responsible only where he knew or had reason to know that his subordinates were about commit to or had committed the acts referred to under Articles 2 to 5 of the Statute. The Chamber concluded that a superior may possess the *mens rea* required to incur criminal liability where: (1) he had actual knowledge, established through direct or circumstantial evidence, that his subordinates were committing or about to commit crimes referred to under Article 2 to 5 of the Statute, or (2) where he had in his possession information of a nature, which at the least, would put him on notice of the risk of such offences by indicating the need for additional investigation in order to ascertain whether such crimes were committed or were about to be committed by his subordinates.[293]

In the absence of direct evidence of the superior's knowledge of the offences committed by his subordinates, such knowledge cannot be presumed, but must be established by way of circumstantial evidence. In determining whether a superior, despite pleas to the contrary, in fact must have possessed the requisite knowledge, a Trial Chamber may consider, *inter alia,* the following indicia, listed by the Commission of Experts in its Final Report:

(a) The number of illegal acts;

(b) The type of illegal acts;

(c) The scope of illegal acts;

(d) The time during which the illegal acts occurred;

(e) The number and type of troops involved;

(f) The logistics involved, if any;

(g) The geographical location of the acts;

(h) The widespread occurrence of the acts;

(i) The tactical tempo of operations;

(j) The modus operandi of similar illegal acts;

(k) The officers and staff involved;

(l) The location of the commander at the time.[294]

---

[293] Para. 383.
[294] Para. 386.

Duty of a Superior to Remain Informed of the Activities of his Subordinates

The Chamber ruled that a superior has a duty to remain informed of the activities of his subordinates. A superior is not permitted to remain wilfully blind to the acts of his subordinates. A superior who simply ignores information within his actual possession compelling the conclusion that criminal offences are being committed, or are about to be committed, by his subordinates commits a most serious dereliction of duty for which he may be held criminally responsible under the doctrine of superior responsibility. The Chamber, in its construction of Article 7(3), gave full consideration to the standard established by article 86 of Additional Protocol I, in addition to judicial precedents from the Second World War.[295]

Rejection of the "Mental" Standard

The Chamber observed that Article 86 underwent considerable change during the drafting of Protocol I, and the drafters explicitly rejected the proposed inclusion of a mental standard according to which a superior would be criminally liable for the acts of his subordinates in situations where he should have had knowledge concerning their activities. The proposed ICRC draft, according to which superiors would be held responsible for the illegal acts of a subordinate "if they *knew or should have known* that he was committing or would commit such a breach and if they did not take measures within their power to prevent or repress the breach" was rejected. In addition, an amended version put forward by the United States employing the formulation "if they *knew or should reasonably have known* in the circumstances at the time" was also not accepted.[296]

The Chamber compared the English and French versions of Article 86. While the English text contains the wording "information which should have enabled them to conclude," the French version, rather than the literal translation "*des information qui auraient dû leur permettre de concluire*", is rendered "*des information leur permettant de concluire*" (literally: information enabling them to conclude). The Chamber observed that the proposition has been made that this discrepancy amounts to a distinction between the English text, which is said to embrace two requirements, one objective (that the superior had certain information) and one subjective (from this information available to the superior he should have drawn certain conclusions), and the French text containing only the objective element. Yet, the Chamber concluded that this discrepancy in language was considered during the drafting of the Protocol, when it was expressly declared by delegates that the difference was not to be considered one of substance.[297]

The Chamber concluded that an interpretation of the terms of Article 86 of the Protocol, as confirmed by the *travaux préparatoires*, means that a superior can be held criminally responsible only if some specific information was in fact available to him that would provide notice of offences committed by his subordinates. This information need not be such that it, by itself, was sufficient to compel the conclusion of the existence of

---

[295] Para. 387.
[296] Para. 391.
[297] Para. 392.

such crimes. It is sufficient that the superior was put on a duty to conduct a further inquiry by the information, or, in other words, that it indicated the need for additional investigation in order to ascertain whether offences were being committed or about to be committed by his subordinates. This standard, which must be considered to reflect the position of customary law at the time of the offences alleged in the indictment, is accordingly controlling for the construction of the *mens rea* standard established in Article 7(3). The Chamber thus made no finding as to the present content of customary law on this point. It was noted, however, that the provision on the responsibility of military commanders in the Rome Statute of the International Criminal Court provides that a commander may be held criminally responsible for failure to act in situations where he knew or should have known of offences committed, or about to be committed, by forces under his effective command and control, or effective authority and control.[298]

Acquiescence: Failure to Prevent or Punish

The Chamber held that the legal duty which rests upon all individuals in positions of superior authority requires them to take all necessary and reasonable measures to prevent the commission of offences by their subordinates or, if such crimes have been committed, to punish the perpetrators thereof. Any evaluation of the action taken by a superior to determine whether this duty has been met is so inextricably linked to the facts of each particular situation that any attempt to formulate a general standard *in abstracto* would not be meaningful.[299]

The Chamber recognized, however, that international law could not oblige a superior to perform the impossible. Hence, a superior may only be held criminally responsible for failing to take such measures as are within his powers. The question then arises of what actions are to be considered to be within the superior's powers in this sense. The Chamber concluded that a superior should be held responsible for failing to take such measures as are within his *material possibility*. The Chamber found that the lack of formal legal competence to take the necessary measures to prevent or repress the crime in question does not necessarily preclude the criminal responsibility of the superior.[300]

Causation

The Chamber observed that causation has not traditionally been postulated as a *conditio sine qua non* for the imposition of criminal liability on superiors for their failure to prevent or punish offences committed by their subordinates. There is no support for the existence of a requirement of proof of causation as a separate element of superior responsibility, either in the existing body of case law, the formulation of the principle in existing treaty law, or, with one exception, in the abundant literature on this subject.[301]

---

[298] Para. 393.
[299] Para. 394.
[300] Para. 395.
[301] Para. 398.

Nonetheless, the Chamber noted that the principle of causality is not without application to the doctrine of command responsibility insofar as it relates to the responsibility of superiors for their failure to prevent the crimes of their subordinates. It considered that recognition of a necessary causal nexus is inherent in the requirement of crimes committed by subordinates and the superior's failure to take the measures within his powers to prevent them. In this situation, the superior may be considered to be causally linked to the offences, in that, but for his failure to fulfil his duty to act, the acts of his subordinates would not have been committed.[302]

In contrast, while a causal connection between the failure of a commander to punish past crimes committed by subordinates and the commission of any such future crimes is not only possible but likely, the Chamber was of the view that no such causal link can possibly exist between an offence committed by a subordinate and the subsequent failure of a superior to punish the perpetrator of that same offence. The very existence of the principle of superior responsibility for failure to punish, therefore, recognised under Article 7(3) and customary law, demonstrates the absence of a requirement of causality as a separate element of the doctrine of superior responsibility.[303]

C. ICTR TRIAL CHAMBERS

Article 6 of the ICTR Statute is identical to Article 7 of the ICTY Statute. The ICTR jurisprudence reported below thus provides an interpretation of identical language.

PROSECUTOR V. AKAYESU, *Judgement,* ICTR-96-4-T, 2 September 1998, Kama, Aspegren & Pillay, JJ.

Distinction Between 6(1) and 6(3) of the Statute

In discussing the distinction between Articles 6(1) and 6(3), the Chamber wrote:

The forms of participation referred to in Article 6(1) cannot render their perpetrator criminally liable where he did not act knowingly, and even where he should have had such knowledge. This differs from Article 6(3) which does not necessarily require that a superior acted knowingly to render him criminally liable; it suffices that he had reason to know that his subordinates were about to commit or had committed a crime and failed to take the necessary or reasonable measures to prevent such acts or punish the perpetrators. In a way this is liability by omission or abstention.[304]

The Chamber found that the principle of superior responsibility derives from the application of the concept in the Nuremberg and Tokyo trials. The principle is codified in Article 86 of Additional Protocol I to Geneva Conventions of 8 June 1977.[305]

---

[302] Para. 399.
[303] Para. 400.
[304] Para. 479.
[305] Para. 486.

The Chamber dealt with the question of whether this section applied to both military and civilian authorities. The Chamber determined that it did, citing the Tokyo jurisprudence, but noting at the same time the dissenting opinion of Judge Röling. The Chamber concluded that in the case of civilians the application of Article 6(3) remains contentious. The Chamber determined that it is appropriate to assess, on a case by case basis, the power or authority actually devolved upon the accused in order to determine whether or not he had power to take all necessary and reasonable measures to prevent the commission of the alleged crimes or to punish the perpetrators thereof.[306]

---

[306] Para. 491.

ARTICLE 8

TERRITORIAL AND TEMPORAL JURISDICTION

THE TERRITORIAL JURISDICTION OF THE INTERNATIONAL TRIBUNAL SHALL EXTEND TO THE TERRITORY OF THE FORMER SOCIALIST FEDERAL REPUBLIC OF YUGOSLAVIA, INCLUDING ITS LAND SURFACE, AIRSPACE AND TERRITORIAL WATERS. THE TEMPORAL JURISDICTION OF THE INTERNATIONAL TRIBUNAL SHALL EXTEND TO A PERIOD BEGINNING ON 1 JANUARY 1991.

ARTICLE 9

CONCURRENT JURISDICTION

1. THE INTERNATIONAL TRIBUNAL AND NATIONAL COURTS SHALL HAVE CONCURRENT JURISDICTION TO PROSECUTE PERSONS FOR SERIOUS VIOLATIONS OF INTERNATIONAL HUMANITARIAN LAW COMMITTED IN THE TERRITORY OF THE FORMER YUGOSLAVIA SINCE 1 JANUARY 1991.

2. THE INTERNATIONAL TRIBUNAL SHALL HAVE PRIMACY OVER NATIONAL COURTS. AT ANY STAGE OF THE PROCEDURE, THE INTERNATIONAL TRIBUNAL MAY FORMALLY REQUEST NATIONAL COURTS TO DEFER TO THE COMPETENCE OF THE INTERNATIONAL TRIBUNAL IN ACCORDANCE WITH THE PRESENT STATUTE AND THE RULES OF PROCEDURE AND EVIDENCE OF THE INTERNATIONAL TRIBUNAL.

I. COMMENTARY

A. PRIMACY

There is in interesting issue in at least one area. In the Decision on the Defence Motion on Jurisdiction in the *Tadić* case, discussed below, the Court discussed the offenses within the Court's jurisdiction as being offenses against customary international law and therefore offenses that transgress all of mankind, not just the domestic law of any one state.

The difficulty, of course, is drawing the line between those offenses that are part of customary international law and those that are not. It has been forcefully argued before the Tribunal, for instance, that the offences set out in Common Article 3 of the Geneva Conventions of 1949 are not part of customary international law. The Tribunal, however, has taken the position that they are incorporated into the Statute under Article 3, and several accused have been convicted pursuant to the common article.[307]

---

[307] This issue is being considered by the Appeals Chamber in the *Delalić* case. The Judgement will probably conclusively decide the issue one way or the other.

II.   TRIBUNAL CASES

A.   APPEALS CHAMBER

1. PRIMACY

PROSECUTOR V. TADIĆ, *Decision on the Defence Motion for Interlocutory Appeal on Jurisdiction*, IT-94-1-AR72, 2 October 1995, Cassese, Li, Deschênes, Abi-Saab & Sidhwa, JJ.

Violation of State Sovereignty

The Trial Chamber, in this case, had decided, relying on the *Eichmann* case, that an individual did not have standing to raise issues of State sovereignty. The Appeals Chamber consulted both the *Eichmann* case and a United States District Court decision in *United States v. Noriega.*[308] These cases were rejected by the Appeals Chamber, writing that an "accused . . . cannot be deprived of a plea so intimately connected with, and grounded in, international law as a defence based on violation of State sovereignty."[309] Having determined that the defendant had a right to raise the issue, the Chamber then went on to reject his contentions, as follows:

> It would be a travesty of law and a betrayal of the universal need for justice, should the concept of State sovereignty be allowed to be raised successfully against human rights. Borders should not be considered as a shield against the reach of the law and as a protection for those who trample underfoot the most elementary rights of humanity.[310]

Jus De Non Evocando

The term *Jus De Non Evocando* is a feature of the constitutions of some States which prohibit a defendant from being removed from the regularly established court to which he is assigned by law to be tried by some special tribunal created for that special purpose. The Chamber found that the principle has no application in the International Tribunal. As the Chamber said:

> . . . one cannot but rejoice at the thought that universal jurisdiction being nowadays acknowledged in the case of international crimes, a person suspected of such offences may finally be brought before an international judicial body for a dispassionate consideration of his indictment by impartial, independent and disinterested judges coming, as it happens here, from all continents of the world.[311]

---

[308] 746 F.Supp. 1506, S.D. Fla. (1990).
[309] Para. 55.
[310] Para. 58.
[311] Para. 62.

ARTICLE 10

NON-BIS-IN-IDEM

1.　NO PERSON SHALL BE TRIED BEFORE A NATIONAL COURT FOR ACTS CONSTITUTING SERIOUS VIOLATIONS OF INTERNATIONAL HUMANITARIAN LAW UNDER THE PRESENT STATUTE, FOR WHICH HE OR SHE HAS ALREADY BEEN TRIED BY THE INTERNATIONAL TRIBUNAL.

2.　A PERSON WHO HAS BEEN TRIED BY A NATIONAL COURT FOR ACTS CONSTITUTING SERIOUS VIOLATIONS OF INTERNATIONAL HUMANITARIAN LAW MAY BE SUBSEQUENTLY TRIED BY THE INTERNATIONAL TRIBUNAL ONLY IF:

(A)　THE ACT FOR WHICH HE OR SHE WAS TRIED WAS CHARACTERIZED AS AN ORDINARY CRIME; OR

(B)　THE NATIONAL COURT PROCEEDINGS WERE NOT IMPARTIAL OR INDEPENDENT, WERE DESIGNED TO SHIELD THE ACCUSED FROM INTERNATIONAL CRIMINAL RESPONSIBILITY, OR THE CASE WAS NOT DILIGENTLY PROSECUTED.

3. IN CONSIDERING THE PENALTY TO BE IMPOSED ON A PERSON CONVICTED OF A CRIME UNDER THE PRESENT STATUTE, THE INTERNATIONAL TRIBUNAL SHALL TAKE INTO ACCOUNT THE EXTENT TO WHICH ANY PENALTY IMPOSED BY A NATIONAL COURT ON THE SAME PERSON FOR THE SAME ACT HAS ALREADY BEEN SERVED.

I.　COMMENTARY

Article 10(2) is an addition to the general principle of *non bis in idem.* The language appears to be fashioned to avoid a situation where a person suspected of violations of international humanitarian law from former Yugoslavia could escape jurisdiction of the Tribunal by being tried in sham proceedings in his home country.

The burden would be on the Prosecutor to show that the national proceedings were as characterized by Rule 10(2)(B).

The other situation covered by Rule 10(B) would be the case, for instance, where someone is tried in a national jurisdiction for one or more murders, as murders under the domestic Penal Code. Presumably 10(2)(A) would not preclude a subsequent trial before the Tribunal for those murders as a crime against humanity.

II.   TRIBUNAL CASES

A.   APPEALS CHAMBER

PROSECUTOR V. TADIĆ, *Decision on the Defence Motion for Interlocutory Appeal on Jurisdiction,* IT-94-1-AR72, 2 October 1995, Cassese, Li, Deschenes, Abi-Saab & Sidwha, JJ.

Tadić contended that the Tribunal did not have jurisdiction in his case since he had been arrested in Germany and was subject to trial before a German Court. At the time, his case in Germany was at the investigation stage. Nevertheless, Tadić asserted that the terms of Article 10 precluded a trial by the Tribunal.

In response the Chamber said:

> This provision has nothing to do with the present case. This is not an instance of an accused being tried anew by this International Tribunal, under the exceptional circumstances described in Article 10 of the Statute. [312]

---

[312] Para. 52.

ARTICLE 11

ORGANIZATION OF THE INTERNATIONAL TRIBUNAL

THE INTERNATIONAL TRIBUNAL SHALL CONSIST OF THE FOLLOWING ORGANS:

(A) THE CHAMBERS, COMPRISING THREE TRIAL CHAMBERS AND AN APPEALS CHAMBER;

(B) THE PROSECUTOR, AND

(C) A REGISTRY, SERVICING BOTH THE CHAMBERS AND THE PROSECUTOR.

ARTICLE 12

COMPOSITION OF THE CHAMBERS

THE CHAMBERS SHALL BE COMPOSED OF ELEVEN INDEPENDENT JUDGES, NO TWO OF WHOM MAY BE NATIONALS OF THE SAME STATE, WHO SHALL SERVE AS FOLLOWS:

  (A)   THREE JUDGES SHALL SERVE IN EACH OF THE TRIAL CHAMBERS;

  (B)   FIVE JUDGES SHALL SERVE IN THE APPEALS CHAMBER.

I.   COMMENTARY

II.   TRIBUNAL CASES

A.   APPEALS CHAMBER

PROSECUTOR V DELALIĆ et. al., Decision on Application for Leave to Appeal (Provisional Release) by Hazim Delić, IT-96-21-PT, 22 November 1996, Cassese, Li & Deschênes, JJ.

The legality of the establishment of a three-member Bench of Judges to entertain applications for leave to appeal

Pursuant to Article 12, the applicant challenged the legality of the establishment of three-member panel of the Appeals Chamber to sit in consideration of issues for leave to appeal pursuant to Rule 72.

The Appeals Chamber ruled that the establishment of the three-member panel to determine whether to grant leave of appeal was consistent with the Rules and broadened the right of appeal provided for under the Statute. Pursuant to the express language of Article 25 of the Statute, appeal is limited to appeals by persons convicted by the Trial Chamber or from the Prosecutor. The Chamber determined that Rule 72 broadened the right to appeal from this very limited right to appeal and thus it enhanced and strengthened the rights of the parties. The Judges through Rule 72 introduced interlocutory appeals *ex novo*. The Chamber found that under the Rules, the Judges set out conditions which the parties must meet to be granted leave before a full five-member appeals bench, where there is no appeal as of right. This "filter mechanism" was set up in the interest of good and expeditious administration of justice, namely for the purpose of promptly rejecting abusive interlocutory appeals while promptly admitting admissible interlocutory appeals. Furthermore, the Judges had the authority to lay down in their jurisprudence the test to be applied for granting leave to appeal.[313]

---

[313] Paras. 20-21.

ARTICLE 13

QUALIFICATIONS AND ELECTION OF JUDGES

1.   THE JUDGES SHALL BE PERSONS OF HIGH MORAL CHARACTER, IMPARTIALITY AND INTEGRITY WHO POSSESS THE QUALIFICATIONS REQUIRED IN THEIR RESPECTIVE COUNTRIES FOR APPOINTMENT TO THE HIGHEST JUDICIAL OFFICES. IN THE OVERALL COMPOSITION OF THE CHAMBERS DUE ACCOUNT SHALL BE TAKEN OF THE EXPERIENCE OF THE JUDGES IN CRIMINAL LAW, INTERNATIONAL LAW, INCLUDING INTERNATIONAL HUMANITARIAN LAW AND HUMAN RIGHTS LAW.

2.   THE JUDGES OF THE INTERNATIONAL TRIBUNAL SHALL BE ELECTED BY THE GENERAL ASSEMBLY FROM A LIST SUBMITTED BY THE SECURITY COUNCIL, IN THE FOLLOWING MANNER:

   (A)   THE SECRETARY-GENERAL SHALL INVITE NOMINATIONS FOR JUDGES OF THE INTERNATIONAL TRIBUNAL FROM STATES MEMBERS OF THE UNITED NATIONS AND NON-MEMBER STATES MAINTAINING PERMANENT OBSERVER MISSIONS AT UNITED NATIONS HEADQUARTERS;

   (B)   WITHIN SIXTY DAYS OF THE DATE OF THE INVITATION OF THE SECRETARY-GENERAL, EACH STATE MAY NOMINATE UP TO TWO CANDIDATES MEETING THE QUALIFICATIONS SET OUT IN PARAGRAPH 1 ABOVE, NO TWO OF WHOM SHALL BE OF THE SAME NATIONALITY;

   (C)   THE SECRETARY-GENERAL SHALL FORWARD THE NOMINATIONS RECEIVED TO THE SECURITY COUNCIL. FROM THE NOMINATIONS RECEIVED THE SECURITY COUNCIL SHALL ESTABLISH A LIST OF NOT LESS THAN TWENTY-TWO AND NOT MORE THAN THIRTY-THREE CANDIDATES, TAKING DUE ACCOUNT OF THE ADEQUATE REPRESENTATION OF THE PRINCIPAL LEGAL SYSTEMS OF THE WORLD;

   (D)   THE PRESIDENT OF THE SECURITY COUNCIL SHALL TRANSMIT THE LIST OF CANDIDATES TO THE PRESIDENT OF THE GENERAL ASSEMBLY. FROM THAT LIST THE GENERAL ASSEMBLY SHALL ELECT THE ELEVEN JUDGES OF THE INTERNATIONAL TRIBUNAL. THE CANDIDATES WHO RECEIVE AN ABSOLUTE MAJORITY OF THE VOTES OF THE STATES MEMBERS OF THE UNITED NATIONS AND OF THE NON-MEMBER STATES MAINTAINING PERMANENT OBSERVER MISSIONS AT UNITED NATIONS HEADQUARTERS, SHALL BE DECLARED ELECTED. SHOULD TWO CANDIDATES OF THE SAME NATIONALITY OBTAIN THE REQUIRED MAJORITY VOTE, THE ONE WHO RECEIVED THE HIGHER NUMBER OF VOTES SHALL BE CONSIDERED ELECTED.

3.   IN THE EVENT OF A VACANCY IN THE CHAMBERS, AFTER CONSULTATION WITH THE PRESIDENTS OF THE SECURITY COUNCIL AND OF THE GENERAL ASSEMBLY, THE

SECRETARY-GENERAL SHALL APPOINT A PERSON MEETING THE QUALIFICATIONS OF PARAGRAPH 1 ABOVE, FOR THE REMAINDER OF THE TERM OF OFFICE CONCERNED.

4. THE JUDGES SHALL BE ELECTED FOR A TERM OF FOUR YEARS. THE TERMS AND CONDITIONS OF SERVICE SHALL BE THOSE OF THE JUDGES OF THE INTERNATIONAL COURT OF JUSTICE. THEY SHALL BE ELIGIBLE FOR RE-ELECTION.

I. COMMENTARY

Reported below is the Appeals Chambers Judgement in Furundžija, which, for the first time, discussed the requirement of impartiality of Judges of the Tribunal.

The *Delalic* holding that the same judges should hear cases to their finality must be reconciled with the *Tadić* re-sentencing decision.[314] Tadić was re-sentenced by the Trial Chamber, after the Appeals Chamber found him guilty of certain offences, for the first time. Judge Robinson, who was not a member of the Trial Chamber in *Tadić*, sat along with Judges McDonald and Vohrah to re-sentence Tadić. The third judge on the original panel at trial, Judge Stephen was no longer a judge at the Tribunal.

II. TRIBUNAL CASES

A. APPEALS CHAMBER

PROSECUTOR V. FURUNDŽIJA, *Judgement*, IT-95-17/1-A, 21 July 2000, Shahabuddeen, Vohrah, Nieto-Navia, Robinson & Pocar, JJ.

Furundžija sought to have Judge Mumba disqualified because she had been a member of the United Nations Commission on the Status of Women (UNCSW) before assuming her duties as a Judge of the Tribunal. She served on the Commission as a representative of the Zambian government, not in her individual capacity. During her tenure, one of he issues that came before the UNCSW was the war in Yugoslavia and the information regarding mass and systematic commission of Rape. This resulted in a resolution of the UNCSW urging the International Tribunal to give priority to and vigorously prosecute such offences. There was also evidence that three authors of an *amicus curiae* brief filed with the Trial Chamber has served on an Expert Group associated with UNCSW where the issue of rape during the war in Yugoslavia was deemed a priority. One of the prosecutors in the case, Patricia Viseur-Sellers attended the meeting of the Expert Group. At that meeting the Expert Group proposed a definition of rape under international law.[315]

Based upon these facts, Furundžija challenged Judge Mumba's ability to sit as a judge in his case, primarily a case involving rape. His challenge was rejected by the Appeals Chamber.

---

[314] Prosecutor v. Tadić, *Sentencing Judgement*, IT-94-T *bis*-R117, 11 November 1999, McDonald, Vohrah & Robinson, JJ.

[315] Paras. 166, 167.

Timing of the Challenge

Furundžija did not raise this issue until some time after the Trial Chamber had rendered its Judgement against him. He explained that he did not learn of Judge Mumba's association with the UNCSW until that time. The Chamber pointed out that they could take the position that the issue would not be considered because it had been raised too late. However, since it is a matter of general importance it would be considered. The Chamber pointed out that this information regarding Judge Mumba had been available for some time in the yearbooks of the Tribunal and through the Public Information Service of the Tribunal. The Chamber did not believe it would have been unduly burdensome for the Appellant to have discovered the qualification of the Presiding Judge at this trial. His failure to do so would be grounds for dismissing this grounds of appeal due to waiver of the issue.

The Requirement of Impartiality

The requirement of impartiality on the part of Judges of the Tribunal is contained within the Tribunal's Statute. The Chamber pointed out:

> The fundamental human right of an accused to be tried before an independent and impartial tribunal is generally recognised as being an integral component of the requirement that an accused should have a fair trial. Article 13(1) of the Statute reflects this, by expressly providing that Judges of the International Tribunal "shall be persons of high moral character, *impartiality* and integrity". This fundamental human right is similarly reflected in Article 21 of the Statute, dealing generally with the rights of the accused and the right to a fair trial. As a result, the Appeals Chamber need look no further than Article 13(1) of the Statute for the source of that requirement.[316]

Although the Statute clearly requires that Judges be impartial, the question becomes one of how to apply that requirement in the context of the ICTY. The Chamber conducted a review of the law regarding the issue. Based upon that review the Chamber formulated a standard to be applied, as follows:

> [T]he Appeals Chamber finds that there is a general rule that a Judge should not only be subjectively free from bias, but also that there should be nothing in the surrounding circumstances which objectively gives rise to an appearance of bias. On this basis, the Appeals Chamber considers that the following principles should direct it in interpreting and applying the impartiality requirement of the Statute:

---

[316] Para. 177.

A. A Judge is not impartial if it is shown that actual bias exists.

B. There is an unacceptable appearance of bias if:

> i) a Judge is a party to the case, or has a financial or proprietary interest in the outcome of a case, or if the Judge's decision will lead to the promotion of a cause in which he or she is involved, together with one of the parties. Under these circumstances, a Judge's disqualification from the case is automatic; or

> ii) the circumstances would lead a reasonable observer, properly informed, to reasonably apprehend bias.[317]

The question then was, what is a "reasonable observer." The Chamber found that a reasonable observer must be:

> an informed person, with knowledge of all the relevant circumstances, including the traditions of integrity and impartiality that form a part of the background and apprised also of the fact that impartiality is one of the duties that Judges swear to uphold.[318]

Furundžija relied on the *Pinochet*[319] case. The Chamber distinguished *Pinochet* from the instant case. While Lord Hoffman, in *Pinochet* was a Director of Amnesty International Charity Limited at the time he heard the *Pinochet* case, Judge Mumba had left her position as her government's representative to the UNCSW before assuming her duties as a Judge at the Tribunal.

Presumption of Impartiality

The Chamber determined that there exists a presumption of impartiality with regard to Judges of the Tribunal. The Chamber explained, as follows:

> This presumption has been recognised in the jurisprudence of the International Tribunal, and has also been recognised in municipal law. For example, the Supreme Court of South Africa in the *South African Rugby Football Union* case found:

> > The reasonableness of the apprehension of bias must be assessed in the light of the oath of office taken by the Judges to administer justice without fear or favour; and their ability to carry out that oath by reason of their training and experience. It must be assumed that they can

---

[317] Para. 189.
[318] Para. 190.
[319] R. v. Bow Street Metropolitan Stipendiary Magistrate and others, *ex parte* Pinochet Ugarte, (No. 2) [1999], 1 All ER 577.

disabuse their minds of any irrelevant personal beliefs or predispositions. They must take into account the fact that they have a duty to sit in any case in which they are not obliged to recuse themselves.[320]

Since there is such a presumption, the burden then is on the one challenging a Judge's impartiality to establish that claim. The threshold is high. It must be firmly established.[321]

With regard to Judge Mumba, the Chamber found that it was significant that she served on the UNCSW not as an individual, but as a representative of her government. She served under instructions from her government and when she spoke, she spoke on behalf of her government.[322]

The Appellant's claim is that by endorsing the view of the UNCSW that rape is an abhorrent crime and should be vigorously prosecuted, Judge Mumba became disqualified from sitting as a Judge in a rape case. The Chamber said that "to endorse the view that rape as a crime is abhorrent and that those responsible for it should be prosecuted within the constraints of the law cannot in itself constitute grounds for disqualification.[323]

B.   TRIAL CHAMBERS

PROSECUTOR V. DELALIĆ et. al., *Decision on the Prosecution's Motion that the Accused State Whether They Will Waive any Objection to the Trial Chamber Sitting after 17 November 1997,* IT-96-21-T, 23 June 1997, Karibi-Whyte, Odio-Benito & Jan, JJ.

Terms and Conditions of Judges

The three judges constituting the Trial Chamber in the *Delalic* case ruled that they owed their four-year tenure as judges of the Tribunal to an election of the General Assembly in May 1993. Their appointment took effect from 17 November 1993.

On 21 May 1997, the General Assembly elected a set of eleven judges to serve on the Tribunal for a term of four years starting on 17 November 1997. The three judges comprising the *Delalić* Trial Chamber were not re-elected. Their tenure as judges expired on 17 November 1997 pursuant to Article 13(4). The issue for determination by the Chamber was whether, despite the fact that their tenure as judges expired on 17 November 1997, they could continue to sit as members of a properly constituted Chamber.

The Chamber made two preliminary observations, before turning to Article 13(4). Under Article 12 the Chamber was properly established and under Article 14 the

---

[320] Para. 196, quoting from President of the Republic of South Africa and Others v. South African Rugby
    Football Union and Others, *Judgement on Recusal Application,* 1999 (7) BCLR 725 (CC), 3 June 1999.
[321] Para. 197.
[322] Para. 199.
[323] Para. 202.

judges were properly assigned to the Chamber.[324] The central issue was determined by reference to Article 13(3) of the ICJ Statute, which provides for the terms and conditions of service of the judges of the ICJ. The Chamber ruled that the three judges in the *Delalić* case shall continue to discharge their duties, despite their non-re-election and, even if replaced, shall finish any cases that they have begun.

Article 13(3) of the ICJ Statute states:

> [T]he members [judges] of the Court shall continue to discharge their duties until their places have been filled. Though replaced, they shall finish any cases which they may have begun.

The Chamber found that Article 13(3) of the ICJ Statute is incorporated into Article 13(4) of the ICTY Statute to ensure continuity and certainty that the same judges hear matters before the Trial Chamber in the interest of judicial efficiency. The interests of justice and public policy have always approved of judges continuing to hear cases to finality even after the expiration of their tenure.

---

[324] Para. 4.

ARTICLE 14

OFFICERS AND MEMBERS OF THE CHAMBERS

1.   THE JUDGES OF THE INTERNATIONAL TRIBUNAL SHALL ELECT A PRESIDENT.

2.   THE PRESIDENT OF THE INTERNATIONAL TRIBUNAL SHALL BE A MEMBER OF THE APPEALS CHAMBER AND SHALL PRESIDE OVER ITS PROCEEDINGS.

3.   AFTER CONSULTATION WITH THE JUDGES OF THE INTERNATIONAL TRIBUNAL, THE PRESIDENT SHALL ASSIGN THE JUDGES TO THE APPEALS CHAMBER AND TO THE TRIAL CHAMBERS. A JUDGE SHALL SERVE ONLY IN THE CHAMBER TO WHICH HE OR SHE WAS ASSIGNED.

4.   THE JUDGES OF EACH TRIAL CHAMBER SHALL ELECT A PRESIDING JUDGE, WHO SHALL CONDUCT ALL OF THE PROCEEDINGS OF THE TRIAL CHAMBER AS A WHOLE.

ARTICLE 15

RULES OF PROCEDURE AND EVIDENCE

THE JUDGES OF THE INTERNATIONAL TRIBUNAL SHALL ADOPT RULES OF PROCEDURE AND EVIDENCE FOR THE CONDUCT OF THE PRE-TRIAL PHASE OF THE PROCEEDINGS, TRIALS AND APPEALS, THE ADMISSION OF EVIDENCE, THE PROTECTION OF VICTIMS AND WITNESSES AND OTHER APPROPRIATE MATTERS.

I. COMMENTARY

At its creation the Tribunal was basically modeled on the "adversary" system. Since then there has been much discussion about whether that was a good idea. It may not have been. All the accused and most of the lawyers representing them come from the "inquisitorial" Civil Law system. This has caused enormous difficulties. For instance, under the system in former Yugoslavia, defendants are encouraged to make statements. The making of a formal statement is part of the investigating magistrate process. At the Tribunal, however, giving a statement to the Prosecution pursuant to Rules 42 and 43 has generally been detrimental to the interests of the accused. There is no practice that provides for a sentence reduction for accused that make statements, unless it amounts to "substantial cooperation with the Prosecutor" under Rule 101.[325]

There have been attempts to create a more hybrid system, combining features from both the inquisitorial and the adversary systems. By and large this has resulted in a creature that is neither one nor the other and in many respects inferior to both.[326]

The differences between the systems was described by one distinguished jurist, as follows:

> To my mind the essence of the adversarial procedure is that the judge listens to the evidence and arguments of the parties, and decides between them; he does not make his own enquiries as to the facts, or adopt conclusions of fact not proposed by either party; nor does he propose or adopt arguments or conclusions of law differing from those which the parties put forward. By contrast, where the procedure is inquisitorial the judge can and does exercise all three of these functions."[327]

---

[325] Erdemović is the only person who has received such credit to date.

[326] With the current President of the Tribunal being from France, one might expect the attempts to intensify.

[327] Staughton, Lord Justice, Common Law and Civil Law Procedures: Which is the more Inquisitorial? A Common Lawyer's Response, *Arbitration International*, (1989), Vol. 5, No. 4, p. 352, as quoted in Jones, John R.W.D., *The Practice of the International Criminal Tribunals for the Former Yugoslavia and Rwanda*, 2d Ed., (Transnational Publishers, 2000), p. 163.

II.   TRIBUNAL CASES

A.   APPEALS CHAMBER

PROSECUTOR V. TADIĆ, *Judgement on Allegations of Contempt Against Prior Counsel, Milan Vujin*, IT-94-1-A-R77, 31 January 2000, Shahabuddeen, Cassese, Nieto-Navia, Mumba & Hunt, JJ.

The Appeals Chamber held that Article 15 does not permit rules to be adopted that constitute *new* offences, but it does permit the judges to adopt *rules of procedure and evidence* for the conduct of matters falling within the inherent jurisdiction of the Tribunal as well as matters within its statutory jurisdiction.
    Two examples given by the Chamber of provisions in the Rules concerning the conduct of a matter falling within the inherent jurisdiction of the Tribunal are Contempt of Court under Rule 77 and False Testimony under Rule 91.[328]

---

[328] Para. 24.

ARTICLE 16

THE PROSECUTOR

1.   THE PROSECUTOR SHALL BE RESPONSIBLE FOR THE INVESTIGATION AND PROSECUTION OF PERSONS RESPONSIBLE FOR SERIOUS VIOLATIONS OF INTERNATIONAL HUMANITARIAN LAW COMMITTED IN THE TERRITORY OF THE FORMER YUGOSLAVIA SINCE 1 JANUARY 1991.

2.   THE PROSECUTOR SHALL ACT INDEPENDENTLY AS A SEPARATE ORGAN OF THE INTERNATIONAL TRIBUNAL. HE OR SHE SHALL NOT SEEK OR RECEIVE INSTRUCTIONS FROM ANY GOVERNMENT OR FROM ANY OTHER SOURCE.

3.   THE OFFICE OF THE PROSECUTOR SHALL BE COMPOSED OF A PROSECUTOR AND SUCH OTHER QUALIFIED STAFF AS MAY BE REQUIRED.

4.   THE PROSECUTOR SHALL BE APPOINTED BY THE SECURITY COUNCIL ON NOMINATION BY THE SECRETARY-GENERAL. HE OR SHE SHALL BE OF HIGH MORAL CHARACTER AND POSSESS THE HIGHEST LEVEL OF COMPETENCE AND EXPERIENCE IN THE CONDUCT OF INVESTIGATIONS AND PROSECUTIONS OF CRIMINAL CASES. THE PROSECUTOR SHALL SERVE FOR A FOUR-YEAR TERM AND BE ELIGIBLE FOR REAPPOINTMENT. THE TERMS AND CONDITIONS OF SERVICE OF THE PROSECUTOR SHALL BE THOSE OF AN UNDER-SECRETARY-GENERAL OF THE UNITED NATIONS.

5.   THE STAFF OF THE OFFICE OF THE PROSECUTOR SHALL BE APPOINTED BY THE SECRETARY-GENERAL ON THE RECOMMENDATION OF THE PROSECUTOR.

I.   COMMENTARY

The Prosecutor of the Tribunal occupies a dual rule.   The Prosecutor functions independently in his or her role as an investigator and in his or her discretion to decide against whom to present indictments.   However, in the role as a Prosecutor before a Chamber the Prosecutor occupies a position of equality with the Defence.   Thus, once an indictment is confirmed, the Prosecutor simply becomes one of the parties to the litigation.

II.   TRIBUNAL CASES

A.   TRIAL CHAMBERS

PROSECUTOR V. KUPREŠKIĆ, *et. al., Decision on Communications Between the Parties and their Witnesses,* IT-95-16-T, 21 September 1998, Cassese, May & Mumba, JJ.

The issue here dealt with an objection raised by Defence counsel regarding communications between the Prosecutor and her witnesses during breaks in their testimony that seemed to be affecting the testimony. This provided the occasion for the following comment by the Chamber regarding the role of the Prosecutor:

> . . . it should be noted that the Prosecutor of the Tribunal is not, or not only, a Party to adversarial proceedings but is an organ of the Tribunal and an organ of international criminal justice whose object is not simply to secure a conviction but to present the case for the Prosecution, which includes not only inculpatory, but also exculpatory evidence, in order to assist the Chamber to discover the truth in a judicial setting.

ARTICLE 17

THE REGISTRY

1.   THE REGISTRY SHALL BE RESPONSIBLE FOR THE ADMINISTRATION AND SERVICING OF THE INTERNATIONAL TRIBUNAL.

2.   THE REGISTRY SHALL CONSIST OF A REGISTRAR AND SUCH OTHER STAFF AS MAY BE REQUIRED.

3.   THE REGISTRAR SHALL BE APPOINTED BY THE SECRETARY-GENERAL AFTER CONSULTATION WITH THE PRESIDENT OF THE INTERNATIONAL TRIBUNAL. HE OR SHE SHALL SERVE FOR A FOUR-YEAR TERM AND BE ELIGIBLE FOR REAPPOINTMENT. THE TERMS AND CONDITIONS OF SERVICE OF THE REGISTRAR SHALL BE THOSE OF AN ASSISTANT SECRETARY-GENERAL OF THE UNITED NATIONS.

4.   THE STAFF OF THE REGISTRY SHALL BE APPOINTED BY THE SECRETARY-GENERAL ON THE RECOMMENDATION OF THE REGISTRAR.

Article 18

Investigation and Preparation of Indictment

1.   The Prosecutor shall initiate investigations ex-officio or on the basis of information obtained from any source, particularly from Governments, United Nations organs, intergovernmental and non-governmental organizations. The Prosecutor shall assess the information received or obtained and decide whether there is sufficient basis to proceed.

2.   The Prosecutor shall have the power to question suspects, victims and witnesses, to collect evidence and to conduct on-site investigations. In carrying out these tasks, the Prosecutor may, as appropriate, seek the assistance of the State authorities concerned.

3.   If questioned, the suspect shall be entitled to be assisted by counsel of his own choice, including the right to have legal assistance assigned to him without payment by him in any such case if he does not have sufficient means to pay for it, as well as to necessary translation into and from a language he speaks and understands.

4.   Upon a determination that a prima facie case exists, the Prosecutor shall prepare an indictment containing a concise statement of the facts and the crime or crimes with which the accused is charged under the Statute. The indictment shall be transmitted to a judge of the Trial Chamber.

I.   COMMENTARY

In the *Decision on Defence Motion to Dismiss the Indictment* from the *Blaškić* case, the Chamber wrote a decision that appears to confuse what is necessary to be included in an indictment for the purposes of providing notice and protection against double jeopardy and what must be disclosed to the Defence during the discovery process. The Chamber seems to have taken the position that if the Prosecutor eventually eliminates any vagueness in the charges and brings specificity to them, then all concerns are satisfied, regardless of whether this happens during the discovery process or even during the presentation of evidence. As a result, this decision stands in isolation from the later jurisprudence on the issues involved.

II.   TRIBUNAL CASES

A.   APPEALS CHAMBER

PROSECUTOR V. FURUNDŽIJA, *Judgement,* IT-95-17/1-A, 21 July 2000, Shahabuddeen, Vohrah, Nieto-Navia, Robinson & Pocar, JJ.

In discussing what it necessary to be included in the indictment, the Appeals Chamber distinguished between the material facts required in the indictment and the evidence that goes to prove those material facts. Furundžija had alleged that evidence was admitted in his case that was not mentioned in his indictment. He contended, as a result, that he was convicted upon evidence as to which he was not provided proper notice in the indictment. The Chamber said:

> In terms of Article 18 of the Statute and Rule 47, the indictment need only contain those material facts and need not set out the evidence that is to be adduced in support of them. In the instant case, the Appeals Chamber can find nothing wrong in the Trial Chamber's admission of this evidence which supports the charge of torture, even though it was not specified in the Amended Indictment. It would obviously be unworkable for an indictment to contain all the evidence that the Prosecutor proposes to introduce at the trial.[329]

B.   TRIAL CHAMBERS

PROSECUTOR V. DOŠEN, *et. al., Decision on Preliminary Motions,* IT-95-8-PT, 10 February 2000. May, Bennouna & Robinson, JJ.

Faced with a contention by the accused that the indictment was vague and lacked sufficient particulars, the Prosecutor filed a document entitled "Attachment A," which set forth additional information as to the time and place of the alleged offences and the identity of victims and co-perpetrators. The Prosecutor argued, however, that the indictment was sufficient standing alone and that "Attachment A" should not be considered a part of the "Amended Indictment." The Trial Chamber disagreed. Not attaching it to and making it a part of the indictment would create uncertainty about its legal status. It was therefore ordered that "Attachment A" should form a part of the Amended Indictment.[330]

It was contended further that even with "Attachment A," the indictment remained vague. The conduct of the accused as to certain counts was not clearly specified. Defendants were charged both for direct responsibility and superior responsibility as shift commanders at Keraterm Camp. The Prosecutor contended that the kind of detail requested by the Defence is unnecessary at this early stage of the proceedings. The Chamber disagreed, saying:

---

[329] Para. 153.
[330] Para. 9.

The form of the alleged participation of the accused in a crime is an material averment which should be clearly laid out in an indictment in order to clarify it and make plain the prosecution case.[331]

The Chamber entered the following Order:

> The Trial Chamber therefore orders the Prosecution to file an amended version of Attachment A. This Attachment will remain confidential and will form part of the Amended Indictment. Against each incident where the victim(s), place and date is named (in the first column), the Prosecution should specify (in the second column) the capacity in which each accused is alleged to have participated and whether his responsibility was:
>
>> (a)   direct pursuant to Article 7, paragraph 1, (and where possible, specifying the form of participation, such as "planning" or "instigating" or "ordering" etc.); or
>>
>> (b)   by virtue of his being on duty as a shift commander pursuant to Article 7, paragraph 3, or, if he was not on duty during that incident, whether there is still an allegation of superior responsibility under Article 7, paragraph 3, for that incident, or
>>
>> (c)   pursuant to Article 7, paragraph 1 and paragraph 3 (with specification as mentioned above).

PROSECUTOR V. KUNARAC, *Decision on the Form of the Indictment*, IT-96-23-PT, 4 November 1999, Mumba, Cassese & Hunt, JJ.

Defendant Kovač filed a Motion regarding the form of the indictment in which he challenged the sufficiency of the indictment in several respects. The Chamber determined that this Article, combined with the language of Article 19(1), provides that in an indictment:

(a)   the Prosecutor does not need to prove the facts alleged before trial and

(b)   the indictment itself must put an accused on sufficient notice of the case against him.[332]

. . . the capacity in which the accused allegedly committed the charged offense must be clearly defined. The indictment must also leave no doubt as to what the accused is alleged to have done at a particular venue on a particular date during a particular time period, with whom, to whom, or to what purpose. It must describe the full conduct complained of which amounts to the crime(s) charged. It must identify with reasonable clarity other persons involved, or affected, where necessary.

---

[331] Para. 12.
[332] Para. 5.

It follows that neither the supporting material nor witness statements made available to an accused under Rule 66 of the Rules of Procedure and Evidence . . . can be used to fill in any gaps in the indictment. An accused could be prejudiced were the Prosecutor to be allowed, for example, to introduce material facts through the calling of additional witnesses at trial instead of applying for leave to amend the indictment.[333]

In addition, the Chamber ordered the Prosecutor to amend and clarify in other respects. For example, paragraphs 11.1 and 11.2 of the Amended indictment refers to "two other women." The indictment was ordered to be amended to disclose the identity of the "two other women," since this was material to a fact to be proved at trial.[334]

PROSECUTOR V. BLAŠKIĆ, *Decision on Defence Motion to Dismiss the Indictment Based Upon Defects in the form Thereof (Vagueness/Lack of Adequate Notice of Charges),* IT-95-14-PT, 4 April 1997, Jorda, Li & Riad, JJ

The Defence filed a motion containing a broad-based attack on the indictment for vagueness and incompleteness. The Chamber agreed with the Defence in some instances. As a general proposition the Chamber concluded that in drafting an indictment, "the Prosecutor is obliged to specify, other than the legal provisions referred to, the facts in support of the indictment."[335]

As to specific counts of the indictment, the Chamber determined that language such as "including, but not limited to" or "among others" are vague expressions and do not belong in an indictment.[336]

With regard to setting out the dates in an indictment, the Judges ruled that the word "about" is overly vague and should be stricken from an indictment. Thus, "from about a certain date to on about a certain date" would not be an appropriate charge.

There was an additional claim that charging conduct as falling within either Article 7(1) or 7(3) brought vagueness to the charge. The Chamber said:

> The Trial Chamber is, however, of the opinion that, in international humanitarian law, more than in any other area, it is incumbent upon the Prosecutor to specify the type of responsibility under which a criminal act falls as promptly and as far as may be practicable as soon as the indictment has been issued.
>
> Nothing prevents the Prosecutor from pleading an alternative responsibility (Article 7(1) or 7(3) of the Statute), but factual allegations supporting either alternative must be sufficiently precise so as to permit the accused to prepare his defence on either or both alternatives. The required level of precision is important, if only in order to permit the accused to demonstrate

---

[333] Para 6, 7.
[334] Para. 18.
[335] Para. 15.
[336] Para. 22

the impossibility of being held responsible both directly for his own deeds and indirectly those of his subordinates.[337]

Counts 12 and 13 of the indictment charged respectively "destruction or wilful damage done to institutions dedicated to religion or education" and "plunder of public or private property." No religious or educational institution was named in the indictment, however. The Chamber ruled that the Prosecutor needed to be more specific in her allegations. But, then, the Chamber went on to find that an exhaustive list could not be required and that during the trial proceedings, the onus would be on the Prosecutor to satisfy the required degree of specificity.[338]

Finally the Chamber discussed the Defence contention that with regard to the charge of taking of hostages, it was improper to charge that offense both under Article 2 and Article 3. The Chamber said:

> Furthermore, the method of concurrent charges used by the Prosecutor has reached its limit here, and it would be appropriate to decide whether the taking of civilians as hostages falls under the precise scope of Article 2 of the Statute or, rather, under the broader scope of Article 3 of the Statute and Common Article 3 of the Geneva Conventions of 1949.
>
> The Trial Chamber invites the Prosecutor to redraft paragraph 14 of the indictment so as to provide the accused with a statement of facts which will permit him to prepare his defence, either under Article 2 or under Article 3 of the Statute. Should both characterisations be chosen - which can be done - it is nonetheless incumbent on the Prosecutor to specify which exchanges of individuals ascribed relate to civilians, which to soldiers, or even which to '(...) inhabitants of an occupied territory, who, on the approach of the enemy spontaneously take up arms to resist the invading forces (...)' (Article 4 (6) of the Geneva Convention on the Treatment of Prisoners of War).[339]

---

[337] Para. 32.
[338] Para. 37.
[339] Para. 38.

ARTICLE 19

REVIEW OF THE INDICTMENT.

1.   THE JUDGE OF THE TRIAL CHAMBER TO WHOM THE INDICTMENT HAS BEEN TRANSMITTED SHALL REVIEW IT. IF SATISFIED THAT A PRIMA FACIE CASE HAS BEEN ESTABLISHED BY THE PROSECUTOR, HE SHALL CONFIRM THE INDICTMENT. IF NOT SO SATISFIED, THE INDICTMENT SHALL BE DISMISSED.

2.   UPON CONFIRMATION OF AN INDICTMENT, THE JUDGE MAY, AT THE REQUEST OF THE PROSECUTOR, ISSUE SUCH ORDERS AND WARRANTS FOR THE ARREST, DETENTION, SURRENDER OR TRANSFER OF PERSONS, AND ANY OTHER ORDERS AS MAY BE REQUIRED FOR THE CONDUCT OF THE TRIAL.

I.   COMMENTARY

In the *Brđanin* case, the issue was raised as to whether any relief could be granted when the supporting material filed with the confirming Judge, along with the indictment does not support the allegations contained in the indictment. The Trial Chamber ruled that there was no possibility of relief in that event.

Although this ruling tends to be in agreement with national systems where a charge is initiated by indictment or information, it may make sense in this Tribunal, where the length of trials and the backlog is so severe to adopt a procedure whereby such a challenge could be made. Among other things it would force the Prosecutor at an early stage to evaluate a case properly and make a determination, based upon materials in its possession whether she can actually establish a *prima facie* case if called upon to do so.

If the supporting material does not establish a *prima facie* case, then what sense is there in going forward with huge expenditures of time and money with a trial only to have the accused acquitted at its end?

II.   TRIBUNAL CASES

B.   TRIAL CHAMBERS

1. ARTICLE 19(1) – MOTION TO DISMISS

PROSECUTOR V. BRĐANIN, *Decision on Motion to Dismiss the Indictment*, IT-99-36-PT, 5 OCTOBER 1999, Hunt, J.

Defendant Brđanin filed a Motion to Dismiss pursuant to Rule 72(A)(i) of the Rules. He contended that the Tribunal was without jurisdiction to proceed on the indictment against him because the supporting material provided to the confirming Judge did not support the allegations of the indictment.

The Pre-Trial Judge ruled on several matters in his written decision. In essence the Judge ruled that the confirmation process is one of form, not substance. The only question that could possibly be considered by a Trial Chamber is whether the confirming Judge followed the proper procedure in the confirmation process.[340]

Article 19.1 of the Statute only requires that the indictment disclose a *prima facie* case, not the supporting material. The Statute makes no reference to supporting materials.[341]

> . . . even if it be accepted for the purposes of argument that the supporting material did not establish the *prima facie* case pleaded in the indictment, the jurisdiction of the Tribunal still depends solely upon what is pleaded in the indictment. Whether there is evidence to support any charge pleaded in the indictment is an issue to be determined – as in both the common law and civil law systems – by the Trial Chamber, at the conclusion of the trial or (if the issue is raised) at the close of the prosecution case.[342]
>
> The Trial Chamber is satisfied that an insufficiency of the supporting material is irrelevant to the issue of the Tribunal's jurisdiction.[343]
>
> There is no provision in the Rules of Procedure and Evidence which permits a Trial Chamber to review the actual decision made by the confirming judge, by way of appeal or in any other way.[344]

---

[340] Para. 8.
[341] Para 12.
[342] Para. 15.
[343] Para. 20.
[344] Para. 21.

ARTICLE 20

COMMENCEMENT AND CONDUCT OF TRIAL PROCEEDINGS

1. THE TRIAL CHAMBERS SHALL ENSURE THAT A TRIAL IS FAIR AND EXPEDITIOUS AND THAT PROCEEDINGS ARE CONDUCTED IN ACCORDANCE WITH THE RULES OF PROCEDURE AND EVIDENCE, WITH FULL RESPECT FOR THE RIGHTS OF THE ACCUSED AND DUE REGARD FOR THE PROTECTION OF VICTIMS AND WITNESSES.

2. A PERSON AGAINST WHOM AN INDICTMENT HAS BEEN CONFIRMED SHALL, PURSUANT TO AN ORDER OR AN ARREST WARRANT OF THE INTERNATIONAL TRIBUNAL, BE TAKEN INTO CUSTODY, IMMEDIATELY INFORMED OF THE CHARGES AGAINST HIM AND TRANSFERRED TO THE INTERNATIONAL TRIBUNAL.

3. THE TRIAL CHAMBER SHALL READ THE INDICTMENT, SATISFY ITSELF THAT THE RIGHTS OF THE ACCUSED ARE RESPECTED, CONFIRM THAT THE ACCUSED UNDERSTANDS THE INDICTMENT, AND INSTRUCT THE ACCUSED TO ENTER A PLEA. THE TRIAL CHAMBER SHALL THEN SET THE DATE FOR TRIAL.

4. THE HEARINGS SHALL BE PUBLIC UNLESS THE TRIAL CHAMBER DECIDES TO CLOSE THE PROCEEDINGS IN ACCORDANCE WITH ITS RULES OF PROCEDURE AND EVIDENCE.

I. COMMENTARY

This article was first discussed by the Tribunal in the *Tadić* case.[345] The Prosecutor had requested various degrees of protection for several of its witnesses and for some of the testimony to occur in closed hearings. The Trial Chamber took the opportunity to draft a comprehensive study of the balancing process between the rights of defendants to fair trials against the rights of victims and witnesses. The Chamber also took into account interest of the public in open hearings.

    See Article 21. Together, Articles 20 and 21 are often referred to as the "fair trial provisions" of the Statute.

II. TRIBUNAL CASES

A. APPEALS CHAMBER

PROSECUTOR V. KOVAČEVIĆ, *Decision Stating Reasons for Appeals Chamber's Order of 29 May 1998,* IT-97-24-AR73, 2 July 1998, McDonald, Shahabuddeen, Wang Tieya, Nieto-Navia & Rodrigues, JJ.

The Appeals Chamber reversed the Trial Chamber prohibiting the Prosecution from amending the indictment. A full report of this decision may be found under Rule 50.

---

[345] The Prosecutor v. Tadić, *Decision on the Prosecutor's Motion Requesting Protective Measures for Victims and Witnesses*, IT-94-1, 10 August 1995.

B.   TRIAL CHAMBERS

1. FAIR TRIAL – 20(1)

A.   WITNESS PROTECTION

PROSECUTOR V. BRĐANIN & TALIC, *Decision on Motion by Prosecution for Protective Measures,* IT-99-36-PT, 3 July 2000, Hunt, Mumba & Pocar, JJ.

In response to her obligations under Rule 66(A)(i), the Prosecutor furnished the Defence with numerous witness statements. However, all identifying information, plus some additional information had been redacted therefrom. This was done without prior authorization from the Trial Chamber. At the same time the Prosecutor filed a Motion for Protective Measures, seeking a number of orders from the Trial Chamber. The Prosecutor asked the Chamber to order the Defence not to disclose any confidential or non-public materials to the media; and, not to disclose to the public, except where necessary for preparation and presentation of the case, the names, identifying information or whereabouts of any witness or potential witness identified to them by the prosecutor, nor any such evidence whether documentary, physical or in the form of statements of witnesses; and, to inform each person amoung the public to whom disclosure is necessary of the material that it is not to be reproduced in any manner, or publicized or shown to any other person and that such material shall be returned to the defence when it is no longer necessary; and, that the defence should maintain a log indicating the name, address and position of anyone to whom such disclosure is made and the date of disclosure; and, if a member of the defence team withdraws from the case all material in their possession should be returned to lead defence counsel; and, at the conclusion of the case all the disclosed material and copies thereof that have not become part of the public record should be returned by counsel to the Registry; and that the Prosecutor is authorized to make limited redactions in the material so furnished concerning the identity and whereabouts of vulnerable victims or witnesses to be disclosed by the Prosecutor only in a reasonable time prior to trial.

In argument for its position, the Prosecutor asserted that it should be entitled to make the redactions from furnished materials because "Bosnia and Herzegovina continues to be a dangerous place, where each ethnic or political group is viewed as the enemy of another, and where 'much of the war is still being fought, with indictees [sic] or suspects and their supporters (as well as supporters of those detained in The Hague) still at large and where witnesses against them are considered "the enemy"'.[346] The Prosecutor also argued that such an order was justified by the circumstances prevailing in this case and for future cases that might come before the Tribunal. The Prosecutor argued:

---

[346] Para. 8.

> If witnesses will not come forward or if witnesses refuse or are otherwise unwilling to testify, there is little evidence to present. Threats, harassment, violence, bribery and other intimidation, interference and obstruction of justice are serious problems, for both the individual witnesses and the Tribunal's ability to accomplish its mission.[347]

The Chamber decided, in reference to the language of Rule 69(A) which requires that non-disclosure may only occur in "exceptional circumstances" as follows:

> In the opinion of the Trial Chamber, the prevailing circumstances within the former Yugoslavia *cannot by themselves* amount to exceptional circumstances. The Tribunal has always been concerned solely with the former Yugoslavia and Rule 69(A) was adopted by the judges against a background of ethnic and political enmities which existed in the former Yugoslavia at the time. . . To be exceptional, the circumstances must therefore go beyond what has been, since before the Tribunal was established, the rule – or the prevailing (or normal) circumstances – in the former Yugoslavia.[348] [Chamber's emphasis]

The Chamber thus concluded that the actions of the Prosecutor in making wholesale redactions in every witness statement furnished under this rule were "both unauthorized and unjustified."[349]

In addition, the Prosecutor sought a procedure that would avoid their making a witness-by-witness application for protection to the Trial Chamber. The Prosecutor suggested that they should, on their own, without permission, perform the redactions they felt necessary and justified. The accused could then, if necessary, make a request of the Prosecutor for disclosure of the identity of certain witnesses or victims to be made earlier than, for instance, 30 days before trial. If the Prosecutor refused the accused would then be in a position to make the request of the Trial Chamber.

The Chamber decided that the Prosecutor's proposal in this regard had two basic defects. First, it assumed that every witness is in danger, at risk or vulnerable, which is simply not so; and, second the proposal would put the onus on the defence instead of the prosecutor where it belongs under the clear language of Rule 69(A). The proposal of the Prosecutor was rejected.[350]

The Prosecutor argued that there is a conflict between Rules 66(A)(i) and 69(A) between the former's obligation to disclose and the latter's protection of victims and witnesses. The Chamber found no such conflict. The Chamber pointed out, relying on Article 20, that "the rights of the accused are made the first consideration, and the need to protect victims and witnesses is a secondary one." The Chamber said the rule should simply be:

---

[347] Para. 9.
[348] Para. 11.
[349] Para. 13.
[350] Paras. 16-18.

If the prosecution is able to demonstrate exceptional circumstances justifying the non-disclosure of the identity of any particular victims or witnesses at this early stage of the proceedings, then its obligations of disclosure under Rule 66(A)(i) will be complied with it if produces copies of the statements with the names and other identifying features of only *those* witnesses redacted.[351] (Chamber's emphasis)

PROSECUTOR V. KOLUNDŽIJA, *Order for Protective Measures*, IT-95-8-PT, 19 October 1999, May, Bennouna & Robinson, JJ.

Protective measures were instituted at the request of the Prosecutor and without objection from the Defence. The Prosecutor was ordered to immediately provide the defence with unredacted copies of the witness statements that formed a part of the supporting materials when the indictment was submitted for confirmation. Neither disclosure of any identifying information regarding these witnesses, nor the substance of their statements was to be made to the public, media or family members and associates of the defendant. The Prosecution and Defence were required to maintain a log indicating the name, address and position of each person or entity to which a copy of the witness statement was delivered along with the date of such disclosure. Persons to whom copies of the statements were delivered were to be instructed not to make any copies of them, and to return them when they were no longer required. The Defence could only contact a witness or potential witness identified by the Prosecutor after reasonable prior written notice to the Prosecutor.

PROSECUTOR V. FURUNDŽIJA, *Decision on Prosecutor's Motion Requesting Protective Measures for Witness "A" and "D" at Trial*, IT-95-17/1-T, 11 June 1998, Mumba, Cassese & May, JJ.

In the case of alleged rape or sexual assault both the Report of the Secretary-General[352] and Tribunal case law[353] acknowledge that protective measures are by and large warranted in the interests of justice, on the basis that tensions and concerns over safety to witnesses and their families continue to exist in the territory of the former Yugoslavia. A request for protective measures in such circumstances satisfies the requirement that there be a showing of exceptional circumstances.

In determining the issue of a request for protective measures for a witness at trial, the Chamber observed that Article 20 and 21 reflect the balance the Tribunal must observe between the right of the accused to a public trial and the protection of victims

---

[351] Para. 21.

[352] Para. 6, citing paragraph 108 of the Report of the Secretary-General.

[353] Prosecutor v. Tadić, *Decision on the Prosecutor's Motion Requesting Protective Measures for Victims and Witnesses*, Case No. IT-94-1-T, 10 August 1995; Prosecutor v. Delalić *et. al.*, *Decision on the Motions by the Prosecution for Protective Measures for the Prosecution Witnesses Pseudonymed "B" through to "M"*, IT-96-21-T, 28 April 1997; Prosecutor v. Delalić *et. al.*, *Decision on the Prosecution's Motion for the Redaction of the Pubic Record*, IT-96-21-T, 5 June 1997.

and witnesses.[354] Further, the Chamber noted that the granting of protective measures is provided for in Rule 75 and Rule 79.

The Chamber noted that an order granting protective measures is consistent with the right to a fair and public hearing pursuant to Article 14(1) of the International Covenant on Civil and Political Rights of 1966 which states, *inter alia*, that the public may be excluded from all or part of a trial "when the interests of the private lives of the parties so requires" or where in special circumstances "publicity would prejudice the interest of justice".[355]

B.   RE-OPENING OF THE PROCEEDINGS

PROSECUTOR V. FURUNDŽIJA, *Judgement*, IT-95-17/1, 10 December 1998, Mumba, Cassese & May, JJ.

After the proceedings and closing submissions had been concluded, but prior to judgement, the Prosecution disclosed for the first time to the Defence a document entitled "Certificate of Psychological Treatment" from Medica, a Womens' Therapy Center in Zenica, dated 11 July 1995. This document related to Witness A and stated that she had contacted Medica on 24 December 1993 in connection with the psychological trauma she had been suffering since she was abused in the Bungalow. Defence Exhibit D37 stated that she had been receiving treatment in the counseling center and that the symptoms of Post-Traumatic Stress Disorder, hereafter "PTSD", had been relieved. The Prosecution also disclosed a statement dated 16 September 1995 from an unidentified witness who stated that she had first seen Witness A on 24 December 1993 at Medica and last saw the witness on 11 July 1995.[356]

The Chamber rejected a motion filed by the Defence to strike out the testimony of Witness A because of the late disclosure by the Prosecution, or alternatively to order a new trial, in the event of a conviction.[357] The Chamber ruled that the interests of justice required a re-opening of the proceedings as the only available means to remedy the prejudice suffered by the Defence. The Chamber held that in the circumstances of this case, the late-disclosed material was considered to be relevant to the issue of credibility of Witness A's testimony. The prejudice to the accused stemmed from the fact that the Defence was unable to fully cross-examine relevant Prosecution witnesses and to call evidence to deal with the issues raised by the Medica documents.[358] The Chamber re-opened the proceeding solely in regards to any medical, psychological or psychiatric treatment or counseling received by Witness A after May 1993. The central issue was whether the reliability of the evidence of Witness A had been or may have been affected by any psychological disorder from which she may have suffered as a result of her ordeal. The defence was permitted to recall Prosecution witnesses for cross-examination and to

---

[354] Para. 4.
[355] Para. 5.
[356] Para. 90.
[357] Para. 91.
[358] Para. 92

call evidence on these issues and the Prosecution was allowed to call evidence in rebuttal.

The Chamber found that the provisions of Article 20 and 21 mandate the Chamber to ensure that the accused receives a fair trial. The Chamber ruled that the accused was entitled to explore every possible defence within the provisions of the Statute and by applying the "interests of justice" test inherent in its powers, the Chamber decided to re-open the proceedings to allow the Defence to remedy the prejudice suffered.[359]

---

[359] Para. 93.

ARTICLE 21

RIGHTS OF THE ACCUSED

1.	ALL PERSONS SHALL BE EQUAL BEFORE THE INTERNATIONAL TRIBUNAL.

2.	IN THE DETERMINATION OF CHARGES AGAINST HIM, THE ACCUSED SHALL BE ENTITLED TO A FAIR AND PUBLIC HEARING, SUBJECT TO ARTICLE 22 OF THE STATUTE.

3.	THE ACCUSED SHALL BE PRESUMED INNOCENT UNTIL PROVED GUILTY ACCORDING TO THE PROVISIONS OF THE PRESENT STATUTE.

4.	IN THE DETERMINATION OF ANY CHARGE AGAINST THE ACCUSED PURSUANT TO THE PRESENT STATUTE, THE ACCUSED SHALL BE ENTITLED TO THE FOLLOWING MINIMUM GUARANTEES, IN FULL EQUALITY:

(A)	TO BE INFORMED PROMPTLY AND IN DETAIL IN A LANGUAGE WHICH HE UNDERSTANDS OF THE NATURE AND CAUSE OF THE CHARGE AGAINST HIM;

(B)	TO HAVE ADEQUATE TIME AND FACILITIES FOR THE PREPARATION OF HIS DEFENCE AND TO COMMUNICATE WITH COUNSEL OF HIS OWN CHOOSING;

(C)	TO BE TRIED WITHOUT UNDUE DELAY;

(D)	TO BE TRIED IN HIS PRESENCE, AND TO DEFEND HIMSELF IN PERSON OR THROUGH LEGAL ASSISTANCE OF HIS OWN CHOOSING; TO BE INFORMED, IF HE DOES NOT HAVE LEGAL ASSISTANCE, OF THIS RIGHT; AND TO HAVE LEGAL ASSISTANCE ASSIGNED TO HIM, IN ANY CASE WHERE THE INTERESTS OF JUSTICE SO REQUIRE, AND WITHOUT PAYMENT BY HIM IN ANY SUCH CASE IF HE DOES NOT HAVE SUFFICIENT MEANS TO PAY FOR IT;

(E)	TO EXAMINE, OR HAVE EXAMINED, THE WITNESSES AGAINST HIM AND TO OBTAIN THE ATTENDANCE AND EXAMINATION OF WITNESSES ON HIS BEHALF UNDER THE SAME CONDITIONS AS WITNESSES AGAINST HIM;

(F)	TO HAVE THE FREE ASSISTANCE OF AN INTERPRETER IF HE CANNOT UNDERSTAND OR SPEAK THE LANGUAGE USED IN THE INTERNATIONAL TRIBUNAL;

(G)	NOT TO BE COMPELLED TO TESTIFY AGAINST HIMSELF OR TO CONFESS GUILT.

I.   COMMENTARY

A.   EQUALITY OF ARMS

Two important decisions have addressed the issue of the meaning and the scope of the principle of equality of arms under Article 20 and 21 of the Statute, the so-called fair trial provisions, both arising out of the *Tadić* case.[360]

B.   CROSS EXAMINATION

In the *Blaškić* case,[361] the Trial Chamber interpreted Article 21(4)(e) as applying only to those witnesses actually called before the Trial Chamber and not to the statements of witnesses admitted as hearsay. Considering that Statutes should be interpreted by their plain meaning, it seems that this is a curious decision indeed. The Article clearly says that the defendant has a right to cross-examine the witnesses against him. It does not distinguish between those who appear in court and those whose statements are admitted as hearsay. Hearsay is traditionally defined as "an out-of-court statement offered to prove the truth of the matter asserted." If the statement of an out-of-court declarant is offered for the purpose of proving the truth of the matter asserted, then the right of cross-examination requires the presence of the witness in court or the statement is inadmissible. The fundamental right of the accused to cross-examine witnesses against him is framed in absolute terms by the Statute. To attach a narrow interpretation to this right which cannot be found in the plain language of the provision affects the fundamental fairness of proceedings.

Of course the out-of-court statement may be admitted without objection. But, where objection is lodged and the witness cannot be made available for cross-examination it seems that the statement could not be admitted because of this Article.

II.   TRIBUNAL CASES

A.   APPEALS CHAMBER

1. EQUALITY OF ARMS

PROSECUTOR V. TADIĆ, *Judgement*, IT-94-1-A, 15 July 1999, Shahabuddeen, Cassese, Tieya, Nieto-Navia & Mumba, JJ.

On appeal, Tadić argued that he did not receive a fair trial because relevant and admissible evidence was not presented due to a lack of cooperation of the authorities of *Republika Srpska* in securing attendance of certain witnesses. In rejecting this ground of appeal, the Appeals Chamber stated that the Trial Chamber had used all the powers at its

---

[360] See, Prosecutor v. Tadić, *Separate Opinion of Judge Vohrah on Prosecution Motion for Production of Defence Witness Statements*, IT-94-1-T, 27 November 1996 and Prosecutor v. Tadić, *Judgement*, IT-94-1-A, 15 July 1999, Shahabuddeen, Cassese, Tieya, Nieto-Navia & Mumba, JJ.

[361] Prosecutor v. Blaškić, *Decision on Standing Objection of the Defence to the Admission of Hearsay with no Inquiry as to its Reliability*, IT-95-14, 21 January 1998, Jorda, Riad & Shahabuddeen, JJ.

disposal under the Rules and Statute to ensure a fair trial, particularly in securing the attendance of defence witnesses. The Trial Chamber responded to requests for assistance made by the defence; namely there was a long adjournment prior to the presentation of the defence case; protective measures for defence witnesses were granted; some testimony was given by video-link; certain witnesses were provided with confidential and safe passage; and, at the request of the Trial Chamber, a letter was sent by the President of the Tribunal to the Acting President of *Republika Srpska* to urge the presence of witnesses at trial.[362]

However, the Appeals Chamber did acknowledge that the right to a fair trial might be violated when a central witness to the defence case does not appear due to the obstructionist efforts of a State. The Defence may bring a motion for a stay of proceedings after exhausting all other measures provided for in the Rules for facilitating the presentation of evidence (subpoena, video-link, etc).[363] In addition, in such circumstances, the Chamber stated that a stay of proceedings occasioned by the frustrations of a fair trial would amount to "exceptional circumstances," justifying provisional release under Rule 65.[364] The Defence must bring these problems to the attention of the Trial Chamber forthwith and not remain silent and raise them for the first time on appeal.[365]

The Chamber held that the fair trial guarantee provided for in Article 20(1) of the Statute includes the principle of "equality of arms":

> The parties do not dispute that the right to a fair trial guaranteed by the Statute covers the principle of equality of arms. This interpretation accords with findings of the Human Rights Committee ("HRC") under the ICCPR. The HRC stated in *Morael v. France* that a fair hearing under Article 14(1) of the ICCPR must at a minimum include, *inter alia*, equality of arms. Similarly, in *Robinson v. Jamaica* and *Wolf v. Panama* the HRC found that there was inequality of arms in violation of the right to a fair trial under Article 14(1) of the ICCPR. Likewise, the case law under the ECHR cited by the Defence accepts that the principle is implicit in the fundamental right of the accused to a fair trial. The principle of equality of arms between the prosecutor and accused in a criminal trial goes to the heart of the fair trial guarantee. The Appeals Chamber finds that there is no reason to distinguish the notion of fair trial under Article 20(1) of the Statute from its equivalent in the ECHR and ICCPR, as interpreted by the relevant judicial and supervisory treaty bodies under those instruments. Consequently, the Chamber holds that the principle of equality of arms falls within the fair trial guarantee under the Statute.[366]

---

[362] Paras. 53 and 54.
[363] Para. 52.
[364] Since this decision was handed down, Rule 65 has been amended and a showing of "exceptional circumstances" is no longer a requirement for the granting of provisional release.
[365] Para. 55.
[366] Para. 44.

The Chamber found that the relationship between Article 20 and 21 of the Statute is that of the general to the particular and that, as a minimum, a fair trial guaranteed by Article 20(1) must entitle the accused to "adequate time and facilities for his defence" as provided for under Article 21(4)(b).[367]

As to the scope of the application of the principle of equality of arms, the Chamber found that the Prosecution and the Defence must be equal before the Trial Chamber and that the Trial Chamber should provide every practicable facility it is capable of granting under the Rules and Statute when faced with a request by a party for assistance in presenting its case.[368]

In referring to the case law under the *European Convention on Human Rights*, the Chamber found that "equality of arms obligates a judicial body to ensure that neither party is put at a disadvantage when presenting its case." The Chamber cited with approval the decision of the European Court of Human Rights in *Delacourt v. Belgium*,[369] wherein the Court held that in a criminal proceeding, the principle of equality of arms entitled both parties to full equality of treatment, maintaining that the conditions of trial must not "put the accused unfairly at a disadvantage."[370]

However, the scope of the principle of equality of arms is limited to the powers of a judicial body to control matters that could materially affect the fairness of the trial.[371]

Specifically on the question of equal access to witnesses, the Chamber found that under Rule 54, Chambers are empowered to issue such orders, summonses, subpoenas, warrants and transfer orders as may be necessary for the purposes of an investigation or for the preparation or conduct of the trial. This includes the power to:

(1)   adopt witness protection measures, ranging from partial to full protection;

(2)   take evidence by video-link or by way of deposition;

(3)   summon witnesses and order their attendance;

(4)   issue binding orders to States for, *inter alia*, the taking and production of evidence;

(5)   issue binding orders to States to assist a party or to summon a witness and order his or her attendance under the Rules;

(6)   for the President of the Tribunal to send, at the instance of the Trial Chamber, a request to the State authorities in question for their assistance in securing the attendance of a witness; and

---

[367] Para. 47.
[368] Para. 52.
[369] Eur. Court H.R., Judgement of 17 January 1970, Series A, no. 11.
[370] Para. 48.
[371] Paras. 49 and 51.

    (7)   order that proceedings be adjourned or, if the circumstances so require, that they be stayed.

PROSECUTOR V. ALEKSOVSKI, *Decision on Prosecutor's Appeal on Admissibility of Evidence,* IT-95-14/1-A, 16 February 1999, May, Tieya, Hunt, Bennouna & Robinson, JJ.

The Appeals Chamber held that the principle of equality of arms and of a fair trial enunciated in Article 20 and 21 of the Statute means equality between the Prosecution and the Defence. Relying on a number of judgements of the European Court of Human Rights, the Chamber approved of the requirement of equality of arms as providing a "fair balance" between the parties and as implying that each party must be afforded a reasonable opportunity to present his case – including his evidence – under conditions that do not place him at a substantial disadvantage *vis-à-vis* his opponent.[372] The Chamber added that the principle of equality of arms applied in favour of both parties is justified because the Prosecution acts on behalf of the interests of the international community, including those of the victims of the offences charged and the accused benefits from fundamental protections under general law or the Statute with which strict compliance is mandatory.[373]

2. RIGHT OF APPEAL

PROSECUTOR V. ALEKSOVSKI, *Judgement,* IT-95-14/1-A, 24 March 2000, May, Mumba, Hunt, Tieya & Robinson, JJ.

The Appeals Chamber ruled that the right of appeal is a component of the fair trial requirement of Article 21(4). The Chamber observed that the right of appeal is both a rule of treaty law under Article 14 of the International Covenant of Civil and Political Rights and a rule of customary international law, highlighted in the Report of the Secretary-General at paragraph 116.[374]

3. MISCELLANEOUS

PROSECUTOR V. KUPREŠKIĆ, *et. al., Decision on Appeal by Dragan Papić Against Ruling to Proceed by Deposition,* IT-95-16, 15 July 1999, Vohrah, Wang Tieya, Nieto-Navia, Hunt & Bennouna, JJ.

The Appellant challenged the proposition that the deposition procedure of Rule 71 could be used to circumvent the normal procedure in the event of the illness of a Judge as set forth in Rule 15. He contended that the illness of a Judge was not an "exceptional circumstance" within the spirit of this rule.

---

[372] Para. 24.
[373] Para. 25.
[374] Paras. 100, 104.

The Chamber said:

> In considering the issues raised by this ground of the appeal, the Appeals Chamber deems it necessary to recall one of the fundamental principles governing the giving of evidence before the Trial Chambers, namely the principle that witnesses shall as a general rule be heard directly by the Judges of the Trial Chambers. This principle is laid down in Article 21(4) of the Statute which grants to every accused person appearing before the Tribunal as one of the "minimum guarantees, in full equality", the right to examine, or have examined, the witnesses against him and to obtain the attendance and examination of witnesses on his behalf under the same conditions as witnesses against him. Sub-rule 90(A) embodies that same principle and specifically prescribes that witnesses shall in principle be heard directly by the Chambers. Furthermore, this principle is a predominant feature in the criminal procedure of national legal systems, underpinned as it is by the compelling reason of facilitating the determination of the charges against an accused person. One of the consequences of this principle is the advantage that all three Judges of a Trial Chamber shall have of observing the demeanour of the witness in person while he or she is being examined by the parties, apart from their ability to put questions to the witness under solemn circumstances in order to best ascertain the truth in respect of the crimes with which an accused is being charged.375

See a full report on this decision under Rule 71.

PROSECUTOR V. KOVAČEVIĆ, *Decision Stating Reasons for Appeals Chamber's Order of 29 May 1998,* IT-97-24-AR73, 2 July 1998, McDonald, Shahabuddeen, Wang Tieya, Nieto-Navia & Rodrigues, JJ.

The Appeals Chamber reversed a decision of the Trial Chamber prohibiting the Prosecution from amending the indictment. A full report of this decision is reported under Rule 50.

PROSECUTOR V. DELALIĆ, *Decision on Prosecution's Application for leave to Appeal Pursuant to Rule 73,* IT-96-21, 16 December 1997, McDonald, Vohrah & Nieto-Navia, JJ.

This decision is based on what is now Sub-rule 73(B)(ii), which at that time was Sub-rule 73(b).

    The Prosecution appealed against the decision of the Trial Chamber to preclude the Prosecution from calling an expert witness in relation to handwriting. (Oral decision on 3 December 1997)

    The Appeals Chamber observed that this Application might be considered of general importance to proceedings before the Tribunal because the issues at its heart are

---

375 Para. 18.

issues of fairness to the accused and the proper conduct of international criminal proceedings.[376]

The Prosecution sought leave call the handwriting expert on 18 November 1997. The Trial Chamber had issued an Order on 25 January 1997 requiring the parties to give notice of their potential expert witnesses. The Order stipulated that "good cause" must be shown for a party to call an expert, notice óf whose testimony is given after that date. The Appeals Chamber found that the Prosecution failed to show good cause why it should be permitted to call the handwriting expert.[377]

The Chamber found that allowing the Prosecution to call a handwriting expert at this stage in the case would have prejudiced the accused's right to a fair trial, guaranteed in Article 21 of the Statute and Article 14 of the International Covenant on Civil and Political Rights.[378]

In particular, the Chamber pointed out that the Prosecution had known since June 1997 that the Trial Chamber would require strict proof of the authorship of the documents beyond the documents *per se*. The Prosecution was not precluded from attempting to secure independent proof of the authorship of the documents. There was no indication that a handwriting expert was unavailable at an earlier stage.[379]

Moreover, the Chamber observed that the accused's right to a prompt and fair trial became paramount in light of the fact that the Prosecution was ready to close its case. With greater assiduity the Prosecution could have called a handwriting expert earlier. The accused had been in detention for 20 months.[380]

B.   TRIAL CHAMBERS

1. FAIR PUBLIC HEARING

PROSECUTOR V. TADIĆ, *Decision on the Prosecutor's Motion Requesting Protective Measures for Victims and Witnesses*, IT-94-1-T, 10 August 1995, McDonald, Stephen & Vohrah, JJ.

In the first decision on the issue of protective measures for victims and witnesses the Chamber took the opportunity to write at length on the subject. One of the issues raised was the extent to which the "fair public hearing" guaranteed to the accused by this rule could be circumscribed by the need to protect victims and witnesses. The Article seems to make the "fair and public hearing" specifically subject to the protection of victims and witnesses provided for in Article 22. That Article specifically contemplates *in camera* hearings.

---

[376] Para. 6.
[377] Para. 8.
[378] Para. 12.
[379] Paras. 11-12.
[380] Para. 13.

The Chamber decided that:

> [T]he Statute . . . does provide that the protection of victims and witnesses is an acceptable reason to limit the accused's right to a public trial. . . the Trial Chamber must interpret the provisions of the Statute and Rules within the context of its own unique framework. . . the Statute authorizes limits to the right to a public trial to protect victims and witnesses.[381]

Judge Stephen wrote separately regarding this issue. He expressed concern that it would be possible to read the Article so as to make both the fairness and the public nature of the hearing subject to Article 22's witness protection language. As is shown by the following, he felt very strongly that the Article should not be read that way:

> That phrase "subject to Article 22" itself repays analysis. What it is in Article 21(2) that is to be subject to Article 22 can scarcely be the combined concept which precedes that phrase, the concept of "a fair and public hearing." It must rather be only one component of that concept, the public quality of the hearing and not its fairness, that is made subject to Article 22,m and this for two reasons: first, because, while Article 22 specifically contemplates non-public hearings, it certainly dopes not contemplate unfair hearings; secondly, because Article 20(1) itself, unqualifiedly and quite separately from Article 21 requires a Trial Chamber to ensure that a trial is "fair." If this understanding of the phrase "subject to Article 22" be correct and it is primarily the public quality, not the fairness, of a hearing that may have to give way to the need to protect victims and witnesses, that in turn suggests that the kind of protection being though of in Article 22 is essentially those measures that will affect the public nature of the trial, rather than its fairness.[382]

Importantly, Judge Stephen also noted that the only right of the accused contained in this Article that is subject to Article 22 is the protection of victims and witnesses. Thus, the remainder of the Article, in his view, is not subject to concerns for the protection of victims and witnesses and the rights enumerated therein cannot be so qualified.[383]

2. EQUALITY OF ARMS

PROSECUTOR V DELALIĆ et. al., *Decision on the Prosecution's Motion for an Order requiring advance Disclosure of Witnesses by the Defence*, IT-96-21-T, 4 February 1998, Karibi-Whyte, Jan & Odio-Benito, JJ.

The Trial Chamber disapproved of the comments by Judge Vohrah in *Tadić*[384], where the Judge wrote that in criminal proceedings the application of equality of arms should be

---

[381] Para. 36.
[382] Page 7, Web edition, www.un.org/icty.
[383] *Ibid.*
[384] Prosecutor v. Tadić, *Separate Opinion of Judge Vohrah on Prosecution Motion for Production of Defence Witness Statements*, IT-94-1-T, 27 November 1996.

inclined in favour of the Defence acquiring parity with the Prosecution in the presentation of the Defence case before the Court to preclude any injustice against the accused.

The Chamber held that procedural equality means· equality between the Prosecution and the Defence and to favour the Defence would result in inequality of arms.[385]

In this case, the Chamber interpreted Article 21(4)(e) to mean that there must be procedural equality between the accused and the Prosecution and, since the Prosecution must provide a witness list pre-trial, the Defence must provide a witness list prior to the commencement of its case, so that the defence witnesses can be examined "under the same conditions" as the defence examined Prosecution witnesses.[386]

PROSECUTOR V. TADIĆ, *Separate Opinion of Judge Vohrah on Prosecution Motion for Production of Defence Witness Statements*, IT-94-1-T, 27 November 1996.

The Separate Opinion of Judge Vohrah is a concurring opinion – forming part of the majority opinion – along with Judge Stephen in holding that the doctrine of legal professional privilege applies and protects the Defence from disclosing the prior statements their witnesses. In regard to the issue of equality of arms, Judge Vohrah rejected the Prosecution submission that the principle of equality of arms requires the Defence to grant the Prosecution access to prior statements made by its witnesses for purposes of impeachment.

Judge Vohrah reviewed decisions brought under both the *European Convention of Human Rights* and the *International Covenant on Civil and Political Rights*. He concluded that the principle of equality of arms is inherent in the notion of a fair trial and that it is intended to ensure that the Defence has the means to prepare and present its case equal to those available to the Prosecution. In addition, Judge Vohrah wrote that this approach to the principle of equality of arms is derived from international covenants and international case law:

> This proposition that the equality of arms principle was intended to elevate the Defence to the level of the Prosecution, as much as possible, in its ability to prepare and present its case is evident in the case law arising out of the European Convention for the Protection of Human Rights and Fundamental Freedoms 1950 ("the ECHR") and the International Covenant on Civil and Political Rights 1966 ("the ICCPR"), both of which incorporate the principle of equality of arms in the concept of a fair trial. *See* Van Dijk and Van Hoof, *supra* at 319-320; *Delacourt v. Belgium*, 11 Eur. Ct. H.R. (ser. A) [1970] 1 at 15; Manfred Nowak, *U.N. Covenant on Civil and Political Rights, CCPR Commentary* (1993) at 244.

---

[385] Para. 48-49. The Trial Chamber apparently mis-interpreted the statement of Judge Vohrah. All he said was that the principle should be interpreted to favour the defence and the prosecution being equal before the Trial Chamber, not that the principle favours the Defence.

[386] Para. 22.

Judge Vohrah wrote that the application of the equality of arms principle in criminal proceedings should be inclined in favour of the Defence acquiring parity with the Prosecution in the presentation of the Defence case before the Court to preclude any injustice against the accused.[387]

3. TRANSLATION OF DOCUMENTS INTO THE LANGUAGE OF THE ACCUSED

PROSECUTOR V. DELALIĆ, *et al, Decision on Defence Application for Forwarding Documents in the Language of the Accused,* IT-96-21-PT, 25 September 1996, McDonald, Stephen & Vohrah, JJ.

In this case the Trial Chamber was called upon to decide which Tribunal documents needed to be translated into the language of the accused, in this case, Bosnian. The guarantees contained in Article 21(1) and 4(a) require that all evidence submitted by either party must be made available in one of the working languages and in the language of the accused. All discovery provided by the Prosecutor, however, need not be provided in the language of the accused. All papers filed with the Registrar must be in either English or French and need not be translated into the language of the accused.

Transcripts of the proceedings are provided in one or both of the working languages simply as an *aide mémoire* and, thus, need not be translated into the language of the accused. All Decisions and Orders are provided in both working languages and in the language of the accused.

PROSECUTOR V. DELALIĆ *et al, Decision on the Applications for Adjournment of the Trial Date,* IT-96-21-PT, 3 February 1997, Karibi-Whyte, Odio-Benito & Jan, JJ.

A delay in providing discovery can result in a delay in starting a trial. In this case, the Trial Chamber, granted a delay, having found that the Prosecutor had failed to comply with fixed dates for disclosure of witness statements. Many of the late witness statements were provided in English, not translated into the language of the accused. The Chamber said:

> The Trial Chamber is cognizant of the fact that unless there is prompt and proper disclosure to the Defence, the Defence cannot make a decision on what evidence it will use at trial, and cannot therefore be adequately prepared for trial. This is especially so in this case where the disclosure was in English, making translation into the language of the accused necessary.[388]

---

[387] Page 7.
[388] Para. 22.

PROSECUTOR V. DELALIĆ *et al, Order on Zdravko Mucić's Oral Request for Serbo-Croatian Interpretation*, IT-96-21-T, 23 June 1997, Karibi-Whyte, Odio-Benito & Jan, JJ.

The accused, Mucić requested interpretation of the trial proceeding into the Croatian language.

The Trial Chamber found that the rights of the accused under Article 21(4)(f) were not violated. The Language and Conference Services Unit of the Tribunal ensures that all hearings are simultaneously translated into Serbo-Croatian for the benefit of the accused and other trial participants. Reports by two linguistic experts found that varieties of Serbo-Croatian are intelligible to all citizens of the former Yugoslavia. The Chamber noted that the accused had only raised the issue of the Croatian language in an oral motion on 11 June 1997, some three months after the commencement of the trial and over a year since his initial appearance.

4. Presumption of Innocence

PROSECUTOR V. KUPREŠKIĆ *et. al., Judgement*, IT-95-16-T, 14 January 2000, Cassese, May & Mumba, JJ.

The Trial Chamber stated that the accused must be presumed innocent until proved guilty. The burden of proof is on the Prosecution and before the defendant may be convicted of any offence the Prosecution must convince the Trial Chamber beyond any reasonable doubt of the defendant's guilt.[389]

5. No Negative Inference to be Drawn from the Silence of the Accused

PROSECUTOR V. KUPREŠKIĆ *et. al., Judgement*, IT-95-16-T, 14 January 2000, Cassese, May & Mumba, JJ.

It is the right of the accused not to give evidence at trial and no adverse inference can be drawn from the fact he did not testify. The Trial Chamber refers to Article 21(3) that guarantees the right to the presumption of evidence and Article 21(4)(g) which provides that the accused cannot be compelled to testify against himself.[390]

---

[389] Para. 339(a). Rule 87(A) states, *inter alia*: "A finding of guilt may be reached only when a majority of the Trial Chamber is satisfied that guilt has been proved beyond reasonable doubt".
[390] Para. 339(d).

6. SUFFICIENCY OF THE INDICTMENT

PROSECUTOR V. BLAŠKIĆ, *Decision Rejecting a Motion of the Defence to Dismiss Counts 4, 7, 10, 14, 16 and 18 Based on the Failure to Adequately Plead the Existence of an International Armed Conflict*, IT-95-14-PT, 4 April 1997, Jorda, Li & Riad, JJ.

Article 21(A)(4) provides that an accused shall "be informed promptly and in detail in a language which he understands of the nature and cause of the charge against him." The Defence in this case contended that a simple allegation that the conflict was at all times international was not a sufficient pleading, and that the indictment must set forth both factual and legal grounds supporting this allegation. Each of the Counts was brought under Article 2 of the Statute and thus required a showing of an international armed conflict to establish jurisdiction in the Tribunal. The Chamber held that the pleading in the indictment was sufficient. Whether an international armed conflict existed could only be considered on the merits at the conclusion of the trial. It is not incumbent upon the Prosecutor to prove the existence of an international armed conflict pre-trial so as to establish jurisdiction in the Chamber to try the case.[391]

7. RIGHT OF CROSS EXAMINATION

PROSECUTOR V. BLAŠKIĆ, *Decision on Standing Objection of the Defence to the Admission of Hearsay with no Inquiry as to its Reliability*, IT-95-14-T, 21 January 1998, Jorda, Riad & Shahabuddeen, JJ.

The Defence sought a ruling from the Trial Chamber on the admissibility of hearsay. Amoung the objections to its admissibility was the contention that it precluded cross-examination of the initial declarant, which violated this Article.

     The Chamber said that since the principle supporting admission of hearsay had already been decided in the *Tadić*[392] case, any objection to the absence of cross-examination would go to weight of the evidence, not its admissibility. The Chamber ruled further that the right to cross-examination guaranteed by Article 21(4)(e) of the Statute applies to the witness testifying before the Trial Chamber and not to the initial declarant whose statement has been transmitted to this Trial Chamber by the witness.

---

[391] Paras. 7, 8.
[392] Prosecutor v. Tadić, *Decision on Hearsay*, IT-95-14 T, 5 August 1996.

8. RIGHTS OF A SUSPECT

PROSECUTOR V DELALIĆ *et. al., Decision on the Motions for the Exclusion of Evidence by the Accused, Zejnil Delalić*, IT-96-21-T, 25 September 1997, Karibi-Whyte, Odio-Benito & Jan, JJ.

The Chamber held that the rights guaranteed by Article 21(4)(d) are the rights of an "accused" person, and are not available to a "suspect" during questioning pursuant to Rule 42. The right of a suspect to legal assistance, guaranteed by Article 18(3), finds expression in Rule 42. In the instant matter, the *Decision on the Motion on the Exclusion and Restitution of Evidence and Other Material Seized from the Accused Zejnil Delalić*, 9 October 1996 held that Rule 42 was not violated.[393]

---

[393] Para. 36.

ARTICLE 22

PROTECTION OF VICTIMS AND WITNESSES

THE INTERNATIONAL TRIBUNAL SHALL PROVIDE IN ITS RULES OF PROCEDURE AND EVIDENCE FOR THE PROTECTION OF VICTIMS AND WITNESSES. SUCH PROTECTION MEASURES SHALL INCLUDE, BUT SHALL NOT BE LIMITED TO, THE CONDUCT OF IN CAMERA PROCEEDINGS AND THE PROTECTION OF THE VICTIM'S IDENTITY.

I. COMMENTARY

This Article was first discussed by the Tribunal in the *Tadić* case.[394] The Prosecutor had requested various degrees of protection for several of its witnesses and requests for closed hearings in some instances. The Trial Chamber took the opportunity to draft a comprehensive study of the balancing process between the rights of defendants to fair trials against the rights of victims and witnesses. The interest of the public in open hearings was also a consideration in the decision.

For a full report see Article 20.

---

[394] Prosecutor v. Tadić, *Decision on the Prosecutor's Motion Requesting Protective Measures for Victims and Witnesses*, IT-94-1, 10 August 1995.

ARTICLE 23

JUDGEMENT.

1.   THE TRIAL CHAMBERS SHALL PRONOUNCE JUDGEMENTS AND IMPOSE
SENTENCES AND PENALTIES ON PERSONS CONVICTED OF SERIOUS VIOLATIONS OF
INTERNATIONAL HUMANITARIAN LAW.

2.   THE JUDGEMENT SHALL BE RENDERED BY A MAJORITY OF THE JUDGES OF THE
TRIAL CHAMBER, AND SHALL BE DELIVERED BY THE TRIAL CHAMBER IN PUBLIC. IT
SHALL BE ACCOMPANIED BY A REASONED OPINION IN WRITING, TO WHICH SEPARATE OR
DISSENTING OPINIONS MAY BE APPENDED.

II.   TRIBUNAL CASES

A.   APPEALS CHAMBER

PROSECUTOR V. FURUNDŽIJA, *Judgement*, IT-95-17/1-A, 21 July 2000,
Shahabuddeen, Vohrah, Nieto-Navia, Robinson & Pocar, JJ.

During the testimony in Furundžija's trial two witnesses, "A" and "D" testified about the
same incidents. There were apparently discrepancies between their accounts. Furundžija
contended that the Trial Chamber failed to resolve these discrepancies that resulted in his
not receiving a fair trial in the spirit of Articles 21(2) and 23(2) of the Statute.
Specifically, Furundžija contended that the Trial Chamber failed to provide a "reasoned
opinion" as required by Article 23(2).

This claim enabled the Appeals Chamber to discuss, for the first time, the
meaning of Article 23(2)'s requirement of a "reasoned opinion in writing."

The Chamber wrote, as follows:

> The right of an accused under Article 23 of the Statute to a reasoned opinion is
> an aspect of the fair trial requirement embodied in Articles 20 and 21 of the
> Statute. The case-law that has developed under the European Convention on
> Human Rights establishes that a reasoned opinion is a component of the fair
> hearing requirement, but that "the extent to which this duty . . . applies may vary
> according to the nature of the decision" and "can only be determined in the light
> of the circumstances of the case."[395] The European Court of Human Rights has
> held that a "tribunal' is not obliged to give a detailed answer to every
> argument.[396]

---

[395] Citing,Case of *Ruiz Torija v. Spain, Judgment of 9 December 1994,* Publication of the European Court of
Human Rights ("Eur.Ct.H.R."), Series A, vol. 303, para. 29.
[396] Para. 69. Citing, Case of *Van de Hurk v. The Netherlands, Judgment of 19 April 1994,* Eur.Ct.H.R., Series A,
vol. 288, para. 61.

The Chamber reviewed the testimony of witnesses "A" and "D" and, although conflicting on some points, the Chamber found that it was not conflicting on the points upon which the Trial Chamber drew its conclusions as to the culpability of Furundžija.[397]

---

[397] Para. 73.

ARTICLE 24

PENALTIES

1.　THE PENALTY IMPOSED BY THE TRIAL CHAMBER SHALL BE LIMITED TO IMPRISONMENT. IN DETERMINING THE TERMS OF IMPRISONMENT, THE TRIAL CHAMBERS SHALL HAVE RECOURSE TO THE GENERAL PRACTICE REGARDING PRISON SENTENCES IN THE COURTS OF THE FORMER YUGOSLAVIA.

2.　IN IMPOSING THE SENTENCES, THE TRIAL CHAMBERS SHOULD TAKE INTO ACCOUNT SUCH FACTORS AS THE GRAVITY OF THE OFFENCE AND THE INDIVIDUAL CIRCUMSTANCES OF THE CONVICTED PERSON.

3.　IN ADDITION TO IMPRISONMENT, THE TRIAL CHAMBERS MAY ORDER THE RETURN OF ANY PROPERTY AND PROCEEDS ACQUIRED BY CRIMINAL CONDUCT, INCLUDING BY MEANS OF DURESS, TO THEIR RIGHTFUL OWNERS.

I.　COMMENTARY

See, Rule 101.

ARTICLE 25

APPELLATE PROCEEDINGS

1.   THE APPEALS CHAMBER SHALL HEAR APPEALS FROM PERSONS CONVICTED BY
THE TRIAL CHAMBERS OR FROM THE PROSECUTOR ON THE FOLLOWING GROUNDS:

   (A)   AN ERROR ON A QUESTION OF LAW INVALIDATING THE DECISION; OR

   (B)   AN ERROR OF FACT WHICH HAS OCCASIONED A MISCARRIAGE OF
           JUSTICE.

2.   THE APPEALS CHAMBER MAY AFFIRM, REVERSE OR REVISE THE DECISIONS
TAKEN BY THE TRIAL CHAMBERS.

I.   COMMENTARY

There is a section below which deals with advisory opinions. Advisory opinions are those
rendered when there is actually no case or controversy. Ordinarily courts will not render
opinions in the absence of a case or controversy. However, the Chambers of the Tribunal
have done so on more than one occasion. This may be justified where the interpretation
of various portions of the Statute and Rules are significant to the future practice before
the Tribunal. However, only where there is a genuine controversy does the in-depth
briefing occur which can assist the Chamber in arriving at the correct decision. One
supposes that as the jurisprudence grows the occasion for issuing advisory opinions will
disappear.

II.   TRIBUNAL CASES

A.   APPEALS CHAMBER

1. MISCELLANEOUS

PROSECUTOR V. FURUNDŽIJA, *Judgement,* IT-95-17/1-A, 21 July 2000,
Shahabuddeen, Vohrah, Nieto-Navia, Robinson & Pocar, JJ.

    The Chamber discussed the power of an Appeals Chamber in light of the
language of Article 25(1)(A) and (B). As to "errors of law" it is not completely
incumbent on a party to carry the burden of establishing that such an error has occurred.
The Appeals Chamber has the power to correct errors of law whether appropriately raised
by a party or not. The Judges wrote:

> Errors of law do not raise a question as to the standard of review as directly as
> errors of fact. Where a party contends that a Trial Chamber made an error of
> law, the Appeals Chamber, as the final arbiter of the law of the Tribunal, must
> determine whether there was such a mistake. A party alleging that there was an
> error of law must be prepared to advance arguments in support of the contention;

> but, if the arguments do not support the contention, that party has not failed to discharge a burden in the sense that a person who fails to discharge a burden automatically loses his point. The Appeals Chamber may step in and, for other reasons, find in favour of the contention that there is an error of law.[398]

It is not, however, just any error of law which will permit reversal or revision of a Trial Chamber's Judgement. It must be one that would render the Trial Chamber's Judgement invalid. As the Chamber explained:

> Furthermore, this Chamber is only empowered to reverse or revise a decision of the Trial Chamber on the basis of Article 25(1)(a) when there is an error of law that invalidates that decision. It is not any error of law that leads to a reversal or revision of the Trial Chamber's decision; rather, the appealing party alleging an error of law must also demonstrate that the error renders the decision invalid.[399]

Presumably the Appeals Chamber could, on it own, even if not properly raised by a party, determine that there was an error of law rendering the Trial Chamber Judgement invalid and reverse or revise.[400]

With regard to "errors of fact" the Appeals Chamber adopted the reasoning from the Rwanda Trial Chamber's decision in *Serushago*[401], as follows:

> Under the Statute and the Rules of the Tribunal, a Trial Chamber is required as a matter of law to take account of mitigating circumstances. But the question of whether a Trial Chamber gave due weight to any mitigating circumstance is a question of fact. In putting forward this question as a ground of appeal, the Appellant must discharge two burdens. He must show that the Trial Chamber did indeed commit the error, and, if it did, he must go on to show that the error resulted in a miscarriage of justice.[402]

2. ERROR ON A QUESTION OF FACT

PROSECUTOR V. TADIĆ, *Judgement*, IT-94-1-T, 15 July 1999, Shahabuddeen, Cassese, Wang Tieya, Nieto-Navia & Mumba, JJ.

The Appeals Chamber wrote:

> The task of hearing, assessing and weighing the evidence presented at trial is left to the Judges sitting in a Trial Chamber. Therefore, the Appeals Chamber must give a margin of deference to a finding of fact reached by a Trial Chamber. It is only where the evidence relied on by the Trial Chamber could not reasonably

---

[398] Para. 35
[399] Para. 36.
[400] The *Erdemović Judgement* assert this proposition rather forcefully.
[401] Prosecutor v. Serushago, *Reasons for Judgement*, ICTR-98-39-A, 6 April 2000, para. 22.
[402] Para. 37.

have been accepted by any reasonable person that the Appeals Chamber can substitute its own finding for that of the Trial Chamber. It is important to note that two judges, both acting reasonably, can come to different conclusions on the basis of the same evidence.[403]

3. ADVISORY OPINIONS

PROSECUTOR V. TADIĆ, *Judgement,* IT-94-1-T, 15 July 1999, Shahabuddeen, Cassese, Wang Tieya, Nieto-Navia & Mumba, JJ.

The Prosecutor appealed the Trial Chamber's finding that a crime against humanity may not be committed for purely personal reasons. Both parties agreed that this finding did not affect the verdict, although the Prosecutor argued that it was important to the jurisprudence of the Tribunal. In effect, the Chamber was being asked to render an advisory opinion. The Chamber stated:

> Neither Party asserts that the Trial Chamber's finding that crimes against humanity cannot be committed for purely personal motives had a bearing on the verdict in terms of Article 25(1) of the Tribunal Statute. Nevertheless this is a matter of general significance for the Tribunal's jurisprudence. It is therefore appropriate for the Appeals Chamber to set forth its views on this matter.[404]

In addition, in its Cross-Appeal, the Prosecutor complained about the failure of the Trial Chamber to order the production of defence witness statements after the witnesses had testified on direct examination. Even though the parties agreed that the ruling had no bearing on the verdict of the Trial Chamber, the Appeals Chamber determined that it was a matter of general importance and therefore should be dealt with. In that regard the Chamber made the following observation:

> The Appeals Chamber has no power under Article 25 of the Statute to pass, one way or another, on the decision of the Trial Chamber as if the decision was itself under appeal. But the point of law which is involved is one of importance and worthy of an expression of opinion by the Appeals Chamber.

4. INHERENT POWERS OF APPEALS CHAMBER

PROSECUTOR V. TADIĆ, *Judgement,* IT-94-1-T, 15 July 1999, Shahabuddeen, Cassese, Wang Tieya, Nieto-Navia & Mumba, JJ.

The Prosecutor contended that the power of the Trial Chamber to order the disclosure of defence witness statements is implicit in Rule 89(B).

---

[403] Page 28.
[404] Para. 247.

The Appeals Chamber determined that it was within the discretion of the Trial Chambers to order such disclosure on a case-by-case basis. The Chamber ruled, as follows:

> With regard to the present case, once a Defence witness has testified, it is for a Trial Chamber to ascertain the credibility of his or her testimony. If he or she has made a prior statement, a Trial Chamber must be able to evaluate the testimony in the light of this statement, in its quest for the truth and for the purpose of ensuring a fair trial. Rather than deriving from the sweeping provisions of Sub-rule 89(B), this power is inherent in the jurisdiction of the International Tribunal, as it is within the jurisdiction of any criminal court, national or international. In other words, this is one of those powers mentioned by the Appeals Chamber in the *Blaškić* (Subpoena) decision which accrue to a judicial body even if not explicitly or implicitly provided for in the statute or rules of procedure of such a body, because they are essential for the carrying out of judicial functions and ensuring the fair administration of justice.405

PROSECUTOR V. ERDEMOVIĆ, *Judgement*, IT-96-22-A, 7 October 1997, Cassese, McDonald, Stephen, Vohrah & Li, JJ.

The Appeals Chamber determined that it could raise issues *proprio motu* once it is seized of an appeal as part of its inherent powers. The Chamber found "nothing in the Statute or Rules, nor in practices of international institutions or national judicial systems, which would confine its consideration to the appeal of issues raised formally by the parties."[406]

5. THE RIGHT TO APPEAL

PROSECUTOR V. TADIĆ, *Judgement in Sentencing Appeals*, IT-94-1-A and IT-94-1-A*bis*, 26 January 2000, Shahabuddeen, Mumba, Cassese, Tieya & Nieto-Navia, JJ.

The Chamber found the right to appeal a judgement of a Trial Chamber resulting in conviction is established under Article 25 and must be accorded substantial weight. The right to appeal so established reflects the position in the general corpus of international human rights law. (See, in particular, the International Covenant on Civil and Political Rights, Article 14(5), the European Convention for the Protection of Human Rights and Fundamental Freedoms, Protocol 7, Article 2, and the American Convention on Human Rights, Article 8(2)(h)). The Chamber held that a Trial Chamber should not impose undue encumbrances that could deter a convicted person from pursuing an appeal.[407]

In addition, the Chamber ruled that fundamental fairness requires that an accused or a convicted person not be punished for the exercise of a procedural right. The

---

[405] Para. 322.
[406] Para. 16.
[407] Para. 29.

Chamber accepted the view of the United States Supreme Court that "[a] court is 'without right to ... put a price on an appeal. A defendant's exercise of a right of appeal must be free and unfettered ... [I]t is unfair to use the great power given to the court to determine sentence to place a defendant in the dilemma of making an unfree choice."[408]

6. SUFFICIENCY OF THE EVIDENCE

PROSECUTOR V. FURUNDŽIJA, *Judgement,* IT-95-17/1-A, 21 July 2000, Shahabuddeen, Vohrah, Nieto-Navia, Robinson & Pocar, JJ.

Furundžija asserted in his appeal that the evidence admitted at the trial was insufficient, as a matter of law, to support his conviction. The Appeals Chamber considered how it should deal with claims of insufficiency of the evidence. Furundžija argued, based on the *Tadić* Appeals Judgement that the Appeals Chamber needs to determine whether the Trial Chamber correctly applied the standard of proof beyond a reasonable doubt. He contended that it was incumbent on the Appeals Chamber to conduct a review of the evidence, both from a sufficiency and quality standpoint and upon that review determine whether a reasonable fact finder could have found an inference or hypothesis consistent with innocence. It was Furundžija's position that he could only be convicted if his guilt was the only fair and rational hypothesis that could be concluded from a review of the evidence.

The Chamber first determined that Furundžija had misinterpreted the decision of the *Tadić* Appeals Chamber. The *Tadić* Judges did not disturb the fact-findings of the Trial Chamber but concluded, only, that the Trial Chamber did not properly apply those facts to the law.

The Chamber disagreed with Furundžija's contentions as to the legal standard of review when a question of evidentiary insufficiency is raised. The Chamber said:

> The Appeals Chamber finds no merit in the Appellant's submission which it understands to mean that the scope of the appellate function should be expanded to include *de novo* review. This Chamber does not operate as a second Trial Chamber. The role of the Appeals Chamber is limited, pursuant to Article 25 of the Statute, to correcting errors of law invalidating a decision, and errors of fact which have occasioned a miscarriage of justice.[409]

---

[408] Para. 30. Citing North Carolina v. Pearce, 395 U.S. 711, 724 (1969) (quoting Worcester v. Commissioner, 370 F.2d. 713, 718).
[409] Para. 40.

ARTICLE 26

REVIEW PROCEEDINGS

WHERE A NEW FACT HAS BEEN DISCOVERED WHICH WAS NOT KNOWN AT THE TIME OF THE PROCEEDINGS BEFORE THE TRIAL CHAMBERS OR THE APPEALS CHAMBER AND WHICH COULD HAVE BEEN A DECISIVE FACTOR IN REACHING THE DECISION, THE CONVICTED PERSON OR THE PROSECUTOR MAY SUBMIT TO THE INTERNATIONAL TRIBUNAL AN APPLICATION FOR REVIEW OF THE JUDGEMENT.

ARTICLE 27

ENFORCEMENT OF SENTENCES

IMPRISONMENT SHALL BE SERVED IN A STATE DESIGNATED BY THE INTERNATIONAL TRIBUNAL FROM A LIST OF STATES WHICH HAVE INDICATED TO THE SECURITY COUNCIL THEIR WILLINGNESS TO ACCEPT CONVICTED PERSONS. SUCH IMPRISONMENT SHALL BE IN ACCORDANCE WITH THE APPLICABLE LAW OF THE STATE CONCERNED, SUBJECT TO THE SUPERVISION OF THE INTERNATIONAL TRIBUNAL.

I. COMMENTARY

To date seven States have entered into agreements with the Tribunal to accept sentenced persons into their prison systems for service of the sentence. These are: Italy, Finland, Norway, Sweden, Austria, France and Spain.

II. TRIBUNAL CASES

B. TRIAL CHAMBERS

PROSECUTOR V. ERDEMOVIĆ, *Sentencing Judgment*, IT-96-22, 29 November 1996, Mumba, Shahabuddeen & Wang Tieya, JJ.

The Trial Chamber became concerned with the language of Rule 27 providing that imprisonment should be in accordance with the applicable law of the State to which a convicted person would be sent to serve his sentence. The Chamber recognized that different States have different rules regarding release dates. The Chamber felt it important to assure that persons convicted and sentenced by the Tribunal serve their entire sentences and thus said: "the Trial Chamber is of the opinion that no measure which a State might take could have the effect of terminating a penalty or subverting it by reducing its length."[410]

---

[410] Para. 73. But see, Article 28.

ARTICLE 28

PARDON OR COMMUTATION OF SENTENCES

IF, PURSUANT TO THE APPLICABLE LAW OF THE STATE IN WHICH THE CONVICTED PERSON IS IMPRISONED, HE OR SHE IS ELIGIBLE FOR PARDON OR COMMUTATION OF SENTENCE, THE STATE CONCERNED SHALL NOTIFY THE INTERNATIONAL TRIBUNAL ACCORDINGLY. THE PRESIDENT OF THE INTERNATIONAL TRIBUNAL, IN CONSULTATION WITH THE JUDGES, SHALL DECIDE THE MATTER ON THE BASIS OF THE INTERESTS OF JUSTICE AND THE GENERAL PRINCIPLES OF LAW.

I.   COMMENTARY

See Commentary and *Erdemović* Sentencing Judgement report under Article 27.

ARTICLE 29

COOPERATION AND JUDICIAL ASSISTANCE

1.   STATES SHALL COOPERATE WITH THE INTERNATIONAL TRIBUNAL IN THE INVESTIGATION AND PROSECUTION OF PERSONS ACCUSED OF COMMITTING SERIOUS VIOLATIONS OF INTERNATIONAL HUMANITARIAN LAW.

2.   STATES SHALL COMPLY WITHOUT UNDUE DELAY WITH ANY REQUEST FOR ASSISTANCE OR AN ORDER ISSUED BY A TRIAL CHAMBER, INCLUDING, BUT NOT LIMITED TO:

(A)   THE IDENTIFICATION AND LOCATION OF PERSONS;

(B)   THE TAKING OF TESTIMONY AND THE PRODUCTION OF EVIDENCE;

(C)   THE SERVICE OF DOCUMENTS;

(D)   THE ARREST OR DETENTION OF PERSONS;

(E)   THE SURRENDER OR THE TRANSFER OF THE ACCUSED TO THE INTERNATIONAL TRIBUNAL.

I.   COMMENTARY

In *Blaškić*,[411] the Appeals Chamber wrote at length on the subpoena power of the ICTY. In summary, the Chamber found "that the International Tribunal is empowered to issue binding orders and requests to States, which are obliged to comply with them pursuant to Article 29 of the Statute and that, in case of non-compliance, a Trial Chamber may make a specific judicial finding to this effect and request the President of the International Tribunal to transmit it to the United Nations Security Council..."

Second, the Chamber found "that the International Tribunal may not address binding orders under Article 29 to State officials acting in their official capacity."

Third, the Chamber found "that the International Tribunal may summon, subpoena or address other binding orders to individuals acting in their private capacity and that, in case of non-compliance, either the relevant State may take enforcement measures as provided in its legislation, or the International Tribunal may instigate contempt proceedings."

Fourth, the Chamber found "that States are not allowed, on the claim of national security interests, to withhold documents and other evidentiary material requested by the International Tribunal; however, practical arrangements may be adopted by a Trial Chamber to make allowance for legitimate and bona fide concerns of States."

This comprehensive decision formed the basis for the later adoption of Rule 54 *bis*, which crystallizes the primary holdings in the decision. The decision is included here in detail since it is a useful interpretive device when dealing with issue under Rule 54 *bis*.

---

[411] Prosecutor v. Blaškić, *Judgement on the Request of the Republic of Croatia for Review of the Decision of Trial Chamber II of 18 July 1997*, 29 October 1997, Cassese, Karibi-Whyte, Li, Stephen & Vohrah, JJ.

For additional material on Rule 29 issues, see, Tribunal cases under Rules 9, 54 and 54 *bis* of the Rules of Procedure and Evidence.

See, Rule 55, re: *Decision on the motion for release by the accused Slavko Dokmanovic.*

II. TRIBUNAL CASES

B. APPEALS CHAMBER

PROSECUTOR V. BLAŠKIĆ, *Judgement on the Request of the Republic of Croatia for Review of the Decision of Trial Chamber II of 18 July 1997*, IT-95-14, 29 October 1997, Cassese, Karibi-Whyte, Li, Stephen & Vohrah, JJ.

On 15 January 1997, Judge McDonald, as confirming Judge on the *Blaškić* Indictment, issued a *subpoena duces tecum* to the Republic of Croatia and its Defence Minister, Mr. Gojko Sušak. The issue found its way to the Trial Chamber that upheld the McDonald subpoena on 18 July 1977. The Republic of Croatia then appealed this to the Appeals Chamber. The Appeals Chamber took jurisdiction of the issues and set up a briefing schedule. In addition, the Chamber invited *amici curiae* to submit briefs addressed to the following issues:

1. The power of a Judge or Trial Chamber of the International Tribunal to issue a *subpoena duces tecum;*

2. the power of a Judge or Trial Chamber of the International Tribunal to make a request or issue a *subpoena duces tecum* to high government officials of a State;

3. the appropriate remedies to be taken if there is non-compliance with a *subpoena duces tecum* or request issued by a Judge or Trial Chamber; and

4. any other issue concerned in this matter, such as the question of the national security interests of a sovereign State.[412]

The meaning of the term *"Subpoena"*

The Chamber found that "the meaning of certain terms in the rules of the ICTY is not pre-determined by the interpretation of these terms in the legal culture from which they originate but must be ascertained independently in the context of the specific framework of the tasks and purposes of the ICTY."[413] The Chamber concluded, in this regard, that:

Since . . . the International Tribunal is not empowered to issue binding orders under threat of penalty to States or to State officials, it is consonant with the spirit of the Statute and the rules to place a narrow interpretation on the term of

---

[412] Para. 15.
[413] Para. 21.

art at issue and construe it as referring only and exclusively to binding orders addressed by the International Tribunal, under threat of penalty, to individuals acting in their private capacity.[414]

Advisory Opinions

The Trial Chamber had determined in its decision that the question of legal remedies in the event of non-compliance with the subpoena was not "ripe for consideration," and thus did not write on that issue. This view was based on the practice in the United States and several other States where courts will only deal with actual cases or controversies and not issue advisory opinions. The Appeals Chamber disagreed by stating that the doctrine relied on by the Trial Chamber has no place in international criminal proceedings. According to the Chamber: "[D]omestic judicial views or approaches should be handled with the greatest caution at the international level, lest one should fail to make due allowance for the unique characteristics of international criminal proceedings."[415] Beyond that, since Croatia was bound to comply with the subpoena, it would be relevant for Croatia to know what remedies and sanctions might be available should it choose to ignore the subpoena.

Subpoenas to States

The Chamber determined that subpoenas could not be addressed to States. The Tribunal has no power to take enforcement measures against States. If the Security Council had "intended to vest the International Tribunal with such a power, they would have expressly provided for it."[416] It cannot be seen as an inherent power since "under current international law States can only be the subject of countermeasures taken by other States or of sanctions visited upon them by the organized international community, *i.e.,* the United Nations or other intergovernmental organizations."[417]

Binding Orders to States

As to this question, the Chamber ruled:

> Article 29 imposes an obligation on Member States [of the UN] towards all other Members or , in other words, an "obligation *erga omnes partes.*" By the same token Article 29 posits a community interest in its observance. In other words, every Member State of the United Nations has a legal interest in the fulfilment of the obligation laid down in Article 29.[418]

Thus, the Chamber held that the Tribunal has the power to issue binding orders and requests to States. However, the discharge of the Tribunal's primary function requires voluntary cooperation of States wherever that is achievable. Thus it is "regarded as sound

---

[414] Para. 21.

[415] Para. 23.

[416] Could the same not be said for the power to prosecute persons for violations of Common Article 3 of the Geneva Conventions?

[417] Para. 25.

[418] Para. 26.

policy for the Prosecutor, as well as defence counsel, first to seek, through cooperative means, the assistance of States, and only if they decline to lend support, then to request a Judge or Trial Chamber to have recourse to the mandatory action provided for in Article 29."[419]

Content of Binding Orders

The Chamber set out the parameters of a request for a binding order. Such a request must:

> (i)   identify specific documents and not broad categories. . . documents must be identified as far as possible and in addition be limited in number. The Trial Chamber may, however, considering the need to ensure a fair trial, to allow omission of those details if it is satisfied that the party requesting the order, acting bona fide, has no means of providing those particulars;

> (ii)   set out succinctly the reasons why documents are deemed relevant to the trial; if that party considers that setting for the reasons for the request might jeopardise its prosecutorial or defence strategy it should say so and at least indicate the general grounds on which its request rests;

> (iii)   not be unduly onerous.

> (iv)   give the requested State sufficient time for compliance.[420]

Legal Remedies in the Event of Non-Compliance

The Chamber determined that the Tribunal had the power to make a judicial finding regarding non-compliance by a State and the further power to submit those findings to the Security Council. In doing so, the Chambers must not include suggestions or recommendations to the Security Council. The power to make the judicial finding is an inherent power. In that connection the Chamber said that:

> . . . the International Tribunal must possess the power to make all those judicial determinations that are necessary for the exercise of its primary jurisdiction. The inherent power inures to the benefit of the International Tribunal in order that its basic judicial function may be fully discharged and its judicial role safeguarded.[421]

Subpoena of State Officials

State officials, acting in their official capacity, are not subject to subpoena by the Tribunal. Such an action would be tantamount to issuing a subpoena to a State, which cannot be done. Officials are instruments of the State.[422]

---

[419] Para. 31.
[420] Para. 32. Not quoted in its entirety and paraphrased in some instances.
[421] Para. 33. See Rule 7 *bis* which sets out the powers of the Chambers in the event of non-compliance.
[422] Para. 38

Binding Orders to State Officials

The Chamber found that both under international law and the Statute of the Tribunal it did not have the power to issue binding orders to State officials. The orders may only be directed to the State and it is up to the State to determine the organs or officials responsible for carrying out that order.[423]

On a practical note, however, the Chamber said:

> . . . it might be a useful practice for the Registrar of the International Tribunal to notify the relevant State officials of the order sent to the State. This notification would serve exclusively to inform State officials who, according to the Prosecutor or defence counsel, may hold the documents, of the order sent to the State. If the central authorities are prepared and willing to comply with Article 29, this practical procedure may speed up the internal process for production of documents.[424]

Binding Orders to Individuals in their Private Capacity

The Chamber determined that the Tribunal clearly does have this power. The Tribunal has jurisdiction over individuals other than those whom it may prosecute. Anyone who may be of assistance to the Tribunal, as a witness or otherwise, may be called upon by the Tribunal as long as they are not an Official of the concerned State acting in their official capacity.

The issue of whether they were acting in their "official capacity" came in for some comment. For instance, if a State official were to witness the commission of a war crime outside his or her official capacity, then the mere fact that he or she is a State official does not bar the Tribunal from summoning them as a witness. The Chamber set out another scenario where a State official would not be protected, as follows:

> Following the issue of a binding order to . . . a State for the production of documents necessary for trial, a State official, who holds that evidence in his official capacity, having been requested by his authorities to surrender it to the International Tribunal may refuse to do so, and the central authorities may not have the legal or factual means available to enforce the International Tribunal's request. In this scenario, the State official is no longer behaving as an instrumentality of his State apparatus. For the limited purposes of criminal proceedings, it is sound practice to "downgrade" as it were, the State official to the rank of an individual acting in a private capacity and apply to him all the remedies and sanctions available against non-complying individuals . . . he may be subpoenaed and, if he does not appear in court, proceedings for contempt of the International Tribunal could be instituted against him.[425]

---

[423] Para. 43.
[424] Para. 45.
[425] Para. 51.

Direct Contact with Individuals

The issue discussed in this portion of the Judgement was whether an individual should be subpoenaed directly or through the appropriate State apparatus. As a preliminary matter, the Chamber determined that there must be a distinction between States upon whose territory suspected crimes had been committed; in this case former Yugoslavia, and other States. In the States of the former Yugoslavia, direct contact is permissible. The Chamber reasoned:

> . . . to go through the official channels for identifying, summoning and interviewing witnesses, or to conduct on-site investigations, might jeopardise investigations by the Prosecutor or defence counsel. In particular, the presence of State officials at the interview of a witness might discourage the witness from speaking the truth, and might also imperil not just his own life or personal integrity but possibly those of his relatives. It follows that it would be contrary to the very purpose and function of the International Tribunal to have State officials present on such occasions. The States and Entities of the former Yugoslavia are obliged to cooperate with the International Tribunal in such a manner as to enable the International Tribunal to discharge it functions. This obligation (which, it should be noted, was restated in the Dayton and Paris Accords), also requires them to allow the Prosecutor and the defence to fulfil their tasks free from any possible impediment or hindrance.[426]

Outside the former Yugoslavia, however, the Chamber determined that it should go through the appropriate organs of a State in order to address a subpoena to an individual. The Chamber described two situations where the Tribunal may enter directly into contact with a private individual:

(i)   when this is authorized by the legislation of the State concerned;

(ii)   when the authorities of the State or Entity concerned, having been requested to comply with an order of the International Tribunal, prevent the International Tribunal from fulfilling its functions.[427]

Legal Remedies for Non-Compliance

The Chamber determined that there were two categories of remedies; those that could be enforced by the State where the individual is located; and, those that can be enforced by the Tribunal. Normally, the Tribunal should turn to the State in which the individual resides to seek enforcement of the subpoena. Failing that, the Tribunal itself can hold the reluctant witness or document custodian in contempt. "It should be added that, if the subpoenaed individual who fails to deliver documents or appear in court also fails to attend contempt proceedings, *in absentia* proceedings should not be ruled out."[428]

---

[426] Para. 53.
[427] Para. 55.
[428] Para. 59.

. . . generally speaking, it would not be appropriate to hold *in absentia* proceedings against persons falling under the primary jurisdiction of the International Tribunal (i.e., persons accused of crimes provided for in Articles 2-5 of the Statute). Indeed, even when the accused has clearly waived his right to be tried in his presence (Article 21, paragraph 4 (d), of the Statute), it would prove extremely difficult or even impossible for an international criminal court to determine the innocence or guilt of that accused. By contrast, *in absentia* proceedings may be exceptionally warranted in cases involving contempt of the International Tribunal, where the person charged fails to appear in court, thus obstructing the administration of justice. These cases fall within the ancillary or incidental jurisdiction of the International Tribunal.[429]

National Security Concerns

Finally, the Chamber dealt with national security concerns. Croatia contended that the Tribunal could not interfere with States in matters involving national security. The Chamber disagreed: "to allow national security considerations to prevent the International Tribunal from obtaining documents that might prove of decisive importance to the conduct of trials would be tantamount to undermining the very essence of the International Tribunal's functions."[430]

However, the Chamber recognized that legitimate security concerns need to be dealt with in a special manner due to the sensitivity of the information. Practical methods and procedures for dealing with these concerns need to be established.

First, the Chamber indicated that a Trial Chamber faced with this issue should determine whether the State concerned has acted and is acting *bona fide*. Is the State operating in good faith in claiming national security?

Second, "the State at issue may be invited to submit the relevant documents to the scrutiny of one Judge of the Trial Chamber." This should increase the confidence of the State in revealing the documents.

Third, if the documents are not in English or French, the State could provide certified translations so that Tribunal translators would not see the documents.

Fourth, the Judge could scrutinize the documents *in camera,* in *ex parte* proceedings, and no transcripts would be made.

Fifth, the documents that the Judge considers irrelevant would be returned to the State without their being filed with the Registry. As to relevant documents the State may be permitted to redact irrelevant parts, attaching an affidavit briefly explaining the reasons for the redaction.

Finally, a State may consider one or two documents too sensitive from a national security point of view and of scant relevance to the proceedings. If operating in good faith, the State involved could submit an affidavit by a responsible official indicating that he has personally examined the documents concerned, describing their contents, setting out why the State believes they are of scant relevance, and stating the principal reasons

---

[429] *Ibid.*
[430] Para. 64.

why the State is reluctant to produce them. The Judge will then be in a position to appraise the affidavit. He could request a more detailed affidavit or request the document. If he requests the document and it is not provided then the enforcement mechanisms would come into play.

B.   TRIAL CHAMBERS

PROSECUTOR V. DOKMANOVIĆ, *Order to the Federal Republic of Yugoslavia for the Service of Documents*, IT-95-13a-PT, 19 December 1997, Cassese, May & Mumba, JJ.

Slavko Dokmanović was in the custody of the Tribunal and the other three co-accused in the same indictment were still at large. The Prosecution filed a Motion for an Order for Publication of Newspaper Advertisement and an Order for Service of Documents. Pursuant to Article 29(2)(c), the Chamber ordered *inter alia*, the Federal Republic of Yugoslavia to affect personal service of certain documents of the three co-accused who were at large, to notify the Registrar of the Tribunal of such service and to affect their arrest pursuant to an outstanding arrest warrant.

ARTICLE 30

THE STATUS, PRIVILEGES AND IMMUNITIES OF THE INTERNATIONAL TRIBUNAL

1. THE CONVENTION ON THE PRIVILEGES AND IMMUNITIES OF THE UNITED NATIONS OF 13 FEBRUARY 1946 SHALL APPLY TO THE INTERNATIONAL TRIBUNAL, THE JUDGES, THE PROSECUTOR AND HIS STAFF, AND THE REGISTRAR AND HIS STAFF.

2. THE JUDGES, THE PROSECUTOR AND THE REGISTRAR SHALL ENJOY THE PRIVILEGES AND IMMUNITIES, EXEMPTIONS AND FACILITIES ACCORDED TO DIPLOMATIC ENVOYS, IN ACCORDANCE WITH INTERNATIONAL LAW.

3. THE STAFF OF THE PROSECUTOR AND OF THE REGISTRAR SHALL ENJOY THE PRIVILEGES AND IMMUNITIES ACCORDED TO OFFICIALS OF THE UNITED NATIONS UNDER ARTICLES V AND VII OF THE CONVENTION REFERRED TO IN PARAGRAPH 1 OF THIS ARTICLE.

4. OTHER PERSONS, INCLUDING THE ACCUSED, REQUIRED AT THE SEAT OF THE INTERNATIONAL TRIBUNAL SHALL BE ACCORDED SUCH TREATMENT AS IS NECESSARY FOR THE PROPER FUNCTIONING OF THE INTERNATIONAL TRIBUNAL.

ARTICLE 31

SEAT OF THE INTERNATIONAL TRIBUNAL

THE INTERNATIONAL TRIBUNAL SHALL HAVE ITS SEAT AT THE HAGUE.

ARTICLE 32

EXPENSES OF THE INTERNATIONAL TRIBUNAL

THE EXPENSES OF THE INTERNATIONAL TRIBUNAL SHALL BE BORNE BY THE REGULAR BUDGET OF THE UNITED NATIONS IN ACCORDANCE WITH ARTICLE 17 OF THE CHARTER OF THE UNITED NATIONS.

ARTICLE 33

WORKING LANGUAGES

THE WORKING LANGUAGES OF THE INTERNATIONAL TRIBUNAL SHALL BE ENGLISH AND FRENCH.

ARTICLE 34

ANNUAL REPORT

THE PRESIDENT OF THE INTERNATIONAL TRIBUNAL SHALL SUBMIT AN ANNUAL REPORT OF THE INTERNATIONAL TRIBUNAL TO THE SECURITY COUNCIL AND TO THE GENERAL ASSEMBLY.

RULES OF PROCEDURE AND EVIDENCE

(ADOPTED 11 FEBRUARY 1994)
(AS AMENDED 5 MAY 1994)
(AS FURTHER AMENDED 4 OCTOBER 1994)
(AS AMENDED 30 JANUARY 1995)
(AS AMENDED 3 MAY 1995)
(AS FURTHER AMENDED 15 JUNE 1995)
(AS AMENDED 6 OCTOBER 1995)
(AS FURTHER AMENDED 18 JANUARY 1996)
(AS AMENDED23 APRIL 1996)
(AS AMENDED 25 JUNE AND 5 JULY 1996)
(AS AMENDED 3 DECEMBER 1996)
(AS FURTHER AMENDED 25 JULY 1997)
(AS REVISED 20 OCTOBER AND 12 NOVEMBER 1997)
(AS AMENDED 9 & 10 JULY 1998)
(AS AMENDED 4 DECEMBER 1998)
(AS AMENDED 23 FEBRUARY 1999)
(AS AMENDED 2 JULY 1999)
(AS AMENDED 17 NOVEMBER 1999)
(AS AMENDED 2 AUGUST 2000)

PART ONE

GENERAL PROVISIONS

RULE 1

ENTRY INTO FORCE

THESE RULES OF PROCEDURE AND EVIDENCE, ADOPTED PURSUANT TO ARTICLE 15 OF THE STATUTE OF THE TRIBUNAL, SHALL COME INTO FORCE ON 14 MARCH 1994.

RULE 2

DEFINITIONS

(A)   IN THE RULES, UNLESS THE CONTEXT OTHERWISE REQUIRES, THE FOLLOWING TERMS SHALL MEAN:

RULES:	THE RULES OF PROCEDURE AND EVIDENCE IN FORCE;
STATUTE:	THE STATUTE OF THE TRIBUNAL ADOPTED BY SECURITY COUNCIL RESOLUTION 827 OF 25 MAY 1993;
TRIBUNAL:	THE INTERNATIONAL TRIBUNAL FOR THE PROSECUTION OF PERSONS RESPONSIBLE FOR SERIOUS VIOLATIONS OF INTERNATIONAL HUMANITARIAN LAW COMMITTED IN THE TERRITORY OF THE FORMER YUGOSLAVIA SINCE 1991, ESTABLISHED BY SECURITY COUNCIL RESOLUTION 827 OF 25 MAY 1993.
ACCUSED:	A PERSON AGAINST WHOM ONE OR MORE COUNTS IN AN INDICTMENT HAVE BEEN CONFIRMED IN ACCORDANCE WITH RULE 47;
ARREST:	THE ACT OF TAKING A SUSPECT OR AN ACCUSED INTO CUSTODY PURSUANT TO A WARRANT OF ARREST OR UNDER RULE 40;
BUREAU:	A BODY COMPOSED OF THE PRESIDENT, THE VICE-PRESIDENT AND THE PRESIDING JUDGES OF THE TRIAL CHAMBERS;
DEFENCE:	THE ACCUSED, AND/OR THE ACCUSED'S COUNSEL;
INVESTIGATION:	ALL ACTIVITIES UNDERTAKEN BY THE PROSECUTOR UNDER THE STATUTE AND THE RULES FOR THE COLLECTION OF INFORMATION AND EVIDENCE, WHETHER BEFORE OR AFTER AN INDICTMENT IS CONFIRMED;
PARTIES:	THE PROSECUTOR AND THE DEFENCE;
PRESIDENT:	THE PRESIDENT OF THE TRIBUNAL;
PROSECUTOR:	THE PROSECUTOR APPOINTED PURSUANT TO ARTICLE 16 OF THE STATUTE;
REGULATIONS:	THE PROVISIONS FRAMED BY THE PROSECUTOR PURSUANT TO SUB-RULE 37 (A) FOR THE PURPOSE OF DIRECTING THE FUNCTIONS OF THE OFFICE OF THE PROSECUTOR;
STATE:	A STATE MEMBER OR NON-MEMBER OF THE UNITED NATIONS OR A SELF-PROCLAIMED ENTITY DE FACTO EXERCISING GOVERNMENTAL FUNCTIONS, WHETHER RECOGNISED AS A STATE OR NOT;

SUSPECT: A PERSON CONCERNING WHOM THE PROSECUTOR POSSESSES RELIABLE INFORMATION WHICH TENDS TO SHOW THAT THE PERSON MAY HAVE COMMITTED A CRIME OVER WHICH THE TRIBUNAL HAS JURISDICTION;

TRANSACTION: A NUMBER OF ACTS OR OMISSIONS WHETHER OCCURRING AS ONE EVENT OR A NUMBER OF EVENTS, AT THE SAME OR DIFFERENT LOCATIONS AND BEING PART OF A COMMON SCHEME, STRATEGY OR PLAN;

VICTIM: A PERSON AGAINST WHOM A CRIME OVER WHICH THE TRIBUNAL HAS JURISDICTION HAS ALLEGEDLY BEEN COMMITTED.

(B)   IN THE RULES, THE MASCULINE SHALL INCLUDE THE FEMININE AND THE SINGULAR THE PLURAL, AND VICE-VERSA.

II.   TRIBUNAL CASES

B.   TRIAL CHAMBERS

1. ARREST

PROSECUTOR V. DOKMANOVIĆ, *Decision on the motion for release by the accused Slavko Dokmanović*, IT-95-13a-PT, 22 October 1997, Cassese, May & Mumba, JJ.

The Trial Chamber found that an arrest occurs when, by physical restraint or conduct, or by words, an individual is made aware that he is not free to leave.[431]
    Dokmanović was not arrested until he arrived at the Erdut United Nations Transitional Administration for Eastern Slavonia, Baranja and Western Sirmium ("UNTAES") base. He was removed from the vehicle by UNTAES and handcuffed. An OTP investigator at the base informed him of his rights and the nature of the charges against him.[432] Dokmanović's firm belief that he was on his way to a meeting, until he arrived at the base, provides evidence that UNTAES officials had not created the type of environment in which a "person knows he is not free", until the accused got out of the vehicle at the Erdut base.[433]

2. STATE

PROSECUTOR V. SIMIĆ, *et. al.*, *Decision on Simo Zarić's Application for Provisional Release*, IT-95-9-PT, 4 April 2000, Robinson, Hunt & Bennouna, JJ

---

[431] Paras. 28-29, 50.
[432] Para. 33.
[433] Para. 31.

The Trial Chamber held that the Government of *Republika Srpska* is competent to issue guarantees in relation to provisional release. Rule 2 defines "State" as including any "self-proclaimed entity *de facto* exercising governmental functions, whether recognised as a State or not." The Chamber observed that under the Constitution of Bosnia and Herzegovina, the *Republika-Srpska* is one of two Entities comprising the State of Bosnia and Herzegovina. Article II, paragraph 8 of the Constitution states: "All competent authorities in Bosnia and Herzegovina shall cooperate with and provide unrestricted access to ... the International Tribunal for the Former Yugoslavia". Further, Article III, paragraph 2 (c) of the Constitution provides: "The Entities shall provide a safe and secure environment for all persons in their respective jurisdictions, by maintaining civilian law enforcement agencies [...]." Further, in granting provisional release to Milan Simić, Trial Chamber I accepted the guarantees of the authorities of the *Republika Srpska* without objection from the Prosecution. *See Prosecutor v. Simić et al.,* Case No. IT-95-9-PT, Decision on Provisional Release of the Accused (Milan Simić), 26 March 1998.[434]

---

[434] Page. 8.

RULE 3

LANGUAGES

(A)   THE WORKING LANGUAGES OF THE TRIBUNAL SHALL BE ENGLISH AND FRENCH.

(B)   AN ACCUSED SHALL HAVE THE RIGHT TO USE HIS OR HER OWN LANGUAGE.

(C)   OTHER PERSONS APPEARING BEFORE THE TRIBUNAL, OTHER THAN AS COUNSEL, WHO DO NOT HAVE SUFFICIENT KNOWLEDGE OF EITHER OF THE TWO WORKING LANGUAGES, MAY USE THEIR OWN LANGUAGE.

(D)   COUNSEL FOR AN ACCUSED MAY APPLY TO THE PRESIDING JUDGE OF A CHAMBER FOR LEAVE TO USE A LANGUAGE OTHER THAN THE TWO WORKING ONES OR THE LANGUAGE OF THE ACCUSED. IF SUCH LEAVE IS GRANTED, THE EXPENSES OF INTERPRETATION AND TRANSLATION SHALL BE BORNE BY THE TRIBUNAL TO THE EXTENT, IF ANY, DETERMINED BY THE PRESIDENT, TAKING INTO ACCOUNT THE RIGHTS OF THE DEFENCE AND THE INTERESTS OF JUSTICE.

(E)   THE REGISTRAR SHALL MAKE ANY NECESSARY ARRANGEMENTS FOR INTERPRETATION AND TRANSLATION INTO AND FROM THE WORKING LANGUAGES.

(F)   IF:

(I)   A PARTY IS REQUIRED TO TAKE ANY ACTION WITHIN A SPECIFIED TIME AFTER THE FILING OR SERVICE OF A DOCUMENT BY ANOTHER PARTY; AND

(II)   PURSUANT TO THE RULES, THAT DOCUMENT IS FILED IN A LANGUAGE OTHER THAN ONE OF THE WORKING LANGUAGES OF THE TRIBUNAL, TIME SHALL NOT RUN UNTIL THE PARTY REQUIRED TO TAKE ACTION HAS RECEIVED FROM THE REGISTRAR A TRANSLATION OF THE DOCUMENT INTO ONE OF THE WORKING LANGUAGES OF THE TRIBUNAL.

II.   TRIBUNAL CASES

A.   APPEALS CHAMBER

PROSECUTOR V. ALEKSOVSKI, *Decision on Prosecutor's Appeal on Admissibility of Evidence,* IT-95-14/1-A, 16 February 1999, May, Tieya, Hunt, Bennouna & Robinson, JJ.

The Appeals Chamber ruled that the period of seven days within which Rule 73(C) provides for the filing of an application for leave to appeal runs from (but does not include) the day upon which the written decision is filed, in whichever of the two working languages of the Tribunal – English or French – the written decision is given.

When a party receives a decision that is written in an official language of the Tribunal, with which he or she is unfamiliar, an application must be made under Rule 127 for a variation of time limits. This, however, is not the case for a document filed in a language other than an official language of the Tribunal pursuant to Rule 3(F).[435] In such circumstances, the time for calculating time limits under Rule 127 commences when the document is translated into one of the official languages and filed.

B.   TRIAL CHAMBERS

PROSECUTOR V. DELALIĆ, *et. al., Decision on Defence Application for Forwarding Documents in the Language of the Accused*, IT-96-21-T, 25 September 1996, Karibi-Whyte, Odio-Benito & Jan, JJ.

In this case the Trial Chamber was called upon to decide which Tribunal documents were required to be translated into the language of the accused, in this case, Bosnian. The guarantees contained in Article 21(1) and 4(a) of the Statute require that all evidence submitted by either party must be made available in one of the working languages and in the language of the accused. All discovery provided by the Prosecutor, however, need not be provided in the language of the accused. All papers filed with the Registrar must be in either English or French and need not be translated into the language of the accused.

Transcripts of the proceedings are provided in one or both of the working languages simply as an *aide mémoire* and, thus, need not be translated into the language of the accused. All Decisions and Orders are provided in both working languages and in the language of the accused.

PROSECUTOR V. DELALIĆ *et. al., Decision on the Applications for Adjournment of the Trial Date*, IT-96-21-T, 3 February 1997, Karibi-Whyte, Odio-Benito & Jan, JJ.

A delay in providing discovery can result in a delay in starting a trial. The Trial Chamber found that the Prosecutor had failed to comply with fixed dates for disclosure of witness statements. Many of the statements were provided in English, not translated into the language of the accused. The Chamber said:

> The Trial Chamber is cognizant of the fact that unless there is prompt and proper disclosure to the Defence, the Defence cannot make a decision on what evidence it will use at trial, and cannot therefore be adequately prepared for trial. This is especially so in this case where the disclosure was in English, making translation into the language of the accused necessary.[436]

---

[435] Para. 13.
[436] Para. 22.

RULE 4

MEETINGS AWAY FROM THE SEAT OF THE TRIBUNAL

A CHAMBER MAY EXERCISE ITS FUNCTIONS AT A PLACE OTHER THAN THE SEAT OF THE TRIBUNAL, IF SO AUTHORISED BY THE PRESIDENT IN THE INTERESTS OF JUSTICE.

RULE 5

NON-COMPLIANCE WITH RULES

(A)   WHERE AN OBJECTION ON THE GROUND OF NON-COMPLIANCE WITH THE RULES OR REGULATIONS IS RAISED BY A PARTY AT THE EARLIEST OPPORTUNITY, THE TRIAL CHAMBER SHALL GRANT RELIEF IF IT FINDS THAT THE ALLEGED NON-COMPLIANCE IS PROVED AND THAT IT HAS CAUSED MATERIAL PREJUDICE TO THAT PARTY.

(B)   WHERE SUCH AN OBJECTION IS RAISED OTHERWISE THAN AT THE EARLIEST OPPORTUNITY, THE TRIAL CHAMBER MAY IN ITS DISCRETION GRANT RELIEF IF IT FINDS THAT THE ALLEGED NONCOMPLIANCE IS PROVED AND THAT IT HAS CAUSED MATERIAL PREJUDICE TO THE OBJECTING PARTY.

(C)   THE RELIEF GRANTED BY A TRIAL CHAMBER UNDER THIS RULE SHALL BE SUCH REMEDY AS THE TRIAL CHAMBER CONSIDERS APPROPRIATE TO ENSURE CONSISTENCY WITH THE FUNDAMENTAL PRINCIPLES OF FAIRNESS.

II.   TRIBUNAL CASES

B.   TRIAL CHAMBERS

PROSECUTOR V DOKMANOVIĆ, *Decision on the motion for release by the accused Slavko Dokmanović*, IT-95-13a-PT, 22 October 1997, McDonald, Odio-Benito & Jan, JJ.

The Trial Chamber observed that Rule 5 of the Rules states that any action that is in non-compliance with the Rules shall only be declared null if it occasioned a miscarriage of justice and if it was inconsistent with the fundamental principles of fairness.[437]

---

[437] Para. 52.

RULE 6

AMENDMENT OF THE RULES

(A)   PROPOSALS FOR AMENDMENT OF THE RULES MAY BE MADE BY A JUDGE, THE PROSECUTOR OR THE REGISTRAR AND SHALL BE ADOPTED IF AGREED TO BY NOT LESS THAN NINE JUDGES AT A PLENARY MEETING OF THE TRIBUNAL CONVENED WITH NOTICE OF THE PROPOSAL ADDRESSED TO ALL JUDGES.

(B)   AN AMENDMENT TO THE RULES MAY BE OTHERWISE ADOPTED, PROVIDED IT IS UNANIMOUSLY APPROVED BY THE JUDGES.

(C)   PROPOSALS FOR AMENDMENT OF THE RULES MAY OTHERWISE BE MADE IN ACCORDANCE WITH THE PRACTICE DIRECTION ISSUED BY THE PRESIDENT.

(D)   AN AMENDMENT SHALL ENTER INTO FORCE SEVEN DAYS AFTER THE DATE OF ISSUE OF AN OFFICIAL TRIBUNAL DOCUMENT CONTAINING THE AMENDMENT, BUT SHALL NOT OPERATE TO PREJUDICE THE RIGHTS OF THE ACCUSED IN ANY PENDING CASE.

II.   TRIBUNAL CASES

A.   APPEALS CHAMBER

1. RETROACTIVE APPLICATION OF NEW OR AMENDED RULES

PROSECUTOR V. BLAŠKIĆ, *Decision on Prosecution's Motion to Set Aside the Decision of the Appeals Chamber of 29 July 1997*, IT-95-14-AR, 12 August 1997, Cassese, Karibi-Whyte, Li, Stephen & Vohrah, JJ.

The Prosecutor raised a question about the retroactive effect of new rule 108 *bis*. With regard to retroactivity, the Appeals Chamber held:

> First, the purpose of amendment of a Rule or adoption of a new rule is to create conditions which are more conducive to the proper administration of justice. Hence Rule 6(C) [earlier version] prescribes that "an amendment shall enter into force immediately", without any limitation of its application other than that of not prejudicing the rights of the accused. Therefore, except in cases where the amendment explicitly states that it is not to have retroactive effect for certain particular reasons, the general rule is that it has retroactive as well as prospective effect. Second, Rule 108*bis* is in any event a procedural rule and no general principle precludes procedural rules from applying retroactively.[438]

---

[438] Page 4, Web Document, www.un.org/icty.

B.   TRIAL CHAMBERS

PROSECUTOR V BLAŠKIĆ, *Decision on the Prosecutor's Motion for Seven (7) Days Advance Disclosure of Defence Witnesses and Defence Witness Statements,* IT-95-14-T, 3 September 1998, Jorda, Riad & Shahabuddeen, JJ.

The Prosecutor sought an order compelling the Defence to disclose their witnesses and witness statements seven days in advance of the day upon which the witness would testify, pursuant to the provision of Rule 73 *ter.* The Defence resisted on the grounds that the Rule was adopted at the plenary session of 9 and 10 July 1998, well after the trial had commenced. It was contended that the application of the new rule to this case would prejudice the defendant and that Rule 6 bars such application.

      The Chamber determined that it was not necessary to determine this issue since under Rule 54, the Chamber has the power to enter any order which will ensure that "truth is ascertained in a fair and expeditious trial." However, the Chamber held that Rule 73 *ter* does create a high water mark regarding what may be ordered disclosed by the Defence, and did not grant the Prosecutor's request for witness statements.

      The Defence was ordered to disclose "the names and identifying information (given names, date of birth, domicile, and profession) in respect of each witness it intended to call, as well as the summary of all the facts about which the said witness will testify, at least seven days prior to the date of their appearance."

PROSECUTOR V. BLAŠKIĆ, *Decision on the Defence Motion to Compel the Disclosure of Rule 66 and 68 Material Relating to Statements Made by a Person Known as "X",* IT-95-14-T, 15 July 1998, Jorda, Riad & Shahabuddeen, JJ.

During the presentation of its case, the Prosecutor was able to elicit from witnesses statements allegedly made by a person named "X". The Defence made a motion to require the Prosecutor to disclose all statements made by "X" in her possession and all documents provided by "X" to SFOR. The Defence theory was that "X" had, in effect, become a witness in the case by the admission of his hearsay statements and that as a result this rule mandated disclosure. The Prosecutor disagreed "that the introduction of hearsay evidence, which the Trial Chamber has ruled is admissible, triggers a concomitant obligation under Rule 66(A) to produce all statements of the hearsay declarant." The Prosecutor contended that the Rule imposes such an obligation only with respect to witnesses the Prosecutor intends to call to testify at trial.

      The Defence contended that it would be improper to apply Rule 66(A)(ii) to this situation since it was amended during the course of the proceedings and under Rule 6(C) (now 6(D)) no amendment should operate to prejudice the rights of the accused in any pending case.

      The Chamber rejected this argument, holding:

> The Trial Chamber is of the opinion that that amendment does not constitute a restriction of the rights of the Defence to obtain discovery of witness

statements but rather a clarification of the spirit of the rule that is the source of the obligation.[439]

---

[439] Para. 8.

RULE 7

AUTHENTIC TEXTS

THE ENGLISH AND FRENCH TEXTS OF THE RULES SHALL BE EQUALLY AUTHENTIC. IN CASE OF DISCREPANCY, THE VERSION WHICH IS MORE CONSONANT WITH THE SPIRIT OF THE STATUTE AND THE RULES SHALL PREVAIL.

PART TWO

PRIMACY OF THE TRIBUNAL

RULE 7 *BIS*

NON-COMPLIANCE WITH OBLIGATIONS

(A)   IN ADDITION TO CASES TO WHICH RULE 11, RULE 13, RULE 59 OR RULE 61 APPLIES, WHERE A TRIAL CHAMBER OR A JUDGE IS SATISFIED THAT A STATE HAS FAILED TO COMPLY WITH AN OBLIGATION UNDER ARTICLE 29 OF THE STATUTE WHICH RELATES TO ANY PROCEEDINGS BEFORE THAT CHAMBER OR JUDGE, THE CHAMBER OR JUDGE MAY ADVISE THE PRESIDENT, WHO SHALL REPORT THE MATTER TO THE SECURITY COUNCIL.

(B)   IF THE PROSECUTOR SATISFIES THE PRESIDENT THAT A STATE HAS FAILED TO COMPLY WITH AN OBLIGATION UNDER ARTICLE 29 OF THE STATUTE IN RESPECT OF A REQUEST BY THE PROSECUTOR UNDER RULE 8, RULE 39 OR RULE 40, THE PRESIDENT SHALL NOTIFY THE SECURITY COUNCIL THEREOF.

RULE 8

REQUEST FOR INFORMATION

WHERE IT APPEARS TO THE PROSECUTOR THAT A CRIME WITHIN THE JURISDICTION OF THE TRIBUNAL IS OR HAS BEEN THE SUBJECT OF INVESTIGATIONS OR CRIMINAL PROCEEDINGS INSTITUTED IN THE COURTS OF ANY STATE, THE PROSECUTOR MAY REQUEST THE STATE TO FORWARD ALL RELEVANT INFORMATION IN THAT RESPECT, AND THE STATE SHALL TRANSMIT SUCH INFORMATION TO THE PROSECUTOR FORTHWITH IN ACCORDANCE WITH ARTICLE 29 OF THE STATUTE.

RULE 9

PROSECUTOR'S REQUEST FOR DEFERRAL

WHERE IT APPEARS TO THE PROSECUTOR THAT IN ANY SUCH INVESTIGATIONS OR CRIMINAL PROCEEDINGS INSTITUTED IN THE COURTS OF ANY STATE:

(I)   THE ACT BEING INVESTIGATED OR WHICH IS THE SUBJECT OF THOSE PROCEEDINGS IS CHARACTERIZED AS AN ORDINARY CRIME;

(II)   THERE IS A LACK OF IMPARTIALITY OR INDEPENDENCE, OR THE INVESTIGATIONS OR PROCEEDINGS ARE DESIGNED TO SHIELD THE ACCUSED FROM INTERNATIONAL CRIMINAL RESPONSIBILITY, OR THE CASE IS NOT DILIGENTLY PROSECUTED; OR

(III)   WHAT IS IN ISSUE IS CLOSELY RELATED TO, OR OTHERWISE INVOLVES, SIGNIFICANT FACTUAL OR LEGAL QUESTIONS WHICH MAY HAVE IMPLICATIONS FOR INVESTIGATIONS OR PROSECUTIONS BEFORE THE TRIBUNAL, THE PROSECUTOR MAY PROPOSE TO THE TRIAL CHAMBER DESIGNATED BY THE PRESIDENT THAT A FORMAL REQUEST BE MADE THAT SUCH COURT DEFER TO THE COMPETENCE OF THE TRIBUNAL.

II.   TRIBUNAL CASES

B.   TRIAL CHAMBERS

PROSECUTOR V. DUSKO TADIĆ, *Decision of the Trial Chamber on the Application by the Prosecutor for a Formal Request for Deferral to the Competence of the International Criminal Tribunal for the Former Yugoslavia in the Matter of Duško Tadić (Pursuant to Rule 9 and 10 of the Rules of Procedure and Evidence)*, IT-94-1-D, 8 November 1994, McDonald, Stephen & Vohrah, JJ.

Duško Tadić was in custody in the Federal Republic of Germany pursuant to an investigation for war crimes allegedly committed in the Prijedor area of Bosnia and Herzegovina. In this Decision, the Trial Chamber granted the request of the Prosecutor to request the Federal Republic of Germany to defer its prosecution against Tadić to the ICTY. The Chamber held that to successfully seek a deferral in this case it was necessary for the Prosecutor to establish three things: (a) there is an investigation currently being conducted by the Prosecutor into crimes within the jurisdiction of the International Tribunal alleged to have taken place in the Prijedor region of Bosnia-Herzegovina; (b) a national investigation or criminal proceeding has been instigated against the said Duško Tadić by the Government of the Federal Republic of Germany in respect of crimes alleged to have taken place in the said Prijedor region; (c) the issue in the national investigation or criminal proceedings is closely related to, or may have implications and common significant factual or legal questions, for the Prosecutor.

RULE 10

FORMAL REQUEST FOR DEFERRAL

(A)   IF IT APPEARS TO THE TRIAL CHAMBER SEISED OF A PROPOSAL FOR DEFERRAL THAT, ON ANY OF THE GROUNDS SPECIFIED IN RULE 9, DEFERRAL IS APPROPRIATE, THE TRIAL CHAMBER MAY ISSUE A FORMAL REQUEST TO THE STATE CONCERNED THAT ITS COURT DEFER TO THE COMPETENCE OF THE TRIBUNAL.

(B)   A REQUEST FOR DEFERRAL SHALL INCLUDE A REQUEST THAT THE RESULTS OF THE INVESTIGATION AND A COPY OF THE COURT'S RECORDS AND THE JUDGEMENT, IF ALREADY DELIVERED, BE FORWARDED TO THE TRIBUNAL.

(C)   WHERE DEFERRAL TO THE TRIBUNAL HAS BEEN REQUESTED BY A TRIAL CHAMBER, ANY SUBSEQUENT TRIAL SHALL BE HELD BEFORE ANOTHER TRIAL CHAMBER.

RULE 11

NON-COMPLIANCE WITH A REQUEST FOR DEFERRAL

IF, WITHIN SIXTY DAYS AFTER A REQUEST FOR DEFERRAL HAS BEEN NOTIFIED BY THE REGISTRAR TO THE STATE UNDER WHOSE JURISDICTION THE INVESTIGATIONS OR CRIMINAL PROCEEDINGS HAVE BEEN INSTITUTED, THE STATE FAILS TO FILE A RESPONSE WHICH SATISFIES THE TRIAL CHAMBER THAT THE STATE HAS TAKEN OR IS TAKING ADEQUATE STEPS TO COMPLY WITH THE REQUEST, THE TRIAL CHAMBER MAY REQUEST THE PRESIDENT TO REPORT THE MATTER TO THE SECURITY COUNCIL.

RULE 11 *BIS*

SUSPENSION OF INDICTMENT IN CASE OF PROCEEDINGS BEFORE NATIONAL COURTS

(A)   WHERE, ON APPLICATION BY THE PROSECUTOR OR *PROPRIO MOTU*, IT APPEARS TO THE TRIAL CHAMBER THAT:

(I)   THE AUTHORITIES OF THE STATE IN WHICH AN ACCUSED WAS ARRESTED ARE PREPARED TO PROSECUTE THE ACCUSED IN THEIR OWN COURTS; AND

(II)   IT IS APPROPRIATE IN THE CIRCUMSTANCES FOR THE COURTS OF THAT STATE TO EXERCISE JURISDICTION OVER THE ACCUSED, THE TRIAL CHAMBER, AFTER AFFORDING THE OPPORTUNITY TO AN ACCUSED ALREADY IN THE CUSTODY OF THE TRIBUNAL TO BE HEARD, MAY ORDER THAT THE INDICTMENT AGAINST THE ACCUSED BE SUSPENDED, PENDING THE PROCEEDINGS BEFORE THE NATIONAL COURTS.

(B)   IF AN ORDER IS MADE UNDER THIS RULE:

(I)   THE ACCUSED, IF IN THE CUSTODY OF THE TRIBUNAL, SHALL BE TRANSFERRED TO THE AUTHORITIES OF THE STATE CONCERNED;

(II)   THE PROSECUTOR MAY TRANSMIT TO THE AUTHORITIES OF THE STATE CONCERNED SUCH INFORMATION RELATING TO THE CASE AS THE PROSECUTOR CONSIDERS APPROPRIATE;

(III)   THE PROSECUTOR MAY DIRECT TRIAL OBSERVERS TO MONITOR PROCEEDINGS BEFORE THE NATIONAL COURTS ON THE PROSECUTOR'S BEHALF.

(C)   AT ANY TIME AFTER THE MAKING OF AN ORDER UNDER THIS RULE AND BEFORE THE ACCUSED IS CONVICTED OR ACQUITTED BY A NATIONAL COURT, THE TRIAL CHAMBER MAY, UPON THE PROSECUTOR'S APPLICATION AND AFTER AFFORDING AN OPPORTUNITY TO THE AUTHORITIES OF THE STATE CONCERNED TO BE HEARD, RESCIND THE ORDER AND ISSUE A FORMAL REQUEST FOR DEFERRAL UNDER RULE 10.

(D)   IF AN ORDER UNDER THIS RULE IS RESCINDED BY THE TRIAL CHAMBER, THE TRIAL CHAMBER MAY FORMALLY REQUEST THE STATE CONCERNED TO TRANSFER THE ACCUSED TO THE SEAT OF THE TRIBUNAL, AND THE STATE SHALL COMPLY WITHOUT UNDUE DELAY IN ACCORDANCE WITH ARTICLE 29 OF THE STATUTE. THE TRIAL CHAMBER OR A JUDGE MAY ALSO ISSUE A WARRANT FOR THE ARREST OF THE ACCUSED.

RULE 12

DETERMINATIONS OF COURTS OF ANY STATE

SUBJECT TO ARTICLE 10, PARAGRAPH 2, OF THE STATUTE, DETERMINATIONS OF COURTS OF ANY STATE ARE NOT BINDING ON THE TRIBUNAL.

RULE 13

NON-BIS-IN-IDEM

WHEN THE PRESIDENT RECEIVES RELIABLE INFORMATION TO SHOW THAT CRIMINAL PROCEEDINGS HAVE BEEN INSTITUTED AGAINST A PERSON BEFORE A COURT OF ANY STATE FOR A CRIME FOR WHICH THAT PERSON HAS ALREADY BEEN TRIED BY THE TRIBUNAL, A TRIAL CHAMBER SHALL, FOLLOWING *MUTATIS MUTANDIS* THE PROCEDURE PROVIDED IN RULE 10, ISSUE A REASONED ORDER REQUESTING THAT COURT PERMANENTLY TO DISCONTINUE ITS PROCEEDINGS. IF THAT COURT FAILS TO DO SO, THE PRESIDENT MAY REPORT THE MATTER TO THE SECURITY COUNCIL.

PART THREE

ORGANIZATION OF THE TRIBUNAL

RULE 14

SOLEMN DECLARATION

(A)   BEFORE TAKING UP DUTIES EACH JUDGE SHALL MAKE THE FOLLOWING SOLEMN DECLARATION:

> "I SOLEMNLY DECLARE THAT I WILL PERFORM MY DUTIES AND EXERCISE MY POWERS AS A JUDGE OF THE INTERNATIONAL TRIBUNAL FOR THE PROSECUTION OF PERSONS RESPONSIBLE FOR SERIOUS VIOLATIONS OF INTERNATIONAL HUMANITARIAN LAW COMMITTED IN THE TERRITORY OF THE FORMER YUGOSLAVIA SINCE 1991 HONOURABLY, FAITHFULLY, IMPARTIALLY AND CONSCIENTIOUSLY".

(B)   THE DECLARATION SHALL BE SIGNED BY THE JUDGE AND WITNESSED BY, OR BY A REPRESENTATIVE OF, THE SECRETARY-GENERAL OF THE UNITED NATIONS. THE DECLARATION SHALL BE KEPT IN THE RECORDS OF THE TRIBUNAL.

(C)   A JUDGE WHOSE SERVICE CONTINUES WITHOUT INTERRUPTION AFTER EXPIRY OF A PREVIOUS PERIOD OF SERVICE SHALL NOT MAKE A NEW DECLARATION.

RULE 15

DISQUALIFICATION OF JUDGES

(A)   A JUDGE MAY NOT SIT ON A TRIAL OR APPEAL IN ANY CASE IN WHICH THE JUDGE HAS A PERSONAL INTEREST OR CONCERNING WHICH THE JUDGE HAS OR HAS HAD ANY ASSOCIATION WHICH MIGHT AFFECT HIS OR HER IMPARTIALITY. THE JUDGE SHALL IN ANY SUCH CIRCUMSTANCE WITHDRAW, AND THE PRESIDENT SHALL ASSIGN ANOTHER JUDGE TO THE CASE.

(B)   ANY PARTY MAY APPLY TO THE PRESIDING JUDGE OF A CHAMBER FOR THE DISQUALIFICATION AND WITHDRAWAL OF A JUDGE OF THAT CHAMBER FROM A TRIAL OR APPEAL UPON THE ABOVE GROUNDS. THE PRESIDING JUDGE SHALL CONFER WITH THE JUDGE IN QUESTION, AND IF NECESSARY THE BUREAU SHALL DETERMINE THE MATTER. IF THE BUREAU UPHOLDS THE APPLICATION, THE PRESIDENT SHALL ASSIGN ANOTHER JUDGE TO SIT IN PLACE OF THE DISQUALIFIED JUDGE.

(C)   THE JUDGE OF THE TRIAL CHAMBER WHO REVIEWS AN INDICTMENT AGAINST AN ACCUSED, PURSUANT TO ARTICLE 19 OF THE STATUTE AND RULES 47 OR 61, SHALL NOT BE DISQUALIFIED FOR SITTING AS A MEMBER OF THE TRIAL CHAMBER FOR THE TRIAL OF THAT ACCUSED. SUCH A JUDGE SHALL ALSO NOT BE DISQUALIFIED FOR SITTING AS A MEMBER OF THE APPEALS CHAMBER, OR AS A MEMBER OF A BENCH OF THREE JUDGES APPOINTED PURSUANT TO RULES 65 (D), 72(B)(II), 73(B), OR 77(J), TO HEAR ANY APPEAL IN THAT CASE.

(D)

        (I)   NO JUDGE SHALL SIT ON ANY APPEAL OR AS A MEMBER OF A BENCH OF THREE JUDGES APPOINTED PURSUANT TO RULES 65 (D), 72 (B)(II), 73 (B) OR 77 (J) IN A CASE IN WHICH THAT JUDGE SAT AS A MEMBER OF THE TRIAL CHAMBER.

        (II)   NO JUDGE SHALL SIT ON ANY STATE REQUEST FOR REVIEW PURSUANT TO RULE 108 *BIS* IN A MATTER IN WHICH THAT JUDGE SAT AS A MEMBER OF THE TRIAL CHAMBER WHOSE DECISION IS TO BE REVIEWED.

I.   COMMENTARY

A.   GENERAL

In the *Delalić* decision, reported below, the Bureau appears to have made a distinction between the appearance of a lack of impartiality and actual impartiality. They rejected the argument that the election and swearing in of Judge Odio-Benito as Vice-President of Costa Rica created the appearance of lack of impartiality within the meaning of Rule 15(A). The Bureau accepted the undertaking of Judge Odio-Benito that she not assume the duties of Vice-President until her judicial duties were completed as evidence of a guarantee "sufficient to exclude any legitimate doubt" in respect of her impartiality and as a guarantee "against outside pressures" which could bring her independence into question.

II.   TRIBUNAL CASES

A.   APPEALS CHAMBER

PROSECUTOR V. FURUNDŽIJA, *Judgement,* IT-95-17/1-A, 21 July 2000, Shahabuddeen, Vohrah, Nieto-Navia, Robinson & Pocar, JJ.

The Chamber discussed at length the requested disqualification of Judge Mumba. This decision is reported in detail in Article 13.

C.   BUREAU

PROSECUTOR V. DELALIĆ, *et. al., Decision of the Bureau on Motion to Disqualify Judges Pursuant to Rule 15 or in the Alternative That Certain Judges Recuse Themselves,* IT-96-21-T, 25 October 1999, McDonald, Shahabuddeen, Cassese, Jorda & May, JJ.

All appellants with the exception of Zejnil Delalić filed this Motion with the Appeals Chamber which in turn referred it to the Bureau.

The issue raised by the Motion was whether, pursuant to both Rules 14 and 15, Judge Odio-Benito was qualified to sit as a Judge in the *Delalić* trial due to her election as Vice-President of Costa Rica during the course of the trial.

The Bureau was of the view that two major issues were raised by the motion and set them out, as follows:

> The two issues set out so far are different. The first issue relates to the question of whether or not a Judge possesses all the necessary requirements for serving as a Judge of the Tribunal. This is a matter of an administrative nature, internal to the Tribunal. It can only be settled by the relevant bodies of the Tribunal. If these bodies are satisfied that the Judge does not fulfil one of the requisite conditions, for instance because he or she has engaged in political or administrative functions incompatible with the judicial function, the Judge is duty bound either to abandon those incompatible functions or to resign from the position of Judge.

> By contrast, the other issue is a judicial matter, which may be raised not only by the Judge concerned but also by any party to the proceedings before a Trial Chamber or the Appeals Chamber. It relates to the right of a Judge to sit in a specific case. If the Judge does not fulfil the requirements referred to in Rule

15(B), he or she is disqualified from hearing that particular case, although he or she is fully entitled to continue to exercise the functions of a Judge of the Tribunal and sit in other cases.[440]

The Bureau then traced the history of this issue with Judge Odio-Benito at the Tribunal:

> It must be noted that the question of whether the position of Vice-President of Costa Rica was compatible with the discharge of the judicial functions by Judge Odio Benito was raised, at the administrative level, by the then President Cassese on 23 May 1997, in a meeting with Judge Odio Benito, when it became known that she was running as a candidate for that position. Judge Odio Benito responded to President Cassese in a letter of 16 October 1997 in which she specified that, if elected, she would not take office before the end of her functions as a Judge sitting in Čelebići and in addition undertook, if elected, to fulfil her judicial functions on a full time basis. In the light of this commitment, the then President Cassese decided that Judge Odio Benito was entitled to run as a candidate for the position of Vice-President. Nevertheless, he felt that it was advisable to submit the matter to the Plenary. This was done in October 1997. The Fourteenth Plenary assembly of all Judges, in the discharge of *administrative functions*, endorsed the decision of the President. (Bureau's emphasis)

> The matter arose again in March 1998, after the election, on 1 February 1998, of Judge Odio Benito to the position of Second Vice-President of Costa Rica. President McDonald noted the renewed commitment of Judge Odio Benito not to assume the functions of Second Vice-President nor, in case of permanent or temporary absence of the President or the First Vice-President, the functions of President of Costa Rica, prior to the termination of her tenure as a Judge. Judge Odio Benito further undertook not to be diverted by anything from the fulfilment of her mandate as a Judge until November 1998. In light of these commitments, President McDonald decided that there was no incompatibility between Judge Odio Benito's judicial duties and her new status of Second Vice-President of Costa Rica. President McDonald too felt it was advisable to submit the matter to the Seventeenth Plenary. This was done on 11 March 1998. The Plenary assembly of Judges, again exercising its *administrative* functions, unanimously endorsed President McDonald's decision.[441] (Bureau's emphasis)

Having set out this history, the Bureau made a distinction between "administrative" and "judicial" functions of Tribunal judges. This motivated the following holding:

> In light of the above, the Bureau holds the view that the fulfilment by a Judge of his or her duty to take part in a collegiate decision of an administrative nature on the administrative issue discussed so far cannot amount to a ground for subsequently disqualifying such a Judge, sitting in the Appeals Chamber, from

---

[440] Para. 9.
[441] Para. 12.

discharging a judicial function (i.e., pronouncing upon the question, raised by the three appellants in their appeal against conviction, of whether Judge Odio Benito, by her election as Second Vice-President of Costa Rica, became disqualified from sitting in Čelebići and whether her impartiality could in any event be perceived as having been compromised).[442] (Bureau's emphasis)

The Bureau therefore considers that the appellants have failed to satisfy the requirements set out in Sub-Rule 15(A). In particular, they have failed to show that Judges Riad, Wang and Nieto-Navia have a personal interest in the question of whether Judge Odio Benito was entitled to sit in Čelebići or have any association with this question which might affect their impartiality.[443]

PROSECUTOR V FURUNDŽIJA, *Decision on Post-Trial Application by Anto Furundžija to the Bureau of the Tribunal for Disqualification of Presiding Judge Mumba, Motion to Vacate Conviction and Sentence, and Motion for a New Trial,* IT-95-17/1, 11 March 1998, McDonald, Jorda, Rodrigues, Hunt & Bennouna, JJ.

Furundžija applied to the Bureau for the disqualification of Presiding Judge Mumba asserting that a judge may not sit on a trial in any case in which the judge has a personal interest or concerning which the judge has or has had any association which might affect his or her impartiality. In the instant case, Furundžija advanced the argument that Judge Mumba's role on the United Nations Commission on the Status of Women and the positions she had taken in relation to rape as a war crime required her to be disqualified as Presiding Judge in the Furundžija trial where the central issues were rape and sexual assault as war crimes.[444]

The Bureau decided that Rule 15(B), so far as it relates to the disqualification of a judge of a Trial Chamber, applies only to an application for disqualification made during the course of the trial and up to the time when judgement is given.

In dismissing the application and motion, the Bureau noted that they were made after the trial had concluded and judgement had been handed down. Furthermore, the Bureau noted that the issue whether the trial was a fair one is not an issue that the Bureau has competence to decide. The Bureau considered that the issue of Judge Mumba's disqualification was a matter that could be dealt with on appeal against the judgement.

---

[442] Para. 15.
[443] Para. 16.
[444] See, Defendant's Post-Trial Application to the Bureau of the Tribunal for the Disqualificaiton of Presiding Judge Mumba, Motion to Vacate Conviction and Sentence, and Motion for a New Trial, 3 February 1999.

PROSECUTOR V DELALIĆ *et. al.*, *Decision of the Bureau on Motion on Judicial Independence*, IT-96-21-T, 4 September 1998, McDonald, Shahabuddeen, Cassesse & Jorda, JJ.

Judge Odio-Benito was elected and sworn in as Vice-President of the Republic of Costa Rica while she sat as a Judge of the Trial Chamber hearing the *Delalić* Case. Prior to taking office, Judge Odio-Benito gave an undertaking to the Plenary Session of the Tribunal that she would not assume the functions or duties of Vice-President.

The central issue for determination was whether, having regard to the fact that Judge Odio-Benito held the office of Second Vice-President of Costa Rica, the requirements of impartiality and possession of the qualifications for appointment to the highest judicial offices in Costa Rica were not being met and she was not qualified to sit as a Judge of the Tribunal pursuant to Article 13(1). There was no challenge to Judge Odio-Benito's "high moral character" and "integrity" in the context of Article 13(1).

Judicial Independence: impartiality and independence as a judge

The Bureau determined the issue of Judge Odio-Benito sitting as a Judge of a Trial Chamber by examining the question of the incompatibility of being a member of the Executive of Costa Rica and a Judge of the Tribunal. Two issues were central to this determination: impartiality and independence as a judge.

The Bureau found that there was a two-part test of impartiality: a subjective element that asks whether a judge is impartial because of a personal conviction that the judge has in a given case; and, an objective element that asks whether the judge offered guarantees sufficient to exclude any legitimate doubt in this respect.[445]

The Bureau ruled that the mere fact that a person who exercises judicial functions is to some extent subject, in another capacity, to executive supervision, is not by itself enough to impair judicial independence.[446] The test for measuring independence consists of examining, *inter alia*, the manner of appointment of Judges, the duration of their term of office, the existence of guarantees against outside pressures and whether the body presents an appearance of independence.[447]

The Bureau ruled that the fact that Judge Odio-Benito held the office of Vice-President of Costa Rica, while sitting, as a Judge of the Tribunal, did not prevent her from being impartial within the meaning of Rule 15(A). The Bureau found that the issue is not whether there is a prohibition against the exercise of any political or administrative function, but whether Judge Odio-Benito was exercising such a function. Merely holding the office of Vice-President of Costa Rica did not create the appearance of impartiality. The Bureau found that Judge Odio-Benito held the office of Vice-President "in name only" from the day she was sworn in and her commitment not to take up the duties of her

---

[445] Page 7.
[446] Page 9.
[447] Page 8.

post until she completed her judicial duties showed that she was not exercising such functions at the same time as she sat as a Judge of the Tribunal.[448]

---

[448] Pages 9-11.

Rule 15 *bis*

Absence of a Judge

(A)   If

     (i)   a Judge is, for illness or other urgent personal reasons, unable to continue sitting in a part-heard case for a period which is likely to be of short duration, and

     (ii)   the remaining Judges of the Chamber are satisfied that it is in the interests of justice to do so,

those remaining Judges of the Chamber may order that the hearing of the case continue in the absence of that Judge for a period of not more than three days.

(B)   If

     (i)   a Judge is, for illness or urgent personal reasons, unable to continue sitting in a part-heard case for a period which is likely to be of short duration, and

     (ii)   the remaining Judges of the Chamber are not satisfied that it is in the interests of justice to order that the hearing of the case continue in the absence of that Judge, then

         (a)   those remaining Judges of the Chamber may nevertheless conduct those matters which they are satisfied it is in the interests of justice that they be disposed of notwithstanding the absence of that Judge, and

         (b)   the Presiding Judge may adjourn the proceedings.

(C)   If a Judge is, for any reason, unable to continue sitting in a part-heard case for a period which is likely to be longer than of a short duration, the Presiding Judge shall report to the President who may assign another Judge to the case and order either a rehearing or continuation of the proceedings from that point. However, after the opening statements provided for in Rule 84, or the beginning of the presentation of evidence pursuant to Rule 85, the continuation of the proceedings can only be ordered with the consent of the accused.

(D)   In case of illness or an unfilled vacancy or in any other similar circumstances, the President may, if satisfied that it is in the interests of justice to do so, authorise a Chamber to conduct routine matters, such as the delivery of decisions, in the absence of one or more of its members.

I.   COMMENTARY

This Rule allows for continuation of proceedings in the event a judge is absent. The absence of a Judge under this rule is divided into one of either "a short duration" or "longer than a short duration." A "short duration" is a period not exceeding three days.

RULE 16

RESIGNATION

A JUDGE WHO DECIDES TO RESIGN SHALL COMMUNICATE THE RESIGNATION IN WRITING TO THE PRESIDENT WHO SHALL TRANSMIT IT TO THE SECRETARY -GENERAL OF THE UNITED NATIONS.

RULE 17

PRECEDENCE

(A)   ALL JUDGES ARE EQUAL IN THE EXERCISE OF THEIR JUDICIAL FUNCTIONS, REGARDLESS OF DATES OF ELECTION, APPOINTMENT, AGE OR PERIOD OF SERVICE.

(B)   THE PRESIDING JUDGES OF THE TRIAL CHAMBERS SHALL TAKE PRECEDENCE ACCORDING TO AGE AFTER THE PRESIDENT AND THE VICE-PRESIDENT.

(C)   JUDGES ELECTED OR APPOINTED ON DIFFERENT DATES SHALL TAKE PRECEDENCE ACCORDING TO THE DATES OF THEIR ELECTION OR APPOINTMENT; JUDGES ELECTED OR APPOINTED ON THE SAME DATE SHALL TAKE PRECEDENCE ACCORDING TO AGE.

(D)   IN CASE OF RE-ELECTION, THE TOTAL PERIOD OF SERVICE AS A JUDGE OF THE TRIBUNAL SHALL BE TAKEN INTO ACCOUNT.

RULE 18

ELECTION OF THE PRESIDENT

(A)   THE PRESIDENT SHALL BE ELECTED FOR A TERM OF TWO YEARS, OR SUCH SHORTER TERM AS SHALL COINCIDE WITH THE DURATION OF HIS OR HER TERM OF OFFICE AS A JUDGE. THE PRESIDENT MAY BE RE-ELECTED ONCE.

(B)   IF THE PRESIDENT CEASES TO BE A MEMBER OF THE TRIBUNAL OR RESIGNS FROM OFFICE BEFORE THE EXPIRATION OF HIS OR HER TERM, THE JUDGES SHALL ELECT FROM AMONG THEIR NUMBER A SUCCESSOR FOR THE REMAINDER OF THE TERM.

(C)   THE PRESIDENT SHALL BE ELECTED BY A MAJORITY OF THE VOTES OF THE JUDGES COMPOSING THE TRIBUNAL. IF NO JUDGE OBTAINS SUCH A MAJORITY, THE SECOND BALLOT SHALL BE LIMITED TO THE TWO JUDGES WHO OBTAINED THE GREATEST NUMBER OF VOTES ON THE FIRST BALLOT. IN THE CASE OF EQUALITY OF VOTES ON THE SECOND BALLOT, THE JUDGE WHO TAKES PRECEDENCE IN ACCORDANCE WITH RULE 17 SHALL BE DECLARED ELECTED.

RULE 19

FUNCTIONS OF THE PRESIDENT

(A)   THE PRESIDENT SHALL PRESIDE AT ALL PLENARY MEETINGS OF THE TRIBUNAL. THE PRESIDENT SHALL COORDINATE THE WORK OF THE CHAMBERS AND SUPERVISE THE ACTIVITIES OF THE REGISTRY AS WELL AS EXERCISE ALL THE OTHER FUNCTIONS CONFERRED ON THE PRESIDENT BY THE STATUTE AND THE RULES.

(B)   THE PRESIDENT MAY FROM TIME TO TIME, AND IN CONSULTATION WITH THE BUREAU, THE REGISTRAR AND THE PROSECUTOR, ISSUE PRACTICE DIRECTIONS, CONSISTENT WITH THE STATUTE AND THE RULES, ADDRESSING DETAILED ASPECTS OF THE CONDUCT OF PROCEEDINGS BEFORE THE TRIBUNAL.

II.   TRIBUNAL CASES

C.   THE PRESIDENT

1. PRACTICE DIRECTIONS

PROSECUTOR V. KOVAČEVIĆ, *et. al., Decision on the Application of the Defence to the President of the Tribunal of 8 July 1998*, Case No. IT-97-24, Shahabuddeen, J.

The Vice President, in the absence of the President, considered an appeal brought by the Defendant complaining of a ruling of Trial Chamber II that only lead counsel and co-counsel are permitted to be heard during the trial. The Vice President determined that the competence given to the President by this section to issue Practice Directions, does not include the competence to entertain an appeal from a ruling in a case.

RULE 20

THE VICE-PRESIDENT

(A)   THE VICE-PRESIDENT SHALL BE ELECTED FOR A TERM OF TWO YEARS, OR SUCH SHORTER TERM AS SHALL COINCIDE WITH THE DURATION OF HIS OR HER TERM OF OFFICE AS A JUDGE. THE VICE PRESIDENT MAY BE RE-ELECTED ONCE.

(B)   THE VICE-PRESIDENT MAY SIT AS A MEMBER OF A TRIAL CHAMBER OR OF THE APPEALS CHAMBER.

(C)   SUB-RULES 18 (B) AND (C) SHALL APPLY *MUTATIS MUTANDIS* TO THE VICE-PRESIDENT.

RULE 21

FUNCTIONS OF THE VICE-PRESIDENT

SUBJECT TO SUB-RULE 22 (B), THE VICE-PRESIDENT SHALL EXERCISE THE FUNCTIONS OF THE PRESIDENT IN CASE OF THE LATTER'S ABSENCE OR INABILITY TO ACT.

RULE 22

REPLACEMENTS

(A)   IF NEITHER THE PRESIDENT NOR THE VICE-PRESIDENT CAN CARRY OUT THE FUNCTIONS OF THE PRESIDENT, THESE SHALL BE ASSUMED BY THE SENIOR JUDGE, DETERMINED IN ACCORDANCE WITH RULE 17.

(B)   IF THE PRESIDENT IS UNABLE TO EXERCISE THE FUNCTIONS OF PRESIDING JUDGE OF THE APPEALS CHAMBER, THAT CHAMBER SHALL ELECT A PRESIDING JUDGE FROM AMONG ITS NUMBER.

RULE 23

THE BUREAU

(A)   THE BUREAU SHALL BE COMPOSED OF THE PRESIDENT, THE VICE-PRESIDENT AND THE PRESIDING JUDGES OF THE TRIAL CHAMBERS.

(B)   THE PRESIDENT SHALL CONSULT THE OTHER MEMBERS OF THE BUREAU ON ALL MAJOR QUESTIONS RELATING TO THE FUNCTIONING OF THE TRIBUNAL.

(C)   A JUDGE MAY DRAW THE ATTENTION OF ANY MEMBER OF THE BUREAU TO ISSUES THAT THE JUDGE CONSIDERS OUGHT TO BE DISCUSSED BY THE BUREAU OR SUBMITTED TO A PLENARY MEETING OF THE TRIBUNAL.

(D)   IF ANY MEMBER OF THE BUREAU IS UNABLE TO CARRY OUT ANY OF THE FUNCTIONS OF THE BUREAU, THESE SHALL BE ASSUMED BY THE SENIOR JUDGE DETERMINED IN ACCORDANCE WITH RULE 17.[449]

II.   TRIBUNAL CASES

B.   THE BUREAU

PROSECUTOR V. DELIĆ, *et. al., Bureau Decision on the "Emergency Motion Filed on Behalf of Various Accused Directed to the Bureau [. . .] to Declare the Registry's 'Modifications of Remuneration for Counsel, Assignment Practice for Support Staff' to be in Violation of Articles 20 and 21 of the Statute of the ICTY and in Violation of the Principle of Equality of Arms Between the Prosecution and the Defence,* IT-00-38-MISC.4, 8 June 2000, Jorda, Mumba, Hunt, May & Rodrigues, JJ.

On 7 April 2000, the Registrar issued a Memorandum setting forth important changes in the remuneration of counsel assigned by the Registry to the accused. In essence the new scheme dramatically reduced the number of compensable hours that counsel and support staff could devote to a case.

     Assigned counsel for most of the detainees joined together and drafted and filed a Motion seeking to immediately suspend the new scheme and to have it declared violative of Articles 20 and 21 of the Statute and in violation of the international law principle of Equality of Arms.

     This Motion was filed with the Bureau based on the language of Rule 23(B) that permits the Bureau to consider "all major questions relating to the functioning of the Tribunal."

     The Bureau, however, found that, based upon this rule, they were not competent to rule on the Motion. The Bureau determined, that "the fundamental issues of remuneration of Defence Counsel and Defence support staff raised in the Motions merit

---

[449] March 1999 Amendment.

review by all the Judges in plenary in accordance with Řule 24 of the Rules." The matter was referred to the plenary of July 2000.

In addition, having decided that this was a fundamental issue deserving attention of the plenary, the Bureau suspended the application of the new scheme "until such time as a more thorough review of the issue raised in the Motions had been conducted."

RULE 24

PLENARY MEETINGS OF THE TRIBUNAL

THE JUDGES SHALL MEET IN PLENARY TO:

    (I)   ELECT THE PRESIDENT AND VICE-PRESIDENT;

    (II)   ADOPT AND AMEND THE RULES;

    (III)   ADOPT THE ANNUAL REPORT PROVIDED FOR IN ARTICLE 34 OF THE STATUTE;

    (IV)   DECIDE UPON MATTERS RELATING TO THE INTERNAL FUNCTIONING OF THE CHAMBERS AND THE TRIBUNAL;

    (V)   DETERMINE OR SUPERVISE THE CONDITIONS OF DETENTION;

    (VI)   EXERCISE ANY OTHER FUNCTIONS PROVIDED FOR IN THE STATUTE OR IN THE RULES.

RULE 25

DATES OF PLENARY SESSIONS

(A)   THE DATES OF THE PLENARY SESSIONS OF THE TRIBUNAL SHALL NORMALLY BE AGREED UPON IN JULY OF EACH YEAR FOR THE FOLLOWING CALENDAR YEAR.

(B)   OTHER PLENARY MEETINGS SHALL BE CONVENED BY THE PRESIDENT IF SO REQUESTED BY AT LEAST EIGHT JUDGES, AND MAY BE CONVENED WHENEVER THE EXERCISE OF THE PRESIDENT'S FUNCTIONS UNDER THE STATUTE OR THE RULES SO REQUIRES.

RULE 26

QUORUM AND VOTE

(A)   THE QUORUM FOR EACH PLENARY MEETING OF THE TRIBUNAL SHALL BE NINE JUDGES.

(B)   SUBJECT TO SUB-RULES 6 (A) AND (B) AND SUB-RULE 18 (C), THE DECISIONS OF THE PLENARY MEETINGS OF THE TRIBUNAL SHALL BE TAKEN BY THE MAJORITY OF THE JUDGES PRESENT. IN THE EVENT OF AN EQUALITY OF VOTES, THE PRESIDENT OR THE JUDGE ACTING IN THE PLACE OF THE PRESIDENT SHALL HAVE A CASTING VOTE.

RULE 27

ROTATION

(A)   JUDGES SHALL ROTATE ON A REGULAR BASIS BETWEEN THE TRIAL CHAMBERS AND THE APPEALS CHAMBER. ROTATION SHALL TAKE INTO ACCOUNT THE EFFICIENT DISPOSAL OF CASES.

(B)   THE JUDGES SHALL TAKE THEIR PLACES IN THEIR NEW CHAMBER AS SOON AS THE PRESIDENT THINKS IT CONVENIENT, HAVING REGARD TO THE DISPOSAL OF PART-HEARD CASES.

(C)   THE PRESIDENT MAY AT ANY TIME TEMPORARILY ASSIGN A MEMBER OF A TRIAL CHAMBER OR OF THE APPEALS CHAMBER TO ANOTHER CHAMBER.

RULE 28

REVIEWING AND DUTY JUDGE

(A)   ON RECEIPT OF AN INDICTMENT FOR REVIEW FROM THE PROSECUTOR, THE REGISTRAR SHALL CONSULT WITH THE PRESIDENT WHO SHALL DESIGNATE ONE OF THE TRIAL CHAMBER JUDGES FOR THE REVIEW.

(B)   THE PRESIDENT, IN CONSULTATION WITH THE JUDGES, SHALL MAINTAIN A ROSTER DESIGNATING ONE JUDGE AS DUTY JUDGE FOR THE ASSIGNED PERIOD OF SEVEN DAYS. THE DUTY JUDGE SHALL BE AVAILABLE AT ALL TIMES, INCLUDING OUT OF NORMAL REGISTRY HOURS, FOR DEALING WITH APPLICATIONS PURSUANT TO SUB-RULES (C) AND (D) BUT MAY REFUSE TO DEAL WITH ANY APPLICATION OUT OF NORMAL REGISTRY HOURS IF NOT SATISFIED AS TO ITS URGENCY. THE ROSTER OF DUTY JUDGES SHALL BE PUBLISHED BY THE REGISTRAR.

(C)   ALL APPLICATIONS IN A CASE NOT OTHERWISE ASSIGNED TO A CHAMBER, OTHER THAN THE REVIEW OF INDICTMENTS, SHALL BE TRANSMITTED TO THE DUTY JUDGE. WHERE ACCUSED ARE JOINTLY INDICTED, A SUBMISSION RELATING ONLY TO AN ACCUSED WHO IS NOT IN THE CUSTODY OF THE TRIBUNAL SHALL BE TRANSMITTED TO THE DUTY JUDGE, NOTWITHSTANDING THAT THE CASE HAS ALREADY BEEN ASSIGNED TO A CHAMBER IN RESPECT OF SOME OR ALL OF THE CO-ACCUSED OF THAT ACCUSED. THE DUTY JUDGE SHALL ACT PURSUANT TO RULE 54 IN DEALING WITH APPLICATIONS UNDER THIS RULE.

(D)   THE DUTY JUDGE MAY, IN HIS OR HER DISCRETION, IF SATISFIED AS TO THE URGENCY OF THE MATTER, DEAL WITH AN APPLICATION IN A CASE ALREADY ASSIGNED TO A CHAMBER OUT OF NORMAL REGISTRY HOURS AS AN EMERGENCY APPLICATION. IN SUCH CASE, THE REGISTRY SHALL ALSO SERVE COPIES OF THE APPLICATION AND OF ANY ORDER OR DECISION ISSUED BY THE DUTY JUDGE IN CONNECTION THEREWITH ON THE CHAMBER TO WHICH THE MATTER IS ASSIGNED.

(E)   DURING PERIODS OF COURT RECESS, REGARDLESS OF THE CHAMBER TO WHICH HE OR SHE IS ASSIGNED, THE DUTY JUDGE MAY:

(I)   TAKE DECISIONS ON PROVISIONAL DETENTION PURSUANT TO RULE 40 *BIS*;

(II)   CONDUCT THE INITIAL APPEARANCE OF AN ACCUSED PURSUANT TO RULE 62.

THE REGISTRY SHALL SERVE A COPY OF ALL ORDERS OR DECISIONS ISSUDED BY THE DUTY JUDGE IN CONNECTION THEREWITH ON THE CHAMBER TO WHICH THE MATTER IS ASSIGNED.

I.   COMMENTARY

Rule 28 provides for the assignment of "reviewing judges" and "duty judges." Pursuant to Rule 28(A), the reviewing judge is designated by the President to review indictments.

Pursuant to Rule 28(C), the powers of the duty judge are not limited to the review of indictments. All other applications in a case not assigned to a Chamber are transmitted to the duty judge. Rules 28(B), (C) and (D) specify the powers of the duty judge and his or her discretionary powers to hear applications. Rule 28(E) sets out the powers of the duty judge during periods of court recess.

RULE 29

DELIBERATIONS

THE DELIBERATIONS OF THE CHAMBERS SHALL TAKE PLACE IN PRIVATE AND REMAIN SECRET.

RULE 30

APPOINTMENT OF THE REGISTRAR

THE PRESIDENT SHALL SEEK THE OPINION OF THE JUDGES ON THE CANDIDATES FOR THE POST OF REGISTRAR, BEFORE CONSULTING WITH THE SECRETARY-GENERAL OF THE UNITED NATIONS PURSUANT TO ARTICLE 17, PARAGRAPH 3, OF THE STATUTE.

RULE 31

APPOINTMENT OF THE DEPUTY REGISTRAR AND REGISTRY STAFF

THE REGISTRAR, AFTER CONSULTATION WITH THE BUREAU, SHALL MAKE RECOMMENDATIONS TO THE SECRETARY-GENERAL OF THE UNITED NATIONS FOR THE APPOINTMENT OF THE DEPUTY REGISTRAR AND OTHER REGISTRY STAFF.

RULE 32

SOLEMN DECLARATION

(A) BEFORE TAKING UP DUTIES, THE REGISTRAR SHALL MAKE THE FOLLOWING DECLARATION BEFORE THE PRESIDENT:

"I SOLEMNLY DECLARE THAT I WILL PERFORM THE DUTIES INCUMBENT UPON ME AS REGISTRAR OF THE INTERNATIONAL TRIBUNAL FOR THE PROSECUTION OF PERSONS RESPONSIBLE FOR SERIOUS VIOLATIONS OF INTERNATIONAL HUMANITARIAN LAW COMMITTED IN THE TERRITORY OF THE FORMER YUGOSLAVIA SINCE 1991 IN ALL LOYALTY, DISCRETION AND GOOD CONSCIENCE AND THAT I WILL FAITHFULLY OBSERVE ALL THE PROVISIONS OF THE STATUTE AND THE RULES OF PROCEDURE AND EVIDENCE OF THE TRIBUNAL".

(B) BEFORE TAKING UP DUTIES, THE DEPUTY REGISTRAR SHALL MAKE A SIMILAR DECLARATION BEFORE THE PRESIDENT.

(C) EVERY STAFF MEMBER OF THE REGISTRY SHALL MAKE A SIMILAR DECLARATION BEFORE THE REGISTRAR.

RULE 33

FUNCTIONS OF THE REGISTRAR

(A)   THE REGISTRAR SHALL ASSIST THE CHAMBERS, THE PLENARY MEETINGS OF THE TRIBUNAL, THE JUDGES AND THE PROSECUTOR IN THE PERFORMANCE OF THEIR FUNCTIONS. UNDER THE AUTHORITY OF THE PRESIDENT, THE REGISTRAR SHALL BE RESPONSIBLE FOR THE ADMINISTRATION AND SERVICING OF THE TRIBUNAL AND SHALL SERVE AS ITS CHANNEL OF COMMUNICATION.

(B)   THE REGISTRAR, IN THE EXECUTION OF HIS OR HER FUNCTIONS, MAY MAKE ORAL AND WRITTEN REPRESENTATIONS TO CHAMBERS ON ANY ISSUE ARISING IN THE CONTEXT OF A SPECIFIC CASE WHICH AFFECTS OR MAY AFFECT THE DISCHARGE OF SUCH FUNCTIONS, INCLUDING THAT OF IMPLEMENTING JUDICIAL DECISIONS, WITH NOTICE TO THE PARTIES WHERE NECESSARY.

I.   COMMENTARY

A.   GENERAL

In the *Delalić* case, the Trial Chamber had ruled that on the basis of Rule 33 and Rule 85 of the *Rules of Detention*, a decision by the Registrar affecting the conditions of detention of the accused at the UNDU must be remitted to the President.

In the *Simić* case, the Trial Chamber ordered certain phone restrictions to be imposed on the accused. The Commander of the UNDU communicated to the Deputy Registrar that such phone restrictions were unmanageable. The Deputy Registrar issued a document stating that it was impossible to implement the Trial Chamber's Order. The Trial Chamber modified its Order.

Query: Can the Trial Chamber or only the President modify phone privileges of a detainee?

II.   TRIBUNAL CASES

C.   PRESIDENT

PROSECUTOR V. DELALIĆ *et. al., Decision of the President on the Prosecutor's Motion for the Production of Notes Exchanged between Zejnil Delalić and Zdravko Mucić,* IT-96-21-PT, 11 November 1996, President Cassese

Detention Matters

Decisions taken by the Registrar, which affect matters relating to detention or arising therefrom, are not within the jurisdiction of a Trial Chamber and they should be submitted to the President for review and final determination.[450] In such circumstances,

---

[450] Para. 9.

as Head of the Detention Unit, the Registrar acts "under the authority of President" within the meaning of Rule 33.

Rule 66 of the *Rules of Detention* reads as follows:

A.   The Prosecutor may request the Registrar or, in cases of emergency, the Commanding Officer, to prohibit, regulate or set conditions for contact between a detainee and any other person if the Prosecutor has reasonable grounds for believing that such contact:

     i.   is for the purposes of attempting to arrange the escape of the detainee from the detention unit;

     ii.   could prejudice or otherwise affect the outcome of:

         a.   the proceedings against the detainee; or,

         b.   any other investigation;

     iii.   could be harmful to the detainee or any other person; or,

     iv.   could be used by the detainee to breach an order for non-disclosure made by a Judge or a Chamber pursuant to Rule 53 or Rule 75 of the Rules of Procedure and Evidence.

B.   If the request is made to the Commanding Officer on grounds of urgency, the Prosecutor shall immediately inform the Registrar of the request, together with the reasons therefor. The detainee shall immediately be informed of the fact of any such request.

C.   A detainee may at any time request the President to deny or reverse a request for prohibition of contact made by the Prosecutor under this rule.

The President held that in Rule 66(A) of the *Rules of Detention*, the phrase "contact between a detainee and any other person" means a detainee and another person on the outside and does not apply to contact between detainees within the Detention Unit. Rule 66 is contained in the Section of the *Rules of Detention* entitled "Communication and Visits" (Rules 60-66) and Rule 60 expressly states that "subject to Rule 66" detainees shall be entitled to "communicate with their families and other persons with whom it is in their legitimate interest to correspond by letter and by telephone".[451]

Furthermore, the President held that an oral request by the Prosecutor to the Registrar did not amount to a valid request under Rule 66. Such a request may only be granted when the conditions in Rule 66(A) are satisfied; namely, that the Prosecutor has reasonable grounds for believing that contact between a detainee and another person is for the purposes of attempting to arrange the escape of the detainee from the detention unit, or could prejudice or otherwise affect the outcome of the proceedings against the detainee or of any other investigation, or that such contact could be harmful to the detainee, or any other person.[452]

Rules 40-44: Rules of Detention

Rules 40-44 of the *Rules of Detention* pertain to the segregation of detainees. Pursuant to Rule 40, the Registrar may, on the request of the Prosecutor or on his own initiative and

---

[451] Para. 20.
[452] Paras. 13-14.

after seeking medical advice, order that detainees be segregated, *i.e.*, kept in separate accommodation and not permitted to meet or exercise together. The President held that the Registrar is duty bound under Rules 40-44 to take all measures which ensure the proper administration of justice and prevent the obstruction of justice, including the segregation of detainees for the purpose of preventing any communication between them.[453] The President found that this regime for segregation was different from the putative measures under Rule 66 that restrict freedom of communication between detainees and persons outside the Detention Unit.[454]

Having ruled that Rule 66 only applies to communications between a detainee and a person outside the Detention Unit, the President found that the *ratio legis* of Rule 66 applies *mutatis mutandis* to communications between detainees, whenever they are segregated pursuant to Rules 40-44. The Registrar may thus, as part of his or her duty to prevent the obstruction of justice, confiscate notes passed surreptitiously between detainees in violation of a segregation order. Written communications between segregated detainees must go through the official channels of the Detention Unit for review before being passed along to their recipient.[455]

Discretion of the Registrar to Disclose Notes to the Prosecutor

The President found that the Registrar had the authority and the duty to confiscate notes, exchanged between detainees, contrary to a segregation order.[456] In addition, the President ruled that whenever the Registrar confiscates material in the Detention Unit, because they were produced, circulated or communicated in breach of *Rules of Detention* or Regulations, it lies in his or her discretion whether to provide such material to the Prosecution.[457]

In exercising this discretion, pursuant to Rule 54, the Registrar must apply a test of whether the material requested by the Prosecutor is necessary (not simply useful or helpful) for the purposes of the investigation or for the preparation or conduct of the trial.[458] This is a two part test: an order of the Tribunal is necessary for the Prosecutor to obtain such material and the material sought must be relevant to an investigation or prosecution being conducted by the Prosecutor. The President noted that with any search or seizure, the Prosecutor could not simply conduct "fishing expeditions" through the Registrar's records.[459]

---

[453] Para. 17.
[454] Para. 16.
[455] Paras. 22.
[456] Para. 27.
[457] Para. 31.
[458] Para. 38.
[459] Para. 39.

RULE 34

VICTIMS AND WITNESSES UNIT

(A)   THERE SHALL BE SET UP UNDER THE AUTHORITY OF THE REGISTRAR A VICTIMS
AND WITNESSES UNIT CONSISTING OF QUALIFIED STAFF TO:

(I)   RECOMMEND PROTECTIVE MEASURES FOR VICTIMS AND WITNESSES IN
ACCORDANCE WITH ARTICLE 22 OF THE STATUTE; AND

(II)   PROVIDE COUNSELLING AND SUPPORT FOR THEM, IN PARTICULAR IN
CASES OF RAPE AND SEXUAL ASSAULT.

(B)   DUE CONSIDERATION SHALL BE GIVEN, IN THE APPOINTMENT OF STAFF, TO THE
EMPLOYMENT OF QUALIFIED WOMEN.

II.   TRIBUNAL CASES

B.   TRIAL CHAMBERS

PROSECUTOR V DELALIĆ *et. al., Decision on Confidential Motion for Protective Measures for Defence Witnesses,* IT-96-21-T, 25 September 1997, Karibi-Whyte, Odio-Benito & Jan, JJ.

Protective Measures and Relocation

The Trial Chamber found that it is empowered to grant protective measures to victims and witnesses on the basis of Article 22 and Rules 69, 75, and 79. However, the issue of relocation of a witness and negotiations with the Victims and Witnesses Unit is not a matter to be decided by a Trial Chamber. Relocation is a matter for the Victims and Witnesses Section[460] that is established under Rule 34, acting under the authority of the Registrar. The Trial Chamber added that in certain circumstances a Trial Chamber should be informed of such arrangements.[461]

PROSECUTOR V DELALIĆ *et. al., Decision on the Prosecution's Oral Request for the Admission of Exhibit 155 into evidence and for an Order to compel the Accused, Zdravko Mucić, to provide a handwriting sample,* IT-96-21-T, 19 January 1998, Karibi-Whyte, Odio-Benito & Jan, JJ.

The Trial Chamber ruled that the Victims and Witnesses Unit is neutral. Its primary function is the protection of victims and witnesses. It may legitimately, under its statutory mandate pursuant to Rule 34, inform a Trial Chamber or the Prosecution, if a witness receives what he considers to be a threat.[462]

---

[460] When this decision was handed down Victims and Witnesses was a "Section". Now it is a "Unit".
[461] Para. 6.
[462] Paras. 36-37.

RULE 35

MINUTES

EXCEPT WHERE A FULL RECORD IS MADE UNDER RULE 81, THE REGISTRAR, OR REGISTRY STAFF DESIGNATED BY THE REGISTRAR, SHALL TAKE MINUTES OF THE PLENARY MEETINGS OF THE TRIBUNAL AND OF THE SITTINGS OF THE CHAMBERS, OTHER THAN PRIVATE DELIBERATIONS.

RULE 36

RECORD BOOK

THE REGISTRAR SHALL KEEP A RECORD BOOK WHICH SHALL LIST, SUBJECT TO ANY PRACTICE DIRECTION UNDER RULE 19 OR ANY ORDER OF A JUDGE OR CHAMBER PROVIDING FOR THE NON-DISCLOSURE OF ANY DOCUMENT OR INFORMATION, ALL THE PARTICULARS OF EACH CASE BROUGHT BEFORE THE TRIBUNAL. THE RECORD BOOK SHALL BE OPEN TO THE PUBLIC.

RULE 37

FUNCTIONS OF THE PROSECUTOR

(A)   THE PROSECUTOR SHALL PERFORM ALL THE FUNCTIONS PROVIDED BY THE STATUTE IN ACCORDANCE WITH THE RULES AND SUCH REGULATIONS, CONSISTENT WITH THE STATUTE AND THE RULES, AS MAY BE FRAMED BY THE PROSECUTOR. ANY ALLEGED INCONSISTENCY IN THE REGULATIONS SHALL BE BROUGHT TO THE ATTENTION OF THE BUREAU TO WHOSE OPINION THE PROSECUTOR SHALL DEFER.

(B)   THE PROSECUTOR'S POWERS AND DUTIES UNDER THE RULES MAY BE EXERCISED BY STAFF MEMBERS OF THE OFFICE OF THE PROSECUTOR AUTHORISED BY THE PROSECUTOR, OR BY ANY PERSON ACTING UNDER THE PROSECUTOR'S DIRECTION.

II.   TRIBUNAL CASES

B.   TRIAL CHAMBERS

PROSECUTOR V. DELALIĆ *et. al., Decision on the Motions for the Exclusion of Evidence by the Accused, Zejnil Delalić*, IT-96-21-T, 25 September 1997, Karibi-Whyte, Odio-Benito & Jan, JJ.

The Chamber ruled that under Rule 37(B), investigators authorized by and acting on behalf of the Prosecutor are, for such purposes, performing the functions of the Prosecutor in accordance with Rule 37(A). Investigators acting under such authorization are competent to carry out interrogations in the same manner as Prosecutors.

RULE 38

DEPUTY PROSECUTOR

(A)   THE PROSECUTOR SHALL MAKE RECOMMENDATIONS TO THE SECRETARY-GENERAL OF THE UNITED NATIONS FOR THE APPOINTMENT OF A DEPUTY PROSECUTOR.

(B)   THE DEPUTY PROSECUTOR SHALL EXERCISE THE FUNCTIONS OF THE PROSECUTOR IN THE EVENT OF THE LATTER'S ABSENCE FROM DUTY OR INABILITY TO ACT OR UPON THE PROSECUTOR'S EXPRESS INSTRUCTIONS.

PART FOUR

INVESTIGATIONS AND RIGHTS OF SUSPECTS

RULE 39

CONDUCT OF INVESTIGATIONS

IN THE CONDUCT OF AN INVESTIGATION, THE PROSECUTOR MAY:

(I)   SUMMON AND QUESTION SUSPECTS, VICTIMS AND WITNESSES AND RECORD THEIR STATEMENTS, COLLECT EVIDENCE AND CONDUCT ON-SITE INVESTIGATIONS;

(II)   UNDERTAKE SUCH OTHER MATTERS AS MAY APPEAR NECESSARY FOR COMPLETING THE INVESTIGATION AND THE PREPARATION AND CONDUCT OF THE PROSECUTION AT THE TRIAL, INCLUDING THE TAKING OF SPECIAL MEASURES TO PROVIDE FOR THE SAFETY OF POTENTIAL WITNESSES AND INFORMANTS;

(III)   SEEK, TO THAT END, THE ASSISTANCE OF ANY STATE AUTHORITY CONCERNED, AS WELL AS OF ANY RELEVANT INTERNATIONAL BODY INCLUDING THE INTERNATIONAL CRIMINAL POLICE ORGANIZATION (INTERPOL); AND

(IV)   REQUEST SUCH ORDERS AS MAY BE NECESSARY FROM A TRIAL CHAMBER OR A JUDGE.

RULE 40

PROVISIONAL MEASURES

IN CASE OF URGENCY, THE PROSECUTOR MAY REQUEST ANY STATE:

    (I)   TO ARREST A SUSPECT OR AN ACCUSED PROVISIONALLY;

    (II)   TO SEIZE PHYSICAL EVIDENCE;

    (III)   TO TAKE ALL NECESSARY MEASURES TO PREVENT THE ESCAPE OF A SUSPECT OR AN ACCUSED, INJURY TO OR INTIMIDATION OF A VICTIM OR WITNESS, OR THE DESTRUCTION OF EVIDENCE.

THE STATE CONCERNED SHALL COMPLY FORTHWITH, IN ACCORDANCE WITH ARTICLE 29 OF THE STATUTE.

PROSECUTOR V. DELALIĆ *et. al., Decision on the Motions for the Exclusion of Evidence by the Accused, Zejnil Delalić*, IT-96-21-T, 25 September 1997, Karibi-Whyte, Odio-Benito & Jan, JJ.

The Chamber held that pursuant to Rule 40, the Prosecutor might in good faith, in the course of investigations request that a State arrest a suspect provisionally. Rule 40 states the type of requests that may be made, not the reasons why the Prosecutor requests the intervention of a State. A suspect may be interrogated under Rules 42 and 43 following a provisional arrest under Rule 40. The ability of the Prosecutor to question a suspect is thus not dependant on an arrest warrant being served under Rule 55(d). The Chamber ruled that there is no distinction made between suspects arrested pursuant to Rule 40 and other suspects and the fact that Rule 40 makes no specific mention of the Prosecutor cannot be taken to mean that the Prosecution is prevented from carrying on with its investigation in any lawful manner it deems fit by interrogating the suspect.[463]

---

[463] Paras. 38-39.

RULE 40 *BIS*

TRANSFER AND PROVISIONAL DETENTION OF SUSPECTS

(A)   IN THE CONDUCT OF AN INVESTIGATION, THE PROSECUTOR MAY TRANSMIT TO THE REGISTRAR, FOR AN ORDER BY A JUDGE ASSIGNED PURSUANT TO RULE 28, A REQUEST FOR THE TRANSFER TO AND PROVISIONAL DETENTION OF A SUSPECT IN THE PREMISES OF THE DETENTION UNIT OF THE TRIBUNAL. THIS REQUEST SHALL INDICATE THE GROUNDS UPON WHICH THE REQUEST IS MADE AND, UNLESS THE PROSECUTOR WISHES ONLY TO QUESTION THE SUSPECT, SHALL INCLUDE A PROVISIONAL CHARGE AND A SUMMARY OF THE MATERIAL UPON WHICH THE PROSECUTOR RELIES.

(B)   THE JUDGE SHALL ORDER THE TRANSFER AND PROVISIONAL DETENTION OF THE SUSPECT IF THE FOLLOWING CONDITIONS ARE MET:

   (I)   THE PROSECUTOR HAS REQUESTED A STATE TO ARREST THE SUSPECT PROVISIONALLY, IN ACCORDANCE WITH RULE 40, OR THE SUSPECT IS OTHERWISE DETAINED BY STATE AUTHORITIES;

   (II)   AFTER HEARING THE PROSECUTOR, THE JUDGE CONSIDERS THAT THERE IS A RELIABLE AND CONSISTENT BODY OF MATERIAL WHICH TENDS TO SHOW THAT THE SUSPECT MAY HAVE COMMITTED A CRIME OVER WHICH THE TRIBUNAL HAS JURISDICTION; AND

   (III)   THE JUDGE CONSIDERS PROVISIONAL DETENTION TO BE A NECESSARY MEASURE TO PREVENT THE ESCAPE OF THE SUSPECT, INJURY TO OR INTIMIDATION OF A VICTIM OR WITNESS OR THE DESTRUCTION OF EVIDENCE, OR TO BE OTHERWISE NECESSARY FOR THE CONDUCT OF THE INVESTIGATION.

(C)   THE ORDER FOR THE TRANSFER AND PROVISIONAL DETENTION OF THE SUSPECT SHALL BE SIGNED BY THE JUDGE AND BEAR THE SEAL OF THE TRIBUNAL. THE ORDER SHALL SET FORTH THE BASIS OF THE APPLICATION MADE BY THE PROSECUTOR UNDER SUB-RULE (A), INCLUDING THE PROVISIONAL CHARGE, AND SHALL STATE THE JUDGE'S GROUNDS FOR MAKING THE ORDER, HAVING REGARD TO SUB-RULE (B). THE ORDER SHALL ALSO SPECIFY THE INITIAL TIME-LIMIT FOR THE PROVISIONAL DETENTION OF THE SUSPECT, AND BE ACCOMPANIED BY A STATEMENT OF THE RIGHTS OF A SUSPECT, AS SPECIFIED IN THIS RULE AND IN RULES 42 AND 43.

(D)   THE PROVISIONAL DETENTION OF A SUSPECT SHALL BE ORDERED FOR A PERIOD NOT EXCEEDING THIRTY DAYS FROM THE DATE OF THE TRANSFER OF THE SUSPECT TO THE SEAT OF THE TRIBUNAL. AT THE END OF THAT PERIOD, AT THE PROSECUTOR'S REQUEST, THE JUDGE WHO MADE THE ORDER, OR ANOTHER JUDGE OF THE SAME TRIAL CHAMBER, MAY DECIDE, SUBSEQUENT TO AN INTER PARTES HEARING OF THE PROSECUTOR AND THE SUSPECT ASSISTED BY COUNSEL, TO EXTEND THE DETENTION FOR A PERIOD NOT EXCEEDING THIRTY DAYS, IF WARRANTED BY THE NEEDS OF THE INVESTIGATION. AT THE END OF THAT EXTENSION, AT THE PROSECUTOR'S

REQUEST, THE JUDGE WHO MADE THE ORDER, OR ANOTHER JUDGE OF THE SAME TRIAL CHAMBER, MAY DECIDE, SUBSEQUENT TO AN INTER PARTES HEARING OF THE PROSECUTOR AND THE SUSPECT ASSISTED BY COUNSEL, TO EXTEND THE DETENTION FOR A FURTHER PERIOD NOT EXCEEDING THIRTY DAYS, IF WARRANTED BY SPECIAL CIRCUMSTANCES. THE TOTAL PERIOD OF DETENTION SHALL IN NO CASE EXCEED NINETY DAYS, AT THE END OF WHICH, IN THE EVENT THE INDICTMENT HAS NOT BEEN CONFIRMED AND AN ARREST WARRANT SIGNED, THE SUSPECT SHALL BE RELEASED OR, IF APPROPRIATE, BE DELIVERED TO THE AUTHORITIES OF THE REQUESTED STATE.

(E)   THE PROVISIONS IN RULES 55 (B) TO 59 BIS SHALL APPLY *MUTATIS MUTANDIS* TO THE EXECUTION OF THE TRANSFER ORDER AND THE PROVISIONAL DETENTION ORDER RELATIVE TO A SUSPECT.

(F)   AFTER BEING TRANSFERRED TO THE SEAT OF THE TRIBUNAL, THE SUSPECT, ASSISTED BY COUNSEL, SHALL BE BROUGHT, WITHOUT DELAY, BEFORE THE JUDGE WHO MADE THE ORDER, OR ANOTHER JUDGE OF THE SAME TRIAL CHAMBER, WHO SHALL ENSURE THAT THE RIGHTS OF THE SUSPECT ARE RESPECTED.

(G)   DURING DETENTION, THE PROSECUTOR AND THE SUSPECT OR THE SUSPECT'S COUNSEL MAY SUBMIT TO THE TRIAL CHAMBER OF WHICH THE JUDGE WHO MADE THE ORDER IS A MEMBER, ALL APPLICATIONS RELATIVE TO THE PROPRIETY OF PROVISIONAL DETENTION OR TO THE SUSPECT'S RELEASE.

(H)   WITHOUT PREJUDICE TO SUB-RULE (D), THE RULES RELATING TO THE DETENTION ON REMAND OF ACCUSED PERSONS SHALL APPLY *MUTATIS MUTANDIS* TO THE PROVISIONAL DETENTION OF PERSONS UNDER THIS RULE.

RULE 41

RETENTION OF INFORMATION

THE PROSECUTOR SHALL BE RESPONSIBLE FOR THE RETENTION, STORAGE AND SECURITY OF INFORMATION AND PHYSICAL EVIDENCE OBTAINED IN THE COURSE OF THE PROSECUTOR'S INVESTIGATIONS.

RULE 42

RIGHTS OF SUSPECTS DURING INVESTIGATION

(A)   A SUSPECT WHO IS TO BE QUESTIONED BY THE PROSECUTOR SHALL HAVE THE FOLLOWING RIGHTS, OF WHICH THE PROSECUTOR SHALL INFORM THE SUSPECT PRIOR TO QUESTIONING, IN A LANGUAGE THE SUSPECT SPEAKS AND UNDERSTANDS:

   (I) THE RIGHT TO BE ASSISTED BY COUNSEL OF THE SUSPECT'S CHOICE OR TO BE ASSIGNED LEGAL ASSISTANCE WITHOUT PAYMENT IF THE SUSPECT DOES NOT HAVE SUFFICIENT MEANS TO PAY FOR IT;

   (II) THE RIGHT TO HAVE THE FREE ASSISTANCE OF AN INTERPRETER IF THE SUSPECT CANNOT UNDERSTAND OR SPEAK THE LANGUAGE TO BE USED FOR QUESTIONING; AND

   (III) THE RIGHT TO REMAIN SILENT, AND TO BE CAUTIONED THAT ANY STATEMENT THE SUSPECT MAKES SHALL BE RECORDED AND MAY BE USED IN EVIDENCE.

(B)   QUESTIONING OF A SUSPECT SHALL NOT PROCEED WITHOUT THE PRESENCE OF COUNSEL UNLESS THE SUSPECT HAS VOLUNTARILY WAIVED THE RIGHT TO COUNSEL. IN CASE OF WAIVER, IF THE SUSPECT SUBSEQUENTLY EXPRESSES A DESIRE TO HAVE COUNSEL, QUESTIONING SHALL THEREUPON CEASE, AND SHALL ONLY RESUME WHEN THE SUSPECT HAS OBTAINED OR HAS BEEN ASSIGNED COUNSEL.

I. COMMENTARY

See, Rule 43.

II. TRIBUNAL CASES

B. TRIAL CHAMBERS

PROSECUTOR V. DELALIĆ *et. al., Decision on the Motion on the Exclusion and Restitution of Evidence and Other Material Seized from the Accused Zejnil Delalić*, IT-96-21-PT, 9 October 1996, McDonald, Stephen & Vohrah, JJ.

This decision disposes of two motions filed by Delalić. The motions sought the suppression of evidence obtained in two separate events. The first was the questioning of Delalić by two investigators from the OTP in Munich, Germany on 18 and 19 March 1996. Delalić contended that his rights under Rules 42 and 43 were violated during this questioning. The second event was the seizure of items in Munich and Vienna by German and Austrian authorities from Delalić's apartments and from the BH Society and a business premises in Vienna.

The supplementary Motion dealing with the seizures was brought by Delalić under Rule 73(A)(iii) for "the exclusion of evidence obtained from the accused or having belonged to him."[464]

The Interview in Munich

The Chamber first pointed out that it was clear from the transcript of the interview that, before answering questions, the text of Rules 42 and 43 had been read verbatim to Delalić, following which he was asked if he had any questions regarding his rights under these rules. He was not told, however, whether he was being questioned as a "suspect" or an "accused." The Defence contended that this was important. The Chamber could find no support in any of the rules for the proposition that Delalić was entitled to be informed of his status. Further, the Chamber said:

> Although it is true that at no stage in the Transcript of Interview did the interviewer expressly inform the accused Zejnil Delalić of his status as a suspect, the interviewer did however inform Zejnil Delalić that the rights he was reading out pursuant to Rule 42 "deal[t] with the rights of suspects during investigation." He then proceeded to ask the accused whether he understood those rights. Similarly, when referring to Rule 43, the interviewer stated that the Rule "deals with the recording and questioning of suspects." This was sufficient to inform Zejnil Delalić that he was a suspect and that the purpose of reading out those Rules was to ensure that he was aware of his rights as such. Accordingly, the Trial Chamber finds that there was no violation during the conduct of this interview of the rights of the accused pursuant to Sub-rule 42(A).[465]

With regard to Rule 42(B), the Defence contended that Delalić should have been questioned only in the presence of his counsel. The Chamber found that Delalić had waived his right to counsel explicitly and voluntarily.[466]

The Defence argued further that on the second day of the interview, Delalić asked for a lawyer to be present and as a result everything from there forward, at least, should be suppressed. The Chamber pointed out that after requesting counsel, Delalić, was asked if he was willing to go forward until counsel arrived, and he agreed. He was reminded that he could change his mind at any time.[467]

Finally, the Defence contended that during the questioning there was a break and that during that break information was elicited from Delalić that led to further questioning after the break. The Chamber determined that if this allegation were correct, then a violation of Rule 43 would be established. The question was deferred, however, until a point in the trial when the Prosecutor attempted to introduce the statement at which time this issue could be litigated and would be ripe for consideration.[468]

---

[464] This ground for bring a preliminary motion was deleted from the Rules in the Revised Rules of 20 October and 12 November 1997.
[465] Para. 11.
[466] Para. 13.
[467] Para. 14.
[468] Para. 15.

The Supplementary Motion

The supplementary motion dealt with the seizures in Munich and Vienna. The Chamber simply ordered the Prosecutor to return any of the seized items that were not relevant to these proceedings and agreed to entertain a further motion should the Prosecutor fail to return such evidence.[469]

PROSECUTOR V. DELALIĆ *et. al., Decision on Zdravko Mucić's Motion for the Exclusion of Evidence,* IT-96-21-T, 2 September 1997, Karibi-Whyte, Odio-Benito & Jan, JJ.

Defendant Mucić was arrested by the Austrian Police in Vienna. The Austrian Police questioned him on 18 March 1996 over a period of about 4 ¾ hours. Subsequently, on 19, 20 and 21 March, investigators from the OTP questioned him. It was conceded that under applicable Austrian Law, he was not entitled to have a lawyer present during the questioning by the Austrian Police, but could only consult with a lawyer following questioning if certain conditions were met and if time would allow. The Defence argued that instead of treating the Vienna Police and the OTP interviews as separate events, they should be considered as one interview extending over parts of four days. Part of the advice the defendant received from the Austrian Police was that a confession could help him in his case, since it could be taken into account in mitigating the sentence. This is correct under Austrian law but incorrect under the practice of the Tribunal. The defendant contended that the advice given by the Austrian Police amounted to an impermissible inducement to confess.

The objections to the admissibility of the statements were based essentially on the violations of the human rights of the suspect, founded on Rules 42 and 43.

The Trial Chamber relied specifically on Rule 89 and Rule 95 in determining the admissibility of the two statements. The Trial Chamber made the following observations regarding Rules 89 and 95. Rule 89(A) states that the Rules set out in Part 6, Section 3 of the Rules – Rules 89-98 – govern the proceedings and that national rules of evidence are not binding on the Trial Chamber. Rule 89(B) implies that a Trial Chamber may apply such national rules of evidence, provided they best favour a fair determination of the matter before it and they are consonant with the spirit of the Statute and the general principles of law. Rule 89(C) contains the general rule that evidence is admissible, if it is relevant and has probative value. The admissibility of evidence is subject to Rule 89(D), which provides that evidence may be excluded when its probative value, is substantially outweighed by the need to ensure a fair trial, and Rule 95, which states that evidence shall not be admitted if obtained by methods which cast substantial doubt on its reliability or if its admission is antithetical to, and would seriously damage, the integrity of the proceedings.[470]

---

[469] Para. 17.
[470] Para. 34, 35.

The Chamber ruled that the exclusion of evidence under Rule 89(D) is *discretionary* whereas under Rule 95 it is *mandatory*. Furthermore, a corollary to these two rules is Rule 89(E) that gives a Trial Chamber the *discretion* to request verification of the authenticity of evidence obtained out of court. Although a discretionary power, Rule 89(E) addresses the issue of authenticity, which goes to the heart of the question of "probative value" under Rule 89(D), the methods used to obtain evidence which may cast substantial doubt on its reliability under Rule 95, and, in certain circumstances, the question whether its admission is antithetical to, and would seriously damage, the integrity of proceedings under Rule 95.

The Chamber concluded that the interviews conducted by the Austrian Police and the Prosecutor constituted two independent and separate interviews. Different teams conducted the interviews. The Austrian interview was conducted under Austrian Law and the Prosecutor's interview under the Rules. The interviews had different purposes: the Austrian interview concerned extradition and the Prosecutor's interview concerned violations of humanitarian law.[471]

Burden of Proof

The Chamber ruled that the burden of proof of voluntariness or absence of oppressive conduct in obtaining a statement is on the Prosecution and it must be proven beyond reasonable doubt.[472] The Chamber stated:

> The Rules insist that all evidence which are reliable and have probative value are admissible. For evidence to be reliable it must be related to the subject matter of the dispute and be obtained under circumstances which should cast no doubt on its nature and character, and the fact that no rules of the fundamental rights have been breached. This can be done if the evidence is obtained in accordance with Rule 95, by methods which are not antithetical to and would not seriously damage, the integrity of the proceedings. There is no doubt statements obtained from suspects which are not voluntary, or which seem to be voluntary but are obtained by oppressive conduct, cannot pass the test under Rule 95.[473]

The Chamber found that Rule 42 governs the interview of a suspect whether the Prosecutor or others conduct the questioning. The Chamber stated that Rule 42 must be read along with Rule 95 to protect the integrity of proceedings. In this regard, the Chamber stated:

> Rule 42 embodies the essential provisions of the right to a fair hearing as enshrined in Article 14(3) of the International Covenant on Civil and Political Rights and Article 6(3)(c) of the European Convention on Human Rights. These are the internationally accepted basic and fundamental rights accorded to the individual to enable the enjoyment of a right to a fair hearing during trial. It seems to us extremely difficult for a statement taken in violation of Rule 42 to

---

[471] Para. 40.
[472] Para. 42.
[473] Para. 41.

fall within Rule 95 which protects the integrity of the proceedings by the non-admissibility of evidence obtained by methods which cast substantial doubts on its reliability.[474]

The Chamber determined that Rule 95 is a residual exclusionary provision which summarizes the provisions in the Rules and which enables the exclusion of evidence antithetical and damaging to the integrity of proceedings.[475]

Austrian Law and the Interview

The Trial Chamber made the following findings:

- Under Austrian law there is no right to counsel during questioning; and a suspect may not have legal counsel present when he is questioned for a criminal offence. On the contrary such rights are guaranteed under Article 18(3) and Rule 42(A)(i).

- Under Austrian law the accused is encouraged to speak, rather than remain silent which is no violation of the accused rights. Suggesting to a suspect to make a confession which goes to mitigation is not inducement. The Chamber held that this did not amount to threats of danger or promise of favour.[476]

The Chamber held that the Austrian interview was inadmissible on the basis of Article 18, Rules 42(A)(i) and 42(B), and Rule 95, namely the denial of the right to counsel that amounted to a violation of Rule 95.[477]

The Chamber found that the inducement to confess, although undesirable and offensive conduct, was not sufficient by itself to require exclusion of the statement. The Chamber stated that although the rules relating to silence and confession are contradictory to the relevant rules in Rule 42, they do not fall below fundamental fairness, thus making it antithetical to or seriously damaging to the integrity of proceedings under Rule 95.[478]

The Chamber found that there is no duty on the questioning investigator to explain to the accused the consequences of waiving his right to have counsel present or his right to remain silent. The provisions of Rule 42 and Rule 43 must be read to the accused in a language he understands. Article 42 is an adaptation of Article 6(3) of the European Convention on Human Rights and Article 14(3) of the International Covenant on Civil and Political Rights that embody elementary and fundamental provisions of universally protected human rights.[479]

---

[474] Para. 43.
[475] Para. 44.
[476] Para. 53, 54.
[477] Para. 55.
[478] *Ibid.*
[479] Paras. 58-60.

The Chamber found that in the OTP interview the accused understood his right to counsel during the interview and that he voluntarily waived that right.[480]

Oppression

The Chamber found that the Austrian Police interview lasted for more than four and three-quarter hours and was conducted by a total of about five inter-changing interrogators.[481]

The Chamber held that, even if the accused was tired, there was no evidence of oppressive questioning, such as to deprive him of the ability to make rational decisions. There is evidence that, notwithstanding the inordinate duration of the interview, there was nothing oppressive. The Accused was given refreshments during the exercise and he had the opportunity to rest at intervals. There was no evidence that the duration of the interview excited in him hopes of release or any fears that made his will crumble thereby prompting statements he otherwise would not have made. From all the evidence, it seems clear that the accused was in complete control and was master of the situation.[482]

To determine whether the circumstances surrounding the questioning of an individual is oppression, the Chamber stated that the following factors are relevant:

> [T]he duration of the questioning and the manner of the exercise of the questioning. The facilities provided such as refreshments or rests between periods of questioning are material considerations. What may be regarded as oppressive with respect to a child, old man or invalid or someone inexperienced in the ways of the administration of justice may not be oppressive with a mature person, familiar with the police or judicial process. The effect is, therefore, relative.[483]

PROSECUTOR V. DELALIĆ *et. al., Decision on Hazim Delić's Motions Pursuant to Rule 73,* IT-96-21-T, 1 September 1997, Karibi-Whyte, Odio-Benito & Jan, JJ.

The Trial Chamber found that only voluntary statements are admissible and that confessions made by accused persons in the absence of their volition and arising from threats, inducement or hope of favour by persons in authority are inadmissible in evidence.[484] The Chamber stated that involuntary statements are excluded because the will of the maker of the statements is constrained, coerced or reduced by inducement. Such statements are therefore unreliable and ought not to be taken seriously in the making of a judicial determination.

The Chamber rejected the proposition that if the accused had known the implications of his Rule 42 waiver, he would not have waived his rights, and thus his waiver was involuntary in that he did not knowingly and intelligently waive those rights

---

[480] Para. 63.
[481] Para. 64.
[482] Para. 70.
[483] Para. 67.
[484] Ibrahim v. The King [1914] A.C. 599.

234

with the full understanding of the result of such waiver.[485] The Chamber ruled that the accused:

> . . . acted voluntarily in respect of the instructions read out to him. His perception of the facts as he understood them was quite different from the consequence which ensued. He undoubtedly, knowingly and intelligently, even if mistakenly, waived his right to silence. A person's conscious, uncoerced and voluntary exercise of his rights cannot, within our jurisprudence, be regarded as involuntary.[486]

PROSECUTOR V. DELALIĆ *et. al., Decision on the Motions for the Exclusion of Evidence by the Accused, Zejnil Delalić*, IT-96-21-T, 25 September 1997, Karibi-Whyte, Odio-Benito & Jan, JJ.

The Trial Chamber decided that the issue of violations of Rule 42, in particular, the right to counsel had been previously decided in *Decision on the Motion on the Exclusion and Restitution of Evidence and Other Material Seized from the Accused Zejnil Delalić*, 9 October 1996 and could not be revisited.[487]

The Chamber is not an appellate or review entity and once it has decided a matter it is *functus officio* and no measure of repetition or re-cloaking of an argument can authorise it to act in excess of its jurisdiction.[488]

Rule 43

The Chamber held that to exclude a statement on the grounds of a violation of Rule 43, the defence must show that an irregularity occurred because some unrecorded information was obtained from the accused and this irregularity led to a violation of the accused's rights.[489]

The usual practice appears to be that questioning of an accused is both video and audio-recorded. A written transcript is then prepared from the audio recording of the interview. In the *Delalić* case, a written transcript was prepared from listening to both audio recordings and video recordings with audio. The irregularities complained of by the defence were that there was neither a complete audio nor video recording of the interview. However, the Chamber found that a complete transcript of the statement existed and was admissible. Relying on Rule 95, the Chamber ruled that

> [I]t cannot be said that the difficulties in recording the Statements cast a "substantial doubt on ... [their] reliability" or that admitting them into evidence will be "antithetical to, and would seriously damage, the integrity of the [present] proceedings.[490]

---

[485] Para. 16.
[486] Para. 18.
[487] Para. 35.
[488] Para. 43.
[489] Para. 44.
[490] Para. 45.

The transcript and not the irregular audio or video recordings were admitted into evidence.[491]

Article 21(4)(d)

The Chamber held that the rights guaranteed by Article 21(4)(d) are the rights of an "accused" person, and are not available to a "suspect" during questioning pursuant to Rule 42. The right of a suspect to legal assistance, guaranteed by Article 18(3), finds expression in Rule 42. In the instant matter, the *Decision on the Motion on the Exclusion and Restitution of Evidence and Other Material Seized from the Accused Zejnil Delalić*, 9 October 1996 held that Rule 42 was not violated.[492]

Rules 37(A) and 37(B)

The Chamber ruled that under Rule 37(B), investigators authorized by and acting on behalf of the Prosecutor are, for such purposes, performing the functions of the Prosecutor in accordance with Rule 37(A). Investigators acting under such authorization are competent to carry out interrogations in the same manner as Prosecutors.

Rule 40: Provisional measures

The Chamber held that pursuant to Rule 40, the Prosecutor might in good faith, in the course of investigations request that a State arrest a suspect provisionally. Rule 40 states the type of requests that may be made, not the reasons why the Prosecutor requests the intervention of a State. A suspect may be interrogated under Rules 42 and 43 following a provisional arrest under Rule 40. The ability of the Prosecutor to question a suspect is thus not dependant on an arrest warrant being served under Rule 55(d). The Chamber ruled that there is no distinction made between suspects arrested pursuant to Rule 40 and other suspects and the fact that Rule 40 makes no specific mention of the Prosecutor cannot be taken to mean that the Prosecution is prevented from carrying on with its investigation in any lawful manner it deems fit by interrogating the suspect.[493]

---

[491] There is potential for very real problems in regards to the transcript of the interviews that may eventually be admitted into evidence. Normally, representatives of the OTP who speak English or French will question an accused, ordinarily in a language other than the one understood by the accused. The questioning of the accused will therefore be done by way of simultaneous interpretation. Great care must be taken to ensure that the transcript of the interview, which will be made in English or French, the two working languages of the Tribunal, accurately reflects each question and answer and other relevant comments made during the interview. For example, if the investigator speaks English and the accused speaks BCS, the question will be posed in English, translated into BCS for the accused. The answer given by the accused will be in BCS and translated into English for the investigator. The first step is to ensure that questions and answers are correctly interpreted. The second step is to ensure that the written transcript of the interview is a complete verbatim account of what was said during the interview. The Judges will only use the English and French transcript of the interview, if an interview is admitted into evidence. Without careful review of the simultaneous translations of the interview, followed by a review of the transcript of the interview against the audio recording of the interview, the Judges may have a transcript that does not accurately reflect what was said.

[492] Para. 36.

[493] Paras. 38-39.

Voluntariness

The Chamber adopted the test for voluntariness that is used by and large in the common law world:

> It has long been established as a positive rule of English criminal law that no statement by an accused is admissible in evidence against him unless it is shown by the prosecution to have been a voluntary statement, in the sense that it has not been obtained from him either by fear of prejudice or hope of advantage exercised or held out by a person in authority. The principle is as old as Hale.[494]

The rule is that where the admissibility of a statement is challenged on the ground that it is not made voluntarily, the judge must determine whether the prosecution has established that it was made voluntarily.[495]

The Chamber found that pursuant to Rule 89(B), a Trial Chamber may hold a "trial within a trial" or *voir dire* to determine whether or not a statement made by an accused was made voluntarily. The *voir dire* procedure can only be used by a Trial Chamber where a statement is challenged on the ground that it is involuntary, namely where it is alleged to have been obtained either from fear of prejudice or hope of advantage held out by a person in authority over the accused.[496]

When a *voir dire* is held, the Chamber determined that the burden of proof rests on the Prosecution to show beyond a reasonable doubt that the statements of an accused person were made voluntarily, and that they were not obtained either by fear of prejudice or hope of advantage held out by interrogators. It is not sufficient for the prosecution to show that there was no intention to extract a confession or that there was no impropriety in the inducement held out. Whether an implicit threat, promise or inducement, the consequence is the same and the statement obtained thereby will be inadmissible.[497]

---

[494] Ibrahim v. R (1914) A.C. 609.
[495] Para. 30.
[496] Para. 40.
[497] Para. 32.

RULE 43

RECORDING QUESTIONING OF SUSPECTS

WHENEVER THE PROSECUTOR QUESTIONS A SUSPECT, THE QUESTIONING SHALL BE AUDIO-RECORDED OR VIDEO-RECORDED, IN ACCORDANCE WITH THE FOLLOWING PROCEDURE:

(I)   THE SUSPECT SHALL BE INFORMED IN A LANGUAGE THE SUSPECT SPEAKS AND UNDERSTANDS THAT THE QUESTIONING IS BEING AUDIO-RECORDED OR VIDEO-RECORDED;

(II) IN THE EVENT OF A BREAK IN THE COURSE OF THE QUESTIONING, THE FACT AND THE TIME OF THE BREAK SHALL BE RECORDED BEFORE AUDIO-RECORDING OR VIDEO-RECORDING ENDS AND THE TIME OF RESUMPTION OF THE QUESTIONING SHALL ALSO BE RECORDED;

(III) AT THE CONCLUSION OF THE QUESTIONING THE SUSPECT SHALL BE OFFERED THE OPPORTUNITY TO CLARIFY ANYTHING THE SUSPECT HAS SAID, AND TO ADD ANYTHING THE SUSPECT MAY WISH, AND THE TIME OF CONCLUSION SHALL BE RECORDED;

(IV) THE TAPE SHALL THEN BE TRANSCRIBED AS SOON AS PRACTICABLE AFTER THE CONCLUSION OF QUESTIONING AND A COPY OF THE TRANSCRIPT SUPPLIED TO THE SUSPECT, TOGETHER WITH A COPY OF THE RECORDED TAPE OR, IF MULTIPLE RECORDING APPARATUS WAS USED, ONE OF THE ORIGINAL RECORDED TAPES; AND

(V)   AFTER A COPY HAS BEEN MADE, IF NECESSARY, OF THE RECORDED TAPE FOR PURPOSES OF TRANSCRIPTION, THE ORIGINAL RECORDED TAPE OR ONE OF THE ORIGINAL TAPES SHALL BE SEALED IN THE PRESENCE OF THE SUSPECT UNDER THE SIGNATURE OF THE PROSECUTOR AND THE SUSPECT.

I.   COMMENTARY

See, Rule 42.

RULE 44

APPOINTMENT, QUALIFICATIONS AND DUTIES OF COUNSEL

(A)   COUNSEL ENGAGED BY A SUSPECT OR AN ACCUSED SHALL FILE A POWER OF ATTORNEY WITH THE REGISTRAR AT THE EARLIEST OPPORTUNITY. A COUNSEL SHALL BE CONSIDERED QUALIFIED TO REPRESENT A SUSPECT OR ACCUSED IF THE COUNSEL SATISFIES THE REGISTRAR THAT THE COUNSEL IS ADMITTED TO THE PRACTICE OF LAW IN A STATE, OR IS A UNIVERSITY PROFESSOR OF LAW, AND SPEAKS ONE OF THE TWO OFFICAL LANGUAGES OF THE TRIBUNAL.

(B)   AT THE REQUEST OF THE SUSPECT OR ACCUSED AND WHERE THE INTERESTS OF JUSTICE SO DEMAND, THE REGISTRAR MAY ADMIT A COUNSEL WHO DOES NOT SPEAK EITHER OF THE TWO WORKING LANGUAGES OF THE TRIBUNAL BUT WHO SPEAKS THE NATIVE LANGUAGE OF THE SUSPECT OR ACCUSED. THE REGISTRAR MAY IMPOSE SUCH CONDITIONS AS DEEMED APPROPRIATE. A SUSPECT OR ACCUSED MAY APPEAL A DECISION OF THE REGISTRAR TO THE PRESIDENT.

(C)   IN THE PERFORMANCE OF THEIR DUTIES COUNSEL SHALL BE SUBJECT TO THE RELEVANT PROVISIONS OF THE STATUTE, THE RULES, THE RULES OF DETENTION AND ANY OTHER RULES OR REGULATIONS ADOPTED BY THE TRIBUNAL, THE HOST COUNTRY AGREEMENT, THE CODE OF CONDUCT AND THE CODES OF PRACTICE AND ETHICS GOVERNING THEIR PROFESSION AND, IF APPLICABLE, THE DIRECTIVE ON THE ASSIGNMENT OF DEFENCE COUNSEL.

(D)   AN ADVISORY PANEL SHALL BE ESTABLISHED TO ASSIST THE PRESIDENT AND THE REGISTRAR IN ALL MATTERS RELATING TO DEFENCE COUNSEL. THE PANEL MEMBERS SHALL BE SELECTED FROM REPRESENTATIVES OF PROFESSIONAL ASSOCIATIONS AND FROM COUNSEL WHO HAVE APPEARED BEFORE THE TRIBUNAL. THEY SHALL HAVE RECOGNIZED LEGAL EXPERIENCE. THE COMPOSITION OF THE ADVISORY PANEL SHALL BE REPRESENTATIVE OF THE DIFFERENT LEGAL SYSTEMS. A DIRECTIVE OF THE REGISTRAR SHALL SET OUT THE STRUCTURE AND AREAS OF RESPONSIBILITY OF THE ADVISORY PANEL.

I.   COMMENTARY

The *Code of Professional Conduct for Defence Counsel Appearing Before the International Tribunal* can be found in the Appendix of this book.

In the *Simić* case, the Prosecutor raised case a very interesting question of conflict of interest. The Trial Chamber, after consideration, ordered the affected attorney to get a waiver from his client. The client provided the written consent requested by the Trial Chamber and Defence counsel continued to act for him.

II.   TRIBUNAL CASES

A.   APPEALS CHAMBER

PROSECUTOR V. DELALIĆ, *et. al., Order Regarding Esad Landžo's Request for Removal of John Ackerman as Counsel on Appeal for Zejnil Delalić*, IT-96-21-A, Nieto-Navia, Wang Tieya, Rodrigues, Hunt, Bennouna, JJ.

Between 25 May 1997 and 16 March 1998, John Ackerman acted as lead counsel for Esad Landžo in the trial of the *Delalić* case. Mr. Ackerman departed at the conclusion of the Prosecution's case against the defendants. On 4 December 1998, the Registrar assigned Mr. Ackerman as counsel on appeal for Zejnil Delalić, effective 26 November 1998.

Landžo, through his counsel, requested that Ackerman be removed as counsel for Delalić due to his previous representation of Landžo. The application contended that Ackerman was privy to confidential matters that could be detrimental to Landžo's appeal and that inconsistent defenses had existed at trial between Landžo and Delalić. In addition, Landžo argued that Ackerman was in violation of the Texas Rules of Disciplinary Conduct by accepting the representation of Delalić on the appeal.

The Chamber determined that "the material before it does not disclose the existence of a conflict of interest or any other ground for holding that John Ackerman is in contravention of the standards of conduct set out in Sub-rule 44(B) of the Rules." The Chamber further found that Ackerman's representation of Delalić on appeal "does not appear to obstruct the proper conduct of proceedings."

B.   TRIAL CHAMBERS

PROSECUTOR V. SIMIĆ, *Decision on the Prosecution Motion to Resolve Conflict of Interest Regarding Attorney Borislav Pisarević*, IT-95-9-PT, 25 March 1999, May, Bennouna & Robinson, JJ.

The Trial Chamber ruled that because of the intimate involvement and personal knowledge of Defence counsel Borislav Pisarević in relation to events relevant to the charges alleged in the indictment, his participation in the trial as Defence counsel for the accused, Simo Zarić raised a conflict of interest. The Chamber disposed of the matter by ordering that for Pisarević to continue his representation of the accused, he must obtain, within 7 days of this decision, Zarić's full and informed written consent, and transmit it to the Trial Chamber. This waiver from the accused was ordered pursuant to Article 9(5) of the *Code of Professional Conduct.*

The Prosecution brought a motion seeking to resolve the alleged conflict of interest, prior to the commencement of the trial, by determining whether he is likely to be called as a witness at trial. Four examples were cited in these proceedings to illustrate the possibility of conflict arising from the Defence counsel being called as either a Prosecution or Defence witness:

1. Defence counsel allegedly concealed a prospective Prosecution witness in his home on the night of the alleged Serb attack on the town of Bosanski Šamac or shortly thereafter and he spoke with two of the accused about whether this individual should surrender to the Serb authorities. The Prosecution stated that Defence counsel was present when another of the co-accused allegedly arrested this individual at gunpoint.

2. Defence counsel was a leading citizen in Bosanski Šamac, and participated in the governmental and political affairs of the municipality as President of the Party of Democratic Changes (SDP). In this capacity, the Prosecution alleged that Defence counsel attended several meetings where political issues were discussed among the ethnic groups. The Prosecution asserted that some of their witnesses would testify at trial that Defence counsel frequently took the side of the Serbs and that he had advance knowledge of the alleged Serb attack on Bosanski Šamac. Accordingly, the Prosecution claimed that Defence counsel was a witness to and participant in the ongoing power struggle between the parties to the conflict, and that his presence makes him a potential witness to the preparation, planning or execution of the offence of persecution.

3. Defence counsel represented a prospective Prosecution witness in a Serb military court in Bijelina, and a false confession was alleged to have been forcibly obtained from that individual by Defence counsel's client before the International Tribunal. The Prosecution asserted that this individual would testify at trial *inter alia*, about how this confession was taken from him and used as evidence against him. Consequently, according to the Prosecution, Defence counsel will have to cross-examine a witness whom he may have previously represented in a sham proceeding before a Serb military court.

4. Defence counsel not only represented some of the prospective Prosecution witnesses before the war, but he also saw two of these individuals in the custody of one of the co-accused after they were alleged to have been beaten by this co-accused, among others. The Prosecution argued that both this co-accused and the Prosecution could call Defence counsel to deny or to corroborate the testimony of these witnesses. The Prosecution further submitted that the two witnesses in question saw Defence counsel wearing a uniform, suggesting his association with the Serb forces occupying the town.

The Chamber held that a conflict of interest between an attorney and a client arises in any situation where, by reason of certain circumstances, representation by such an attorney prejudices, or could prejudice, the interests of the client and the wider interests of justice.

Relying on Articles 9(1) and 9(2) of the *Code of Professional Conduct for Defence Counsel Appearing before the International Tribunal*, the Chamber found that counsel must act at all times in the best interests of the client and exercise all care to ensure that a conflict of interest does not arise in the course of representing a client.

In the instant case, the Chamber found that there exists a potential for conflict arising at trial between Defence counsel and his client. The Chamber observed that it is left with a picture that Defence counsel as an attorney who had personal knowledge of and was intimately involved in many of the events that will be at issue at trial. The Chamber found that Defence counsel, who denied some but not all of the factual allegations made by the Prosecution, had run afoul of Article 16 of the *Code of Professional Conduct*, since he is likely to be a necessary witness in relation to contested issues.

The Chamber disposed of the matter according to the mechanism set out in Article 9(5) of the *Code of Professional Conduct* for dealing with conflict of interest. Article 9(5) reads as follows:

Where a conflict of interest does arise, Counsel must-

(a) promptly and fully inform each potentially affected Client of the nature and extent of the conflict; and

(b) either:

(i) take all steps necessary to remove the conflict; or

(ii) obtain the full and informed consent of all potentially affected Clients to continue the representation, so long as Counsel is able to fulfil all other obligations under this Code.

The Chamber found that pursuant to Rule 9(5)(b)(ii), the consent of Defence counsel's client is compatible with the continued discharge of counsel's obligations under the *Code of Professional Conduct*. In ordering that the client must provide a full and informed written consent in order for his counsel to continue to represent him, the Chamber observed that its decision gave due weight to the right of the accused to counsel of his choice pursuant to Article 21(4)(b).

RULE 45

ASSIGNMENT OF COUNSEL

(A)   WHENEVER THE INTERESTS OF JUSTICE SO DEMAND, COUNSEL SHALL BE ASSIGNED TO SUSPECTS OR ACCUSED WHO LACK THE MEANS TO REMUNERATE SUCH COUNSEL. SUCH ASSIGNEMENTS SHALL BE TREATED IN ACCORDANCE WITH THE PROCEDURE ESTABLISHED IN A DIRECTIVE SET OUT BY THE REGISTRAR AND APPROVED BY THE JUDGES.

(B)   A LIST OF COUNSEL WHO, IN ADDITION TO FULFILLING THE REQUIREMENTS OF RULE 44, HAVE SHOWN THAT THEY POSSESS REASONABLE EXPERIENCE IN CRIMINAL AND/OR INTERNATIONAL LAW AND HAVE INDICATED THEIR WILLINGNESS TO BE ASSIGNED BY THE TRIBUNAL TO ANY PERSON DETAINED UNDER THE AUTHORITY OF THE TRIBUNAL LACKING THE MEANS TO REMUNERATE COUNSEL, SHALL BE KEPT BY THE REGISTRAR.

(C)   IN PARTICULAR CIRCUMSTANCES, UPON THE REQUEST A PERSON LACKING THE MEANS TO REMUNERATE COUNSEL, THE REGISTRAR MAY ASSIGN COUNSEL WHOSE NAME DOES NOT APPEAR ON THE LIST BUT WHO OTHERWISE FULFILS THE REQUIREMENTS OF RULE 44.

(D)   IF A REQUEST IS REFUSED, A FURTHER REQUEST MAY BE MADE BY A SUSPECT OR AN ACCUSED TO THE REGISTRAR.

(E)   THE REGISTRAR SHALL, IN CONSULTATION WITH THE JUDGES, ESTABLISH THE CRITERIA FOR THE PAYMENT OF FEES TO ASSIGNED COUNSEL.

(F)   WHERE A PERSON IS ASSIGNED COUNSEL AND IS SUBSEQUENTLY FOUND NOT TO BE LACKING THE MEANS TO REMUNERATE COUSNEL, THE CHAMBER MAY MAKE AN ORDER OF CONTRIBUTION TO RECOVER THE COST OF PROVIDING COUNSEL.

(G)   A SUSPECT OR AN ACCUSED ELECTING TO CONDUCT HIS OR HER OWN DEFENCE SHALL SO NOTIFY THE REGISTRAR IN WRITING AT THE FIRST OPPORTUNITY.

I.   COMMENTARY

The facts and findings in *Dokmanović*, appear to be case specific. Nonetheless, the Trial Chamber outlined the relevant provisions of the Directive and Rules as well as the powers of the Trial Chamber when a decision of the Registrar to deny counsel is challenged.

II.   TRIBUNAL CASES

B.   TRIAL CHAMBERS

1. INDIGENT ACCUSED

PROSECUTOR V. KUPREŠKIĆ, *et. al., Decision on the Registrar's Withdrawal of the Assignment of Defence Counsel*, IT-95-16-T, 3 September 1999, Cassese, May & Mumba, JJ.

The Registrar learned from a media report that the defendants in this case were receiving substantial financial assistance from auctions at which paintings made by them had been sold. The media report indicated that 4.300.000 DM had been raised in this manner. Based solely on this media report the Registrar withdrew the assignment of counsel for all defendants in this case. At this point the trial was nearing a conclusion, with its final hearing period having been scheduled.

The accused made complaint directly to the President, who referred the matter to the Trial Chamber for resolution. The Chamber took the matter up immediately without requiring the filing of formal Motions due to the imminence of the next hearing period in the trial.

Relying on Articles 13(C) and 19(D) of the *Directive on Assignment of Defence Counsel*[498], the Chamber overruled the Registrar and re-instated all assigned counsel on the following reasoning:

> The Trial Chamber finds that the burden of proof shifts depending on the stage at which the decision is to be made. Articles 8 to 10 of the Directive deal with the declaration of financial means and information relating thereto to be submitted by the accused to the Registrar. At the initial stage the accused must satisfy the Registrar that he fulfils the requirements of Article 5 of the Directive. Thus the burden of proof is upon him. Article 19 of the Directive deals with the withdrawal of the assignment of counsel, after an initial showing of indigency has been made to the satisfaction of the Registrar. In this case the Registrar takes away a benefit which had already been granted to the accused. The burden of proof for the withdrawal is upon her.499
>
> To decide the question of whether the accused are still indigent and whether the alleged payments may be taken into account for the purposes of determining that issue, the Trial Chamber must satisfy itself that the evidence before the Registrar is sufficient. Having considered the evidence before the

---

[498] The Directive on Assignment of Defence Counsel (Directive No. 1/94, as amended 1 August 1997, IT/73/Rev. 4) is found in the Appendix.

[499] Para. 6.

Registrar, the Trial Chamber finds that the evidence is not sufficient. Media reports may serve as a first step to launch an investigation into the veracity of the reported facts. That newspapers and other kinds of media are very often a highly unreliable source of information is common knowledge. Their reports, unsubstantiated by other material, cannot by themselves be sufficient evidence for a court of law.[500]

PROSECUTOR V. DOKMANOVIĆ, *Decision on Defence Preliminary Motion on the Assignment of Counsel,* IT-95-13a-PT, 30 September 1997, McDonald, Odio-Benito & Jan, JJ.

In this case, there was a dispute between the accused and the Registrar over the issue of whether the accused was indigent. The Registrar found that the Accused had sufficient means to engage counsel of his choice and, therefore, decided that Mr. Toma Fila was not to be assigned as defence counsel by the Registry. The Registrar had temporarily assigned Mr. Fila on 30 June 1997, for a 30-day period, while the determination of indigency of the Accused was made.[501]

The Chamber ruled that the determination of indigency of an accused person and the assignment of counsel is within the competence of the Registrar and is regulated by the *Directive on Assignment of Defence Counsel.*[502]

The Accused challenged the determination by the Registrar, based on the Declaration of Means submitted pursuant to Article 8 of the Directive and other information gathered by her concerning his financial situation.[503]

The Chamber interpreted Article 13(C) of the Directive and Rule 73, which provided that an accused person may raise an objection against a decision of the Registrar not to assign counsel, when such objection is filed as a preliminary motion within 60 days.[504]

The dispute between the accused and the Registrar centered on whether the accused or his wife owned certain property, the valuation of the property and the ability of the accused to dispose of the property. The Chamber ruled that until the questions over the value of the property and its disposability are resolved within the Registry, it was appropriate to exclude this property from the calculation of the financial means of the accused. On that basis, the Chamber found that the accused was indigent and that he had the right to counsel assigned by the Registrar. When further information became available, the Chamber ruled that it might reconsider this Decision.[505]

---

[500] Para. 7
[501] The Directive on Assignment of Defence Counsel (Directive No. 1/94, as amended 1 August 1997, IT/73/Rev. 4) is found in the Appendix.
[502] Para. 10.
[503] Para. 7.
[504] Para. 10. See, Rule 72(A)(iv).
[505] Para. 12.

Furthermore, the Chamber observed that since a motion by the Defence was pending, it would be a violation of the right of the accused to be represented by counsel, if he were precluded from being assisted in the preparation for the hearing on this motion by the effect of a decision of the Registrar to deny assignment of counsel.

RULE 46

MISCONDUCT OF COUNSEL

(A)   A CHAMBER MAY, AFTER A WARNING, REFUSE AUDIENCE TO COUNSEL IF, IN ITS OPINION, THE CONDUCT OF THAT COUNSEL IS OFFENSIVE, ABUSIVE OR OTHERWISE OBSTRUCTS THE PROPER CONDUCT OF THE PROCEEDINGS.

(B)   A JUDGE OR A CHAMBER MAY ALSO, WITH THE APPROVAL OF THE PRESIDENT, COMMUNICATE ANY MISCONDUCT OF COUNSEL TO THE PROFESSIONAL BODY REGULATING THE CONDUCT OF COUNSEL IN THE COUNSEL'S STATE OF ADMISSION OR, IF A PROFESSOR AND NOT OTHERWISE ADMITTED TO THE PROFESSION, TO THE GOVERNING BODY OF THAT COUNSEL'S UNIVERSITY.

(C)   UNDER THE SUPERVISION OF THE PRESIDENT, THE REGISTRAR SHALL PUBLISH AND OVERSEE THE IMPLEMENTATION OF A CODE OF PROFESSIONAL CONDUCT FOR DEFENCE COUNSEL.

II.   TRIBUNAL CASES

B.   TRIAL CHAMBERS

PROSECUTOR V. DELALIĆ, *et. al., Order,* IT-96-21-T, 16 June 1998, Karibi-Whyte, Odio Benito & Jan, JJ.

In response to an Order requiring the Defence to file a list of Defence witnesses, counsel for Mucić filed a list that was totally unacceptable. As a result, the Chamber ordered counsel to file an appropriate list. When counsel failed to do so, the Chamber entered an Order requesting for a second time that an appropriate list be filed, along with a warning pursuant to Rule 46(A), which read, in part:

> ... counsel for Mr. Mucić that he has already been warned twice pursuant to Sub-rule 46(A) of the Rules and that, should the present Order not be complied with in full, to the satisfaction of the Trial Chamber, counsel will be refused audience, the necessary consequence thus being that he will be withdrawn from representing Mr. Mucić and the defence case will be continued by co-counsel, with the assistance of such other counsel as the Registrar shall assign.

PART FIVE

PRE-TRIAL PROCEEDINGS

RULE 47

SUBMISSION OF INDICTMENT BY THE PROSECUTOR

(A)   AN INDICTMENT, SUBMITTED IN ACCORDANCE WITH THE FOLLOWING PROCEDURE, SHALL BE REVIEWED BY A JUDGE DESIGNATED IN ACCORDANCE WITH RULE 28 FOR THIS PURPOSE.

(B)   THE PROSECUTOR, IF SATISFIED IN THE COURSE OF AN INVESTIGATION THAT THERE IS SUFFICIENT EVIDENCE TO PROVIDE REASONABLE GROUNDS FOR BELIEVING THAT A SUSPECT HAS COMMITTED A CRIME WITHIN THE JURISDICTION OF THE TRIBUNAL, SHALL PREPARE AND FORWARD TO THE REGISTRAR AN INDICTMENT FOR CONFIRMATION BY A JUDGE, TOGETHER WITH SUPPORTING MATERIAL.

(C)   THE INDICTMENT SHALL SET FORTH THE NAME AND PARTICULARS OF THE SUSPECT, AND A CONCISE STATEMENT OF THE FACTS OF THE CASE AND OF THE CRIME WITH WHICH THE SUSPECT IS CHARGED.

(D)   THE REGISTRAR SHALL FORWARD THE INDICTMENT AND ACCOMPANYING MATERIAL TO THE DESIGNATED JUDGE, WHO WILL INFORM THE PROSECUTOR OF THE DATE FIXED FOR REVIEW OF THE INDICTMENT.

(E)   THE REVIEWING JUDGE SHALL EXAMINE EACH OF THE COUNTS IN THE INDICTMENT, AND ANY SUPPORTING MATERIALS THE PROSECUTOR MAY PROVIDE, TO DETERMINE, APPLYING THE STANDARD SET FORTH IN ARTICLE 19, PARAGRAPH 1, OF THE STATUTE, WHETHER A CASE EXISTS AGAINST THE SUSPECT.

(F)   THE REVIEWING JUDGE MAY:

   (I)   REQUEST THE PROSECUTOR TO PRESENT ADDITIONAL MATERIAL IN SUPPORT OF ANY OR ALL COUNTS, OR TO TAKE ANY FURTHER MEASURES WHICH APPEAR APPROPRIATE;

   (II)   CONFIRM EACH COUNT;

   (III)   DISMISS EACH COUNT; OR

   (IV)   ADJOURN THE REVIEW SO AS TO GIVE THE PROSECUTOR THE OPPORTUNITY TO MODIFY THE INDICTMENT.

(G)   THE INDICTMENT AS CONFIRMED BY THE JUDGE SHALL BE RETAINED BY THE REGISTRAR, WHO SHALL PREPARE CERTIFIED COPIES BEARING THE SEAL OF THE TRIBUNAL. IF THE ACCUSED DOES NOT UNDERSTAND EITHER OF THE OFFICIAL LANGUAGES OF THE TRIBUNAL AND IF THE LANGUAGE UNDERSTOOD IS KNOWN TO THE REGISTRAR, A TRANSLATION OF THE INDICTMENT IN THAT LANGUAGE SHALL ALSO BE

PREPARED, AND SHALL BE INCLUDED AS PART OF EACH CERTIFIED COPY OF THE INDICTMENT.

(H)   UPON CONFIRMATION OF ANY OR ALL COUNTS IN THE INDICTMENT,

      (I)   THE JUDGE MAY ISSUE AN ARREST WARRANT, IN ACCORDANCE WITH SUB-RULE 55 (A), AND ANY ORDERS AS PROVIDED IN ARTICLE 19 OF THE STATUTE, AND

      (II)   THE SUSPECT SHALL HAVE THE STATUS OF AN ACCUSED.

(I)   THE DISMISSAL OF A COUNT IN AN INDICTMENT SHALL NOT PRECLUDE THE PROSECUTOR FROM SUBSEQUENTLY BRINGING AN AMENDED INDICTMENT BASED ON THE ACTS UNDERLYING THAT COUNT IF SUPPORTED BY ADDITIONAL EVIDENCE.

I.   COMMENTARY

A.   CUMULATIVE CHARGES

The propriety or otherwise of charging more than one offence based on the same set of facts, has been addressed several times by both the International Tribunal for the former Yugoslavia and Rwanda. There are three questions that properly arise out of the issue:

      1.   Is it permissible for the Prosecution to indict someone with several offences, each of which arises out of the same set of facts?

      2.   If it is permissible so to indict someone, is it then permissible or desirable to convict someone of each such offence?

      3.   What are the consequences for sentencing of allowing such offences to be indicted and convictions entered for several such offences?

The observation made by the Trial Chamber when faced with a Motion challenging the form of the indictment in the *Kupreškić* case, raised the question of which offences might be thought to protect different values and which offences had unique legal elements not required by other offences, so justifying, if the Prosecutor deemed it appropriate, the submission of an indictment alleging cumulative charges. Given the frequency with which this issue was to resurface at both ICTY and ICTR, it is perhaps unfortunate that this chance was allowed to slip by. Trial Chamber II, however, was to return to this issue in much greater detail in their Judgment in this case.

      A fair reading of all the cases on this subject reported below leads one to certain conclusions.

Drafting of Indictments

The current position would appear to be that the Prosecution *may* (but is not obliged to do so) lay *cumulative* charges, provided it can meet all the other criteria for drafting indictments:

      (1)   Whenever it contends that the facts charged violate simultaneously two or more provisions of the Statute in accordance with the criteria discussed

above. The Prosecution *should* charge *in the alternative* rather than cumulatively whenever an offence appears to be in breach of more than one provision, depending on the elements of the crime the Prosecution is able to prove; or

(2)   Where the provisions creating the offences protect different interests; or

(3)   Where it is necessary to record a conviction for both offences in order fully to describe what the accused did.

Conversely the Prosecution *should refrain* as much as possible from making charges based on the same facts but under excessive multiple heads, whenever it would not seem warranted to contend, in line with the principles set out above in the section on the applicable law, that the same facts are simultaneously in breach of various provisions of the Statute.

Amendment of Indictments

It may happen that, in the course of the trial, the Prosecutor finds that she has not proved beyond reasonable doubt the commission of the crime charged, but that a *different offence*, not charged in the indictment, has been proved which has different objective or subjective elements. In these cases the Prosecutor must, if it is desired to seek a conviction for that offence, move the Trial Chamber to be granted leave to amend the indictment so as to afford the Defence the opportunity to contest the charge. The later this Motion is made, the harder it will be to justify it.

During the course of the trial, the Prosecutor may conclude that *a more serious offence* than that charged in the Indictment has been or may be proved. Clearly, once again the Prosecutor must, if it is desired to seek a conviction for that offence, request leave to amend the indictment, so as to avoid any jeopardy to the rights of the accused. The accused must be put in a position to contest the charges and to this end he must be informed promptly and in detail of the "nature and cause of the charge against him."[506] The same concept applies to the Trial Chamber, should it consider that a more serious offence has been proved in court.

The Prosecutor may conclude during the trial that a *lesser-included offence*, not charged in the Indictment, may be or has been proved in court. Given that the Chamber may convict of such an offence, there is no need to apply to amend the Indictment. It would seem advisable, however, that prompt notice be given by the Prosecutor to the Defence and the Chamber that she proposes to submit that the lesser but not the greater offence has been committed, so that the accused may know the particulars of the case against him or her. In any event, any careful defence advocate should have appreciated by the close of the Prosecution's case that some vital element of the more serious offence is lacking and that only some lesser offence has been notionally proved and thus should not be taken by surprise.

Powers of the Trial Chamber

In the event that the Trial Chamber were to conclude that the more serious offence had

---

[506] Statute of the ICTY, Article 21(4)(a).

not been proved, it is sufficient for it to make this finding in its judgement, without ordering the Prosecutor to amend the Indictment and to convict the Defendant of the lesser offence.

The Chamber may conclude that the facts proven by the Prosecutor do not show that the accused is guilty of having perpetrated a war crime; they show instead that he aided and abetted the commission of the crime. In this case, the Chamber may classify the offence in a manner different from that suggested by the Prosecutor, without previously notifying the Defence of the change in the *nomen iuris*.

If instead the Chamber finds in the course of trial that the evidence conclusively shows that the accused has committed a more serious crime than the one charged, it may call upon the Prosecutor to consider amending the indictment.

It may decide to convict the accused of the lesser offence charged. The Chamber should take the same course of action in the event the Prosecutor should decide not to accede to the Chamber's request that the indictment be amended.

If the Chamber finds in the course of trial that only a different offence has been proved, it should ask the Prosecutor to amend the indictment. If the Prosecutor does not comply with this request, the Trial Chamber shall have no choice but to dismiss the charge.

Sentencing

If under the principles set out above a Chamber finds that by a single act or omission the accused has perpetrated two offences under two distinct provisions of the Statute, and that the offences contain elements uniquely required by each provision, the Chamber shall find the accused guilty on two separate counts. In that case the sentences consequent upon the convictions for the same act shall be served concurrently, but the Chamber *may* (depending on whether it is appropriate to do so or not) aggravate the sentence for the more serious offence if it considers that the less serious offence committed by the same conduct significantly adds to the *heinous nature* of the prevailing offence, for instance because the less serious offence is characterised by distinct, highly reprehensible elements of its own (*e.g.* the use of poisonous weapons in conjunction with the more serious crime of genocide).

In the event, however, that a Chamber finds under the principles set out above that by a single act or omission the accused has not perpetrated two offences under two distinct provisions of the Statute but only one offence, then the Chamber will have to decide on the appropriate conviction for that offence only. For example, if the more specialised offence, *e.g.* genocide in the form of murder, is made out on the evidence beyond a reasonable doubt, then a conviction should be recorded for that offence and not for the offence of murder as a war crime. In that case only one conviction will be recorded and only one sentence will be imposed.

II.   TRIBUNAL CASES

B.   TRIAL CHAMBERS

PROSECUTOR V. DOŠEN, *et. al.*, *Decision on Preliminary Motions*, IT-95-8-PT, 10 February 2000, May, Bennouna & Robinson, JJ.

Faced with a contention by the accused that the indictment was vague and lacked sufficient particulars, the Prosecutor filed a document entitled "Attachment A," which set forth additional information as to the time and place of the alleged offences and the identity of victims and co-perpetrators. The Prosecutor argued, however, that the indictment was sufficient standing alone and that "Attachment A" should not be considered a part of the Amended Indictment. The Trial Chamber disagreed. Not attaching it to and making it a part of the indictment would create uncertainty about its legal status. It was therefore ordered that "Attachment A" should form a part of the Amended Indictment.[507]

It was contended further that even with "Attachment A," the indictment remained vague. The conduct of the accused as to certain counts was not clearly specified. Defendants were charged both for direct responsibility and superior responsibility as shift commanders at Keraterm Camp. The Prosecutor contended that the kind of detail requested by the Defence is unnecessary at this early stage of the proceedings. The Trial Chamber disagreed, saying:

> The form of the alleged participation of the accused in a crime is an material averment which should be clearly laid out in an indictment in order to clarify it and make plain the prosecution case.[508]

The Chamber entered the following Order:

> The Trial Chamber therefore orders the Prosecution to file an amended version of Attachment A. This Attachment will remain confidential and will form part of the Amended Indictment. Against each incident where the victim(s), place and date is named (in the first column), the Prosecution should specify (in the second column) the capacity in which each accused is alleged to have participated and whether his responsibility was:
>
> > (a)   direct pursuant to Article 7, paragraph 1, (and where possible, specifying the form of participation, such as "planning" or "instigating" or "ordering" etc.); or

---

[507] Para. 9.
[508] Para. 12.

252

(b)   by virtue of his being on duty as a shift commander pursuant to Article 7, paragraph 3, or, if he was not on duty during that incident, whether there is still an allegation of superior responsibility under Article 7, paragraph 3, for that incident, or

(c)   pursuant to Article 7, paragraph 1 and paragraph 3 (with specification as mentioned above).

1. CUMULATIVE CHARGES

PROSECUTOR V. TADIĆ, *Decision on Defence Motion on Form of the Indictment,* IT-94-1-T, 14 November 1995, McDonald, Stephen & Vohrah, JJ.

The issue of cumulative charging was first raised, somewhat obliquely, in this case in Trial Chamber II who observed:

> In any event, since this is a matter that will only be relevant insofar as it might affect penalty, it can best be dealt with if and when matters of penalty fall for consideration. What can, however, be said with certainty is that penalty cannot be made to depend upon whether offences arising from the same conduct are alleged cumulatively or in the alternative. What is to be punished by penalty is proven criminal conduct and that will not depend upon technicalities of pleading.[509]

This approach presages a practical approach to sentencing, the rationale of which is to sentence an offender for what he has done rather than to worry unduly about the labels which have been placed upon such conduct through "the technicalities of pleading".

PROSECUTOR V. DELALIĆ, *et. al., Decision on Motion by the Accused Zejnil Delalić Based on Defects in the Form of the Indictment,* IT-96-21-T, 2 October 1996, McDonald, Stephen & Vohrah, JJ.

An identically composed bench to that in the *Tadić* case reported above dealt afresh with the issue in this case. The Trial Chamber concluded that no different considerations applied and that they would follow the course they had taken in *Tadić*.[510]

PROSECUTOR V. KUPREŠKIĆ *et. al., Decision on Defence Challenges to Form of the Indictment,* IT-95-16-PT, 15 May 1998, Cassese, May & Mumba, JJ.

In the course of deciding on a Preliminary Motion on the indictment, Trial Chamber II visited the issue briefly. The Chamber observed that:

---

[509] Page 10.
[510] Para. 24. See also, The Prosecutor v Zejnil Delalić, *et. al., Decision on Application for Leave to Appeal by Hazim Delić (Defects in the Form of the Indictment),* IT-96-21-PT, 6 December 1996, Para. 32 *et seq.*

...the Prosecutor may be justified in bringing cumulative charges when the Articles of the Statute referred to are designed to protect different values and when each Article requires proof of a legal element not required by the others.

PROSECUTOR V KRNOJELAC, *Decision on the Defence Preliminary Motion on the Form of the Indictment,* IT-97-25-PT, 24 February 1999, Hunt, Cassese & Mumba, JJ

Trial Chamber II returned to the issue in this Decision on a Preliminary Motion. Making it plain that the issue turned upon and was relevant only to the question of penalty, the objections on this ground were dismissed. The Defence had raised the issue as a breach of the so-called "double jeopardy principle." The Chamber indicated that the issue had nothing, in reality, to do with "double jeopardy" which was "concerned with *successive* prosecutions upon different charges arising out of the same (or substantially the same) facts, and not with the prosecution of such charges in the *same* trial." In rejecting the Motion on this point, the Chamber said:

> The prosecution must be allowed to frame charges within the one indictment on the basis that the tribunal of fact may not accept a particular element of one charge which does not have to be established for the other charges, and in any event in order to reflect the totality of the accused's criminal conduct, so that the punishment imposed will do the same. Of course, great care must be taken in sentencing that an offender convicted of different charges arising out of the same or substantially the same facts is not punished more than once for his commission of the individual acts (or omissions) which are common to two or more of those charges. But there is no breach of the double jeopardy principle by the inclusion in the one indictment of different charges arising out of the same or substantially the same facts.[511]

PROSECUTOR V KVOČKA, *et. al., Decision on Defence Motions on the Form of the Indictment,* IT-98-30-PT, 12 April 1999, May, Bennouna & Robinson JJ.

A defence objection to cumulative charges was summarily dismissed, relying on the *Tadić* and *Krnolejac* decisions discussed above[512].

PROSECUTOR V KUPREŠKIĆ, *et. al., Judgement,* IT-95-16-T, 14 January 2000, Cassese, May & Mumba JJ.

The Trial Chamber conducted a comprehensive review of the subject of cumulative charging and came to a number of important conclusions, considering that:

---

[511] Para 5, *et. seq.*
[512] Para. 47.

this issue has a broad import and great relevance, all the more so because it has not been dealt with in depth by an international criminal court. [513]

The Chamber identified two important areas in which the issue has importance:

(a)   to *substantive* international criminal law; and

(b)   to *procedural* international criminal law.

As regards (a) the Chamber posed two questions:

(i)   whether and on what conditions the same act or transaction may infringe two or more rules of international criminal law; and

(ii)   in case of a double conviction for a single action, how this should be reflected in sentencing.

As regards (b) the Chamber posed three questions:

(i)   when and on what conditions can the Prosecutor opt for cumulative charges for the same act or transaction?; and

(ii)   when should the Prosecutor instead put forward alternative charges?; and

(iii)   with what powers is a Trial Chamber vested when faced with a charge that has been wrongly formulated by the Prosecutor?[514]

The Chamber reviewed the position that had been taken at the International Military Tribunal at Nuremberg (IMT) and found that many Defendants had been convicted of both war crimes and crimes against humanity arising from the same acts.

In considering the issue of substantive criminal law, the Chamber advanced the proposition that it is possible for various elements of a general criminal transaction to infringe different provisions, citing instances from the Inter-American Court of Human Rights, The European Commission of Human Rights and the European Court of Human Rights.[515] It concluded that there could exist distinct offences:

. . . that is, an accumulation of separate acts, each violative of a different provision. In civil law systems this situation is referred to as *concours réel d'infractions*, *Realkonkurrenz* , *concorso reale di reati*, etc. These offences may be grouped together into one general transaction on the condition that it is clear that the transaction consists of a cluster of offences.[516]

By contrast the Chamber found that the position differs with regard to the case of one and the same act or transaction simultaneously breaching two or more provisions, the European Court having repeatedly held that "one and the same fact may fall foul of more

---

[513] Para. 637.
[514] Para. 639.
[515] Para. 647.
[516] *Ibid.*

than one provision of the Convention and Protocols."[517] Concerning this type of situation, the Trial Chamber identified two distinct categories of acts or transactions:

> (a)   an act or transaction that breaches one provision in some respects and another provision in other respects; and

> (b)   acts or transactions that are fully covered by both provisions.

Cumulative Charges and Domestic Law

The Chamber referred to a number of tests which exist in national jurisdictions to identify into which category any act or transaction may fall. In *Morey v. The Commonwealth* [518] The Supreme Court of the State of Massachusetts held:

> A single act may be an offence against two statutes: and if each statute requires proof of an additional fact which the other does not, an acquittal or conviction under either statute does not exempt the defendant from prosecution and punishment under the other.

Subsequently in *Blockburger v United States of America*[519] the Supreme Court of the United States held:

> The applicable rule is that where the same act or transaction constitutes a violation of two distinct statutory provisions, the test to be applied to determine whether there are two offences or only one, is whether each provision requires proof of an additional fact which the other does not.

If this test ("the *Blockburger* test") is not met the Chamber held that it follows that one of the offences falls entirely within the ambit of the other offence (since it does not possess any element which the other lacks) in which case the relationship between the two provisions can be described as that between concentric circles, in that one has a broader scope and completely encompasses the other.

As to the position in the Civil Law, the choice between the two provisions was considered to be governed by the maxim *in toto iure generi per speciem derogatur* (or *lex specialis derogat generali*), whereby the more specific or less sweeping provision should be chosen, the rationale of this being that if an action is legally regulated both by a general provision and by a specific one, the latter prevails as most appropriate, being more specifically directed towards that action. The Chamber found it logical to assume that the national or international law-making body intended to give the provision governing the action more directly and in greater detail the dominant position. This principle was recognised also by international law. Civil law courts tend to speak in these circumstances of "reciprocal speciality" which the Chamber equated with the *Blockburger* test.[520]

---

[517] Para. 648.
[518] 108 Mass. 433,434, (1871).
[519] 284 U.S. 299,304; 52 S.Ct. 180, (1932).
[520] Para. 647 *et seq.*

In other cases, although the provisions cannot be said to be in a *lex specialis - lex generalis* relationship, it would nonetheless appear unsound to apply both provisions, such a notion corresponding to the common law doctrine of the "lesser included offence." The Chamber noted, however, that in civil law jurisdictions, a double conviction is ruled out in such cases by the so-called principle of "consumption," its *ratio* being that when all the legal requirements for a lesser offence are met in the commission of a more serious one, a conviction in respect of the more serious count fully encompasses the criminality of the conduct.

Cumulative Charging and the European Convention on Human Rights

It was held that a similar principle exists in international law, notably in the case-law of the European Commission and Court of Human Rights concerning the application of Article 3 of the European Convention on Human Rights, although the Chamber observed that the European Commission and Court had never applied the three provisions cumulatively.

The Chamber noted how the *Aksoy* case[521] illustrated the application of Article 3 as the two international bodies have applied it. In this case, the European Court, after finding that the facts complained of amounted to torture, held that:

> in view of the gravity of this conclusion, it was not necessary for the Court to examine the applicant's complaints of other forms of ill-treatment.

The Chamber identified what it believed to be the rationale behind this approach as being twofold, namely: (1) the European Commission and Court have applied a principle analogous to that of consumption; and (2) they have considered that the various norms of Article 3 all pursue the same goal and safeguard the same basic values. The latter rationale produced a further test, which consists in ascertaining whether the various provisions at stake protect different values, of which traces could be found in both the common law and civil law systems.

This test was:

> if an act or transaction is simultaneously in breach of two criminal provisions protecting different values, it may be held that that act or transaction infringes *both* criminal provisions.

A review of national case law suggested, however, that the test is hardly ever used other than in conjunction with and to support the other tests mentioned above in *Blockburger* and reciprocal speciality, as well as the principles of speciality and consumption. This test was considered unlikely to alter the conclusions reached through the application of these principles.

---

[521] Eur. Court HR, *Aksoy v. Turkey,* Judgment of 18 Dec. 1996, Reports of Judgments and Decisions, 1996-VI, p. 2279.

Cumulative Charging and the Statute

By way of exemplifying how these tests work out in practice, the Chamber proceeded to examine a number of specific relationships between sets of offences.

As to the relationship between "Murder" under Article 3 (War Crimes) and "Murder" under Article 5(a) (Crimes Against Humanity) the Chamber concluded that:

> ... the relevant question here is whether murder as a war crime requires proof of facts which murder as a crime against humanity does not require, and *vice versa* (the *Blockburger* test). Another relevant question is whether the prohibition of murder as a war crime protects different values from those safeguarded by the prohibition of murder as a crime against humanity.

> With regard to the former question, while murder as a crime against humanity requires proof of elements that murder as a war crime does not require (the offence must be part of a systematic or widespread attack on the civilian population), this is not reciprocated. As a result, the *Blockburger* test is not fulfilled, or in other words the two offences are not in a relationship of reciprocal speciality. The prohibition of murder as a crime against humanity is *lex specialis* in relation to the prohibition of murder as a war crime.

> In addressing the latter question, it can generally be said that the substantive provisions of the Statute pursue the same general objective (deterring serious breaches of humanitarian law and, if these breaches are committed, punishing those responsible for them). In addition, they protect the same general values in that they are designed to ensure respect for human dignity. Admittedly, within this common general framework, Articles 3 and 5 may pursue some specific aims and protect certain specific values.

> However, as under Article 5 of the Statute, crimes against humanity fall within the Tribunal's jurisdiction only when committed in armed conflict, the difference between the values protected by Article 3 and Article 5 would seem to be inconsequential.[522]

The Chamber therefore held that, given also the marginal difference in values protected, it could convict the Defendant of violating the prohibition of murder as a crime against humanity only if it finds that the requirements of murder under both Article 3 and under Article 5 are proved.

The Chamber next examined the relationship between "Persecution" under Article 5(h) (Crimes Against Humanity) and "Murder" under Article 5(a) (Crimes Against Humanity). On the grounds set out above, the Chamber held that "persecution" may comprise not only murder carried out with a discriminatory intent but also crimes other than murder.

As to the relationship between murder as a crime against humanity and persecution as a crime against humanity, the Chamber observed that persecution requires

---

[522] Paras. 668-672.

a discriminatory element that murder, albeit as a crime against humanity, does not. The Chamber concluded therefore that there is reciprocal speciality between these crimes; indeed, both may have unique elements. An accused may be guilty of persecution for destroying the homes of persons belonging to another ethnic group and expelling the occupants, without however being found guilty of any acts of killing. The destruction of homes and the expulsion of persons, if carried out with the requisite discriminatory intent may in and of themselves be sufficient to constitute persecution. On the other hand, an accused may commit a murder that lacked the requisite discriminatory intent as part of a widespread attack on a civilian population that, because it is non-discriminatory, fails to satisfy the definition of persecution. These, then, are two separate offences, which may be equally charged.

If an accused is found guilty of persecution, *inter alia* because of the commission of a murder, it was held that he should only be found guilty of persecution, and not of murder *and* persecution, because in that case the *Blockburger* test would not be met: Murder is, in that case, already encompassed within persecution as a form of aggravated murder, and it did not possess any elements which the persecutory murders do not. Hence, in that case, murder may be seen as either falling under *lex generalis* or as a lesser-included offence, and a conviction should not ensue when there is already a conviction under *lex specialis* for the more serious offence, *i.e.* persecutory murder.

A further different state of affairs was envisaged by the Chamber, namely where a person is charged both with murder as a crime against humanity and with persecution (including murder) as a crime against humanity. In that case the same acts of murder may be material to both crimes. This is so if it is proved that (i) murder as a form of persecution meets both the requirement of discriminatory intent and that of the widespread or systematic practice of persecution, and (ii) murder as a crime against humanity fulfils the requirement for the wilful taking of life of innocent civilians and that of a widespread or systematic practice of murder of civilians. If these requirements are met, we are clearly faced with a case of reciprocal speciality or in other words the requirements of the *Blockburger* test are fulfilled. Consequently, murder would constitute an offence under both Articles 5(h) and (a) of the Statute.

Looking at the "different values test" it was held that it was clear that the criminalisation of murder and persecution might serve different values. The prohibition of murder aims at protecting innocent civilians from being obliterated on a large scale. More generally, it intends to safeguard human life in times of armed conflicts. On the other hand, the ban on persecution intends to safeguard civilians from severe forms of discrimination. This ban is designed to reaffirm and impose respect for the principle of equality between groups and human beings.

This test therefore supported the result achieved by using the other test. Under the conditions described above, the test based on protection of values leads to the conclusion that the same act or transaction (murder) may infringe two different provisions of Article 5 of the Statute.[523]

---

[523] Paras. 673-678.

As to the relationship between "Inhumane Acts" under Article 5(i) (Crimes Against Humanity) and "Cruel Treatment" under Article 3 (War Crimes) it was evident that, in the particular way in which the Indictment in this case had been drawn, these two crimes had been pleaded as alternatives and should therefore be considered so to be.

The Chamber held that every time an inhumane act under Article 5(i) is committed, *ipso facto* cruel treatment under Article 3 is inflicted but that the reverse was not true; cruel treatment under Article 3 may not be covered by Article 5(i) if the element of widespread or systematic practice is missing. Thus, if the evidence proves the commission of the facts in question, a conviction should only be recorded for one of these two offences; inhumane acts, if the background conditions for crimes against humanity are satisfied, and if they are not, cruel treatment as a war crime. In such circumstances it was deemed not strictly necessary to consider the "different values test", since the *Blockburger* test was ultimately conclusive of the issue.[524]

Finally the Chamber examined the relationship between the charges for Inhumane Acts (or Cruel Treatment) and the charges for Murder in the particular circumstances of this case: Not only were the elements different but in reality different victims were alleged and therefore these were clearly different and separate offences. Thus, implicitly, the Chamber did not see the need for any further evaluation.[525]

Cumulative Charges and Sentencing

The Chamber now turned to the practical consequences of the results of conducting these various tests upon the sentences to be imposed in the event of more than one conviction for a single act. It was common ground between the parties that a defendant should not suffer two distinct penalties, to be served consecutively, for the same act or transaction. Nevertheless the Chamber declared that it was under a duty to apply the provisions of the Statute and customary international law.

Faced with some divergence between international law and national law, the Chamber concluded that:

> . . . a fair solution can be derived both from the object and purpose of the provisions of the Statute as well as the general concepts underlying the Statute, and from "the general principles of justice applied by jurists and practised by military courts" referred to by the International Military Tribunal at Nuremberg.

In consequence the Chamber offered the following two propositions:

> 1.   If under the principles set out above a Trial Chamber finds that by a single act or omission the accused has perpetrated two offences under two distinct provisions of the Statute, and that the offences contain elements uniquely required by each provision, the Trial Chamber shall find the accused guilty on two separate counts. In that case the sentences consequent upon the convictions for the same act shall be served concurrently, but the Trial Chamber may aggravate the sentence for the more serious offence if it considers that the

---

[524] Para. 711.
[525] Para. 712.

less serious offence committed by the same conduct significantly adds to the *heinous nature* of the prevailing offence, for instance because the less serious offence is characterised by distinct, highly reprehensible elements of its own (*e.g.* the use of poisonous weapons in conjunction with the more serious crime of genocide).

2.   On the other hand, if a Trial Chamber finds under the principles set out above that by a single act or omission the accused has not perpetrated two offences under two distinct provisions of the Statute but only one offence, then the Trial Chamber will have to decide on the appropriate conviction for that offence only. For example, if the more specialised offence, *e.g.* genocide in the form of murder, is made out on the evidence beyond a reasonable doubt, then a conviction should be recorded for that offence and not for the offence of murder as a war crime. In that case only one conviction will be recorded and only one sentence will be imposed. [526]

Cumulative Charges and Procedural Criminal Law

Consequent upon its conclusions as to the position of substantive international criminal law, the Chamber now turned to issues of Procedural Criminal Law.

Dealing firstly with the power of the Prosecutor to opt for cumulative or alternative charges, the Chamber held that the approach currently adopted ·by the Prosecution creates an onerous situation for the Defence, on the grounds that the same facts are often cumulatively classified under different headings, frequently under *two* different heads (war crimes, and crimes against humanity), and in other cases before the Tribunal under three (or even possibly four) different heads.

The onerous situation envisaged by the Chamber might well be, for example, facing a defence advocate with the dilemma of asking a particular question or raising a particular issue that was highly relevant and helpful on one charge but unhelpful and highly damaging on another charge. It also leads to long and unwieldy documents being produced which frequently seem to bear the hallmarks of the scattergun approach rather than that required by Rule 47(c).

Noting that neither the Statute nor the Rules establish how the charges must be brought by the Prosecutor, the Chamber held that, generally speaking, if under the principles set out above, the facts allegedly committed by the accused are in breach of only one provision of the Statute, the Prosecutor should present only one charge. If, however, in the Prosecutor's view, the alleged facts simultaneously infringe more than one provision of the Statute, the Prosecutor should present cumulative charges under each relevant provision.

The Chamber concluded that in any given situation the issue must be settled in the light of two basic but apparently conflicting requirements:

---

[526] Paras. 713-719.

(a)   that the rights of the accused be fully safeguarded.

(b)   that the Prosecutor be granted all the powers consistent with the Statute to enable her to fulfil her mission efficiently and in the interests of justice.

An example of the former was the right of the accused to be "informed promptly and in detail….of the nature and cause of the charge against him."[527] It follows that the accused is entitled to know the specifics of the charges against him, namely (a) the facts of which he is accused and (b) the legal classification of those facts. In particular, as far as this legal element is concerned, he must be put in a position to know the legal ingredients of the offence charged. Another might be the right of the accused to a fair trial under Articles 20 and 21 of the Statute. For example the overloading of an Indictment might in certain circumstances amount to oppression and thereby unfairness.

It was suggested that the latter requirement (that relating to the functions of the Prosecutor) implies that legal technicalities concerning classification of international offences should not be allowed to thwart the mission of the Prosecutor, which is to prosecute persons responsible for serious violations of international humanitarian law. The efficient fulfilment of the Prosecution's mission favours a system that is not hidebound by formal requirements of pleading in the indictment.[528]

The Chamber set some parameters, as follows:

1.   The Prosecution:

(a) *may* make *cumulative* charges whenever it contends that the facts charged violate simultaneously two or more provisions of the Statute in accordance with the criteria discussed above;

(b) *should* charge *in the alternative* rather than cumulatively whenever an offence appears to be in breach of more than one provision, depending on the elements of the crime the Prosecution is able to prove. (emphasis added)

As a practical suggestion the Chamber stated that in a doubtful case it is appropriate from a Prosecutorial viewpoint to suggest that a certain act falls under a stricter and more serious provision of the Statute, adding however that if proof to this effect is not convincing, the act falls under a less serious provision.

The Chamber now turned to the question of the obligations of the Prosecutor when she decides to change the legal classification of facts in the course of trial and the power of a trial chamber when it disagrees with the prosecutor's legal classification of the facts.

The Chamber conducted an exhaustive review of national legal systems in an effort to determine if there was any consensus regarding this issue.

---

[527] Statute of the ICTY, Article 21(4)(a).
[528] This is a worrying suggestion which implies that precision of pleading (and thus accurate drawing of offences known to the law) can be swept aside if it conflicts with the Prosecutor's duty as he or she sees it.

It was concluded from that review that no general principle of criminal law common to all major legal systems of the world could be found and that it therefore fell to the Chamber to look for a general principle of law consonant with the fundamental features and the basic requirements of international criminal justice.

In so doing the Chamber identified two basic requirements having paramount importance on account of the present status of international criminal law:

(1)   the requirement that the rights of the accused be fully safeguarded.

(2)   The requirement that the Prosecutor and, more generally, the International Tribunal be in a position to exercise all the powers expressly or implicitly deriving from the Statute, or inherent in their functions, that are necessary for them to fulfil their mission efficiently and in the interests of justice.

As to the first requirement the Chamber emphasised again that, at present, international criminal rules are still in a rudimentary state. They need to be elaborated and rendered more specific either by international law-making bodies or by international case law so as to gradually give rise to general rules. In this state of flux the rights of the accused would not be satisfactorily safeguarded were one to adopt an approach akin to that of some civil law countries. Were the Chamber allowed to convict persons of a specific crime as well as any other crime based on the same facts, of whose commission the Chamber might be satisfied at trial, the accused would not be able to prepare his defence with regard to a well-defined charge. The task of the defence would become exceedingly onerous, given the aforementioned uncertainties that still exist in international criminal law.

Hence, even though the *iura novit curia* principle is normally applied in international judicial proceedings, under present circumstances it would be inappropriate for this principle to be followed in proceedings before international criminal courts, where the rights of an individual accused are at stake. It would also violate Article 21(4)(a) of the Statute, which provides that an accused shall be informed "promptly and in detail" of the "nature and cause of the charge against him".

As to the second requirement, it was held that the efficient discharge of the Tribunal's functions in the interest of justice warrants the conclusion that any possible errors of the Prosecution should not stultify criminal proceedings whenever a case nevertheless appears to have been made by the Prosecution and the flaws in the formulation of the charge are not such as to impair or curtail the rights of the Defence.

C.   ICTR Trial Chambers

PROSECUTOR V AKAYESU, *Judgement*, ICTR-96-4-T, 2 September 1998, Kama P., Aspegren & Pillay, JJ.

In the first Judgement delivered by the Rwanda Tribunal, the Learned Judges posed this question:

....whether, if the Chamber is convinced beyond a reasonable doubt that a given factual allegation set out in the Indictment has been established, it may find the accused guilty of all of the crimes charged in relation to those facts or only one. The reason for posing this question is that it might be argued that the accumulation of criminal charges offends against the principle of double jeopardy or a substantive *non bis in idem* principle in criminal law. Thus an accused who is found guilty of both genocide and crimes against humanity in relation to the same set of facts may argue that he has been twice judged for the same offence, which is generally considered impermissible in criminal law.[529]

It is clear that the practice of concurrent sentencing ensures that the accused is not twice punished for the same acts. Notwithstanding this absence of prejudice to the accused, it is still necessary to justify the prosecutorial practice of accumulating criminal charges.[530]

In concluding that such charging of cumulative offences is acceptable, the Trial Chamber had recourse to the Penal Code of Rwanda, Chapter VI:

> Concurrent offences:
>
> Article 92: Where a person has committed several offences prior to a conviction on any such charges, such offences shall be concurrent.
>
> Article 93: Notional plurality of offences occurs:
>
>> 1. Where a single conduct may be characterized as constituting several offences;
>>
>> 2. Where a conduct includes acts which, though constituting separate offences, are interrelated as deriving from the same criminal intent or as constituting lesser included offences of one another.
>>
>> 3. In the former case, only the sentence prescribed for the most serious offence shall be passed while, in the latter case, only the sentence provided for the most severely punished offence shall be passed, the maximum of which may be exceeded by half"[531]

The Chamber promulgated three circumstances where such cumulative charging would be acceptable:

1.   where the offences have different elements; or

2.   where the provisions creating the offences protect different interests; or

3.   where it is necessary to record a conviction for both offences in order fully to describe what the accused did.

---

[529] Para. 461, *et.seq.*
[530] *Ibid.*
[531] *Ibid.*

The Chamber, however, concluded that it was not justifiable to convict an accused of two offences in relation to the same set of facts where (a) one offence is a lesser included offence of the other, or (b) where one offence charges accomplice liability and the other offence charges liability as a principal.

The Chamber concluded that, having regard to Tribunal's Statute, genocide, crimes against humanity, and violations of article 3 common to the Geneva Conventions and of Additional Protocol II all have different elements and were intended to protect different interests.

Conversely, the Chamber did not consider that any of genocide, crimes against humanity, and violations of article 3 common to the Geneva Conventions and of Additional Protocol II are lesser-included forms of each other:

> The ICTR Statute does not establish a hierarchy of norms, but rather all three offences are presented on an equal footing. While genocide may be considered the gravest crime, there is no justification in the Statute for finding that crimes against humanity or violations of common article 3 and Additional Protocol II are in all circumstances alternative charges to genocide and thus lesser included offences. As stated, and it is a related point, these offences have different constituent elements. Again, this consideration renders multiple convictions for these offences in relation to the same set of facts permissible.[532]

PROSECUTOR V. KAYISHEMA AND RUZINDANA, *Judgement*, ICTR-95-1-T, 21 May 1999, Sekule & Ostrovsky JJ., Khan J. dissenting.[533]

The majority Judges held that:

> It is only acceptable to convict an accused of two or more offences in relation to the same set of facts in the following circumstances: (1) where offences have differing elements, or (2) where the laws in question protect differing social interests. To address the issue of concurrence, that is whether two or more crimes charged in the Indictment could be considered the same offence, the Trial Chamber examines two factors: Firstly, whether the crimes as charged contain the same elements, and secondly, whether the laws in question protect the same social interests.

Omitting reference to the third reason for the acceptability of cumulative charging offered in *Akayesu*,[534] the majority proceeded to declare that many of the offences charged had overlapping elements and protected similar social interests, and that convictions on all counts charged could not therefore be justified. Three crimes, genocide, murder and extermination were thus found to be, in effect, the same offence and therefore it would be improper to charge them in the same indictment.

---

[532] Para. 470.
[533] Para. 625 *et seq.*
[534] See above.

In a dissenting opinion, Khan J. reviewed the pertinent authorities and concluded:

> Thus, the line of international jurisprudence has evolved to hold that where the prosecution has charged such different crimes based upon the same facts, the matter falls for consideration once an accused is ultimately found guilty. And, the consequence of cumulative charges can be suitably dealt with at the stage of sentencing, rather than at verdict. In my view, this approach applies equally well to matters where the elements of the crimes, as proved, also overlap.[535]

PROSECUTOR V RUTAGANDA, *Judgement*, ICTR-96-13-T, 6 December 1999, Pillay, Kama & Aspegren, JJ.

In this Judgement, Trial Chamber I rejected the majority's approach in *Kayishema* and expressed their approval of and adherence to the dissenting opinion of Khan, J. in the latter case.[536]

PROSECUTOR V MUSEMA, *Judgement*, 27 January 2000, Pillay, Kama & Aspegren, JJ.

In this Judgement, Trial Chamber I rejected the majority's approach in *Kayishema* and expressed their approval of and adherence to the dissenting opinion of Khan, J. in the latter case.[537]

---

[535] Para. 23.
[536] Paras. 108-119 and Paras. 289-299 respectively.
[537] Paras. 108-119 and Paras. 289-299 respectively.

RULE 48

JOINDER OF ACCUSED

PERSONS ACCUSED OF THE SAME OR DIFFERENT CRIMES COMMITTED IN THE COURSE OF THE SAME TRANSACTION MAY BE JOINTLY CHARGED AND TRIED.

III.   TRIBUNAL CASES

B.   TRIAL CHAMBERS

PROSECUTOR V. KUNARAC, *et. al., Decision on Joinder of Trials*, IT-96-23-PT, 9 February 2000, Mumba, Hunt & Pocar, JJ.

Defendant Zoran Vuković filed a Motion asking that his trial be joined with that of Kunarac and Kovač and requesting a postponement of that trial from 20 March 2000 until 2 May 2000. The Chamber determined that under Rule 48 it had discretion to decide whether an accused should be joined with others, but there is no obligation that they be tried jointly. In this case the Chamber concluded that joinder would not be in the interests of justice. The Chamber said:

> It appears that the postponement of the trial at this stage will be an inevitable consequence of a joinder. The trial was originally scheduled to commence on 1 February 2000, but in order to give Radomir Kovač – who was arrested in August 1999 – the opportunity to properly prepare his defence, the Trial Chamber in December 1999 postponed the starting date of the trial to 20 March 2000. Dragoljub Kunarac surrendered to the Tribunal as long ago as March 1998. Another delay cannot be allowed. The Trial Chamber, the Prosecutor and the two co-accused have gone past the point of preparation for trial where any further postponement would be in the interests of justice. For example, as a result of various meeting between the Prosecutor and the two co-accused, the Prosecutor has, on 1 February 2000, filed a document on the admissions by the parties and contested and uncontested matters. It would appear from the said document that the agreement reached might shorten the trial in some important respects. Were Zoran Vuković to be tried together with the two co-accused, he might want to contest the agreed upon issues referred to, or worse, those negotiations and agreements would have to be reopened altogether.[538]

The Chamber determined that should Vuković decide that he could be ready for trial on 20 March 2000, he could re-apply for joinder.[539]

---

[538] Para. 10.
[539] Para. 13.

PROSECUTOR V. KVOČKA, *et. al.*, IT-98-30-PT & PROSECUTOR V. KOLUNDŽIJA, IT-95-8-PT, *Decision on Prosecutor's Motion for Joinder*, 19 October 1999, May, Bennouna & Robinson, JJ.

The Prosecutor sought to join Kolundžija with the Omarska case, IT-98-30. The Trial Chamber declined to do so. The Chamber held that "joining the accused Dragan Kolundžija to Indictment IT-98-30 is not in the interests of justice as it would delay the proceedings against the other accused charged in that indictment."

PROSECUTOR V. KOVAČEVIĆ, KVOČKA, RADIĆ, & ŽIGIĆ, *Decision on Motion for Joinder of Accused and Concurrent Presentation of Evidence*, IT-97-24-PT & IT-98-30-PT, 14 May 1998, May, Cassese & Mumba, JJ.

The Prosecutor made a Motion to join the cases of Kvočka, Radić and Žigić with that of Kovačević. Kvočka, Radić and Žigić were assigned to a different Trial Chamber. In effect, the Prosecutor wanted to try separate indictments at once with a concurrent presentation of evidence.

The Trial Chamber denied the motion, finding that its practical effect would be to order joint trials of all the accused. The Chamber ruled as follows:

> The Trial Chamber considers that the course requested by the Prosecution may endanger the rights of all accused to a fair trial, because it may lead to conflict of interests between the accused in conducting their defence. Such conflict would cause serious prejudice to all the accused. Rule 82(B) empowers a Trial Chamber to separate trials if "it considers it necessary to avoid a conflict of interests that might cause serious prejudice to an accused . . .". Had the four accused been jointly indicted in this case, the Trial Chamber would have had to consider separating their trials.[540]

In addition the Chamber determined that the granting of such a motion would result in a violation of Kovačević's right to an expeditious trial. Such a "violation is not justified by the argument that joinder may expedite the trials of the other accused."[541]

---

[540] Para. 10.
[541] *Ibid.*

RULE 49

JOINDER OF CRIMES

TWO OR MORE CRIMES MAY BE JOINED IN ONE INDICTMENT IF THE SERIES OF ACTS COMMITTED TOGETHER FORM THE SAME TRANSACTION, AND THE SAID CRIMES WERE COMMITTED BY THE SAME ACCUSED.

RULE 50

AMENDMENT OF INDICTMENT

(A)   (I)   THE PROSECUTOR MAY AMEND AN INDICTMENT:

           (A)   AT ANY TIME BEFORE ITS CONFIRMATION, WITHOUT LEAVE;

           (B)   BETWEEN ITS CONFIRMATION AND THE ASSIGNMENT OF THE CASE TO A TRIAL CHAMBER, WITH THE LEAVE OF THE JUDGE WHO CONFIRMED THE INDICTMENT, OR A JUDGE ASSIGNED BY THE PRESIDENT; AND

           (C)   AFTER THE ASSIGNMENT OF THE CASE TO A TRIAL CHAMBER, WITH THE LEAVE OF THAT TRIAL CHAMBER OR A JUDGE OF THAT CHAMBER, AFTER HAVING HEARD THE PARTIES.

        (II)   AFTER THE ASSIGNMENT OF THE CASE TO A TRIAL CHAMBER IT SHALL NOT BE NECESSARY FOR THE AMENDED INDICTMENT TO BE CONFIRMED.

        (III)   RULE 47(G) AND RULE 53 *BIS* APPLY *MUTATIS MUTANDIS* TO THE AMENDED INDICTMENT.

(B)   IF THE AMENDED INDICTMENT INCLUDES NEW CHARGES AND THE ACCUSED HAS ALREADY APPEARED BEFORE A TRIAL CHAMBER IN ACCORDANCE WITH RULE 62, A FURTHER APPEARANCE SHALL BE HELD AS SOON AS PRACTICABLE TO ENABLE THE ACCUSED TO ENTER A PLEA ON THE NEW CHARGES.

(C)   THE ACCUSED SHALL HAVE A FURTHER PERIOD OF THIRTY DAYS IN WHICH TO FILE PRELIMINARY MOTIONS PURSUANT TO RULE 72 IN RESPECT OF THE NEW CHARGES AND, WHERE NECESSARY, THE DATE FOR TRIAL MAY BE POSTPONED TO ENSURE ADEQUATE TIME FOR THE PREPARATION OF THE DEFENCE.

II.   TRIBUNAL CASES

A.   APPEALS CHAMBER

PROSECUTOR V. KOVAČEVIĆ, *Decision Stating Reasons for Appeals Chamber's Order of 29 May 1998,* IT-97-24-AR73, 2 July 1998, McDonald, Shahabuddeen, Wang Tieya, Nieto-Navia & Rodrigues, JJ.

This decision reverses the Trial Chamber's prohibition of an Amendment of the Indictment. The Defendant was arrested and transferred to the Tribunal on 10 July 1997. The indictment charged him with one count of Complicity in Genocide. As early as 11 July 1997 the Prosecutor informed defence counsel that they intended to amend the indictment. The Prosecutor again mentioned their intention to amend at a status conference on 24 November 1997. The Prosecutor's Request to Amend was not filed, however, until 28 January 1998, when she sought to add an additional fourteen counts to the original one count. The Defence objected to the Amendment on various grounds and on 5 March 1998, the Chamber refused the request to amend. The trial was set to begin on 11 May 1998. The accused announced that if the amendment were permitted he would need an additional seven months preparation time.

The Trial Chamber denied the request, as follows:

> First, the new counts involved an unacceptable increase in the size of the original indictment. Secondly, they led to undue delay. Thirdly, the accused was not informed promptly of the additional charges. Before this Chamber, the defence raised the point whether the addition of the new counts was barred by the speciality principle of extradition law.[542]

The Appeals Chamber said:

> No doubt, size can be taken into account in considering whether any injustice would be caused to the accused; but, provided other relevant requirements are met, a court would not be slow to deny the prosecution a right to amend on that ground only. The Trial Chamber did not consider whether any possible injustice could be remedied by disallowing only some of the amendments, in which case, the prosecution could have been asked to indicate its preferences: it rejected the whole.[543]

> In the circumstances of this case, this Chamber is not satisfied that the size of the amendments was objectionable.[544]

The Chamber decided that it needed to determine whether a 7-month delay would be reasonable in light of the right of the accused to a fair and expeditious trial as mandated by Articles 20 and 21 of the Statute.

The Chamber's consideration of this issue follows:

> The right of an accused to be informed promptly of the nature and cause of the charges against him, enshrined in similar terms in Article 6(3)(a) of the ECHR, Article 14(3)(a) of the ICCPR and Article 21, subparagraph 4(a) of the Statute of the International Tribunal, constitutes one element of the general requirement of fairness that is a fundamental aspect of a right to a fair trial. The following common general principles which may be derived from the practice of the European Court of Human Rights in relation to Article 6 of the ECHR provides some guidance as to how to interpret the requirements set out in Article 21, sub-paragraphs 4 (a) and (c) of the Tribunal's Statute: firstly, that the accused's right to be informed promptly of the charges against him has to be assessed in the light of the general requirement of fairness to the accused; secondly, that the information provided to the accused must enable him to prepare an effective defence; thirdly, that the accused must be tried without undue delay; and fourthly, that the requirement must be interpreted according to the special

---

[542] Para. 21.
[543] Para. 24.
[544] Para. 25.

features of each case. This is consistent with the provisions of the Statute, which in Article 21, subparagraph 2 provides that all accused are entitled to a fair and public hearing, and thereafter in sub-paragraph 4 sets out the right of the accused to be informed promptly of the charge against him, and to be tried without undue delay, as part of the specific minimum guarantees necessary to ensure that this general requirement of fairness is met.[545]

As it relates to the present Appeal, the timeliness of the Prosecutor's request for leave to amend the Indictment must thus be measured within the framework of the overall requirement of the fairness of the proceedings. Based upon the estimates of the defence, which were accepted by the Trial Chamber, it would take an additional seven months for the defence to prepare to defend against the charges in the Amended Indictment. Considering the complexity of the case, the omission of the defence to object to the prosecution's motion to schedule consideration of the request for leave to amend the Indictment until after the motion for provisional release had been decided, and the Trial Chamber's decision accepting the prosecution's proposal, the extension of the proceedings, even by a period of seven months, would not constitute undue delay and would afford the accused a fair trial.[546]

In addition, the Chamber found that Article 20 of the Statute of the International Tribunal requires that an arrestee be informed promptly of the charges contained in the indictment against him, not other possible charges. The Chamber says this is the meaning of the ICCPR and the meaning of the Tribunal's Statute.[547]

Based on the principle of speciality, the Defence contended that the Defendant could only be tried for those offences which were contained in the indictment at the time of his arrest in Bosnia and Herzegovina and that additional charges could not be added once he was in the custody of the Tribunal. The Chamber rejected this argument: "the fundamental relations between requested and requesting state [sic] have no counterpart in the arrangements relating to the International Tribunal."[548]

---

[545] Para. 30.

[546] Para. 31.

[547] Paras. 34-36. The principle of speciality provides that when a State requests the extradition of an accused from another state, it cannot, once extradition has been granted, then charge the accused with offenses for which he was not specifically extradited.

[548] Para. 37. This decision was based on a previous version of this rule. Under the current version the application for leave to amend would have been made to the original confirming judge or, if no longer available, to a judge assigned by the President. The rule change does not change the substance of the issue considered by the Appeals Chamber.

RULE 51

WITHDRAWAL OF INDICTMENT

(A)   THE PROSECUTOR MAY WITHDRAW AN INDICTMENT, WITHOUT LEAVE, AT ANY TIME BEFORE ITS CONFIRMATION, BUT THEREAFTER, UNTIL THE INITIAL APPEARANCE OF THE ACCUSED BEFORE A TRIAL CHAMBER PURSUANT TO RULE 62, ONLY WITH LEAVE OF THE JUDGE WHO CONFIRMED IT. AT OR AFTER SUCH INITIAL APPEARANCE AN INDICTMENT MAY ONLY BE WITHDRAWN BY MOTION BEFORE THAT TRIAL CHAMBER PURSUANT TO RULE 73.

(B)   THE WITHDRAWAL OF THE INDICTMENT SHALL BE PROMPTLY NOTIFIED TO THE SUSPECT OR THE ACCUSED AND TO THE COUNSEL OF THE SUSPECT OR ACCUSED.

RULE 52

PUBLIC CHARACTER OF INDICTMENT

SUBJECT TO RULE 53, UPON CONFIRMATION BY A JUDGE OF A TRIAL CHAMBER, THE INDICTMENT SHALL BE MADE PUBLIC.

RULE 53

NON-DISCLOSURE

(A)   IN EXCEPTIONAL CIRCUMSTANCES, A JUDGE OR A TRIAL CHAMBER MAY, IN THE INTERESTS OF JUSTICE, ORDER THE NON-DISCLOSURE TO THE PUBLIC OF ANY DOCUMENTS OR INFORMATION UNTIL FURTHER ORDER.

(B)   WHEN CONFIRMING AN INDICTMENT THE JUDGE MAY, IN CONSULTATION WITH THE PROSECUTOR, ORDER THAT THERE BE NO PUBLIC DISCLOSURE OF THE INDICTMENT UNTIL IT IS SERVED ON THE ACCUSED, OR, IN THE CASE OF JOINT ACCUSED, ON ALL THE ACCUSED.

(C)   A JUDGE OR TRIAL CHAMBER MAY, IN CONSULTATION WITH THE PROSECUTOR, ALSO ORDER THAT THERE BE NO DISCLOSURE OF AN INDICTMENT, OR PART THEREOF, OR OF ALL OR ANY PART OF ANY PARTICULAR DOCUMENT OR INFORMATION, IF SATISFIED THAT THE MAKING OF SUCH AN ORDER IS REQUIRED TO GIVE EFFECT TO A PROVISION OF THE RULES, TO PROTECT CONFIDENTIAL INFORMATION OBTAINED BY THE PROSECUTOR, OR IS OTHERWISE IN THE INTERESTS OF JUSTICE.

(D)   NOTWITHSTANDING SUB-RULES (A), (B) AND (C), THE PROSECUTOR MAY DISCLOSE AN INDICTMENT OR PART THEREOF TO THE AUTHORITIES OF A STATE OR AN APPROPRIATE AUTHORITY OR INTERNATIONAL BODY WHERE THE PROSECUTOR DEEMS IT NECESSARY TO PREVENT AN OPPORTUNITY FOR SECURING THE POSSIBLE ARREST OF AN ACCUSED FROM BEING LOST.

II.   TRIBUNAL CASES

B.   TRIAL CHAMBERS

PROSECUTOR V. DOKMANOVIĆ, *Decision on the motion for release by the accused Slavko Dokmanović*, IT-95-13a-PT, 22 October 1997, Cassese, May & Mumba, JJ.

On 3 April 1996, the name of Dokmanović was added to the indictment against three other accused persons, subject to an order for non-disclosure as provided for in Rule 53. The Office of the Prosecutor had adopted this approach of requesting orders for non-disclosure due to the non-cooperation of some States in executing arrest warrants issued by the Tribunal.[549] The Chamber found that Rule 53 is in clear and absolute terms and the non-disclosure of an indictment does not constitute good grounds for a challenge to the arrest of an accused.[550]

---

[549] Para. 53.
[550] Para. 54.

RULE 53 *BIS*

SERVICE OF INDICTMENT

(A)   SERVICE OF THE INDICTMENT SHALL BE EFFECTED PERSONALLY ON THE ACCUSED AT THE TIME THE ACCUSED IS TAKEN INTO CUSTODY OR AS SOON AS REASONABLY PRACTICABLE THEREAFTER.

(B)   PERSONAL SERVICE OF AN INDICTMENT ON THE ACCUSED IS EFFECTED BY GIVING THE ACCUSED A COPY OF THE INDICTMENT CERTIFIED IN ACCORDANCE WITH RULE 47 (G).

RULE 54

GENERAL RULE

AT THE REQUEST OF EITHER PARTY OR *PROPRIO MOTU*, A JUDGE OR A TRIAL CHAMBER MAY ISSUE SUCH ORDERS, SUMMONSES, SUBPOENAS, WARRANTS AND TRANSFER ORDERS AS MAY BE NECESSARY FOR THE PURPOSES OF AN INVESTIGATION OR FOR THE PREPARATION OR CONDUCT OF THE TRIAL.

I.   COMMENTARY

This rule is used as a residual clause by the Tribunal to support powers not specifically granted by the Statute or Rules. It must be kept in mind, however, that the Tribunal cannot use it rule-making power under Article 15 to grant itself powers which would exceed those granted by the Statute.

The *Blaškić* case provides a good example of the use of the powers conferred by this rule. The Appeals Chamber wrote at length on the subpoena power of the ICTY. The Decision is reported in detail under Article 29.

II.   TRIBUNAL CASES

A.   APPEALS CHAMBER

1. MISCELLANEOUS

PROSECUTOR V. BLAŠKIĆ, *Judgement on the Request of the Republic of Croatia for Review of the Decision of Trial Chamber II of 18 July 1997*, IT-95-14, Cassese, Karibi-Whyte, Li, Stephen & Vohrah, JJ.

On 15 January 1997, Judge McDonald, as confirming Judge on the *Blaškić* Indictment, issued a *subpoena duces tecum* to the Republic of Croatia and its Defence Minister, Mr. Gojko Sušak. The issue found its way to the Trial Chamber which upheld the McDonald subpoena on 18 July 1977. This was then appealed to the Appeals Chamber by the Republic of Croatia. The Appeals Chamber took jurisdiction of the issues and set up a briefing schedule. In addition, the Chamber invited *amici curiae* to submit briefs addressed to the following issues:

1.   The power of a Judge or Trial Chamber of the International Tribunal to issue a *subpoena duces tecum;*

2.   the power of a Judge or Trial Chamber of the International Tribunal to make a request or issue a *subpoena duces tecum* to high government officials of a State;

3.   the appropriate remedies to be taken if there is non-compliance with a *subpoena duces tecum* or request issued by a Judge or Trial Chamber; and

4.   any other issue concerned in this matter, such as the question of the national security interests of a sovereign State.[551]

A complete report on this decision may be found under Rule 29.

PROSECUTOR V. SIMIĆ, *et. al., Decision on Application for Leave to Appeal Against Trial Chamber Decision of 7 March 2000*, IT-95-9-AR73.3, 3 May 2000, Nieto-Navia, Vohrah & Pocar, JJ.

In rejecting the application for leave to appeal, the Appeals Chamber held, *inter alia*, that the Trial Chamber is clearly endowed with the power to issue orders *proprio motu* by virtue of Rule 54 and that in the circumstances of the particular disclosure requested by the Defence, there was nothing improper in the fact that it utilised this power, being satisfied that it was necessary and in the interests of justice to do so for the purposes of the evidentiary hearing on the legality of the arrest of the accused. The Chamber ruled moreover that Rule 66(B) of the Rules did not relate to the material sought by the accused, as it does not relate to the trial of the accused but rather to the issue of the jurisdiction of the Tribunal to try him.[552]

2. RETURN OF MATERIALS DISCLOSED BY THE PROSECUTOR

PROSECUTOR V. KOVAČEVIĆ, *Order Refusing Leave to Appeal*, IT-97-24, 24 September 1998, Shahabuddeen, Wang Tieya & Nieto-Navia, JJ.

The Trial Chamber refused a request by the Prosecutor that all materials furnished by the Prosecutor to the Defence in this case be returned, since the case had concluded. The Prosecutor then sought leave to appeal. A Bench of the Appeals Chamber denied leave to appeal. The Appeals Chamber determined that Rule 73(B) presupposed that the decision was made in a pending case. Since this case was terminated by the death of the accused, the decision complained of could not be appealed. The Chamber was without jurisdiction to hear the appeal. The Bench pointed out that they were not called upon to decide whether there is a right of appeal without leave in this situation.

---

[551] Para. 15.
[552] Page 7.

B.   TRIAL CHAMBERS

1. SUBPOENAS

PROSECUTOR V. KOVAČEVIĆ, *Decision on Defence Motion to Issue Subpoena to United Nations Secretariat*, IT-97-24-T, 1 July 1998, May, Cassese & Mumba, JJ.

The Defence requested the Trial Chamber to issue a Subpoena on the Secretariat of the United Nations for certain documents. The Chamber first determined that the request appeared to be related to matters that were either irrelevant or peripheral to the issues in the case and declined to issue a subpoena or any other kind of binding order. However, the Chamber suggested that the Defence should first request the materials from the United Nations Secretariat, providing them with enough information to be able to identify and locate the documentary items sought. In addition the Chamber ordered:

> If the material is not forthcoming, the Defence may raise the matter again before the Trial Chamber, providing full details of the items sought, their relevance to the matter before the Trial Chamber and their known or presumed location, together with written confirmation of the views of the United Nations Secretariat as to their production.

PROSECUTOR V. KOVAČEVIĆ, *Decision Refusing Defence Motion for Subpoena*, IT-97-24-T, 23 June 1998, May, Cassese & Mumba, JJ.

The Defence requested that a subpoena be issued for the production of documents to the OSCE Mission in Bosnia. The Registry had learned that the OSCE Mission took the position that documents would not be provided to individuals. The Chamber determined that the "International Tribunal has no authority to issue such a subpoena to the OSCE, it being an international organization and not a State.

PROSECUTOR V. DELALIĆ, *et. al., Decision on the Motion Ex Parte by the Defence of Zdravko Mucić concerning the Issue of Subpoena to an Interpreter*, IT-96-21-T, 8 July 1997, Karibi-Whyte, Odio-Benito, & Jan, JJ.

Pursuant to Rule 54, the Trial Chamber held that when a party seeks an Order "for the purposes of an investigation or for the preparation or conduct or the trial," the party seeking the order must satisfy two conditions: it must be necessary for the party to obtain the material and the material must be relevant to the investigation, preparation or conduct of a trial. The Chamber held that the applicant must demonstrate that the evidence sought by way of order must be necessary – not merely useful or helpful –and that there is no other way to obtain the evidence sought.[553]

---

[553] Para. 13. Citing, Prosecutor v Zejnil Delalić *et al, Decision on the Prosecutor's Motion for the Production of*

PROSECUTOR V. DELALIĆ *et. al., Order on the Prosecution's Request for the Issuance of Subpoenae ad testificandum and for an Order to the Government of Bosnia and Herzegovina,* IT-96-21-T, 16 October 1997, Karibi-Whyte, Odio-Benito & Jan, JJ.

This order was made prior to the Subpoena decision in *Blaškić.*[554]

Request to B-H Government

However, the Trial Chamber issued a Request to the Government of Bosnia and Herzegovina (*Request to the Government of Bosnia and Herzegovina,* 16 October 1997) in the following terms:

- To serve *subpoenae ad testificandum* on certain individuals;
- To seek the appearance of these individuals before the Trial Chamber;
- To have a representative of the Government of B-H appear before the Trial Chamber in the event of non-compliance with these requests, to explain why the Requests had not been satisfied.

PROSECUTOR V. DELALIĆ, *et. al., Order on the Motion of the Defence for Hazim Delić for the issuance of Subpoenas,* IT-96-21-T, 25 June 1998, Karibi-Whyte, Odio-Benito & Jan, JJ.

Relying on Rule 54, the Trial Chamber held that it may issue a subpoena to an individual acting in his or her private capacity.

Relying on Article 29 and the *Blaškić* subpoena decision,[555] the Chamber found that a Trial Chamber may make requests to a State seeking assistance in ensuring the presence of an individual ordered to appear before the Trial Chamber by way of a subpoena, failing which the State representative may be called upon by the Trial Chamber to explain the reasons why the individual has not appeared.

The Chamber relied on the following passage from the *Blaskić* subpeona decision:

... The implementing legislation of the International Tribunal's Statute enacted by some States provides that any order or request of the International Tribunal should be addressed to a specific central body of the country, which then channels it to the relevant prosecutorial or judicial agencies. It may be inferred from this that any order or request should therefore be addressed to that central national body.

Notes Exchanged Between Zejnil Delalić and Zdravko Mucić, IT-96-21-T, 11 November 1996.
[554] Prosecutor v. Blaškić, *Judgement on the Request of the Republic of Croatia for Review of the Decision of Trial Chamber II of 18 July 1997,* IT-95-14, 29 October 1997.
[555] *Ibid.*

2. SAFE CONDUCT

PROSECUTOR V DOKMANOVIĆ, *Order on Defence Motion for Safe Conduct,* IT-95-13a-T, 12 June 1998, Cassese, May & Mumba, JJ.

The Trial Chamber cited with approval a decision in the *Tadić* case[556] that established that safe conduct, although not provided for in the Statute, could be ordered under the general power of Rule 54.

The Chamber considered that the physical presence of witnesses before the International Tribunal is of fundamental importance to the administration of justice. The Chamber entered the following Order:

Order

The Witness shall not be prosecuted, detained or subject to any other restriction on his personal liberty while in the Netherlands, or in transit, for the purpose of testifying before the International Tribunal, by or on behalf of the Prosecution, in respect of acts within the jurisdiction of the International Tribunal and allegedly committed prior to his departure from his home country;

The safe conduct shall be limited in time to seven days prior to and seven days after the giving of testimony, subject to the Witness no longer being required by the International Tribunal. In case of illness which prevents the Witness from leaving the Netherlands, the Witness will retain the safe conduct until he is able to travel again and for a period of seven days thereafter, which is required for his return to his home country;

The Witness shall be restricted to travelling between the port of entry or of exit and his or her lodgings, limited movements around the vicinity of the place of lodging, and between the lodgings and the International Tribunal.

PROSECUTOR V. DELALIĆ, *et. al., Order Granting Safe Conduct to Defence Witnesses,* IT-96-21-T, 25 June 1998, Karibi-Whyte, Odio-Benito & Jan, JJ.

This Decision refers to and relies on safe conduct Orders in two other cases.[557]

The Trial Chamber observed that safe conduct is not provided for expressly in the Rules, but it can be ordered under Rule 54. Relying on the *Tadić* Decision, the Chamber found that "an order for safe conduct grants only a very limited immunity from prosecution" and only "with respect to crimes within the jurisdiction of the International Tribunal committed before the witness' arrival at the International Tribunal and only for the time during which the witness is present at the seat of the International Tribunal for the purpose of giving testimony".

The Chamber entered the following Order:

---

[556] Prosecutor v. Tadić, *Decision on Defence Motions to Summon and Protect Defence Witnesses, and on the Giving of Evidence by Video-Link,* IT-94-1-T, 25 June 1996.

[557] Prosecutor v. Tadić, *Decision on the Defence Motion to Summon and Protect Defence Witnesses, and on the Giving of Evidence by Video-Link,* IT-94-1, 25 June 1996, Safe conduct – 15 days prior to and 15 days after the giving of evidence and Prosecutor v. Dokmanović, *Order on Defence Motion for Safe Conduct,* IT-94-13a, 12 June 1998, Safe conduct – 7 days prior to and 7 days after the giving of evidence.

Order

(1) the witnesses named in the Annex to the Motion shall not be prosecuted, detained or subjected to any other restriction on their personal liberty while in the Netherlands, or in transit, for the purpose of testifying in the present case, by or on behalf of the Prosecution, in respect of acts within the jurisdiction of the International Tribunal and allegedly committed prior to their departure from their home country;

(2) the summonses served on the witnesses shall contain the clause that safe conduct does not bar prosecution for offences which the witnesses might commit after their departure from their home country and during their stay in the Netherlands and a further clause which stipulates that no immunity is granted concerning their testimony before the Trial Chamber and that any statement which they give will be recorded and may later be used in evidence against them, subject to the provisions of Sub-Rule 90(F) of the Rules;

(3) the safe conduct shall be limited in time to seven days prior to and seven days after the giving of testimony by each witness, subject to the witnesses no longer being required by the International Tribunal. In case of illness which prevent them from leaving the Netherlands, the witnesses will retain the safe conduct until they are able to travel again and for a period of seven days thereafter, which is required for their return to their home country. If any of the witnesses are detained for a crime which they allegedly committed while in the Netherlands, the safe conduct will run from the date they are released from prison for a period of seven days thereafter, which are required for their return to their home country;

(4) the witnesses shall be restricted to travelling between the port of entry or of exit and their lodgings, limited movements around the vicinity of their place of lodging, and between their lodgings and the International Tribunal.

3. EXPERT WITNESSES – PRODUCTION

PROSECUTOR V. KOVAČEVIĆ, *Decision on Defence Request to Cross-Examine the Prosecutor's Expert Witness*, IT-97-24-T, 3 July 1998, May, Cassese & Mumba, JJ.

The Defence filed a Motion seeking *inter alia,* that expert witness Sophie Hanne Greve be present for purposes of cross-examination; for English language translations of her publications; for the names of witnesses interviewed by her and the times they were interviewed; and for the contemporaneous notes of those interviews.

The Chamber granted the request, in part, as follows:

1.   Sophie Hanne Greve shall be called to testify in person;

2.   the expert witness shall provide to the Defence copies of her publications in the English language as she may be able to locate and produce at the time she testifies;

3.   the expert is not required to disclose the names and times of interview of the witnesses upon whose statements she relied in preparing her report; and

4.   there being no contemporaneous notes of the interviews, the expert cannot be required to disclose them.

4. MOTIONS TO RECONSIDER

PROSECUTOR V. KOVAČEVIĆ, *Decision on Defence Motion to Reconsider,* IT-97-24-T, 30 June 1998, May, Cassese & Mumba, JJ.

The Defence filed a "Motion to Reconsider the Decision to Refuse Defence Motion for Subpoena."
       The Chamber held that "motions to reconsider do not form part of the procedures of the International Tribunal and are not provided for in the Rules of Procedure and Evidence of the International Tribunal."

5. RETURN OF MATERIALS DISCLOSED BY PROSECUTOR

PROSECUTOR V. BRĐANIN & TALIĆ, *Decision on Motion by Prosecution for Protective Measures,* IT-99-36-PT, 3 July 2000, Hunt, Mumba & Pocar, JJ.

The Chamber rejected the request of the Prosecutor that the defence be ordered to return to the Registry all non-public documents provided to it by the Prosecutor at the close of the proceedings. The Chamber ruled that once such documents are disclosed to the Defence and have notes made upon them by counsel, they become "work product" and are therefore privileged documents. In addition, the Chamber wrote:

> The Trial Chamber does not accept that the likely risk of either deliberate or unintentional disclosure after the conclusion of the case is of such significance as to justify the unwieldy and possibly unfair consequences of an order that the documents be returned in every case. The fact that orders for the return of statements have been made in similarly general terms in other cases does not impress the Trial Chamber, as the present case appears to be the first in which objection has been taken to orders of the nature sought in this case, and the first in which there has been any examination of what is involved in those orders.

>   The Trial Chamber is prepared to make an order . . . that if a member of the Brđanin and Talić Defence team withdraws from the case, all the material in his or her possession shall be returned to the lead defence counsel.[558]

---

[558] Paras. 43-44.

The Chamber did acknowledge that there might be instances when document return orders are appropriate, but it should be considered only at the end of the trial when the risk involved may be more easily identified.[559]

PROSECUTOR V. KOVAČEVIĆ, *Order Denying Request for Return of Materials*, IT-97-24, 24 August 1998, May, Cassese & Mumba, JJ.

After the proceedings against Kovačević were terminated, the Prosecutor filed a Motion asking the Chamber to order the return of all materials provided by the Prosecutor to the Defence pursuant to Rule 66 and 68 of the Rules of Procedure and Evidence. The Chamber denied the request as not being "in keeping with the usual practice of the Tribunal or domestic jurisdictions." The Chamber further noted that no notice was given to the Defence that the materials would need to be returned in the event that the trial did not proceed. Finally, the Chamber said "it would now be difficult and time-consuming for the Defence to comply with the Request, especially since the Defence may have marked or otherwise annotated the materials."[560]

6. JUDICIAL ASSISTANCE

PROSECUTOR V. SIMIĆ, *et. al., Order on Defence Requests for Judicial Assistance for the Production of Information*, IT-95-9-PT, 7 March 2000, Robinson, Hunt & Bennouna, JJ

Pursuant to Rule 54, the Trial Chamber ordered the Prosecution to disclose information and documents in connection with an evidentiary hearing to be held regarding the legality of the arrest of the accused Todorović and his application for an order directing the Prosecutor to forthwith return him to the country of refuge and his Petition for a Writ of *Habeas Corpus*. The Order issued by the Chamber provided, *inter alia*, that the Prosecution must disclose to the defence the following items relating to the initial detention and arrest of Todorović on or about 26 and 27 September 1998, at the Tuzla Air Force base in Bosnia and Herzegovina: all correspondence and reports of SFOR relating to the apprehension of Todorović; all audio and video tapes made by SFOR of the initial detention and arrest of Todorović; all audio or video tapes made by the Prosecution of the detention and arrest of Todorović; all SFOR pre- and post-arrest operations reports relating to the arrest and detention of Todorović; the identity of the individual or individuals who transported Todorović by helicopter to the Tuzla Air Force base, who placed him under arrest and served him with an arrest warrant from the International Tribunal and who represented the Prosecutor at time of his arrest.[561]

    The Chamber granted the request for disclosure on the basis that the accused had made a *prima facie* showing that the requested evidence was in the custody or control of the Prosecution, he identified expressly and precisely the legitimate forensic purpose for

---

[559] Para 44.
[560] The Prosecutor made an effort to appeal this decision. See the report above.
[561] Pg. 3.

which access is sought and he demonstrated that production of the material is likely to assist materially in the presentation of the case relating to his arrest and his request for release.[562]

7. DOCUMENTS USED BY A WITNESS IN PREPARATION FOR TESTIMONY

PROSECUTOR V. BLAŠKIĆ, *Order for the Production of Documents Used to Prepare for Testimony,* IT-95-14, 22 April 1999, Jorda, Shahabuddeen & Rodrigues, JJ.

At trial, the defendant, Blaškić, testified at length and in great detail. During the testimony Blaškić revealed that in preparation for his testimony he relied on a war diary prepared by his deputy and a military log of his activities at his headquarters.

On its own, the Trial Chamber ordered the production of the war diary and the military log by the Defence. The Chamber said that it "deems it appropriate, in the interest of justice and so that it be better able to ascertain the truth" that it should have the war diary and military log produced. The Chamber ordered both the Defence and the Federation of Bosnia and Herzegovina to produce the documents.

---

[562] Pg. 3.

RULE 54 *BIS*

ORDERS DIRECTED TO STATES FOR THE PRODUCTION OF DOCUMENTS

(A)   A PARTY REQUESTING AN ORDER UNDER RULE 54 THAT A STATE PRODUCE DOCUMENTS OR INFORMATION SHALL APPLY IN WRITING TO THE RELEVANT JUDGE OR TRIAL CHAMBER AND SHALL:

       (I)   IDENTIFY AS FAR AS POSSIBLE THE DOCUMENTS OR INFORMATION TO WHICH THE APPLICATION RELATES;

       (II)   INDICATE HOW THEY ARE RELEVANT TO ANY MATTER IN ISSUE BEFORE THE JUDGE OR TRIAL CHAMBER AND NECESSARY FOR A FAIR DETERMINATION OF THAT MATTER; AND

       (III)   EXPLAIN THE STEPS THAT HAVE BEEN TAKEN BY THE APPLICANT TO SECURE THE STATE'S ASSISTANCE.

(B)   THE JUDGE OR TRIAL CHAMBER MAY REJECT AN APPLICATION UNDER SUB-RULE (A) *IN LIMINE* IF SATISFIED THAT:

       (I) THE DOCUMENTS OR INFORMATION ARE NOT RELEVANT TO ANY MATTER IN ISSUE IN THE PROCEEDINGS BEFORE THEM OR ARE NOT NECESSARY FOR A FAIR DETERMINATION OF ANY SUCH MATTER; OR

       (II) NO REASONABLE STEPS HAVE BEEN TAKEN BY THE APPLICANT TO OBTAIN THE DOCUMENTS OR INFORMATION FROM THE STATE.

(C)   A DECISION BY A JUDGE OR A TRIAL CHAMBER UNDER SUB-RULE (B) TO REJECT AN APPLICATION SHALL BE SUBJECT TO APPEAL PURSUANT TO RULE 116 *BIS*.

(D)   EXCEPT IN CASES WHERE A DECISION HAS BEEN TAKEN PURSUANT TO SUB-RULE (B), OR SUB-RULE (E), THE STATE CONCERNED SHALL BE GIVEN NOTICE OF THE APPLICATION, AND NOT LESS THAN FIFTEEN DAYS' NOTICE OF THE HEARING OF THE APPLICATION, AT WHICH THE STATE SHALL HAVE AN OPPORTUNITY TO BE HEARD.

(E)   IF, HAVING REGARD TO ALL CIRCUMSTANCES, THE JUDGE OR TRIAL CHAMBER HAS GOOD REASONS FOR SO DOING, THE JUDGE OR TRIAL CHAMBER MAY MAKE AN ORDER TO WHICH THIS RULE APPLIES WITHOUT GIVING THE STATE CONCERNED NOTICE OR THE OPPORTUNITY TO BE HEARD UNDER SUB-RULE (D), AND THE FOLLOWING PROVISIONS SHALL APPLY TO SUCH AN ORDER:

       (I)   THE ORDER SHALL BE SERVED ON THE STATE CONCERNED;

       (II)   SUBJECT TO PARAGRAPH (IV), THE ORDER SHALL NOT HAVE EFFECT UNTIL FIFTEEN DAYS AFTER SUCH SERVICE;

       (III)   A STATE MAY, WITHIN FIFTEEN DAYS OF SERVICE OF THE ORDER, APPLY BY NOTICE TO THE JUDGE OR TRIAL CHAMBER TO HAVE THE ORDER SET ASIDE, ON THE GROUNDS THAT DISCLOSURE WOULD PREJUDICE NATIONAL SECURITY INTERESTS. SUB-RULE (F) SHALL APPLY TO SUCH A NOTICE AS IT DOES TO A NOTICE OF OBJECTION;

(IV)   WHERE NOTICE IS GIVEN UNDER PARAGRAPH (III), THE ORDER SHALL THEREUPON BE STAYED UNTIL THE DECISION ON THE APPLICATION;

(V)   SUB-RULES (F) AND (G) SHALL APPLY TO THE DETERMINATION OF AN APPLICATION MADE PURSUANT TO PARAGRAPH (III) AS THEY DO TO THE DETERMINATION OF AN APPLICATION OF WHICH NOTICE IS GIVEN PURSUANT TO SUB-RULE (D);

(VI)   THE STATE AND THE PARTY WHO APPLIED FOR THE ORDER SHALL, SUBJECT TO ANY SPECIAL MEASURES MADE PURSUANT TO A REQUEST UNDER SUB-RULES (F) OR (G), HAVE AN OPPORTUNITY TO BE HEARD AT THE HEARING OF AN APPLICATION MADE PURSUANT TO PARAGRAPH (III) OF THIS SUB-RULE.

(F)   THE STATE, IF IT RAISES AN OBJECTION PURSUANT TO SUB-RULE (D), ON THE GROUNDS THAT DISCLOSURE WOULD PREJUDICE ITS NATIONAL SECURITY INTERESTS, SHALL FILE A NOTICE OF OBJECTION NOT LESS THAN FIVE DAYS BEFORE THE DATE FIXED FOR THE HEARING, SPECIFYING THE GROUNDS OF OBJECTION. IN ITS NOTICE OF OBJECTION THE STATE:

(I)   SHALL IDENTIFY, AS FAR AS POSSIBLE, THE BASIS UPON WHICH IT CLAIMS THAT ITS NATIONAL SECURITY INTERESTS WILL BE PREJUDICED; AND

(II)   MAY REQUEST THE JUDGE OR TRIAL CHAMBER TO DIRECT THAT APPROPRIATE PROTECTIVE MEASURES BE MADE FOR THE HEARING OF THE OBJECTION, INCLUDING IN PARTICULAR:

(A)   HEARING THE OBJECTION IN CAMERA AND *EX PARTE*;

(B)   ALLOWING DOCUMENTS TO BE SUBMITTED IN REDACTED FORM, ACCOMPANIED BY AN AFFIDAVIT SIGNED BY A SENIOR STATE OFFICIAL EXPLAINING THE REASONS FOR THE REDACTION;

(C)   ORDERING THAT NO TRANSCRIPTS BE MADE OF THE HEARING AND THAT DOCUMENTS NOT FURTHER REQUIRED BY THE TRIBUNAL BE RETURNED DIRECTLY TO THE STATE WITHOUT BEING FILED WITH THE REGISTRY OR OTHERWISE RETAINED.

(G)   WITH REGARD TO THE PROCEDURE UNDER SUB-RULE (F) ABOVE, THE JUDGE OR TRIAL CHAMBER MAY ORDER THE FOLLOWING PROTECTIVE MEASURES FOR THE HEARING OF THE OBJECTION:

(I)   THE DESIGNATION OF A SINGLE JUDGE FROM A CHAMBER TO EXAMINE THE DOCUMENTS OR HEAR SUBMISSIONS; AND/OR

(II)   THAT THE STATE BE ALLOWED TO PROVIDE ITS OWN INTERPRETERS FOR THE HEARING AND ITS OWN TRANSLATIONS OF SENSITIVE DOCUMENTS.

(H)   REJECTION OF AN APPLICATION MADE UNDER THIS RULE SHALL NOT PRECLUDE A SUBSEQUENT APPLICATION BY THE REQUESTING PARTY IN RESPECT OF THE SAME DOCUMENTS OR INFORMATION IF NEW CIRCUMSTANCES ARISE.

(I)   AN ORDER UNDER THIS RULE MAY PROVIDE FOR THE DOCUMENTS OR INFORMATION IN QUESTION TO BE PRODUCED BY THE STATE UNDER APPROPRIATE ARRANGEMENTS TO PROTECT ITS INTERESTS, WHICH MAY INCLUDE THOSE ARRANGEMENTS SPECIFIED IN SUB-RULES (F)(II) OR (G).

I.   COMMENTARY

This Rule came in to force on 7 December 1999. The Rule creates procedures for requesting the production of documents from States. It sets out the manner in which such a request shall be made, the appeal procedures, and the rights of parties, including States to be heard. It is derived directly from the *Blaškić* Decision regarding subpoenas, reported in detail under Article 29.

RULE 55

EXECUTION OF ARREST WARRANTS

(A)   A WARRANT OF ARREST SHALL BE SIGNED BY A JUDGE. IT SHALL INCLUDE AN ORDER FOR THE PROMPT TRANSFER OF THE ACCUSED TO THE TRIBUNAL UPON THE ARREST OF THE ACCUSED.

(B)   THE ORIGINAL WARRANT SHALL BE RETAINED BY THE REGISTRAR, WHO SHALL PREPARE CERTIFIED COPIES BEARING THE SEAL OF THE TRIBUNAL.

(C)   EACH CERTIFIED COPY SHALL BE ACCOMPANIED BY A COPY OF THE INDICTMENT CERTIFIED IN ACCORDANCE WITH RULE 47 (G) AND A STATEMENT OF THE RIGHTS OF THE ACCUSED SET FORTH IN ARTICLE 21 OF THE STATUTE, AND IN RULES 42 AND 43 *MUTATIS MUTANDIS*. IF THE ACCUSED DOES NOT UNDERSTAND EITHER OF THE OFFICIAL LANGUAGES OF THE TRIBUNAL AND IF THE LANGUAGE UNDERSTOOD BY THE ACCUSED IS KNOWN TO THE REGISTRAR, EACH CERTIFIED COPY OF THE WARRANT OF ARREST SHALL ALSO BE ACCOMPANIED BY A TRANSLATION OF THE STATEMENT OF THE RIGHTS OF THE ACCUSED IN THAT LANGUAGE.

(D)   SUBJECT TO ANY ORDER OF A JUDGE OR CHAMBER, THE REGISTRAR MAY TRANSMIT A CERTIFIED COPY OF A WARRANT OF ARREST TO THE PERSON OR AUTHORITIES TO WHICH IT IS ADDRESSED, INCLUDING THE NATIONAL AUTHORITIES OF A STATE IN WHOSE TERRITORY OR UNDER WHOSE JURISDICTION THE ACCUSED RESIDES, OR WAS LAST KNOWN TO BE, OR IS BELIEVED BY THE REGISTRAR TO BE LIKELY TO BE FOUND.

(E)   THE REGISTRAR SHALL INSTRUCT THE PERSON OR AUTHORITIES TO WHICH A WARRANT IS TRANSMITTED THAT AT THE TIME OF ARREST THE INDICTMENT AND THE STATEMENT OF THE RIGHTS OF THE ACCUSED BE READ TO THE ACCUSED IN A LANGUAGE THAT HE OR SHE UNDERSTANDS AND THAT THE ACCUSED BE CAUTIONED IN THAT LANGUAGE THAT THE ACCUSED HAS THE RIGHT TO REMAIN SILENT, AND THAT ANY STATEMENT HE OR SHE MAKES SHALL BE RECORDED AND MAY BE USED IN EVIDENCE.

(F)   NOTWITHSTANDING SUB-RULE (E), IF AT THE TIME OF ARREST THE ACCUSED IS SERVED WITH, OR WITH A TRANSLATION OF, THE INDICTMENT AND THE STATEMENT OF RIGHTS OF THE ACCUSED IN A LANGUAGE THAT THE ACCUSED UNDERSTANDS AND IS ABLE TO READ, THESE NEED NOT BE READ TO THE ACCUSED AT THE TIME OF ARREST.

(G)   WHEN AN ARREST WARRANT ISSUED BY THE TRIBUNAL IS EXECUTED BY THE AUTHORITIES OF A STATE, OR AN APPROPRIATE AUTHORITY OR INTERNATIONAL BODY, A MEMBER OF THE OFFICE OF THE PROSECUTOR MAY BE PRESENT AS FROM THE TIME OF THE ARREST.

II.   TRIBUNAL CASES

B.   TRIAL CHAMBERS

PROSECUTOR V. DOKMANOVIĆ, *Decision on the Motion for Release by the Accused Slavko Dokmanović*, IT-95-13a-PT, 22 October 1997, McDonald, Odio-Benito & Jan, JJ.

The Trial Chamber found that the Statute and the Rules provide for alternative procedures for securing the presence of accused persons before the Tribunal.[563] Pursuant to Article 29 and Rule 55 the primary method of arrest and transfer of persons to the Tribunal is through State cooperation. The Chamber found that Article 29 imposes a binding obligation on States to cooperate with the Tribunal by affording it complete judicial assistance. This does not, however, preclude the arrest and transfer of accused persons by other methods. Rule 59 *bis* was adopted within the parameters of Articles 19 and 20 of the Statute to provide for a mechanism additional to that of Rule 55. The Chamber observed that although the Rules cannot extend the powers of the Tribunal beyond those envisaged in the Statute, the enactment of a Rule that is not in violation of the Statute and comports with its spirit could only be regarded as legitimate.[564]

Article 29 sets out the general obligation of all States to cooperate with the Tribunal and afford it complete judicial assistance. Pursuant to United Nations Security Council Resolution 827 (25 May 1993), which adopted the Statute of the Tribunal, all States are required to cooperate with the Tribunal and take all necessary measures under their domestic law to implement the Statute and comply with those orders issued by a Trial Chamber under Article 29.[565]

In addition, Article 29(2)(d) and (e) provides that States must comply with orders for the arrest or detention of persons and their surrender or transfer. The Chamber referred to the Report of the Secretary-General which emphasizes that the establishment of the Tribunal on the basis of a Chapter VII decision creates a binding obligation on all States to take whatever steps are required to implement the decision and that an order by a Trial Chamber for the surrender or transfer of persons to the custody of the Tribunal shall be considered to be the application of an enforcement measure under Chapter VII of the Charter of the United Nations.[566]

Rule 59 *bis* provides that once an arrest warrant has been transmitted to an international authority, an international body, or the Office of the Prosecutor, the accused person named therein may be taken into custody without the involvement of the State in which he or she is located. The Chamber found that the procedure established by Rule 59 *bis* is valid and fully supported by the terms of the Statute.[567]

---

[563] Para. 34.
[564] Para. 35 and 40.
[565] Para. 35.
[566] Para. 35.
[567] Para. 36.

The Judges observed that Article 19(2) confers upon the Judge who has confirmed an indictment the power to issue orders and warrants for arrest, detention, surrender or transfer of persons, and any other orders as may be required for the conduct of the trial. This power, phrased in discretionary terms, indicates that Article 19(2) does not contemplate that arrest warrants may only be directed to States. The Chamber regarded Rule 59 *bis* as giving effect to Article 19(2). It permits a decision by the confirming Judge that requires that entities other than States receive and execute warrants for the arrest, detention and transfer of accused persons.[568]

The Chamber found that Rule 59 *bis* could be applied in the light of the provision of Article 20(2) regarding the procedure to be followed after the confirmation of an indictment. The Chamber observed that the plain language of Article 20(2) only contemplates that an accused person shall be taken into custody, informed of the charges against him, and transferred to the Tribunal. No mention is made of States, nor is any limitation placed upon the authority of an international body or the Prosecutor to participate in the arrest process.[569]

The Chamber concluded that Rule 59 *bis* is clear in its terms and is supported by the Statute of the Tribunal. It must, therefore, be considered to be valid and supplementary to Rule 55. Indeed, Rule 59 *bis* explicitly provides that it applies "notwithstanding Rules 55 to 59," indicating further that what was contemplated was an additional mechanism.[570]

The accused had complained that his arrest by UNTAES was illegal. The Chamber determined that UNTAES is an international authority within the meaning of Rule 59 *bis* and it was executing its mandate to cooperate with the Tribunal by affecting the arrest of the accused.[571]

The arrest in this case was accomplished pursuant to Rule 59 *bis* and the presence of the OTP when the arrest was executed is also explicitly contemplated in Rule 55(C). Although the arrest warrant directs UNTAES to search for, arrest and transfer the accused to the Tribunal and to inform him promptly of his rights and the nature of the charges against him, it was actually the OTP that informed the accused of his rights and of the nature of the charges. What is imperative, however, is that the accused be informed of his rights and the charges against him and this was done. Clearly the OTP has the authority to do this.[572]

The Chamber noted that neither the Statute nor the Rules entitle the accused to receive a copy of the warrant for his arrest in his own language. Under Rule 55, the accused must be read the indictment and his rights in a language that he understands and be cautioned in that language. Under Rule 59 *bis* the accused is entitled to be informed of the charges against him in a language that he understands, and of the fact that he is being transferred to the Tribunal, when he is taken into custody. Upon his transfer he must have the indictment, a statement of his rights, and his caution read to him in such a language.

---

[568] Para. 37.
[569] Para. 38.
[570] Para. 41.
[571] Para. 49.
[572] Para. 51.

The fact that the Prosecution provided the accused with a copy of the arrest warrant was a matter solely at its discretion. Furthermore, the official version of an arrest warrant is signed by a judge of the Tribunal in one of the official languages of the Tribunal and the translation into Serbo-Croatian bears no official status.[573]

Method of Arrest

The Chamber found that the use of trickery and ruse to lure an indictee into a situation where he may be arrested does not amount to a forcible abduction or kidnapping and such techniques for affecting arrest are consistent with principles of international law.[574]

The accused entered the UNTAES Vehicle that carried him to the Erdut base in Croatia of his own free will. He was actually eager to get into the vehicle due to his belief that he was going to a meeting to discuss his property rights in the UNTAES administered territory of Eastern Slavonia.

Since the Chamber found that the particular method used to arrest and detain the accused was justified and legal, it did not decide whether the International Tribunal has the authority to exercise jurisdiction over a defendant illegally obtained from abroad.[575]

---

[573] Para. 56.
[574] Para. 57.
[575] Para. 78.

RULE 56

COOPERATION OF STATES

THE STATE TO WHICH A WARRANT OF ARREST OR A TRANSFER ORDER FOR A WITNESS IS TRANSMITTED SHALL ACT PROMPTLY AND WITH ALL DUE DILIGENCE TO ENSURE PROPER AND EFFECTIVE EXECUTION THEREOF, IN ACCORDANCE WITH ARTICLE 29 OF THE STATUTE.

RULE 57

PROCEDURE AFTER ARREST

UPON ARREST, THE ACCUSED SHALL BE DETAINED BY THE STATE CONCERNED WHICH SHALL PROMPTLY NOTIFY THE REGISTRAR. THE TRANSFER OF THE ACCUSED TO THE SEAT OF THE TRIBUNAL SHALL BE ARRANGED BETWEEN THE STATE AUTHORITIES CONCERNED, THE AUTHORITIES OF THE HOST COUNTRY AND THE REGISTRAR.

RULE 58

NATIONAL EXTRADITION PROVISIONS

THE OBLIGATIONS LAID DOWN IN ARTICLE 29 OF THE STATUTE SHALL PREVAIL OVER ANY LEGAL IMPEDIMENT TO THE SURRENDER OR TRANSFER OF THE ACCUSED OR OF A WITNESS TO THE TRIBUNAL WHICH MAY EXIST UNDER THE NATIONAL LAW OR EXTRADITION TREATIES OF THE STATE CONCERNED.

RULE 59

FAILURE TO EXECUTE A WARRANT OR TRANSFER ORDER

(A)   WHERE THE STATE TO WHICH A WARRANT OF ARREST OR TRANSFER ORDER HAS BEEN TRANSMITTED HAS BEEN UNABLE TO EXECUTE THE WARRANT, IT SHALL REPORT FORTHWITH ITS INABILITY TO THE REGISTRAR, AND THE REASONS THEREFOR.

(B)   IF, WITHIN A REASONABLE TIME AFTER THE WARRANT OF ARREST OR TRANSFER ORDER HAS BEEN TRANSMITTED TO THE STATE, NO REPORT IS MADE ON ACTION TAKEN, THIS SHALL BE DEEMED A FAILURE TO EXECUTE THE WARRANT OF ARREST OR TRANSFER ORDER AND THE TRIBUNAL, THROUGH THE PRESIDENT, MAY NOTIFY THE SECURITY COUNCIL ACCORDINGLY.

RULE 59 *BIS*

TRANSMISSION OF ARREST WARRANTS

(A)   NOTWITHSTANDING RULES 55 TO 59, ON THE ORDER OF A JUDGE, THE REGISTRAR SHALL TRANSMIT TO AN APPROPRIATE AUTHORITY OR INTERNATIONAL BODY OR THE PROSECUTOR A COPY OF A WARRANT FOR THE ARREST OF AN ACCUSED, ON SUCH TERMS AS THE JUDGE MAY DETERMINE, TOGETHER WITH AN ORDER FOR THE PROMPT TRANSFER OF THE ACCUSED TO THE TRIBUNAL IN THE EVENT THAT THE ACCUSED BE TAKEN INTO CUSTODY BY THAT AUTHORITY OR INTERNATIONAL BODY OR THE PROSECUTOR.

(B)   AT THE TIME OF BEING TAKEN INTO CUSTODY AN ACCUSED SHALL BE INFORMED IMMEDIATELY, IN A LANGUAGE THE ACCUSED UNDERSTANDS, OF THE CHARGES AGAINST HIM OR HER AND OF THE FACT THAT HE OR SHE IS BEING TRANSFERRED TO THE TRIBUNAL. UPON SUCH TRANSFER, THE INDICTMENT AND A STATEMENT OF THE RIGHTS OF THE ACCUSED SHALL BE READ TO THE ACCUSED AND THE ACCUSED SHALL BE CAUTIONED IN SUCH A LANGUAGE.

(C)   NOTWITHSTANDING SUB-RULE (B), THE INDICTMENT AND STATEMENT OF RIGHTS OF THE ACCUSED NEED NOT BE READ TO THE ACCUSED IF THE ACCUSED IS SERVED WITH THESE, OR WITH A TRANSLATION OF THESE, IN A LANGUAGE THE ACCUSED UNDERSTANDS AND IS ABLE TO READ.

I.   COMMENTARY

See, Rule 55, re: Prosecutor v. Dokmanović, *Decision on the motion for release by the accused Slavko Dokmanović*, IT-95-13a-PT, 22 October 1997.

RULE 60

ADVERTISEMENT OF INDICTMENT

AT THE REQUEST OF THE PROSECUTOR, A FORM OF ADVERTISEMENT SHALL BE TRANSMITTED BY THE REGISTRAR TO THE NATIONAL AUTHORITIES OF ANY STATE OR STATES, FOR PUBLICATION IN NEWSPAPERS OR FOR BROADCAST VIA RADIO AND TELEVISION, NOTIFYING PUBLICLY THE EXISTENCE OF AN INDICTMENT AND CALLING UPON THE ACCUSED TO SURRENDER TO THE TRIBUNAL AND INVITING ANY PERSON WITH INFORMATION AS TO THE WHEREABOUTS OF THE ACCUSED TO COMMUNICATE THAT INFORMATION TO THE TRIBUNAL.

RULE 61

PROCEDURE IN CASE OF FAILURE TO EXECUTE A WARRANT

(A)   IF, WITHIN A REASONABLE TIME, A WARRANT OF ARREST HAS NOT BEEN EXECUTED, AND PERSONAL SERVICE OF THE INDICTMENT HAS CONSEQUENTLY NOT BEEN EFFECTED, THE JUDGE WHO CONFIRMED THE INDICTMENT SHALL INVITE THE PROSECUTOR TO REPORT ON THE MEASURES TAKEN. WHEN THE JUDGE IS SATISFIED THAT:

   (I)   THE REGISTRAR AND THE PROSECUTOR HAVE TAKEN ALL REASONABLE STEPS TO SECURE THE ARREST OF THE ACCUSED, INCLUDING RECOURSE TO THE APPROPRIATE AUTHORITIES OF THE STATE IN WHOSE TERRITORY OR UNDER WHOSE JURISDICTION AND CONTROL THE PERSON TO BE SERVED RESIDES OR WAS LAST KNOWN TO THEM TO BE; AND

   (II)   IF THE WHEREABOUTS OF THE ACCUSED ARE UNKNOWN, THE PROSECUTOR AND THE REGISTRAR HAVE TAKEN ALL REASONABLE STEPS TO ASCERTAIN THOSE WHEREABOUTS, INCLUDING BY SEEKING PUBLICATION OF ADVERTISEMENTS PURSUANT TO RULE 60, THE JUDGE SHALL ORDER THAT THE INDICTMENT BE SUBMITTED BY THE PROSECUTOR TO THE TRIAL CHAMBER OF WHICH THE JUDGE IS A MEMBER.

(B)   UPON OBTAINING SUCH AN ORDER THE PROSECUTOR SHALL SUBMIT THE INDICTMENT TO THE TRIAL CHAMBER IN OPEN COURT, TOGETHER WITH ALL THE EVIDENCE THAT WAS BEFORE THE JUDGE WHO INITIALLY CONFIRMED THE INDICTMENT. THE PROSECUTOR MAY ALSO CALL BEFORE THE TRIAL CHAMBER AND EXAMINE ANY WITNESS WHOSE STATEMENT HAS BEEN SUBMITTED TO THE CONFIRMING JUDGE. IN ADDITION, THE TRIAL CHAMBER MAY REQUEST THE PROSECUTOR TO CALL ANY OTHER WITNESS WHOSE STATEMENT HAS BEEN SUBMITTED TO THE CONFIRMING JUDGE.

(C)   IF THE TRIAL CHAMBER IS SATISFIED ON THAT EVIDENCE, TOGETHER WITH SUCH ADDITIONAL EVIDENCE AS THE PROSECUTOR MAY TENDER, THAT THERE ARE REASONABLE GROUNDS FOR BELIEVING THAT THE ACCUSED HAS COMMITTED ALL OR ANY OF THE CRIMES CHARGED IN THE INDICTMENT, IT SHALL SO DETERMINE. THE TRIAL CHAMBER SHALL HAVE THE RELEVANT PARTS OF THE INDICTMENT READ OUT BY THE PROSECUTOR TOGETHER WITH AN ACCOUNT OF THE EFFORTS TO EFFECT SERVICE REFERRED TO IN SUB-RULE (A) ABOVE.

(D)   THE TRIAL CHAMBER SHALL ALSO ISSUE AN INTERNATIONAL ARREST WARRANT IN RESPECT OF THE ACCUSED WHICH SHALL BE TRANSMITTED TO ALL STATES. UPON REQUEST BY THE PROSECUTOR OR *PROPRIO MOTU*, AFTER HAVING HEARD THE PROSECUTOR, THE TRIAL CHAMBER MAY ORDER A STATE OR STATES TO ADOPT PROVISIONAL MEASURES TO FREEZE THE ASSETS OF THE ACCUSED, WITHOUT PREJUDICE TO THE RIGHTS OF THIRD PARTIES.

(E)   IF THE PROSECUTOR SATISFIES THE TRIAL CHAMBER THAT THE FAILURE TO EFFECT PERSONAL SERVICE WAS DUE IN WHOLE OR IN PART TO A FAILURE OR REFUSAL OF A STATE TO COOPERATE WITH THE TRIBUNAL IN ACCORDANCE WITH ARTICLE 29 OF THE STATUTE, THE TRIAL CHAMBER SHALL SO CERTIFY. AFTER CONSULTING THE PRESIDING JUDGES OF THE CHAMBERS, THE PRESIDENT SHALL NOTIFY THE SECURITY COUNCIL THEREOF IN SUCH MANNER AS THE PRESIDENT THINKS FIT.

I.   COMMENTARY

When the Rule 61 mechanism is triggered, a hearing may be held, during which evidence is brought by the Prosecution which may result in a finding by the Trial Chamber that there are reasonable grounds for believing that the accused committed the crime(s) charged. The Chamber then issues an international arrest warrant for the accused and may request the President to notify the Security Council that the State which has received the warrant for the arrest and transfer has not complied with its obligations. Such notification has occurred in relation to the *Nikolić* case (IT-94-Z-R6 1) (non-cooperation of the Bosnian Serb administration), the *Rajić* case (IT-95-12-R61) (non-cooperation. of Bosnia and Herzegovina and the Republic of Croatia), the *Karadžić* and *Mladić* case (IT-95 I I-R6 1 and IT-95- 1 S-R6 1) (non-cooperation of the FRY and the *Republika Srpska*). The *Mrksić, Radić and Sljivancanin* case (IT-95-l3-R61), (non-cooperation of the FRY) and the *Martić* case (IT-95-l I-R61).

RULE 62

INITIAL APPEARANCE OF ACCUSED

UPON TRANSFER OF AN ACCUSED TO THE SEAT OF THE TRIBUNAL, THE PRESIDENT SHALL FORTHWITH ASSIGN THE CASE TO A TRIAL CHAMBER. THE ACCUSED SHALL BE BROUGHT BEFORE THAT TRIAL CHAMBER WITHOUT DELAY, AND SHALL BE FORMALLY CHARGED. THE TRIAL CHAMBER OR THE JUDGE SHALL:

(I)   SATISFY HIMSELF OR HERSELF THAT THE RIGHT OF THE ACCUSED TO COUNSEL IS RESPECTED;

(II)   READ OR HAVE THE INDICTMENT READ TO THE ACCUSED IN A LANGUAGE THE ACCUSED SPEAKS AND UNDERSTANDS, AND SATISFY HIMSELF OR HERSELF THAT THE ACCUSED UNDERSTANDS THE INDICTMENT;

(III)   INFORM THE ACCUSED THAT, WITHIN THIRTY DAYS OF THE INITIAL APPEARANCE, HE OR SHE WILL BE CALLED UPON TO ENTER A PLEA OF GUILTY OR NOT GUILTY ON EACH COUNT, BUT THAT, SHOULD THE ACCUSED SO REQUEST, HE OR SHE MAY IMMEDIATELY ENTER A PLEA OF GUILTY OR NOT GUILTY ON ONE OR MORE COUNT;

(IV)   IF THE ACCUSED FAILS TO ENTER A PLEA AT THE INITIAL OR ANY FURTHER APPEARANCE, ENTER A PLEA OF NOT GUILTY ON THE ACCUSED'S BEHALF,

(V)   IN CASE OF A PLEA OF NOT GUILTY, INSTRUCT THE REGISTRAR TO SET A DATE FOR TRIAL;

(VI)   IN CASE OF A PLEA OF GUILTY:

     (A)   IF BEFORE THE TRIAL CHAMBER, ACT IN ACCORDANCE WITH RULE 62 *BIS*, OR

     (B)   IF BEFORE A JUDGE, REFER THE PLEA TO THE TRIAL CHAMBER SO THAT IT MAY ACT IN ACCORDANCE WITH RULE 62 *BIS*;

(VII)   INSTRUCT THE REGISTRAR TO SET SUCH OTHER DATES AS APPROPRIATE.

I.   COMMENTARY

The Appeals Chamber Judgement in the *Erdemović* case is notable for many reasons, not least of which was the disagreement amoung the judges with regard to several issues. There was no single majority opinion of all the judges. The judgement, as a result, has limited precedential value other than with regard to those specific legal issues upon which a majority of the judges were in agreement. There is an opinion by Judges McDonald and Vohrah. There are dissenting opinions of Judge Li, Judge Cassese and

Judge Stephen. There is no opinion signed by a majority of the Judges. Four Judges agreed, for different reasons, that the plea was not informed and that a new sentencing hearing was necessary. Three Judges supported the proposition enunciated by McDonald and Vohrah that the plea was not equivocal.

II.   TRIBUNAL CASES

A.   APPEALS CHAMBER

PROSECUTOR V. ERDEMOVIĆ, *Judgement,* IT-96-22-A, 7 October 1997, McDonald, Cassese, Stephen, Vohrah & Li, JJ.

Guilty Pleas

Voluntariness

On this appeal Judges McDonald and Vohrah first considered the issue of whether a guilty plea is voluntary. They first determined that all common law jurisdictions require that a guilty plea be voluntary. According to these judges, voluntariness requires two elements. First, "an accused person must have been mentally competent to understand the consequences of his actions when pleading guilty;" and second, "the plea must not have been the result of any threat or inducement other than the expectation of receiving credit for a guilty plea by way of some reduction of sentence."[576]

Informed Plea

"[A]n accused who pleads guilty must understand the nature and consequences of his plea and to what precisely he is pleading guilty."[577] According to Judges McDonald and Vohrah, an informed plea is one in which it can be shown that the accused: (1) understands "the nature of the charges against him and the consequences of pleading guilty generally; and" (2) "the nature and distinction between the alternative charges and the consequences of pleading guilty to one rather than the other."[578] Judges McDonald and Vohrah, joined by Judges Stephen and Cassese held that the Defendant did not enter an informed plea in that it was not clear to him the difference between the seriousness of a war crime and a crime against humanity. Having pleaded guilty to a crime against humanity he unwittingly pleaded guilty to the more serious crime.[579]

Equivocal Plea

An equivocal guilty plea is one in which, while pleading guilty, the defendant offers an

---

[576] Para. 10.
[577] Para. 14.
[578] *Ibid.*
[579] Para. 27.

explanation for his conduct that, if established, would amount to a complete defence against the charge. Erdemović, during his guilty plea, indicated that he committed the acts charged while under duress. If duress were a complete defence, the plea would have been equivocal and should not have been accepted by the Trial Chamber. Three Judges, McDonald, Vohrah and Li found that duress is not a complete defence while two judges, Cassese and Stephen, felt otherwise. In that context, it was the Judgment of the Chamber that the plea was not equivocal.[580]

---

[580] Para. 31.

RULE 62 *BIS*

GUILTY PLEAS

IF AN ACCUSED PLEADS GUILTY IN ACCORDANCE WITH RULE 62 (VI), OR REQUESTS TO CHANGE HIS OR HER PLEA TO GUILTY AND THE TRIAL CHAMBER IS SATISFIED THAT:

(I)   THE GUILTY PLEA HAS BEEN MADE VOLUNTARILY;

(II)   THE GUILTY PLEA IS INFORMED;

(III)   THE GUILTY PLEA IS NOT EQUIVOCAL; AND

(IV)   THERE IS A SUFFICIENT FACTUAL BASIS FOR THE CRIME AND THE ACCUSED'S PARTICIPATION IN IT, EITHER ON THE BASIS OF INDEPENDENT INDICIA OR ON LACK OF ANY MATERIAL DISAGREEMENT BETWEEN THE PARTIES ABOUT THE FACTS OF THE CASE, THE TRIAL CHAMBER MAY ENTER A FINDING OF GUILT AND INSTRUCT THE REGISTRAR TO SET A DATE FOR THE SENTENCING HEARING.

RULE 63

QUESTIONING OF ACCUSED

(A)   QUESTIONING BY THE PROSECUTOR OF AN ACCUSED, INCLUDING AFTER THE INITIAL APPEARANCE, SHALL NOT PROCEED WITHOUT THE PRESENCE OF COUNSEL UNLESS THE ACCUSED HAS VOLUNTARILY AND EXPRESSLY AGREED TO PROCEED WITHOUT COUNSEL PRESENT. IF THE ACCUSED SUBSEQUENTLY EXPRESSES A DESIRE TO HAVE COUNSEL, QUESTIONING SHALL THEREUPON CEASE, AND SHALL ONLY RESUME WHEN THE ACCUSED'S COUNSEL IS PRESENT.

(B)   THE QUESTIONING, INCLUDING ANY WAIVER OF THE RIGHT TO COUNSEL, SHALL BE AUDIO-RECORDED OR VIDEO-RECORDED IN ACCORDANCE WITH THE PROCEDURE PROVIDED FOR IN RULE 43. THE PROSECUTOR SHALL AT THE BEGINNING OF THE QUESTIONING CAUTION THE ACCUSED IN ACCORDANCE WITH RULE 42 (A)(III).

RULE 64

DETENTION ON REMAND

UPON BEING TRANSFERRED TO THE SEAT OF THE TRIBUNAL, THE ACCUSED SHALL BE DETAINED IN FACILITIES PROVIDED BY THE HOST COUNTRY, OR BY ANOTHER COUNTRY. IN EXCEPTIONAL CIRCUMSTANCES, THE ACCUSED MAY BE HELD IN FACILITIES OUTSIDE OF THE HOST COUNTRY. THE PRESIDENT MAY, ON THE APPLICATION OF A PARTY, REQUEST MODIFICATION OF THE CONDITIONS OF DETENTION OF AN ACCUSED.

RULE 65

PROVISIONAL RELEASE

(A)　ONCE DETAINED, AN ACCUSED MAY NOT BE RELEASED EXCEPT UPON AN ORDER OF A TRIAL CHAMBER.

(B)　RELEASE MAY BE ORDERED BY A TRIAL CHAMBER ONLY AFTER HEARING THE HOST COUNTRY AND ONLY IF IT IS SATISFIED THAT THE ACCUSED WILL APPEAR FOR TRIAL AND, IF RELEASED, WILL NOT POSE A DANGER TO ANY VICTIM, WITNESS OR OTHER PERSON.

(C)　THE TRIAL CHAMBER MAY IMPOSE SUCH CONDITIONS UPON THE RELEASE OF THE ACCUSED AS IT MAY DETERMINE APPROPRIATE, INCLUDING THE EXECUTION OF A BAIL BOND AND THE OBSERVANCE OF SUCH CONDITIONS AS ARE NECESSARY TO ENSURE THE PRESENCE OF THE ACCUSED FOR TRIAL AND THE PROTECTION OF OTHERS.

(D)　ANY DECISION RENDERED UNDER THIS RULE SHALL BE SUBJECT TO APPEAL IN CASES WHERE LEAVE IS GRANTED BY A BENCH OF THREE JUDGES OF THE APPEALS CHAMBER, UPON GOOD CAUSE BEING SHOWN. SUBJECT TO SUB-RULE (F) BELOW, APPLICATIONS FOR LEAVE TO APPEAL SHALL BE FILED WITHIN SEVEN DAYS OF THE IMPUGNED DECISION. WHERE SUCH DECISION IS RENDERED ORALLY, THE APPLICATION SHALL BE FILED WITHIN SEVEN DAYS OF THE ORAL DECISION, UNLESS

(I)　THE PARTY CHALLENGING THE DECISION WAS NOT PRESENT OR REPRESENTED WHEN THE DECISION WAS PRONOUNCED, IN WHICH CASE THE TIME-LIMIT SHALL RUN FROM THE DATE ON WHICH THE CHALLENGING PARTY IS NOTIFIED OF THE ORAL DECISION; OR

(II)　THE TRIAL CHAMBER HAS INDICATED THAT A WRITTEN DECISION WILL FOLLOW, IN WHICH CASE THE TIME-LIMIT SHALL RUN FROM FILING OF THE WRITTEN DECISION.

(E)　THE PROSECUTOR MAY APPLY FOR A STAY OF A DECISION BY THE TRIAL CHAMBER TO RELEASE AN ACCUSED ON THE BASIS THAT THE PROSECUTOR INTENDS TO APPEAL THE DECISION, AND SHALL MAKE SUCH AN APPLICATION AT THE TIME OF FILING HIS OR HER RESPONSE TO THE INITIAL APPLICATION FOR PROVISIONAL RELEASE BY THE ACCUSED.

(F)　WHERE THE TRIAL CHAMBER GRANTS A STAY OF ITS DECISION TO RELEASE AN ACCUSED, THE PROSECUTOR SHALL FILE HIS OR HER APPEAL NOT LATER THAN ONE DAY FROM THE RENDERING OF THAT DECISION.

(G)　WHERE THE TRIAL CHAMBER ORDERS A STAY OF ITS DECISION TO RELEASE THE ACCUSED PENDING AN APPEAL BY THE PROSECUTOR, THE ACCUSED SHALL NOT BE RELEASED UNTIL EITHER:

(I)　THE TIME-LIMIT FOR THE FILING OF AN APPLICATION FOR LEAVE TO APPEAL BY THE PROSECUTOR HAS EXPIRED, AND NO SUCH APPLICATION IS FILED;

(II)   A BENCH OF THREE JUDGES OF THE APPEALS CHAMBER REJECTS THE APPLICATION FOR LEAVE TO APPEAL;

(III)   THE APPEALS CHAMBER DISMISSES THE APPEAL; OR

(IV)   A BENCH OF THREE JUDGES OF THE APPEALS CHAMBER OR THE APPEALS CHAMBER OTHERWISE ORDERS.

(H)   IF NECESSARY, THE TRIAL CHAMBER MAY ISSUE A WARRANT OF ARREST TO SECURE THE PRESENCE OF AN ACCUSED WHO HAS BEEN RELEASED OR IS FOR ANY OTHER REASON AT LIBERTY. THE PROVISIONS OF SECTION 2 OF PART FIVE SHALL APPLY MUTATIS MUTANDIS.

I.   COMMENTARY

Pursuant to an amendment to Rule 65(B) in December 1999, an accused no longer needs to show "special circumstances" when applying for provisional release. The two requirements which must be established are that the accused will appear for trial and pose no danger to any victim, witness or other person.

In July 2000, Rule 65 was further amended to provide that a request for provisional release may occur either before or after judgement. Prior to judgement, such requests are made to a Trial Chamber. Follow judgement, such a request is made to the Appeals Chamber. Rule 65(I) states that a convicted person may apply for provisional release pending appeal. In addition to the two requirements which must be established by the applicant under Rule 65(B) – appearance for trial and posing no danger – a third criterion must be satisfied – special circumstances warranting such release.

II.   TRIBUNAL CASES

A.   APPEALS CHAMBER

PROSECUTOR V. SIMIĆ, *et. al.*, *Decision on Application for Leave to Appeal (Provisional Release)*, IT-95-9-AR65, 19 April 2000, Vohrah, Nieto-Navia & Pocar, JJ.

The Appeals Chamber rejected the appeal brought by the Prosecution under Rule 65(D), against decisions granting provisional release to two accused. The Chamber held that the Prosecution failed to show "good cause" within the meaning of Rule 65(D) which requires the party seeking leave to appeal to satisfy the Bench of the Appeals Chamber that the Trial Chamber may have erred in making the impugned decision.

The Prosecution had argued that "good cause" existed on the grounds that the decision of the Trial Chamber represented one of the first interpretations and applications of amended Rule 65(B) and that the Trial Chamber erred in ruling that it was satisfied that, if released, the accused would not pose a danger to victims, witnesses or other persons and that they would appear for trial. In addition, the Prosecution argued that the decisions granting provisional release will cause irreparable prejudice to the Prosecutor and that the Trial Chamber misapplied the legal principles governing provisional release.[581]

PROSECUTOR V. SIMIĆ, *et. al., Decision Relating to the Trial Chamber's Ruling on the Basis of Written Submissions prior to Holding Oral Argument as Scheduled,* IT-95-9, 28 July 1999, McDonald, Shahabuddeen, Tieya, Nieto-Navia & Mumba, JJ.

The Appeals Chamber ordered the Trial Chamber to hold an oral hearing on the Request for provisional release.

Trial Chamber III had ordered that oral arguments be heard on the Request for Provisional Release at a hearing on 23 and 24 February 1999. However, the Trial Chamber denied the Request in a written Decision of 15 February 1999, without a prior hearing of the parties.

The Appeals Chamber considered that the Application for Leave to Appeal raised the issue of whether a Trial Chamber, having ordered that oral arguments be heard on a matter pending before it, may properly issue its decision on that matter solely on the basis of the written submissions of the parties. In granting leave to appeal, the Chamber found that this issue is of general importance to proceedings before the International Tribunal within the meaning of Sub-rule 73(B)(ii).

The Chamber considered that by scheduling an oral hearing the Trial Chamber created an expectation on the part of the Defence to have an oral hearing on its Request for Provisional Release prior to the issuance of a decision on the request and that the decision was rendered contrary to this expectation.

B.   TRIAL CHAMBERS

PROSECUTOR V. BRĐANIN & TALIĆ, *Decision on Motion by Radoslav Brđanin for Provisional Release,* IT-99-36-PT, 25 July 2000, Hunt, Mumba & Daqun, JJ.

The Trial Chamber denied Brđanin's motion for provisional release. In the course of doing so a number of important issues were discussed.

Interpretation of Rule 65

The Chamber found that despite the amendment to Rule 65, which no longer requires the accused to show "exceptional circumstances," there is no presumption that provisional release will be the norm. The particular circumstances of each case must be considered in light of the provisions of Rule 65 as it now stands.[582]

---

[581] Pgs. 2-3.
[582] Para. 12.

At all times, the accused bears the onus of establishing that if released, he will appear for trial and pose no danger to any victim, witness or other person. Furthermore, once the accused makes an evidentiary showing[583] that the he will return for trial and not intimidate witnesses, the burden does not shift to the Prosecutor to demonstrate "exceptional circumstances" to justify continued detention.[584]

Appearance for Trial

The Chamber ruled that Brđanin had not shown that if granted provisional release, he would appear for trial. The Government of Republika Srpska had issue a guarantee to the Tribunal on Brđanin's behalf. The Chamber discussed the effect of such a guarantee. The history of Republika Srpska is not one that would give the Tribunal confidence that their guarantees would be honored because no single accused had been arrested by the Republika Srpska upon indictments issued by the Tribunal. Furthermore, the Judges reasoned that since Brđanin had once been a high government official, the possibility that he may, in mitigation, decided to cooperate with the Prosecutor provides a disincentive for the government to honour its guarantee. The Chamber added that the weight to be given a guarantee by the Government of Republika Srpska may be different where it is not a high level indicted person who would have to be returned.[585]

In addition, the Chamber ruled that the seriousness of the charges against the accused is a factor to be considered in relation to the issue of whether the accused will appear for trial. The Chamber determined that "the more serious the charge, and the greater the likely sentence if convicted, the greater the reason for not appearing at trial."[586] Further, the Judges said:

> Brđanin has reason enough for not wanting to appear. . . . [C]ommon experience suggests that any person in his position, even if he is innocent, is likely to take advantage of the refuge which Republika Srpska presently provides to other high-level indicted persons.[587]

Finally, the Chamber stated that a substantial burden – falling short of establishing exceptional circumstances – rests with the applicant to show that he will appear for trial, given the fact that the Tribunal does not have any power to execute its arrest warrants and it must rely on the local authorities or international bodies to effect arrests for failure to appear at trial.[588]

---

[583] In this case that showing consisted of a sworn statement from one witness and the in-court testimony of another.

[584] Para. 13.

[585] Para. 15.

[586] Para. 16.

[587] *Ibid.*

[588] Para. 18.

Interference with Witnesses

Having ruled that Brđanin had not satisfied the Chamber that he would appear for trial, no finding was made upon the issue whether he would pose a danger to anyone, if released.

However, the Chamber made several observations in relation to this second prong of the test under Rule 65. First, the fact that an accused may be released to an area where crimes are alleged to have been committed does not by itself suggest that he will exert pressure on victims and witnesses or pose a danger to them. Furthermore, the mere ability to exert pressure on Prosecution witnesses, because of the fact that the accused received unredacted materials in support of the indictment and statements of the witnesses it intends to call at trial as part of the disclosure provisions of Rule 66, cannot form the basis for denying provisional release.[589]

Second, the mere possibility that the willingness of witnesses to testify would be affected by the provisional release of an accused does not constitute "danger" within the meaning of Rule 65. The Chamber stated that if the applicant can establish that he will not pose a danger to a witness, the Prosecution must reassure its witnesses in accused's case as well as in other cases.[590]

Judicial Discretion under Rule 65

In general, a Chamber has the discretion "to refuse" an application for provisional release notwithstanding that the applicant has established the two conditions under Rule 65, and it is not a discretion "to grant" the order notwithstanding that the applicant has failed to satisfy one or both conditions.[591] A showing of family hardship and difficulties in case preparation caused by detention were seen as very real considerations to the accused, but they did not justify provisional release where the Chamber was not satisfied that he would appear for trial.[592]

Voluntary Surrender

Brđanin was arrested upon a sealed indictment and as a result did not have any opportunity to voluntarily surrender to the Tribunal. The Chamber observed that, under ordinary circumstances, voluntary surrender is a favourable factor to be considered. However, in the context of this case, where he never had the opportunity to demonstrate his willingness to voluntarily surrender, the fact that he did not do so, did not militate against his application for provisional release.[593]

---

[589] Para. 19.
[590] Para. 20.
[591] Para. 22.
[592] Para. 23.
[593] Para. 17.

Pre-Trial Detention

The Chamber did not decide whether the length of pre-trial detention is relevant to applications for provisional release. The Chamber observed however that the reasonableness of pre-trial detention is logically a matter relevant to the exercise of judicial discretion under Rule 65 and it must be interpreted according to the circumstances in which the Tribunal operates. Two factors identified by the Chamber which may affect the length of pre-trial detention were the necessity of the Tribunal to rely on local authorities or international bodies to effect arrest warrants and the fact that the serious nature of the crimes prosecuted by the Tribunal would be very unlikely to produce sentences of a duration which would be less than an expected pre-trial detention. In the instant case, Brđanin had been in custody since 6 July 1999 and the Prosecution estimated that he was likely to be in pre-trial detention for a period of nineteen to twenty months. The Chamber found that the likely period of pre-trial detention for Brđanin had not been demonstrated to be unreasonable.[594]

PROSECUTOR V. SIMIĆ, *et. al., Decision on Simo Zarić's Application for Provisional Release*, IT-95-9-PT, 4 April 2000, Robinson Hunt & Bennouna, JJ.[595]

Pursuant to Rule 65(E), when the Prosecution applies for a stay of any decision granting an accused's motion for provisional release, the order of release, if granted, is stayed such that the accused shall not be released for one full day from the rendering of the decision, at the earliest and, if the Prosecution files an application for leave to appeal the decision granting provisional release within that time, then, pursuant to Rule 65(G), the Accused shall not be released until either:

(i)   a bench of three Judges of the Appeals Chamber rejects the application for leave to appeal;

(ii)   the Appeals Chamber dismisses the appeal; or

(iii)   a bench of three Judges of the Appeals Chamber or the Appeals Chamber otherwise orders.

In granting the application for provisional release, the Trial Chamber considered that Rule 65(B), as amended, no longer requires an accused to demonstrate exceptional circumstances before release may be ordered. The Chamber found that under Rule 65(B), a determination as to whether release is to be granted must be made in the light of the particular circumstances of each case, and may be granted only if the Trial Chamber is satisfied that the accused "will appear for trial and, if released, will not pose a danger to any victim, witness or other person."[596]

---

[594] Paras. 24-28.
[595] See, Prosecutor v. Simic *et. al., Decision on Miroslav Tadić's Application for Provisional Release*, IT-95-9-PT, 4 April 2000, Robinson, Hunt, & Bennouna, JJ.
[596] Pg. 7.

The Chamber rejected the contention of the Prosecution that the amendment to Rule 65(B), removing the requirement of exceptional circumstances, is *ultra vires* the Statute. The Chamber ruled that Rule 65(B), as amended, is not inconsistent with any provision in the Statute and is wholly consistent with the internationally recognised standards regarding the rights of the accused that the International Tribunal is obliged to respect.[597]

In the instant case, the Chamber considered the following factors determinative in granting provisional release to the accused. He voluntarily surrendered to the custody of the International Tribunal. Both on his own behalf, and through the Government of the *Republika Srpska*, he provided the guarantees required by the Trial Chamber. The Trial Chamber was satisfied that the accused, if released, would appear for trial and that he would not pose a danger to victims, witnesses or other persons. Finally, at the time of making his application for provisional release, the accused had been held in detention, awaiting trial, for more than two years, and that there was no likelihood of an early date being fixed for the commencement of his trial.[598]

The Chamber ordered the provisional release of the accused under the following terms and conditions:

1. The Accused shall be transported to Schiphol airport in the Netherlands by the Dutch authorities;

2. At Schiphol airport, the Accused shall be provisionally released into the custody of the designated official of Bosnia and Herzegovina, Trivun Jovičić (or such other designated official as the Trial Chamber may, by order, accept), who shall accompany the Accused for the remainder of his travel to Bosnia and Herzegovina;

3. On his return flight, the Accused shall be accompanied by the same designated official of Bosnia and Herzegovina, Trivun Jovičić (or by such other designated official as the Trial Chamber may, by order, accept), who shall deliver the Accused into the custody of the Dutch authorities at Schiphol airport at a date and time to be determined by the Trial Chamber, and the Dutch authorities shall then transport the Accused back to the United Nations Detention Unit;

4. During the period of his provisional release, the Accused shall abide by, and the authorities of the Republika Srpska, including the local police in Bosanski Šamac, shall ensure compliance with, the following conditions:

   a) to remain within the confines of the municipality of Bosanski Šamac;

   b) to surrender his passport to the International Police Task Force (IPTF) in Oraska or to the Office of the Prosecutor in Sarajevo;

   c) to report each day to the local police in Bosanski Šamac;

   d) to consent to having the IPTF check with the local police about his presence and to the making of occasional, unannounced visits by the IPTF to the Accused;

   e) not to have any contact with any other co-accused in the case;

---

[597] Pgs. 7-8.
[598] Pg. 8.

    f)   not to have any contact whatsoever nor in any way interfere with any persons who may testify at his trial;

    g)   not to discuss his case with anyone other than his counsel;

    h)   to assume responsibility for all expenses concerning transport from Schiphol airport to Bosanski Šamac and back;

    i)   to comply strictly with any order of this Trial Chamber varying the terms of or terminating his provisional release.[599]

In addition, the Chamber ordered the Registrar to consult with the Ministry of Justice of the Netherlands as to the practical arrangements for his release and requested that the authorities of all States through which he would travel to hold the Accused in custody for any time he spends in transit at the airport and to arrest and detain the Accused pending his return to the United Nations Detention Unit, should he attempt to escape. Finally, the Chamber ordered that the Accused should be immediately detained should he breach any of the foregoing terms and conditions of his provisional release.[600]

PROSECUTOR V. KUNARAC, *et. al., Decision on Request for Provisional Release of Dragoljub Kunarac,* IT-96-23-PT, 11 November 1999, Mumba, Cassese & Hunt, JJ.[601]

Defendant Kunarac filed a Motion for Provisional Release. He listed several factors as "exceptional circumstances" justifying his release. They were:

    a.   his voluntary surrender to the International Tribunal;

    b.   the resolution of the preliminary proceedings concerning him;

    c.   his co-operation with the Prosecutor during the pre-trial proceedings;

    d.   his readiness to proceed to trial, together with his co-accused Mr. Radomir Kovač;

    e.   the possible postponement of the commencement of the joint trial to enable his co-accused to adequately prepare his defence;

    f.   there being no danger of him escaping or not appearing for trial;

    g.   him not posing a danger to any victim, witness or other person or destroying the evidence against him;

    h.   the completion of the gathering of evidence against him;

---

[599] Pg. 9.

[600] Pg. 10.

[601] This case was decided prior to a change in the rule removing the requirement for the accused to show "exceptional circumstances" before he could be granted release. The Rule was amended to comply with the International Covenant on Civil and Political Rights.

i.   his need to undergo medical rehabilitation relating to the disability with his arm, and that the medical rehabilitation could be done while his co-accused is preparing for trial;

j.   the positive influence his provisional release would have on other indictees to voluntary surrender themselves to the International Tribunal; and

k.   his readiness to give undertakings to the International Tribunal relating to his willingness to appear for trial, stay in the Detention Unit during the course of the trial and to respect any conditions for his provisional release imposed by the Trial Chamber in accordance with the Rules.[602]

The Chamber denied his release. The Chamber determined that voluntary surrender is not an exceptional circumstance. Persons who know they are indicted should surrender. It is not exceptional. Neither is it exceptional that the preliminary proceedings concerning him are concluded; that he cooperated with the prosecutor during pre-trial proceedings; that he is ready to proceed to trial; nor that the Prosecutor has completed the gathering of evidence against him. As to factor (e) the Chamber stated that the trial would commence in early February 2000 and saw no reason why it could be further postponed. As to (f), (g) and (k), the defendant's willingness to give personal undertakings does not create an exceptional circumstance where other indictees are still at large.

Finally, the Chamber stated:

> The Trial Chamber is of the view that the Prosecutor's submission is justified that were the accused to be released this close to the intended commencement of the trial, such action could have a negative impact on the willingness of her witnesses to participate. In the circumstances of the case, a reasonable danger might arise that potential witnesses would feel reluctant to participate in the trial.[603]

Six days later on 17 November 1999, the Chamber issued a further decision after having been made aware of guarantees for Kunarac from *Republika Srpska*. The Chamber decided that its prior decision was not affected by the government guarantees for the reasons set out in their original decision.[604]

---

[602] Para. 3.
[603] Para. 7.
[604] See Further Decision on Request for Provisional Release of Dragoljub Kunarac, 17 November 1999.

RULE 65 *BIS*

STATUS CONFERENCES

(A)   A TRIAL CHAMBER OR A TRIAL CHAMBER JUDGE SHALL CONVENE A STATUS CONFERENCE WITHIN ONE HUNDRED AND TWENTY DAYS OF THE INITIAL APPEARANCE OF THE ACCUSED AND THEREAFTER WITHIN ONE HUNDRED AND TWENTY DAYS AFTER THE LAST STATUS CONFERENCE:

    (I)   TO ORGANIZE EXCHANGES BETWEEN THE PARTIES SO AS TO ENSURE EXPEDITIOUS PREPARATION FOR TRIAL,

    (II)   TO REVIEW THE STATUS OF HIS OR HER CASE AND TO ALLOW THE ACCUSED THE OPPORTUNITY TO RAISE ISSUES IN RELATION THERETO, INCLUDING THE MENTAL AND PHYSICAL CONDITION OF THE ACCUSED.

(B)   THE APPEALS CHAMBER OR AN APPEALS CHAMBER JUDGE SHALL CONVENE A STATUS CONFERENCE, WITHIN ONE HUNDRED AND TWENTY DAYS OF THE FILING OF A NOTICE OF APPEAL AND THEREAFTER WITHIN ONE HUNDRED AND TWENTY DAYS AFTER THE LAST STATUS CONFERENCE, TO ALLOW ANY PERSON IN CUSTODY PENDING APPEAL THE OPPORTUNITY TO RAISE ISSUES IN RELATION THERETO, INCLUDING THE MENTAL AND PHYSICAL CONDITION OF THAT PERSON.

RULE 65 *TER*

PRE-TRIAL JUDGE

(A)   THE PRESIDING JUDGE OF THE TRIAL CHAMBER SHALL, NO LATER THAN SIXTY DAYS AFTER THE INITIAL APPEARANCE OF THE ACCUSED, DESIGNATE FROM AMONG ITS MEMBERS A JUDGE RESPONSIBLE FOR THE PRE-TRIAL PROCEEDINGS (HEREINAFTER "PRE-TRIAL JUDGE").

(B)   THE PRE-TRIAL JUDGE SHALL, UNDER THE AUTHORITY AND SUPERVISION OF THE TRIAL CHAMBER SEISED OF THE CASE, COORDINATE COMMUNICATION BETWEEN THE PARTIES DURING THE PRE-TRIAL PHASE. THE PRE-TRIAL JUDGE SHALL ENSURE THAT THE PROCEEDINGS ARE NOT UNDULY DELAYED AND SHALL TAKE ANY MEASURE NECESSARY TO PREPARE THE CASE FOR A FAIR AND EXPEDITIOUS TRIAL.

(C)   THE PRE-TRIAL JUDGE SHALL SET APPROPRIATE DEADLINES, PARTICULARLY WHERE THE PROSECUTOR REQUESTS TIME FOR FURTHER INVESTIGATION.

(D)   THE PRE-TRIAL JUDGE MAY BE ENTRUSTED BY THE TRIAL CHAMBER WITH ALL OR PART OF ANY PRE-TRIAL FUNCTIONS SET FORTH IN RULE 66, RULE 73 AND RULE 73 *BIS*, OR WITH ALL OR PART OF THE PRE-DEFENCE FUNCTIONS SET FORTH IN RULE 73 *TER*.

(E)   ONCE DISCLOSURE PURSUANT TO RULES 66 AND 68 IS COMPLETED AND ANY EXISTING PRELIMINARY MOTIONS FILED WITHIN THE TIME-LIMIT PROVIDED BY RULE 72 ARE DISPOSED OF, THE PRE-TRIAL JUDGE SHALL ORDER THE PROSECUTOR, WITHIN A TIME-LIMIT SET BY THE PRETRIAL JUDGE AND BEFORE THE PRE-TRIAL CONFERENCE REQUIRED BY RULE 73 *BIS*, TO FILE THE FOLLOWING:

(I)   A PRE-TRIAL BRIEF ADDRESSING THE FACTUAL AND LEGAL ISSUES, INCLUDING A WRITTEN STATEMENT SETTING OUT THE NATURE OF HIS OR HER CASE;

(II)   ADMISSIONS BY THE PARTIES AND A STATEMENT OF MATTERS WHICH ARE NOT IN DISPUTE;

(III)   A STATEMENT OF CONTESTED MATTERS OF FACT AND LAW;

(IV)   A LIST OF WITNESSES THE PROSECUTOR INTENDS TO CALL WITH:

(A)   THE NAME OR PSEUDONYM OF EACH WITNESS;

(B)   A SUMMARY OF THE FACTS ON WHICH EACH WITNESS WILL TESTIFY;

(C)   THE POINTS IN THE INDICTMENT AS TO WHICH EACH WITNESS WILL TESTIFY, INCLUDING SPECIFIC REFERENCES TO COUNTS AND RELEVANT PARAGRAPHS IN THE INDICTMENT; AND

(D)   THE ESTIMATED LENGTH OF TIME REQUIRED FOR EACH WITNESS; AND

(V)   A LIST OF EXHIBITS THE PROSECUTOR INTENDS TO OFFER STATING WHERE POSSIBLE WHETHER THE DEFENCE HAS ANY OBJECTION AS TO AUTHENTICITY.

THE PRE-TRIAL JUDGE SHALL GIVE DIRECTIONS TO THE PARTIES REQUIRING THEM TO MEET AND DISCUSS THE ISSUES RELEVANT TO THE PREPARATION OF THE CASE FOR TRIAL SO THAT THE PROSECUTOR MAY COMPLY WITH SUB-RULES (E)(II), (III) AND (V).

(F)   AFTER THE SUBMISSION BY THE PROSECUTOR OF THE ITEMS MENTIONED IN SUB-RULE (E), THE PRE-TRIAL JUDGE SHALL ORDER THE DEFENCE, WITHIN A TIME-LIMIT SET BY THE PRETRIAL JUDGE, AND NOT LATER THAN SEVEN DAYS BEFORE THE PRE-TRIAL CONFERENCE, TO FILE A PRE-TRIAL BRIEF ADDRESSING THE FACTUAL AND LEGAL ISSUES, AND INCLUDING A WRITTEN STATEMENT SETTING OUT:

(I)   IN GENERAL TERMS, THE NATURE OF THE ACCUSED'S DEFENCE;

(II)   THE MATTERS WITH WHICH THE ACCUSED TAKES ISSUE IN THE PROSECUTOR'S PRE-TRIAL BRIEF; AND

(III)   IN THE CASE OF EACH SUCH MATTER, THE REASON WHY THE ACCUSED TAKES ISSUE WITH IT.

(G)   AFTER THE CLOSE OF THE PROSECUTOR'S CASE AND BEFORE THE COMMENCEMENT OF THE DEFENCE CASE, THE PRE-TRIAL JUDGE SHALL ORDER THE DEFENCE TO FILE THE FOLLOWING:

(I)   A LIST OF WITNESSES THE DEFENCE INTENDS TO CALL WITH:

(A)   THE NAME OR PSEUDONYM OF EACH WITNESS;

(B)   A SUMMARY OF THE FACTS ON WHICH EACH WITNESS WILL TESTIFY;

(C)   THE POINTS IN THE INDICTMENT AS TO WHICH EACH WITNESS WILL TESTIFY; AND

(D)   THE ESTIMATED LENGTH OF TIME REQUIRED FOR EACH WITNESS; AND

(II)   A LIST OF EXHIBITS THE DEFENCE INTENDS TO OFFER IN ITS CASE, STATING WHERE POSSIBLE WHETHER THE PROSECUTOR HAS ANY OBJECTION AS TO AUTHENTICITY.

(H)   THE PRE-TRIAL JUDGE SHALL RECORD THE POINTS OF AGREEMENT AND DISAGREEMENT ON MATTERS OF LAW AND FACT. IN THIS CONNECTION, HE OR SHE MAY ORDER THE PARTIES TO FILE WRITTEN SUBMISSIONS WITH EITHER THE PRE-TRIAL JUDGE OR THE TRIAL CHAMBER.

(I)   IN ORDER TO PERFORM HIS OR HER FUNCTIONS, THE PRE-TRIAL JUDGE MAY *PROPRIO MOTU* HEAR THE PARTIES. THE PRE-TRIAL JUDGE MAY HEAR THE PARTIES IN HIS OR HER PRIVATE ROOM, IN WHICH CASE MINUTES OF THE MEETING SHALL BE TAKEN BY A REPRESENTATIVE OF THE REGISTRY.

(J)   THE PRE-TRIAL JUDGE SHALL KEEP THE TRIAL CHAMBER REGULARLY
INFORMED, PARTICULARLY WHERE ISSUES ARE IN DISPUTE AND MAY REFER SUCH
DISPUTES TO THE TRIAL CHAMBER.

(K)

(I)   AFTER THE FILINGS BY THE PROSECUTOR PURSUANT TO SUB-RULE
(E), THE PRE-TRIAL JUDGE SHALL SUBMIT TO THE TRIAL CHAMBER A
COMPLETE FILE CONSISTING OF ALL THE FILINGS OF THE PARTIES,
TRANSCRIPTS OF STATUS CONFERENCES AND MINUTES OF MEETINGS
HELD IN THE PERFORMANCE OF HIS OR HER FUNCTIONS PURSUANT TO
THIS RULE.

(II)   THE PRE-TRIAL JUDGE SHALL SUBMIT A SECOND FILE TO THE TRIAL
CHAMBER AFTER THE DEFENCE FILINGS PURSUANT TO SUB-RULE (G).

(L)   THE TRIAL CHAMBER MAY *PROPRIO MOTU* EXERCISE ANY OF THE FUNCTIONS
OF THE PRE-TRIAL JUDGE.

II.   TRIBUNAL CASES

B.   TRIAL CHAMBERS

1. POWERS OF THE PRE-TRIAL JUDGE

PROSECUTOR V. KUNARAC, *et. al., Order for Clarification of the Powers of the Pre-Trial Judge,* Case No. IT-96-23-PT, 5 January 2000, Mumba, Cassese & Hunt, JJ.

Judge Mumba had been appointed Pre-Trial Judge with regard to one or more of the Defendants in this case. By way of clarification, the Chamber ordered as follows:

> . . . the appointment of Judge Mumba as Pre-Trial Judge with the extended powers under Rule 65 *ter* of the Rules of Procedure and Evidence applies to the whole of Case Number IT-96-23 against all remaining seven accused and any subsequent case number derived therefrom.

RULE 66

DISCLOSURE BY THE PROSECUTOR

(A)   SUBJECT TO THE PROVISIONS OF RULES 53 AND 69, THE PROSECUTOR SHALL MAKE AVAILABLE TO THE DEFENCE IN A LANGUAGE WHICH THE ACCUSED UNDERSTANDS

  (I)   WITHIN THIRTY DAYS OF THE INITIAL APPEARANCE OF THE ACCUSED, COPIES OF THE SUPPORTING MATERIAL WHICH ACCOMPANIED THE INDICTMENT WHEN CONFIRMATION WAS SOUGHT AS WELL AS ALL PRIOR STATEMENTS OBTAINED BY THE PROSECUTOR FROM THE ACCUSED, AND

  (II)   WITHIN THE TIME-LIMIT PRESCRIBED BY THE TRIAL CHAMBER OR BY THE PRE-TRIAL JUDGE APPOINTED PURSUANT TO RULE 65 *TER*, COPIES OF THE STATEMENTS OF ALL WITNESSES WHOM THE PROSECUTOR INTENDS TO CALL TO TESTIFY AT TRIAL, AND COPIES OF ALL AFFIDAVITS AND FORMAL STATEMENTS REFERRED TO IN RULE 94 *TER*; COPIES OF THE STATEMENTS OF ADDITIONAL PROSECUTION WITNESSES SHALL BE MADE AVAILABLE TO THE DEFENCE WHEN A DECISION IS MADE TO CALL THOSE WITNESSES.

(B)   THE PROSECUTOR SHALL ON REQUEST, PERMIT THE DEFENCE TO INSPECT ANY BOOKS, DOCUMENTS, PHOTOGRAPHS AND TANGIBLE OBJECTS IN THE PROSECUTOR'S CUSTODY OR CONTROL, WHICH ARE MATERIAL TO THE PREPARATION OF THE DEFENCE, OR ARE INTENDED FOR USE BY THE PROSECUTOR AS EVIDENCE AT TRIAL OR WERE OBTAINED FROM OR BELONGED TO THE ACCUSED.

(C)   WHERE INFORMATION IS IN THE POSSESSION OF THE PROSECUTOR, THE DISCLOSURE OF WHICH MAY PREJUDICE FURTHER OR ONGOING INVESTIGATIONS, OR FOR ANY OTHER REASONS MAY BE CONTRARY TO THE PUBLIC INTEREST OR AFFECT THE SECURITY INTERESTS OF ANY STATE, THE PROSECUTOR MAY APPLY TO THE TRIAL CHAMBER SITTING IN CAMERA TO BE RELIEVED FROM THE OBLIGATION UNDER THE RULES TO DISCLOSE THAT INFORMATION. WHEN MAKING SUCH APPLICATION THE PROSECUTOR SHALL PROVIDE THE TRIAL CHAMBER (BUT ONLY THE TRIAL CHAMBER) WITH THE INFORMATION THAT IS SOUGHT TO BE KEPT CONFIDENTIAL.

I.   COMMENTARY

Prosecutor v. Blaškić, *Opinion Further to the Decision of the Trial Chamber Seized of the Case The Prosecutor v. Dario Kordić and Mario Čerkez*, 12 November 1998

Kordić and Čerkez sought access to non-public materials in the *Blaškić* case in the course of preparing their own case for trial.

In this Opinion, the Chamber characterized the issue as one of discovery under Rules 66 and 68. In fact, the issue is one of the obligations of the defence to conduct a full and complete investigation of whatever evidence might be available to assist their client. Such material may include the non-public testimony and documents from other Tribunal cases. This is not a discovery issue dealing with the nature and scope of materials that the Prosecutor must provide to the Defence. It is submitted that in an Appeals Chamber decision from the *Aleksovski* case, the Appeals Chamber correctly framed the issue in the following manner:

> The Appeals Chamber, however, points out that there is a firm obligation placed upon those representing an accused person to make proper inquiries as to what evidence is available in that person's defence. In the circumstances of this case, the evidence led by the accused person in the *Blaškić* trial was very obviously a primary source of such enquiry by those representing Zlatko Aleksovski.[605]

Prosecutor v. Blaškić, *Decision on the Defence Motion to Compel the Disclosure of Rule 66 and 68 Material Relating to Statements Made by a Person Know as "X"*, 15 July 1998.

In this decision there was apparently significant testimony in the trial of statements made by a person know as "X". "X" never appeared as a witness in the trial. Thus the testimony of this witness made it into the record and presumably was considered by the Judges without his statements ever having been tested by cross-examination. This seems to be a clear violation of Article 21(4)(e) which states that it is the right of an accused "to examine, or have examined, the witnesses against him." That clearly could not be done, and was not done with witness "X". It is not clear from the decision the nature of the "X" statements. Although there is precedent for the admission of hearsay evidence, such evidence should not be admitted under conditions where cross-examination could expose its flaws. For instance the testimony of a witness who observed certain activities that are the subject matter of the charges against a defendant should not come into the record as hearsay. Such a witness should be available for cross-examination, or the evidence should not be heard.

It does not ameliorate the unfairness of such a procedure to understand that the Judges are professional Judges who can take into account the fact that the witness' statement was admitted as hearsay and make credibility and relevance judgments based on that fact. If the witness is never subjected to cross-examination, his or her testimony is never tested and there is no basis upon which any Judge could make reasonable and rational judgments regarding credibility. Such judgments are best made from observing the witness during his testimony. It is virtually impossible to make a credibility judgment from a transcript, let alone a witness' report of what some third person has said. There is simply no basis upon which to judge the credibility of that third person.

Finally, it must be always kept in mind, that the witnesses in the cases tried in this Tribunal are mostly of a different ethnic background from the accused and testify in

---

[605] Prosecutor v. Aleksovski, *Decision on Prosecutor's Appeal on Admissibility of Evidence,* IT-95-14/1, 16 February 1999, Para. 18.

relation to events arising out of a war in which they were involved. This should raise special concerns regarding credibility. It is just the issue of credibility that can be so effectively determined if the witness is present in court and subject to cross-examination.

Prosecutor v. Delalić, et. al., Order on the Prosecutor's Application to Delay Production of Material to the Accused Delalić, 18 june 1996

In this case, it appears that the Trial Chamber sought a compromise between the Prosecutor's concern to determine whether any of the four co-accused would give other statements to the Prosecution and the right of the accused requesting the statement of the co-accused to receive information that was material to the preparation of his defence.

Prosecutor v. Brđanin & Talić, Decision on Motion by Prosecution for Protective Measures, 3 July 2000

In a far-reaching and comprehensive decision, the Trial Chamber analysed and ruled on a number of questions regarding the obligations of the Prosecutor under Rules 66 and the protection of witnesses under Rule 69. The Chamber determined that in considering these issues the rights of the accused must always be paramount. Any protection scheme must adequately take the defendant's rights under Rule 20 into account as a primary consideration. Under no circumstances is the Prosecutor permitted to redact materials provided to the defence without leave of the Trial Chamber. To obtain leave the Prosecutor must show "exceptional circumstances" which are always something more than the prevailing conditions in former Yugoslavia or Tribunal experience with other lawyers in other cases.

Significantly, the decision, if followed by other Chambers, would bring to an end the onerous task of keeping logs of each person to whom protected materials are given. The Chamber decided that such a practice is simply not justified. It also would impact the practice of requiring defence counsel to return all non-public documents at the conclusion of a case. Finally, it sets guidelines limiting confidential filings. In certain cases the Chamber, on a trial basis, will set out certain types of materials that may be filed confidentially. Beyond that, leave of the Chamber will be required before a document may be confidentially filed.

II.   TRIBUNAL CASES

B.   TRIAL CHAMBERS

1. RULE 66(A) AND (B)

PROSECUTOR V. BRĐANIN & TALIĆ, *Decision on Motion by Prosecution for Protective Measures,* IT-99-36-PT, 3 July 2000, Hunt, Mumba & Pocar, JJ.

In response to her obligations under Rule 66(A)(i), the Prosecutor furnished the Defence with numerous witness statements. However, all identifying information, plus some additional information had been redacted therefrom. This was done without prior authorisation from the Trial Chamber. At the same time, the Prosecutor filed a Motion for protective measures, seeking a number of orders from the Trial Chamber. The Prosecutor asked the Chamber to order the Defence:

- not to disclose to the public, except where necessary for preparation and presentation of the case, the names, identifying information or whereabouts of any witness or potential witness identified to them by the prosecutor, nor any such evidence whether documentary, physical or in the form of statements of witnesses;

- to inform each person among the public to whom disclosure is necessary of the material that it is not to be reproduced in any manner, or publicized or shown to any other person and that such material shall be returned to the defence when it is no longer necessary;

- to maintain a log indicating the name, address and position of anyone to whom such disclosure is made and the date of disclosure; and, if a member of the defence team withdraws from the case all material in their possession should be returned to lead defence counsel; and, at the conclusion of the case all the disclosed material and copies thereof should be returned by counsel to the Registry that have not become part of the public record; and that the Prosecutor is authorized to make limited redactions in the material so furnished concerning the identity and whereabouts of vulnerable victims or witnesses to be disclosed by the Prosecutor only in a reasonable time prior to trial.

The Prosecutor argued that she should be entitled to make the redactions from the materials because "Bosnia and Herzegovina continues to be a dangerous place, where each ethnic or political group is viewed as the enemy of another, and where much of the war is still being fought, with indictees [sic] or suspects and their supporters (as well as supporters of those detained in The Hague) still at large and where witnesses against them are considered 'the enemy'".[606] The Prosecutor also argued that such an order was justified not just by the circumstances prevailing in this case but for future cases that might come before the Tribunal. The Prosecutor argued:

> If witnesses will not come forward or if witnesses refuse or are otherwise unwilling to testify, there is little evidence to present. Threats, harassment, violence, bribery and other intimidation, interference and obstruction of justice are serious problems, for both the individual witnesses and the Tribunal's ability to accomplish its mission.[607]

The Chamber interpreted the language of Rule 69(A), that requires that non-disclosure may only occur in "exceptional circumstances," as follows:

> In the opinion of the Trial Chamber, the prevailing circumstances within the former Yugoslavia *cannot by themselves* amount to exceptional circumstances. The Tribunal has always been concerned solely with the former Yugoslavia and Rule 69(A) was adopted by the judges against a background of ethnic and political enmities which existed in the former Yugoslavia at the time. . . To be

---

[606] Para. 8.
[607] Para. 9.

exceptional, the circumstances must therefore go beyond what has been, since before the Tribunal was established, the rule – or the prevailing (or normal) circumstances – in the former Yugoslavia.[608] (Chamber's emphasis)

The Chamber concluded that the wholesale redactions in every witness statement disclosed to the Defence under Rule 69 was "both unauthorized and unjustified."[609]

The Chamber rejected a procedure proposed by the Prosecutor according to which the Prosecutor could, without leave, make the redactions she felt were necessary and justified and the accused could then, if necessary, make a reasonable request for the identity of certain witnesses or victims to be revealed earlier than, for instance, 30 days before trial. The Chamber decided that this proposal had two basic defects. First, it assumed that every witness is in danger, at risk or vulnerable, which is simply not so; and, second the proposal puts the onus on the defence instead of the prosecutor where it belongs under the clear language of Rule 69(A).[610]

The Chamber ruled that there is no conflict regarding the obligation to disclose under Rules 66(A)(i) and the protection of victims and witnesses under Rule 69(A). Relying on Article 20, the Chamber pointed out: "the rights of the accused are made the first consideration, and the need to protect victims and witnesses is a secondary one." The Chamber said the rule should simply be:

> If the prosecution is able to demonstrate exceptional circumstances justifying the non-disclosure of the identity of any particular victims or witnesses at this early stage of the proceedings, then its obligations of disclosure under Rule 66(A)(i) will be complied with it if produces copies of the statements with the names and other identifying features of only *those* witnesses redacted.[611] (Chamber's emphasis)[612]

PROSECUTOR V BLAŠKIĆ, *Decision on the Defence Motion to Compel the Disclosure of Rule 66 and 68 Material Relating to Statements Made by a Person Know as "X"*, IT-95-14-T, 15 July 1998, Jorda, Riad & Shahabuddeen, JJ.

During the presentation of its case, the Prosecutor was able to elicit from witnesses, statements made by a person named "X". The Defence made a motion to require the Prosecutor to disclose all statements made by "X" in her possession and all documents provided by "X" to SFOR. The Defence theory was that "X" had, in effect, become a witness in the case by the admission of his hearsay statements and that as a result this rule mandated disclosure. The Prosecutor disagreed "that the introduction of hearsay evidence, which the Trial Chamber has ruled is admissible, triggers a concomitant

---

[608] Para. 11.
[609] Para. 13.
[610] Paras. 16-18.
[611] Para. 21.
[612] See also Rule 69 for a report on this decision.

obligation under Rule 66(A) to produce all statements of the hearsay declarant." The Prosecutor contended that the Rule imposes such an obligation only with respect to witnesses the Prosecutor intends to call to testify at trial.

As a side and related issue the Defence contended that it would be improper to apply Rule 66(A)(ii) to this situation since it was amended during the course of the proceedings and under Rule 6(C) no amendment should operate to prejudice the rights of the accused in any pending case.[613]

The Chamber rejected the contention of the Defence on the basis that Rule 66 is very clear in that it only applies to witnesses *whom the Prosecutor intends to call to testify*. The Chamber did go on to explain:

> The Trial Chamber notes the concern expressed by the Defence regarding the credibility of the statements of "X", but, in the spirit of its decision on hearsay evidence, recalls that all the evidence required to evaluate such credibility will be taken into consideration by the Judges when they determine what weight to give to the said statements, and, in particular, the fact that they are the results of hearsay testimony and that, as such, they were not the subject of cross-examination.

PROSECUTOR V. KUPREŠKIĆ et. al., Decision on the Prosecution Motion to Delay Disclosure of Witness Statements, IT-95-16-T, 21 May 1998, Cassese, May & Mumba, JJ.

The Prosecutor sought leave of the Chamber to delay the disclosure of 28 of 40 witness statements to the Defence. The Prosecutor contended that there had been allegations of witness intimidation and that reducing the time for disclosure until 8 days before their appearance would narrow the scope for such abuses.

The Chamber denied the Motion.

Rule 66(A)(ii) provides for disclosure not less than sixty days before trial.[614] Article 21(4)(b) of the Statute provides that an accused shall "have adequate time and facilities for the preparation of his defence." In that context, if the statements are not produced until 8 days before the witness appears, it would not be possible for the Defence to adequately prepare its case for trial. In that event a request for adjournment would be justified

Having denied the Prosecutor's Motion, the Chamber then went on to make some orders providing for additional protection for the witnesses, which incorporated contempt powers under Rule 77, if those orders were in any way violated.

---

[613] See report under Rule 6 for the resolution of this issue

[614] Rule 66(A)(ii) now provides that the Trial Chamber or the Pre-Trial Judge prescribes the time limit for disclosure.

PROSECUTOR V DELALIĆ *et. al., Decision on the Motion by the Accused Zejnil Delalić for the Disclosure of Evidence*, IT-96-21-PT, 25 September 1996, McDonald, Sidhwa & Vohrah, JJ.

Since the *Delalić* Decision, the wording of Rule 66(A) has changed. At the time, the Prosecutor had to disclose three types of material to the defence under Rule 66(A).

Today, the wording of current Rule 66(A)(i) requires the Prosecution to disclose two types of material, within thirty days of the initial appearance of the accused. The wording of Rule 66(A) in regard to those requirements has remained unchanged and the *Delalić* Decision remains applicable. The Prosecutor must therefore disclose the following materials pursuant to Rule 66(A)(i):

> 1.   Copies of supporting material which accompanied the indictment, which includes all supporting material, including any witness statements, given to the confirming judge.

> 2.   All prior statements of the accused that the Prosecution has in its possession.[615]

Rule 66(A)(ii) appears to be modeled on the *Delalić* Decision where the Trial Chamber held that the obligation to disclose "all prior statements obtained by the Prosecution ... from prosecution witnesses" meant that:

> ... once the Prosecution makes a determination that it intends to call an individual as a witness at trial, it is obliged to disclose, "as soon as practicable," any statement taken prior to the time that the witness testifies at trial. This obligation on the Prosecution is also continuing and, as the Prosecution decides on each witness, it must disclose the prior statement of that witness.

Rule 66(B) remains unchanged since the *Delalić* Decision.

The Trial Chamber held that pursuant to Rule 66(B), the Defence is entitled to inspect three categories of materials:

> 1.   documents material to the preparation of the defence;

> 2.   those intended for use by Prosecution as evidence at trial;

> 3.   those that were obtained from or belonged to the accused.

In regard to the second and third categories, the Chamber ruled that the Prosecution must provide materials that fall within these categories to the Defence on request. In particular, the obligation on the Prosecution to allow the defence to inspect material it intends to use at trial is a continuing obligation throughout the proceedings and the materials obtained from or belonging to the accused can be identified without great difficulty.

The Chamber observed that the first category refers to materials that cannot be defined abstractly. In its analysis of the phrase "material to the preparation of the

---

[615] Para. 4.

defence," the Chamber noted that it is similar to Rule 16(a)(1)(c) of the United States' Federal Rules of Criminal Procedure and the test for materiality of evidence in English Criminal Law[616]. By reference to these two national legal systems, the Chamber ruled that the Prosecution is initially the party responsible for deciding what evidence in its possession may be material to the preparation of the Defence. If the Defence believes that the Prosecution has withheld evidence material to its preparation, it must make a *prima facie* showing of materiality and demonstrate that the requested evidence is in the custody or control of the Prosecution. In this regard, the Chamber held that the Defence should be guided by the definitions of materiality from American and English case law, which it cited with approval in its decision. The United States District Court made the following statement:

> The phrase "material to the preparation of the defendant's defense" is one that causes practical problems on both sides of the discovery equation. On the one hand, a defendant's counsel cannot know in most cases the precise nature of all the documents that should be available, but the defence counsel is going to be hard pressed to specifically argue materiality of individual documents. On the other hand, it is equally clear that the discovery rules do not require "open file" discovery with the defendant being allowed to browse at will through the prosecution files. [citation omitted] Moreover, a good deal of inculpatory evidence will have already been turned over as evidence that the government will be using in its case-in-chief. The problem here is to define "materiality" in such a way that it does not merely duplicate other discovery information definitions. Rule 16(a)(1)(C) was not intended to impose a completely redundant discovery obligation.[617]

The English Court of Appeal described the test for materiality in the following terms:

> that which can be seen on a sensible appraisal by the prosecution;
>
> (1) to be relevant or possibly relevant to an issue in the case;
>
> (2) to raise or possibly raise a new issue whose existence is not apparent from the evidence the prosecution proposes to use;
>
> (3) to hold out a real, as opposed to fanciful, prospect of providing a lead on evidence which goes to (1) or (2).

---

[616] *R. v. Keane*, 99 CR. App. R. 1 (Court of Appeal).
[617] *United States v. Liquid Sugars, Inc. & Mooney*, 158 F.R.D. 466 (U.S. Dist. Ct. E.D. Cal. 1994).

PROSECUTOR V. DELALIĆ *et. al., Decision on Motion by the Defendants on the Production of Evidence by the Prosecution*, IT-96-21-T, 8 September 1997, Karibi-Whyte, Odio Benito & Jan, JJ.

The Chamber ruled on the obligation on the Prosecutor to disclose statements:

> The wording of Sub-rule 66(A) is clear and unequivocal. The Prosecution has a duty to disclose to the Defence all statements taken from the accused or any of the Prosecution witnesses. This obligation has been emphasized by Trial Chamber I in its *Decision on the Production of Discovery Materials*, of 27 January 1997, in the Blaškić case (The Prosecutor v. Tihomir Blaškić, IT-95-14-PT, (RP D3177-D3203), para. 38), in which it stated that all previous statements of all Prosecution witnesses, in whatever form, must be disclosed to the Defence.[618]

2. *EX PARTE* APPLICATIONS FOR NON-DISCLOSURE

PROSECUTOR V DELALIĆ *et. al., Order on the Prosecutor's Application to Delay Production of Material to the Accused Delalić*, IT-96-21-PT, 18 June 1996, McDonald, Sidhwa & Vohrah, JJ.

Pursuant to Rule 66(B), the Prosecutor is required to allow the Defence to inspect any books, documents, photographs and tangible objects in the Prosecutor's custody or control, which are material to the preparation of the defence, or are intended for use by the Prosecutor as evidence at trial or were obtained from or belonged to the accused.

However, under Rule 66(C), the Prosecutor may apply *ex parte* to a Trial Chamber for non-disclosure of information falling under Rule 66(B), if the disclosure of information "may prejudice further or ongoing investigations, or for any other reasons may be contrary to the public interest or affect the security interests of any State".

In the instant case, the Prosecutor applied under Rule 66(C) to withhold the statement that a co-accused had given to the Prosecutor. This statement was material to the preparation of the defence of the accused requesting disclosure of the statement, but the Prosecution sought to delay its production on the basis of the public interest of discovering the truth, until the Prosecutor could determine whether any of the four co-accused would provide additional or initial interviews.

The Chamber held that since all four co-accused were in detention at the United Nations Detention Unit, the Prosecutor was required to disclose the statement of the co-accused within 14 days.

---

[618] Para. 10.

3. DELAY IN PROVIDING DISCOVERY

PROSECUTOR V. DELALIĆ *et al, Decision on the Applications for Adjournment of the Trial Date*, IT-96-21-T, 3 February 1997, Karibi-Whyte, Odio-Benito & Jan, JJ.

A delay in providing discovery can result in a delay in starting a trial. The Chamber found that the Prosecutor had failed to comply with fixed dates for disclosure of witness statements. The Chamber said:

> The Trial Chamber is cognizant of the fact that unless there is prompt and proper disclosure to the Defence, the Defence cannot make a decision on what evidence it will use at trial, and cannot therefore be adequately prepared for trial. This is especially so in this case where the disclosure was in English, making translation into the language of the accused necessary.[619]

4. SUPPORTING MATERIALS FROM OTHER CASES

PROSECUTOR V. BLAŠKIĆ, *Decision on the Production of Discovery Materials,* IT-95-14-T, 27 January 1997, Jorda, Deschênes & Riad, JJ.

The Defense requested the production of the material filed by the Prosecutor in support of the indictments against Ivica Rajić, Zoran Marinić and Zoran Kupreškić on the theory that the allegations also arose out of events in the Lašva Valley and were, therefore, similar to the Blaškić indictment. The defence contended that there would likely be exculpatory evidence contained within the supporting materials.

The Chamber refused to order such production on the grounds that it "would mean disclosing confidential information, not strictly required for General Blaškić's defence, which concerns [in the case of Rajić] another accused who is a fugitive from international justice and for whom prosecutorial proceedings have not reached the same stage of development."[620] The Chamber pointed out that the legitimate objective of the defence, the discovery of exculpatory evidence, could be achieved by reminding the Prosecutor of her obligation of disclosure of exculpatory evidence pursuant to Rule 68.[621]

---

[619] Para. 22.
[620] Para. 28.
[621] *Ibid.*

5. NON-PUBLIC TESTIMONY AND EXHIBITS FROM OTHER CASES

PROSECUTOR V. BLAŠKIĆ, *Opinion Further to the Decision of the Trial Chamber Seized of the Case The Prosecutor v. Dario Kordić and Mario Čerkez Dated 12 November 1998*, IT-95-14-T, 16 December 1998, Jorda, Riad & Shahabuddeen, JJ.

Kordić and Čerkez were charged in an indictment similar to that of General Blaškić for events which occurred in the Lašva Valley. In preparation for their defence the Kordić and Čerkez counsel requested access to the non-public testimony and exhibits in the *Blaškić* case.

 This Trial Chamber determined that the request should be considered under the provisions of Rules 66 and 68. From that standpoint, the Chamber pointed out that the Prosecutor "is obligated to disclose to the Defence certain documents, with no distinction made on the basis of the non-public nature." The Chamber said that the "statement of a witness in one case and, where appropriate, the exhibits tendered on that occasion constitute statements or evidence within the meaning of Rules 66 and 68 of the Rules."

 Based on this analysis, the Chamber ruled that the Prosecutor should determine which witnesses who testified in *Blaškić* would be called in *Kordić* and *Čerkez*. All of these, including exhibits admitted during their testimony should be disclosed. In addition, to the extent there is non-public testimony or documents that fall within the exculpatory evidence provisions of Rule.68 they should likewise be disclosed.

 The Chamber then went on to enter additional protective measures regarding this material.

6. STATEMENTS OF THE ACCUSED

PROSECUTOR V. BLAŠKIĆ, *Decision on the Production of Discovery Materials*, IT-95-14-PT, 27 January 1997, Jorda, Deschênes & Riad, JJ.

The Defence made a request for discovery of all statements of the accused in the possession of the Prosecutor. The Prosecutor contended that this provision of the rule should be interpreted narrowly and should only include "official" statements of the accused either given under oath or, at least, signed and recognized by the accused. The Prosecutor would exempt from the rule all letters, notes, books, orders or other documents written by the accused or produced by him.

 The Chamber disagreed with the Prosecutor's narrow interpretation. The Chamber ruled: "all the previous statements of the accused which appear in the Prosecutor's file, whether collected by the Prosecution or originating from any other source, must be disclosed to the Defence immediately."[622]

 The Chamber did point out, however, that Rule 66(C) would permit the Prosecutor to apply for relief from disclosure where such disclosure "may prejudice

---

[622] Para. 37.

further or ongoing investigations or be contrary to the public interest or affect the security interests of any State." In addition Rule 70(A) protects work product, *e.g.*, "reports, memoranda, or other internal documents prepared by a party, its assistants or representatives in connection with the investigation or preparation of the case."[623]

---

[623] Para. 39.

RULE 67

RECIPROCAL DISCLOSURE

(A)   AS EARLY AS REASONABLY PRACTICABLE AND IN ANY EVENT PRIOR TO THE COMMENCEMENT OF THE TRIAL:

  (I)   THE PROSECUTOR SHALL NOTIFY THE DEFENCE OF THE NAMES OF THE WITNESSES THAT THE PROSECUTOR INTENDS TO CALL IN PROOF OF THE GUILT OF THE ACCUSED AND IN REBUTTAL OF ANY DEFENCE PLEA OF WHICH THE PROSECUTOR HAS RECEIVED NOTICE IN ACCORDANCE WITH SUB-RULE (II) BELOW;

  (II)   THE DEFENCE SHALL NOTIFY THE PROSECUTOR OF ITS INTENT TO OFFER:

     (A)   THE DEFENCE OF ALIBI; IN WHICH CASE THE NOTIFICATION SHALL SPECIFY THE PLACE OR PLACES AT WHICH THE ACCUSED CLAIMS TO HAVE BEEN PRESENT AT THE TIME OF THE ALLEGED CRIME AND THE NAMES AND ADDRESSES OF WITNESSES AND ANY OTHER EVIDENCE UPON WHICH THE ACCUSED INTENDS TO RELY TO ESTABLISH THE ALIBI;

     (B)   ANY SPECIAL DEFENCE, INCLUDING THAT OF DIMINISHED OR LACK OF MENTAL RESPONSIBILITY; IN WHICH CASE THE NOTIFICATION SHALL SPECIFY THE NAMES AND ADDRESSES OF WITNESSES AND ANY OTHER EVIDENCE UPON WHICH THE ACCUSED INTENDS TO RELY TO ESTABLISH THE SPECIAL DEFENCE.

(B)   FAILURE OF THE DEFENCE TO PROVIDE NOTICE UNDER THIS RULE SHALL NOT LIMIT THE RIGHT OF THE ACCUSED TO TESTIFY ON THE ABOVE DEFENCES.

(C)   IF THE DEFENCE MAKES A REQUEST PURSUANT TO SUB-RULE 66 (B), THE PROSECUTOR SHALL BE ENTITLED TO INSPECT ANY BOOKS, DOCUMENTS, PHOTOGRAPHS AND TANGIBLE OBJECTS, WHICH ARE WITHIN THE CUSTODY OR CONTROL OF THE DEFENCE AND WHICH IT INTENDS TO USE AS EVIDENCE AT THE TRIAL.

(D)   IF EITHER PARTY DISCOVERS ADDITIONAL EVIDENCE OR MATERIAL WHICH SHOULD HAVE BEEN PRODUCED EARLIER PURSUANT TO THE RULES, THAT PARTY SHALL PROMPTLY NOTIFY THE OTHER PARTY AND THE TRIAL CHAMBER OF THE EXISTENCE OF THE ADDITIONAL EVIDENCE OR MATERIAL.

II. TRIBUNAL CASES

A. APPEALS CHAMBER

1. DEFENCES

A. DURESS

PROSECUTOR V. ERDEMOVIĆ, *Judgement*, IT-96-22-A, 7 October 1997, Cassese, McDonald, Li, Stephen & Vohrah

Upon his original plea of guilty, Erdemović offered the explanation that he had been forced to commit the offenses to which he was pleading. This raised the issue of duress as a defence. The Appeals Chamber determined that if duress were a complete defence, then the plea would have been equivocal and should be set aside.[624]

Judges McDonald and Vohrah, in their separate opinion conducted a very detailed and lengthy survey of case law from both national and international jurisdictions. They concluded that although many jurisdictions and cases accept duress as a complete defence, there is no *opinio juris* of a magnitude sufficient to satisfy the requirements of establishing a principle of customary international law.[625]

Judge Li, in a separate opinion arrived at the same position after conducting his own analysis of relevant law. He thus joined Judges McDonald and Vohrah to make up a majority of the Chamber.

Judge Cassese in his separate and dissenting opinion took the position that Judges McDonald and Vohrah overstepped their bounds by conducting a policy analysis. He suggested that once those judges had discovered that there is no specific international rule regarding the defence of duress, they should then have relied on the general rule of duress that provides that in certain circumstances it can be a complete defence. In his criticism of the majority's discussion of "practical policy considerations," Judge Cassese wrote, as follows:

> This International Tribunal is called upon to apply international law, in particular our Statute and principles and rules of international humanitarian law and international criminal law. Our International Tribunal is a court of law; it is bound only by international law. It should therefore refrain from engaging in meta-legal analyses. In addition, it should refrain from relying exclusively on notions, policy considerations or the philosophical underpinnings of common-law countries, while disregarding those of civil-law countries or other systems of law. What is even more important, a policy-oriented approach in the area of criminal law runs contrary to the fundamental customary principle *nullum crimen sine lege*. On the strength of international principles and rules my

---

[624] Para. 31.
[625] Paras. 32 – 87.

conclusions on duress differ widely from those of the majority of the Appeals Chamber.[626]

Judge Cassese concluded, as follows:

> (1) under international criminal law duress may be generally urged as a defence, provided certain strict requirements are met; when it cannot be admitted as a defence, duress may nevertheless be acted upon as a mitigating circumstance; (2) with regard to war crimes or crimes against humanity whose underlying offence is murder or more generally the taking of human life, no special rule of customary international law has evolved on the matter; consequently, even with respect to these offences the *general rule on duress* applies; it follows that duress may amount to a defence provided that its stringent requirements are met. For offences involving killing, it is true, however, that one of the requirements . . . – proportionality – would usually not be fulfilled. Nevertheless, in exceptional circumstances this requirement might be met, for example, when the killing would be *in any case* perpetrated by persons other than the one acting under duress (since then it is not a question of saving your own life by killing another person, but of simply saving your own life when the other person will inevitably die, which may not be 'disproportionate' as a remedy).[627] (Chamber's emphasis).

B.   NECESSITY

PROSECUTOR V. ALEKSOVSKI, *Judgement,* IT-95-14/1-A, 24 March 2000, May, Mumba, Hunt, Tieya, & Robinson, JJ.

The Appeals Chamber declined to consider whether necessity constitutes a defence under international law, whether it is the same as the defence of duress or whether the principle *iura novit curia* should be applied in this case.[628]

C.   TIMELINESS OF A DEFENCE

PROSECUTOR V. ALEKSOVSKI, *Judgement,* IT-95-14/1-A, 24 March 2000, May, Mumba, Hunt, Tieya, & Robinson, JJ.

The Appeals Chamber considered that, in general, the accused before this Tribunal have to raise all possible defences, where necessary in the alternative, during the trial, and where so required under the Rules of Procedure and Evidence. In particular, Rules 67(A) and (B) require notice in relation to alibi and special defences, including that of diminished or lack of mental capacity. Rule 65 *ter* (F) reads, in part: "the pre-trial Judge shall order the defence ... to file a pre-trial brief addressing factual and legal issues, and

---

[626] Para. 11.
[627] Para. 12.
[628] Para. 55.

including a written statement setting out: (i) in general terms, the nature of the accused's defence; (ii) the matters with which the accused takes issue in the Prosecutor's pre-trial brief; and (iii) in the case of each such matter, the reason why the accused takes issue with it."[629]

The Chamber observed that an accused, generally, cannot raise a defence for the first time on appeal.[630] The Chamber found that this general obligation to raise all possible defences during trial stems from the Rules – in particular Rules *65ter* and 67, as well as the obligation upon the accused to plead to the charges against him at his initial appearance pursuant to Rule 62. By not raising a defence in a timely fashion it would preclude the Prosecution the opportunity to cross-examine witnesses testifying in support of any defence put forward and to call rebuttal witnesses, if necessary. It would also create difficulty for the Appeals Chamber in properly assessing a Trial Chamber's judgement where the Defence failed to raise a defence expressly, despite evidence having been led that may support such a defence.[631]

A.   TU QUOQUE

PROSECUTOR V. KUPREŠKIĆ, *et, al., Judgement,* IT-95-16-T, 14 January 2000, Cassese, May & Mumba, JJ.

The Trial Chamber rejected the suggestion made by the Defence that attacks committed against Muslims by Croats could be justified because similar attacks had allegedly been perpetrated by Muslims against the Croat population.

The Chamber rejected the proposition that the conduct of the enemy can justify or legitimize reciprocity or reprisal by the other side. According to the *tu quoque* principle, the fact that the adversary has committed similar crimes offers a valid defence to the individuals accused. The Chamber stated categorically the irrelevance of reciprocity, particularly in relation to obligations found within international humanitarian law that have an absolute and non-derogable character.[632]

In examining the *tu quoque* principle, the Chamber drew a distinction between the proposition that breaches of international humanitarian law, committed by the enemy, which can justify similar breaches by a belligerent and breaches, perpetrated by the adversary, which can legitimize similar breaches by a belligerent in response to, or in retaliation to, such violations by the enemy. The Chamber decided to confine its analysis of the *tu quoque* principle to the first proposition on the basis that response or retaliation coincides more conveniently with the doctrine of reprisals.[633] A difference between *tu quoque* and reprisal is that under *tu quoque*, reciprocation against another's violation of international law could be allowed even when such actions are not justifiable as reprisals.

---

[629] Para. 51.
[630] See, The Prosecutor v. Dusko Tadic, "Judgement" Case No. IT-94-1-A, Appeals Chamber, 15 July 1999, para. 55; The Prosecutor v. Zlatko Aleksovski, "Decision on Prosecutor's Appeal on Admissibility of Evidence", Case No.: IT-95-14/1-AR73, Appeals Chamber, 16 Feb. 2000, paras. 18-20.
[631] Para. 51.
[632] Para. 511.
[633] Para. 515.

According to the *tu quoque* principle, once a norm of the law of war is violated, it no longer applies to the relations between the warring parties.[634] It is precisely on the view that the norms of humanitarian law are not based on a bilateral exchange of rights and obligations that the Chamber rejected the *tu quoque* principle.[635]

The principle was rejected for two reasons. First, the *tu quoque* principle had been rejected by the courts which tried those charged with war crimes following the Second World War on the basis that an accused cannot exculpate himself from a crime by showing that another has committed a similar crime.[636]

Second, and more importantly, the Chamber pointed out that the norms of international humanitarian law are absolute and unconditional and they are not based on reciprocity or contingent upon the adherence to these norms by the other party or parties to a conflict. The Chamber pointed out that most norms of international humanitarian law prohibiting war crimes, crimes against humanity and genocide are peremptory norms of *jus cogens*, which by definition are non-derogable. The Chamber ruled that certain treaty rules are considered so fundamental that they may not be the subjects of reprisal action. The Vienna Convention on the Law of Treaties (1969) at Article 60 provides that provisions relating to the protection of the human person contained in treaties of a humanitarian character, in particular provisions prohibiting any form of reprisals against persons protected by such treaties, may not be revoked for prior material breaches. Despite the fact that crimes against humanity are not a part of treaty law, the Chamber found that there are clearly peremptory norms of *jus cogens* and the *tu quoque* principle is not available either as an excuse or a mitigating factor for the commission of crimes against humanity[637].

B. TRIAL CHAMBERS

1. RULE 67(A)(I)

PROSECUTOR V. DELALIĆ *et. al., Decision on the Defence Motion to Compel the Discovery of Identity and Location of Witnesses*, IT-96-21-T, 18 March 1997, Karibi-Whyte, Odio-Benito & Jan, JJ.

The Chamber ruled that the obligation of the Prosecutor to disclose the "identity" of its witnesses does not necessarily include the present addresses of the witnesses. Substantial identifying information for each witness includes sex, date of birth, names of parents, place of origin and the town or village where the witness resided at the time relevant to the charges. Such information provides the Defence with adequate notice concerning those whom the Prosecution deems essential to the proof of its case against the accused and it allows the Defence to adequately conduct its own investigations. The Chamber ruled that this information allows the Defence to have a proper appreciation of

---

[634] See, also, Bassiouni, Crimes Against Humanity, (1999), pages 502-503.
[635] Para. 517.
[636] Para. 516.
[637] See, also, Bassiouni, Crimes Against Humanity, (1999) pages 504-505.

Prosecution witnesses to prepare its defence and to avoid a mere blind confrontation with the witness in the courtroom. However, under the Rules and Statute, the Defence does not have a right to the current address of a Prosecution witness for the purposes of conducting pre-trial interviews.

The Chamber struck a balance between the right of the Accused to examine witnesses under Article 21(4)(e), the obligation on the Prosecutor to disclose the identify of its witnesses to the Defence under Rule 69(C), the provisions of Article 20(1) which require the appropriate balance between the "full respect" of the rights of the accused and "due regard" for the protection of victims and witnesses, and the power of the Trial Chamber to order measures for the privacy and protection of victims and witnesses provided that the measures are consistent with the rights of the accused under Sub-rule 75(A).

The Chamber stated that it is not for the Prosecution to provide assurances to witnesses once it has decided that these witnesses will be called to give testimony before the Tribunal. The granting of any necessary protective measures is solely a matter for determination by the Trial Chamber.

PROSECUTOR V. BLAŠKIĆ, *Decision on the Production of Discovery Materials,* IT-95-14-PT, 27 January 1997, Jorda, Deschênes & Riad, JJ.

The Defence requested a list from the Prosecutor of all the witnesses the Prosecutor intended to call during the trial. The Prosecutor responded that she was producing the list as quickly as possible.

The Chamber wrote the following:

> The Trial Chamber notes that Sub-rule 67(A) does not refer to an official list. However, by stipulating that the Prosecution has the obligation to inform the Defence of the names of the prosecution witnesses "as early as reasonably practicable and in any event prior to the commencement of the trial," the Rules support the idea that all names of the prosecution witnesses must be disclosed at the same time in a comprehensive document which thus permits the Defence to have a clear and cohesive view of the Prosecution's strategy and to make the appropriate preparations.[638]

---

[638] Para. 22.

2. ALIBI

PROSECUTOR V DELALIĆ *et. al., Decision on the Motion to Compel the Disclosure of the Addresses of the Witnesses,* IT-96-21-T, 13 June 1997, Karibi-Whyte, Odio-Benito & Jan, JJ.

The Trial Chamber ruled that the language of Rule 67(A)(ii) is clear and unambiguous and it imposes an obligation on the defence to disclose the names and addresses of all witnesses which they intend to call in relation to the defence of alibi and any special defence, such as diminished or lack of mental responsibility.

    Rule 67(A)(ii) is clearly distinguishable from the obligation upon the Prosecution under Rule 67(A)(i), which does not include disclosure of the present address of its witnesses.[639]

3. DIMINISHED OR LACK OF MENTAL RESPONSIBILITY

PROSECUTOR V. DELALIĆ *et. al., Judgement,* IT-96-21-T, 16 November 1998, Karibi-Whtye, Odio-Benito & Jan, JJ.

The Trial Chamber made the following observations in regards to the defence of diminished responsibility:

> ...the accused must be suffering from an abnormality of mind which has substantially impaired his mental responsibility for his acts or omissions. The abnormality of mind must have arisen from a condition of arrested or retarded development of the mind, or inherent causes induced by disease or injury. These categories clearly demonstrate that the evidence is restricted to those which can be supported by medical evidence. Consequently, killings motivated by emotions, such as those of jealousy, rage or hate, appear to be excluded.[640]

The Chamber added that an essential requirement of the defence of diminished responsibility is that the accused's abnormality of mind should substantially impair his ability to control his actions. The question of the substantiality of impairment is subjective and is one of fact and need not amount to total impairment. The Chamber considered it pertinent to observe that the ability to exercise self-control in relation to one's physical acts, which is relevant to the defence of diminished responsibility, is distinct from the ability to form a rational judgement which must mean that it is distinct from the level of intelligence of the accused.[641] Finally, the Chamber stated that the defence of diminished responsibility is more likely to be accepted if there is expert

---

[639] It seems that any policy which justifies precluding the Defence from obtaining the present addresses of Prosecution witnesses should apply with equal reason to the Prosecution obtaining the present address of Defence witnesses. It is an equality of arms issue that may, in fact, render these conflicting provisions of the rules violative of the Statute.

[640] Para. 1166.

[641] Para. 1169.

evidence of the accused's mental abnormality which has substantially impaired his mental responsibility.[642]

PROSECUTOR V. DELALIĆ *et. al., Order on Esad Landžo's Submission Regarding Diminished or Lack of Mental Responsibility*, IT-96-21-T, 18 June 1998, Karibi-Whyte, Odio-Benito & Jan, JJ.

The Trial Chamber ruled that the accused offering a special defence of diminished or lack of mental responsibility carries the burden of proving this defence on the balance of probabilities.

The Trial Chamber declined to provide a definition of this defence.

PROSECUTOR V. DELALIĆ *et. al., Order on Edad Landžo's Request for Definition of Diminished or Lack of Mental Capacity*, IT-96-21-T, 15 July 1998, Karibi-Whtye, Odio-Benito & Jan, JJ.

The Trial Chamber referred to its decision *Order on Esad Landžo's Submission Regarding Diminished or Lack of Mental Responsibility*, 18 June 1998, where it reserved decision on the definition of diminished or lack of mental capacity to final judgement and declared itself *functus officio* in respect of the issue of whether it will determine "diminished or lack of mental capacity" prior to judgement.

4. RECIPROCAL DISCOVERY

PROSECUTOR V. DELALIĆ *et. al., Decision on Motion to Specify the Documents Disclosed by the Prosecutor that Delalić's Defence Intends to Use as Evidence*, IT-96-21-T, 8 September 1997, Karibi-Whtye, Odio-Benito & Jan, JJ.

In regards to the Rule 67(C) the Trial Chamber ruled, as follows:

> [S]ub-rule 67(C) deals with the reciprocal obligation on the defence to allow the Prosecution to inspect any books, documents, photographs and tangible objects which it intends to use at trial. In other words, the Sub-rule provides that, if the defence is going to use a certain document at trial and it has previously asked for similar disclosure from the Prosecution under Sub-rule 66(B), it is obliged to allow the Prosecution to inspect those documents beforehand.

The Chamber found that the defence received all the documents relevant to this matter from the Prosecution itself. The Prosecution thus had an opportunity to inspect those documents. The Chamber found that the Prosecution was attempting to gain insight into the defence strategy at trial, rather that obtain disclosure.

---

[642] Para. 1170.

RULE 68

DISCLOSURE OF EXCULPATORY EVIDENCE

THE PROSECUTOR SHALL, AS SOON AS PRACTICABLE, DISCLOSE TO THE DEFENCE THE EXISTENCE OF EVIDENCE KNOWN TO THE PROSECUTOR WHICH IN ANY WAY TENDS TO SUGGEST THE INNOCENCE OR MITIGATE THE GUILT OF THE ACCUSED OR MAY AFFECT THE CREDIBILITY OF PROSECUTION EVIDENCE.

II. TRIBUNAL CASES

B. TRIAL CHAMBERS

1. EXCULPATORY EVIDENCE

PROSECUTOR V BRĐANIN & TALIĆ, *Decision on Motion by Momir Talić for Disclosure of Evidence,* IT-99-36-PT, Hunt, Mumba & Daqun, JJ.

Defendant Talić filed a Motion seeking disclosure of materials pursuant to Rule 68. At the time, a Motion for Protective Measures in which the Prosecutor sought leave to redact certain material from the supporting materials submitted to the confirming Judge was pending.[643] In setting out the Prosecutor's obligations under this rule, the Chamber said:

> The obligation of the prosecution to disclose to the accused the existence of any evidence known to it which in any way tends to suggest the innocence of, or mitigates the guilt of, the accused or which may affect the credibility of prosecution evidence must be discharged "as soon as practicable." The word "evidence" in Rule 68 must be interpreted very widely. It is not restricted to material which is in a form that would be admissible in evidence. It includes all information which in any way tends to suggest the innocence of, or mitigates the guilt of, the accused or which may affect the credibility of prosecution evidence. The obligation is a continuing one, and one which does not depend upon the imposition of any time-limit. If the prosecution knows of the existence of any such evidence at the present time, it must disclose it to the accused "as soon as practicable." The prosecution's response that it is presently premature for it to do so, and that it should be permitted to wait until the decision in the Protective Measures Motion has been given, is rejected.[644]

---

[643] This Motion has now been decided and is reported extensively herein. See Rule 69.
[644] Para. 8.

PROSECUTOR V. BLAŠKIĆ, *Decision on the Production of Discovery Materials,* IT-95-14-PT, 27 January 1997, Jorda, Deschênes & Riad, JJ.

As a component of exculpatory evidence, the Defence requested disclosure by the Prosecutor of a lack of inculpatory evidence regarding any element of any offence contained in the indictment. By the time the motion was argued, it appears that the Defence had limited its request to one that would permit it to raise the issue at trial as the evidence developed. This was in keeping with the Prosecutor's response. The Trial Chamber concurred that the time and place for raising arguments as to the lack of inculpatory evidence was during the trial on the merits.[645]

In its request, the Defence submitted a list of 50 types of materials, asserting that the Defence knew of the existence of the materials and its belief that the Prosecutor had the materials in her possession and had not disclosed them.

The Chamber held that when presented with a specific request such as the one in this case, the Prosecutor must state:

- whether the materials are in fact in her possession;

- whether the materials contain exculpatory evidence;

- whether she believes that although she does possess exculpatory materials, Sub-rule 66(C) or any other relevant provision require that their confidentiality be protected.[646]

PROSECUTOR V DELALIĆ *et. al., Decision on the Request of the Accused Hazim Delić pursuant to Rule 68 for Exculpatory Information,* IT-96-21-T, 24 June 1997, Karibi-Whyte, Odio-Benito & Jan, JJ.

The Trial Chamber defined "exculpatory information" as such material that is known to the Prosecutor and is favourable to the accused in the sense that it tends to suggest the innocence or mitigate the guilt of the accused or may affect the credibility of prosecution evidence.[647]

The Chamber held that the Defence must show that the Prosecutor knows of the existence of the material and that it is in the possession of the Prosecutor. Relying on a decision from the *Blaškić case*, the Chamber found that the Defence is required to make a *prima facie* showing of the exculpatory nature of the material that the Prosecutor possesses.[648]

The Chamber read the provisions of Rule 68 into the general duty of the Prosecutor to disclose information to the Defence pursuant to Rule 66(B), namely the disclosure of evidence in the custody or control of the Prosecutor that is material to the

---

[645] Para. 25.
[646] Para. 47
[647] Para. 12.
[648] Para. 13. Citing, Prosecutor v. Blaškić, *Decision on the Production of Discovery Materials*, IT-95-14-PT, 27 January 1997, para. 50.

preparation of the Defence. Relying on the *Decision on the Motion by the Accused Zejnil Delalić for the Disclosure of Evidence*, 25 September 1996, which dealt with Rule 66(B). The Chamber ruled that the Defence must specify the material it regards as exculpatory.[649]

2. SUPPORTING MATERIALS FROM OTHER CASES

PROSECUTOR V. BLAŠKIĆ, *Decision on the Production of Discovery Materials,* IT-95-14-PT, 27 January 1997, Jorda, Deschênes & Riad, JJ.

The Defense requested the production of the material filed by the Prosecutor in support of the indictments against Ivica Rajić, Zoran Marinić and Zoran Kupreškić on the theory that the allegations also arose out of event in the Lašva Valley and were, therefore, similar to the *Blaškić* indictment. The defence contended that there would likely be exculpatory evidence contained within the supporting materials.

The Chamber refused to order such production on the grounds that it "would mean disclosing confidential information, not strictly required for General Blaškić's defence, which concerns [in the case of Rajić] another accused who is a fugitive from international justice and for whom prosecutorial proceedings have not reached the same stage of development."[650] The Chamber pointed out that the legitimate objective of the defence, the discovery of exculpatory evidence, could be achieved by reminding the Prosecutor of her obligation of disclosure of exculpatory evidence pursuant to Rule 68.[651]

3. EFFECT OF FAILURE TO COMPLY

PROSECUTOR V. BLAŠKIĆ, *Decision on the Defence Motion for Sanctions for the Prosecutor's Continuing Violation of Rule 68,* IT-95-14-T, 25 September 1998, Jorda, Riad & Shahabuddeen, JJ.

The Defence filed a motion seeking sanctions against the Prosecutor for continuing violations of the obligation to disclose pursuant to Rule 68. The Defence, as a sanction, suggested the dismissal of what was apparently a discovery motion filed by the Prosecutor. The Chamber held that a "violation by one party of its disclosure obligations in no way relieves the other party of its own disclosure obligations." In considering the remedy the Chamber said that "possible violations of Rule 68 are governed less by a system of "sanctions" than by the Judges' definitive evaluation of the evidence presented by either of the parties, and the possibility which the opposing party will have had to contest it."

---

[649] Para. 14.
[650] Para. 28.
[651] *Ibid.*

RULE 69

PROTECTION OF VICTIMS AND WITNESSES

(A)   IN EXCEPTIONAL CIRCUMSTANCES, THE PROSECUTOR MAY APPLY TO A TRIAL CHAMBER TO ORDER THE NON-DISCLOSURE OF THE IDENTITY OF A VICTIM OR WITNESS WHO MAY BE IN DANGER OR AT RISK UNTIL SUCH PERSON IS BROUGHT UNDER THE PROTECTION OF THE TRIBUNAL.

(B)   IN THE DETERMINATION OF PROTECTIVE MEASURES FOR VICTIMS AND WITNESSES, THE TRIAL CHAMBER MAY CONSULT THE VICTIMS AND WITNESSES SECTION.

(C)   SUBJECT TO RULE 75, THE IDENTITY OF THE VICTIM OR WITNESS SHALL BE DISCLOSED IN SUFFICIENT TIME PRIOR TO THE TRIAL TO ALLOW ADEQUATE TIME FOR PREPARATION OF THE DEFENCE.

I.   COMMENTARY

Prosecutor v. Brđanin & Talić, *Decision on Motion by Prosecution for Protective Measures*, 3 July 2000

In a far-reaching and comprehensive decision the Trial Chamber analysed and ruled on a number of questions regarding the obligations of the Prosecutor under Rules 66 and the protection of witnesses under Rule 69. The Chamber determined that in considering these issues the rights of the accused must always be paramount. Any protection scheme must adequately take the defendant's rights under Rule 20 into account as a primary consideration. Under no circumstances is the Prosecutor permitted to redact materials provided to the defence without leave of the Trial Chamber. To obtain leave the Prosecutor must show "exceptional circumstances" which are always something more than the prevailing conditions in former Yugoslavia or Tribunal experience with other lawyers in other cases.

II.   TRIBUNAL CASES

B.   TRIAL CHAMBERS

PROSECUTOR V. BRĐANIN & TALIĆ, *Decision on Motion by Prosecution for Protective Measures,* IT-99-36-PT, 3 July 2000, Hunt, Mumba & Pocar, JJ.

In response to her obligations under Rule 66(A)(i), the Prosecutor furnished the Defence with numerous witness statements. However, all identifying information, plus some additional information had been redacted therefrom. This was done without prior authorisation from the Trial Chamber. At the same time the Prosecutor filed a Motion for

343

protective measures, seeking a number of orders from the Trial Chamber. The Chamber authored a comprehensive decision regarding the disclosure obligations of the Prosecutor vis-à-vis the protection of witnesses.

The Prosecutor requested that the Defence be ordered:

- not to disclose any confidential or non-public materials to the media;
- not to disclose to the public, except where necessary for preparation and presentation of the case, the names, identifying information or whereabouts of any witness or potential witness identified to them by the prosecutor, nor any such evidence whether documentary, physical or in the form of statements of witnesses;
- to inform each person among the public to whom disclosure is necessary of the material that it is not to be reproduced in any manner, or publicized or shown to any other person and that such material shall be returned to the defence when it is no longer necessary;
- to maintain a log indicating the name, address and position of anyone to whom such disclosure is made and the date of disclosure; and, if a member of the defence team withdraws from the case all material in their possession should be returned to lead defence counsel; and, at the conclusion of the case all the disclosed material and copies thereof should be returned by counsel to the Registry that have not become part of the public record; and that the Prosecutor is authorized to make limited redactions in the material so furnished concerning the identity and whereabouts of vulnerable victims or witnesses to be disclosed by the Prosecutor only in a reasonable time prior to trial.

The Prosecutor argued that she should be entitled to make the redactions from the materials because "Bosnia and Herzegovina continues to be a dangerous place, where each ethnic or political group is viewed as the enemy of another, and where "much of the war is still being fought, with indictees [sic] or suspects and their supporters (as well as supporters of those detained in The Hague) still at large and where witnesses against them are considered 'the enemy'".[652] The Prosecutor also argued that such an order was justified not just by the circumstances prevailing in this case but also to safeguard future cases that might come before the Tribunal. The Prosecutor argued:

> If witnesses will not come forward or if witnesses refuse or are otherwise unwilling to testify, there is little evidence to present. Threats, harassment, violence, bribery and other intimidation, interference and obstruction of justice are serious problems, for both the individual witnesses and the Tribunal's ability to accomplish its mission.[653]

The Chamber interpreted the language of Rule 69(A), that requires that non-disclosure may only occur in "exceptional circumstances" as follows:

---

[652] Para. 8.
[653] Para. 9.

In the opinion of the Trial Chamber, the prevailing circumstances within the former Yugoslavia *cannot by themselves* amount to exceptional circumstances. The Tribunal has always been concerned solely with the former Yugoslavia and Rule 69(A) was adopted by the judges against a background of ethnic and political enmities which existed in the former Yugoslavia at the time. . . To be exceptional, the circumstances must therefore go beyond what has been, since before the Tribunal was established, the rule – or the prevailing (or normal) circumstances – in the former Yugoslavia.[654] [Chamber's emphasis]

The Chamber concluded that the wholesale redactions in every witness statement disclosed to the Defence under Rule 69 was "both unauthorized and unjustified."[655]

The Chamber rejected a procedure proposed by the Prosecutor according to which the Prosecutor could, without leave, make the redactions she felt were necessary and justified and the accused could then, if necessary, make a request for the identity of certain witnesses or victims to be revealed earlier than, for instance, 30 days before trial. The Chamber decided that this proposal had two basic defects. First, it assumed that every witness is in danger, at risk or vulnerable, which is simply not so; and, second the proposal puts the onus on the defence instead of the prosecutor where it belongs under the clear language of Rule 69(A).[656]

The Chamber ruled that there is no conflict regarding the obligation to disclose under Rules 66(A)(i) and the protection of victims and witnesses under Rule 69(A). Relying on Article 20, the Chamber pointed out: "the rights of the accused are made the first consideration, and the need to protect victims and witnesses is a secondary one." The Chamber said the rule should simply be:

> If the prosecution is able to demonstrate exceptional circumstances justifying the non-disclosure of the identity of any particular victims or witnesses at this early stage of the proceedings, then its obligations of disclosure under Rule 66(A)(i) will be complied with it if produces copies of the statements with the names and other identifying features of only *those* witnesses redacted.[657] (Chamber's emphasis)

Non-Disclosure Orders

The Judges interpreted the phrase "until such person is brought under the protection of the Tribunal" in Rule 69(A). The language implies some sort of witness protection program, but, in fact, none exists. It is clear, however, that the Rule does empower the Chamber to make the "usual non-disclosure orders in relation to particular victims and witnesses once exceptional circumstances have been shown."[658]

---

[654] Para. 11.
[655] Para. 13.
[656] Paras. 16-18.
[657] Para. 21.
[658] Para. 23.

One of the justifications advanced by the Prosecutor for making redactions in this case was that some of the witnesses had expressed a fear that they might be in danger or at risk if they agreed to testify and their identity became known. The Chamber responded to this explanation, as follows:

> It is, however, important to recall the terms of the rule under which the prosecution seeks a non-disclosure order. Rule 69(A) applies only to the "non-disclosure of the identity of a victim or witness who may be in danger or at risk." Any fears expressed by potential witnesses themselves that they may be in danger or at risk are *not in themselves* sufficient to establish any real *likelihood* that they may be in danger or at risk. Something more than that must be demonstrated to warrant an interference with the rights of the accused which these redactions represent.[659] (Chamber's emphasis)

> The Trial Chamber accepts that, once the defence commences (quite properly) to investigate the background of the witnesses whose identity has been disclosed to them, there is a risk that those to whom the defence has spoken may reveal to others the identity of those witnesses, with the consequential risk that the witnesses will be interfered with. But it does not accept that, absent specific evidence of such a risk relating to a particular witness, the likelihood that the interference will eventuate in this way is sufficiently great as to justify the extraordinary measures which the prosecution seeks in this case in relation to every witness.[660]

> Whilst the Tribunal must make it clear to prospective victims and witnesses in other cases that it will exercise its powers to protect them from, *inter alia,* interference or intimidation where it is possible to do so, the rights of the accused in the case in which the order is sought remain the first consideration. It is not easy to see how those rights can properly be reduced to any significant extent because of a fear that the prosecution may have difficulties in finding witnesses who are willing to testify in other cases.[661]

Once the Chamber determines, upon the Prosecutor's showing of "exceptional circumstances" that grounds exist for non-disclosure of identifying information, the question then becomes at what point in the process must such information be disclosed. The Prosecutor suggested that thirty days prior to trial might be the appropriate choice. The Prosecutor argued that the name of the witness provides very little in terms of the preparation activities of the defence.

The Chamber responded:

> There can be no assumption by counsel for the accused that these [protected] witnesses will be telling the truth. There are well-documented cases where, upon a careful investigation, witnesses called by the prosecution have turned out not

---

[659] Para. 26.
[660] Para. 28.
[661] Para. 30

346

to have been where they say they were, or have subsequently retracted their evidence.[662] The Appeals Chamber has placed a firm obligation upon those representing an accused person to make proper inquiries into what evidence is available in that person's defence.[663] Some of the prosecution witnesses are likely to be of such importance that it will be necessary for at least the final stage of the investigation into those witnesses to be done by counsel who is to appear for the accused at the trial. That is obvious to anyone with experience of criminal trials. The earlier stages can be conducted by the investigator(s) retained for the accused in the field. Many more than one person may well need to be spoken to before appropriate information becomes available.[664]

Return of Documents

The Chamber rejected the request of the Prosecutor that the defence be ordered to return to the Registry all non-public documents provided to it by the Prosecutor at the close of the proceedings. The Chamber ruled that once such documents are disclosed to the Defence and have notes made upon them by counsel, they become "work product" and are therefore privileged documents. In addition, the Chamber wrote:

> The Trial Chamber does not accept that the likely risk of either deliberate or unintentional disclosure after the conclusion of the case is of such significance as to justify the unwieldy and possibly unfair consequences of an order that the documents be returned in every case. The fact that orders for the return of statements have been made in similarly general terms in other cases does not impress the Trial Chamber, as the present case appears to be the first in which objection has been taken to orders of the nature sought in this case, and the first in which there has been any examination of what is involved in those orders.
>
> The Trial Chamber is prepared to make an order . . . that if a member of the Brđanin and Talić Defence team withdraws from the case, all the material in his or her possession shall be returned to the lead defence counsel.[665]

The Chamber did acknowledge that there might be instances when document return orders are appropriate, but it should be considered only at the end of the trial when the risk involved may be more easily identified.[666]

---

[662] At this point the Chamber outlined several instances in Tribunal cases where witnesses were found not to be truthful.

[663] Citing, *Prosecutor v. Aleksovski, Decision on Prosecutor's Appeal on Admissibility of Evidence*, IT-95-14/1-AR73, 16 Feb. 1999, par. 18.

[664] Para. 36.

[665] Paras. 43-44.

[666] Para 44.

Maintaining a Log

The Chamber ruled that the Defence does not need to maintain logs of each person to whom the protected material was divulged and the date upon which that was done. The Judges analysed the issue, as follows:

> It is significant, in the view of the Trial Chamber, that the review of this log is contemplated only in the event of a "perceived violation" of the non-disclosure order. As that order is binding only upon the Brđanin and Talić Defence (which term is limited by its definition to the accused themselves, their counsel and all staff assigned to them by the Tribunal), Order (4) [of the Prosecutor's proposed order] appears to be intended specifically to provide the basis for "appropriate" action against only those persons responsible for maintaining the log. The "appropriate" action could well include prosecution for contempt of the Tribunal.[667]
>
> If, however, any member of the defence team is to be prosecuted for contempt, it is perhaps disingenuous of the prosecution to assert that the log will not be disclosed to it, as it would be the prosecution to which the Trial Chamber would necessarily have to turn for assistance in proceedings for contempt pursuant to Rule 77. Again, if any member of the defence team is to be prosecuted for contempt, he or she is entitled to the same presumption of innocence and right to silence which any other accused person has. The obligation to keep the log upon which such a prosecution is to be based would require that accused person to provide evidence against him or herself; contrary to Article 21 of the Tribunal's Statute. Such a procedure could be justified only where the situation were so grave that substantial damage was being caused by improper disclosures. The Trial Chamber is not satisfied that such a situation exists here.[668]

PROSECUTOR V. KOLUNDŽIJA, *Order for Protective Measures*, IT-95-8-PT, 19 October 1999, May, Bennouna & Robinson, JJ.

Protective measures were instituted at the request of the Prosecutor and without objection from the Defence. The Prosecutor was ordered to immediately provide the defence with unredacted copies of the witness statements that formed a part of the supporting materials when the indictment was submitted for confirmation. Neither disclosure of any identifying information regarding these witnesses, nor the substance of their statements was to be made to the public, media or family members and associates of the defendant. The Prosecution and Defence were required to maintain a log indicating the name, address and position of each person or entity to which a copy of the witness statement is delivered along with the date of such disclosure. Persons to whom copies of the

---

[667] Para. 47.
[668] Para. 48

statements are delivered were to be instructed not to make any copies of them, and to return them when they are no longer required. The Defence was permitted to contact a witness or potential witness identified by the Prosecutor only after reasonable prior written notice to the Prosecutor.

RULE 70

MATTERS NOT SUBJECT TO DISCLOSURE

(A)   NOTWITHSTANDING THE PROVISIONS OF RULES 66 AND 67, REPORTS, MEMORANDA, OR OTHER INTERNAL DOCUMENTS PREPARED BY A PARTY, ITS ASSISTANTS OR REPRESENTATIVES IN CONNECTION WITH THE INVESTIGATION OR PREPARATION OF THE CASE, ARE NOT SUBJECT TO DISCLOSURE OR NOTIFICATION UNDER THOSE RULES.

(B)   IF THE PROSECUTOR IS IN POSSESSION OF INFORMATION WHICH HAS BEEN PROVIDED TO THE PROSECUTOR ON A CONFIDENTIAL BASIS AND WHICH HAS BEEN USED SOLELY FOR THE PURPOSE OF GENERATING NEW EVIDENCE, THAT INITIAL INFORMATION AND ITS ORIGIN SHALL NOT BE DISCLOSED BY THE PROSECUTOR WITHOUT THE CONSENT OF THE PERSON OR ENTITY PROVIDING THE INITIAL INFORMATION AND SHALL IN ANY EVENT NOT BE GIVEN IN EVIDENCE WITHOUT PRIOR DISCLOSURE TO THE ACCUSED.

(C)   IF, AFTER OBTAINING THE CONSENT OF THE PERSON OR ENTITY PROVIDING INFORMATION UNDER THIS RULE, THE PROSECUTOR ELECTS TO PRESENT AS EVIDENCE ANY TESTIMONY, DOCUMENT OR OTHER MATERIAL SO PROVIDED, THE TRIAL CHAMBER, NOTWITHSTANDING RULE 98, MAY NOT ORDER EITHER PARTY TO PRODUCE ADDITIONAL EVIDENCE RECEIVED FROM THE PERSON OR ENTITY PROVIDING THE INITIAL INFORMATION, NOR MAY THE TRIAL CHAMBER FOR THE PURPOSE OF OBTAINING SUCH ADDITIONAL EVIDENCE ITSELF SUMMON THAT PERSON OR A REPRESENTATIVE OF THAT ENTITY AS A WITNESS OR ORDER THEIR ATTENDANCE. A TRIAL CHAMBER MAY NOT USE ITS POWER TO ORDER THE ATTENDANCE OF WITNESSES OR TO REQUIRE PRODUCTION OF DOCUMENTS IN ORDER TO COMPEL THE PRODUCTION OF SUCH ADDITIONAL EVIDENCE.

(D)   IF THE PROSECUTOR CALLS A WITNESS TO INTRODUCE IN EVIDENCE ANY INFORMATION PROVIDED UNDER THIS RULE, THE TRIAL CHAMBER MAY NOT COMPEL THAT WITNESS TO ANSWER ANY QUESTION RELATING TO THE INFORMATION OR ITS ORIGIN, IF THE WITNESS DECLINES TO ANSWER ON GROUNDS OF CONFIDENTIALITY.

(E)   THE RIGHT OF THE ACCUSED TO CHALLENGE THE EVIDENCE PRESENTED BY THE PROSECUTION SHALL REMAIN UNAFFECTED SUBJECT ONLY TO THE LIMITATIONS CONTAINED IN SUB-RULES (C) AND (D).

(F)   THE TRIAL CHAMBER MAY ORDER UPON AN APPLICATION BY THE ACCUSED OR DEFENCE COUNSEL THAT, IN THE INTERESTS OF JUSTICE, THE PROVISIONS OF THIS RULE SHALL APPLY *MUTATIS MUTANDIS* TO SPECIFIC INFORMATION IN THE POSSESSION OF THE ACCUSED.

(G)   NOTHING IN SUB-RULE (C) OR (D) ABOVE SHALL AFFECT A TRIAL CHAMBER'S POWER UNDER RULE 89 (D) TO EXCLUDE EVIDENCE IF ITS PROBATIVE VALUE IS SUBSTANTIALLY OUTWEIGHED BY THE NEED TO ENSURE A FAIR TRIAL.

II.　　TRIBUNAL CASES

B.　　Trial Chambers

1. Documents Used by a Witness in Preparation for Testimony

PROSECUTOR V. BLAŠKIĆ, *Order for the Production of Documents Used to Prepare for Testimony,* IT-95-14-T, 22 April 1999, Jorda, Shahabuddeen & Rodrigues, JJ.

At trial, the defendant Blaškić testified at length and in great detail. During the testimony, he revealed that in preparation for his testimony he relied on a war diary prepared by his deputy and a military log of his activities at his headquarters.

On its own, without request by the Prosecutor, the Trial Chamber ordered the production of the war diary and the military log by the Defence. The Chamber determined that it "deems it appropriate, in the interest of justice and so that it be better able to ascertain the truth" that it should have the war diary and military log produced. The Chamber ordered both the Defence and the Federation of Bosnia and Herzegovina to produce the documents.

The Chamber specifically found that the documents "could not be said to constitute internal or other documents within the meaning of" Rule 70.

2. Witnesses called under this Rule

PROSECUTOR V. BLAŠKIĆ, *Decision of Trial Chamber I on the Prosecutor's Motion for Video Deposition and Protective Measures,* IT-95-14-T, 11 November 1997, Jorda, Riad & Shahabuddeen, JJ.

By Motion, the Prosecutor sought to present the testimony of Witness A by video deposition under the provisions of this rule. The Defence objected on several grounds, including the suggested limitations on cross-examination.

The Chamber first determined that the proposed testimony of Witness A actually fell within the provisions of this rule. This required a finding that the information is in the possession of the Prosecutor and that it was provided confidentially for the sole purpose of generating new evidence. It is important that the condition of confidentially not be one imposed by the Prosecutor but by the entity furnishing the confidential information to the Prosecutor.

Having made the threshold findings the Chamber went on to order:

- Witness A shall be heard at a closed session;

- classified documents, the provision of which was sought by the Defence, shall not be provided to it unless the Government concerned should decide to provide them on its own initiative;

-the scope of the Defence cross-examination shall be restricted to the scope of the direct examination, the Chamber reserving for itself the right to rule in any dispute in this respect;

- in accordance with Sub-rule 70(D), Witness A may decline to answer a question about the information involved or about its origin on the grounds of confidentiality;

- a representative of the Government concerned may be present in the courtroom at the time of Witness A's deposition.

With respect to the rights of the Defendant, the Trial Chamber stated:

. . . the Statute of the Tribunal as well as the latter's Rules of Procedure and Evidence guarantee the accused a fair trial and that the provisions of Sub-rule 70(G), in particular, enable the Chamber to exclude any evidence whose probative value would be substantially outweighed by the needs of a fair trial.

RULE 71

DEPOSITIONS

(A)   WHERE IT IS IN THE INTERESTS OF JUSTICE TO DO SO, A TRIAL CHAMBER MAY ORDER, *PROPRIO MOTU* OR AT THE REQUEST OF A PARTY, THAT A DEPOSITION BE TAKEN FOR USE AT TRIAL, WHETHER OR NOT THE PERSON WHOSE DEPOSITION IS SOUGHT IS ABLE PHYSICALLY TO APPEAR BEFORE THE TRIBUNAL TO GIVE EVIDENCE. THE TRIAL CHAMBER SHALL APPOINT A PRESIDING OFFICER FOR THAT PURPOSE.

(B)   THE MOTION FOR THE TAKING OF A DEPOSITION SHALL INDICATE THE NAME AND WHEREABOUTS OF THE PERSON WHOSE DEPOSITION IS SOUGHT, THE DATE AND PLACE AT WHICH THE DEPOSITION IS TO BE TAKEN, A STATEMENT OF THE MATTERS ON WHICH THE PERSON IS TO BE EXAMINED, AND OF THE CIRCUMSTANCES JUSTIFYING THE TAKING OF THE DEPOSITION.

(C)   IF THE MOTION IS GRANTED, THE PARTY AT WHOSE REQUEST THE DEPOSITION IS TO BE TAKEN SHALL GIVE REASONABLE NOTICE TO THE OTHER PARTY, WHO SHALL HAVE THE RIGHT TO ATTEND THE TAKING OF THE DEPOSITION AND CROSS-EXAMINE THE PERSON WHOSE DEPOSITION IS BEING TAKEN.

(D)   DEPOSITION EVIDENCE MAY BE TAKEN EITHER AT OR AWAY FROM THE SEAT OF THE TRIBUNAL, AND IT MAY ALSO BE GIVEN BY MEANS OF A VIDEO-CONFERENCE.

(E)   THE PRESIDING OFFICER SHALL ENSURE THAT THE DEPOSITION IS TAKEN IN ACCORDANCE WITH THE RULES AND THAT A RECORD IS MADE OF THE DEPOSITION, INCLUDING CROSS-EXAMINATION AND OBJECTIONS RAISED BY EITHER PARTY FOR DECISION BY THE TRIAL CHAMBER. THE PRESIDING OFFICER SHALL TRANSMIT THE RECORD TO THE TRIAL CHAMBER.

I.   COMMENTARY

A number of changes were made to this rule, effective 7 December 1999. The old Rule 71(A) provided that only the parties could request that depositions be taken and that an order for deposition evidence could be granted in "exceptional circumstances." Under the amended Rule 71(A), either party may make an application or the Trial Chamber *proprio motu* may order that depositions be taken. The words "exceptional circumstances" were deleted. Furthermore, under Rule 71(A), depositions may be taken from an individual whether or not he or she is able physically to appear before the Tribunal. Rule 71(D), as amended, provides that depositions may be taken at or away from the seat of the Tribunal or by video-conference pursuant to Rule 71 *bis*.

The decision of the Appeals Chamber in the *Kupreškić* case under the old version of Rule 71, *Decision on Appeal by Dragan Papić Against Ruling to Proceed by Deposition* of 15 July 1999, reported below, appears to have influenced the amendment to Rule 71.

Although decided under the old version of Rule 71, the *Kvočka* decision is an example of the procedure that may be adopted for taking depositions.

II.   TRIBUNAL CASES

A.   APPEALS CHAMBER

PROSECUTOR V. KUPREŠKIĆ, *et. al., Decision on Appeal by Dragan Papić Against Ruling to Proceed by Deposition,* IT-95-16, 15 July 1999, Vohrah, Wang Tieya, Nieto-Navia, Hunt & Bennouna, JJ.

During the defence presentation in the trial of this case one of the Judges became ill. The Presiding Judge informed the parties that the Judge would likely be absent for the remainder of the week. The Presiding Judge then asked if either of the parties was prepared to make a request to continue taking the testimony of defence witnesses by deposition pursuant to Rule 71. The Prosecutor made the request orally. Counsel for Appellant opposed the deposition procedure. In spite of this objection, the Presiding Judge ruled that the depositions would proceed. The testimonies of two witnesses were taken by deposition. During the testimony by deposition of the third witness the Judges were informed that Dragan Papić had filed a Motion for Leave to Appeal at which point the deposition was stopped.

The Appellant raised four grounds in this appeal. He first contended that the ruling is flawed since it was made by only two judges and not by the Trial Chamber, which according to the Statute, Article 12, is composed of three judges. He also argued that the ruling was rendered in response to an oral request only and that the rule provides for a written request and can relate only to the requesting party's own witnesses. Here the Prosecutor orally requested that depositions be taken of Defence witnesses. Third, he contended that the procedure violated the provisions of Rules 15(E) and 15(F). Finally, he contended that the ruling was inconsistent with his right to have his witnesses examined under the same conditions as the witnesses against him pursuant to Article 21(4)(e) of the Statute. The full Trial Chamber heard all the witnesses for the Prosecutor, none by deposition.

In regards to the first ground of appeal, the Chamber ruled:

> As to the first ground of appeal, namely that the ruling was illegal since it was not rendered by a properly constituted Trial Chamber as required by Rule 71 but by two Judges, it is clear from the transcript that the decision to proceed by way of deposition was taken in direct response to the Prosecution's oral request, prompted by the Presiding Judge, and in the face of the Appellant's express opposition to the granting of that request. The transcripts of the proceedings do not in any way indicate that the two sitting Judges had discussed the matter in advance with the absent Judge. On the basis of the record of proceedings, it must be concluded that the ruling was in fact rendered by only the two sitting Judges.[669]

---

[669] Para. 13.

Rule 71 provides that a Trial Chamber may order that a deposition be taken, whilst Article 12 of the Statute stipulates that a Trial Chamber shall be composed of three Judges. Given the plain and ordinary meaning of the latter provision, a Trial Chamber is only competent to act as a Trial Chamber *per se* if it comprises three Judges. Consequently, the requirement in Rule 71 that an order for depositions to be taken may only be rendered by a Trial Chamber has not been met. That a written decision confirming the ruling was issued by the Trial Chamber the following day could not *ipso facto* cure this illegality. Where the Statute or the Rules prescribe that a matter is to be decided by a *Trial Chamber*, two sitting Judges may not do so on the part of the Trial Chamber, save in the case where the Trial Chamber has received prior authorisation by the President. Such authorisation may, however, only be given in respect of routine matters pursuant to Sub-rule 15(E). In the present case, no such authorisation had been given by the President, and, in any event, the making of a decision to proceed by way of deposition with regard to the examination of witnesses giving evidence on facts relating to the specific charges made against an accused, thereby having a direct bearing on the determination of the guilt or innocence of the accused, does not, in the view of the Appeals Chamber, constitute "routine matters" within the meaning of Sub-rule 15(E). This is amply supported by the two examples provided in the provision having no bearing whatsoever on any determination of the culpability or otherwise of the accused.

The Appeals Chamber, therefore, finds that the ruling was null and void since it was rendered without jurisdiction with regard to defence witnesses Pero Papić and Goran Males, both of whom were heard pursuant to the ruling. .[670]

As to the second ground of appeal, the Chamber ruled that the oral motion by the Prosecutor– as opposed to a written motion as prescribe by Rule 71 – was purely a technical non-compliance with the rule and had no adverse affects upon the rights of the accused or the integrity of the proceedings. All parties were present and given the opportunity to voice their views of the matter.[671]

In relation to the third ground of appeal – the proposition that the deposition procedure of Rule 71 could be used to circumvent the normal procedure in the event of the illness of a Judge as set forth in Rule 15 and that the illness of a Judge was not an "exceptional circumstance" within the spirit of this rule – the Chamber said:

> In considering the issues raised by this ground of the appeal, the Appeals Chamber deems it necessary to recall one of the fundamental principles governing the giving of evidence before the Trial Chambers, namely the principle that witnesses shall as a general rule be heard directly by the Judges of the Trial Chambers. This principle is laid down in Article 21(4) of the Statute which grants to every accused person appearing before the Tribunal as one of the "minimum guarantees, in full equality", the right to examine, or have

---

[670] Para. 14
[671] Para. 15

examined, the witnesses against him and to obtain the attendance and examination of witnesses on his behalf under the same conditions as witnesses against him. Sub-rule 90(A) embodies that same principle and specifically prescribes that witnesses shall in principle be heard directly by the Chambers. Furthermore, this principle is a predominant feature in the criminal procedure of national legal systems, underpinned as it is by the compelling reason of facilitating the determination of the charges against an accused person. One of the consequences of this principle is the advantage that all three Judges of a Trial Chamber shall have of observing the demeanour of the witness in person while he or she is being examined by the parties, apart from their ability to put questions to the witness under solemn circumstances in order to best ascertain the truth in respect of the crimes with which an accused is being charged.[672]

The Appeals Chamber is also alive to the need to avoid an overly restrictive interpretation of the Rules so as to allow the Trial Chambers to respond to the varied circumstances with which they are faced and to ensure the efficient functioning of the Tribunal. Notwithstanding these considerations, the Appeals Chamber takes the view that Rule 71 must be construed strictly and in accordance with its original purpose of providing an exception, with special conditions, to the general rule for direct evidence to be furnished, especially in the context of a criminal trial. In the result, any relaxation of Rule 71 or deviation from the purpose for which it was originally designed must require the consent of the accused.[673]

The Chamber did indicate, however, that the deposition procedure could be used in this context where an accused gave his consent to such procedure.[674]

Finally, an analysis of Article 21(4) and its source in the European Convention on Human Rights, led the Chamber to the conclusion that the Appellant's contention that he had a right to have his witnesses heard under the same conditions as the Prosecutor's witnesses did not require that the witnesses for all parties give their evidence in exactly the same manner. The contention was found to be without merit.[675]

B.   TRIAL CHAMBERS

PROSECUTOR V. KVOČKA *et. al.*, *Decision to Proceed by Way of Deposition Pursuant to Rule 71*, IT-98-30-PT, 15 November 1999, May, Bennouna & Robinson, JJ.

In this case, the parties provided the Chamber with a list of witness for whom it was agreed that deposition evidence could be taken, together with the current whereabouts of those witnesses. The Chamber then entered the following order:

---

[672] Para. 18.
[673] Para. 19.
[674] Para. 22.
[675] Para. 24.

1. The evidence of the witnesses listed in the Confidential Annex to this Decision will be taken by way of deposition pursuant to Rule 71;

2. Ms. Yvonne Featherstone, Senior Legal Officer, is appointed as Presiding Officer in respect of the depositions, under the terms of Rule 71(A);

3. The Presiding Officer shall call the parties in this case to a conference to consider matters relating to the taking of the depositions, including dates, venue, travel and accommodation;

4. The Presiding Officer is empowered, in consultation with the Registry, to make all practical arrangements in respect of the depositions, except that deposition evidence shall be taken in closed session and the accused shall not be present;

5. The Presiding Officer shall present the Trial Chamber with a written report on the status of the deposition proceedings every other month and further, shall report immediately any difficulties in the implementation of this Decision to the Trial Chamber; and

Any applications for protective measures, including safe conduct, in respect of individual witnesses whose evidence will be taken by way of deposition, must be filed with the Trial Chamber by 15 December 1999.

RULE 71 *BIS*

TESTIMONY BY VIDEO-CONFERENCE LINK

AT THE REQUEST OF EITHER PARTY, A TRIAL CHAMBER MAY, IN THE INTERESTS OF JUSTICE, ORDER THAT TESTIMONY BE RECEIVED VIA VIDEO-CONFERENCE LINK.

II. TRIBUNAL CASES

B. TRIAL CHAMBERS

PROSECUTOR V. DELALIĆ *et. al., Decision on the Motion to Allow Witness K, L and M to give their Testimony by Means of Video-link Conference*, IT-96-21-T, 28 May 1997, Karibi-Whyte, Odio-Benito & Jan, JJ.

This matter was decided under Rule 75(B)(iii). The Trial Chamber observed that evidence by video-link is not provided for in the Rules. The conditions under which such evidence may be given were determined by relying on the provisions of the Rules governing evidence generally and the jurisprudence of major legal systems, as reflective of "general principles of law" in accordance with Sub-rule 89(B).

     The Chamber observed that video-link evidence is an exception to the right of having the witness physically present in the courtroom as guaranteed the accused under Article 21(4)(e). The accused may confront the witness by cross-examination and the Trial Chamber may observe the witness during his or her testimony. The Chamber held that video-conferencing is an extension of the Chamber to the location of the witness.[676] Such evidence may be given away from the seat of the Tribunal or by means of one-way closed circuit television from an isolated location at the Tribunal.

     In determining whether evidence could be given by video-link, the Chamber applied the two conditions articulated in the *Tadić* case,[677] and added a third criterion. The three-pronged test the party requesting video-link must satisfy is the following:

1. The testimony of the witness must be shown to be sufficiently important to make it unfair to proceed without it;

2. The witness must be unable or unwilling for good reason to come to the International Tribunal at The Hague; and

3. The accused must not be prejudiced in the exercise of his right to confront the witness.[678]

---

[676] Para. 15.

[677] Prosecutor v. Tadić, *Decision on the Defence Motions to Summon and Protect Defence Witnesses, and on the Giving of Evidence by Video-Link*, IT-94-1, 25 June 1996, paragraph 21.

[678] Para. 17.

The Chamber observed that the evidentiary value of testimony provided by video-link is not as weighty as testimony given in the courtroom. The fact that the witness is not physically present in the courtroom may detract from the reliance placed upon his or her evidence. But, the credibility of the witness is a matter for the Chamber to determine when evaluating the evidence as a whole.[679]

In addition, the Chamber adopted the guidelines from the *Tadić*[680] case to ensure that testimony given by video-link conference is practicable and reliable:

> The Trial Chamber acknowledges the need to provide for guidelines to be followed in order to ensure the orderly conduct of the proceedings when testimony is given by video-link. First, the party making the application for video-link testimony should make arrangements for an appropriate location from which to conduct the proceedings. The venue must be conducive to the giving of truthful and open testimony. Furthermore, the safety and solemnity of the proceedings at the location must be guaranteed. The non-moving party and the Registry must be informed at every stage of the efforts of the moving party and they must be in agreement with the proposed location. Where no agreement is reached on an appropriate location, the Trial Chamber shall hear the parties and the Registry, and make a final decision. The following locations should preferably be used: (i) an embassy or consulate, (ii) offices of the International Tribunal in Zagreb or Sarajevo, or, (iii) a court facility. Second, the Trial Chamber will appoint a Presiding Officer to ensure that the testimony is given freely and voluntarily. The Presiding Officer will identify the witnesses and explain the nature of the proceedings and the obligation to speak the truth. He will inform the witnesses that they are liable to prosecution for perjury in case of false testimony, will administer the taking of the oath and will keep the Trial Chamber informed at all times of the conditions at the location. Third, unless the Trial Chamber decides otherwise, the testimony shall be given in the physical presence only of the Presiding Officer and, if necessary, of a member of the Registry technical staff. Fourth, the witnesses must, by means of a monitor, be able to see, at various times, the Judges, the accused and the questioner, similarly the Judges, the accused and the questioner must each be able to observe the witness on their monitor. Fifth, a statement made under solemn declaration by a witness shall be treated as having been made in the courtroom and the witness shall be liable to prosecution for perjury in exactly the same way as if he had given evidence at the Seat of the International Tribunal.

---

[679] Para. 18.
[680] Prosecutor v. Tadić, *Decision on the Defence Motions to Summon and Protect Defence Witnesses, and on the Giving of Evidence by Video-Link*, IT-94-1, 25 June 1996.

PROSECUTOR V. DOKMANOVIĆ, *Decision on the Prosecutor's Motion for Deposition Evidence,* IT-95-13a-T, 11 March 1998, Cassese, May & Mumba, JJ.

The Prosecution sought protective measures for a witness under Rule 79 and applied for the witness to give evidence by deposition under Rule 71. The Chamber found that the Prosecution had established that the testimony of this witness was sufficiently important as to make it unfair to proceed without it and that the witness was unable or unwilling for good reason to come to the International Tribunal. The Defence did not object to the protective measures sought or to the testimony of the witness being given in this fashion.

The Chamber ruled that the Witness should testify by video-link and not by way of deposition under Rule 71. The Chamber observed that it prefers that witnesses be heard directly whenever possible or by video-conference link if that is not possible.

The Chamber approved of the guidelines for the giving of evidence by video-conference link laid down in the *Tadić* case:[681]

Order:

1. Witness D may give testimony through video-conference link provided that the necessary equipment can be made available to the International Tribunal;

2. The name, address, whereabouts and other identifying data concerning the person given pseudonym D shall not be disclosed to the public or to the media;

3. The name, address, whereabouts and other identifying information concerning witness D shall be sealed and not included in any of the public records of the International Tribunal;

4. To the extent the name of, or other identifying data concerning witness D is contained in existing public documents of the International Tribunal, that name and other identifying data shall be expunged from those documents;

5. Documents of the International Tribunal identifying this witness shall not be disclosed to the public or the media;

6. The pseudonym D shall be used whenever referring to this witness in proceedings before the International Tribunal and in discussions among parties to the trial;

7. The accused, the defence counsel and their representatives who are acting pursuant to their instructions or requests shall not disclose the name of this witness or other identifying data concerning this witness to the public or to the media, except to the limited extent such disclosure to members of the public is necessary to investigate the witness adequately;

8. Any such disclosure shall be done in such a way as to minimise the risk of the witness's name being divulged to the public at large or to the media;

9. The public and the media shall not photograph, video-record or sketch the protected witness while the witness is in the precincts of the International Tribunal; and

---

[681] Prosecutor v. Tadić, *Decision on the Defence Motions to Summon and Protect Defence Witnesses, and on the Giving of Evidence by Video-Link*, IT-94-1, 25 June 1996.

HEREBY DIRECTS the Registrar to take all reasonable steps in the circumstances of the present case to ensure that the guidelines established in the *Tadić Decision* are followed.

RULE 72

PRELIMINARY MOTIONS

(A)   PRELIMINARY MOTIONS, BEING MOTIONS WHICH

    (I)   CHALLENGE JURISDICTION;

    (II)   ALLEGE DEFECTS IN THE FORM OF THE INDICTMENT;

    (III)   SEEK THE SEVERANCE OF COUNTS JOINED IN ONE INDICTMENT UNDER RULE 49 OR SEEK SEPARATE TRIALS UNDER RULE 82 (B); OR

    (IV)   RAISE OBJECTIONS BASED ON THE REFUSAL OF A REQUEST FOR ASSIGNMENT OF COUNSEL MADE UNDER RULE 45 (C)

SHALL BE IN WRITING AND BE BROUGHT NOT LATER THAN THIRTY DAYS AFTER DISCLOSURE BY THE PROSECUTOR TO THE DEFENCE OF ALL MATERIAL AND STATEMENTS REFERRED TO IN RULE 66 (A)(I) AND SHALL BE DISPOSED OF NOT LATER THAN SIXTY DAYS AFTER THEY WERE FILED AND BEFORE THE COMMENCEMENT OF THE OPENING STATEMENTS PROVIDED FOR IN RULE 84..

(B)   DECISIONS ON PRELIMINARY MOTIONS ARE WITHOUT INTERLOCUTORY APPEAL SAVE

    (I)   IN THE CASE OF MOTIONS CHALLENGING JURISDICTION, WHERE AN APPEAL BY EITHER PARTY LIES AS OF RIGHT;

    (II)   IN OTHER CASES WHERE LEAVE TO APPEAL IS, UPON GOOD CAUSE BEING SHOWN, GRANTED BY A BENCH OF THREE JUDGES OF THE APPEALS CHAMBER.

(C)   APPLICATIONS UNDER SUB-RULE (B)(I) SHALL BE FILED WITHIN FIFTEEN DAYS AND APPLICATIONS FOR LEAVE TO APPEAL UNDER SUB-RULE (B)(II) SHALL BE FILED WITHIN SEVEN DAYS OF FILING OF THE IMPUGNED DECISION. WHERE SUCH DECISION IS RENDERED ORALLY, THE APPLICATION SHALL BE FILED WITHIN SEVEN DAYS OF THE ORAL DECISION, UNLESS

    (I)   THE PARTY CHALLENGING THE DECISION WAS NOT PRESENT OR REPRESENTED WHEN THE DECISION WAS PRONOUNCED, IN WHICH CASE THE TIME-LIMIT SHALL RUN FROM THE DATE ON WHICH THE CHALLENGING PARTY IS NOTIFIED OF THE ORAL DECISION; OR

    (II)   THE TRIAL CHAMBER HAS INDICATED THAT A WRITTEN DECISION WILL FOLLOW, IN WHICH CASE THE TIME-LIMIT SHALL RUN FROM FILING OF THE WRITTEN DECISION.

I. COMMENTARY

In 1996, at the time of a series of preliminary motions in the *Delalić* case, Rule 73 – Other Motions – did not exist. An interlocutory appeal by Delalić under Rule 72(B)(ii) seeking redress from the decision of the Trial Chamber, which had refused his request for provisional release, was dismissed because it did not satisfy the first branch of the test under Rule 72(B)(ii) – an application relating to one of the issues covered by the Rule relating to preliminary motions.[682]

Today, an appeal against a refusal to grant provisional release or any other matter not covered by Rule 72 may be brought pursuant to Rule 73 – Other Matters – after the case has been assigned to a Trial Chamber.

II. TRIBUNAL CASES

A. APPEALS CHAMBER

1. JURISDICTIONAL QUESTIONS

PROSECUTOR V. BRĐANIN, *Decision on Interlocutory Appeal from Decision on Motion to Dismiss Indictment Filed Under Rule 72*, IT-99-36-AR72, 16 November 1999, Bennouna, Shahabuddeen, Vohrah, Tieya & Nieto-Navia, JJ.

Defendant Brđanin filed a Motion to dismiss the indictment pending against him. In the motion, he contended that since there was no evidence in the supporting material that supported a *prima facie* case under the indictment, the Trial Chamber was without jurisdiction to proceed.

The Trial Chamber denied the Motion.

Brđanin then filed an Interlocutory Appeal, challenging the Trial Chamber's decision.

The Appeals Chamber rejected the Interlocutory Appeal as improperly filed:

> . . . assuming *arguendo* the existence of a substantive error in the *prima facie* assessment of the material before him by the confirming Judge, such an error could not be considered as going to jurisdiction within the meaning of Rule 72(B)(i).[683]

---

[682] Prosecutor v. Delalić et. al., *Decision on Application for Leave to Appeal (Provisional Release)*, IT-96-21-PT, 15 October 1996.

[683] Page 3.

PROSECUTOR V. DELALIĆ et. al., *Decision on Application for Leave to Appeal (Provisional Release) by Hazim Delić*, IT-96-21-PT, 22 November 1996, Cassese, Li & Deschênes, JJ.

The Legality of the Establishment of a Three-Member Bench of Judges to Entertain Applications for Leave to Appeal

The applicant challenged the legality of the establishment of a three-member panel of the Appeals Chamber to sit in consideration of an application for leave to appeal. Article 12 of the Statute states that "five judges shall serve in the Appeals Chamber".

The Chamber ruled that the establishment of the three-member panel to determine whether to grant leave to appeal was consistent with the Rules and broadened the right of appeal provided for under the Statute. Pursuant to the express language of Article 25 of the Statute, appeal is limited to appeals by persons convicted by the Trial Chamber or by the Prosecutor. The Chamber determined that Rule 72 broadened the right to appeal from this very limited right to appeal and thus it enhanced and strengthened the rights of the parties. The Judges through Rule 72 introduced interlocutory appeals *ex novo*. The Chamber found that, under the Rules, the Judges set out conditions which the parties must meet to be granted leave before a full five-member appeals bench, where there is no appeal as of right. This "filter mechanism" was set up in the interest of good and expeditious administration of justice, namely for the purpose of promptly rejecting abusive interlocutory appeals while promptly admitting admissible interlocutory appeals. Furthermore, the Judges had the authority to lay down in their jurisprudence the test to be applied for granting leave to appeal.[684]

B.   TRIAL CHAMBERS

1. JURISDICTIONAL QUESTIONS

PROSECUTOR V. BRĐANIN, *Decision on Motion to Dismiss the Indictment*, IT-99-36-PT, 5 October 1999, Hunt, PTJ

Defendant Brđanin filed a Motion to Dismiss the Indictment pursuant to Rule 72(A)(i) of the Rules. He contended that the Tribunal was without jurisdiction to proceed on the indictment against him because the supporting material provided to the confirming Judge did not support the allegations of the indictment.

The Pre-Trial Judge, determined several things in his written decision. In essence, the Judge ruled that the confirmation process is one of form, not substance. The only question that could possibly be considered by a Trial Chamber is whether the confirming Judge followed the proper procedure in the confirmation process.[685]

---

[684] Paras. 20-21.
[685] Para. 8.

Article 19(1) of the Statute only requires that the indictment disclose a *prima facie* case, not the supporting material. The Statute makes no reference to supporting materials.[686] The Pre-Trial Judge made the following findings:

> . . . even if it be accepted for the purposes of argument that the supporting material did not establish the *prima facie* case pleaded in the indictment, the jurisdiction of the Tribunal still depends solely upon what is pleaded in the indictment. Whether there is evidence to support any charge pleaded in the indictment is an issue to be determined – as in both the common law and civil law systems – by the Trial Chamber, at the conclusion of the trial or (if the issue is raised) at the close of the prosecution case.[687]

> The Trial Chamber is satisfied that an insufficiency of the supporting material is irrelevant to the issue of the Tribunal's jurisdiction.[688]

> There is no provision in the Rules of Procedure and Evidence which permits a Trial Chamber to review the actual decision made by the confirming judge, by way of appeal or in any other way.[689]

2. INTERLOCUTORY APPEALS: GOOD CAUSE

PROSECUTOR V DELALIĆ *et. al., Decision on Motion by Esad Landžo pursuant to Rule 73*, IT-96-21-T, 1 September 1997, Karibi-Whyte, Odio-Benito & Jan, JJ.

There is a discussion in this Decision regarding the meaning of "good cause".
In Rule 72(B)(ii), leave to appeal may be granted "upon good cause being shown."
The *Landžo* decision provides some insight into the meaning of "good cause." It is reasonable to say that "good cause" indicates the discretionary nature of the power vested in a Trial Chamber to grant the relief sought on a case-by-case basis. The applicant must show that there are good and substantial reasons why his application should be entertained.[690]

PROSECUTOR V. DELALIĆ *et. al., Decision on Zdravko Mucić's Motion for Leave to File an out-of-time Application pursuant to Rule 73*, IT-96-21-T, 1 September 1997, Karibi-Whyte, Odio-Benito & Jan, JJ.

This Decision is similar to the preceding Landžo Decision.
It was held that Mucić established good cause that enabled the Trial Chamber to exercise its discretion to grant relief from waiver under Rule 73(B).
Mucić did not bring a preliminary motion within the prescribed time limits to

---

[686] Para 12.
[687] Para. 15.
[688] Para. 20.
[689] Para. 21.
[690] Paras. 14-17.

challenge the admissibility of the statement he gave to the Prosecutor. The Chamber found that there was good cause to grant relief from waiver, since the accused was alleging that his statement was obtained in oppressive circumstances. The reason for granting the waiver was to enable the Prosecution to satisfy the Trial Chamber that there was no oppression in obtaining the statement; that is to show that the statement was offered voluntarily by the accused.

PROSECUTOR V. DELALIĆ *et. al., Decision on Hazim Delić's Motions Pursuant to Rule 73*, IT-96-21-T, 1 September 1997, Karibi-Whyte, Odio-Benito & Jan, JJ.

Like the previous decisions, the phrase "good cause" is commented upon by the Trial Chamber in the context of the old Rule 73(C), "showing of good cause" for a grant of relief of waiver to file an out-of-time preliminary motion.

In regard to the phrase "good cause", the Trial Chamber stated:

> The most important hurdle in the compliance with Sub-rule 73(C) is the determination of what constitutes good cause to persuade the Trial Chamber to exercise its discretion in favour of the applicant. The phrase good cause used in Sub-rule 73(C) is an ordinary English expression commonly used in judicial legislation enabling the Judge in the exercise of his discretion where the applicant has lost or forfeited his right. The determination of the meaning of the phrase good cause is a question of fact depending upon the particular facts and circumstances of the case within the context of the rights in respect of which the application is brought. Accordingly, although it is difficult to prescribe a general rule as to what should constitute good cause it seems to the Trial Chamber that a combination of circumstances may be relevant. For instance, where the reason for the application would be defeated if the discretion is not exercised in favour of the applicant, the fact that the right pursued is very substantial and likely to succeed, or the delay is not inordinate will constitute a good cause for the exercise of discretion.[691]

---

[691] Para. 6.

RULE 73

OTHER MOTIONS

(A) AFTER A CASE IS ASSIGNED TO A TRIAL CHAMBER, EITHER PARTY MAY AT ANY TIME MOVE BEFORE THE CHAMBER BY WAY OF MOTION, NOT BEING A PRELIMINARY MOTION, FOR APPROPRIATE RULING OR RELIEF SUCH MOTIONS MAY BE WRITTEN OR ORAL, AT THE DISCRETION OF THE TRIAL CHAMBER.

(B) DECISIONS ON SUCH MOTIONS ARE WITHOUT INTERLOCUTORY APPEAL SAVE WITH THE LEAVE OF A BENCH OF THREE JUDGES OF THE APPEALS CHAMBER WHICH MAY GRANT SUCH LEAVE

    (I)   IF THE DECISION IMPUGNED WOULD CAUSE SUCH PREJUDICE TO THE CASE OF THE PARTY SEEKING LEAVE AS COULD NOT BE CURED BY THE FINAL DISPOSAL OF THE TRIAL INCLUDING POST-JUDGEMENT APPEAL; OR

    (II)   IF THE ISSUE IN THE PROPOSED APPEAL IS OF GENERAL IMPORTANCE TO PROCEEDINGS BEFORE THE TRIBUNAL OR IN INTERNATIONAL LAW GENERALLY.

(C) APPLICATIONS FOR LEAVE TO APPEAL SHALL BE FILED WITHIN SEVEN DAYS OF THE FILING OF THE IMPUGNED DECISION. WHERE SUCH DECISION IS RENDERED ORALLY, THE APPLICATION SHALL BE FILED WITHIN SEVEN DAYS OF THE ORAL DECISION, UNLESS

    (I)   THE PARTY CHALLENGING THE DECISION WAS NOT PRESENT OR REPRESENTED WHEN THE DECISION WAS PRONOUNCED, IN WHICH CASE THE TIME-LIMIT SHALL RUN FROM THE DATE ON WHICH THE CHALLENGING PARTY IS NOTIFIED OF THE ORAL DECISION; OR

    (II)   THE TRIAL CHAMBER HAS INDICATED THAT A WRITTEN DECISION WILL FOLLOW, IN WHICH CASE THE TIME-LIMIT SHALL RUN FROM FILING OF THE WRITTEN DECISION.

II.   TRIBUNAL CASES

A.   APPEALS CHAMBER

1. RULE 73(B)(II): INTERLOCUTORY APPEALS

PROSECUTOR V. KOVAČEVIĆ, *Order Refusing Leave to Appeal,* IT-97-24, 24 September 1998, Shahabuddeen, Wang Tieya & Nieto-Navia, JJ.

The Trial Chamber refused a request by the Prosecutor that all materials furnished by the Prosecutor to the Defence in this case be returned, since the case had concluded. The Prosecutor then sought leave to appeal. A Bench of the Appeals Chamber denied leave to appeal. The Chamber determined that Rule 73(B) presupposes that the decision was made in a pending case. Since this case was terminated by the death of the accused, the impugned decision could not be appealed. The Chamber was without jurisdiction to hear the appeal. The Bench pointed out that they were not called upon to decide whether there is a right of appeal without leave in this situation.[692]

PROSECUTOR V. DELALIĆ *et. al., Decision on Prosecution's Application for leave to Appeal Pursuant to Rule 73,* IT-96-21-T, 16 December 1997, McDonald, Vohrah & Nieto-Navia, JJ.

The Prosecution appealed against the decision of the Trial Chamber to preclude the Prosecution from calling an expert witness in relation to handwriting. (Oral decision on 3 December 1997, *Order on the Motion to seek leave to call additional expert witness concerning handwriting,* 20 January 1998).

The Appeals Chamber considered the Application of general importance to proceedings before the Tribunal because the issues at its heart were issues of fairness to the accused and the proper conduct of international criminal proceedings.[693]

The Prosecution sought leave to call a handwriting expert on 18 November 1997. The Trial Chamber had issued an Order on 25 January 1997 requiring the parties to give notice of their potential expert witnesses. The Order stipulated that "good cause" must be shown for a party to call an expert, notice of whose testimony is given after that date. The Chamber found that the Prosecution failed to show good cause why it should be permitted to call the handwriting expert.[694]

The Appeals Chamber found that allowing the Prosecution to call a handwriting expert at this stage in the case would prejudice the accused's right to a fair trial, guaranteed in Article 21 of the Statute and Article 14 of the International Covenant on Civil and Political Rights.[695]

In particular, the Chamber pointed out that the Prosecution had known since June 1997 that the Trial Chamber would require strict proof of the authorship of documents. The Prosecution was not precluded from attempting to secure independent proof of the authorship of the documents. There was no indication that a handwriting expert was unavailable at an earlier stage.[696]

Moreover, the Chamber observed that the accused's right to a prompt and fair trial became paramount in light of the fact that the Prosecution was ready to close its case. With greater assiduity the Prosecution could have called a handwriting expert earlier. The accused had been in detention for 20 months.[697]

---

[692] See the full report of the Trial Chamber Decision under Rule 54.
[693] Para. 6.
[694] Para. 8.
[695] Para. 12.
[696] Paras. 11-12.
[697] Para. 13.

2. INTERLOCUTORY APPEAL: ISSUE OF GENERAL IMPORTANCE

PROSECUTOR V. SIMIĆ, *Decision on Application by Miroslav Tadić for Leave to Appeal against Decision on Provisional Release*, IT-95-9-PT, 8 June 1999, Shahabuddeen, Tieya & Nieto-Navia, JJ.

The Appeals Chamber granted leave to appeal pursuant to Rule 73(B)(ii).

Trial Chamber III ordered that oral arguments be heard on the Request for Provisional Release at a hearing on 23 and 24 February 1999. However, the Trial Chamber denied the provisional release request in a written decision of 15 February 1999, without a prior hearing of the parties.

The Chamber considered that the Application for Leave to Appeal raised the issue of whether a Trial Chamber, having ordered that oral arguments be heard on a matter pending before it, may properly issue its decision on that matter solely on the basis of the written submissions of the parties. In granting leave to appeal, the Chamber found that this issue is of general importance to proceedings before the Tribunal within the meaning of Rule 73(B)(ii).

The Chamber did not pronounce on whether the Decision could cause such prejudice to the case of the Appellant Tadić as could not be cured by the final disposal of the trial including post-judgement appeal.

3. INTERLOCUTORY APPEAL: ISSUE WHICH COULD NOT BE CURED BY FINAL DISPOSAL OF THE TRIAL INCLUDING POST-JUDGEMENT APPEAL

PROSECUTOR V. SIMIĆ, *Decision on Application by Stevan Todorović for Leave to Appeal against the Oral Decision of Trial Chamber III of 4 March 1999*, IT-95-9-PT 1 July 1999, McDonald, Shahabuddeen & Cassese, JJ.

The Appeals Chamber granted leave to appeal pursuant to Rule 73(B).

The Chamber observed that the Defence sought an evidentiary hearing and an order directing the Prosecution to afford discovery, as a preliminary step to a subsequent request for the dismissal of the indictment against the accused Todorović and his release from detention.

The Chamber found that in these circumstances the Trial Chamber's decision not to grant the Defence requests could cause such prejudice to the accused Todorović as could not be cured by the final disposition of the trial including post-judgement appeal within the meaning of Rule 73(B)(i).

The Chamber decided to grant leave to appeal on the issue of whether the Trial Chamber erred in denying the Defence request for an evidentiary hearing and an order directing the Prosecution to afford discovery.

B. TRIAL CHAMBERS

1. LAWFULNESS OF DETENTION

PROSECUTOR V. BRĐANIN, *Decision on Petition for a Writ of Habeas Corpus on Behalf of Radoslav Brđanin,* IT-99-36-PT, 8 December 1999, Hunt, JJ.

Defendant Brđanin filed a Petition for a Writ of *Habeas Corpus* in an attempt to challenge the lawfulness of his detention, contending that the supporting material accompanying the indictment did not support a *prima facie* case against him. The Trial Chamber held:

> This Tribunal has no power to issue writs in the name of any Sovereign or other head of state, and it is not a court of civil jurisdiction which can hear the proceedings commenced by such a writ. But the Tribunal certainly does have both the power and the procedure to resolve a challenge to the lawfulness of a detainee's detention.[698]

Since the Chamber decided that *habeas corpus* was not an appropriate method to challenge the lawfulness of detention, it treated the Petition for a Writ of *Habeas Corpus* as a motion pursuant to Rule 73. The Chamber detailed the process by which the indictment had been filed and confirmed and the arrest procedure, all in accordance with the Statute and Rules. The Chamber rejected the contention that such a challenge to lawfulness should be resolved by a review by the Chamber of the supporting material attached to the indictment to determine the existence of a *prima facie* case. The Chamber stated that "such material is manifestly irrelevant to any issue shown to have arisen in the present case concerning the lawfulness of the Accused's detention."[699]

2. MISCELLANEOUS

PROSECUTOR V. SIMIĆ, *et. al., Decision on the Prosecution Motion under Rule 73 for a Ruling Concerning the Testimony of a Witness,* IT-95-9-PT, 27 July 1999, Robinson, Hunt & Bennouna, JJ

In this decision, the Trial Chamber ruled, on an *ex parte* and confidential basis, that the ICRC has an unqualified right to non-disclosure in judicial proceedings of information in the possession of its employees relating to its activities.[700] The decision related to a witness who was a former employee of the ICRC, whom the prosecution had intended to call, and who was prepared voluntarily to give evidence that was apparently relevant to this prosecution. The Chamber held that the evidence of the former employee of the

---

[698] Para. 5.

[699] Para. 16.

[700] Paras. 73-74, 76. The confidentiality of that decision was lifted by an order of the Trial Chamber on 1 October, following the agreement of the parties reached after the decision had been delivered, *Order Releasing Ex Parte Confidential Decision of the Trial Chamber*, IT-95-9-PT, 1 October 1999.

ICRC sought to be presented by the Prosecutor should not be given. The ruling relates only to information obtained by employees of the ICRC in the course of performing their official functions.[701]

---

[701] Para. 36.

RULE 73 *BIS*

PRE-TRIAL CONFERENCE

(A)   PRIOR TO THE COMMENCEMENT OF THE TRIAL, THE TRIAL CHAMBER SHALL HOLD A PRE-TRIAL CONFERENCE.

(B)   IN THE LIGHT OF THE FILE SUBMITTED TO THE TRIAL CHAMBER BY THE PRE-TRIAL JUDGE PURSUANT TO RULE 65 *TER* (K)(I), THE TRIAL CHAMBER MAY CALL UPON THE PROSECUTOR TO SHORTEN THE ESTIMATED LENGTH OR THE EXAMINATION-IN-CHIEF FOR SOME WITNESSES.

(C)   IN THE LIGHT OF THE FILE SUBMITTED TO THE TRIAL CHAMBER BY THE PRE-TRIAL JUDGE PURSUANT TO RULE 65 *TER* (K)(I), THE TRIAL CHAMBER MAY CALL UPON THE PROSECUTOR TO REDUCE THE NUMBER OF WITNESSES IF IT CONSIDERS THAT AN EXCESSIVE NUMBER OF WITNESSES ARE BEING CALLED TO PROVE THE SAME FACTS.

(D)   AFTER COMMENCEMENT OF THE TRIAL, THE PROSECUTOR MAY, IF HE OR SHE CONSIDERS IT TO BE IN THE INTERESTS OF JUSTICE, FILE A MOTION TO REINSTATE THE LIST OF WITNESSES OR TO VARY HIS OR HER DECISION AS TO WHICH WITNESSES ARE TO BE CALLED.

RULE 73 *TER*

PRE-DEFENCE CONFERENCE

(A)   PRIOR TO THE COMMENCEMENT BY THE DEFENCE OF ITS CASE THE TRIAL CHAMBER MAY HOLD A CONFERENCE.

(B)   IN THE LIGHT OF THE FILE SUBMITTED TO THE TRIAL CHAMBER BY THE PRE-TRIAL JUDGE PURSUANT TO RULE 65 *TER* (K)(II), THE TRIAL CHAMBER MAY CALL UPON THE DEFENCE TO SHORTEN THE ESTIMATED LENGTH OF THE EXAMINATION-IN-CHIEF FOR SOME WITNESSES.

(C)   IN THE LIGHT OF THE FILE SUBMITTED TO THE TRIAL CHAMBER BY THE PRE-TRIAL JUDGE PURSUANT TO RULE 65 *TER* (K)(II), THE TRIAL CHAMBER MAY CALL UPON THE DEFENCE TO REDUCE THE NUMBER OF WITNESSES IF IT CONSIDERS THAT AN EXCESSIVE NUMBER OF WITNESSES ARE BEING CALLED TO PROVE THE SAME FACTS.

(D)   AFTER COMMENCEMENT OF THE DEFENCE CASE, THE DEFENCE MAY, IF IT CONSIDERS IT TO BE IN THE INTERESTS OF JUSTICE FILE A MOTION TO REINSTATE THE LIST OF WITNESSES OR TO VARY ITS DECISION AS TO WHICH WITNESSES ARE TO BE CALLED.

PART SIX

PROCEEDINGS BEFORE TRIAL CHAMBERS

RULE 74

AMICUS CURIAE

A CHAMBER MAY, IF IT CONSIDERS IT DESIRABLE FOR THE PROPER DETERMINATION OF THE CASE, INVITE OR GRANT LEAVE TO A STATE, ORGANIZATION OR PERSON TO APPEAR BEFORE IT AND MAKE SUBMISSIONS ON ANY ISSUE SPECIFIED BY THE CHAMBER.

RULE 74 *BIS*

MEDICAL EXAMINATION OF THE ACCUSED

A TRIAL CHAMBER MAY, *PROPRIO MOTU* OR AT THE REQUEST OF A PARTY, ORDER A MEDICAL, PSYCHIATRIC OR PSYCHOLOGICAL EXAMINATION OF THE ACCUSED. IN SUCH CASE, THE REGISTRAR SHALL ENTRUST THIS TASK TO ONE OR SEVERAL EXPERTS WHOSE NAMES APPEAR ON A LIST PREVIOUSLY DRAWN UP BY THE REGISTRY AND APPROVED BY THE BUREAU.

II. TRIBUNAL CASES

B. TRIAL CHAMBERS

PROSECUTOR V. KVOČKA *et. al., Decision on Defence Request for Assignment of Experts for the Accused, Dragoljub Prcać*, IT-98-30/1-T, 18 May 2000, Rodriguez, Riad & Wald, JJ.

On the request of the accused, the Chamber ordered that a psychological and medical-psychiatric examination of the accused be conducted with a view, *inter alia*, of establishing the following:

    1.   Giving information regarding the past and present physical and mental ability of the accused;

    2. Making any necessary observations on the mental state of the accused during the commission of the alleged crimes and interpreting the resulted obtained;

    3.   Giving information on the present psychological state of the accused and on his potential ability to be reintegrated into society, and formulating any needed recommendations in this regard.

A psychological and a medical-psychiatric expert were ordered to file a joint written report of the evaluations, observations and recommendations with the Chamber, which might be taken into consideration, if and where appropriate, for sentencing purposes.

RULE 75

MEASURES FOR THE PROTECTION OF VICTIMS AND WITNESSES

(A)   A JUDGE OR A CHAMBER MAY, *PROPRIO MOTU* OR AT THE REQUEST OF EITHER PARTY, OR OF THE VICTIM OR WITNESS CONCERNED, OR OF THE VICTIMS AND WITNESSES UNIT, ORDER APPROPRIATE MEASURES FOR THE PRIVACY AND PROTECTION OF VICTIMS AND WITNESSES, PROVIDED THAT THE MEASURES ARE CONSISTENT WITH THE RIGHTS OF THE ACCUSED.

(B)   A CHAMBER MAY HOLD AN IN CAMERA PROCEEDING TO DETERMINE WHETHER TO ORDER:

    (I)   MEASURES TO PREVENT DISCLOSURE TO THE PUBLIC OR THE MEDIA OF THE IDENTITY OR WHEREABOUTS OF A VICTIM OR A WITNESS, OR OF PERSONS RELATED TO OR ASSOCIATED WITH A VICTIM OR WITNESS BY SUCH MEANS AS:

        (A)   EXPUNGING NAMES AND IDENTIFYING INFORMATION FROM THE CHAMBER'S PUBLIC RECORDS;

        (B)   NON-DISCLOSURE TO THE PUBLIC OF ANY RECORDS IDENTIFYING THE VICTIM;

        (C)   GIVING OF TESTIMONY THROUGH IMAGE- OR VOICE-ALTERING DEVICES OR CLOSED CIRCUIT TELEVISION; AND

        (D)   ASSIGNMENT OF A PSEUDONYM;

    (II)   CLOSED SESSIONS, IN ACCORDANCE WITH RULE 79;

    (III)   APPROPRIATE MEASURES TO FACILITATE THE TESTIMONY OF VULNERABLE VICTIMS AND WITNESSES, SUCH AS ONE-WAY CLOSED CIRCUIT TELEVISION.

(C) A CHAMBER SHALL, WHENEVER NECESSARY, CONTROL THE MANNER OF QUESTIONING TO AVOID ANY HARASSMENT OR INTIMIDATION.

(D)   ONCE PROTECTIVE MEASURES HAVE BEEN ISSUED IN RESPECT OF A VICTIM OR WITNESS, ONLY THE CHAMBER GRANTING SUCH MEASURES MAY VARY OR RESCIND THEM OR AUTHORISE THE RELEASE OF PROTECTED MATERIAL TO ANOTHER CHAMBER FOR USE IN OTHER PROCEEDINGS. IF, AT THE TIME OF THE REQUEST FOR VARIATION OR RELEASE, THE ORIGINAL CHAMBER IS NO LONGER CONSTITUTED BY THE SAME JUDGES, THE PRESIDENT MAY AUTHORISE SUCH VARIATION OR RELEASE.

I.   COMMENTARY

In the *Kunarac Order on Defence Experts*, the Chamber denied a request to have certain witnesses medically examined. It was the opinion of the Chamber that medical evidence with regard to the offenses alleged in the indictment was not needed and rarely relevant. An example was given of a situation where it could be relevant, however. If a witness were claiming a cigarette burn caused a scar, it would be appropriate to call an expert to say that it was caused by a surgical procedure. This would, of course impeach the witness. The burden to obtain an examination is placed squarely on the Defendant to show that there is a reasonable likelihood, in the particular case, that it will assist the accused. It is difficult to imagine how the Defendant could have convinced the Chamber that a witness with a scar should be medically examined, since he would not know until completion of the examination whether the scar was caused by a cigarette burn or surgery. In proceedings before this Tribunal, often the defence does not know the whereabouts of the witness and is therefore unable to interview persons who know the witness.

II.   TRIBUNAL CASES

B.   TRIAL CHAMBERS

PROSECUTOR V. KUNARAC, *et. al., Order on Defence Experts,* IT-96-23-T, 29 March 2000, Mumba, Hunt & Pocar, JJ.

The three defendants in this case filed a joint motion requesting that they be authorized to share the protected statements of five witnesses with three medical experts and to permit the experts to examine the witnesses. The Prosecutor did not oppose the statements being given to the experts as long as it was clear that they were under the same non-disclosure obligations as counsel in the case. The Prosecutor opposed the requested medical examinations and the Chamber agreed:

> Expert medical evidence is not required in relation to the evidence of witnesses in relation to crimes such as rape, torture, outrages upon personal dignity and enslavement, and the circumstances in which expert medical evidence would even be relevant are rare. An example where such evidence may be relevant would be where a witness claims that a particular scar resulted from a cigarette burn, but where the expert was able to say that the scar was the result of a surgical procedure....However, it would not be appropriate to permit a medical examination unless there is shown to be a reasonable likelihood in the particular case that it will assist the accused.[702]

---

[702] Paras. 5, 6.

The Defence also suggested that it might be helpful to the Chamber to hear from a psychoanalyst regarding the credibility of a witness who had given four conflicting statements in relation to the same events. The Chamber stated that it was "not persuaded from what has been said so far that such evidence would be admissible."[703]

PROSECUTOR V. DOŠEN *et. al., Order on Motion of Accused Kolundžija for Access to Certain Confidential Materials,* IT-95-8-PT, 3 February 2000, May, Bennouna & Robinson, JJ.

Defendant Kolundžija sought an order from the Chamber permitting him access to certain confidential material regarding the issue of post-traumatic stress disorder from the *Furundžija* case. The Prosecutor objected on the grounds that Rule 75(D) provides that such a request must be made to the Trial Chamber that instituted the protective measures in the first instance, or if no longer constituted of the same judges, to the President. The Chamber agreed and dismissed the Motion.

PROSECUTOR V. FURUNDŽIJA, *Request Concerning the Release of Transcripts of Closed Session Testimony of Witnesses,* IT-95-17/1-T, 10 February 1998, Cassese, May & Mumba, JJ.

The Trial Chamber in the *Furundžija* case was seized of the Decision on the Motion of the Accused for Access to Non-public Materials in the Lašva Valley and Related Cases, issued by the Chamber hearing the case of the *Prosecutor v. Dario Kordić and Mario Čerkez.*[704] The Defence in the *Kordić and Čerkez* trial applied to have access to the testimony of those witnesses who testified in the *Furundžija* trial in closed session. Only the Trial Chamber that had made the order could modify the order for protective measures granted in the *Furundžija* case.

    The Trial Chamber in the *Furundžija* case decided that due to the possible safety concerns of each witness, the closed session testimony of only the witnesses *in casu* who consented thereto should be released for possible use in another case before the Tribunal. The Chamber requested the Victims and Witnesses Unit to make investigations and seek the consent of the protected witnesses to redacted transcripts of their closed-session testimony being released to the accused and defence counsel in other pending and future cases before the Tribunal.[705]

    The Victims and Witnesses Unit informed the Chamber that three of five witnesses had consented to having the transcript of their testimony released. The Chamber decided to release to the Trial Chamber seized of the *Kordić and Čerkez* case the transcript of the closed session testimony of the witnesses who had consented to such

---

[703] Para. 7.
[704] The Prosecutor v. Kordić *et. al.*, Case No. IT-95-14/2.
[705] Prosecutor v. Furundžija, *Order*, IT-95-17/1-T, 10 December 1998

release. In deciding to release the transcripts, the Chamber considered that the protected witnesses should continue to enjoy at least an equivalent level of protection. The Chamber ordered the Registrar to release the transcripts of this testimony to the *Kordić and Čerkez* Trial Chamber.

PROSECUTOR V. SIMIĆ, *Order permitting Contact with Witness in the Matter of Contempt Allegations against an Accused and his Counsel,* IT-95-9-R77, 14 October 1999, Robinson, Hunt & Bennouna, JJ.

The Trial Chamber had ordered that a witness was not to have any contact with the Prosecution until his testimony was completed nor was he to discuss the case with anyone until then.

Pursuant to Rule 75, The Chamber amended this Order and allowed members of the Prosecution, including those who have already testified in the proceedings [*i.e.* Investigators] to have contact with the witness, during a recess in proceedings and prior to the completion of his testimony, provided that such contact shall be limited to social and non-case related matters and the testimony of the witness shall not be discussed in any fashion. The Chamber emphasized that breach of this condition would constitute a contempt punishable under Rule 77.

The Chamber considered that this Order struck a balance between the health and well being of the witness and the rights of the accused.

PROSECUTOR V DELALIĆ *et. al., Decision on the Motions by the Prosecution for Protective Measures for the Prosecution Witnesses Pseudonymed "B" through to "M",* IT-96-21-T, 28 April 1997, Karibi-Whyte, Odio-Benito & Jan, JJ.

The Trial Chamber undertook a detailed analysis of all the statutory and rules provisions governing the issue of witness protections. At the outset, the Chamber observed that the Statute and Rules attempt to strike a balance between the rights of the accused and the protection of victims and witnesses.

Article 20(1) of the Statute provides for a fair trial in accordance with the Rules and with full respect for the rights of the accused and due regard for the protection of victims and witnesses. Article 20(4) favours public hearings. Article 21(2) favours a public trial, subject only to Article 22. Article 22 does, however, allow *in camera* hearings to protect the identity of a victim. The Secretary-General in his report to the Security Council called for the protection of victims and witnesses, especially in cases of rape and sexual assault.

In reviewing the Rules adopted for the protections of victims and witnesses, the Chamber noted that Rule 69 allows for non-disclosure to the press, public and accused at the pre-trial stage of the identity of a victim or witness who may be in danger until that witness is brought under the protection of the Tribunal.[706] Rule 75 permits appropriate

---

[706] Para. 36.

protective measures that are consistent with the rights of the accused.[707] Rule 79 provides for the exclusion of the press and public from part of the proceedings on the grounds of public order or morality, the safety or non-disclosure of the identity of a victim or witness or the protection of the interests of justice.[708]

Confidentiality as a protective measure seeks the non-disclosure of identifying information to the public or the media.[709] An order of confidentiality impinges on the right of the accused to a public hearing guaranteed under Article 20(4) and Article 21(2). However, both of these provisions make allowances for a Trial Chamber to hold closed sessions or take other measures designed to protect victims and witnesses. Article 20(4) simply states that a hearing shall be public unless the Trial Chamber decides to close the proceedings in accordance with the Rules. Article 21(2) qualifies the right to a public hearing by making express reference to Article 22 which states that the Rules shall include, but not be limited to, the conduct of in camera proceedings and the protection of the victim's identity to ensure the protection of victims and witnesses.

The Chamber held that the Rules provide for the protection of victims and witnesses in a manner that is consistent with the Statute. Rule 69 (Protection of Victims and Witnesses) allows for non-disclosure to the press, public and accused at the pre-trial stage of the identity of a victim or witness who may be in danger until the witness is brought under the protection of the Tribunal.[710] Rule 75 (Measures for the Protection of Victims and Witnesses) provides for appropriate protective measures that are consistent with the rights of the accused.[711]

Furthermore, Rule 78 (Open Sessions) and Rule 79 (Closed Sessions) reflect the right of the accused to a public hearing and the circumstances in which that right can be limited on the basis that a closed session is necessary for the protection of victims and witnesses. Rule 79(A)(ii) makes specific reference to Rule 75 (Measures for the Protection of Victims and Witnesses) the contents of which were enacted pursuant to Article 22.[712] Rule 79 enables the exclusion of the press and public from the proceedings for various reasons, including safety by the non-disclosure of the identity of a victim and witness. The application of this Rule requires the Chamber to strike a balance between the right of the accused to a public hearing and the right of the witness to protection in the interests of justice.[713]

The Chamber ruled that the testimony of a witness in regard to allegations of having been a victim of sexual assault might be heard in closed sessions pursuant to Rule 79. In regard to this type of testimony, the Chamber made reference to paragraph 108 of the Report of the Secretary-General, which reads as follows:

---

[707] Para. 36.
[708] Para. 36.
[709] Para. 30.
[710] Para. 36.
[711] Para. 36.
[712] Para. 33.
[713] Para. 35.

In the light of the particular nature of the crimes committed in the former Yugoslavia, it will be necessary for the International Tribunal to ensure the protection of victims and witnesses. Necessary protection measures should therefore be provided in the rules of procedure and evidence for victims and witnesses, especially in cases of rape or sexual assault. Such measures should include, but should not be limited to the conduct of in camera proceedings and the protection of the victim's identity.

After surveying the law of many national jurisdictions, the Chamber found that for reasons of public order or morality, under Rule 79(A)(i), the non-disclosure to the public and the media of the identity of a witness giving evidence involving sexual assault was an appropriate measure.[714]

In certain circumstances, a Chamber may order that a witness testify in closed session pursuant to Rule 79, where there is a demonstrable fear of reprisals against that person or his or her family, taking into account the community in which the witnesses and their families live. For fear to constitute a basis for hearing evidence in closed session, the party seeking such relief must present the Chamber with some objective criteria upon which it can base its decision whether to grant or refuse the request for protection. In particular, that party must demonstrate that the witness' testimony is crucial, thus making the witness vulnerable to acts of retaliation.[715]

Without an objective showing of a reason to fear reprisal, a Chamber may order protective measures that are less comprehensive than hearing evidence in closed session under Rule 79. Such a measure may include shielding the witnesses from visual recognition by the public and media. These measures are provided for in Rule 75(B)(i)(c).[716]

Anonymity of a witness means non-disclosure of identity to the public and media, along with protection from face to face confrontation in the courtroom with the accused. The grant of anonymity affects both the right of the accused to a public hearing under Article 20(4) and Article 21(2) and the right to confrontation under Article 21(4)(e). The Chamber held that the general rule is that all evidence, as much as possible, should be produced in the presence of the accused at the hearing with a view to confrontation with the accused. This right cannot be compromised except in the public interest and to uphold public policy.[717]

The Chamber determined that the factors that the party seeking an order of anonymity must satisfy are the following:

(a)   first and foremost, there must be real fear for the safety of the witness or his or her family;

---

[714] Paras. 41-44.
[715] Paras. 46-48.
[716] Para. 49. See, also Prosecutor v. Tadić, *Decision on the Prosecutor's Motion Requesting Protective Measures for Witness R*, IT-94-1, 31 July 1996.
[717] Para. 54-55.

(b)   secondly, the testimony of the witness must be important to the case of the Prosecutor;

(c)   the Trial Chamber must be satisfied that there is no *prima facie* evidence that the witness is untrustworthy;

(d)   the ineffectiveness or non-existence of a witness protection programme by the Tribunal; and

(e)   the protective measures taken should be necessary.

Furthermore, the Chamber held that the issue of balance between the rights of the accused and the protection of victims and witnesses should be examined in the light of the following passage from the dissenting opinion of Judge Stephen in the *Tadić* Trial[718], which was subsequently quoted with approval in the *Blaškić* Trial[719]:

> The philosophy which imbues the Statute and the Rules of the Tribunal appears clear: The victims and witnesses merit protection, even from the accused, during the preliminary proceedings and continuing until a reasonable time before the start of the trial itself. From that time forth, however, the right of the accused to an equitable trial must take precedence and require that the veil of anonymity be lifted in his favour, even if the veil must continue to obstruct the view of the public and the media.

In an application to preclude the witness from seeing the accused or the accused from seeing the witness on the grounds that the witness will be re-traumatised if he or she sees the accused person, the Chamber held that retraumatisation is essentially a medical, psychological condition which requires proof of the specific condition of the witness. Without presenting such evidence to a Trial Chamber, the right of the accused to confrontation with the witness under Article 21(4)(e) prevails. The Chamber noted that other appropriate measures could be ordered to facilitate the testimony of vulnerable victims and witnesses pursuant to Sub-rule 75(B)(iii).[720]

PROSECUTOR V. DELALIĆ *et. al., Decision on the Prosecution's Motion for the Redaction of the Public Record*, IT-96-21-T, 5 June 1997, Karibi-Whyte, Odio-Benito & Jan, JJ.

The issue for determination in this case was whether statements made by a witness regarding her abortion, in the course of her testimony about rape, are admissible into evidence.

The Trial Chamber held that pursuant to Rule 96(iv), any reference made by the witness during the course of her testimony to her having had an abortion must be

---

[718] Decision on the Prosecutor's Motion requesting protective measures for victims and witnesses, 10 August 1995.

[719] Decision on the Application of the Prosecutor dated 19 October 1996 requesting protective measures for victims and witnesses, 5 November 1996.

[720] Paras. 65-66.

removed from the transcript, audio-recordings and video recordings of the Tribunal.

The Chamber held, further, that Rule 75 is not applicable for the resolution of this matter.

The Chamber observed that proceedings before the Tribunal are public and they are transmitted by television to the public gallery of the courtroom, the press lobby and other locations within the Tribunal. Under Order,[721] there is a thirty-minute delay mechanism on the transmission of the proceedings to every monitor other than the monitor in the public gallery. This means that if in the course of open session, a witness or any of the court participants accidentally disclose information of a confidential nature, a party could request the redaction of such information so that, in the subsequent public broadcast, the information would not be included.[722]

The Chamber observed that, pursuant to Rule 79, the press and the public may be excluded from all or part of the proceedings when the Chamber considers that public order, morality, safety and security or non-disclosure of the identity of a victim or witness, and/or the protection of the interests of justice so require. Closed sessions are designed, *inter alia*, to encourage and facilitate the giving of evidence by vulnerable witnesses. Access to the records of closed sessions is restricted to the parties and the Chamber.[723]

Pursuant to Rule 81(B), the disclosure of records of closed sessions may only be ordered by a Trial Chamber when the reasons for their confidentiality no longer exists.

Relying on one of its decisions in *Delalić*,[724] the Chamber observed that the protection of victims and witnesses permits a departure from the general principle of public proceedings. The balance between a public hearing and the protection of victims and witnesses must be assessed within the context of the circumstances of each case.[725]

The Chamber found that Rule 75 envisages protection of potential witnesses by providing the necessary safeguards to facilitate and encourage their appearance before the Tribunal at any stage of trial proceedings. The grounds on which measures to protect victims and witnesses are requested differ as the proceedings unfold.[726]

The measures that a Trial Chamber may order to protect victims and witnesses are wide ranging and may include the protection of their privacy. These measures must be consistent with the rights of the accused and may encompass the non-disclosure to the public and the media of the identity or whereabouts of the victim or witness or his or her family, either by the use of a pseudonym, the expurgation of names and identifying information from the public record, or by any other means which the Chamber may deem appropriate to secure the protection of the victim or witness.[727]

---

[721] Prosecutor v. Delalić et. al., *Order on the Prosecutor's Motion for Delayed Release of Transcripts and Video and Audio Tapes of Proceedings*, 1 October 1996.

[722] Para. 5.

[723] Para. 27.

[724] Prosecutor v. Delalić, *et al, Decision on the Motions by the Prosecution for Protective Measures for the Prosecution Witnesses Pseudonymed "B" through to "M"*, 28 April 1997.

[725] Para. 28.

[726] Para. 30.

[727] Para. 31.

A Chamber may order the redaction of information in the record regarding names or other identifying information of a witness who has been granted protection under Rule 75. In the case of the accidental disclosure of witness identification during proceedings, such information is struck from the public record but it continues to form a part of the full confidential record which cannot be made public unless disclosure is ordered by a Trial Chamber pursuant to Sub-rule 81(B). The rationale for expunging the disclosure of such information is that a preexisting protective order precluded it from becoming public.[728]

However, the power of a Chamber to redact the record does not extend to a situation where witnesses make public the private and potentially embarrassing detail themselves. The Chamber noted that regardless of the sentiments of the witness concerning the public dissemination of private information, a public fact couldn't be transformed into a private one by virtue of an order.[729]

In the instant case, the testimony of the witness took place in open session and was heard by those in the public gallery and it was broadcast to the public over the television network at the Tribunal.[730]

PROSECUTOR V DELALIĆ *et. al.*, *Decision on Confidential Motion for Protective Measures for Defence Witnesses*, IT-96-21-T, 25 September 1997, Karibi-Whyte, Odio-Benito & Jan, JJ.

Protective Measures and Relocation

A Trial Chamber is empowered to grant protective measures to victims and witnesses on the basis of Article 22 and Rules 69, 75, and 79. However, the issue of relocation of a witness and negotiations with the Victims and Witnesses Unit is not a matter to be decided by a Trial Chamber. Relocation is a matter for the Victims and Witnesses Unit that is established under Rule 34, acting under the authority of the Registrar. The Chamber added that in certain circumstances a Trial Chamber should be informed of such arrangements.[731]

Ex Parte Application by the Defence

Normally, an application for protective measures is not brought *ex parte*. However, when the Defence brought this application, there was no obligation to disclose the identity of its witnesses to the Prosecution under Rule 67(A)(i). The Chamber viewed this witness to be a "potential witness" and the measures granted by the Chamber were seen as "interim measures for a potential witness." Only if the individual testified would he be identified to the Prosecution and the Prosecution would be permitted to make submissions in regards to the application for protective measures for the witness.[732]

---

[728] Para. 33.
[729] Paras. 35-36.
[730] Para. 37.
[731] Para. 6.
[732] Para. 9.

PROSECUTOR V. BLAŠKIĆ, *Decision on the Requests of the Prosecutor of 12 and 14 May 1997 in Respect of the Protection of Witnesses*, IT-95-14-PT, 6 June 1997, Jorda, Deschênes & Riad, JJ.

In this case the statement of a witness was disclosed to the media. The Chamber found that since there was no protection order regarding this witness, no investigation would be conducted, as requested by the Prosecutor. However, since the Prosecutor used the occasion to request additional and more restrictive protective measures, the Chamber determined they were justified. As a result, the Chamber ordered the Prosecution and the Defence to:

> 1)   maintain a log indicating the name, address and position of each individual who has received a copy of a witness' statement as well as the date such statement was given and to submit the log to the Trial Chamber whenever the Trial Chamber so requests;

> 2)   instruct those individuals who have received a copy of the statements not to reproduce them – under pain of being held in contempt of the Tribunal – and to return the documents as soon as they are no longer required; and

> 3)   verify that those individuals comply strictly with the above orders.[733]

---

[733] Para. 10.

RULE 76

SOLEMN DECLARATION BY INTERPRETERS AND TRANSLATORS

BEFORE PERFORMING ANY DUTIES, AN INTERPRETER OR A TRANSLATOR SHALL SOLEMNLY DECLARE TO DO SO FAITHFULLY, INDEPENDENTLY, IMPARTIALLY AND WITH FULL RESPECT FOR THE DUTY OF CONFIDENTIALITY.

I.   COMMENTARY

In the decision regarding the subpoena of an interpreter the Chamber declared that interpreters are immune from being summoned to give testimony regarding their official duties. It was contended in this instance that irregularities had occurred during the OTP's taking of a statement from the accused. It seems that in the interest of seeking the truth, there should be an exception to this granted immunity, in the event of a claim of such irregularities. In another context, the Tribunal has determined that government officials may not be subpoenaed to testify regarding the performance of their official duties. However, if that official acquires relevant evidence outside his official duties, he may be summoned to testify. It seems that the same logic would apply to the interpreter who sees irregularities occurring during the course of a statement being taken from an accused. The observation of such irregularities is not within the official duties of that interpreter.

       On the other hand, it seems appropriate that the interpreter be protected from being summoned to testify about the interpretation process itself since those activities are within his or her official duties.

II.   TRIBUNAL CASES

B.   TRIAL CHAMBERS

PROSECUTOR V DELALIĆ *et. al., Decision on the Motion Ex Parte by the Defence of Zdravko Mucić concerning the Issue of Subpoena to an Interpreter,* IT-96-21-T, 8 July 1997, Karibi-Whyte, Odio-Benito & Jan, JJ.

In this case, defendant Mucić sought to subpoena a Tribunal interpreter for the purpose of developing evidence as to matters that had occurred during the taking of a statement from him by the OTP.

       The Chamber held that when a party seeks an order "for the purposes of an investigation or for the preparation or conduct of the trial," under Rule 54 the party seeking the order must satisfy two conditions: it must be necessary for the party to obtain the material and the material must be relevant to an investigation or the preparation or conduct of a trial. The Judges held that the applicant must demonstrate that the evidence sought by way of order must be necessary – not merely useful or helpful – for the purpose of the investigation or for the preparation or conduct of the trial and that there is no other way, but by means of an order, to obtain the evidence sought.[734]

The word "interpreter" is not defined in the Statute and Rules, but the Chamber held that it may be defined as one who interprets from either an official or un-official language of the International Tribunal into the official languages of the International Tribunal and *vice versa* in judicial proceedings or proceedings related thereto.[735]

The duties of an interpreter are enumerated in Rule 76 and require the interpreter to interpret faithfully, independently and impartially and with full respect for the duty of confidentiality.[736] The Chamber found that the essence of the declaration under Rule 76 is to ensure the maintenance of the position of impartiality owed to the parties that is an essential prerequisite of the interpreter's function. The declaration emphasises the independence of the interpreter from either party in the proceedings and the confidentiality of the subject matter interpreted. The interpreter or translator merely passes information to either party of what the other has said in the proceedings and the fact that he or she has no duty to keep a record of what is said by either party makes his/her position extremely difficult if invited to testify as to what exactly was said.[737]

The Chamber held that in the administration of justice, interpreters and other functionaries of the Tribunal – such as clerks or registrars of the court – should be immune from having to testify in respect of matters arising from the discharge of their duties. The Chamber found that an interpreter has the status of an impartial third party in furtherance of the administration of justice. An interpreter is an officer of the Trial Chamber when providing interpretation before the Trial Chamber and an officer of the Tribunal when interpretation is related to judicial proceedings.[738]

---

[734] Para. 13. Citing, Prosecutor v Delalić et al, *Decision on the Prosecutor's Motion for the Production of Notes Exchanged Between Zejnil Delalić and Zdravko Mucić*, IT-96-21-T, 11 November 1996.
[735] Para. 9.
[736] Para. 10.
[737] Para. 19.
[738] Paras. 10, 18, 20.

RULE 77

CONTEMPT OF THE TRIBUNAL

(A)   ANY PERSON WHO:

    (I)   BEING A WITNESS BEFORE A CHAMBER, CONTUMACIOUSLY REFUSES OR FAILS TO ANSWER A QUESTION,

    (II)   DISCLOSES INFORMATION RELATING TO THOSE PROCEEDINGS IN KNOWING VIOLATION OF AN ORDER OF A CHAMBER, OR

    (III)   WITHOUT JUST EXCUSE FAILS TO COMPLY WITH AN ORDER TO ATTEND BEFORE OR PRODUCE DOCUMENTS BEFORE A CHAMBER,

    (IV)   COMMITS A CONTEMPT OF THE TRIBUNAL.

(B)   ANY PERSON WHO THREATENS, INTIMIDATES, CAUSES ANY INJURY OR OFFERS A BRIBE TO, OR OTHERWISE INTERFERES WITH, A WITNESS WHO IS GIVING, HAS GIVEN, OR IS ABOUT TO GIVE EVIDENCE IN PROCEEDINGS BEFORE A CHAMBER, OR A POTENTIAL WITNESS, COMMITS A CONTEMPT OF THE TRIBUNAL.

(C)   ANY PERSON WHO THREATENS, INTIMIDATES, OFFERS A BRIBE TO, OR OTHERWISE SEEKS TO COERCE ANY OTHER PERSON, WITH THE INTENTION OF PREVENTING THAT OTHER PERSON FROM COMPLYING WITH AN OBLIGATION UNDER AN ORDER OF A JUDGE OR CHAMBER, COMMITS A CONTEMPT OF THE TRIBUNAL.

(D)   INCITEMENT TO COMMIT, AND ATTEMPTS TO COMMIT, ANY OF THE ACTS PUNISHABLE UNDER THIS RULE ARE PUNISHABLE AS CONTEMPTS OF THE TRIBUNAL WITH THE SAME PENALTIES.

(E)   NOTHING IN THIS RULE AFFECTS THE INHERENT POWER OF THE TRIBUNAL TO HOLD IN CONTEMPT THOSE WHO KNOWINGLY AND WILFULLY INTERFERE WITH ITS ADMINISTRATION OF JUSTICE.

(F)   WHEN A CHAMBER HAS REASON TO BELIEVE THAT A PERSON MAY BE IN CONTEMPT OF THE TRIBUNAL, IT MAY, *PROPRIO MOTU*, INITIATE PROCEEDINGS AND CALL UPON THAT PERSON THAT HE OR SHE MAY BE FOUND IN CONTEMPT, GIVING NOTICE OF THE NATURE OF THE ALLEGATIONS AGAINST THAT PERSON. AFTER AFFORDING SUCH PERSON AN OPPORTUNITY TO APPEAR AND ANSWER PERSONALLY OR BY COUNSEL, THE CHAMBER MAY, IF SATISFIED BEYOND REASONABLE DOUBT, FIND THE PERSON TO BE IN CONTEMPT OF THE TRIBUNAL.

(G)   ANY PERSON SO CALLED UPON SHALL, IF THAT PERSON SATISFIES THE CRITERIA FOR DETERMINATION OF INDIGENCY ESTABLISHED BY THE REGISTRAR, BE ASSIGNED COUNSEL IN ACCORDANCE WITH RULE 45.

(H)   THE MAXIMUM PENALTY THAT MAY BE IMPOSED ON A PERSON FOUND TO BE IN CONTEMPT OF THE TRIBUNAL:

    (I)   UNDER SUB-RULES (A) AND (E) ABOVE IS A TERM OF IMPRISONMENT NOT EXCEEDING TWELVE MONTHS, OR A FINE NOT EXCEEDING DFL. 40,000, OR BOTH;

> (II)   UNDER SUB-RULES (B), (C) OR (D) ABOVE IS A TERM OF
>   IMPRISONMENT NOT EXCEEDING SEVEN YEARS, OR A FINE NOT
>   EXCEEDING DFL. 200,000, OR BOTH.

(I)   PAYMENT OF A FINE SHALL BE MADE TO THE REGISTRAR TO BE HELD IN A
SEPARATE ACCOUNT.

(J)   ANY DECISION RENDERED BY A TRIAL CHAMBER UNDER THIS RULE SHALL BE
SUBJECT TO APPEAL IN CASES WHERE LEAVE IS GRANTED BY A BENCH OF THREE
JUDGES OF THE APPEALS CHAMBER, UPON GOOD GROUNDS BEING SHOWN.
APPLICATIONS FOR LEAVE TO APPEAL SHALL BE FILED WITHIN SEVEN DAYS OF THE
IMPUGNED DECISION. WHERE SUCH DECISION IS RENDERED ORALLY, THE APPLICATION
SHALL BE FILED WITHIN SEVEN DAYS OF THE ORAL DECISION, UNLESS

> (I)   THE PARTY CHALLENGING THE DECISION WAS NOT PRESENT OR
>   REPRESENTED WHEN THE DECISION WAS PRONOUNCED, IN WHICH
>   CASE THE TIME-LIMIT SHALL RUN FROM THE DATE ON WHICH THE
>   CHALLENGING PARTY IS NOTIFIED OF THE ORAL DECISION; OR

> (II)   THE TRIAL CHAMBER HAS INDICATED THAT A WRITTEN DECISION WILL
>   FOLLOW, IN WHICH CASE THE TIME-LIMIT SHALL RUN FROM FILING OF
>   THE WRITTEN DECISION.

I.   COMMENTARY

II.   TRIBUNAL CASES

A.   APPEALS CHAMBER

PROSECUTOR V. TADIĆ, *Judgement on Allegations of Contempt Against Prior
Counsel, Milan Vujin*, IT-94-1-A-R77, 31 January 2000, Shahabuddeen,
Cassese, Nieto-Navia, Mumba & Hunt, JJ.

The Appeals Chamber found Tadić's former Defence counsel Milan Vujin guilty of
contempt for putting forward to the Chamber, in support of a Rule 115 application, a case
which was known to him to be false and for manipulating witnesses by having them give
statements which avoided any identification of persons who may have been responsible
for the crimes for which Tadić had been convicted so as to avoid the identification of
other persons who may have had exposure.[739]
      Vujin was ordered to pay a fine of Dfl 15,000 and the Registrar was directed to
consider striking him off the list of assigned counsel and to report his conduct to his
professional body.[740] The Chamber stated that it determined the punishment to be

---

[739] Para. 160.
[740] Para. 174.

imposed upon Vujin on the basis that the Registrar in the reasonable exercise of her power would necessarily strike him off the list of assigned counsel and report his conduct to his professional body.[741]

The Chamber held that the power to deal with contempt under Rule 77 is within the inherent jurisdiction of the Tribunal. The Chamber stated that a power to punish conduct that tends to obstruct, prejudice or abuse the administration of justice of the Tribunal is necessary in order to ensure that the exercise of its jurisdiction under the Statute is not frustrated and that its basic judicial functions are safeguarded. Without elaborating on the point, the Chamber added that the Tribunal's powers to deal with contempt or conduct interfering with the administration of justice are not in every situation the same as those possessed by domestic courts, because as an international court must take into account its different setting within the basic structure of the international community.[742]

The Chamber observed that Rule 77 was enacted by the Judges at Plenary meetings pursuant to Article 15 of the Statute that empowers the judges to adopt rules of procedure and evidence for the conduct of matters, *inter alia*, falling within the inherent jurisdiction of the Tribunal. The Chamber stated that Rule 77 was adopted on that basis and not as a new offence, which would be *ultra vires* the power of the judges under the Statute.[743]

In contempt proceedings, it is a matter for the Respondent to allegations of contempt to decide if and when he will give evidence. The Chamber stated that if the Respondent testified after his own witnesses gave testimony, it would take into account the fact that he heard that evidence before giving his own evidence.[744]

Furthermore, the Chamber found that defence counsel appearing in matters before the Tribunal are bound by the *Code of Professional Conduct for Defence Counsel Appearing Before the International Tribunal*, which according to Article 19, prevails where there is any inconsistency between it and any other code which counsel may be bound to honour.[745]

Under Rule 45, the Registrar keeps a list of assigned counsel. The Registrar has the power pursuant to Article 20 of the *Directive on Assignment of Defence Counsel* to strike any counsel off that list where he or she has been refused audience by a Chamber in accordance with Rule 46, and to notify the professional body to which that counsel belongs of the action taken in relation to his or her conduct.

In these proceedings, the Chamber was of the view that Vujin's conduct was substantially worse than what would permit the Registrar to strike counsel off the list pursuant to Article 20 of the Directive. However, the misconduct of counsel provisions of Rule 46 do not apply when counsel is no longer appearing as counsel before the Tribunal, as was the case with Vujin.[746] Nonetheless, the Chamber was of the view that the

---

[741] Para. 164.
[742] Para. 18.
[743] Para. 24.
[744] Paras. 11 and 129.
[745] Para. 163.
[746] Paras. 170-171.

Registrar had power generally to strike Vujin off the list of assigned counsel because of his serious professional misconduct as demonstrated by the Chamber's findings. The Chamber directed the Registrar to consider striking Vujin off the list and reporting his conduct as found by the Chamber to the professional body to which he belongs.[747]

B.   TRIAL CHAMBERS

PROSECUTOR V. FURUNDŽIJA, *The Trial Chamber's Formal Complaint to the Prosecutor Concerning the Conduct of the Prosecution*, IT-95-17/1-T, 5 June 1998, Cassese, May & Mumba JJ.

The complaint against the Prosecution arose as a result of a consistent pattern of non-compliance by the Prosecution with orders of the Trial Chamber, the failure of the Prosecution to comply with obligations imposed by the Rules of Procedure and Evidence, late and/or last minute filing of substantial motions by the Prosecution and the failure of the Prosecution to provide the Trial Chamber with satisfactory reasons for such conduct.[748] The Chamber considered the cumulative effect of the conduct of the Prosecution as being close to negligent.[749]

The Chamber highlighted a number of instances that demonstrated the conduct causing grave concern and which culminated in the formal complaint. The Prosecution failed to comply with certain orders of the Chamber for filing and failed to satisfy the Chamber of a justifiable reason for its conduct.[750] An order to, *inter alia*, supply the Chamber with the statements of witnesses and other documentary material on which the Prosecution intended to rely at trial "as expeditiously as possible" was only satisfied more than three months after it was issued.[751] The Prosecution failed to comply with oral undertakings given to the Chamber to file certain witness statements within a certain period.[752] The Prosecution did not address satisfactorily issues specifically requested by the Chamber regarding alleged violations of Article 7(1) of the Statute in a timely fashion.[753] The Prosecution failed to comply with its Rule 66 disclosure obligations. Finally, the Prosecution failed in its obligation to provide, "not later than sixty days before the date set for trial," copies of the statements of all witnesses whom the Prosecution intends to call to testify at trial.[754] In particular, the Prosecution either before or shortly after the accused had come into the custody of the International Tribunal had received the testimony of the relevant witnesses. The Chamber found it deeply disturbing to discover that a witness statement from the main witness against the accused was only disclosed to the Defence on 22 May 1998, having been received in the office of the Prosecution on 1 November 1997. Furthermore, although the Defence had been able to

---

[747] Para. 164.
[748] Para. 2.
[749] Para. 3.
[750] Para. 9(a).
[751] Para. 9(b).
[752] Para. 9(c).
[753] Para. 9(d).
[754] Para. 9(e).

locate and interview an important Prosecution witness, the Prosecution only discovered this person's whereabouts at the end of April 1998 and interviewed the witness on 19 and 20 May 1998. The decision whether to call this witness as part of the Prosecution case had not been made by 29 May 1998, a little over a week before the trial was scheduled to begin.[755]

The Chamber made specific reference to Article 21 of the Statute in making its complaint about the conduct of the Prosecution. The Chamber observed that its role in protecting the rights of the accused enshrined in Article 21 is of the utmost importance. In particular, the Chamber emphasized that an accused held in detention is presumed innocent until proven guilty and he has a right to have his case dealt with as a priority, in a fair and expeditious manner.[756]

The Chamber observed that counsel who appears before the Tribunal must demonstrate the highest standards of integrity, competence and professionalism. All counsel appearing before the Tribunal are bound by their respective national codes of conduct. In addition, Defence Counsel are bound by the *Code of Conduct for Defence Counsel Appearing Before the International Tribunal.*[757] A Trial Chamber has no jurisdiction to consider the matter of a Code of Conduct for the Prosecution[758] or any express powers of discipline over members of the Prosecution that falls short of contempt under Rule 77.[759]

The Chamber refused to condone inaction, inefficiency, shoddiness and incompetence of any sort from the parties appearing before it. In particular, the Chamber observed that professionalism requires the Prosecution to be particularly diligent, for example, in searching its evidence, records and databases for information relevant to the case in hand and locating witnesses as a matter of urgency.[760]

The Chamber went on to say that it encourages fairness, honesty and professional courtesy between the parties who appear before it. The Chamber observed that this might, in certain circumstances, entail assistance to the other party that may not, on a rigid and narrow reading, be technically required by the Rules. The discovery process exists to enable the accused to examine, in advance of trial, the evidence against him and to build his defence to the allegations against him. In particular, it appeared to the Chamber that Defence Counsel could reasonably expect to be informed by the

---

[755] Para. 9(e). The practice allowing the Prosecutor to delay production of a witness' statement until the Prosecutor decides whether or not she will call him provides an opportunity for the unscrupulous prosecutor to avoid providing witness statements until virtually the last minute. It seems that the rule should be that the statement be provided if it is relevant to any issue in the case. The Defence would then have a much better opportunity of being prepared in the event the witness is called.

[756] Para. 5.

[757] IT/125, 12 June 1997

[758] Para. 4. Citing Prosecutor v. Milan Kovačević, *Order on Defendant's Motion for a Prosecutorial Code of Conduct*, IT-97-24-PT, 12 May 1998. It seems incongruous that there should be a Code of Conduct that applies only to the Defence. Again, this is potentially a violation of equality of arms. If the issue is one of independence of the Prosecutor, then she should draft a Code of Conduct for the Prosecutors and make it public. Otherwise the appearance to the public is that the Tribunal has determined that only Defence counsel are likely to behave unethically or exhibit unprofessional conduct.

[759] Para. 11-12.

[760] Para. 6.

Prosecution if witnesses called to testify against his or her client have testified in other proceedings. Provision of the transcripts of such evidence, if the testimony was given to the Tribunal, should be considered to be within the remit of the discovery process and treated as an obligation upon the Prosecution.[761]

The Chamber held that Rule 77 only covers the most extreme of cases where there has been interference with the course and administration of justice. The Chamber considered that the misconduct of the Prosecution fell short of knowing and wilful interference with the administration of justice, and therefore fell outside the inherent contempt powers recognised in Rule 77(F).[762]

C.   THE PRESIDENT

PROSECUTOR V. DELALIĆ, *et. al., Decision of the President on the Prosecutor's Motion for the Production of Notes Exchanged between Zejnil Delalić and Zdravko Mucić,* IT-96-21-PT, 11 November 1996, Cassese, P.

The President held that the Judges of the Tribunal in Plenary Session adopted Rule 77 by virtue of the inherent powers of the Judges to control proceedings before a Chamber of the Tribunal. The Prosecutor or the Defence may bring allegations of contempt to the attention of a Trial Chamber or a Trial Chamber may *proprio motu* initiate contempt proceedings. The decision whether the matter will be prosecuted lies in the discretion of the Trial Chamber.[763] Under Rule 77, the Prosecutor has no power to prosecute for contempt.

---

[761] Para. 7.
[762] Para. 11.
[763] Para. 34.

RULE 77 *BIS*

PAYMENT OF FINES

(A)   IN IMPOSING A FINE UNDER RULE 77 OR RULE 91, A JUDGE OR CHAMBER SHALL SPECIFY THE TIME FOR ITS PAYMENT.

(B)   WHERE A FINE IMPOSED UNDER RULE 77 OR RULE 91 IS NOT PAID WITHIN THE TIME SPECIFIED, THE JUDGE OR CHAMBER IMPOSING THE FINE MAY ISSUE AN ORDER REQUIRING THE PERSON ON WHOM THE FINE IS IMPOSED TO APPEAR BEFORE, OR TO RESPOND IN WRITING TO, THE TRIBUNAL TO EXPLAIN WHY THE FINE HAS NOT BEEN PAID.

(C)   AFTER AFFORDING THE PERSON ON WHOM THE FINE IS IMPOSED AN OPPORTUNITY TO BE HEARD, THE JUDGE OR CHAMBER MAY MAKE A DECISION THAT APPROPRIATE MEASURES BE TAKEN, INCLUDING:

   (I)   EXTENDING THE TIME FOR PAYMENT OF THE FINE;

   (II)   REQUIRING THE PAYMENT OF THE FINE TO BE MADE IN INSTALLMENTS;

   (III) IN CONSULTATION WITH THE REGISTRAR, REQUIRING THAT THE MONEYS OWED BE DEDUCTED FROM ANY OUTSTANDING FEES OWING TO THE PERSON BY THE TRIBUNAL WHERE THE PERSON IS A COUNSEL RETAINED BY THE TRIBUNAL PURSUANT TO THE DIRECTIVE ON THE ASSIGNMENT OF DEFENCE COUNSEL;

   (IV)   CONVERTING THE WHOLE OR PART OF THE FINE TO A TERM OF IMPRISONMENT NOT EXCEEDING TWELVE MONTHS.

(D)   IN ADDITION TO A DECISION UNDER SUB-RULE (C), THE JUDGE OR CHAMBER MAY FIND THE PERSON IN CONTEMPT OF THE TRIBUNAL AND IMPOSE A NEW PENALTY APPLYING RULE 77 (H)(I), IF THAT PERSON WAS ABLE TO PAY THE FINE WITHIN THE SPECIFIED TIME AND HAS WILFULLY FAILED TO DO SO. THIS PENALTY FOR CONTEMPT OF THE TRIBUNAL SHALL BE ADDITIONAL TO THE ORIGINAL FINE IMPOSED.

(E)   THE JUDGE OR CHAMBER MAY, IF NECESSARY, ISSUE AN ARREST WARRANT TO SECURE THE PERSON'S PRESENCE WHERE HE OR SHE FAILS TO APPEAR BEFORE OR RESPOND IN WRITING PURSUANT TO AN ORDER UNDER SUB-RULE (B). A STATE OR AUTHORITY TO WHOM SUCH A WARRANT IS ADDRESSED, IN ACCORDANCE WITH ARTICLE 29 OF THE STATUTE, SHALL ACT PROMPTLY AND WITH ALL DUE DILIGENCE TO ENSURE PROPER AND EFFECTIVE EXECUTION THEREOF. WHERE AN ARREST WARRANT IS ISSUED UNDER THIS SUB-RULE, THE PROVISIONS OF RULES 45, 57, 58, 59, 59 *BIS*, AND 60 SHALL APPLY *MUTATIS MUTANDIS*. FOLLOWING THE TRANSFER OF THE PERSON CONCERNED TO THE TRIBUNAL, THE PROVISIONS OF RULES 64, 65 AND 99 SHALL APPLY *MUTATIS MUTANDIS*.

(F)   WHERE UNDER THIS RULE A PENALTY OF IMPRISONMENT IS IMPOSED, OR A FINE IS CONVERTED TO A TERM OF IMPRISONMENT, THE PROVISIONS OF RULES 102, 103 AND 104 AND PART NINE SHALL APPLY *MUTATIS MUTANDIS*.

(G)   ANY FINDING OF CONTEMPT OR PENALTY IMPOSED UNDER THIS RULE SHALL BE SUBJECT TO APPEAL AS ALLOWED FOR IN RULE 77 (J).

RULE 78

OPEN SESSIONS

ALL PROCEEDINGS BEFORE A TRIAL CHAMBER, OTHER THAN DELIBERATIONS OF THE CHAMBER, SHALL BE HELD IN PUBLIC, UNLESS OTHERWISE PROVIDED.

RULE 79

CLOSED SESSIONS

(A)   THE TRIAL CHAMBER MAY ORDER THAT THE PRESS AND THE PUBLIC BE EXCLUDED FROM ALL OR PART OF THE PROCEEDINGS FOR REASONS OF:

      (I)   PUBLIC ORDER OR MORALITY;

      (II)   SAFETY, SECURITY OR NON-DISCLOSURE OF THE IDENTITY OF A VICTIM OR WITNESS AS PROVIDED IN RULE 75; OR

      (III)   THE PROTECTION OF THE INTERESTS OF JUSTICE.

(B)   THE TRIAL CHAMBER SHALL MAKE PUBLIC THE REASONS FOR ITS ORDER.

I.   COMMENTARY

In the *Kunarac* case, the Trial Chamber had an opportunity to visit generally the issue of closed hearings. The Chamber said that non-public hearings should be the exception, "the public should have the opportunity to assess the fairness of the proceedings. Justice should not only be done, it should also be seen to be done."[764]

II.   TRIBUNAL CASES

B.   TRIAL CHAMBERS

PROSECUTOR V. KUNARAC, *et. al., Order on Defence Motion Pursuant to Rule 79, IT-96-23-T, 22 March 2000, Mumba, Hunt & Pocar, JJ.*

The Defence filed a motion asking that the press and public be excluded during the testimony of certain Prosecution witnesses. The Defence was concerned that the giving of their testimony in open session could influence its quality, and that the nature of the testimony could violate the morality of the witnesses and the public. It was contended that such an order would be in the interests of justice, since witnesses must feel secure to testify correctly as to certain relevant facts.

      The Chamber rejected the request. The Prosecutor had already requested and obtained protection of the nature requested for certain witnesses where it was clearly justified. That was enough.

---

[764] Para. 5.

With regard to the issue of closed hearings, the Chamber said:

> The Trial Chamber is of the view that it is of great importance that proceedings before this Tribunal should be public as far as possible. Non-public proceedings should be the exception and will be allowed only in accordance with the Statute and the Rules that do provide for certain limited instances where proceedings may be non-public. Over and above the reasons that public proceedings facilitate public knowledge and understanding and may have a general deterrent effect, the public should have the opportunity to assess the fairness of the proceedings. Justice should not only be done, it should also be seen to be done.765

PROSECUTOR V DOKMANOVIĆ, *Decision on Prosecutor's Motion to Modify Order Relating to Videotape of the Arrest of the Accused and Motion for Non-Disclosure of the Contents of the Videotape,* IT-95-13a-PT, 26 September 1997, Cassese, May & Mumba, JJ.

The arrest of the accused by UNTAES personnel in Eastern Slovonia, Croatia was video and audio-recorded and subsequently a transcript of the arrest was prepared. Portions of the audiotapes and the transcript that reflected the arrest of the accused had been made public in connection with a Motion filed by the Defence challenging the legality of the arrest of the accused. However, the Prosecution opposed disclosing the videotape of the arrest to the public, the media and the Defence. The Chamber ordered the Prosecution to file the videotape, under seal, with the Registry. The Judges viewed the videotape in chambers, in the presence of both the Prosecution and the Defence, the Prosecution having that day confirmed in writing to the Chamber that it did not in fact object to the Defence being present and seeing the contents of the videotape in a controlled environment.

The issue for determination was whether the public and the media should be entitled to view the contents of the videotape.

The Chamber held that the videotape of the arrest of the accused must not be disclosed to the public or media, nor could a copy of it be provided to the Defence. A copy of the videotape, which was filed under seal with the Registrar, could be viewed by the Defence, within the precincts of the Tribunal, upon request being made at least two days in advance of the desired time of viewing.

The portions of the audiotapes and the transcripts that had become public exhibits for the purposes of the resolution of the legality of arrest motion filed by the Defence satisfied the requirements of a public trial and the transparency of the judicial process and thus the videotape served no additional function in this regard.[766]

Having considered Rule 78 and 79, the Chamber accepted that release of the videotape to the public could jeopardize the safety of personnel who were still in the region where the arrest occurred and future operations, by revealing the methods and techniques utilised in the execution of arrest warrants. The Chamber observed:

---

[765] Para. 5.
[766] Para. 21.

Given that the region has only recently emerged from a brutal armed conflict and is an area still deemed to require administration by an international authority in order for the peace-building process to remain on track, it is reasonable for that international authority to have some concerns for the safety of its personnel. It is indeed the contention of the Defence that the arrest of the accused met with some outcry on the part of the Serb population of the area and the Prosecution's position that there may be those who wish to harm personnel involved in the arrest does not, therefore, seem entirely unwarranted.[767]

In addition, the Chamber noted that this was the first time that an international body and the Prosecution had executed an arrest warrant issued by the Tribunal and, given the failure of some States to fulfil their obligations to execute arrests themselves, the techniques and methods utilised by such forces are of immense interest to those who seek to evade capture.[768]

PROSECUTOR V DOKMANOVIĆ, *Order for Closed Session*, IT-95-13a-T, 28 May 1998, Cassese, May & Mumba, JJ.

Pursuant to Rule 79, with the agreement of the parties, the Trial Chamber ruled *proprio muto*, in the interests of justice, that the testimony of a defence expert witness regarding the health and personal circumstances of the accused would be given in closed session.

---

[767] Para. 18.
[768] Para. 19.

RULE 80

CONTROL OF PROCEEDINGS

(A)   THE TRIAL CHAMBER MAY EXCLUDE A PERSON FROM THE COURTROOM IN ORDER TO PROTECT THE RIGHT OF THE ACCUSED TO A FAIR AND PUBLIC TRIAL, OR TO MAINTAIN THE DIGNITY AND DECORUM OF THE PROCEEDINGS.

(B)   THE TRIAL CHAMBER MAY ORDER THE REMOVAL OF AN ACCUSED FROM THE COURTROOM AND CONTINUE THE PROCEEDINGS IN THE ABSENCE OF THE ACCUSED IF THE ACCUSED HAS PERSISTED IN DISRUPTIVE CONDUCT FOLLOWING A WARNING THAT SUCH CONDUCT MAY WARRANT THE REMOVAL OF THE ACCUSED FROM THE COURTROOM.

RULE 81

RECORDS OF PROCEEDINGS AND EVIDENCE

(A)   THE REGISTRAR SHALL CAUSE TO BE MADE AND PRESERVE A FULL AND ACCURATE RECORD OF ALL PROCEEDINGS, INCLUDING AUDIO RECORDINGS, TRANSCRIPTS AND, WHEN DEEMED NECESSARY BY THE TRIAL CHAMBER, VIDEO RECORDINGS.

(B)   THE TRIAL CHAMBER MAY ORDER THE DISCLOSURE OF ALL OR PART OF THE RECORD OF CLOSED PROCEEDINGS WHEN THE REASONS FOR ORDERING ITS NON-DISCLOSURE NO LONGER EXIST.

(C)   THE REGISTRAR SHALL RETAIN AND PRESERVE ALL PHYSICAL EVIDENCE OFFERED DURING THE PROCEEDINGS SUBJECT TO ANY PRACTICE DIRECTION OR ANY ORDER WHICH A CHAMBER MAY AT ANY TIME MAKE WITH RESPECT TO THE CONTROL OR DISPOSITION OF PHYSICAL EVIDENCE OFFERED DURING PROCEEDINGS BEFORE THAT CHAMBER.

(D)   PHOTOGRAPHY, VIDEO-RECORDING OR AUDIO-RECORDING OF THE TRIAL, OTHERWISE THAN BY THE REGISTRAR, MAY BE AUTHORISED AT THE DISCRETION OF THE TRIAL CHAMBER.

II.   TRIBUNAL CASES

B.   TRIAL CHAMBERS

PROSECUTOR V DELALIĆ *et. al., Order on the Prosecutor's Motion for Delayed Release of Transcripts and Video and Audio Tapes of Proceedings*, IT-96-21-T, 1 October 1996, Karibi-Whyte, Odio-Benito & Jan, JJ.

The Chamber entered the following Order:

PURSUANT TO RULES 54 and 81

HEREBY GRANTS the MOTION AND ORDERS as follows:

(1) there shall be no simultaneous video or audio transmission of any of the proceedings in this case;

(2) transmission of the recording of the proceedings shall be delayed for a period of thirty minutes unless extended by order of the Trial Chamber;

(3) any party may object to the subsequent release of such transmission and, subject to the decision of the Trial Chamber, may request that the transmission be edited prior to release to the public and the media, in which case the transmission may be further delayed to permit such editing to take place;

(4) in the absence of any such objection, the delayed transmission shall automatically be released at the expiration of the agreed period;

(5) the transcripts of all public proceedings will be released in draft format as soon as practicable after redaction of all matters agreed by the Trial Chamber during the period of delayed transmission;

(6) the final transcript of all public proceedings in this matter will be made available as soon as practicable after review by the parties and incorporation of any corrections accepted by the Trial Chamber.[769]

---

769 Final Transcripts were never provided. The *Čelebići* appeal was conducted on the basis of a Draft Transcript.

RULE 82

JOINT AND SEPARATE TRIALS

(A)   IN JOINT TRIALS, EACH ACCUSED SHALL BE ACCORDED THE SAME RIGHTS AS IF SUCH ACCUSED WERE BEING TRIED SEPARATELY.

(B)   THE TRIAL CHAMBER MAY ORDER THAT PERSONS ACCUSED JOINTLY UNDER RULE 48 BE TRIED SEPARATELY IF IT CONSIDERS IT NECESSARY IN ORDER TO AVOID A CONFLICT OF INTERESTS THAT MIGHT CAUSE SERIOUS PREJUDICE TO AN ACCUSED, OR TO PROTECT THE INTERESTS OF JUSTICE.

I.   COMMENTARY

Although Rule 82 seems to be limited to severance of trials, it should be noted that Rule 107 provides that the rules of evidence and procedure governing proceedings in the Trial Chamber apply *mutatis mutandis* to proceedings in the Appeals Chamber.

II.   TRIBUNAL CASES

A.   APPEALS CHAMBER

1. SEVERANCE

PROSECUTOR V. DELALIĆ, *et. al., Order on Motion by Zejnil Delalić to Sever His Appeal from that of Other Čelebići Appellants*, IT-96-21-A, 29 July 1999, Nieto-Navia, Tieya, Rodriguez, Hunt & Bennouna, JJ.

At trial, Delalić was acquitted while his co-defendants were all convicted. The Prosecution appealed the acquittal of Delalić. He was released from custody immediately following his acquittal. He sought to sever his appeal from that of his co-defendants in an effort to expedite a final judgement. The Chamber in previous rulings determined that it would wait until briefing was completed before deciding the issue.

After consulting the briefs filed by all the parties, the Chamber concluded:

> . . . the issue of command responsibility arises in three of the four appeals filed, and since the Appeals Chamber would wish to reserve its judgment upon that issue until it had heard the other appeals upon that issue, severance of the prosecution appeal against Zejnil Delalić's acquittal from the other appeals would not expedite judgement in that appeal.

B.   TRIAL CHAMBERS

1. JOINT TRIALS

PROSECUTOR V. KUPREŠKIĆ et. al., *Judgement*, IT-95-16-T, 14 January 2000, Cassese, May & Mumba, JJ.

In a joint trial, Chamber must give separate consideration to the case of each accused.[770]

PROSECUTOR V DELALIĆ *et. al., Decision on the Motion by Defendant Delalić Requesting Procedures for Final Determination of the Charges Against Him*, IT-96-21-T, 1 July 1998, Karibi-Whyte, Odio-Benito & Jan, JJ.

The Trial Chamber held that in a joint trial, the first accused cannot conclude his evidence, make closing arguments and have the Chamber render a judgement and possibly a sentence before the second accused starts his defence.

Furthermore, The Chamber observed that the practical effect of attempting to render a verdict in relation to the first accused, before the second accused begins his evidence, impacts directly on the proper conduct of proceedings and ultimately deliberations. Under the Rules, for each accused, the Prosecution may call rebuttal evidence, the accused may call rejoinder evidence and the Trial Chamber may call evidence *proprio motu*. Acceding to the request of the first accused would cause delays in the defence cases of the other accused and result in the Chamber not considering the evidence at trial, as a whole.

The Chamber held that once co-accused are properly joined pursuant to Rule 48, severance of a joint trial can only be ordered under Rule 82(B), as a preliminary motion under Rule 72(A)(iii).

The Chamber found that on a reading of Rule 82(A) and Rules 83, 84, 86 and 87 there was no basis for granting the relief sought by the first accused.

Severance of Persons Jointly Indicted

Rule 82(B) enables severance of crimes joined in one indictment or for separate trials of persons so joined. A motion for severance must be brought as a Preliminary Motion under Rule 72(A)(iii)

The conditions under which a Trial Chamber may order a separate trial are set out in Rule 82(B):

- If the Trial Chamber considers it necessary in order to avoid conflicts of interest that might cause prejudice to an accused; or
- To protect the interest of justice.

The Chamber observed that if either condition is satisfied, a Trial Chamber might order separate trials for the accused.[771] The Chamber stated that the provisions of Rule 82(B) give wide discretion to a Trial Chamber in determining whether an accused

---

[770] Para. 339(b).
[771] Para. 34.

jointly charged should be granted a separate trial. The application of the two conditions set out in Rule 82(B) involves the exercise of judicial discretion.[772]

The Chamber observed that the rationale underpinning joint trials is to save in expense and time, to have the same verdict and treatment of all persons tried jointly in relation to the same transaction, and to avoid discrepancies and inconsistencies which could flow from separate trials of joint offenders.[773]

The Chamber stated that a Trial Chamber may *proprio motu* order a separate trial if satisfied that any of the accused in a joint trial may be seriously prejudiced due to conflicts of interests arising from such a trial. A separate trial may be ordered where evidence admissible against one of the accused is inadmissible against the others or where a separate trial would enable the Prosecution to call an accomplice.[774]

Same Transaction

In construing Rule 48, the word "transaction" should be read in the light of the definition in Rule 2 and Rule 82(B)[775]

Construction of Rules 82 to 87

The Trial Chamber held that an accused tried jointly under Rule 82(B) maintains all the rights of a single accused person, including those enumerated in Articles 20 and 21 and Rules 83 to 87.

Pursuant to Rule 86, closing arguments follow the same order as the presentation of evidence under Rule 85. The Chamber held that an accused person in a joint trial, though vested individually with all the rights of an accused person in a single trial, is subject to the collective rights of the group in the overall interests of justice for ensuring an expeditious and fair trial.[776]

The Chamber read the framework set out in Rules 84-86 in connection with the deliberation of the Trial Chamber in a joint trial, following closing arguments, by the parties:

> [A]n accused in a joint trial will make his opening statement before the presentation of evidence and his closing arguments after the presentation of all the evidence (Rule 86). The presentation of all the evidence in Rule 86 in a joint trial means all evidence on the part of the Prosecution and the Defence of each accused, as a whole. It is not confined to all the evidence of each accused person in the Defence. When Rule 87 refers to both parties completing their presentation of the case it means the Prosecution and all the accused persons as a Defence in a joint accused trial. The Presiding Judge shall declare the hearing closed and the Trial Chamber shall deliberate in private. It is not intended in a multiple accused trial to close the case for each accused person by conducting a

---

[772] Para. 35.

[773] Para. 35.

[774] Para. 36.

[775] Paras. 30-32. Citing, Prosecutor v. Delalić et. al., *Decision on Motions for Separate Trial filed by the Accused Zejnil Delalić and the Accused Zdravko Mucić*, IT-96-21-PT, 25 September 1996.

[776] Para. 41.

separate closing address for this purpose (Rule 87). The trial is a joint trial of all the accused persons on the indictment which has not been severed.[777]

The Chamber found that to be judged separately means that each accused, having been charged with a distinct offence, even if the same, in different counts, ought to be considered separately in accordance with the supporting evidence. Under Rule 87, deliberation is held on the trial as a whole, but voting on each charge is separate as are the findings in respect of each accused tried together under Rule 48.[778]

2. SEPARATE TRIALS

PROSECUTOR V. SIMIĆ *et. al., Decision on Defence Motion to Sever Defendants and Counts,* IT-95-9-PT, 15 March 1999, May, Bennouna & Robinson, JJ.

The Trial Chamber denied the Motion by the Defendant Todorović for severance.

The Chamber ruled that the co-accused were properly joined pursuant to Rule 48, according to the well-established practice of the Tribunal. The alleged events occurred in the "same transaction" in and around the municipalities of Bosanski Šamac and Odžak from approximately 1 September 1991 through 31 December 1993.

The Defendant Todorović argued that a conflict of interest which might cause prejudice to him could be caused in the following situations: (1) if the co-accused choose to testify they might incriminate Todorović; (2) if the co-accused choose not to testify but if their pre-trial statements, which the accused says incriminate him, were to be entered into evidence, he would be deprived of the right to confront and cross-examine "his accusers"; and (3) if the accused himself were to testify on certain counts but remain silent on others, adverse inferences could be drawn against him.

The Chamber held that the possibility of "mutually antagonistic defences" among co-accused does not constitute a conflict of interest capable of causing serious prejudice to an accused within the meaning of Rule 82(B).

PROSECUTOR V DELALIĆ et. al., Decision on Motions for Separate Trial filed by the Accused Zejnil Delalić and the Accused Zdravko Mucić, IT-96-21-PT, 25 September 1996, McDonald, Stephen & Vohrah, JJ.

The Chamber held that the rules relevant to the issue of separate trial must be interpreted in relation to the definition of "transaction" in Rule 2 and Rule 82(B).

When co-accused are jointly charged in one indictment under Rule 48, with acts which are allegedly committed in the same transaction under Rule 2, a Trial Chamber may order the accused to be tried separately if one of two requirements of Rule 82(B) are fulfilled, namely to avoid a conflict of interest that might cause serious prejudice to an accused or to protect the interests of justice.

---

[777] Para. 42.
[778] Paras. 43-44.

In the instant case, the Chamber found that there was an absence of conflict of interest.

In regard to the second prong of the test in Rule 82(B), the Chamber found that it would be contrary to the interests of justice to grant separate trials. Separate trials would result in multiple trials that would cause considerable delays, especially for the accused not tried first. It would require the Judges to hear the same witnesses giving the same evidence more than once.

The Chamber held that the Rules do not provide for a preliminary or separate trial, confined to a sole issue, to held be held prior to the trial on indictment. In the instant case, the accused Delalić sought such a preliminary trial on the issue of his status as a superior under Article 7(3), prior to the commencement of the trial on the indictment in which Delalić was charged along with three other co-accused, three of whom were charged with having committed various violations of Article 2 and Article 3 of the Statute.[779]

Furthermore, the Chamber observed that a preliminary trial confined to one matter would not necessarily result in a speedier outcome than would a joint trial, if the issue determined by way of a preliminary trial was a finding of guilt. In these circumstances, the other co-accused who had to await the outcome of the preliminary trial would suffer considerable delay in the commencement of their trial and witnesses may have to undergo the hardship and inconvenience of testifying in both the preliminary trial and the trial on the indictment.[780]

Joint and Separate Trial

The Chamber held that no conflict of interests was shown to exist between the co-accused.[781]

The Chamber found that a severance of the indictment would be contrary to the interests of justice. A severance would result in two or three trials, instead of just one joint trial, which would entail delay for the accused that was not tried first. Separate trials would involve much duplication of evidence and great hardship on traumatised witnesses. There would be repetition of witnesses between joint trials. The Judges would have to hear the same witnesses giving the same testimony on at least two, and probably more, occasions and on each occasion would have to try to consider the evidence with minds unaffected by their prior conclusions regarding that evidence reached on earlier occasions.[782]

---

[779] Para. 3a.
[780] Para. 8.
[781] Para. 4.
[782] Paras. 5-7.

RULE 83

INSTRUMENTS OF RESTRAINT

INSTRUMENTS OF RESTRAINT, SUCH AS HANDCUFFS, SHALL BE USED ONLY ON THE ORDER OF THE REGISTRAR AS A PRECAUTION AGAINST ESCAPE DURING TRANSFER OR IN ORDER TO PREVENT AN ACCUSED FROM SELF-INJURY, INJURY TO OTHERS OR TO PREVENT SERIOUS DAMAGE TO PROPERTY. INSTRUMENTS OF RESTRAINT SHALL BE REMOVED WHEN THE ACCUSED APPEARS BEFORE A CHAMBER OR A JUDGE.

RULE 84

OPENING STATEMENTS

BEFORE PRESENTATION OF EVIDENCE BY THE PROSECUTOR, EACH PARTY MAY MAKE AN OPENING STATEMENT. THE DEFENCE MAY, HOWEVER, ELECT TO MAKE ITS STATEMENT AFTER THE CONCLUSION OF THE PROSECUTOR'S PRESENTATION OF EVIDENCE AND BEFORE THE PRESENTATION OF EVIDENCE FOR THE DEFENCE.

RULE 84 *BIS*

STATEMENT OF THE ACCUSED

(A)   AFTER THE OPENING STATEMENTS OF THE PARTIES OR, IF THE DEFENCE ELECTS TO DEFER ITS OPENING STATEMENT PURSUANT TO RULE 84, AFTER THE OPENING STATEMENT OF THE PROSECUTOR, IF ANY, THE ACCUSED MAY, IF HE OR SHE SO WISHES, AND THE TRIAL CHAMBER SO DECIDES, MAKE A STATEMENT UNDER THE CONTROL OF THE TRIAL CHAMBER. THE ACCUSED SHALL NOT BE COMPELLED TO MAKE A SOLEMN DECLARATION AND SHALL NOT BE EXAMINED ABOUT THE CONTENT OF THE STATEMENT.

(B)   THE TRIAL CHAMBER SHALL DECIDE ON THE PROBATIVE VALUE, IF ANY, OF THE STATEMENT.

Rule 85

Presentation of Evidence

(A)   EACH PARTY IS ENTITLED TO CALL WITNESSES AND PRESENT EVIDENCE. UNLESS OTHERWISE DIRECTED BY THE TRIAL CHAMBER IN THE INTERESTS OF JUSTICE, EVIDENCE AT THE TRIAL SHALL BE PRESENTED IN THE FOLLOWING SEQUENCE:

(I)   EVIDENCE FOR THE PROSECUTION;

(II)   EVIDENCE FOR THE DEFENCE;

(III) PROSECUTION EVIDENCE IN REBUTTAL;

(IV)   DEFENCE EVIDENCE IN REJOINDER;

(V)   EVIDENCE ORDERED BY THE TRIAL CHAMBER PURSUANT TO RULE 98; AND

(VI)   ANY RELEVANT INFORMATION THAT MAY ASSIST THE TRIAL CHAMBER IN DETERMINING AN APPROPRIATE SENTENCE IF THE ACCUSED IS FOUND GUILTY ON ONE OR MORE OF THE CHARGES IN THE INDICTMENT.

(B)   EXAMINATION-IN-CHIEF, CROSS-EXAMINATION AND RE-EXAMINATION SHALL BE ALLOWED IN EACH CASE. IT SHALL BE FOR THE PARTY CALLING A WITNESS TO EXAMINE SUCH WITNESS IN CHIEF, BUT A JUDGE MAY AT ANY STAGE PUT ANY QUESTION TO THE WITNESS.

(C)   IF THE ACCUSED SO DESIRES, THE ACCUSED MAY APPEAR AS A WITNESS IN HIS OR HER OWN DEFENCE.

II.   TRIBUNAL CASES

B.   TRIAL CHAMBERS

1. ORDER OF PRESENTATION

PROSECUTOR V. KUPREŠKIĆ, *et. al., Decision on Order of Presentation of Evidence,* IT-95-16-T, 21 January 1999, Cassese, May & Mumba, JJ.

During an oral hearing in the Chamber, Defence counsel requested leave of the Chamber to conduct re-examination of witnesses whom they had not called, but had been called by other defence counsel. The Chamber denied the request and followed the oral ruling with a written decision.

With regard to the general concept of re-examination the Chamber, quoting from Peter Murphy, *A Practical Approach to Evidence,* 3rd Ed., p. 460, said:

Very little need be said about re-examination. It is the process whereby a party calling a witness may seek to explain or clarify any points that arose in cross-examination and appear to be unfavourable to his case. Re-examination is, therefore, possible only where there has been cross-examination and is limited to matters raised in cross-examination: it is not an opportunity to adduce further evidence in chief.

The Chamber acknowledged and accepted a decision from the *Delalić* case[783] in which the Chamber determined that re-cross-examination may sometimes be allowed where new material is introduced during re-examination. In addition, if new material is developed during questioning by the Judges, then a party is entitled to further examine on the new matters.

The Chamber made it clear, however, that re-examination is limited to the party calling the witness, not counsel for co-defendants.

The Chamber also ruled that should the Prosecutor intend to introduce documents in the cross-examination of a witness, those documents must be disclosed to defence counsel at the earliest available opportunity and, at the latest, prior to cross-examination.

Thus, the order of presentation was determined to be: examination-in-chief by the accused calling the witness, cross-examination by other accused, cross-examination by the Prosecution, and re-examination by the accused calling the witness.

PROSECUTOR V. DELALIĆ *et. al., Order on the Prosecutor's Motion on the Order of Appearance of Defence Witnesses and the order of cross-examination by the Prosecution and Counsel for the Co-Accused,* IT-96-21-T, 3 April 1998, Karibi-Whyte, Odio-Benito & Jan, JJ.

Relying on its earlier decision[784] the Chamber ruled that for each defence witness in a joint trial, when the defence complete their respective examination-in-chief and cross-examinations, the Prosecutor may then proceed with cross-examination.

There is no right to "re-cross-examination" under Rule 85, but where, during re-examination new material is introduced, the opposing party is entitled to further cross-examine the witness on such new material.

As between themselves, the co-accused may cross-examine a defence witness in an order other than the order in which the names of the accused appear on the indictment, provided there is unanimous agreement, on a witness by witness basis, among the co-accused.

PROSECUTOR V. DELALIĆ *et. al., Decision on the Motion on Presentation of Evidence by the Accused, Esad Landžo,* IT-96-21-T, 1 May 1997, Karibi-Whyte, Odio-Benito & Jan, JJ.

---

[783] See, below.

[784] Prosecutor v. Delalic, *et. al., Decision on the Motion on Presentation of Evidence by the Accused, Esad Landžo,* IT-96-21, 1 May 1997.

The issue in this case was whether, as a general rule, the right to examine-in-chief, cross-examine, re-examine and re-cross-examine, exists in each case where evidence is presented.

The Chamber held that under Rule 85(B), there shall be examination-in-chief, cross-examination, and re-examination in each case of presentation of evidence by the Prosecution and the Defence. Accordingly, as a general rule, the testimony of a witness ends with his re-examination, absent any new matter arising during re-examination. However, Rule 85(B) also provides that a Judge may at any stage put questions to a witness to clarify issues that remain unclear after an answer by the witness. Thus, if new matters are raised during re-examination or during questioning by the Judges, the Chamber may permit re-cross-examination, in the exercise of its discretion.

The Chamber found the wording of Rules 85(A) and 85(C) to be clear and unambiguous. Rule 85(A) deals with the order of presentation of evidence. Unless otherwise directed by the Chamber in the interests of justice, evidence is presented by the parties in the order provided for in Rule 85(A)(i)-(iv), which may be followed by evidence ordered by the Trial Chamber pursuant to Rule 85(A)(v).

2. TESTIMONY OF THE ACCUSED

PROSECUTOR V. TADIĆ, *Judgement on Allegations of Contempt Against Prior Counsel, Milan Vujin*, IT-94-1-A-R77, 31 January 2000, Shahabuddeen, Cassese, Nieto-Navia, Mumba & Hunt, JJ.

In contempt proceedings, it is a matter for the Respondent to allegations of contempt to decide if and when he will testify. The Chamber stated that in evaluating the testimony given by a Respondent who waits until after the testimony of his witnesses, it would take into account the fact that he heard that testimony before giving his own testimony.[785]

PROSECUTOR V. KVOČKA *et. al., Oral Decision on Having the Accused Testimony Prior to the Calling of the First Prosecution Witness*, IT-98-30-T, 28 February 2000, Rodriguez, Riad & Wald, JJ.

Following a pre-trial request by three of the accused to testify prior to the calling of the first Prosecution witness, the Chamber held that such a procedure would be adopted in these proceeding "in the interests of justice" pursuant to Rule 85(A). Furthermore, the Chamber ruled that the cross-examination of the accused that had testified would occur after all the Prosecution evidence-in-chief had been presented. The accused would be cross-examined by counsel for the other co-accused and then by the Prosecution.

---

[785] Paras. 11 and 129.

PROSECUTOR V. DELALIĆ *et. al., Order on the Prosecutor's Motion on the Order of Appearance of Defence Witnesses and the Order of Cross-examination by the Prosecution and Counsel for the Co-Accused*, IT-96-21-T, 3 April 1998, Karibi-Whyte, Odio-Benito & Jan, JJ.

The Chamber held that Rule 85(C) states that the accused may, if he so desires, appear as a witness in his own defence and it does not in any way restrict this right of the accused to a particular stage of his defence.[786]

3. REBUTTAL EVIDENCE AND FRESH EVIDENCE

PROSECUTOR V. DELALIĆ *et. al., Decision on the Prosecution's Alternative Request to Reopen the Prosecution's Case*, IT-96-21-T, 19 August 1998, Karibi-Whyte, Odio-Benito & Jan, JJ.

After the close of the Prosecution case under Rule 85(A)(i) and the Defence case under Rule 85(A)(ii), the Trial Chamber has the discretion whether to allow the parties to call additional evidence.

The Chamber stated that Rule 85 contains the well-settled rule of practice that evidence should be called at the proper time. In particular, the Chamber observed that matters probative of the guilt of the accused should be adduced as part of the case of the Prosecution under Rule 85(A)(i), bearing in mind that the Prosecution may elicit such evidence through cross-examination of defence witnesses, if any, or the accused, should he testify. To depart from the premise that the Prosecution should be able to discharge the onus of proving the guilt of the accused beyond reasonable doubt at the close of the case of the parties and allow the Prosecution to lead further evidence is exceptional and cannot merely be done in order to reinforce evidence already brought or to call evidence previously deemed unnecessary.[787]

The principle that the Prosecution cannot re-open its case to present rebuttal evidence or fresh evidence is not without exception. The Trial Chamber observed that the situations in which the parties may call additional evidence cannot be precisely defined, but a number of circumstances can be identified which are important to the determination of this issue.

Rebuttal

The Chamber held that Rule 85(A)(iii) provides expressly for the possibility of the Prosecution calling evidence in rebuttal. The Chamber described the limits on the ability of the Prosecution to call such evidence. The Rule must not be construed as a *carte blanche* for the Prosecution to adduce evidence at a later stage in the proceedings that should properly have been presented as part of its original case under Rule 85(A)(i).[788]

---

[786] Pg. 3.
[787] Para. 18.
[788] Para. 22.

The Chamber noted that the essence of the presentation of rebuttal evidence is to refute a particular piece of evidence that has been presented by the Defence during its case in chief. Rebuttal evidence is thus evidence limited to matters that arise directly and specifically out of defence evidence. In general, leave to present rebuttal evidence will be denied when the evidence is being proposed by the Prosecution to fill a perceived gap in its evidence against the accused. The Prosecution cannot call additional evidence merely because its case has been contradicted. An important factor for a Trial Chamber to consider is the circumstance surrounding the means by which the Prosecution obtained the evidence it attempts to call in rebuttal. A Chamber should exercise its discretion in allowing rebuttal evidence to be called in relation to matters arising *ex improviso*. However, evidence available to the Prosecution *ab initio*, the relevance of which does not arise *ex improviso*, and which remedies a defect in the Prosecution case is generally not admissible.[789]

Rejoinder

The Chamber ruled that the ability of the Defence to respond to rebuttal evidence, by way of rejoinder evidence, under Rule 85(A)(iv) is subject to the same conditions as the Prosecutor's ability to present rebuttal evidence under Rule 85(A)(iii). The accused is not entitled to revisit the defence case as a whole in presenting rejoinder evidence. This evidence is confined to presenting evidence that is directed to contradicting matters arising directly and specifically out of the evidence brought in rebuttal.[790]

Formal and Non-Contentious Evidence

The Chamber held that a party might adduce evidence of a purely formal and non-contentious nature after the close of the case of the parties. For example, if the Prosecution has omitted to tender a material statutory instrument during its case, no prejudice is caused to the accused by allowing the Prosecution to re-open its case to ensure that the trial record is complete. However, the Chamber was of the view that evidence relating to the substance of a charge against the accused, such as identity, is not admissible, since such evidence goes directly to an allegation and it would be unjust to call upon the accused to answer at that stage in the proceedings.[791]

Fresh Evidence

Fresh evidence is new evidence which was not in the possession of the party seeking to introduce it at the time of the conclusion of its case and which, by exercise of all reasonable diligence, could not have been obtained by that party before that time. The burden of establishing that the evidence sought to be adduced is fresh evidence, rests on the party seeking to present it.[792]

---

[789] Para. 23.
[790] Para. 24.
[791] Para. 25.
[792] Para. 26.

The Chamber identified the following factors that it considered relevant, amoung others, in exercising its discretion to allow the Prosecution to call additional evidence. The later in the trial the Prosecution seeks to adduce further evidence, the less likely a Chamber is to accede to the request. The Chamber will consider the delay to proceedings that are likely to be caused by allowing the Prosecution to re-open its case and the suitability of adjournments in the overall context of the trial. The nature of the evidence must be considered. The probative value of the evidence must outweigh any prejudice caused to the accused.[793]

The Chamber determined, in this instance, that the Prosecution did not meet the burden of demonstrating that, with reasonable diligence, the proposed evidence could not have been previously obtained and presented as part of the Prosecution case.[794]

Documents that the Prosecution sought to present were relevant but had no probative value. These documents existed *ab initio*. The failure of the Prosecution to obtain this evidence during its case was not satisfactorily explained. The admission of the evidence would further protract proceedings – new evidence, followed by defence evidence and perhaps rebuttal and rejoinder evidence. The evidence was founded on inference and did not point unequivocally at the establishment of the Prosecution case.

4. EYEWITNESS IDENTIFICATION EVIDENCE

PROSECUTOR V. KUPREŠKIĆ, *et, al., Judgement*, IT-95-16-T, 14 January 2000, Cassese, May & Mumba, JJ.

The Trial Chamber sounded a word of caution with regard to eyewitness identification evidence in cases where a witness obtains no more than a fleeting glance of a suspect. The Chamber cited with approval a decision of the Court of Appeal of England that stands for the proposition that a witness can easily be mistaken about identification and that an honest but mistaken witness can be a convincing one.[795]

5. ADMISSION OF EVIDENCE – GENERAL PRINCIPLES

PROSECUTOR V. BLAŠKIĆ, *Judgement*, IT-95-14-T, 3 March 2000, Jorda, Rodrigues & Shahabuddeen, JJ.

The Trial Chamber discussed generally the admission of evidence before the Tribunal. According to this Chamber:

---

[793] It is submitted that the foregoing comments on "factors regarding discretion" apply to both "rebuttal evidence" and "fresh evidence", if the Prosecution is allowed to "re-open its case". It is important to keep in mind the difference between "rebuttal evidence" and "fresh evidence" within the context of Rule 85. If the Prosecution calls "rebuttal evidence", the defence may be entitled to call "rejoinder evidence". On the other hand, if the Prosecution re-opens its case the defence may re-open its case and in addition rebuttal and rejoinder evidence may follow.

[794] Paras. 29-30.

[795] Para. 339(c). *R. v. Turnbull* [1977] QB 224.

The principle embodied by the case-law of the Trial Chamber on the issue is the one of extensive admissibility of evidence – questions of credibility or authenticity being determined according to the weight given to each of the materials by the Judges at the appropriate time.[796]

In this respect, it is appropriate to point out that the Trial Chamber authorised the presentation of evidence without its being submitted by a witness. The Trial Chamber relied on various criteria for this. At the outset, it is appropriate to observe that the proceedings were conducted by professional Judges with the necessary ability for first hearing a given piece of evidence and then evaluating it so as to determine its due weight with regard to the circumstances in which it was obtained, it actual contents and its credibility in light of all the evidence tendered. Secondly, the Trial Chamber could thus obtain much material of which it might otherwise have been deprived. Lastly, the proceedings restricted the compulsory resort to a witness serving only to present documents. In summary, this approach allowed the proceedings to be expedited whilst respecting the fairness of the trial and contributing to the ascertainment of the truth.[797]

6. EVIDENCE OF GOOD CHARACTER

PROSECUTOR V. KUPREŠKIĆ, et. al., *Decision on Evidence of the Good Character of the Accused and the Defence of Tu Quoque*, IT-95-16-T, 17 February 1999, Cassese, May & Mumba, JJ.

At the trial level, defence Counsel for Zoran Kupreškić filed a Motion seeking leave of the Chamber to introduce evidence of good character. Among other things, the Prosecutor announced that she would not contest that prior to the events alleged in the indictment all the defendants were persons of good character. With regard to evidence of good character the Chamber, however, made the following observations:

> [G]enerally speaking, evidence of the accused's character prior to the events for which he is indicted before the International Tribunal is not a relevant issue inasmuch as (a) by their nature as crimes committed in the context of widespread violence and during a national or international emergency, war crimes and crimes against humanity may be committed by persons with no prior convictions or history of violence, and that consequently evidence of prior good, or bad, conduct on the part of the accused before the armed conflict began is rarely of any probative value before the International Tribunal, and (b) as a general principle of criminal law, evidence as to the character of an accused is generally inadmissible to show the accused's propensity to act in conformity therewith.

---

[796] Para. 34.
[797] Para. 35.

RULE 86

CLOSING ARGUMENTS

(A)   AFTER THE PRESENTATION OF ALL THE EVIDENCE, THE PROSECUTOR MAY PRESENT A CLOSING ARGUMENT; WHETHER OR NOT THE PROSECUTOR DOES SO, THE DEFENCE MAY MAKE A CLOSING ARGUMENT. THE PROSECUTOR MAY PRESENT A REBUTTAL ARGUMENT TO WHICH THE DEFENCE MAY PRESENT A REJOINDER.

(B)   NOT LATER THAN FIVE DAYS PRIOR TO PRESENTING A CLOSING ARGUMENT, A PARTY SHALL FILE A FINAL TRIAL BRIEF WITH THE TRIAL CHAMBER.

(C)   THE PARTIES SHALL ALSO ADDRESS MATTERS OF SENTENCING IN CLOSING ARGUMENTS.

RULE 87

DELIBERATIONS

(A)   WHEN BOTH PARTIES HAVE COMPLETED THEIR PRESENTATION OF THE CASE, THE PRESIDING JUDGE SHALL DECLARE THE HEARING CLOSED, AND THE TRIAL CHAMBER SHALL DELIBERATE IN PRIVATE. A FINDING OF GUILT MAY BE REACHED ONLY WHEN A MAJORITY OF THE TRIAL CHAMBER IS SATISFIED THAT GUILT HAS BEEN PROVED BEYOND REASONABLE DOUBT.

(B)   THE TRIAL CHAMBER SHALL VOTE SEPARATELY ON EACH CHARGE CONTAINED IN THE INDICTMENT. IF TWO OR MORE ACCUSED ARE TRIED TOGETHER UNDER RULE 48, SEPARATE FINDINGS SHALL BE MADE AS TO EACH ACCUSED.

(C)   IF THE TRIAL CHAMBER FINDS THE ACCUSED GUILTY ON ONE OR MORE OF THE CHARGES CONTAINED IN THE INDICTMENT, IT SHALL AT THE SAME TIME DETERMINE THE PENALTY TO BE IMPOSED IN RESPECT OF EACH FINDING OF GUILT.

II.   TRIBUNAL CASES

B.   TRIAL CHAMBERS

PROSECUTOR V. DELALIĆ *et. al., Judgement*, IT-96-21-T, 16 November 1998, Karibi-Whyte, Odio-Benito & Jan, JJ.

Proof Beyond a Reasonable Doubt

The Trial Chamber found that the Prosecution is bound in law to prove the case alleged against the accused beyond reasonable doubt. At the conclusion of the case the accused is entitled to the benefit of the doubt as to whether the offence has been proved.[798]

The Chamber observed that the provisions of Article 21(3) of the Statute presume the innocence of the accused until he or she is proven guilty. It is a fundamental requirement of any judicial system that the person who has invoked its jurisdiction and desires the tribunal or court to take action on his behalf must prove his case to its satisfaction. As a matter of common sense, therefore, the legal burden of proving all facts essential to their claims rests upon the prosecutor in criminal proceedings.[799]

The Chamber quoted with approval from English case law, *Miller v. Minister of Pensions,* in which Lord Denning explained that the expression "proof beyond reasonable doubt" should be understood as follows:

> It need not reach certainty but it must carry a high degree of probability. Proof beyond a reasonable doubt does not mean proof beyond the shadow of a doubt. The law would fail to protect the community if it admitted fanciful possibilities

---

[798] Para. 601.
[799] Para. 599.

to deflect the course of justice. If the evidence is so strong against a man as to leave only a remote possibility in his favour, which can be dismissed with the sentence, 'of course it is possible, but not in the least probable', the case is proved beyond reasonable doubt, but nothing short of that will suffice.[800]

The Chamber stated that if, at the conclusion of the proceedings, there is any doubt that the Prosecution has established the case against the accused, the accused is entitled to the benefit of the doubt and, thus, acquittal.[801]

---

[800] Para. 600.
[801] Para. 603.

RULE 89

GENERAL PROVISIONS

(A)   THE RULES OF EVIDENCE SET FORTH IN THIS SECTION SHALL GOVERN THE PROCEEDINGS BEFORE THE CHAMBERS. THE CHAMBERS SHALL NOT BE BOUND BY NATIONAL RULES OF EVIDENCE.

(B)   IN CASES NOT OTHERWISE PROVIDED FOR IN THIS SECTION, A CHAMBER SHALL APPLY RULES OF EVIDENCE WHICH WILL BEST FAVOUR A FAIR DETERMINATION OF THE MATTER BEFORE IT AND ARE CONSONANT WITH THE SPIRIT OF THE STATUTE AND THE GENERAL PRINCIPLES OF LAW.

(C)   A CHAMBER MAY ADMIT ANY RELEVANT EVIDENCE WHICH IT DEEMS TO HAVE PROBATIVE VALUE.

(D)   A CHAMBER MAY EXCLUDE EVIDENCE IF ITS PROBATIVE VALUE IS SUBSTANTIALLY OUTWEIGHED BY THE NEED TO ENSURE A FAIR TRIAL.

(E)   A CHAMBER MAY REQUEST VERIFICATION OF THE AUTHENTICITY OF EVIDENCE OBTAINED OUT OF COURT.

I.   COMMENTARY

In the *Decision on the Motion of the Prosecution for the Admissibility of Evidence*, in the *Delalić* case, the Chamber discussed at length the issue of hearsay evidence and its treatment as to admissibility and weight. When a hearsay statement is admitted, clearly the author of the statement has never appeared before the tribunal and the statement has never been subject to the scrutiny of cross-examination. At trial, it is therefore important to review the record with an eye for determining which evidence is first hand and which is second hand,

Moreover, the question of the "alleged author not appearing as a witness" affects the right of the accused to confrontation pursuant to Article 21(4)(e). As with hearsay evidence, the admissibility of evidence under Rule 89(C) has been found not to violate Article 21(4)(e). However, as the *Decision on the Motion of the Prosecution for the Admissibility of Evidence*, 19 January 1998 and the *Judgement* indicate, the fact that the author of a piece of evidence does not testify in court precludes the accused from confronting him through cross-examination and the weight to be accorded such evidence may be minimal, if any.

II.   TRIBUNAL CASES

A.   APPEALS CHAMBER

PROSECUTOR V. ALEKSOVSKI, *Judgement*, IT-95-14/1-A, 24 March 2000, May, Mumba, Hunt, Tieya & Robinson, JJ.

Application of the Standard of Proof Beyond a Reasonable Doubt

The Appeals Chamber found that the Trial Chamber did not err, as a matter of law or act unreasonably in relying on witness testimonies without medical reports or scientific evidence as proof of the suffering experienced by witnesses. Furthermore, the Chamber found no error by the Trial Chamber in the exercise of its discretion when it evaluated the testimony of various witnesses at trial. The Trial Chamber had accepted such testimony as sufficient and credible and applied the standard of proof beyond reasonable doubt correctly.[802]

The Chamber held that the only Rule directly relevant to the issue at hand is Rule 89. In particular, Rule 89(C) states that a Chamber "may admit any relevant evidence which it deems to have probative value", and Rule 89(D) states that a Chamber "may exclude evidence if its probative value is substantially outweighed by the need to ensure a fair trial". The Chamber also observed that neither the Statute nor the Rules oblige a Trial Chamber to require medical reports or other scientific evidence as proof of a material fact. Similarly, the testimony of a single witness on a material fact does not require, as a matter of law, any corroboration.[803]

As for discretion in evaluating evidence presented at trial, the Chamber ruled that Trial Chambers are best placed to hear, assess and weigh the evidence, including witness testimonies, presented at trial. Depending on the various factors that have to be assessed in the circumstances of each case, a Trial Chamber may rely on single witness testimony as proof of a material fact. The Trial Chamber must consider whether a witness is reliable and whether evidence presented is credible. The Chamber held that it may overturn the Trial Chamber's finding of fact only where the evidence relied on could not have been accepted by any reasonable tribunal or where the evaluation of the evidence is wholly erroneous.[804]

---

[802] Para. 64.
[803] Para. 62.
[804] Para. 63.

PROSECUTOR V. ALEKSOVSKI, *Decision on Prosecutor's Appeal on Admissibility of Evidence,* IT-95-14/1-A, 16 February 1999, May, Tieya, Hunt, Bennouna & Robinson, JJ.

Zlatko Aleksovski and Tihomir Blaškić were originally indicted together, along with five others, for events that occurred during the armed conflict in the Lašva Valley of Bosnia and Herzegovina in 1993. The accused were charged *inter alia* with war crimes under Article 2 and Article 3 of the Statute. A request for a separate trial made by Aleksovski was granted and Aleksovski and Blaškić were tried separately. Separate Trial Chambers tried them and, for the purposes of determination of the matter on appeal in this case, their trial proceedings were being conducted in parallel. During the defence case in the *Blaškić* trial, Admiral Davor Domazet gave expert testimony concerning causes, course and conduct of the armed conflict in the Lašva Valley. The evidence of Admiral Domazet related to whether the armed conflict was international in character, which evidence was relevant to the application of Article 2 and Article 3 of the Statute. By this time, in the *Aleksovski* trial, both the Prosecution and the Defence had closed their cases, but the Prosecution and the Defence had yet to call their respective rebuttal and rejoinder evidence.

On the basis of Rule 89(C), the Trial Chamber in *Aleksovski* granted a request by the Defence to present as evidence the transcript, video-recording and accompanying exhibits of the evidence of Admiral Domazet in the *Blaškić* trial. However, the Chamber denied a request by the Prosecution to rebut the evidence of Admiral Domazet with the transcript of evidence of a confidential witness who had testified during the Prosecution case in chief in *Blaškić* regarding the nature of the armed conflict in the Lašva Valley.

The Appeals Chamber reversed the decision of the Trial Chamber, in part, and ruled that the evidence tendered by the Prosecution to rebut the evidence of General Domazet was admissible in the *Aleksovski* trial. The Chamber arrived at this conclusion after reviewing the Tribunal case law on the admissibility of hearsay evidence.

Hearsay Evidence

The Appeals Chamber defined hearsay evidence as follows: "the statement of a person made otherwise than in the proceedings in which it is being tendered, but nevertheless being tendered in those proceedings in order to establish the truth of what that person says".[805]

The Chamber found that under Rule 89(C), it is well settled in the practice of the Tribunal that a Trial Chamber has a broad discretion to admit relevant hearsay evidence

---

[805] Para. 14.

which is considered to have probative value.[806] The Chamber noted that for hearsay evidence to be admitted to prove the truth of its contents, a Trial Chamber must be satisfied that it is reliable for that purpose, in the sense of being voluntary, truthful and trustworthy. In regard to the reliability of the hearsay evidence, the Trial Chamber may consider both the content of the hearsay statement and the circumstances under which the evidence arose. In other words, the probative value of a hearsay statement will depend upon the context and character of the evidence in question. The absence of the opportunity to cross-examine the person who made the statements, and whether the hearsay is "first-hand" or more removed, are also relevant to the probative value of the evidence. The fact that the evidence is hearsay does not necessarily deprive it of probative value, but it is acknowledged that the weight or probative value to be afforded to that evidence will usually be less than that given to the testimony of a witness who has given it under a form of oath and who has been cross-examined, although even this will depend upon the infinitely variable circumstances which surround hearsay evidence.[807]

For the purposes of the *Aleksovski* trial, General Domazet was considered a witness under Rule 90 in the *Blaškić* trial. He gave an oral statement on oath and his testimony was taken within the provisions of Rule 90. He was not considered a witness in the *Aleksovski* trial and the statement he made during the *Blaškić* proceedings was admitted as hearsay pursuant to Rule 89(C).[808] The Chamber ruled that the Trial Chamber properly exercised its discretion in admitting the evidence under Rule 89(C), even though the Defence offered it into evidence after the close of its case.

In addition, the Chamber observed that there is a firm obligation placed upon those representing an accused person to make proper enquiries as to what evidence is available in that person's defence. In the circumstances of this case, the evidence led by the accused person in the *Blaškić* trial was obviously a primary source of such enquiry by those representing Aleksovski.[809]

The party wishing to tender a statement from other proceedings is not required to demonstrate that the witness is not immediately available to testify. A Trial Chamber is entitled to take account of the stage of the trial, the length of time the accused has been in custody and whether the witness is immediately available in exercising its discretion to admit the evidence.[810]

The cross-examination of Admiral Domazet by the Prosecution in the *Blaškić* trial satisfied the need to cross-examine him in the *Aleksovski* proceedings. It was common ground that the alleged events out of which both men were charged took place in the same area, the Lašva Valley area, and that the two proceedings (which arose out of the same indictment) had much in common in both their legal and factual aspects. In those circumstances, the cross-examination of the witness in the first trial will suffice for

---

[806] See, Prosecutor v. Tadić, *Decision on the Defence Motion on Hearsay*, IT-94-1-T, 5 August 1996 and Prosecutor v. Blaškić, *Decision on Standing Objection of the Defence to the Admission of Hearsay with no Inquiry as to its Reliability*, IT-95-14-T, 26 January 1998.
[807] Para. 15.
[808] Para. 17.
[809] Para. 18.
[810] Para. 19.

the second trial, unless it can be shown that any particular line of cross-examination that would have been both relevant and significant to the second trial was not pursued in the first trial. Furthermore, if there is no objection made to the cross-examination of the witness on the issue of credit being curtailed during the initial proceedings, that objection must be made to the Trial Chamber in the subsequent proceedings where the statement is being tendered into evidence.[811]

A party is entitled to respond in kind to the evidence of the other party on the basis of the principle of equality of arms.[812]

If the witness who gave testimony in the first trial was subject to a protective order, the party wishing to adduce that evidence may apply to the Chamber trying the first case for a waiver or amendment of the protective measures in relation to the witness to enable the witness's evidence to be disclosed in the second trial. The Chamber observed that this is the practice in the Tribunal and once the evidence is disclosed, it can be admitted in the subsequent proceedings subject to suitable protective measures.[813]

The fact that the admission of the transcript of evidence of a confidential witness cannot be cross-examined does not preclude it from being admitted into evidence under Rule 89(C). In all cases where hearsay evidence is admitted, the opposing party is precluded from cross-examining the witness. The Chamber indicated that where there are common legal and factual aspects between the two trials, the disadvantage of not being able to cross-examination the witness may be tempered by the fact the witness might have been cross-examined in the first trial.[814]

PROSECUTOR V. TADIĆ, *Judgement on Allegations of Contempt Against Prior Counsel, Milan Vujin*, IT-94-1-A-R77, 31 January 2000, Shahabuddeen, Cassese, Nieto-Navia, Mumba & Hunt, JJ.

Admissibility of Prior Out-of-Court-Statement

The Appeals Chamber held that a statement made by a witness out of court which is inconsistent with his or her evidence in court is admissible for the truth of its contents, but the weight to be given to the prior statement – as hearsay material – will depend upon the infinitely variable circumstances which surround hearsay material. The Chamber observed that it is now well settled in the practice of the Tribunal that hearsay material having probative value is admissible for the truth of its contents. However, the weight to be afforded to that material will usually be less than that of the testimony of a witness who has testified under oath and who has been cross-examined.[815]

---

[811] Para. 20.
[812] Para. 26.
[813] Para. 26.
[814] Para. 27.
[815] Para. 93.

PROSECUTOR V. TADIĆ, *Judgment*, IT-94-1-A, 15 July 1999, Shahabuddeen, Cassese, Tieya, Nieto-Navia & Mumba

In its Cross-Appeal, the Prosecutor complained about the failure of the Trial Chamber to order the production of defence witness statements after the witnesses had testified on direct examination. Even though the parties agreed that the ruling had no bearing on the verdict of the Trial Chamber, the Chamber determined that it was a matter of general importance and therefore dealt with it. In that regard the Chamber made the following observation:

> The Appeals Chamber has no power under Article 25 of the Statute to pass, one way or another, on the decision of the Trial Chamber as if the decision was itself under appeal. But the point of law which is involved is one of importance and worthy of an expression of opinion by the Appeals Chamber.

The Prosecutor contended that the power of the Trial Chamber to order such disclosure is implicit in Rule 89(B).

The Appeals Chamber determined that it was within the discretion of the Trial Chambers to order such disclosure on a case-by-case basis. The Chamber ruled, as follows:

> With regard to the present case, once a Defence witness has testified, it is for a Trial Chamber to ascertain the credibility of his or her testimony. If he or she has made a prior statement, a Trial Chamber must be able to evaluate the testimony in the light of this statement, in its quest for the truth and for the purpose of ensuring a fair trial. Rather than deriving from the sweeping provisions of Sub-rule 89(B), this power is inherent in the jurisdiction of the International Tribunal, as it is within the jurisdiction of any criminal court, national or international. In other words, this is one of those powers mentioned by the Appeals Chamber in the Blaškić (Subpoena) decision which accrue to a judicial body even if not explicitly or implicitly provided for in the statute or rules of procedure of such a body, because they are essential for the carrying out of judicial functions and ensuring the fair administration of justice.[816]

---

[816] Para. 332.

B.   TRIAL CHAMBERS

1. HEARSAY

PROSECUTOR V. BLAŠKIĆ, *Decision on Standing Objection of the Defence to the Admission of Hearsay with no Inquiry as to its Reliability*, IT-95-14-T, 21 January 1998, Jorda, Riad & Shahabuddeen, JJ.

The Defence filed a general motion opposing the admission of hearsay evidence without an inquiry into its reliability. The Defence contended that the Trial Chamber should admit hearsay only upon a showing of its reliability following a detailed investigation. To a great extent the Defence relied upon the laws of national jurisdictions and the European Court of Human Rights. In that regard the Chamber said:

> The International Tribunal is, in fact, a *sui generis* institution with its own rules of procedure which do not merely constitute a transposition of national legal systems. The same holds for the conduct of the trial which, contrary to the Defence arguments, is not similar to an adversarial trial, but is moving towards a more hybrid system.[817]

Relying on the previous decision of the Trial Chamber in *Tadić*[818], the Chamber explained:

> The Trial Chamber therefore considers that the admissibility of hearsay evidence may not be subject to any prohibition in principle since the proceedings are conducted before professional Judges who possess the necessary ability to begin by hearing hearsay evidence and then to evaluate it so that they may make a ruling as to its relevance and probative value.[819]

Finally the Chamber pointed out that the Defence was always free to argue that hearsay should be excluded because its probative value is insufficient.

---

[817] Para. 5.
[818] Prosecutor v. Tadić, *Decision on the Defence Motion on Hearsay*, IT-94-1-T, 5 August 1996.
[819] Para. 10

2. MISCELLANEOUS

PROSECUTOR V. KVOČKA et. al., Oral Decision on Confrontation of a Witness during Examination-in-chief, IT-98-30/1-T, 10 July 2000, Rodriguez, Riad & Wald, JJ.

A party leading a witness through examination-in-chief may use his or her prior out-of-court statement to confront the witness with an inconsistency in relation to that prior statement and attempt to establish the reason why the witness has changed his statement, without calling into question the credibility of the witness. The Chamber ruled that in such circumstances, the relevant parts of the prior statement might be read to the witness.[820]

PROSECUTOR V. KVOČKA et. al., Oral Decision on the Admissibility of Prior out-of-court Statements, IT-98-30/1-T, 4 July 2000, Rodriguez, Riad & Wald, JJ.

The Trial Chamber made three rulings in regards to the admissibility of prior out-of-court statements.[821]

　　The Chamber rejected the request of the Prosecution to admit, as an exhibit, a prior-out-of court statement made by a witness appearing before the Chamber. The Chamber was of the view that examination-in-chief could not consist of having the witness authenticate his or her statement, which would then be admitted into evidence for the truth of its contents. The result of such a procedure is that the defence would have to conduct its cross-examination entirely on the basis of a written document. The Chamber held that such a procedure would jeopardize what the Chamber referred to as the principle of orality of debates.

　　In regards to using prior out-of-court statements for impeachment purposes during cross-examination, the Chamber ruled the relevant passages from such statements may be read to the witness during cross-examination, without tendering the statement into evidence. The Chamber reasoned that it is sufficient for the parties to quote, at the hearing, the paragraphs from the statement that they consider relevant to the issue of credibility, which will then be entered into the record.

　　Finally, the Chamber ruled that transcripts of testimony of a witness who testified in other trials before the Tribunal are admissible. The Chamber added that the admission of such transcripts is without prejudice regarding the admission of statements used with a view to challenge the credibility of witnesses.

---

[820] Transcript, pgs. 3802, 3803.
[821] Transcript, pgs. 3510-3514.

428

PROSECUTOR V DELALIĆ *et. al., Decision on the Motion to Allow Witness K, L and M to give their Testimony by Means of Video-link Conference*, IT-96-21-T, 28 May 1997, Karibi-Whyte, Odio-Benito & Jan, JJ.

The Trial Chamber held that the provisions governing the rules of evidence contained in Rules 89-98 are not exhaustive. The Trial Chamber determined moreover that when the Judges of the Tribunal drafted the Rules, they did not attempt to cover every conceivable evidentiary matter that may arise before the Tribunal. In particular, the Chamber relied on Rule 89(B) in holding that a Chamber may resort, in its discretion, to rules of evidence from national legal systems which will best favour the determination of the matter before it.[822]

    Although not bound by national rules of evidence, according to Rule 89(A) a Chamber may apply general principles of municipal law in a manner that is consonant with the Statute.[823] The Chamber interpreted the words "general principles of law" by reference to Article 38(1)(c) of the Statute of the International Court of Justice which provides that one of the sources of international law is "the general principles of law recognized by civilized nations." The Chamber held that the words "general principles of law" have the same substantive meaning in these two provisions and using general principles of domestic law may fill gaps in the Rules.[824]

    In addition, the Chamber adopted the following passage from an opinion of Judge Stephen in *Tadić* on the meaning of Rule 89(B):

> Where a substantial number of well recognized legal systems adopt a particular solution to a problem, it is appropriate to regard that solution as involving some quite general principle of law such as is referred to in Sub-rule 89(B).[825]

PROSECUTOR V. DELALIĆ *et. al., Decision on the Prosecution's Oral Request for the Admission of Exhibit 155 into Evidence and for an Order to Compel the Accused, Zdravko Mucić, to Provide a Handwriting Sample*, IT-96-21-T, 19 January 1998, Karibi-Whyte, Odio-Benito & Jan, JJ.

The Trial Chamber found that primarily Rules 89, 95 and 96(iv), govern the admissibility of evidence. In particular, Rule 89 provides the general framework for the operation of the other Rules contained in this section of the Rules.[826]

    Rule 89(B) is a residuary provision which permits a Trial Chamber to apply rules of evidence that are consistent with the Statute and general principles of law in cases not provided for by the Rules.[827]

---

[822] Paras. 7 and 9.
[823] Para. 10.
[824] Para. 8.
[825] Prosecutor v. Tadić, *Separate Opinion of Judge Stephan on Prosecution Motion for Production of Defence Witness Statements*, IT-94-1-T, 27 November 1996, pg. 6.
[826] Para. 28.
[827] Para. 28.

Rule 89(C)

The Chamber found that the plain words of Rule 89(C) require that evidence be "relevant" and have "probative value" to be admissible. The Chamber noted that there is implicit in "relevancy" an element of "probative value," but the relationship between the two terms and the their respective definitions is not open to an easy and clear definition. Both relevant evidence and probative evidence can be seen as evidence that tends to prove a matter in issue. The Chamber accepted the proposition that for two facts to be relevant there must exist a connection between the two which makes it possible to infer the existence of one from the other. The probative value of a piece of evidence will not always be easy to determine as it is a quality of necessarily variable content and much will depend upon the context and the character of the evidence in question.[828]

Furthermore, the Chamber held that an element of reliability, which it termed "sufficient indicia of reliability" needed to be established as a condition to admissibility under Rule 89(C). The Chamber rejected the proposition that the reliability of documents tendered into evidence by the Prosecution needed to be proved beyond reasonable doubt. The Chamber held that reliability is the invisible golden thread which runs through all the components of admissibility, but the clear and unambiguous language of Rule 89(C) did not allow for any additional conditions of admissibility beyond "relevance" and "probative value" to be read into it.[829]

In short, under Rule 89(C), all relevant evidence for which there is sufficient indicia of reliability may be deemed both relevant and of probative value and therefore admissible, provided such evidence is not affected by an exclusionary rule.

Silence of the Accused and Privilege Against Self-Incrimination

In the instant case, the Prosecution was seeking an Order pursuant to Rule 54 that the accused provide a sample of his handwriting. In regard to the powers of the Trial Chamber to make an order pursuant to Rule 54, the Trial Chamber made the following observation of the interplay between the Statute and Rules:

> Article 14 sub-paragraph 3(g) of the ICCPR is *in pari materia* with Article 21 sub-paragraph 4(g). There is a similar provision in the ACHR, Article 8 sub-paragraph 2(g). The essence of these provisions is to protect an accused person from being compelled to testify against his own interest or to confess guilt. This is also the essence of Article 20 sub-paragraph 1. The exercise of the power of the Trial Chamber under Rule 54 must be consistent with the rights of the accused guaranteed under the Statute. This is because the powers of the Trial Chamber under Rule 54 were granted pursuant to the rule making powers vested in the Judges in Article 15 of the Statute. Thus, the exercise of such powers cannot be inconsistent with the provisions of the Statute. It is a well settled canon for the construction of statutes, which requires no citation of decided cases, that where delegated legislation is inconsistent with its enabling statutory

---

[828] Para. 29.
[829] Para. 31-33.

provision, it is void entirely or *pro tanto.*[830]

The Chamber found that Rule 42(A)(iii) and Rule 63 have addressed the omission of the right to remain silent from Article 21(4)(g). Accordingly, no adverse inference can be drawn from the silence of the accused person.[831]

Furthermore, the Chamber found that where the material factor absent in the incriminating elements is the handwriting sample, the accused could not be compelled to supply the missing element. This would infringe on the protection against self-incrimination guaranteed by Article 21(4)(g). The accused cannot be compelled by order of a Trial Chamber to assist the Prosecution in its investigation and provide evidence that may incriminate him. The situation is different where the accused voluntarily complies on demand without coercion.[832]

In regard to the privilege against self-incrimination, the Chamber adopted the following passage from the Supreme Court of the United States in *Miranda v. Arizona*[833] and stated that no less is required in applying the Statute and Rules:[834]

> [Its] constitutional foundation . . . is the respect a government - state or federal - must accord to the dignity and integrity of its citizens. To maintain a "fair state - individual balance", to require the government "to shoulder the entire load" to respect the inviolability of the human personality, our accusatory system of criminal justice demands that the government seeking to punish an individual, produce the evidence against him by its own independent labors, rather than by the cruel, simple expedient of compelling it from his own mouth.

The Chamber held that the right to remain silent is implicit from the construction of Article 21(4)(g) and provided for expressly in Rule 63 and this right means that the accused person can stay mute without reacting to the allegation. This is a legitimate reaction to a preceding warning of the right to remain silent and it is an exercise of the right to protection against self-incrimination.[835]

The Chamber found that the phrase "to testify against himself" is clear and unambiguous and this privilege from self-incrimination is not qualified in any way. This privilege protects the innocent by insulating them from the effects of coercion from law enforcement authorities, it protects society by conviction of the guilty, and it encourages witnesses to volunteer to testify who might be deterred from doing so out of fear of self-incrimination.[836]

---

[830] Para. 41.
[831] Para. 46.
[832] Para. 47.
[833] 384 U.S. 436, 460 (1966)
[834] Para. 49.
[835] Para. 50.
[836] Para. 58.

PROSECUTOR V DELALIĆ *et. al.*, *Decision on the Motion of the Prosecution for the Admissibility of Evidence*, IT-96-21-T, 19 January 1998, Karibi-Whyte, Odio-Benito & Jan, JJ.

The Chamber observed that the Rules contain ten provisions that regulate all evidentiary matters in proceedings before the Tribunal. The rules on admissibility of evidence are not technical and, pursuant to Rule 89(C), they favour admissibility provided the evidence is relevant and deemed to have probative value.[837]

The Chamber found that evidence might nonetheless be excluded in three specific instances. Rule 89(D) provides that evidence may be excluded if its probative value is substantially outweighed by the need to ensure a fair trial. Rule 95 states that no evidence shall be admissible if obtained by methods that cast substantial doubt on its reliability or if its admission is antithetical to, and would seriously damage, the integrity of the proceedings. Rule 96(iv) states that prior sexual conduct of the victim shall not be admitted in evidence. Such evidence may be redacted from the record if such evidence is elicited from or offered by a witness.

Pursuant to Rule 89(E), a Chamber may request verification of the authenticity of evidence obtained out of court.[838]

Rule 89(B) is a residual clause which permits a Trial Chamber, in cases not otherwise provided for in the Rules, to apply rules of evidence which will best favour a fair determination of the matter before it and are consonant with the spirit of the Statute and the general principles of law.

The Chamber found that on the plain text of Rule 89(C), evidence must be relevant and have probative value to be admissible. The Chamber noted that probative value means evidence that tends to prove an issue and that relevance is a concept that contains an implicit requirement of probative value. The Chamber accepted the proposition that for two facts to be relevant there must exist a connection between the two that makes it possible to infer the existence of one from the other. Recognizing that relevance and probative value are difficult to define *in abstracto*, the Chamber observed that the application of these two concepts call for evaluation based on human experience and logic and will depend upon the particular circumstances of the case and the nature of the evidence sought to be admitted.

---

[837] Paras. 15-16.
[838] Para. 16.

Reliability

Relying on the *Tadić Hearsay Decision,*[839] the Chamber held that reliability is an inherent and implicit component of each element of admissibility and accepted that unreliable evidence has neither relevance nor probative value and is therefore inadmissible under Rule 89(C).[840] However, the Chamber added that a determination of reliability is not a separate, first step in assessing a piece of evidence offered for admission. The Chamber refused to read into the provisions of Rule 89(C) proof of genuineness, authorship or credibility of evidence as a condition precedent to the issue of admissibility. The Chamber ruled that there must be indicia of reliability when assessing the relevance and probative value of evidence at the stage of determining its admissibility.[841]

On the of the issue of reliability, the Chamber drew a distinction between admissibility and weight:

> [T]rials before the International Tribunal are conducted before professional judges, who by virtue of their training and experience are able to consider each piece of evidence which has been admitted and determine its appropriate weight. As noted above, it is an implicit requirement of the Rules that the Trial Chamber give due considerations to indicia of reliability when assessing the relevance and probative value of evidence at the stage of determining its admissibility. However, this terminology may leave some room for misunderstanding, and could possibly be misperceived as demanding that a binding determination be made at this stage as to the genuineness, authorship or credibility of evidence. For this reason the Trial Chamber wishes to make clear that the mere admission of a document into evidence does not in and of itself signify that the statements contained therein will necessarily be deemed to be an accurate portrayal of the facts. Factors such as authenticity and proof of authorship will naturally assume the greatest importance in the Trial Chamber's assessment of the weight to be attached to individual pieces of evidence. The threshold standard for the admission of evidence, however, should not be set excessively high, as often documents are sought to be admitted into evidence, not as ultimate proof of guilt or innocence, but to provide a context and complete the picture presented by the evidence gathered.[842]

Furthermore, the Chamber held that in assessing the weight and probative value of evidence, an important factor would be whether or not the alleged author of the document appears as a witness. Otherwise, the contents of a document remain unauthenticated and not subject to the kind of scrutiny which comes with the cross-examination of a witness.[843]

---

[839] Prosecutor v. Tadić, *Decision on the Defence Motion on Hearsay*, IT-94-1-T, 5 August 1996.
[840] Para. 18.
[841] Para. 19-20.
[842] Para. 20.
[843] Para. 22.

Under Rule 89(C), all relevant evidence for which there is sufficient indicia of reliability may be deemed both relevant and of probative value and therefore admissible, provided such evidence is not affected by an exclusionary rule. The admission of evidence does not in any way constitute a binding determination as to the authenticity or trustworthiness of the evidence sought to be admitted. These matters are to be assessed by the Chamber at a later stage in the course of determining the weight to be attached to the evidence.[844]

PROSECUTOR V DELALIĆ *et. al.*, *Judgement*, IT-96-21-T, 16 November 1998, Karibi-Whyte, Odio-Benito & Jan, JJ.

In this case, there were a number of documents seized by Vienna Police from premises alleged to have been controlled by Delalić. There was significant dispute regarding their admission into evidence. Several members of the Vienna Police testified before the Chamber and there was extensive argument and briefing regarding the documents. In regard to these documents, the Chamber wrote:

> In the Decision on the Motion of the Prosecution for the Admissibility of Evidence of 21 January 1998, this Trial Chamber stated the attitude towards admissibility of the exhibits and their probative value as follows:
>
>> the Trial Chamber wishes to make clear that the mere admission of a document into evidence does not in and of itself signify that the statements contained therein will necessarily be deemed to be an accurate portrayal of the facts. Factors such as authenticity and proof of authorship will naturally assume the greatest importance in the Trial Chamber's assessment of the weight to be attached to individual pieces of evidence.
>
> In that Decision the Trial Chamber stated that in the admission of documents the fact that the alleged authors have not appeared as witnesses is a factor to be taken into account at the stage of assessing the weight and probative value of such exhibits. This is because such documents would not have received and survived the scrutiny involved in the cross-examination of a witness.
>
> The Trial Chamber considers the Vienna documents in accordance with their probative value and the extent to which they have been established in evidence. *Prima facie* they are all relevant to the consideration of the contention that Zejnil Delalić had command authority by virtue of his transactions in relation to the war effort in Bosnia and Herzegovina, and whether he was, at the period relevant to the Indictment, in a position of superior authority in relation to the institutions in the Konjic municipality; and, in particular, over the Čelebići prison-camp, its commander and guards.[845]

---

[844] Para. 31.
[845] Paras. 704-705. (Footnotes omitted)

In regard to documents which were relevant, but for which no witness was called to authenticate them, the Trial Chamber found, as follows:

> There is a peculiar feature of these documents in that, although they are all relevant to the issue at hand, none of them is authenticated as the parties alleged to have created them never gave evidence. Accordingly, it was not possible to expose them to the scrutiny of cross-examination.[846]

The Chamber found that documents, where there was no evidence of authenticity or authorship, were unreliable and attached no weight to them.[847]

PROSECUTOR V DELALIĆ *et. al.*, *Decision on the Tendering of Prosecution Exhibits 104-108*, IT-96-21-T, 9 February 1998, Karibi-Whyte, Odio-Benito & Jan, JJ.

Best Evidence Rule

By reference to Rule 89(B), the Trial Chamber held that the classic statement of the "best evidence rule" from English law can be used by a Trial Chamber as a guide in considering the evidence presented in a case. The best evidence rule was articulated by Lord Hardwicke in the *Omychund v. Barker*[848] case, as follows:

> [t]he judges and sages of the law have laid it down that there is but one general rule of evidence, the best that the nature of the case will allow.

The Chamber added that the principle of a fair trial is dominant when relying on the best evidence available in the circumstances.[849]

---

[846] Para. 709.
[847] Para. 710-711, 713-714.
[848] (1745) 1 Atk. 21 at p. 49.
[849] Para. 15.

RULE 90

TESTIMONY OF WITNESSES

(A)   SUBJECT TO RULES 71 AND 71 *BIS*, WITNESSES SHALL, IN PRINCIPLE, BE HEARD DIRECTLY BY THE CHAMBERS.

(B)   EVERY WITNESS SHALL, BEFORE GIVING EVIDENCE, MAKE THE FOLLOWING SOLEMN DECLARATION: I SOLEMNLY DECLARE THAT I WILL SPEAK THE TRUTH, THE WHOLE TRUTH AND NOTHING BUT THE TRUTH".

(C)   A CHILD WHO, IN THE OPINION OF THE CHAMBER, DOES NOT UNDERSTAND THE NATURE OF A SOLEMN DECLARATION, MAY BE PERMITTED TO TESTIFY WITHOUT THAT FORMALITY, IF THE CHAMBER IS OF THE OPINION THAT HE IS SUFFICIENTLY MATURE TO BE ABLE TO REPORT THE FACTS OF WHICH THE CHILD HAD KNOWLEDGE AND UNDERSTANDS THE DUTY TO TELL THE TRUTH. A JUDGEMENT, HOWEVER, CANNOT BE BASED ON SUCH TESTIMONY ALONE.

(D)   A WITNESS, OTHER THAN AN EXPERT, WHO HAS NOT YET TESTIFIED SHALL NOT BE PRESENT WHEN THE TESTIMONY OF ANOTHER WITNESS IS GIVEN. HOWEVER, A WITNESS WHO HAS HEARD THE TESTIMONY OF ANOTHER WITNESS SHALL NOT FOR THAT REASON ALONE BE DISQUALIFIED FROM TESTIFYING.

(E)   NOTWITHSTANDING SUB-RULE (D), UPON ORDER OF THE CHAMBER, AN INVESTIGATOR IN CHARGE OF A PARTY'S INVESTIGATION SHALL NOT BE PRECLUDED FROM BEING CALLED AS A WITNESS ON THE GROUND THAT HE OR SHE HAS BEEN PRESENT IN THE COURTROOM DURING THE PROCEEDINGS.

(F)   A WITNESS MAY OBJECT TO MAKING ANY STATEMENT WHICH MIGHT TEND TO INCRIMINATE THE WITNESS. THE CHAMBER MAY, HOWEVER, COMPEL THE WITNESS TO ANSWER THE QUESTION. TESTIMONY COMPELLED IN THIS WAY SHALL NOT BE USED AS EVIDENCE IN A SUBSEQUENT PROSECUTION AGAINST THE WITNESS FOR ANY OFFENCE OTHER THAN PERJURY.

(G)   THE TRIAL CHAMBER SHALL EXERCISE CONTROL OVER THE MODE AND ORDER OF INTERROGATING WITNESSES AND PRESENTING EVIDENCE SO AS TO:

      (I)   MAKE THE INTERROGATION AND PRESENTATION EFFECTIVE FOR THE ASCERTAINMENT OF THE TRUTH; AND

      (II)   AVOID NEEDLESS CONSUMPTION OF TIME.

(H)

      (I)   CROSS-EXAMINATION SHALL BE LIMITED TO THE SUBJECT-MATTER OF THE EVIDENCE-IN-CHIEF AND MATTERS AFFECTING THE CREDIBILITY OF THE WITNESS AND, WHERE THE WITNESS IS ABLE TO GIVE RELEVANT EVIDENCE TO THE CASE FOR THE CROSS-EXAMINING PARTY, TO THE SUBJECT-MATTER OF THAT CASE.

(II)   IN THE CROSS-EXAMINATION OF A WITNESS WHO IS ABLE TO GIVE
         EVIDENCE RELEVANT TO THE CASE FOR THE CROSS-EXAMINING
         PARTY, COUNSEL SHALL PUT TO THAT WITNESS THE NATURE OF THE
         CASE OF THE PARTY FOR WHOM THAT COUNSEL APPEARS WHICH IS IN
         CONTRADICTION OF THE EVIDENCE GIVEN BY THE WITNESS.

(III)   THE TRIAL CHAMBER MAY, IN THE EXERCISE OF ITS DISCRETION,
         PERMIT ENQUIRY INTO ADDITIONAL MATTERS.

I.   COMMENTARY

Rules 90 (H)(i) and (ii) sets the potential scope of cross-examination by providing that it
may cover the issue of credibility and matters which are relevant to the case of the cross-
examining party. However, Rule 90 (H)(ii) makes this line of cross-examination subject
to counsel putting "the nature of the case of the party for whom that counsel appears
which is in contradiction of the evidence given by the witness". In addition, Rule
90(H)(iii) provides for the Trial Chamber exercising its discretion to permit enquiry into
additional matters. For example, a fact witness who by virtue of being a lawyer may have
knowledge of laws and regulations which are relevant to the cross-examining party's
case. The witness may not have spoken about these laws or regulations during his
examination-in-chief and adducing such evidence from him will not be contradictory to
the evidence given by him. Yet, such evidence may be relevant to the cross-examining
party's case. In the example given, the fact witness is in essence an expert witness on law
and regulations and although he was not called to give evidence on his expertise, his
testimony may be relevant.

In the *Kupreškić* Decision on Communications between the Parties and their
Witnesses the Trial Chamber was right to identify this matter as an issue of importance,
not just in the instant case but as a matter of general application.

The concerns which exist are twofold:

1. Counsel or an investigator, realising that a witness is not coming up to proof
(i.e. not giving evidence in accordance with their written and attested statement)
may speak to a witness at a break in the proceedings in such a way that, quite
unintentionally, causes the witness to give evidence at variance with evidence
already given. This circumstance, whilst not improper, is highly undesirable.

2. Counsel or an investigator, again realising that a witness is not coming up to
proof, may actively remind a witness of what was stated in a previous written
statement and during the course of conversations between the witness and
themselves engage the witness with a view to influencing their future evidence.
Such a course would almost certainly be an inherent contempt of the Tribunal.

A witness is supposed to testify from their memory. It is not improper to refresh that
memory with a witness' prior statement. However, there is a line between present
recollection refreshed and past recollection recorded. Thus, if a witness is merely

parroting something that appears in his statement that he does not remember, his testimony is hearsay and he cannot be cross-examined on this statement. The real danger of mid-testimony advice to witnesses is that they will present evidence as to which they do not have a present recollection as if they do have such a recollection, thereby thwarting the entire concept of cross-examination as well as jeopardizing the weight the Chamber may attach to the testimony.

It is right to emphasise that in the instant case the Trial Chamber expressly ruled out any act of impropriety or improper influence on the part of the Prosecution.

Anyone, experienced or not, may discuss the nature of the evidence with a witness who has already begun to give evidence in such a way that the witness appreciates, for example, the thrust of the cross-examination, which he or she would not have done without the contact taking place. Having thus realised what is important, the witness then changes or modifies or adds to the evidence in such a way as to affect the integrity of the evidence.

A particular problem may arise given the special circumstances in which witnesses may find themselves in The Hague. They may be away from home, family and a familiar national environment for long periods and may be left in a situation where their evidence is given in two parts, each separated from the other by a break of some days or even, as has happened in some cases, weeks. It is right to recognise that they may well have developed a significant relationship with the party calling them which may have given rise to a degree of dependency and trust.

The Chamber recognised the need to balance the desire to avoid anything happening which might affect the integrity of the evidence with the need to provide appropriate witness support.

Similar orders were made in the cases of *Prosecutor v. Jelisic* and *Prosecutor v. Kvočka et. al.*

The order in the *Kupreškić* case is an excellent example of the application of Rule 89(B). Here was a case in which the Chamber discovered that there was nothing in the Rules that covered this precise problem. The Chamber utilised this wide provision to fashion a sensible Order. It is a matter of some surprise that it has not yet found its way into the Rules as a permanent state of affairs, given that such a practice protects the integrity of the evidence and removes from any party the risk that something they do or say may be misconstrued by the other side or by the Chamber which may lead to an embarrassing enquiry as to what did or did not happen.

II.   TRIBUNAL CASES

B.   TRIAL CHAMBERS

PROSECUTOR V. KUNARAC, *et. al., Order on Rule 90(E),* IT-96-23-T, 15 March 2000, Mumba, Hunt & Pocar, JJ. Courtroom

The Prosecutor requested that one of its investigators be present during the trial without being precluded from being a witness. The Motion was granted with the proviso that the investigator's presence in court could affect the weight given to her testimony.[850]

PROSECUTOR V. KUPREŠKIĆ *et. al., Decision on Communications between the Parties and their Witnesses,* IT-95-16-T, 21 September 1998. Cassese, May, & Mumba, JJ.

The issue of communication between the parties and witnesses, once the witness has taken his or her solemn declaration under Rule 90 (B), was raised by Defence Counsel who discovered that Counsel for the Prosecution had been engaging in out-of-court discussions with Prosecution witnesses during breaks in the proceedings.

The Trial Chamber ordered that the Prosecution and Defence must not, henceforth, communicate with a witness, once he or she has made the solemn declaration provided for in Rule 90(B) and commenced testifying, on the subject of the content of the witness's testimony save with the leave of the Chamber.

The Chamber noted that the Defence had raised a genuine issue of importance since the aforementioned instances have posed a problem for Defence counsel in that it has led to their being confronted during the trial with evidence that had not previously been disclosed to them.

The Chamber went on to state that this is not to imply in any way that the Prosecutor has on any occasion acted with impropriety or exerted any influence on the witnesses in question and that the Chamber fully accepts the Prosecutor's explanation that on each occasion the witness in question has volunteered the information, during the break, which was later the subject of a tender of evidence.

The Chamber held that there was no specific provision in either the Statute or the Rules which specifically dealt with this issue but that Rules 89(B) and 90(G) provided it with sufficient basis to address it.

The rationale for the Chamber's decision was that the Prosecutor is not, or not only, a Party to adversarial proceedings but is an organ of the Tribunal and an organ of international criminal justice whose object is not simply to secure a conviction but to present the case for the Prosecution, which includes not only inculpatory, but also exculpatory evidence, in order to assist the Chamber to discover the truth in a judicial setting.

---

[850] Para. 2.

The Chamber held that a witness who has taken the Solemn Declaration under Rule 90 (B) is a witness of truth before the Tribunal and, inasmuch as he or she is required to contribute to the establishment of the truth, is not strictly a witness for either party.

The Chamber was plainly concerned as a result of its enquiries into what had taken place between the Prosecution and its witnesses that permitting either Party to communicate with a witness after he or she has commenced his or her testimony may lead both witness and Party, albeit unwittingly, to discuss the content of the testimony already given and thereby to influence the witness's further testimony in ways which are not consonant with the spirit of the Statute and Rules of the Tribunal.

The Chamber also indicated that it was aware of potential practical problems that might arise, for example, if a witness should wish to volunteer some information, which had arisen as a result of the course of examination-in-chief or cross-examination, to the party calling him or her. To this end the Chamber decided to utilise the services of the Victims and Witnesses Unit, ordering that if a witness wishes to contact the party which called him or her, he or she shall inform the competent staff of the Victims and Witnesses Unit who will then report the matter to the relevant party. In such circumstances that party may then decide whether or not to request, orally or in writing, the leave of the Chamber [to approach the witness] and will to this effect provide reasons for the request.

The Chamber held that, when granting leave, it might, whenever it deems it appropriate, decide that the contact between the requesting party and the witness must take place in the presence of an official of the Victims and Witnesses Unit. Also being alive to the possible discomfort to a witness who discovers that he or she is unable to communicate with Counsel or an investigator with whom a relationship of trust had been formed, went on to say that the Chamber may direct that a member of the Victims and Witnesses Unit should be present in court during the testimony of a given witness to provide the necessary moral and psychological support to compensate for the withdrawal of this support by the Prosecution or the Defence during the period that the witness testifies.

PROSECUTOR V. FURUNDŽIJA, *Order on Defence Motion Requesting Sequestration of Witnesses,* IT-95-17/1-T, 10 June 1998, Mumba, Cassese & May, JJ.

This is an example of the Notice which is given to witnesses through the Victims and Witnesses Unit of the Registry as a matter of practice:

NOTICE

Rule 90 (D) of the Rules of Evidence and Procedure of the International Tribunal provides:

(D)   A witness, other than an expert, who has not yet testified shall not be present when the testimony of another witness is given. However, a witness who has heard the testimony of another witness shall not for that reason alone be disqualified from testifying.

In addition to the basic instruction to witnesses not to be present in the courtroom when another witness is testifying, the Trial Chamber HEREBY DIRECTS you not to discuss testimony with other potential witnesses both prior to and during the trial.

In practical terms this means that, from the time you are first advised that one of the parties wishes to list you as a potential witness for trial, you should not discuss any matters relating to the trial with persons other than members of the Office of the Prosecutor, counsel for the defence or their designated representatives, or officials of the International Tribunal.

Witnesses must not watch, read or listen to media coverage of the proceedings prior to giving evidence. When the time- comes to give your evidence you may be asked by the Trial Chamber whether you have discussed your testimony with other witnesses and whether you have read about the proceedings in the press or watched the broadcasts on television.

Witnesses giving evidence before the International Tribunal are required to make a solemn declaration that they will speak the truth. A witness who gives false testimony after having made the declaration is liable to a potential fine of up to US $10,000 or imprisonment for up to twelve months or both.

PROSECUTOR V DELALIĆ *et. al., Decision on the Motions by the Prosecution for Protective Measures for the Prosecution Witnesses Pseudonymed "B" through to "M", IT-96-21-T, 28 April 1997, Karibi-Whyte, Odio-Benito & Jan, JJ.*

The Trial Chamber made the following observation in relation to Rule 90(A):

The Trial Chamber rejects the submission of the Defence that Rule 90(A) implies that a witness can only be heard from the courtroom. Direct evidence is evidence presented directly before the Trial Chamber either from the courtroom or, in appropriate circumstances as determined and directed by the Trial Chamber, from the remote witness room. The mandate of the Trial Chamber is to ensure a fair trial, and maintain a balance between the rights of the accused and the protection of the witness.[851]

B.   PRESIDENT

1. ACCUSED AS A WITNESS

PROSECUTOR V DELALIĆ *et. al., Decision of the President on the Prosecutor's Motion for the Production of Notes Exchanged between Zejnil Delalić and Zdravko Mucić, IT-96-21-T, 11 November 1996, Karibi-Whyte, Odio-Benito & Jan, JJ.*

Rule 85(C) provides that "the accused may appear as a witness in his or her own defence". The President found that under Rule 90 an accused who testifies in his defence cannot be considered for all purposes a witness. First, Rule 90(D), which provides that a witness who has not yet testified shall not be present when the testimony of another witness is given, is contrary to the right of the accused to be present throughout the trial

---

[851] Para. 67.

pursuant to Article 21(4)(d). Furthermore, Rule 90(F)[852] states that a witness may be compelled to answer a question which may incriminate him, whereas pursuant to Article 21(4)(g) the accused shall not be compelled to testify against himself or to confess guilt. The Rules have separate definitions and substantive provisions for the accused and other witnesses.[853]

---

[852] At the time of this Decision the relevant provision was Rule 90(E).
[853] Para. 36.

RULE 90 *BIS*

TRANSFER OF A DETAINED WITNESS

(A)   ANY DETAINED PERSON WHOSE PERSONAL APPEARANCE AS A WITNESS HAS BEEN REQUESTED BY THE TRIBUNAL SHALL BE TRANSFERRED TEMPORARILY TO THE DETENTION UNIT OF THE TRIBUNAL, CONDITIONAL ON THE PERSON'S RETURN WITHIN THE PERIOD DECIDED BY THE TRIBUNAL.

(B)   THE TRANSFER ORDER SHALL BE ISSUED BY A JUDGE OR TRIAL CHAMBER ONLY AFTER PRIOR VERIFICATION THAT THE FOLLOWING CONDITIONS HAVE BEEN MET:

(I)   THE PRESENCE OF THE DETAINED WITNESS IS NOT REQUIRED FOR ANY CRIMINAL PROCEEDINGS IN PROGRESS IN THE TERRITORY OF THE REQUESTED STATE DURING THE PERIOD THE WITNESS IS REQUIRED BY THE TRIBUNAL;

(II)   TRANSFER OF THE WITNESS DOES NOT EXTEND THE PERIOD OF DETENTION AS FORESEEN BY THE REQUESTED STATE.

(C)   THE REGISTRAR SHALL TRANSMIT THE ORDER OF TRANSFER TO THE NATIONAL AUTHORITIES OF THE STATE ON WHOSE TERRITORY, OR UNDER WHOSE JURISDICTION OR CONTROL, THE WITNESS IS DETAINED. TRANSFER SHALL BE ARRANGED BY THE NATIONAL AUTHORITIES CONCERNED IN LIAISON WITH THE HOST COUNTRY AND THE REGISTRAR.

(D)   THE REGISTRAR SHALL ENSURE THE PROPER CONDUCT OF THE TRANSFER, INCLUDING THE SUPERVISION OF THE WITNESS IN THE DETENTION UNIT OF THE TRIBUNAL; THE REGISTRAR SHALL REMAIN ABREAST OF ANY CHANGES WHICH MIGHT OCCUR REGARDING THE CONDITIONS OF DETENTION PROVIDED FOR BY THE REQUESTED STATE AND WHICH MAY POSSIBLY AFFECT THE LENGTH OF THE DETENTION OF THE WITNESS IN THE DETENTION UNIT AND, AS PROMPTLY AS POSSIBLE, SHALL INFORM THE RELEVANT JUDGE OR CHAMBER.

(E)   ON EXPIRATION OF THE PERIOD DECIDED BY THE TRIBUNAL FOR THE TEMPORARY TRANSFER, THE DETAINED WITNESS SHALL BE REMANDED TO THE AUTHORITIES OF THE REQUESTED STATE, UNLESS THE STATE, WITHIN THAT PERIOD, HAS TRANSMITTED AN ORDER OF RELEASE OF THE WITNESS, WHICH SHALL TAKE EFFECT IMMEDIATELY.

(F)   IF, BY THE END OF THE PERIOD DECIDED BY THE TRIBUNAL, THE PRESENCE OF THE DETAINED WITNESS CONTINUES TO BE NECESSARY, A JUDGE OR CHAMBER MAY EXTEND THE PERIOD ON THE SAME CONDITIONS AS STATED IN SUB-RULE (B).

RULE 91

FALSE TESTIMONY UNDER SOLEMN DECLARATION

(A)   A CHAMBER, *PROPRIO MOTU* OR AT THE REQUEST OF A PARTY, MAY WARN A WITNESS OF THE DUTY TO TELL THE TRUTH AND THE CONSEQUENCES THAT MAY RESULT FROM A FAILURE TO DO SO.

(B)   IF A CHAMBER HAS STRONG GROUNDS FOR BELIEVING THAT A WITNESS HAS KNOWINGLY AND WILFULLY GIVEN FALSE TESTIMONY, IT MAY DIRECT THE PROSECUTOR TO INVESTIGATE THE MATTER WITH A VIEW TO THE PREPARATION AND SUBMISSION OF AN INDICTMENT FOR FALSE TESTIMONY.

(C)   THE RULES OF PROCEDURE AND EVIDENCE IN PARTS FOUR TO EIGHT SHALL APPLY *MUTATIS MUTANDIS* TO PROCEEDINGS UNDER THIS RULE.

(D)   NO JUDGE WHO SAT AS A MEMBER OF THE TRIAL CHAMBER BEFORE WHICH THE WITNESS APPEARED SHALL SIT FOR THE TRIAL OF THE WITNESS FOR FALSE TESTIMONY.

(E)   THE MAXIMUM PENALTY FOR FALSE TESTIMONY UNDER SOLEMN DECLARATION SHALL BE A FINE OF DFL. 200,000 OR A TERM OF IMPRISONMENT OF SEVEN YEARS, OR BOTH. THE PAYMENT OF ANY FINE IMPOSED SHALL BE PAID TO THE REGISTRAR TO BE HELD IN THE ACCOUNT REFERRED TO IN SUB-RULE 77 (I).

(F)   SUB-RULES (B) TO (E) APPLY *MUTATIS MUTANDIS* TO A PERSON WHO KNOWINGLY AND WILLINGLY MAKES A FALSE STATEMENT IN AN AFFIDAVIT OR FORMAL STATEMENT WHICH THE PERSON KNOWS OR HAS REASON TO KNOW MAY BE USED AS EVIDENCE IN PROCEEDINGS BEFORE THE TRIBUNAL.

RULE 92

CONFESSIONS

A CONFESSION BY THE ACCUSED GIVEN DURING QUESTIONING BY THE PROSECUTOR SHALL, PROVIDED THE REQUIREMENTS OF RULE 63 WERE STRICTLY COMPLIED WITH, BE PRESUMED TO HAVE BEEN FREE AND VOLUNTARY UNLESS THE CONTRARY IS PROVED.

RULE 93

EVIDENCE OF CONSISTENT PATTERN OF CONDUCT

(A)   EVIDENCE OF A CONSISTENT PATTERN OF CONDUCT RELEVANT TO SERIOUS VIOLATIONS OF INTERNATIONAL HUMANITARIAN LAW UNDER THE STATUTE MAY BE ADMISSIBLE IN THE INTERESTS OF JUSTICE.

(B)   ACTS TENDING TO SHOW SUCH A PATTERN OF CONDUCT SHALL BE DISCLOSED BY THE PROSECUTOR TO THE DEFENCE PURSUANT TO RULE 66.

RULE 94

JUDICIAL NOTICE

(A)   A TRIAL CHAMBER SHALL NOT REQUIRE PROOF OF FACTS OF COMMON KNOWLEDGE BUT SHALL TAKE JUDICIAL NOTICE THEREOF.

(B)   AT THE REQUEST OF A PARTY OR *PROPRIO MOTU*, A TRIAL CHAMBER, AFTER HEARING THE PARTIES, MAY DECIDE TO TAKE JUDICIAL NOTICE OF ADJUDICATED FACTS OR DOCUMENTARY EVIDENCE FROM OTHER PROCEEDINGS OF THE TRIBUNAL RELATING TO MATTERS AT ISSUE IN THE CURRENT PROCEEDINGS.

I.   COMMENTARY

Under Rule 94, judicial notice of certain facts may be taken within the exercise of the powers conferred on a Trial Chamber, as a matter of law, as part of the process of determining the facts upon which it may render a final decision on the merits of a case. One way of formulating whether the fact in question can be noticed, without proof, is to ask whether the fact under consideration is not a matter of reasonable dispute between the parties and thought to be capable of immediate and accurate demonstration by reference to an indisputable source of information. The jurisprudence of the International Tribunal indicates that Rule 94 has been relied upon to take judicial notice of official statements or documents from international organisations or governments or in regards to background matters which the parties admit or agree are not in dispute.

Furthermore, Rule 94(B) expands the scope of judicial notice to include adjudicated facts or documentary evidence from other proceedings of the Tribunal. This provision may be seen as an example of a rule incorporating a concept that is specific to the prosecution of cases before the International Tribunal. It sets parameters on the way in which evidence from other proceedings in the Tribunal may be treated in subsequent trials and confines this peculiar species of judicial notice to facts or documentary evidence that have been adjudicated in the system established by the Statute. This includes facts or documentary evidence in respect of which there has been a final determination by a Trial Chamber, where there is no appeal or, in the case of an appeal, by the Appeals Chamber.[854] Without final judicial determination of the facts and documentary evidence from other proceedings of the Tribunal, it would be unsafe and imprudent to admit them without proof in a trial before a Chamber.

In keeping with the rationale that underpins the concept of judicial notice, the types of facts falling under Rule 94(B) must be confined to those which are so notorious as to be beyond any reasonable dispute between people of good faith. Nonetheless, certain adjudicated facts may be disputed and be central to litigation between the parties *inter se* in subsequent proceedings, in which case no judicial notice of those facts can be

---

[854] See, Prosecutor v. Aleksovski, *Dissenting Opinion of Judge Patrick Robinson on the Decision on Prosecutor's Appeal on Admissibility of Evidence*, IT-95-14/1-A, 16 February 1999, paragraph 13-15. Pursuant to Article 25 of the Statute, the Appeals Chamber may hear appeals on matter of law or fact.

taken. In those circumstances, those facts are limited to the acknowledgement that a certain finding of fact has been made in other proceedings, without comment or concession as to its correctness or underlying justice.

A review of the case-law of the Tribunal, indicates that a Chamber may not only take judicial notice of certain facts, it may also enter a ruling that certain legal conclusions may be made at any point in the proceedings. Two decisions reviewed below are important because of approach each Trial Chamber took to the application of the rule of judicial notice and the consequences of taking judicial notice of certain facts. In the *Simić* case, the Trial Chamber declined to take judicial notice of the international character of the armed conflict on the request of the Prosecution. Relying upon the *Tadić Jurisdictional Decision*, the Chamber found that different conflicts of different nature took place in the former Yugoslavia and that it would be for each Chamber, depending on the circumstances of each case, to make its own determination on the nature of the armed conflict, based upon the specific evidence presented to it. The Trial Chamber stated that these findings have no binding force except as between the parties in respect of a particular case ("*effet relatif de la chose jugée*"), that the circumstances of each case are different, and that as regards the controversial issue of the nature of the conflict, which involves an interpretation of facts, both parties should be able to present arguments and evidence on them.

In the *Kvočka case*, the parties had agreed to a large number of adjudicated facts from prior cases before the International Tribunal. The question which faced the Chamber was whether, on the basis of those adjudicated fact, certain elements of the charges could be considered proven beyond reasonable doubt. In ruling that certain legal conclusions could be drawn based on those fact, the Chamber did not appear to be departing from the decision handed down in the *Simić* case. Indeed, in the instance of the *Kvočka case*, the agreement by the parties to adjudicated facts from prior cases amounted to admissions by the parties or a statement of matters which are not in dispute.[855] Once the parties had agreed to certain facts contained in prior judgements of the Tribunal, nothing precluded the Chamber from drawing legal conclusions based on those facts.

However, where a Trial Chamber takes judicial notice of certain facts and does not decide upon the legal charaterisation of those facts, the parties to the proceedings must determine whether further evidence must be adduced in order to establish the point which is suggested or inferred by the judicially noticed facts. For example, the Prosecution must assess whether those facts which are relevant to an ingredient of an offence are sufficient for it to meet its burden of proving guilt beyond reasonable doubt or whether it must present additional evidence on that point.

One of the outstanding issues in relation to judicial notice before the Tribunal is the question of successive indictments and trials which arise out of common geographic or temporal events from the conflicts in the former Yugoslavia, where the parties dispute findings of fact from previous cases. As has been seen, Rule 94(B) broadens the usual parameters of judicial notice by referring to adjudicated facts or documentary evidence from other proceedings of the Tribunal relating to matters at issue in a subsequent trial.

---

[855] See, Rule 65 *ter*.

However, a defendant who was not a party in the original proceeding, where the adjudication took place, should not be bound by those facts where it can be said that there exists a reasonable basis to dispute the facts in question. For example, a party at trial may not have contested certain facts in earlier proceedings. The facts may have been secondary to the ultimate issue of guilt or innocence of the particular accused. The judgement rendered in such a case will make findings of fact based on the evidence presented to it by the parties *inter se*, not in anticipation of subsequent proceedings. In a later trial, however, those very facts may be central to the determination of the guilt or innocence of the accused, in which case those facts are likely to be disputed by the parties and it would be inappropriate to take judicial notice of those facts. This particular issue can only be determined on a case by case basis, for the approach and strategy of a party in a subsequent trial may be entirely different than those advocated by the parties in earlier proceedings.

II. TRIBUNAL CASES

B. TRIAL CHAMBERS

PROSECUTOR V. KVOČKA *et. al.*, *Decision on Judicial Notice*, IT-98-30/1-T, 8 June 2000, Rodriguez, Riad & Wald, JJ.

Pursuant to Rule 94(B), the Trial Chamber took judicial notice of 444 facts from the *Tadić* and *Delalić* judgements that the parties had agreed were adjudicated facts.[856] In addition, on the basis of these facts, the Chamber found certain elements of Article 3 (Violations of the Law and Customs of War) and Article 5 (Crimes Against Humanity) of the Statute had been proven beyond reasonable doubt and that no further evidence needed to be adduced in regards to these issues at trial. The Chamber decided that at the times and places alleged in the indictment, there existed an armed conflict, which included widespread and systematic attack against notably the Muslim and Croat civilian population and that there was a nexus between this armed conflict and the widespread and systematic attack on the civilian population and the existence of the Omarska, Keraterm and Trnopolje camps and the mistreatment of the prisoners therein.

    This finding by the Chamber, on the basis of adjudicated facts, did not mean that the accused were responsible for the commission of any offences alleged in the indictment. The Chamber emphasized that the Prosecution maintained the burden of proving the guilt of the accused beyond reasonable doubt under Article 7(1) and Article 7(3), as charged in the indictment.[857]

---

[856] See, also, Prosecutor v. Kvočka et. al., *Prosecutor's Motion for judicial notice of adjudicated facts*, IT-98-30-PT, 11 January 1999 and Prosecutor v. Kvočka et. al., *Decision on Prosecutor's Motion for judicial notice of adjudicated facts,*. IT-98-30-PT, 19 March 1999.

[857] Pg. 6.

PROSECUTOR V. SIMIĆ, *Decision on the Pre-Trial Motion by the Prosecution Requesting the Trial Chamber to Take Judicial Notice of the International Character of the Conflict in Bosnia-Herzegovina*, IT-95-9-PT, 25 March 1999, May, Bennouna & Robinson, JJ.

The Trial Chamber dismissed the Motion by the Prosecution brought under Rule 94 to take judicial notice of the international character of the conflict in Bosnia and Herzegovina, at least for the period starting on 6 March 1992 or at the latest by 6 April 1992 and ending at the earliest on 19 May 1992.

Pursuant to Rule 94(A), the Chamber, *proprio motu* did take judicial notice of the following facts:

- Bosnia and Herzegovina proclaimed its independence from the Socialist Federal Republic of Yugoslavia on 6 March 1992;
- The independence of Bosnia and Herzegovina as a State was recognised by the European Community on 6 April 1992 and by the United States on 7 April 1992.[858]

The Chamber observed that the purpose of judicial notice under Rule 94 is judicial economy and that it should be interpreted as covering facts that are not subject to reasonable dispute. A balance must be struck between judicial economy and the right of the accused to a fair trial. Rule 94 is intended to cover fact and not legal consequences inferred from those facts. Judicial notice may only be taken of factual findings but not of a legal characterisation as such.

The Prosecution was requesting the Chamber to take judicial notice of the international character of the conflict in Bosnia and Herzegovina either as a fact of common knowledge under Rule 94(A) or an adjudicated fact under Rule 94(B). The request was aimed at permitting the application of the counts in the indictment based on Article 2 of the Statute that require the Prosecution to prove *inter alia* the existence of an international armed conflict. The consequence of taking judicial notice of this issue means that it would preclude examining the evidence on the character of the conflict.

Facts of Common Knowledge

The Chamber rejected the submission that the international character of the conflict in Bosnia and Herzegovina was a fact of common knowledge or an historical fact of common knowledge. Nor was it a fact of common knowledge within the Tribunal because of the jurisprudence of the Tribunal where an international armed conflict has been found to exist as a matter of fact.

---

[858] The Trial Chamber cited the following case in regards to Rule 94(A): Prosecutor v. Kovačević, *Order on Prosecution Request for Judicial Notice*, IT-97-24-PT, 12 May 1998.

Adjudicated Facts

Relying on the *Tadić* Jurisdictional Decision, the Chamber found that different conflicts of different natures took place in the former Yugoslavia and that it would be for each Trial Chamber, depending on the circumstances of each case, to make its own determination on the nature of the armed conflict upon the specific evidence presented to it. In regard to decisions handed down by other Trial Chambers on the issue of the nature of the conflict, the Chamber stated that these findings have no binding force except between the parties in respect of a particular case ("effet relatif de la chose jugée"), that the circumstances of each case are different, and that as regards the controversial issue of the nature of the conflict, which involved an interpretation of facts, both parties should be able to present arguments and evidence on them.

The Defence opposed the request by the Prosecution on two main grounds. First, based on a review of international and national practice, that a Court may only take judicial notice of notorious facts which cannot be reasonably disputed, or capable of immediate and accurate demonstration by resorting to readily accessible sources of indispensable accuracy, and that the issue of judicial notice should be approached in criminal proceedings with great caution and care. Second, judicial notice of the international character of the conflict would jeopardise the rights of the accused under Article 21 of the Tribunal's Statute, in particular their right to a fair trial and right to examine or have examined the evidence presented by the Prosecutor. The accused has a right to an independent determination of the facts at issue.

PROSECUTOR V. ZEJNIL DELALIĆ *et. al.*, *Judgement*, IT-96-21-T, 16 November 1998, Karibi-Whyte, Odio-Benito & Jan, JJ

Res Judicata

The observations of the Trial Chamber seem apposite to the application of the interpretation and application of Rule 94(B). The Chamber held that the principle of *res judicata* (a thing adjudicated is received as the truth) only applies *inter partes* in a case where a matter has already been judicially determined within that case itself. The Chamber observed that as in national criminal systems that employ a public prosecutor in some form, the Prosecution is clearly always a party to cases before the Tribunal. The doctrine of *res judicata* is limited, in criminal cases, to the question of whether, when the previous trial of a particular individual is followed by another of the same individual, a specific matter has already been fully litigated. In national systems where a public prosecutor appears in all criminal cases, the doctrine is clearly not applied so as to prevent the prosecutor from disputing a matter that the prosecutor has argued in a previous, different case. The Chamber added that it is certainly not bound by the Decisions of other Trial Chambers in past cases and must make its findings based on the evidence presented to it and its own interpretation of the law applicable to the case at issue. The circumstances of each case differ significantly and thus also the evidence presented by the Prosecution. The Chamber concluded by pointing out that even should the Prosecution bring evidence that is largely similar to that presented in a previous case, the Chamber's assessment of it might lead to entirely different results.[859]

---

[859] Para. 222.

RULE 94 *BIS*

TESTIMONY OF EXPERT WITNESSES

(A)   NOTWITHSTANDING THE PROVISIONS OF RULE 65 *TER* (E)(IV)(B) AND RULE 65 *TER* (G)(I)(B), THE FULL STATEMENT OF ANY EXPERT WITNESS CALLED BY A PARTY SHALL BE DISCLOSED TO THE OPPOSING PARTY AS EARLY AS POSSIBLE AND SHALL BE FILED WITH THE TRIAL CHAMBER NOT LESS THAN TWENTY-ONE DAYS PRIOR TO THE DATE ON WHICH THE EXPERT IS EXPECTED TO TESTIFY.

(B)   WITHIN FOURTEEN DAYS OF FILING OF THE STATEMENT OF THE EXPERT WITNESS, THE OPPOSING PARTY SHALL FILE A NOTICE INDICATING WHETHER:

      (I)   IT ACCEPTS THE EXPERT WITNESS STATEMENT; OR

      (II)   IT WISHES TO CROSS-EXAMINE THE EXPERT WITNESS.

(C)   IF THE OPPOSING PARTY ACCEPTS THE STATEMENT OF THE EXPERT WITNESS, THE STATEMENT MAY BE ADMITTED INTO EVIDENCE BY THE TRIAL CHAMBER WITHOUT CALLING THE WITNESS TO TESTIFY IN PERSON.

II.   TRIBUNAL CASES

B.   TRIAL CHAMBERS

PROSECUTOR V DELALIĆ *et. al.*, *Order on the Prosecution's Motion for leave to call Additional Expert Witnesses*, IT-96-21-T, 13 November 1997, Karibi-Whyte, Jan, Odio-Benito, JJ.

The Trial Chamber found that the principle of *iura novit curia* (the court knows the law) does not prevent it from being addressed on certain matters of law by either the Prosecution or Defence. In other words, an expert may testify on matters of law that ultimately remain within the exclusive province of the Trial Chamber.

      In the instant case, the Prosecution expert testified in relation to the legal definition of "nationality" in international law. This issue was ultimately determined by the Chamber in relation to the definition of "protected persons" under Article 2 that incorporates the Grave Breaches regime of the Geneva Conventions of 1949 into the Statute.

RULE 94 *TER*

AFFIDAVIT EVIDENCE

TO PROVE A FACT IN DISPUTE, A PARTY MAY PROPOSE TO CALL A WITNESS AND TO SUBMIT IN CORROBORATION OF HIS OR HER TESTIMONY ON THAT FACT AFFIDAVITS OR FORMAL STATEMENTS SIGNED BY OTHER WITNESSES IN ACCORDANCE WITH THE LAW AND PROCEDURE OF THE STATE IN WHICH SUCH AFFIDAVITS OR STATEMENTS ARE SIGNED. THESE AFFIDAVITS OR STATEMENTS ARE ADMISSIBLE PROVIDED THEY ARE FILED PRIOR TO THE GIVING OF TESTIMONY BY THE WITNESS TO BE CALLED AND THE OTHER PARTY DOES NOT OBJECT WITHIN SEVEN DAYS AFTER COMPLETION OF THE TESTIMONY OF THE WITNESS THROUGH WHOM THE AFFIDAVITS ARE TENDERED. IF THE PARTY OBJECTS AND THE TRIAL CHAMBER SO RULES, OR IF THE TRIAL CHAMBER SO ORDERS, THE WITNESSES SHALL BE CALLED FOR CROSS-EXAMINATION.

I.　　COMMENTARY

This Rule provides for either "affidavits or formal statements" to be taken in accordance with the law and procedure of the State in which they are signed. Affidavits are unknown in Civil Law jurisdictions and the reference to formal statements brings the procedure in line with the means for taking a solemn declaration in those jurisdictions.

To be admissible the affidavits or formal statements must be filed prior to the testimony of the witness that they are intended to corroborate.

RULE 95

EXCLUSION OF CERTAIN EVIDENCE

NO EVIDENCE SHALL BE ADMISSIBLE IF OBTAINED BY METHODS WHICH CAST SUBSTANTIAL DOUBT ON ITS RELIABILITY OR IF ITS ADMISSION IS ANTITHETICAL TO, AND WOULD SERIOUSLY DAMAGE, THE INTEGRITY OF THE PROCEEDINGS.

II. TRIBUNAL CASES

B. TRIAL CHAMBERS

PROSECUTOR V. FURUNDŽIJA, *Judgement*, IT-95-17/1-T, 10 December 1998, Mumba, Cassese & May, JJ.

More than once it has been revealed in trials at the Tribunal that witnesses are suffering from Post-Traumatic Stress Disorder. This has, of course, prompted questions regarding their qualification as witnesses.

The Trial Chamber, in this case found that because a person is suffering from PTSD, it does not mean that he or she is necessarily inaccurate in the evidence given. Such a person can be a perfectly reliable witness.[860]

PROSECUTOR V DELALIĆ *et. al., Decision on Zdravko Mucić's Motion for the Exclusion of Evidence*, IT-96-21-T, 2 September 1997, Karibi-Whyte, Odio-Benito & Jan, JJ.

The Trial Chamber held that Rule 95 is a summary of the provisions in the Rules, which enable the exclusion of evidence antithetical to and damaging, and thereby protecting the integrity of the proceedings. Rule 95 is a residual exclusionary provision.[861]

---

[860] Para. 109.
[861] Para. 44.

RULE 96

EVIDENCE IN CASES OF SEXUAL ASSAULT

IN CASES OF SEXUAL ASSAULT:

(I)   NO CORROBORATION OF THE VICTIM'S TESTIMONY SHALL BE REQUIRED;

(II)   CONSENT SHALL NOT BE ALLOWED AS A DEFENCE IF THE VICTIM

(A)   HAS BEEN SUBJECTED TO OR THREATENED WITH OR HAS HAD REASON TO FEAR VIOLENCE, DURESS, DETENTION OR PSYCHOLOGICAL OPPRESSION, OR

(B)   REASONABLY BELIEVED THAT IF THE VICTIM DID NOT SUBMIT, ANOTHER MIGHT BE SO SUBJECTED, THREATENED OR PUT IN FEAR;

(III)   BEFORE EVIDENCE OF THE VICTIM'S CONSENT IS ADMITTED, THE ACCUSED SHALL SATISFY THE TRIAL CHAMBER IN CAMERA THAT THE EVIDENCE IS RELEVANT AND CREDIBLE;

(IV)   PRIOR SEXUAL CONDUCT OF THE VICTIM SHALL NOT BE ADMITTED IN EVIDENCE.

II.   TRIBUNAL CASES

B.   TRIAL CHAMBERS

PROSECUTOR V DELALIĆ *et. al., Decision on the Prosecution's Motion for the Redaction of the Public Record,* IT-96-21-T, 5 June 1997, Karibi-Whyte, Odio-Bentio & Jan, JJ.

The issue for determination in this case was whether statements made by a witness regarding her abortion, in the course of her testimony about rape, are admissible into evidence.

The Chamber determined that any reference made by the witness during the course of her testimony to her having had an abortion must be removed from the transcript, audio-recordings and video recordings of the Tribunal.

This is the first decision of the Tribunal to consider Rule 96(iv). Two main issues were examined: (1) the purpose of Rule 96(iv) and its relationship to other provisions of the Rules governing the admissibility of evidence and (2) the meaning of "prior sexual conduct".

The Chamber found that the rules governing the admissibility of evidence are of a flexible, non-technical nature. Relying primarily on Rules 89(C) and 89(D), the Chamber held that evidence must be relevant and have probative value to be admissible, but relevant evidence may be inadmissible, if its probative value is substantially outweighed by the need to ensure a fair trial.

In addition, the Chamber found that Rule 96 is a specific evidentiary rule that applies to the admissibility of evidence in cases of sexual assault. In particular, Rule 96(iv), provides that evidence concerning past sexual conduct of the victim is inadmissible. The Chamber described the purpose of Rule 96(iv) in the following terms:

> Regarding Sub-rule 96(iv), the Judges considered that the prime objective of this provision is to adequately protect the victims from harassment, embarrassment and humiliation by the presentation of evidence which relates to past sexual conduct. Sub-rule 96(iv) seeks to prevent situations where the admission of certain evidence may lead to a confusion of the issues, therefore offending the fairness of the proceedings. Furthermore, when adopting Sub-rule 96(iv), due regard was given to the fact that in rape or other sexual assault cases, evidence of prior sexual conduct of the victims mainly serves to call the reputation of the victim into question. Moreover, it was considered that the value, if any, of information about the prior sexual conduct of a witness in the context of trials of this nature was nullified by the potential danger of further causing distress and motional damage to the witnesses.[862]

The Chamber concluded that Rule 96(iv) makes a victim's prior sexual history irrelevant.

Prior Sexual Conduct

The Chamber ruled that the phrase "prior sexual conduct" within the meaning of Rule 96(iv) includes information about an abortion the witness had in the past.[863]

The Chamber relied on three factors in coming to this conclusion: the unfettered discretion of Judges to determine the admissibility of evidence under the Rules (in particular, Rule 89), the wide discretion of the Judges to determine what constitutes "prior sexual conduct" under Rule 96(iv), and the persuasive nature of so-called rape shield legislation in many countries which prohibit the admission of evidence of prior sexual conduct, including evidence of the use of contraceptives, evidence of pregnancy, and evidence of abortion.[864]

Furthermore, the Chamber ruled that Rule 96(iv) is an exclusionary rule that forbids the introduction of evidence concerning prior sexual conduct in sexual assault cases and there can be no waiver of its imperative terms.[865]

---

[862] Para. 48.
[863] Para. 59.
[864] Para. 59.
[865] Para. 58.

Finally, in the instant case, it was held that the evidence concerning the abortion was irrelevant. It did not affect the credibility of the witness, and the defence conceded that the evidence had no bearing on its case.[866]

---

[866] Para. 60.

RULE 97

LAWYER-CLIENT PRIVILEGE

ALL COMMUNICATIONS BETWEEN LAWYER AND CLIENT SHALL BE REGARDED AS PRIVILEGED, AND CONSEQUENTLY NOT SUBJECT TO DISCLOSURE AT TRIAL, UNLESS:

(I)   THE CLIENT CONSENTS TO SUCH DISCLOSURE; OR

(II)   THE CLIENT HAS VOLUNTARILY DISCLOSED THE CONTENT OF THE COMMUNICATION TO A THIRD PARTY, AND THAT THIRD PARTY THEN GIVES EVIDENCE OF THAT DISCLOSURE.

RULE 98

POWER OF CHAMBERS TO ORDER PRODUCTION OF ADDITIONAL EVIDENCE

A TRIAL CHAMBER MAY ORDER EITHER PARTY TO PRODUCE ADDITIONAL EVIDENCE. IT MAY *PROPRIO MOTU* SUMMON WITNESSES AND ORDER THEIR ATTENDANCE.

II.   TRIBUNAL CASES

B.   TRIAL CHAMBERS

PROSECUTOR V. BLAŠKIĆ, *Decision of Trial Chamber I on the Appearance of Colonel Robert Stewart,* IT-95-14-T, 25 March 1999, Jorda, Rodrigues & Shahabuddeen, JJ.

This Trial Chamber decided to call a witness on its own initiative. It was ordered, according to the Chamber, "to ascertain the truth in respect of the crimes of which the accused has been charged." The witness was Colonel Robert Stewart, Commander of the UNPROFOR British battalion at the time of the acts mentioned in the amended indictment. In addition, the Chamber ordered the Prosecution and the Defence "to provide under seal and *ex parte* all statements of the Witness or any material in their possession produced or annotated by him and relating to the indictment."

The Chamber set out the conditions for the giving of the testimony as follows:

- the Witness shall testify freely about the matters of which he had knowledge that occurred within the scope of his then mission and that relate to the acts with which the accused has been charged as they appear in the indictment; he shall answer the questions put to him by the Judges;

- the Prosecutor and then the Defence shall have the same limited time for questioning the Witness within the scope of the statements made by the Witness at the hearing and under the control of the Trial Chamber;

RULE 98 *BIS*

MOTION FOR JUDGEMENT OF ACQUITTAL

(A)   AN ACCUSED MAY FILE A MOTION FOR THE ENTRY OF JUDGEMENT OF ACQUITTAL ON ONE OR MORE OFFENCES CHARGED IN THE INDICTMENT WITHIN SEVEN DAYS AFTER THE CLOSE OF THE PROSECUTOR'S CASE AND, IN ANY EVENT, PRIOR TO THE PRESENTATION OF EVIDENCE BY THE DEFENCE PURSUANT TO RULE 85 (A) (II).

(B)   THE TRIAL CHAMBER SHALL ORDER THE ENTRY OF JUDGEMENT OF ACQUITTAL ON MOTION OF AN ACCUSED OR *PROPRIO MOTU* IF IT FINDS THAT THE EVIDENCE IS INSUFFICIENT TO SUSTAIN A CONVICTION ON THAT OR THOSE CHARGES.

I.   COMMENTARY

With the exception of the decision in the *Jelisić* case under Rule 98 *bis*, Tribunal jurisprudence has always determined motions for acquittal at the close of Prosecution's case on the basis of a standard lower than proof beyond a reasonable doubt. As a general rule, Chambers have formulated the test for such a motion by asking the question "whether there was evidence, were it to be accepted by the Chamber, which could lawfully support a conviction of the accused" (*Tadić* case) or whether the Trial Chamber was "satisfied that, as a matter of law, there is evidence before it relating to each of the offences in question for the accused persons to be invited to make their defence" (*Delalić* case).

The *Jelisić* case departed from this standard of proof for the purposes of a motion for acquittal. In that case, the Chamber applied the standard of proof beyond reasonable doubt in dismissing the charge of genocide against Jelisić at the close of the Prosecution's case.

In the *Kordić* and *Čerkez* case, the Chamber declined to follow the test adopted by the Trial Chamber in the *Jelisić* case in ruling on a Rule 98 *bis* application. The Chamber pointed out that the *Jelesić* decision is subject to an appeal and is to be taken as a decision on its own particular facts arrived at in the unusual circumstances of that case.

Rule 98(A) is ambiguous. It provides for a 7-day period within which to file such a motion and then goes on to say that in any case it must be filed before the Defence case begins. The assumption is that if the Defence case is to begin within the 7-day period, then the Motion must be filed earlier than the 7-day requirement. It could, however, be read to permit filing at any time prior to the beginning of the Defence case, Presumably with leave to extend the time limit pursuant to Rule 127.

II.   TRIBUNAL CASES

B.   TRIAL CHAMBERS

PROSECUTOR V. KORDIĆ & ČERKEZ, *Decision on Defence Motions for Judgement of Acquittal*, IT-95-14/2-T, 6 April 2000, May, Bennouna & Robinson, JJ.

The Chamber observed that the broad purpose of Rule 98 *bis* is to determine whether the Prosecution has put forward a case sufficient to warrant the Defence being called upon to answer it. Implicit in Rule 98 *bis* proceedings is the distinction between the determination made at the halfway stage of the trial, and the ultimate decision on the guilt of the accused to be made at the end of the case, on the basis of proof beyond reasonable doubt.[867]

The Test for a Motion for Acquittal under Rule 98 bis

The Chamber held that the test to be applied on a motion for acquittal under Rule 98 *bis* is whether there is evidence on which a reasonable Trial Chamber could convict. The Chamber did not elaborate any further on the meaning of this test other than to say that there must be some evidence that could properly lead to a conviction.[868] However, the Chamber observed that this standard proceeds on the basis that generally the Chamber would not consider questions of credibility and reliability in dealing with a motion under Rule 98 *bis*, leaving those matters to the end of the case. The one situation where the Chamber is obliged to consider such matters is where the Prosecution's case has completely broken down, either on its own presentation or as a result of such fundamental questions being raised through cross-examination as to the reliability and credibility of witnesses that the Prosecution is left without a case.[869]

PROSECUTOR V. JELISIĆ, *Oral Decision on Rule 98 bis Dismissing the Charge of Genocide*, IT-95-10-T, 19 October 1999, Jorda, Riad & Rodriguez, JJ.

Pursuant to Rule 98 *bis*, the Chamber *proprio motu* dismissed the charge of genocide against the accused at the close of the Prosecution case. The Chamber set out the test that it applied to a Rule 98 *bis* motion for judgement of acquittal, in the following terms:

---

[867] Para. 11.
[868] Para. 26.
[869] Para. 28.

The Prosecutor has not provided the sufficient proof which would allow us to establish beyond all reasonable doubt that Jelisić planned, incited, ordered, committed, or in any other way participated, in full consciousness, in the even partial destruction of the Bosnian Muslim population, as a national, ethnic, or religious group, and this doubt which must rebound to the benefit of the accused. Therefore Goran Jelisić cannot be declared guilty of genocide.[870]

PROSECUTOR V. BLASKIĆ, *Decision of the Trial Chamber I on the Defence Motion to Dismiss,* IT-95-14-T, 3 September 1998, Jorda, Riad & Shahabuddeen, JJ.

Although Rule 98 *bis* had been amended by the time the motion was filed in this case, the Defence insisted on having it considered pursuant to the old practice that had grown up around Rule 54 in the *Čelebići* and *Tadić* cases. Nonetheless, the Chamber apparently chose to treat the Motion as one filed pursuant to Rule 98 *bis*. In denying the Motion, the Chamber stated that the test is as follows:

> . . . should the evidence presented be insufficient to justify a conviction for one or several of the crimes ascribed in the indictment, the Trial Chamber, either *proprio motu* or at the request of the accused, may render a judgment of acquittal for that or those crimes; that this means that the Trial Chamber must grant the Motion if it is convinced that, at this stage of the proceedings, the Prosecution has not provided sufficient evidence to justify immediately a judgement of conviction based on the various counts invoked by counsel for the accused.[871]

The Chamber did not foreclose the possibility, however, of considering such a motion at this stage pursuant to Rule 54. In that event the indictment or some counts of it could be dismissed "only if [the Chamber] deemed that the Prosecution has so clearly failed to satisfy its obligation as the prosecuting party, that, commencing with this stage of the proceedings, it is no longer even necessary to review the Defence evidence regarding the counts covered in the Motion."

PROSECUTOR V DELALIĆ *et. al., Order on the Motions to Dismiss the Indictment at the Close of the Prosecutor's Case,* IT-96-21-T, 18 March 1998, Karibi-Whyte, Odio-Benito & Jan, JJ.

This order was issued under Rule 54, prior to the enactment of Rule 98 *bis.*

---

[870] Cited in Prosecutor v. Kordić & Čerkez, *Decision on Defence Motions for Judgement of Acquittal,* IT-95-14/2-T, 6 April 2000, May, Bennouna & Robinson, JJ, para. 16.

[871] This sounds very much like the Jelisić test. If the evidence would not justify finding the defendant guilty beyond a reasonable doubt the charges must be dismissed.

The *Delalić* case was decided according to the test set out in *Tadić*[872]. The Chamber applied the following test: whether the Trial Chamber is satisfied that as a matter of law, there is evidence relating to each element of the offences in question which, were it to be accepted, is such that a reasonable tribunal might convict.

---

[872] Prosecutor v. Tadić, *Decision on Defence Motion to Dismiss Charges*, IT-94-1,13 September 1996, McDonald, Stephen & Vohrah, JJ.

RULE 98 *TER*

JUDGEMENT

(A)   THE JUDGEMENT SHALL BE PRONOUNCED IN PUBLIC, ON A DATE OF WHICH NOTICE SHALL HAVE BEEN GIVEN TO THE PARTIES AND COUNSEL AND AT WHICH THEY SHALL BE ENTITLED TO BE PRESENT, SUBJECT TO THE PROVISIONS OF SUB-RULE 102 (B).

(B)   IF THE TRIAL CHAMBER FINDS THE ACCUSED GUILTY OF A CRIME AND CONCLUDES FROM THE EVIDENCE THAT UNLAWFUL TAKING OF PROPERTY BY THE ACCUSED WAS ASSOCIATED WITH IT, IT SHALL MAKE A SPECIFIC FINDING TO THAT EFFECT IN ITS JUDGEMENT. THE TRIAL CHAMBER MAY ORDER RESTITUTION AS PROVIDED IN RULE 105.

(C)   THE JUDGEMENT SHALL BE RENDERED BY A MAJORITY OF THE JUDGES. IT SHALL BE ACCOMPANIED OR FOLLOWED AS SOON AS POSSIBLE BY A REASONED OPINION IN WRITING, TO WHICH SEPARATE OR DISSENTING OPINIONS MAY BE APPENDED.

(D)   A COPY OF THE JUDGEMENT AND OF THE JUDGES' OPINIONS IN A LANGUAGE WHICH THE ACCUSED UNDERSTANDS SHALL AS SOON AS POSSIBLE BE SERVED ON THE ACCUSED IF IN CUSTODY. COPIES THEREOF IN THAT LANGUAGE AND IN THE LANGUAGE IN WHICH THEY WERE DELIVERED SHALL ALSO AS SOON AS POSSIBLE BE PROVIDED TO COUNSEL FOR THE ACCUSED.

RULE 99

STATUS OF THE ACQUITTED PERSON

(A) SUBJECT TO SUB-RULE (B), IN THE CASE OF AN ACQUITTAL OR THE UPHOLDING OF A CHALLENGE TO JURISDICTION, THE ACCUSED SHALL BE RELEASED IMMEDIATELY.

(B) IF, AT THE TIME THE JUDGEMENT IS PRONOUNCED, THE PROSECUTOR ADVISES THE TRIAL CHAMBER IN OPEN COURT OF THE PROSECUTOR'S INTENTION TO FILE NOTICE OF APPEAL PURSUANT TO RULE 108, THE TRIAL CHAMBER MAY, ON APPLICATION IN THAT BEHALF BY THE PROSECUTOR AND UPON HEARING THE PARTIES, IN ITS DISCRETION, ISSUE AN ORDER FOR THE CONTINUED DETENTION OF THE ACCUSED, PENDING THE DETERMINATION OF THE APPEAL.

II.   TRIBUNAL CASES

B.   TRIAL CHAMBERS

PROSECUTOR V. DELALIĆ *et. al., Judgement*, IT-96-21-T, 16 November 1998, Karibi-Whyte, Odio-Benito & Jan, JJ.

Pursuant to Rule 99, the Trial Chamber ordered that Zejnil Delalić be released immediately from the United Nations Detention Unit following his acquittal on all charges.[873]

    An oral application made by the Prosecution under Rule 99(B) for the continued detention of Delalić pending appeal was denied.

---

[873] Paragraph 1291.

RULE 100

SENTENCING PROCEDURE ON A GUILTY PLEA

(A)   IF THE TRIAL CHAMBER CONVICTS THE ACCUSED ON A GUILTY PLEA, THE PROSECUTOR AND THE DEFENCE MAY SUBMIT ANY RELEVANT INFORMATION THAT MAY ASSIST THE TRIAL CHAMBER IN DETERMINING AN APPROPRIATE SENTENCE.

(B)   THE SENTENCE SHALL BE PRONOUNCED IN A JUDGEMENT IN PUBLIC AND IN THE PRESENCE OF THE CONVICTED PERSON, SUBJECT TO SUB-RULE 102 (B).

RULE 101

PENALTIES

(A)   A CONVICTED PERSON MAY BE SENTENCED TO IMPRISONMENT FOR A TERM UP TO AND INCLUDING THE REMAINDER OF THE CONVICTED PERSON'S LIFE.

(B)   IN DETERMINING THE SENTENCE, THE TRIAL CHAMBER SHALL TAKE INTO ACCOUNT THE FACTORS MENTIONED IN ARTICLE 24, PARAGRAPH 2, OF THE STATUTE, AS WELL AS SUCH FACTORS AS:

    (I)   ANY AGGRAVATING CIRCUMSTANCES;

    (II)   ANY MITIGATING CIRCUMSTANCES INCLUDING THE SUBSTANTIAL COOPERATION WITH THE PROSECUTOR BY THE CONVICTED PERSON BEFORE OR AFTER CONVICTION;

    (III)   THE GENERAL PRACTICE REGARDING PRISON SENTENCES IN THE COURTS OF THE FORMER YUGOSLAVIA;

    (IV)   THE EXTENT TO WHICH ANY PENALTY IMPOSED BY A COURT OF ANY STATE ON THE CONVICTED PERSON FOR THE SAME ACT HAS ALREADY BEEN SERVED, AS REFERRED TO IN ARTICLE 10, PARAGRAPH 3, OF THE STATUTE.

(C)   THE TRIAL CHAMBER SHALL INDICATE WHETHER MULTIPLE SENTENCES SHALL BE SERVED CONSECUTIVELY OR CONCURRENTLY.

(D)   CREDIT SHALL BE GIVEN TO THE CONVICTED PERSON FOR THE PERIOD, IF ANY, DURING WHICH THE CONVICTED PERSON WAS DETAINED IN CUSTODY PENDING SURRENDER TO THE TRIBUNAL OR PENDING TRIAL OR APPEAL.

II.   TRIBUNAL CASES

B.   APPEALS CHAMBERS

PROSECUTOR V. FURUNDŽIJA, *Judgement,* IT-95-17/1-A, 21 July 2000, Shahabuddeen, Vohrah, Nieto-Navia, Robinson & Pocar, JJ.

On Appeal, Furundžija argued that his sentence of ten years for torture and eight years for aiding and abetting an outrage on personal dignity were so excessive as to constitute cruel and unusual punishment. He advanced several arguments in support of this position. First, he contended that since crimes against humanity are more serious than war crimes, his penalty was excessive, not having been convicted of a crime against humanity.

Crimes Against Humanity Not More Serious Than War Crimes

The Chamber referred to its recent decision in *Aleksovski*[874] regarding occasions when the Appeals Tribunal might refuse to follow previous decisions. Deciding that this was not

---

[874] Prosecutor v. Aleksovski, *Judgement*, IT-95-14/1-A, 24 March 2000.

one of those occasions, the Chamber noted its agreement with the *Tadić* Sentencing Appeals Judgement[875] on the issue of the relative seriousness between war crimes and crimes against humanity.[876]

Furundžija next contended that since the Tribunal had established in prior cases that crimes resulting in loss of life are more serious than others, and since his case did not involve a loss of life, his sentence is unnecessarily harsh.

The Chamber agreed with other decisions that a sentence must reflect the gravity of the accused's criminal conduct. Sentencing is a task which is particularly within the discretion of the Trial Chamber. The Chamber said:

> The sentencing provisions in the Statute and the Rules provide Trial Chambers with the discretion to take into account the circumstances of each crime in assessing the sentence to be given. A previous decision on sentence may indeed provide guidance if it relates to the same offence and was committed in substantially similar circumstances; otherwise, a Trial Chamber is limited only by the provisions of the Statute and the Rules. It may impose a sentence of imprisonment for a term up to and including the remainder of the convicted person's life. As a result, an individual convicted of a war crime could be sentenced to imprisonment for a term up to and including the remainder of his life, depending on the circumstances.[877]

Furundžija contended that there was an emerging penal regime within the Tribunal and that his sentence, compared with that emerging regime was clearly excessive. With regard to this the Chamber wrote:

> The Appeals Chamber notes that the practice of the Tribunal with regard to sentencing is still in its early stages. Several sentences have been handed down by different Trial Chambers but these are now subject to appeal. Only three final sentencing judgements have been delivered: one by a Trial Chamber established for sentencing purposes following a successful appeal by the accused in *Erdemović*, and the others by the Appeals Chamber in *Tadić* and *Aleksovsk*i, each of which has resulted in a revision of the sentence imposed by the original Trial Chamber. It is thus premature to speak of an emerging "penal regime", and the coherence in sentencing practice that this denotes. It is true that certain issues relating to sentencing have now been dealt with in some depth; however, still others have not yet been addressed. The Chamber finds that, at this stage, it is not possible to identify an established "penal regime." Instead, due regard must be given to the relevant provisions in the Statute and the Rules which

---

[875] Prosecutor v. Tadić, *Judgement in Sentencing Appeals*, IT-94-1-A and IT-94-1-A *bis*, 26 January 2000.

[876] Para. 243. The controversy over this issue continues, however. Judge Vohrah attached a Declaration to the Judgement in which he continues to argue that crimes against humanity must be characterised as more serious than war crimes. He suggests that the reasoning that got the Chamber to this position must logically require it to take the same position with regard to genocide. Judge Vohrah wonders why a prosecutor would bother attempting to prove the additional elements required for crimes against humanity or genocide if at sentencing the convictions will be treated as war crimes in any event.

[877] Para. 250.

govern sentencing, as well as the relevant jurisprudence of this Tribunal and the ICTR, and of course to the circumstances of each case.[878]

Finally, the Chamber dealt with Furundžija's claim that there was the possibility of innocence hanging over his case and that this was not taken into account in the Trial Chamber's sentence. The Appeals Chamber said:

> [G]uilt or innocence is a question to be determined prior to sentencing. In the event that an accused is convicted, or an Appellant's conviction is affirmed, his guilt has been proved beyond a reasonable doubt. Thus a possibility of innocence can never be a factor in sentencing.[879]

— PROSECUTOR V. ALEKSOVSKI, *Judgement*, IT-95-14/1-A, 24 March 2000, May, Mumba, Hunt, Tieya & Robinson, JJ.

Gravity of the Conduct of the Accused

The Appeals Chamber held that the gravity of the conduct of the accused is the starting point for consideration of an appropriate sentence in the practice of the Tribunal. Citing Article 24(2) of the Statute, the Chamber endorsed the following statements from the *Čelebići* Judgement and the *Kupreškić* Judgement in relation to the gravity of the offence and sentencing. In the *Čelebići* Judgement, the Trial Chamber stated:

> the most important consideration, which may be regarded as the litmus test for the appropriate sentence, is the gravity of the offence.

The Trial Chamber in the *Kupreškić* Judgement held:

> the sentences to be imposed must reflect the inherent gravity of the criminal conduct of the accused. The determination of the gravity of the crime requires a consideration of the particular circumstances of the case, as well as the form and degree of the participation of the accused in the crime.

In the instant case, the Chamber found that the Trial Chamber erred in not having sufficient regard to the gravity of the conduct of the accused. The Chamber pointed to the following factors. The offences were not trivial. As warden of a prison, the accused took part in violence against the inmates. His superior responsibility as a warden seriously aggravated the offences. Instead of preventing it, he involved himself in violence against those whom he should have been protecting, and allowed them to be subjected to psychological terror. He also failed to punish those responsible. Most seriously, by participating in the selection of detainees to be used as human shields and for trench digging, he was putting at risk the lives of those entrusted to his custody. The Chamber summarized the case against Aleksovski as one of a prison warden who personally participated in physical violence against detainees when, by virtue of his rank, he should have taken steps to prevent or punish it. He did more than merely tolerate the crimes as a

---

[878] Para. 237.
[879] Para. 253.

commander. His direct participation provided additional encouragement to his subordinates to commit similar acts. The Chamber concluded by stating the combination of these factors should have resulted in a longer sentence and should certainly not have provided grounds for mitigation.[880]

Deterrence

The Chamber accepted the general importance of deterrence as a consideration in sentencing for international crimes and it concurred with the statement of the Appeals Chamber in the *Tadić* Sentencing Judgement where it is stated that "this factor must not be accorded undue prominence in the overall assessment of the sentences to be imposed on persons convicted by the International Tribunal".[881]

Retribution

The Chamber briefly discussed retribution as an important factor in determining sentence, which is not to be understood as fulfilling a desire for revenge but as duly expressing the outrage of the international community at these crimes. The Chamber observed that a sentence should make plain the condemnation of the international community of the behaviour in question and show that the international community was not ready to tolerate serious violations of international humanitarian law and human rights.[882]

The "Discernable Error" Test

The Chamber held that it should not intervene in the exercise of the Trial Chamber's discretion with regard to sentence unless there is a discernable error.[883] The Chamber defined the discernable error test by stating that a sentence is unduly lenient where it falls outside the range of sentences that the judge, applying his mind to all the relevant factors, could reasonably consider appropriate. It must be demonstrated that the sentencing judge fell into material error of fact or law. Such error may appear in the reasons given by the sentencing judge or the sentence itself may be manifestly excessive or inadequate, thus disclosing error.[884]

In applying the discernable error test to the *Aleksovski* case, the Chamber found that there was a discernible error in the Trial Chamber's exercise of discretion in imposing sentence. That error consisted of giving insufficient weight to the gravity of the conduct of the accused and failing to treat his position as commander as an aggravating feature in relation to his responsibility under Article 7(1) of the Statute. The Chamber concluded that the sentence imposed by the Trial Chamber was manifestly inadequate.[885]

The Chamber imposed a sentence of seven years' imprisonment in lieu of the two and a half years imposed by the Trial Chamber.[886]

---

[880] Para. 183.
[881] Para. 185. See, Prosecutor v. Tadić, *Judgement in Sentencing Appeals*, IT-94-1-A and IT-94-1-A*bis*, 26 January 2000.
[882] Para. 185.
[883] Para. 187.
[884] Para. 186.
[885] Para. 187.
[886] Para. 191.

Double Jeopardy

The Chamber held that when imposing a revised sentence, the element of double jeopardy or double expose to sentencing must be borne in mind. In the case of Aleksovski, he had to appear for sentence twice for the same conduct, suffering the consequent anxiety and distress. He was detained a second time after a period of release of nine months. The Chamber added that had it not been for these factors the sentence would have been considerably longer.[887]

PROSECUTOR V. TADIĆ, *Judgement in Sentencing Appeals,* IT-94-1-A and IT-94-1-A *bis,* 26 January 2000, Shahabuddeen, Mumba, Cassese, Tieya & Nieto-Navia, JJ.

Tadić appealed against the 20 year sentence imposed on him at trial on the basis that is was unfair.

The Appeals Chamber rejected this ground of appeal, stating that it could find no error in the exercise of the Trial Chamber's discretion in regards to sentencing. The Chamber found that the sentence was within the discretionary framework of the Statute.[888]

Sentencing Practice in Former Yugoslavia

The Chamber found no merit in the Appellant's contention that the Trial Chamber failed to sufficiently consider the sentencing practice and in particular the maximum sentences in the former Yugoslavia. The Chamber reiterated that in imposing sentence, a Chamber is not bound by any national system, including the law and practice of the former Yugoslavia. The Chamber found that the reliance by the Appellant on the law of the former Yugoslavia, which prescribed a maximum sentence of 20 years as an alternative to the death penalty, is misplaced. As part of the discretionary power of a Chamber, Rule 101(A) provides that a person may be imprisoned for the remainder of his life.[889]

Recommended Sentence

The Trial Chamber imposed concurrent sentences of imprisonment *inter se* on Tadić ranging from 6 to 20 years. In addition, the Chamber recommended that, unless exceptional circumstances applied, Tadić's sentence should not be commuted or otherwise reduced to a term of imprisonment less than ten years from the date of the Sentencing Judgment or of the final determination of any appeal, whichever is the later.[890]

The Appeals Chamber observed that the Statute and Rules do not provide guidance for judicial discretion with respect to the recommendation of a minimum sentence. The Chamber ruled that the authority for recommending a minimum sentence

---

[887] Para. 190.
[888] Paras. 20 and 21.
[889] Para. 21.
[890] Para. 6. See, Prosecutor v. Tadić, *Sentencing Judgment,* IT-94-1-T, 14 July 1997, para. 76.

flows from the powers inherent in the judicial functions of a Trial Chamber and does not amount to a departure from the Statute or the Rules. This discretion is, however, limited in regards to attaching conditions to sentences. A Trial Chamber may not impose conditions on a sentence which are contrary to fundamental fairness.[891]

In the instant case, the Chamber found that the Trial Chamber erred in recommending that the miminum term of sentence take as its starting point the final determination of appeal. The Chamber held that such a condition could suggest to a prospective appellant that the exercise of the right to appeal could result in enhanced penalties. The consequential discouragement of appeals may preclude substantial questions of law being raised on appeal.[892]

The Chamber ruled that the Trial Chamber did not err in the exercise of its discretion in recommending a minimum term of 10 years, which would run from the date of the Sentencing Judgment, handed down by the Trial Chamber.

Credit for Time Served

Tadić was arrested on 12 February 1994 in the Federal Republic of Germany, where he was living, on suspicion of having committed the offences of torture and abetting the commission of genocide in the former Yugoslavia in June 1992, which are crimes under German law. He was held in custody in Germany, until he was transferred to The Hague on 24 April 1995, where he remained in custody during all trial and appeal proceedings.

The Chamber ruled that under Rule 101(D), an individual is entitled to credit for the time spent in custody in a third country only for the period pending his surrender to the Tribunal. However, the Chamber recognised that the criminal proceedings against Tadić in the Federal Republic of Germany emanated from substantially the same criminal conduct as that for which he was convicted at the Tribunal. Thus, the Chamber found that fairness requires that account be taken of the period that Tadić spent in custody in the Federal Republic of Germany prior to the issuance of the Tribunal's formal request for deferral.

Deterrence

The Chamber rejected the contention that the Trial Chamber erred by placing excessive weight on the factor of deterrence in assessing the sentence to be imposed on Tadić.

The Chamber accepted that deterrence might legitimately be considered in sentencing, but that this factor must not be accorded undue prominence in the overall assessment of the sentences to be imposed on persons convicted by the Tribunal. In the circumstances of the present case, the Chamber was not satisfied that the Trial Chamber gave undue weight to deterrence as a factor in the determination of the appropriate sentence to be imposed on Tadić.[893]

---

[891] Paras. 28 and 32.
[892] Paras. 31 and 32.
[893] Para. 48.

Sentencing Tariff Based on the Relative Position of an Accused

The Chamber ruled that the Trial Chamber failed to adequately consider the need for sentences to reflect the relative significance of the role of Tadić in the broader context of the conflict in the former Yugoslavia. The Chamber recognized that the criminal conduct underlying the charges for which Tadić was convicted were incontestably heinous, his level in the command structure, when compared to that of his superiors, *i.e.* commanders, or the very architects of the strategy of ethnic cleansing, was low.[894]

The Chamber considered that a sentence of more than 20 years' imprisonment for any count of the Indictment on which Tadić stood convicted is excessive and could not stand.

Whether Crimes Against Humanity Should Attract a Higher Sentence than War Crimes

A majority of the Chamber (Shahabuddeen[895], Mumba, Tieya and Nieto-Navia, JJ.) found that there is no basis for a distinction between the seriousness of a crime against humanity and that of a war crime in the Statute or the Rules of the International Tribunal construed in accordance with customary international law. The authorized penalties are also the same, the level in any particular case being fixed by reference to the circumstances of the case. The Chamber found support for this by turning to Article 8(1) of the Rome Statute that takes a similar position.[896]

Judge Cassese rendered a separate opinion in which he dissented from the majority. He wrote that whenever an offence is deemed to be a "crime against humanity" it must be regarded as inherently of greater gravity, all else being equal (*ceteris paribus*), than if it is instead characterised as a "war crime." He added that it must entail a heavier penalty, with the possible impact of extenuating or aggravating circumstances that may in practice have a significant bearing upon the eventual sentence.[897]

B.   TRIAL CHAMBERS

PROSECUTOR V. BLAŠKIĆ, *Judgement,* IT-95-14-T, 3 March 2000, Jorda, Rodrigues & Shahabuddeen, JJ.

Sentencing Practice in Former Yugoslavia

Rule 101(B)(iii) provides that sentencing practices in the former Yugoslavia should be considered in arriving at an appropriate sentence. The Chamber held that reference to Yugoslavian sentencing practices is only "indicative and not binding."[898]

---

[894] Paras. 55-56.
[895] Presiding Judge Shahabuddeen issued a Separate Opinion.
[896] Para. 69.
[897] Separate Opinion of Judge Cassese, para. 16.
[898] Para. 759.

Function of Sentencing

The Chamber adopted the declaration from *Erdemović* in regard to the function of sentencing:

> . . . the International Tribunal sees public reprobation and stigmatization by the international community, which would thereby express its indignation over heinous crimes and denounce the perpetrators, as one of the essential functions of a prison sentence for a crime against humanity.[899]

The Chamber declared that this reasoning is not only applicable to crimes against humanity but to war crimes and other serious violations of international humanitarian law.[900]

Mitigating Circumstances

The Statute and Rules set forth two mitigating circumstances: superior orders under Article 7(4) and substantial cooperation with the Prosecutor under Rule 101(B)(ii). However, the Tribunal has full discretion to consider other mitigating circumstances. In this case the Chamber, considered the following mitigating circumstances:

- The fact that the accused did not directly participate . . . when the accused holds a junior position within the civilian or military command structure.[901]

- Duress, where established, does mitigate the criminal responsibility of the accused when he had no choice or moral freedom in committing the crime.[902]

- Independently of duress, the context in which the crimes were committed, namely the conflict, is usually taken into consideration in determining the sentence to be imposed.[903]

- Article 24(2) of the Statute allows the personal status of the accused to be taken into account in determining the sentence . . . the sanction must fit the crime's perpetrator and not merely the crime itself.[904]

- The mental state of the accused, although not invoked in this case.[905]

---

[899] Para. 763, Quoting Prosecutor v. Erdemović, *Sentencing Judgement,* IT-96-22-T, 29 November 1996, para. 65.
[900] Para. 764.
[901] Para. 768.
[902] Para. 769.
[903] Para. 770.
[904] Para. 771.
[905] Para. 772.

- The accused's conduct after committing the crimes . . . Such conduct includes co-operation with the Prosecutor, remorse, voluntary surrender and pleading guilty.[906]

- The youth of the accused.[907]

- Personal history of the accused.[908]

With regard to this last factor, the personal history of the accused, the Chamber determined that in a case as serious as the *Blaškić* case, the weight of such a consideration "is limited or even non-existent when determining the sentence."[909]

Aggravating Circumstances

The Chamber ruled that the following were the appropriate aggravating circumstances to be considered in assessing the sentence under Rule 101(B)(i):

- How the crime was committed. The fact that a crime was egregious is a qualitative criterion that can be gleaned from its particularly cruel or humiliating nature.

- The number of victims reflects the scale of the crimes committed.

- The motive of the crime when it is particularly flagrant.

- The status of the victims, civilians and/or women.

- The physical and mental effects of the bodily harm meted out to the victims.

- The command position of the accused.

- The form of participation. Direct participation is an aggravating circumstance . . . command position is more of an aggravating circumstance . . . the fact that a commander does not participate directly may not justify a reduction in sentence.

- The premeditation of an accused.[910]

Single Sentence

The Chamber imposed one single sentence of 45 years upon General Blaškić. The Chamber reasoned that this Rule does not preclude a single sentence, although that has not been the general practice at the ICTY. Trial Chamber I of the ICTR has imposed single sentences.[911]

---

[906] Para. 773.
[907] Para. 778
[908] Para. 779.
[909] Para. 782.
[910] Paras. 783-793.
[911] Para. 805.

PROSECUTOR V. KUPREŠKIĆ *et. al.*, *Judgement*, IT-95-16-T, 14 January 2000, Cassese, May & Mumba, JJ.

Gravity of the Offence

The Chamber found that the sentence to be imposed must reflect the inherent gravity of the criminal conduct of the accused. The determination of the gravity of the crime requires a consideration of the particular circumstances of the case, including the form and degree of the participation of the accused in the crime.[912]

Sentencing Practice in Former Yugoslavia

The Chamber noted that it is not bound to follow the sentencing practice of the courts of the former Yugoslavia and that its sentencing practice is an aid in determining the sentences to be imposed by the Chamber.[913]

General Sentencing Policy of the International Tribunal

The Chamber was of the view that, in general, retribution and deterrence are the main purposes to be considered when imposing sentences in cases before the Tribunal. The Chamber observed that retribution, despite the primitive ring that is sometimes associated with it, is a relevant and important consideration in imposing punishment for serious violations of international humanitarian law. Deterrence is directed to specific accused as well as other persons worldwide, including the citizens of Bosnia and Herzegovina, to discourage the commission of crimes in similar circumstances. The Chamber was further of the view that another relevant sentencing purpose is to show the world in general, that there is no impunity for these types of crimes. The Chamber considered this factor important in strengthening the resolve of those involved in preventing crimes against international humanitarian law from being committed and to create trust in and respect for the developing system of international criminal justice.[914]

The Sentence to be Imposed for a Multiple Conviction

The Chamber observed that where an accused has been convicted on more than one count, based on the commission of one or several deeds, the practice of the Tribunal has been to impose sentences on each count to be served concurrently.[915]

The Chamber found that in practice, there is no real difference in effect between the imposition of concurrent sentences for multiple sentences and one composite sentence for multiple offences. The Chamber reasoned that in the unlikely event of there being uncertainty about the length of the concurrent or consecutive sentences to be served, the State of imprisonment could approach the Tribunal for clarification. Similarly, if a convicted person is eligible for pardon or commutation of sentences according to the law of the State of imprisonment, the State must inform the President of the Tribunal, who

---

[912] Para. 852.
[913] Para. 840.
[914] Para. 848.
[915] Para. 866.

will determine whether pardon or commutation is appropriate. Further, in the event of a successful appeal on any count, the Chamber was of the view that there would be no problems with the sentences.[916]

PROSECUTOR V. JELISIĆ, *Judgement*, IT-95-10-T, 14 December 1999, Jorda, Riad & Rodrigues, JJ.

The Chamber considered that the provisions of Rule 101 do not preclude the handing down of a single sentence for several crimes. The accused pleaded guilty to the following: sixteen violations of the laws or customs of war, including twelve for murder, three for cruel treatment and one for plunder plus fifteen violations of crimes against humanity, including twelve counts of murder and three counts of inhumane acts.

The Chamber broke with the practice of other Trial Chambers in imposing multiple penalties and imposed a single sentence of forty years.[917]

PROSECUTOR V. FURUNDŽIJA, *Judgement*, IT-95-17/1-T, 10 December 1998, Mumba, Cassese & May, JJ.

The Chamber relied on Articles 23 and 24 and duly considered Rules 100 and 101.[918]

Aggravating Circumstances

The Chamber found that the accused's role in the tortures was that of fellow perpetrator. His function was to interrogate Witness A in the large room and later in the pantry where he also interrogated Witness D, while Accused B was torturing both. The Chamber ruled that, in such situations, the fellow perpetrator plays a role every bit as grave as the person who actually inflicts the pain and suffering. Torture is one of the most serious offences known to international criminal law and any sentence imposed must take this into account.[919]

The Chamber found the accused did not himself perpetrate acts of rape, but he aided and abetted in the rapes and serious sexual assaults inflicted on Witness A. The circumstances of these attacks were particularly horrifying. A woman was brought into detention, kept naked and helpless before her interrogators and treated with the utmost cruelty and barbarity. The accused, far from preventing these crimes, played a prominent part in their commission.[920]

The Chamber held that this case presents particularly vicious instances of torture and rape. The accused's active role as a commander was considered to be an aggravating factor. Furthermore, the fact that Witness A was a civilian detainee and at the complete mercy of her captors was considered to be a further aggravating circumstance.[921]

---

[916] Para. 867.
[917] Paras. 136-139.
[918] Paras. 277-278.
[919] Para. 281.
[920] Para. 282.
[921] Para. 283.

Mitigating Circumstance

The Chamber considered that the fact that the accused was 23 years of age at the relevant time, that he had no previous convictions and is the father of a young child is true of many accused persons and cannot be given any significant weight in a case of this gravity.[922]

Sentencing Practice in Former Yugoslavia

The Chamber set out the various factors relevant to sentencing which were contained in Article 41(1) of the SFRY Penal Code:

> The court shall weigh the punishment to be imposed on the perpetrator of a criminal offence within the legal limits of the punishment for that offence, keeping in mind the purpose of punishment and taking into consideration all the circumstances which influence the severity of the punishment, and particularly: the degree of criminal responsibility; motives for the commission of the offence; the intensity of threat or injury to the protected object; circumstances of the commission of the offence; the perpetrator's past life; the perpetrator's personal circumstances and his behaviour after the commission of the offence; as well as other circumstances relating to the perpetrator.

The Chamber also cited Article 142 of Chapter XVI of the 1990 SFRY Penal Code entitled "Criminal Offences Against Humanity and International Law":

> Whoever, in violation of international law in time of war, armed conflict or occupation, orders an attack against the civilian population . . . or killings, tortures, or inhuman treatment of the civilian population . . . compulsion to prostitution or rape . . . shall be punished by no less than five years in prison or by death penalty.

The Chamber found that Article 142 allows for the imposition of severe penalties for war crimes, namely "at least five years in prison" or the death penalty. Pursuant to Article 24 the maximum penalty the Tribunal may impose is that of life imprisonment and never the death penalty.[923]

Sentencing Policy

The Chamber considered the specific circumstances and events surrounding the perpetration of the offence as well as the physical pain and suffering and emotional trauma of the victim.[924]

The Chamber held that two important functions of punishment are retribution and deterrence: the individual must be punished because he broke the law and he must be punished so that he and others will no longer break the law.[925]

---

[922] Para. 284.
[923] Para. 286.
[924] Para. 287.
[925] Para. 288.

The Chamber considered that punishment by an international tribunal must serve as a tool of retribution, stigmatisation and deterrence, whose penalties are made more onerous by its international nature, moral authority and impact upon world public opinion.[926]

The Chamber considered that the accused should benefit from rehabilitative programmes in which he may participate while serving his sentence.[927]

Sentencing imposed for Multiple Convictions

Furundžija was found guilty of the two counts with which he was charged. Under one count, he was found guilty of the torture of Witness A by means of serious sexual assault and beatings. The Trial Chamber found that the accused was a fellow perpetrator in a particularly vicious form of torture and imposed a sentence of 10 years. Under the other count, he was found guilty as an aider and abettor to the very serious offence of outrages on personal dignity, including sexual assault and rape and the Chamber imposed a sentence of 8 years.

Pursuant to Rule 101(C), the Chamber ruled that Furundžija would serve his sentence imposed for outrages upon personal dignity including rape concurrently with the sentence imposed for torture.[928]

The Chamber followed the practice of the Tribunal in *Tadić* and *Čelebići* in imposing concurrent sentences.[929]

PROSECUTOR V. DELALIĆ et. al., Judgement, IT-96-21-T, 16 November 1998, Karibi-Whyte, Odio-Benito & Jan, JJ.

The Chamber stated that the most important consideration, which may be regarded as the litmus test for determining the appropriate sentence, is the gravity of the offence.[930]

Sentencing Practice in Former Yugoslavia

Pursuant to Article 24(1), a Trial Chamber may have recourse to the general practice regarding prison sentences in the courts of the former Yugoslavia. The Chamber interpreted the words "have recourse to" to mean that the sentencing practice in the former Yugoslavia could be used as an aid to elucidate the principles to be followed.[931] The Chamber held that there is no jurisprudential or juridical basis for the assertion that the International Tribunal is bound by decisions of the courts of the former Yugoslavia. Article 24(1) of the Statute does not so require. Article 9(2), which vests primacy in the Tribunal over national courts indeed implies the contrary.[932]

---

[926] Paras. 289-290.
[927] Para. 291.
[928] Paras. 292-295.
[929] Para. 296.
[930] Para. 1225.
[931] Para. 1194.
[932] Para. 1212.

Retribution

The Chamber observed that the theory of retribution, which is an inheritance of the primitive theory of revenge, urges retaliation to appease the victim. The policy of the Security Council of the United Nations is directed towards reconciliation of the parties. This is the basis of the Dayton Peace Agreement by which all the parties to the conflict in Bosnia and Herzegovina have agreed to live together. The Chamber stated that a consideration of retribution as the only factor in sentencing is likely to be counter-productive and disruptive of the entire purpose of the Security Council, which is the restoration and maintenance of peace in the territory of the former Yugoslavia. Retributive punishment by itself does not bring justice.[933]

Protection of Society

The Chamber found that the protection of society from the guilty accused is an important factor in the determination of appropriate sentence. The policy of protection depends upon the nature of the offence and the conduct of the accused. The protection of society often involves long sentences of imprisonment to protect society from the hostile, predatory conduct of the guilty accused. The Chamber observed that this factor is relevant and important where the guilty accused is regarded as dangerous to society.[934]

Rehabilitation

The factor of rehabilitation considers the circumstances of reintegrating the guilty accused into society. This is usually the case when younger, or less educated, members of society are found guilty of offences. It therefore becomes necessary to reintegrate them into society so that they can become useful members of it and enable them to lead normal and productive lives upon their release from imprisonment. The age of the accused, his circumstances, his ability to be rehabilitated and availability of facilities in the confinement facility can, and should, be relevant considerations in this regard.[935]

Deterrence

The Chamber observed that deterrence is probably the most important factor in the assessment of appropriate sentences for violations of international humanitarian law. Apart from the fact that the accused should be sufficiently deterred by appropriate sentence from ever contemplating taking part in such crimes again, persons in similar situations in the future should similarly be deterred from resorting to such crimes. Deterrence of high-level officials, both military and civilian, in the context of the former Yugoslavia, by appropriate sentences of imprisonment, is a useful measure to return the area to peace. Although long prison sentences are not the ideal, there may be situations that will necessitate sentencing an accused to long terms of imprisonment to ensure continued stability in the area. Punishment of high-ranking political officials and military

---

[933] Para. 1231.
[934] Para. 1232. For instance, in this case, there was expert evidence that Defendant Landžo was a Sociopath. Sociopaths are seen as persons lacking a social conscience. The condition is virtually untreatable.
[935] Para. 1233.

officers will demonstrate that such officers cannot flout the designs and injunctions of the international community with impunity.[936]

Motives for the Commission of Offences

The Chamber stated that motive is not generally an essential ingredient of liability for the commission of an offence. It is to some extent a necessary factor in the determination of sentence after guilt has been established. For violations of international humanitarian law it is essential to consider the motives of the accused. The motive for committing an act that results in the offence charged may constitute aggravation or mitigation of the appropriate sentence. For instance, where the accused is found to have committed the offence charged with cold, calculated premeditation, suggestive of revenge against the individual victim or group to which the victim belongs, such circumstances necessitate the imposition of aggravated punishment. On the other hand, if the accused is found to have committed the offence charged reluctantly and under the influence of group pressure and, in addition, demonstrated compassion toward the victim or the group to which the victim belongs, these are certainly mitigating factors which the Chamber will take into consideration in the determination of the appropriate sentence.[937]

Concurrence of Sentences

During the pre-trial stage of these proceedings, the Chamber ruled that an accused person could be charged cumulatively.[938] The Chamber agreed with a previous decision issued in the case of the *Prosecutor v. Tadić*, and thus declined to evaluate this argument on the basis that the matter is only relevant to penalty considerations if the accused is ultimately found guilty of the charges in question. It is in this context that the Chamber ruled that each of the sentences is to be served concurrently and that the sentence imposed shall not be consecutive.[939]

---

[936] Para. 1234.
[937] Para. 1235.
[938] Prosecutor v. Delalić, *Decision on motion by the accused Zejnil Delalić based on defects in the form of the Indictment*, IT-96-21-PT, 4 October 1996.
[939] Para. 1286.

RULE 102

STATUS OF THE CONVICTED PERSON

(A)   THE SENTENCE SHALL BEGIN TO RUN FROM THE DAY IT IS PRONOUNCED. HOWEVER, AS SOON AS NOTICE OF APPEAL IS GIVEN, THE ENFORCEMENT OF THE JUDGEMENT SHALL THEREUPON BE STAYED UNTIL THE DECISION ON THE APPEAL HAS BEEN DELIVERED, THE CONVICTED PERSON MEANWHILE REMAINING IN DETENTION, AS PROVIDED IN RULE 64.

(B)   IF, BY A PREVIOUS DECISION OF THE TRIAL CHAMBER, THE CONVICTED PERSON HAS BEEN RELEASED, OR IS FOR ANY OTHER REASON AT LIBERTY, AND IS NOT PRESENT WHEN THE JUDGEMENT IS PRONOUNCED, THE TRIAL CHAMBER SHALL ISSUE A WARRANT FOR THE CONVICTED PERSON'S ARREST. ON ARREST, THE CONVICTED PERSON SHALL BE NOTIFIED OF THE CONVICTION AND SENTENCE, AND THE PROCEDURE PROVIDED IN RULE 103 SHALL BE FOLLOWED.

RULE 103

PLACE OF IMPRISONMENT

(A)   IMPRISONMENT SHALL BE SERVED IN A STATE DESIGNATED BY THE PRESIDENT OF THE TRIBUNAL FROM A LIST OF STATES WHICH HAVE INDICATED THEIR WILLINGNESS TO ACCEPT CONVICTED PERSONS.

(B)   TRANSFER OF THE CONVICTED PERSON TO THAT STATE SHALL BE EFFECTED AS SOON AS POSSIBLE AFTER THE TIME-LIMIT FOR APPEAL HAS ELAPSED.

(C)   PENDING THE FINALISATION OF ARRANGEMENTS FOR HIS OR HER TRANSFER TO THE STATE WHERE HIS OR HER SENTENCE WILL BE SERVED, THE CONVICTED PERSON SHALL REMAIN IN THE CUSTODY OF THE TRIBUNAL.

I.   COMMENTARY

See Article 27 for a list of States that have agreed to accept convicted persons.

RULE 104

SUPERVISION OF IMPRISONMENT

ALL SENTENCES OF IMPRISONMENT SHALL BE SUPERVISED BY THE TRIBUNAL OR A BODY DESIGNATED BY IT.

RULE 105

RESTITUTION OF PROPERTY

(A) AFTER A JUDGEMENT OF CONVICTION CONTAINING A SPECIFIC FINDING AS PROVIDED IN SUB-RULE 98 *TER* (B), THE TRIAL CHAMBER SHALL, AT THE REQUEST OF THE PROSECUTOR, OR MAY, *PROPRIO MOTU*, HOLD A SPECIAL HEARING TO DETERMINE THE MATTER OF THE RESTITUTION OF THE PROPERTY OR THE PROCEEDS THEREOF, AND MAY IN THE MEANTIME ORDER SUCH PROVISIONAL MEASURES FOR THE PRESERVATION AND PROTECTION OF THE PROPERTY OR PROCEEDS AS IT CONSIDERS APPROPRIATE.

(B) THE DETERMINATION MAY EXTEND TO SUCH PROPERTY OR ITS PROCEEDS, EVEN IN THE HANDS OF THIRD PARTIES NOT OTHERWISE CONNECTED WITH THE CRIME OF WHICH THE CONVICTED PERSON HAS BEEN FOUND GUILTY.

(C) SUCH THIRD PARTIES SHALL BE SUMMONED BEFORE THE TRIAL CHAMBER AND BE GIVEN AN OPPORTUNITY TO JUSTIFY THEIR CLAIM TO THE PROPERTY OR ITS PROCEEDS.

(D) SHOULD THE TRIAL CHAMBER BE ABLE TO DETERMINE THE RIGHTFUL OWNER ON THE BALANCE OF PROBABILITIES, IT SHALL ORDER THE RESTITUTION EITHER OF THE PROPERTY OR THE PROCEEDS OR MAKE SUCH OTHER ORDER AS IT MAY DEEM APPROPRIATE.

(E) SHOULD THE TRIAL CHAMBER NOT BE ABLE TO DETERMINE OWNERSHIP, IT SHALL NOTIFY THE COMPETENT NATIONAL AUTHORITIES AND REQUEST THEM SO TO DETERMINE.

(F) UPON NOTICE FROM THE NATIONAL AUTHORITIES THAT AN AFFIRMATIVE DETERMINATION HAS BEEN MADE, THE TRIAL CHAMBER SHALL ORDER THE RESTITUTION EITHER OF THE PROPERTY OR THE PROCEEDS OR MAKE SUCH OTHER ORDER AS IT MAY DEEM APPROPRIATE.

(G) THE REGISTRAR SHALL TRANSMIT TO THE COMPETENT NATIONAL AUTHORITIES ANY SUMMONSES, ORDERS AND REQUESTS ISSUED BY A TRIAL CHAMBER PURSUANT TO SUB-RULES (C), (D), (E) AND (F).

RULE 106

COMPENSATION TO VICTIMS

(A)   THE REGISTRAR SHALL TRANSMIT TO THE COMPETENT AUTHORITIES OF THE STATES CONCERNED THE JUDGEMENT FINDING THE ACCUSED GUILTY OF A CRIME WHICH HAS CAUSED INJURY TO A VICTIM.

(B)   PURSUANT TO THE RELEVANT NATIONAL LEGISLATION, A VICTIM OR PERSONS CLAIMING THROUGH THE VICTIM MAY BRING AN ACTION IN A NATIONAL COURT OR OTHER COMPETENT BODY TO OBTAIN COMPENSATION.

(C)   FOR THE PURPOSES OF A CLAIM MADE UNDER SUB-RULE (B) THE JUDGEMENT OF THE TRIBUNAL SHALL BE FINAL AND BINDING AS TO THE CRIMINAL RESPONSIBILITY OF THE CONVICTED PERSON FOR SUCH INJURY.

PART SEVEN
APPELLATE PROCEEDINGS

RULE 107

GENERAL PROVISION

THE RULES OF PROCEDURE AND EVIDENCE THAT GOVERN PROCEEDINGS IN THE TRIAL CHAMBERS SHALL APPLY *MUTATIS MUTANDIS* TO PROCEEDINGS IN THE APPEALS CHAMBER.

RULE 108

NOTICE OF APPEAL

A PARTY SEEKING TO APPEAL A JUDGEMENT SHALL, NOT MORE THAN FIFTEEN DAYS FROM THE DATE ON WHICH THE JUDGEMENT WAS PRONOUNCED, FILE NOTICE OF APPEAL.

RULE 108 *BIS*

STATE REQUEST FOR REVIEW

(A)   A STATE DIRECTLY AFFECTED BY AN INTERLOCUTORY DECISION OF A TRIAL CHAMBER MAY, WITHIN FIFTEEN DAYS FROM THE DATE OF THE DECISION, FILE A REQUEST FOR REVIEW OF THE DECISION BY THE APPEALS CHAMBER IF THAT DECISION CONCERNS ISSUES OF GENERAL IMPORTANCE RELATING TO THE POWERS OF THE TRIBUNAL.

(B)   THE PARTY UPON WHOSE MOTION THE TRIAL CHAMBER ISSUED THE IMPUGNED DECISION SHALL BE HEARD BY THE TRIAL CHAMBER. THE OTHER PARTY MAY BE HEARD IF THE APPEALS CHAMBER CONSIDERS THAT THE INTERESTS OF JUSTICE SO REQUIRE.

(C) THE APPEALS CHAMBER MAY AT ANY STAGE SUSPEND THE EXECUTION OF THE IMPUGNED DECISION.

(D) RULE 116 BIS SHALL APPLY *MUTATIS MUTANDIS.*

RULE 109

RECORD ON APPEAL

(A)   THE RECORD ON APPEAL SHALL CONSIST OF THE PARTS OF THE TRIAL RECORD, AS CERTIFIED BY THE REGISTRAR, DESIGNATED BY THE PARTIES.

(B)   THE PARTIES, WITHIN THIRTY DAYS OF THE CERTIFICATION OF THE TRIAL RECORD BY THE REGISTRAR, MAY BY AGREEMENT DESIGNATE THE PARTS OF THAT RECORD WHICH, IN THEIR OPINION, ARE NECESSARY FOR THE DECISION ON THE APPEAL.

(C)   SHOULD THE PARTIES FAIL SO TO AGREE WITHIN THAT TIME, THE APPELLANT AND THE RESPONDENT SHALL EACH DESIGNATE TO THE REGISTRAR, WITHIN SIXTY DAYS OF THE CERTIFICATION, THE PARTS OF THE TRIAL RECORD WHICH EACH CONSIDERS NECESSARY FOR THE DECISION ON THE APPEAL.

(D)   THE APPEALS CHAMBER SHALL REMAIN FREE TO CALL FOR THE WHOLE OF THE TRIAL RECORD.

II.   TRIBUNAL CASES

A.   APPEALS CHAMBER

PROSECUTOR V. DELALIĆ, *et. al., Decision on Motion to Preserve and Provide Evidence,* IT-96-21-A, 22 April 1999, Nieto-Navia, Wang Tieya, Rodrigues, Hunt & Bennouna, JJ.

Appellant Landžo, in his Notice of Appeal, raised a contention that he was deprived of a fair trial because the Presiding Judge slept through significant portions of the trial. He filed a Motion with the Appeals Chamber seeking production of the videotapes from a particular courtroom camera that is largely focused on the Judges.

The Appeals Chamber denied this motion. The Chamber held that the mere allegations of counsel as to the Judge's sleeping were insufficient to justify production of the videotapes. The Chamber ruled that it would need "first-hand and detailed evidence citing specific instances . . . in affidavit form." Landžo was, however, invited to file a fresh Motion with the requisite first-hand and detailed evidence attached. The Chamber stated that if the new motion "demonstrates that access to the video recording is likely to materially assist in the presentation of his case on appeal, and if the Appeals Chamber (after considering the submissions of the parties) considers that the evidence falls within that description, relief will be granted."

PROSECUTOR V. DELALIĆ, *et. al., Order on the Second Motion to Preserve and Provide Evidence,* IT-96-21-A, 15 June 1999, Hunt, Riad, Wang Tieya, Nieto-Navia & Bennouna, JJ.

Landžo accepted the invitation of the Appeals Chamber, referred to in the above-reported case and filed a fresh Motion supported with affidavits. The Chamber decided that the affidavits were sufficient. It was ordered that counsel or co-counsel and/or their legal assistants be permitted to view the videotapes requested between 16 June and 13 September 1999 on the premises of the Tribunal. Only Counsel or co-counsel could view proceedings held in closed session. The videotapes could not be removed from the room designated for viewing. No audio or video copies of the tapes could be provided to anyone. In addition, the Appellant was ordered to file a notice providing details of the dates, times and passages from the videotapes upon which he would rely on or before 13 September 1999. The Prosecutor was ordered to file a notice on 17 September 1999 setting forth the amount of time she would need after that date to view the videotapes.

RULE 110

COPIES OF RECORD

THE REGISTRAR SHALL MAKE A SUFFICIENT NUMBER OF COPIES OF THE RECORD ON APPEAL FOR THE USE OF THE JUDGES OF THE APPEALS CHAMBER AND OF THE PARTIES.

I.   COMMENTARY

In practice, this Rule is not enforced. The Registry will not supply the parties with a copy of the Record on Appeal. The Registry simply takes the position that it will provide an index of the filings and it is up to counsel to assemble the record. Counsel must take care to preserve documents with this in mind.

RULE 111

APPELLANT'S BRIEF

AN APPELLANT'S BRIEF OF ARGUMENT SETTING OUT THE GROUNDS OF APPEAL AND AUTHORITIES SHALL BE FILED WITHIN NINETY DAYS OF FILING OF THE NOTICE OF APPEAL PURSUANT TO RULE 108.

RULE 112

RESPONDENT'S BRIEF

A RESPONDENT'S BRIEF OF ARGUMENT AND AUTHORITIES SHALL BE FILED WITHIN THIRTY DAYS OF THE FILING OF THE APPELLANT'S BRIEF.

RULE 113

BRIEF IN REPLY

AN APPELLANT MAY FILE A BRIEF IN REPLY WITHIN FIFTEEN DAYS AFTER THE FILING OF THE RESPONDENT'S BRIEF.

RULE 114

DATE OF HEARING

AFTER THE EXPIRY OF THE TIME-LIMITS FOR FILING THE BRIEFS PROVIDED FOR IN RULES 111, 112 AND 113, THE APPEALS CHAMBER SHALL SET THE DATE FOR THE HEARING AND THE REGISTRAR SHALL NOTIFY THE PARTIES.

RULE 115

ADDITIONAL EVIDENCE

(A)   A PARTY MAY APPLY BY MOTION TO PRESENT BEFORE THE APPEALS CHAMBER ADDITIONAL EVIDENCE WHICH WAS NOT AVAILABLE TO IT AT THE TRIAL. SUCH MOTION MUST BE SERVED ON THE OTHER PARTY AND FILED WITH THE REGISTRAR NOT LESS THAN FIFTEEN DAYS BEFORE THE DATE OF THE HEARING.

(B)   THE APPEALS CHAMBER SHALL AUTHORISE THE PRESENTATION OF SUCH EVIDENCE IF IT CONSIDERS THAT THE INTERESTS OF JUSTICE SO REQUIRE.

II.   TRIBUNAL CASES

A.   APPEALS CHAMBER

PROSECUTOR V. TADIĆ, *Decision on Appellant's Motion for the Extension of the Time-Limits and Admission of Additional Evidence*, IT-94-1-A, 15 October 1998, Shahabuddeen, Cassese, Tieya, Nieto-Navia & Mumba, JJ.

The Requirement of Due Diligence

Additional evidence is not admissible under Rule 115 in the absence of a reasonable explanation as to why it was not available at trial. Such an explanation must include compliance with the requirement that the moving party exercised due diligence.[940]

The Chamber reasoned that by the time proceedings have reached the Appeals Chamber, evidence relevant to the culpability of the accused has already been submitted to a Trial Chamber to enable it to reach a verdict and a sentence, if he is found guilty. The corrective nature of the appeals procedure alone suggests that there is some limitation to any additional evidentiary material being presented to the Appeals Chamber. Otherwise, the unrestricted admission of such material would amount to a fresh trial.[941] In addition, the Chamber held that where an accused person knows of evidence, but he fails through lack of diligence to secure it for the Trial Chamber to consider, he is of his own volition declining to make use of his entitlements under the Statute and he certainly cannot complain of unfairness.[942]

Furthermore, the Chamber found that due diligence is both a matter of criminal procedure regarding admissibility of evidence, and a matter of professional conduct of lawyers. In the context of the Statute and the Rules, unless gross negligence is shown to exist in the conduct of either Prosecution or Defence counsel, due diligence will be presumed.[943] The Chamber added that no counsel can be criticised for lack of due diligence in exhausting all available courses of action, if that counsel makes a reasoned

---

[940] Para. 45.
[941] Para. 42
[942] Para. 44.
[943] Para. 48.

determination that the material in question is irrelevant to the matter in hand, even if that determination turns out to be incorrect. Counsel may have chosen not to present the evidence at trial because of his litigation strategy or because of the view taken by him of the probative value of the evidence. The determination which the Chamber has to make, except in cases where there is evidence of gross negligence, is whether the evidence was available at the time of trial. Subject to that exception, counsel's decision not to call evidence at trial does not serve to make it unavailable.[944]

The Requirement of Availability of the Evidence

The Chamber held that it is only to the extent that it can be shown that the additional evidence in question was not available at trial that it will be necessary to consider whether the admission of the evidence is required by the interests of justice. The Chamber ruled that such an interpretation of Rule 115 is supported by the principle of finality that must be balanced against the need to avoid a miscarriage of justice. When there could be a miscarriage, the principle of finality will not operate to prevent the admission of additional evidence that was not available at trial, if that evidence would assist in the determination of guilt or innocence.[945]

PROSECUTOR V. ERDEMOVIĆ, *Judgement,* IT-96-22-A, 7 October 1997, Cassese, McDonald, Li, Stephen & Vohrah, JJ.

During the Appeals stage of his case, Erdemović sought to introduce additional evidence. He sought the appointment of a distinguished professor of ethics for the purpose of giving an opinion "regarding the possibility of moral choice of an ordinary soldier who is faced with committing a crime when following the orders of a superior in time of war."[946] In addition, he requested that the panel of experts, who had previously examined him, conduct an additional examination to determine his mental condition at the time the offense was committed.

The Chamber rejected these requests and held that the evidence was not relevant to the determination of the appeal. If the Defendant believed the evidence to be relevant, it should have been brought to the attention of the Trial Chamber during the sentencing hearing. The Chamber stated: "the appeal process of the International Tribunal is not designed for the purpose of allowing the parties to remedy their own failings or oversights during trial or sentencing."[947] The Defendant had not filed an affidavit indicating the substance of either of the proposed evidentiary additions.[948]

---

[944] Para. 50.
[945] Para. 35.
[946] Para. 14.
[947] Para. 15.
[948] *Ibid.* Rule 115(A) was added after this decision but it does not affect the Chamber's findings.

RULE 116 *BIS*

EXPEDITED APPEALS PROCEDURE

(A)   AN APPEAL UNDER SUB-RULE 72 (B) OR SUB-RULE 73 (B) OR APPEAL FROM A DECISION RENDERED UNDER RULE 54 *BIS* (C), RULE 65, RULE 77 OR RULE 91 SHALL BE HEARD EXPEDITIOUSLY ON THE BASIS OF THE ORIGINAL RECORD OF THE TRIAL CHAMBER. APPEALS MAY BE DETERMINED ENTIRELY ON THE BASIS OF WRITTEN BRIEFS.

(B)   ALL DELAYS AND OTHER PROCEDURAL REQUIREMENTS SHALL BE FIXED BY AN ORDER OF THE PRESIDING JUDGE ISSUED ON AN APPLICATION BY ONE OF THE PARTIES, OR *PROPRIO MOTU* SHOULD NO SUCH APPLICATION HAVE BEEN MADE WITHIN FIFTEEN DAYS AFTER THE FILING OF THE NOTICE OF APPEAL.

(C)   RULES 109 TO 114 SHALL NOT APPLY TO SUCH APPEALS.

(D)   THE PRESIDING JUDGE, AFTER CONSULTING THE MEMBERS OF THE APPEALS CHAMBER, MAY DECIDE NOT TO APPLY SUB-RULE 117 (D).

RULE 117

JUDGEMENT ON APPEAL

(A)   THE APPEALS CHAMBER SHALL PRONOUNCE JUDGEMENT ON THE BASIS OF THE RECORD ON APPEAL TOGETHER WITH SUCH ADDITIONAL EVIDENCE AS HAS BEEN PRESENTED TO IT.

(B)   THE JUDGEMENT SHALL BE RENDERED BY A MAJORITY OF THE JUDGES. IT SHALL BE ACCOMPANIED OR FOLLOWED AS SOON AS POSSIBLE BY A REASONED OPINION IN WRITING, TO WHICH SEPARATE OR DISSENTING OPINIONS MAY BE APPENDED.

(C)   IN APPROPRIATE CIRCUMSTANCES THE APPEALS CHAMBER MAY ORDER THAT THE ACCUSED BE RETRIED ACCORDING TO LAW.

(D)   THE JUDGEMENT SHALL BE PRONOUNCED IN PUBLIC, ON A DATE OF WHICH NOTICE SHALL HAVE BEEN GIVEN TO THE PARTIES AND COUNSEL AND AT WHICH THEY SHALL BE ENTITLED TO BE PRESENT.

RULE 118

STATUS OF THE ACCUSED FOLLOWING APPEAL

(A)   A SENTENCE PRONOUNCED BY THE APPEALS CHAMBER SHALL BE ENFORCED IMMEDIATELY.

(B)   WHERE THE ACCUSED IS NOT PRESENT WHEN THE JUDGEMENT IS DUE TO BE DELIVERED, EITHER AS HAVING BEEN ACQUITTED ON ALL CHARGES OR AS A RESULT OF AN ORDER ISSUED PURSUANT TO RULE 65, OR FOR ANY OTHER REASON, THE APPEALS CHAMBER MAY DELIVER ITS JUDGEMENT IN THE ABSENCE OF THE ACCUSED AND SHALL, UNLESS IT PRONOUNCES AN ACQUITTAL, ORDER THE ARREST OR SURRENDER OF THE ACCUSED TO THE TRIBUNAL.

PART EIGHT

REVIEW PROCEEDINGS

RULE 119

REQUEST FOR REVIEW

WHERE A NEW FACT HAS BEEN DISCOVERED WHICH WAS NOT KNOWN TO THE MOVING PARTY AT THE TIME OF THE PROCEEDINGS BEFORE A TRIAL CHAMBER OR THE APPEALS CHAMBER, AND COULD NOT HAVE BEEN DISCOVERED THROUGH THE EXERCISE OF DUE DILIGENCE, THE DEFENCE OR, WITHIN ONE YEAR AFTER THE FINAL JUDGEMENT HAS BEEN PRONOUNCED, THE PROSECUTOR, MAY MAKE A MOTION TO THAT CHAMBER FOR REVIEW OF THE JUDGEMENT.

II.   TRIBUNAL CASES

A.   APPEALS CHAMBER

PROSECUTOR V. TADIĆ, *Decision on Appellant's Motion for the Extension of the Time-Limits and Admission of Additional Evidence*, IT-94-1-A, 15 October 1998, Shahabuddeen, Cassese, Tieya, Nieto-Navia & Mumba, JJ.

The Chamber ruled that where an applicant seeks to present a new fact that becomes known only after trial, despite the exercise of due diligence during the trial in discovering it, Rule 119 is the governing provision. In such a case, the Appellant is not seeking to admit additional evidence of a fact that was considered at trial, but rather a new fact. The proper venue for a review application is the Chamber that rendered the final judgement, whether it is a Trial Chamber or an Appeals Chamber.[949]

The Chamber observed that a distinction exists between a fact and evidence of that fact. The mere subsequent discovery of evidence of a fact which was known at trial is not itself a new fact within the meaning of Rule 119. In the instant case, the Chamber stated that the alleged new fact evidence submitted by the Appellant is not evidence of a new fact. Rather, it is additional evidence of facts put in issue at the trial. Some of that additional evidence was not available at the trial that brought the application under Rule 115 rather than Rule 119.[950]

---

[949] Para. 30.
[950] Para. 32.

RULE 120

PRELIMINARY EXAMINATION

IF A MAJORITY OF JUDGES OF THE CHAMBER THAT PRONOUNCED THE JUDGEMENT AGREE THAT THE NEW FACT, IF PROVED, COULD HAVE BEEN A DECISIVE FACTOR IN REACHING A DECISION, THE CHAMBER SHALL REVIEW THE JUDGEMENT, AND PRONOUNCE A FURTHER JUDGEMENT AFTER HEARING THE PARTIES.

RULE 121

APPEALS

THE JUDGEMENT OF A TRIAL CHAMBER ON REVIEW MAY BE APPEALED IN ACCORDANCE WITH THE PROVISIONS OF PART SEVEN.

RULE 122

RETURN OF CASE TO TRIAL CHAMBER

IF THE JUDGEMENT TO BE REVIEWED IS UNDER APPEAL AT THE TIME THE MOTION FOR REVIEW IS FILED, THE APPEALS CHAMBER MAY RETURN THE CASE TO THE TRIAL CHAMBER FOR DISPOSITION OF THE MOTION.

PART NINE

PARDON AND COMMUTATION OF SENTENCES

RULE 123

NOTIFICATION BY STATES

IF, ACCORDING TO THE LAW OF THE STATE OF IMPRISONMENT A CONVICTED PERSON IS ELIGIBLE FOR PARDON OR COMMUTATION OF SENTENCE, THE STATE SHALL, IN ACCORDANCE WITH ARTICLE 28 OF THE STATUTE, NOTIFY THE TRIBUNAL OF SUCH ELIGIBILITY.

RULE 124

DETERMINATION BY THE PRESIDENT

THE PRESIDENT SHALL, UPON SUCH NOTICE, DETERMINE, IN CONSULTATION WITH THE JUDGES, WHETHER PARDON OR COMMUTATION IS APPROPRIATE.

RULE 125

GENERAL STANDARDS FOR GRANTING PARDON OR COMMUTATION

IN DETERMINING WHETHER PARDON OR COMMUTATION IS APPROPRIATE, THE PRESIDENT SHALL TAKE INTO ACCOUNT, *INTER ALIA*, THE GRAVITY OF THE CRIME OR CRIMES FOR WHICH THE PRISONER WAS CONVICTED, THE TREATMENT OF SIMILARLY-SITUATED PRISONERS, THE PRISONER'S DEMONSTRATION OF REHABILITATION, AS WELL AS ANY SUBSTANTIAL COOPERATION OF THE PRISONER WITH THE PROSECUTOR.

PART TEN

TIME

RULE 126

GENERAL PROVISION

WHERE THE TIME PRESCRIBED BY OR UNDER THESE RULES FOR THE DOING OF ANY ACT IS TO RUN AS FROM THE OCCURRENCE OF AN EVENT, THAT TIME SHALL BEGIN TO RUN AS FROM THE DATE ON WHICH NOTICE OF THE OCCURRENCE OF THE EVENT WOULD HAVE BEEN RECEIVED IN THE NORMAL COURSE OF TRANSMISSION BY COUNSEL FOR THE ACCUSED OR THE PROSECUTOR AS THE CASE MAY BE.

RULE 127

VARIATION OF TIME-LIMITS

(A)   SAVE AS PROVIDED BY SUB-RULE (B), A TRIAL CHAMBER MAY, ON GOOD
CAUSE BEING SHOWN BY MOTION,

(I)   ENLARGE OR REDUCE ANY TIME PRESCRIBED BY OR UNDER THESE
RULES;

(II)   RECOGNIZE AS VALIDLY DONE ANY ACT DONE AFTER THE EXPIRATION
OF A TIME SO PRESCRIBED ON SUCH TERMS, IF ANY, AS IS THOUGHT
JUST AND WHETHER OR NOT THAT TIME HAS ALREADY EXPIRED.

(B)   IN RELATION TO ANY STEP FALLING TO BE TAKEN IN CONNECTION WITH AN
APPEAL OR APPLICATION FOR LEAVE TO APPEAL, THE APPEALS CHAMBER OR A BENCH
OF THREE JUDGES OF THAT CHAMBER MAY EXERCISE THE LIKE POWER AS IS
CONFERRED BY SUB-RULE (A) AND IN LIKE MANNER AND SUBJECT TO THE SAME
CONDITIONS AS ARE THEREIN SET OUT.

(C)   THIS RULE SHALL NOT APPLY TO THE TIMES PRESCRIBED IN RULES 40 *BIS* AND
90 *BIS*.

II.   TRIBUNAL CASES

A.   APPEALS CHAMBER

PROSECUTOR V. ALEKSOVSKI, *Decision on Prosecutor's Appeal on
Admissibility of Evidence,* IT-95-14/1-A, 16 February 1999, May, Tieya, Hunt,
Bennouna & Robinson, JJ.

The Appeals Chamber ruled that the period of seven days within which Rule 73(C)
provides for the filing of an application for leave to appeal runs from (but does not
include) the day upon which the written decision is filed, in whichever of the two
working languages of the Tribunal – English or French – the written decision is given.
The Chamber observed that if there is some difficulty for the party wishing to challenge
the decision in filing the application for leave to appeal within that period of seven days,
then that party should move under Rule 127(A) to have the Chamber either enlarge the
time prescribed by Rule 73 or recognise any act done after that time as having been
validly done.[951]
     In the instant case, the impugned decision was written in French and the
Appellant had treated the date when the English translation became available as that from
which the seven-day period under Rule 73 commenced. The Chamber ruled that when a
party receives a decision that is written in one of the two official languages of the

---

[951] Para. 13.

Tribunal and is a language with which he or she is unfamiliar, an application must be made under Rule 127 for a variation of time limits. This, however, is not the case for a document filed in a language other than an official language of the Tribunal pursuant to Rule 3(F).[952] In such circumstances, the time for calculating time limits under Rule 127 commences when the document is translated into one of the official languages and filed.

B.   TRIAL CHAMBERS

PROSECUTOR V. SIMIĆ, *et. al.*, *Decision Denying Request for Modification*, IT-95-9-PT, 15 February 1999, May, Bennouna & Robinson, JJ.

The Pre-Trial Judge refused to grant a request by the Defence seeking modification of an Order such that time-limits for the filing of responses would run from the date on which the last of the defence counsel – in a joint trial – received the originating document.

This issue arose because not all counsel were receiving filings at the same time or soon after the document was filed.

In denying this Request, the Pre-Trial Judge referred to Rule 126 and Rule 127 and ruled that the proper course to follow is to seek a variation under Rule 127 by "showing good cause".

---

[952] Para. 13.

GENERAL PART

This Part contains materials and decisions of the Tribunal that are either not tied to any particular Article or Rule or which are grouped together for the sake of convenience.

BINDING FORCE OF DECISIONS OF THE APPEALS CHAMBER

In the *Aleksovski* case,[953] the Appeals Chamber ruled that on a proper construction of the Statute, taking due account of its text and purpose, it should follow its previous decisions to ensure certainty and predictability, but it should be free to depart from them for cogent reasons in the interests of justice.[954] The Chamber observed that instances where the interests of justice require a departure from a previous decision include cases where the previous decision has been decided on the basis of a wrong legal principle or cases where a previous decision has been given *per incuriam*, that is a judicial decision that has been wrongly decided, usually because the judge or judges were ill-informed about the applicable law.[955]

The Chamber emphasized that the general rule is that previous decisions are to be followed and that departure from them is the exception. A previous decision will not be followed, only after the most careful consideration has been given to it, both as to the law, including the authorities cited and the facts.[956] The Chamber ruled that the principle of *ratio decidendi* – the legal principle – requires that previous decisions be followed. However, the Chamber added that the obligation to follow that principle only applies in similar cases or substantially similar cases. The Chamber elaborated on this point by stating that this means less that the facts are similar or substantially similar, than that the question raised by the facts in the subsequent case is the same as the question decided by the legal principle in the previous decision. There is no obligation to follow previous decisions that may be distinguished for one reason or another from the case before the court.[957] Finally, the Chamber found that when faced with previous decisions that are conflicting, it is obliged to determine which decision it will follow, or whether to depart from both decisions for cogent reasons in the interests of justice.[958]

Appeals Chamber decisions are, however, binding on Trial Chambers. The Chamber gave the following reasons in support:

---

[953] Prosecutor v. Aleksovski, *Judgement*, IT-95-14/1-A, 24 March 2000, May, Mumba, Hunt, Tieya & Robinson, JJ.
[954] Para. 107.
[955] Para. 108.
[956] Para. 109. See, also the Declaration of Judge David Hunt.
[957] Para. 110.
[958] Para. 111.

(i) the Statute establishes a hierarchical structure in which the Appeals Chamber is given the function of settling definitively certain questions of law and fact arising from decisions of the Trial Chambers. Under Article 25, the Appeals Chamber hears an appeal on the ground of an error on a question of law invalidating a Trial Chamber's decision or on the ground of an error of fact which has occasioned a miscarriage of justice, and its decisions are final;

(ii) the fundamental mandate of the Tribunal to prosecute persons responsible for serious violations of international humanitarian law cannot be achieved if the accused and the Prosecution do not have the assurance of certainty and predictability in the application of the applicable law; and

(iii) the right of appeal is ... a component of the fair trial requirement, which is itself a rule of customary international law and gives rise to the right of the accused to have like cases treated alike. This will not be achieved if each Trial Chamber is free to disregard decisions of law made by the Appeals Chamber, and to decide the law as it sees fit. In such a system, it would be possible to have four statements of the law from the Tribunal on a single legal issue - one from the Appeals Chamber and one from each of the three Trial Chambers, as though the Security Council had established not a single, but four tribunals. This would be inconsistent with the intention of the Security Council, which, from a plain reading of the Statute and the Report of the Secretary-General, envisaged a tribunal comprising three trial chambers and one appeals chamber, applying a single, unified, coherent and rational corpus of law. The need for coherence is particularly acute in the context in which the Tribunal operates, where the norms of international humanitarian law and international criminal law are developing, and where, therefore, the need for those appearing before the Tribunal, the accused and the Prosecution, to be certain of the regime in which cases are tried is even more pronounced.[959]

BINDING FORCE OF DECISIONS BETWEEN TRIAL CHAMBERS

In the *Aleksovski* case, the Appeals Chamber ruled that decisions of Trial Chambers, which are bodies of coordinate jurisdiction, have no binding force on each other. However, a Trial Chamber is free to follow the decision of another Trial Chamber if it finds that decision persuasive.[960]

In the *Delalić* case,[961] the Trial Chamber held that prior decisions of a Trial Chamber in another case have no binding force *per se*:

---

[959] Para. 113.
[960] Para. 114.
[961] Prosecutor v. Delalić *et. al., Decision on the Motion to Allow Witness K, L and M to give their Testimony by Means of Video-link Conference*, IT-96-21-T, 28 May 1997, Karibi-Whyte, Odio-Benito & Jan, JJ.

The International Tribunal meets the tasks assigned to it with a spirit of innovation and awareness that each case and situation which it is called to assess presents a unique set of circumstances with its own considerations. It is, however, the case that, where a decision has been rendered on a request, a Trial Chamber called to examine a similar request may look to that previous decision for guidance. If there are reasons to support departures from a previous decision in whole or in part, then the Trial Chamber will do so. If, however, no such reasons exist, the Trial Chamber may find it useful to take the same approach as in the prior decision.[962]

THE INTERNATIONAL TRIBUNAL AND CASE LAW

In the *Kupreškić* case[963], for the first time in its case law, the Trial Chamber addressed the issue of its character as an international court. The Chamber gave three main reasons for holding that that the International Tribunal is an international court.[964] First, pursuant to Security Council Resolution 827 (1993),[965] the Security Council of the United Nations decided to establish an "international tribunal" for the sole purpose of prosecuting persons responsible for serious violations of international humanitarian law in the territory of the former Yugoslavia since 1 January 1991.

Second, the international character of the Tribunal is reflected in its structure and functioning and the status, privileges and immunities of the International Tribunal granted to certain individuals pursuant to Article 30 of the Statute.

Third, the International Tribunal is called upon to apply international law to establish whether serious violations of international humanitarian law have been committed. This obligation flows primarily from the Statute of the Tribunal and the Report of the Secretary-General[966] that was approved by the Security Council in the resolution establishing the Tribunal.

The Chamber ruled that the normative corpus of the International Tribunal – the body of law according to which it must decide principle issues before it – is international law and that the Tribunal may resort to domestic law to fill *lacunae* in the Statute or to international customary law.[967] Thus, the Chamber found that the Tribunal is international in nature and it applies international law *principaliter*. It then decided that, except for the decisions of the Appeals Chamber of the International Tribunal, which are binding upon Trial Chambers, it should use international judicial decision as a subsidiary means for the determination of rules of law in conformity with Article 38 of the Statute of the ICJ.[968] The Chamber ruled that the Tribunal is not bound by precedents of other international criminal courts such as Nuremberg or Tokyo or by national criminal courts that have

---

[962] Para. 16.
[963] Prosecutor v. Kupreškić, *et, al., Judgement*, IT-95-16-T, 14 January 2000, Cassese, May & Mumba, JJ.
[964] Para. 539.
[965] (S/RES/827 (1993)).
[966] Report of Secretary-General pursuant to Paragraph 2 of Security Council Resolution 808 (1993), presented 3 May 1993.
[967] Para. 539.
[968] Para. 540.

adjudicated international crimes.[969] Thus, the doctrine of *stare decisis* – the doctrine of binding precedent – adhered to in common law jurisdiction does not apply to the International Tribunal, since there is no hierarchical judicial system in the international community. However, the Chamber found that judicial decisions may be evidence of *opinio iuris sive necessitatis* or State practice regarding a rule of customary law or they may indicate the emergence of a general principle of international law. At most, such judicial decisions may be persuasive authority for the interpretation of existing law. The Chamber concluded that the Justinian maxim *non exemplis, sed legibus indicandum est* – the courts must adjudicate on the strength of the law, not of cases – applies to the Tribunal.[970]

In evaluating the persuasive authority of judicial decisions, the Chamber found that decisions handed down by international criminal courts are more persuasive than national courts applying international humanitarian law on the basis of national criminal legislation. In particular, the Chamber found that the decisions of the Nuremberg and Tokyo Tribunals as well as the national courts operating under Control Council Law No. 10 applied either existing law or law which had been gradually transformed into customary international law. Decisions from national jurisdictions require a stricter level of scrutiny since they apply and interpret international rules through the prism of national legislation.[971]

THE ROME STATUTE, 1998

The *Tadić* Appeal addressed the issue of the extent to which various provisions of the Rome Statute are codifications of customary international law, or merely new formulations adopted for the purpose of the Statute.[972]

The Chamber observed that the legal weight to be currently attributed to the provisions of the Rome Statute has been correctly set out by Trial Chamber II in *Furundžija*.[973] There the Trial Chamber pointed out that the Statute is still a non-binding international treaty, for it has not yet entered into force. Nevertheless, it already possesses significant legal value. The Statute was adopted by an overwhelming majority of the States attending the Rome Diplomatic Conference and was substantially endorsed by the Sixth Committee of the United Nations General Assembly. This shows that that text is supported by a great number of States and may be taken to express the legal position *i.e.* *opinio juris* of those States.[974]

---

[969] Para. 541.
[970] Para. 540.
[971] Paras. 541-542.
[972] Prosecutor v. Tadić, *Judgement*, IT-94-1-A, 15 July 1999, Shahabuddeen, Cassese, Tieya, Nieto-Navia & Mumba, JJ.
[973] Prosecutor v. Furundžija, *Judgement*, IT-95-17/1-T, 10 December 1998, Mumba, Cassese, & May, JJ, para. 227.
[974] Para. 223.

EFFECT OF NATIONAL LEGISLATION AND CASE LAW

In practice before the Tribunal, legal questions arise which have not been resolved in any international forum. Counsel and the Judges often look to legislation and case law from national legal systems. This raises the issue of the extent to which the Tribunal can apply domestic law.

In the *Tadić Appeal Judgement*[975], the Chamber discussed the value of national legislation and case law when interpreting international law. The Chamber wrote, as follows:

> It should be emphasised that reference to national legislation and case law only serves to show that the notion of common purpose upheld in international criminal law has an underpinning in many national systems. By contrast, in the area under discussion, national legislation and case law cannot be relied upon as a source of international principles or rules, under the doctrine of the general principles of law recognised by the nations of the world: For this reliance to be permissible, it would be necessary to show that most, if not all, countries adopt the same notion of common purpose. More specifically, it would be necessary to show that, in any case, the major legal systems of the world take the same approach to this notion. The above brief survey shows that this is not the case. Nor can reference to national law have, in this case, the scope and purport adumbrated in general terms by the United Nations Secretary-General in his Report, where it is pointed out that "suggestions have been made that the international tribunal should apply domestic law in so far as it incorporates customary international humanitarian law". In the area under discussion, domestic law does not originate from the implementation of international law but, rather, to a large extent runs parallel to, and precedes, international regulation.[976]

The Trial Chamber in the *Furundžija* case[977] held that whenever international criminal rules do not define a notion of criminal law, reliance upon national legislation is justified, subject to the following conditions:

> (i) unless indicated by an international rule, reference should not be made to one national legal system only, say that of common-law or that of civil-law States. Rather, international courts must draw upon the general concepts and legal institutions common to all the major legal systems of the world. This presupposes a process of identification of the common denominators in these legal systems so as to pinpoint the basic notions they share;

> (ii) since "international trials exhibit a number of features that differentiate them from national criminal proceedings", account must be taken of the specificity of

---

[975] Prosecutor v. Tadić, *Judgement*, IT-94-1-A, 15 July 1999, Shahabuddeen, Cassese, Tieya, Nieto-Navia & Mumba, JJ.

[976] Para. 225.

[977] Prosecutor v. Furundžija, *Judgement*, IT-95-17/1-T, 10 December 1998, Mumba, Cassese, & May, JJ.

international criminal proceedings when utilising national law notions. In this way a mechanical importation or transposition from national law into international criminal proceedings is avoided, as well as the attendant distortions of the unique traits of such proceedings.[978]

ANALOGY IN INTERNATIONAL CRIMINAL LAW: SUBSTANTIVE VS. PROCEDURAL LAW

The President stated, as *obiter dictum*, that in international law analogy is normally inadmissible with regard to substantive rules of criminal law, but it may be warranted to fill *lacunae* in the interpretation and application of international rules of criminal procedure or rules governing penitentiary regimes. This view was qualified with the proviso that resorting to analogy should not lead to results contrary to the intent of the law-making body or fall afoul of the basic *ratio* behind the enactment, nor should it result in infringements or unjust restrictions of fundamental human rights.[979]

DEFINITIONS OF OFFENSES

The following section compiles the definitions and elements of selected offences under the jurisdiction of the Tribunal pursuant to Articles 2-5 of the Statute. In some cases, the same act – for instance, murder – may either constitute a war crime, a crime against humanity, or genocide. In this regard the *actus reus* is the same. At one level, what distinguishes the act criminally is the *mens rea* of the accused. For example, certain acts which fall short of the requisite intent for genocide may have the necessary element of discrimination to be considered the crime of persecution. The distinction is thus between the intent to "discriminate" in the case of persecution and to "destroy" in the case of genocide, both of which are issues of criminal intent. In addition, a murder committed without proof of discrimination, may nonetheless constitute a crime against humanity under Article 5(a) provided the other requirements for a crime against humanity are fulfilled, failing which it may be considered a war crime.

1. TORTURE

In the *Furundžija Judgement*,[980] the Chamber noted that the Statute does not contain a definition of torture. The Chamber found that the main elements of the legal definition of torture, which apply to any instance of torture, whether in peacetime or in the context of an armed conflict, are contained in Article 1 of 1984 Torture Convention:

> For the purposes of this Convention, the term 'torture' means any act by which severe pain or suffering, whether physical or mental, is intentionally inflicted on a person for such purposes as obtaining from him or a third person information or a confession, punishing him for an act he or a third person has committed or

---

[978] Para. 178.

[979] Prosecutor v. Delalić, *et. al., Decision of the President on the Prosecutor's Motion for the Production of Notes Exchanged between Zejnil Delalic and Zdravko Mucic*, IT-96-21-PT, 11 November 1996, President Cassese, para. 24.

[980] Prosecutor v. Furundzija, *Judgement*, IT-95-17/1-T, 10 December 1998, Mumba, Cassese, & May, JJ.

is suspected of having committed, or intimidating or coercing him or a third person, or for any reason based on discrimination of any kind, when such pain or suffering is inflicted by or at the instigation of or with the consent or acquiescence of a public official or other person acting in an official capacity. It does not include pain or suffering arising only from, inherent in or incidental to lawful sanctions.[981]

As for specific elements of torture in the context of international criminal law relating to armed conflict, the Chamber defined torture in the as follows:

(i)   torture consists of the infliction, by act or omission, of severe pain or suffering, whether physical or mental; in addition

(ii)   this act or omission must be intentional;

(iii)   it must aim at obtaining information or a confession, or at punishing, intimidating, humiliating or coercing the victim or a third person, or at discriminating, on any ground, against the victim or a third person;

(iv)   it must be linked to an armed conflict;

(v)   at least one of the persons involved in the torture process must be a public official or must at any rate act in a non-private capacity, e.g. as a de facto organ of a State or any other authority- wielding entity.

Humiliation as a Form of Torture

The Chamber considered that the definition of torture might include the humiliation of the victim, since the general spirit of international humanitarian law is to safeguard human dignity. The Chamber furthermore observed that the general provisions of such important international treaties as the Geneva Conventions and Additional Protocols consistently aim at protecting persons not taking part, or no longer taking part, in the hostilities from "outrages upon personal dignity." The Chamber found that the notion of humiliation is, in any event close to the notion of intimidation, which is explicitly referred to in the Torture Convention's definition of torture.[982]

Rape as a Form of Torture

The Trial Chamber held that the use of rape in the course of detention and interrogation may constitute the crime of torture, when rape is resorted to either by the interrogator himself or by other persons associated with the interrogation of a detainee, as a means of punishing, intimidating, coercing or humiliating the victim, or obtaining information, or a confession, from the victim or a third person.[983]

---

[981] Paras. 159-162.
[982] Para. 162.
[983] Para. 163.

Rape as a Distinct Crime under International Criminal Law

The prosecution of rape is explicitly provided for in Article 5 of the Statute as a crime against humanity. Rape may also amount to a grave breach of the Geneva Conventions under Article 2, a violation of the laws or customs of war under Article 3 or an act of genocide under Article 4, if the requisite éléments are satisfied.[984]

The Chamber held that the constituent elements of the crime of rape are the following:

> (i) the sexual penetration, however slight:
>
>> (a) of the vagina or anus of the victim by the penis of the perpetrator or any other object used by the perpetrator; or
>>
>> (b) of the mouth of the victim by the penis of the perpetrator;
>
> (ii) by coercion or force or threat of force against the victim or a third person.[985]

The Chamber found moreover that international criminal rules punish not only rape but also any serious sexual assault falling short of actual penetration. This prohibition embraces all serious abuses of a sexual nature inflicted upon the physical and moral integrity of a person by means of coercion, threat of force or intimidation in a way that is degrading and humiliating for the victim's dignity. The Chamber found that the distinction between these categories of acts is one that is primarily material for the purposes of sentencing.[986]

The Chamber indicated that the definition of rape used in the *Akayesu Judgement*[987] and the *Čelebići Judgement*[988] lacked specificity.[989] Both those Judgements defined rape in the following terms:

> Like torture, rape is used for such purposes as intimidation, degradation, humiliation, discrimination, punishment, control or destruction of a person. Like torture, rape is a violation of personal dignity, and rape in fact constitutes torture when inflicted by or at the instigation of or with the consent or acquiescence of a public official or others person acting in an official capacity. The Chamber defines rape as a physical invasion of a sexual nature, committed on a person under circumstances which are coercive.

---

[984] Para. 172.
[985] Para. 185.
[986] Para. 186.
[987] Case No. ICTR-96-4-T, Para. 597.
[988] Case No. IT-96-21-T, Para. 479.
[989] Paras. 176-177.

2. WILFUL KILLING - MURDER

In the *Delalić Judgement,*[990] the Trial Chamber ruled that there can be no line drawn to distinguish between the term "wilful killing" in Article 2 or "murder" in Article 3. Both wilful killing and murder are considered to have the same *actus reus* and *mens rea.*[991]

The Chamber found that the *actus reus* is clearly established where the death of the victim was the result of the actions or omissions of the accused, and the conduct of the accused was a substantial cause of the death of the victim.[992]

The Chamber determined that the necessary intent, or *mens rea*, required to establish the crimes of wilful killing and murder, is present where there is demonstrated an intention on the part of the accused to kill, or inflict serious injury in reckless disregard of human life.[993]

3. PLUNDER

In the *Delalić Judgement,*[994] the Trial Chamber observed that the offence of the unlawful appropriation of public and private property in armed conflict has varyingly been termed "pillage", "plunder" and "spoliation." Thus, whereas article 47 of the Hague Regulations and Article 33 of Geneva Convention IV by their terms prohibit the act of "pillage," the Nuremberg Charter, Control Council Law No. 10 and the Statute of the International Tribunal all make reference to the war crime of "plunder of public and private property." The Chamber noted that the concept of pillage in the traditional sense implied an element of violence not necessarily present in the offence of plunder. However, the Chamber declined to determine whether, under current international law, these terms are entirely synonymous. The Chamber concluded that the term "plunder," as incorporated in the Statute of the International Tribunal, should be understood to embrace all forms of unlawful appropriation of property in armed conflict for which individual criminal responsibility attaches under international law, including those acts traditionally described as "pillage." The Chamber did not attempt to set out a more comprehensive description of the circumstances under which such criminal responsibility arises.[995]

4. UNLAWFUL CONFINEMENT

In the *Delalić Judgement,*[996] the Trial Chamber held that the confinement of civilians during armed conflict may be permissible in limited cases, but has in any event to be in compliance with the provisions of Articles 42 and 43 of Geneva Convention IV. The security of the State concerned might require the internment of civilians and, furthermore,

---

[990] Prosecutor v. Delalić, *et. al., Judgement*, IT-96-21-T, 16 November 1998, Karibi-Whyte, Odio-Benito & Jan, JJ.

[991] Paras. 420-424.

[992] Para. 424.

[993] Para. 439.

[994] Prosecutor v. Delalić, *et. al., Judgement*, IT-96-21-T, 16 November 1998, Karibi-Whyte, Odio-Benito & Jan, JJ.

[995] Para. 591.

[996] Prosecutor v. Delalić, *et. al., Judgement*, IT-96-21-T, 16 November 1998, Karibi-Whyte, Odio-Benito & Jan, JJ.

the decision of whether a civilian constitutes a threat to the security of the State is largely left to its discretion. However, the Chamber observed that it must be borne in mind that the measure of internment for reasons of security is an exceptional one and can never be taken on a collective basis. An initially lawful internment clearly becomes unlawful if the detaining party does not respect the basic procedural rights of the detained persons and does not establish an appropriate court or administrative board as prescribed in article 43 of Geneva Convention IV.[997]

5. CRIMES AGAINST HUMANITY AND GENOCIDE

In the *Kupreškić Judgement*[998], the Trial Chamber commented on the similarities and differences between persecution and genocide. The elements that distinguish between persecution and genocide are both found in relation to the prohibited acts and the criminal intent behind those acts. The Chamber stated:

> [T]he *mens rea* requirement for persecution is higher than for ordinary crimes against humanity, although lower than for genocide. In this context the Trial Chamber wishes to stress that persecution as a crime against humanity is an offence belonging to the same *genus* as genocide. Both persecution and genocide are crimes perpetrated against persons that belong to a particular group and who are targeted because of such belonging. In both categories what matters is the intent to discriminate: to attack persons on account of their ethnic, racial, or religious characteristics (as well as, in the case of persecution, on account of their political affiliation). While in the case of persecution the discriminatory intent can take multifarious inhumane forms and manifest itself in a plurality of actions including murder, in the case of genocide that intent must be accompanied by the intention to destroy, in whole or in part, the group to which the victims of the genocide belong. Thus, it can be said that, from the viewpoint of *mens rea,* genocide is an extreme and most inhuman form of persecution. To put it differently, when persecution escalates to the extreme form of wilful and deliberate acts designed to destroy a group or part of a group, it can be held that such persecution amounts to genocide.[999]

EX PARTE APPLICATIONS

In the *Simić* case[1000] the Trial Chamber addressed the issue of when a party may seek relief *ex parte.*

---

[997] Para. 583.

[998] Prosecutor v. Kupreškić, *et. al., Judgement,* IT-95-16-T, 14 January 2000, Cassese, May, Mumba, JJ.

[999] Para. 636.

[1000] Prosecutor v. Simić, *et. al., Decision on (1) Application by Stevan Todorović to Re-open the Decision of 27 July 1999, (2) Motion by ICRC to Re-open Scheduling Order of 18 November 1999, and (3) Conditions for Access to Materia,* IT-95-9-PT, 28 February 2000, Robinson, Hunt & Bennouna, JJ.

The Chamber stated that *ex parte* applications are appropriately made in many different circumstances and are warranted only where the disclosure to the other party or parties in the proceedings of the information conveyed by the application, or of the fact of the application itself, would be likely to prejudice unfairly either the party making the application or some person or persons involved in or related to that application. The Chamber observed that such applications are to some extent justified by Article 20(1) of the Tribunal's Statute, which requires Trial Chambers to ensure that a trial is fair and is conducted with full respect for the rights of the accused and with due regard for the protection of victims and witnesses pursuant to Article 22.[1001] The fundamental principle in every case is that *ex parte* proceedings should be entertained only where it is thought to be necessary in the interests of justice to do so – that is, justice to *everyone* concerned.[1002]

The Chamber noted the following Rules that refer expressly or by necessary implication to various circumstances in which *ex parte* proceedings are appropriate.

- Rule 47 requires the prosecution to submit an indictment to a confirming judge for review before an arrest warrant may be issued.

- Rule 50 requires the prosecution to return to the confirming judge in order to obtain leave to amend the indictment whenever leave to amend is sought (and if further confirmation is required) at any time before evidence is presented in the trial.

- The new Rule 54 *bis* enshrines the procedure first discussed in the *Blaškić Subpoena Decision*[1003] for hearing a State in camera and *ex parte* to enable submissions to be made in relation to national security interests concerning the issue of a subpoena.

- Rule 66(C) permits the prosecution to provide the Trial Chamber (and only the Trial Chamber) with information which should otherwise be disclosed to the defence but which is sought to be kept confidential.

- Rule 69 permits the Trial Chamber to consult with the Tribunal's Victims and Witnesses Section before determining the nature of the protective measures to be provided for a witness. This is clearly intended to be on an *ex parte* basis. As a matter of practice, and in accordance with common sense, applications by either party for protective orders are determined on an *ex parte* basis where the persons to be protected would otherwise be identified.

- Rule 77 permits any party to bring to the notice of a Trial Chamber *ex parte* the conduct of a person who may be in contempt of the Tribunal, but that person is called upon by the Trial Chamber in relation to that conduct only if the Trial Chamber has reason to believe that that person may thereby be in contempt.

[1001] Para. 38.
[1002] Para. 41.
[1003] Prosecutor v. Blaškić, *Judgement on the Request of the Republic of Croatia for Review of the Decision of the Trial Chamber II of 18 July 1997*, IT-95-14-AR108 *bis*, 29 October 1997, Cassese, Karibi-Whyte, Li, Stephen & Vohrah.

- Rule 108 *bis* was recently amended to remove the entitlement of the party in the proceedings who was not a party to an application pursuant to Rule 54 *bis* to be heard in a State Request for Review of the decision made in that application.

The Chamber indicated that the reference to the foregoing Rules is merely illustrative of the circumstances where an *ex parte* application may be brought. The Chamber added that it is not possible or appropriate to define the circumstances in which such motions are appropriate by any limiting definition.[1004]

CONFIDENTIAL FILINGS WITH THE REGISTRAR

In the *Brđanin* case,[1005] the Prosecutor filed a Motion for Protective Measures with the Registry declaring it to be confidential. The Trial Chamber lifted the confidentiality of the Order and then reinstated it as to one paragraph after complaint by the Prosecutor. In its decision on the Motion, the Chamber discussed the issue of confidential filings and invited the Registrar to respond to the question whether parties should be permitted to file matters as confidential without prior approval of a Trial Chamber.

The Chamber stated that the public interest in knowing that an application for protection of witnesses has been filed, is the following:

> ... there is a public interest in the workings of courts generally (including this Tribunal) - not just in the hearings, but in everything to do with their working - which should only be excluded if good cause is shown to the contrary. The attitude displayed by the prosecution in the present case appears to be part of an unfortunately increasing trend in proceedings before the Tribunal for matters to be dealt with behind closed doors. When the prosecution seeks to have anything dealt with confidentially, the accused does not usually object because it is in his interest that the less that is made public concerning his case the better. This trend is a dangerous one for the public perception of the Tribunal, and it should be stopped.[1006]

The Chamber proposed a system whereby confidential filings would be prohibited without leave, except (a) all *ex parte* applications whatever their nature, (b) all *inter pares* applications for witness protection which relate to specific persons, and (c) all applications which involve ongoing investigations, pending indictment and sealed indictments and responses to confidential motions filed by the defence or prosecutor and to Trial Chamber decisions which relate to confidential hearings or motions.

Although the Chamber did not rule on the issue, it did indicate that it proposed to give this system a trial in particular cases.[1007]

[1004] Para. 41.
[1005] Prosecutor v. Brđanin & Talić, *Decision on Motion by Prosecution for Protective Measures,* IT-99-36-PT, 3 July 2000, Hunt, Mumba & Pocar, JJ.
[1006] Para. 55.
[1007] Para. 64.

APPENDIX

I.   ## Practice Direction on Procedure for the Filing of Written Submissions in Appeal Proceedings Before the International Tribunal

1 October 1999

PRACTICE DIRECTION ON PROCEDURE FOR THE FILING OF WRITTEN SUBMISSIONS IN APPEAL PROCEEDINGS BEFORE THE INTERNATIONAL TRIBUNAL

INTRODUCTION

In accordance with Sub-rule 19(B) of the Rules of Procedure and Evidence of the International Tribunal for the Prosecution of Persons Responsible for Serious Violations of International Humanitarian Law Committed in the Territory of the Former Yugoslavia since 1991 ("Rules" and "International Tribunal" respectively) and having consulted with the Bureau, the Registrar, the Prosecutor and the Appeals Chamber, I issue this Practice Direction in order to establish a procedure for the filing of written submissions in appeal proceedings before the International Tribunal:

APPEALS AGAINST DECISION'S WHERE INTERLOCUTORY APPEAL LIES AS OF RIGHT

1.   A party wishing to appeal a decision of a Trial Chamber where an interlocutory appeal lies as of right shall file with the Registrar, in accordance with the Rules, an interlocutory appeal containing:

(a)   the precise title and date of the appealed decision;

(b)   a summary of the proceedings before the Trial Chamber relating to the appealed decision;

(c)   the specific provision of the Rules pursuant to which the appeal is filed;

(d)   a concise statement as to why it is contended that the provision relied upon is applicable to the appeal;

(e)   the grounds on which the appeal is made;

(f)   the relief sought.

2.   The opposite party or parties shall file a response within ten days of the filing of the interlocutory appeal. Such a response shall clearly state whether or not the interlocutory appeal is opposed and the grounds therefor. It shall further set out any objection to the applicability of the provision of the Rules relied upon by the appellant as the basis for the appeal.

3.   The appellant may file a reply within four days of the filing of the response. The Appeals Chamber may thereafter decide the appeal without further submissions from the parties.

APPEALS AGAINST DECISIONS WHERE INTERLOCUTORY APPEAL LIES ONLY WITH THE LEAVE OF A BENCH OF THREE JUDGES OF THE APPEALS CHAMBER

4.   A party wishing to appeal an interlocutory decision of a Trial Chamber which may be appealed only with the leave of a bench of three Judges of the Appeals Chamber shall

file with the Registrar, in accordance with the Rules, an application for leave to appeal containing:

(a)   the precise title and date of the decision sought to be appealed;

(b)   a summary of the proceedings before the Trial Chamber relating to the decision sought to be appealed;

(c)   the specific provision of the Rules under which leave to appeal is sought;

(d)   a concise statement as to why it is contended that the applicable criteria for the granting of leave to appeal under the provision relied upon have been met.

5.   The opposite party or parties shall file a response within ten days of the filing of the application for leave to appeal. Such a response shall clearly state whether or not the application for leave to appeal is opposed and the grounds therefor. It shall further indicate any objection to the applicability of the provision of the Rules relied upon by the appellant as the basis for the application for leave to appeal.

6.   The appellant may file a reply within four days of the filing of the response. The bench of three Judges of the Appeals Chamber may thereafter decide the application for leave to appeal without further submissions from the parties.

7.   Where leave to appeal is granted, the appellant shall within ten days of the filing of the decision of the bench of three Judges of the Appeals Chamber file with the Registrar an interlocutory appeal containing:

(a)   the precise title and date of the appealed decision and the decision by a bench of three Judges of the Appeals Chamber granting leave to appeal;

(b)   a summary of the proceedings before the Trial Chamber relating to the appealed decision;

(c)   the specific provision of the Rules pursuant to which the appeal is filed;

(d)   the grounds on which the appeal is made;

(e)   the relief sought.

8.   The opposite party or parties shall file a response within ten days of the filing of the interlocutory appeal. This response shall clearly state whether or not the interlocutory appeal is opposed and the grounds therefor.

Gabrielle Kirk McDonald

President

II. Directive on Assignment of Defence Counsel

DIRECTIVE ON ASSIGNMENT OF DEFENCE COUNSEL

(DIRECTIVE NO.1/94)

(AS AMENDED 30 JANUARY 1995)

(AS AMENDED 25 JUNE 1996)

(AS AMENDED 1 AUGUST 1997)

(AS REVISED 17 NOVEMBER 1997)

(AS AMENDED 10 JULY 1998)

(AS AMENDED 19 JULY 1999)

(IT/73/REV.7)

TABLE OF CONTENTS

PREAMBLE

The Registrar of the Tribunal,

Considering the Statute of the Tribunal as adopted by the Security Council under resolution 827 (1993) of 25 May 1993, and in particular Articles 18 and 21 thereof ;

Considering the Rules of Procedure and Evidence as adopted by the Tribunal on 11 February 1994 and amended on 5 May 1994, and in particular Rules 42, 45 and 55 thereof

Considering the Rules for the Detention of Persons awaiting Trial or Appeal before the Tribunal or otherwise Detained on the Authority of the Tribunal as adopted by the Tribunal on 5 May 1994, and in particular Rule 67 thereof;

Considering the host country agreement between the United Nations and the Kingdom of the Netherlands concerning the seat of the Tribunal signed at New York on 29 July 1994, and in particular Article XX thereof;

Considering the Directive on the Assignment of Defence Counsel as adopted by the Tribunal on 28 July 1994, as subsequently amended;

Considering the amendments to the Directive on the Assignment of Defence Counsel which were adopted at the Twentith Plenary of the Tribunal;

ISSUES REVISION 7 OF THE DIRECTIVE ON THE ASSIGNMENT OF

DEFENCE COUNSEL AS FOLLOWS:

Article 1

Entry into force

This directive lays down the conditions and arrangements for assignment of counsel and shall enter into force on the first day of August nineteen hundred and ninety four (1 August 1994).

Article 2

Definitions

Under this directive, the following terms shall mean:

Code of Conduct: the Code of Professional Conduct for Defence Counsel Appearing Before the International Tribunal as promulgated by the Registrar on 12 June 1997 ;

Counsel: All references in this Directive to "counsel" shall be understood to apply both to lead counsel and co-counsel.

Directive: Directive No. 1/94 on the Assignment of Defence Counsel as approved by the Tribunal on 28 July 1994;

President: the President of the Tribunal;

Registrar: the Registrar of the Tribunal;

Rules: the Rules of Procedure and Evidence adopted by the Tribunal 11 February 1994 ;

Rules of Detention: the Rules for the Detention of Persons Awaiting Trial or Appeal before the Tribunal or otherwise Detained on the Authority of the Tribunal;

Stage of procedure: each of the stages of procedure laid down by the Rules in which the suspect or the accused may be involved (investigation, indictment, proceedings in the Trial Chamber, appeal, review).

Statute: the Statute of the Tribunal adopted by the Security Council under resolution 827 (1993) of 25 May 1993;

Tribunal: the International Tribunal for the Prosecution of Persons Responsible for Serious Violations of International Humanitarian Law Committed in the Territory of the Former Yugoslavia since 1991;

In this Directive, the masculine shall include the feminine and the singular the plural, and vice versa.

Article 3

Right to counsel

(A) Without prejudice to the right of an accused to conduct his own defence, a suspect who is to be questioned by the Prosecutor during an investigation and an accused upon whom personal service of the indictment has been effected shall have the right to be assisted by counsel provided that the person has not expressly waived his right to counsel.

(B) Any person detained on the authority of the Tribunal, including any person detained in accordance with Rule 90 *bis*, also has the right to be assisted by counsel provided that the person has not expressly waived his right to counsel.

(C) All references in this Directive to suspects or accused shall also be understood to apply to any persons detained on the authority of the Tribunal.

Article 4

Person to whom counsel is assigned

Deleted at the thirteenth plenary session

Article 5

Indigency

In accordance with the facts of the individual case, a suspect or an accused shall be considered to be indigent if he does not have sufficient means to retain counsel of his choice.

Article 6

Request for assignment of counsel

Subject to the provisions of Article 22, a suspect or accused who wishes to be assigned counsel shall make a request to the Registrar of the Tribunal by means of the form included in Annex I. A request shall be lodged with the Registry, or transmitted to it, by the suspect or accused himself or by a person authorised by him to do so on his behalf.

Article 7

Applicant's financial situation

(A) A suspect or accused who requests the assignment of counsel, must fulfil the requirement of indigency as defined in Article 5.

(B) In order to determine whether the suspect or accused is indigent, there shall be taken into account means of all kinds of which he has direct or indirect enjoyment or freely disposes, including but not limited to direct income, bank accounts, real or personal property, and stocks, bonds, or ·other assets held, but excluding any family or social benefits to which he may be entitled. In assessing such means, account shall also be taken of the ·means of the spouse of a suspect or accused, as well as those of persons with whom he habitually resides.

(C) Account shall also be taken of the apparent lifestyle of a suspect or accused , and of his enjoyment of any property, movable or immovable, and whether or not he derives income from it.

Article 8

Declaration of means

For the purposes of Article 7, the Registrar shall invite a suspect or accused requesting the assignment of counsel to make a declaration of his means on the form included in Annex II.

Article 9

Certification of the declaration of means

A declaration must, so far as possible, be certified by an appropriate authority , either that of the place where the suspect or accused resides or is found or that of any other place considered appropriate in the circumstances which it shall be for the Registrar to assess. If the declaration is not certified within a reasonable period of time, the Registrar may assign counsel without prejudice to Articles 10 and 19.

Article 10

Information

For the purpose of establishing whether the suspect or accused satisfies the requisite conditions for assignment of counsel, the Registrar may request the gathering of any information, hear the suspect or accused, consider any representation, or request the production of any documents likely to support the request.

Article 11

Decision by the Registrar

(A) After examining the declaration of means laid down in Article 8 and relevant information obtained pursuant to Article 10, the Registrar shall determine if the suspect or accused is indigent or not, and shall decide:

(i) without prejudice to Article 19, either to assign counsel and choose for this purpose a name from the list drawn up in accordance with Article 14; or,

(ii) not to grant the request for assignment of counsel, in which case his decision shall be reasoned.

(B) To ensure that the right to counsel is not affected while the Registrar examines the declaration of means laid down in Article 8 and the information obtained pursuant to Article 10 the Registrar may temporarily assign counsel to a suspect or an accused for a period not exceeding 30 days.

Article 11 *bis*

Assignment of counsel in the interests of justice

If a suspect or an accused,

(i) either requests an assignment of counsel but does not comply with the requirements set out above within a reasonable time,

(ii) or fails to obtain or to request assignment of counsel, or to elect in writing that he intends to conduct his own defence,

the Registrar shall nevertheless assign him counsel in the interests of justice in accordance with Rule 45 (E) of the Rules and without prejudice to Article 19.

Article 12

Notification of the decision

The Registrar shall notify the suspect or accused of his decision, and shall also notify the counsel so assigned and his professional or governing body of his decision .

Article 13

Remedy against a decision not to assign counsel

(A) The suspect whose request for assignment of counsel has been denied may seek the President's review of the decision of the Registrar. The President may either confirm the Registrar's decision or decide that a counsel should be assigned.

(B) The accused whose request for assignment of counsel for his initial appearance has been denied, may make a motion to the Trial Chamber before which he is due to appear for immediate review of the Registrar's decision. The Trial Chamber may either confirm the Registrar's decision or decide that a counsel should be assigned.

(C) After the initial appearance of the accused, an objection against the denial of his request for the assignment of counsel shall take the form of a preliminary motion by him before the Trial Chamber not later than 60 days after his first appearance and, in any event, before the hearing on the merits.

Article 14

Pre-requisites for the assignment of counsel

(A) Any person may be assigned as counsel if the Registrar is satisfied that he fulfils the following pre-requisites:

> (i) he is admitted to the practice of law in a State, or is a University professor of law;
>
> (ii) he speaks one of the two working languages of the Tribunal;
>
> (iii) he agrees to be assigned as counsel by the Tribunal to represent any indigent suspect or accused;
>
> (iv) his name has been included in the list envisaged in Rule 45 (A) of the Rules .

(B) In particular circumstances, a Judge or the Trial Chamber seized of the case may, upon the request of an indigent suspect or accused, authorise the Registrar to assign counsel who speaks the language of the suspect or the accused but does not speak either of the two working languages of the Tribunal.

Article 15

Professional certification

In support of the pre-requisites provided for in Article 14 (A) the Registrar shall be supplied with a certificate of professional qualification issued by the competent professional or governing body and such other documentation the Registrar deems necessary.

Article 16

Scope of the assignment

(A) A suspect or accused shall be entitled to have one counsel assigned to him and that counsel shall deal with all stages of procedure and all matters arising out of the representation of the suspect or accused or of the conduct of his defence , including where two or more crimes are joined in one indictment.

(B) Where persons accused of the same or different crimes are jointly charged or tried, each accused shall be entitled to request assignment of separate counsel.

(C) Under exceptional circumstances and at the request of the person assigned as counsel, the Registrar may, in accordance with Article 14 above, assign a second counsel to assist the lead counsel. The counsel first assigned shall be called the lead counsel.

(D) Lead counsel may request the Registrar to withdraw a co-counsel.

(E) Under the authority of lead counsel, who is responsible for the defence, co- counsel may deal with all stages of the procedure and all matters arising out of the representation of the accused or of the conduct of his defence. Lead counsel shall sign all documents submitted to the Tribunal unless he authorises co-counsel , in writing, to sign on his behalf.

(F) Co-counsel will be remunerated in accordance with Article 25.

(G) Other than in exceptional circumstances, no counsel shall be assigned to more than one suspect or accused at a time.

Article 17

Applicable law

In the performance of their duties counsel assigned shall be subject to the relevant provisions of the Statute, the Rules, the Rules of Detention, this Directive and any other rules or regulations adopted by the Tribunal, the Host Country Agreement , the Code of Conduct and the codes of practice and ethics governing their profession.

Article 18

Responsibility for costs and expenses

(A) Where counsel has been assigned, the costs and expenses of legal representation of the suspect or accused necessarily and reasonably incurred shall be met by the Tribunal subject to the budgetary provisions, rules and regulations, and practice set by the United Nations.

(B) Such costs and expenses to be met by the Tribunal shall include all remuneration due to counsel in accordance with Articles 23 and 30. They shall also include costs relating to legal assistance, investigative assistance, costs relating to the production of evidence for the defence, to the ascertainment of facts, costs relating to temporary consultancy on specific questions, expert opinion paid at the rates established in Annex VI, and accommodation and transportation of witnesses. They shall include travel taxes and similar duties. General office costs are included in the remuneration for counsel. This embraces in any case, but not exclusively expenses for phone and mail or express mail, photocopies, books and journals, lease of office space, purchase of office equipment, office supplies and secretarial support.

(C) When counsel has not been assigned, and if counsel so requests, the Registrar , subject to reservations of paragraph (A), may determine that all or part of the costs and expenses of legal representation of the suspect or accused necessarily and reasonably incurred shall be covered by the Tribunal if such costs and expenses cannot be borne by the suspect or the accused because of his financial situation .

(D) The Financial Officer of the Registry shall reimburse the sums claimed by assigned counsel for the expenses as provided in paragraphs (A) and (B) above on receipt of a statement of expenses made out using the form included in Annexes III and V which must be presented within six months and be approved by the Registrar.

Article 19

Withdrawal of assignment when the suspect or accused is no longer indigent

(A) Assignment of counsel may be withdrawn by the Registrar if:

> (i) after his decision, the suspect or accused comes into means which, had they been available at the time the request in Article 6 was made, would have caused the Registrar not to grant the request;

> (ii) information is obtained which establishes that the suspect or accused has sufficient means to allow him to pay for the cost of his defence;

(B) The decision to withdraw the assignment shall be reasoned and notified to the suspect or accused and to the counsel assigned. Such withdrawal shall take effect from the date of receipt of the notification.

(C) After the notification of the withdrawal of the assignment of counsel, all the costs and expenses incurred by the representation of the suspect or accused shall cease to be met by the Tribunal.

(D) The provisions of Article 13 shall apply mutatis mutandis where there is dissatisfaction against the decision withdrawing the assignment of counsel.

Article 20

Withdrawal of assignment in other situations

(A) In exceptional circumstances, the Registrar may:

(i) at the request of the accused, or his counsel, withdraw the assignment of counsel ;

(ii) at the request of lead counsel withdraw the assignment of co-counsel.

(B) The Registrar shall withdraw the assignment of counsel:

(i) upon the decision by a Chamber to refuse audience to assigned counsel for misconduct under Rule 46 (A);

(ii) where counsel no-longer satisfies the requirements of Article 14 (A).

(iii) Under such circumstances, the Registrar may strike counsel off the list of defence counsel mentioned in Rule 45.

(C) In such cases the withdrawal shall be notified to the accused, to the counsel concerned and to his professional or governing body.

(D) The Registrar shall immediately assign a new counsel to the suspect or accused .

(E) Where a request for withdrawal, made pursuant to paragraph A, has been denied the person making the request may seek the President's review of the decision of the Registrar.

Article 21

Replacement

(A) Where the assignment of counsel is withdrawn by the Registrar or where the services of assigned counsel are discontinued, the counsel assigned may not withdraw from acting until either a replacement counsel has been provided by the Tribunal or by the suspect or accused, or the suspect or accused has declared his intention in writing to conduct his own defence.

(B) In exceptional circumstances, the withdrawn counsel may continue to represent the suspect or the accused for a period of not exceeding 30 days after the date on which their replacement is assigned. During this period the costs and expenses incurred by both counsel shall be met by the Tribunal.

Article 22

Assignment of counsel away from the seat of the Tribunal

(A) Away from the seat of the Tribunal, and in a case of urgency, a suspect who, during the investigation, requests assignment of counsel, may indicate the name of counsel if he knows one who may be assigned in accordance with the provisions of this Directive.

(B) Where the suspect fails to indicate a name, the Prosecutor, or a person authorised by him or acting under his direction, may contact the local Bar Association and obtain the name of counsel who may be assigned in accordance with the provisions of this Directive.

(C) In the situations envisaged in paragraphs (A) and (B), the procedure for assignment of counsel as set out in this Directive shall apply mutatis mutandis but shall be accelerated where necessary.

Article 23

Remuneration paid to assigned counsel

(A) The remuneration paid to assigned counsel for any one case and at any one stage of the procedure shall include:

(i) a fixed rate,

(ii) fees calculated on the basis of a fixed hourly rate applied at any stage of the procedure to the number of hours of work, and

(iii) a daily allowance calculated on the basis of fixed rates as established by the United Nations Schedule of Daily Subsistence Allowance Rates applied to the number of days of work. Counsel is not entitled to DSA while staying at his or her place of residence.

(B) Assigned counsel who receives remuneration from the Tribunal shall not be entitled to receive remuneration from any other source.

Article 24

Fixed rate

The fixed rate envisaged in Article 23 (A) (i) shall be equivalent to four hundred US Dollars (US$ 400.00).

Article 25

Fees

The fixed hourly rate for fees envisaged in Article 23 (A) (ii) shall be assessed by the Registrar on the basis of the seniority and experience of counsel, according to Annex VI. This rate includes general office costs.

Article 26

Daily allowances

(A) The rate for daily allowance provided in Article 23 (A) (iii) above shall be calculated on the basis of the current daily subsistence allowance rates applicable in the country where he is acting as assigned counsel.

(B) In accordance with the regulations in force at the United Nations, the applicable rate shall be lowered after an initial sixty day period by twenty-five percent.

Article 27

Statement of remuneration

(A) Subject to the provisions of Article 28, payment of the fees envisaged in Article 23 (A) shall be made at the conclusion of the relevant stage of procedure, on presentation by counsel of a detailed statement using the form included in Annex IV.

(B) The statement shall indicate, inter alia, the name of the suspect or the accused , the registration number in the Record Book, the stage of the procedure at which assigned counsel was involved and the number of hours of work.

Article 28

Provisional payment

In exceptional circumstances and with the authorisation of the Registrar, a provisional payment of the daily allowance set out in Article 23 (A) (iii) above or expenses of counsel may be made on presentation by counsel of a provisional statement using the forms included in Annexes III or V wether applicable covering the corresponding period or the expenses.

Article 29

Payment *pro rata temporis*

When, during engagement, an assigned counsel is replaced in the same capacity by another assigned counsel for whatever reason, the remuneration shall be paid to each of them *pro rata temporis*.

Article 30

Travel expenses

(A) Travel expenses shall be reimbursed for an assigned counsel who does not usually reside in the territory of the host country or in the country where the particular stage of the procedure is being conducted, on the basis of one economy class round trip air ticket by the shortest route or within limits laid down by the Registrar , on presentation of a statement of travel expenses using the form included in Annex V, accompanied by the original counterfoil of the ticket.

(B) Travel expenses shall be reimbursed to assigned counsel residing in the territory of the country but not in the town where he is serving, on the basis of either first class public transportation tickets or fixed rates as established by the United Nations Schedule of Rates of Reimbursement for Travel by Private Motor Vehicle applicable to different groups of Countries and Territories, per kilometre travelled on the outward and return journeys by the shortest route, on presentation of a statement of travel expenses using the form included in Annex V.

(C) Notwithstanding paragraphs (A) and (B), the Registrar shall assess, after consulting the President and depending on the circumstances of the case, whether the Tribunal , in the interests of justice and in order to ensure the full exercise of defence rights, is required to meet other travel expenses of assigned counsel.

(D) Counsel shall submit all travel requests to the Registry at least one week before their scheduled travel, unless they can demonstrate that circumstances beyond their control prevent them from complying with this requirement. The Registry reserves the right to deduct cancellation fees, arising from changes in travel arrangement , from counsel's remuneration in cases where changes are not sufficiently related to his professional entitlement as assigned counsel.

Article 31

Financial Officer of the Registry

(A) All sums payable to assigned counsel under the provisions of this Directive shall be paid by the Financial Officer of the Registry.

(B) The statement of expenses, the statement of remuneration (be it provisional or final) and the statement of travel expenses envisaged under Articles 18, 27, 28 and 30, must receive the prior approval of the Registrar.

Article 32

Advisory panel

(A) An Advisory Panel shall be set up consisting of two members chosen by the President by ballot from the list referred to in Article 14, two members proposed by the International Bar Association, two members proposed by the Union Internationale des Avocats, and the President of the Nederlandse Orde van Advokaten or his representative. Each member of the Advisory Panel must have a minimum of 10 years legal experience.

(B) The President of the Advisory Panel will be the President of the Nederlandse Orde van Advokaten or his representative. The membership of the Advisory Panel shall come up for appointment every two years on the anniversary date of the entry into force of this Directive.

(C) The Advisory Panel may be consulted as and when necessary by the Registrar or the President on matters relating to assignment of counsel.

(D) The Advisory Panel may also of its own initiative refer to the Registrar any matter relating to the assignment of counsel.

Article 33

Settlement of disputes

In the event of disagreement on questions relating to calculation and payment of remuneration or to reimbursement of expenses, the Registrar shall make a decision , after consulting the President and, if necessary, the Advisory Panel, on an equitable basis.

Article 34

Provision of facilities

At the seat of the Tribunal, assigned counsel may use the libraries and the documentation centre used by the Judges of the Tribunal.

ANNEX VI

Fixed gross hourly rate for Counsel in US $

(general office costs are included in this sum)

Lead Counsel

20 years' professional experience or more 110 US$

15-19 years' professional experience 100 US$

10-14 years' professional experience 90 US$

0-9 years' professional experience 80 US$

Co-counsel

Fixed rate of 80 US$

Fixed gross hourly rate for allotments to

Legal Assistants and Investigators in German Marks

(general office costs are included in this sum)

10 years' professional experience or more 50 DM

5-9 years' professional experience 40 DM

0-4 years' professional experience 30 DM

III.   The Code of Professional Conduct for Defence Counsel Appearing
         Before the International Tribunal

THE CODE OF PROFESSIONAL CONDUCT FOR DEFENCE COUNSEL APEARING
BEFORE THE INTERNATIONAL TRIBUNAL

PREAMBLE

This Code is made in the belief that:

1. As legal practitioners, Counsel must maintain high standards of professional conduct.

2. The role of Counsel as specialist advocates in the administration of justice requires them to act honestly, fairly, skilfully, diligently and courageously.

3. Counsel have an overriding duty to defend their client's interests, to the extent that they can do so without acting dishonestly or by improperly prejudicing the administration of justice.

4. Counsel may be subject to disciplinary proceedings under Rule 46 of the Rules of Procedure and Evidence of the Tribunal. It is therefore necessary that Counsel be aware of their rights and obligations toward the Tribunal.

To these ends, this Code and its Articles of conduct have been formulated.

PRELIMINARY

Article 1.

Definitions

(1) In this Code, unless a different interpretation is required by the provisions of the Code or the context in which they appear, the following terms shall mean:

"Client"   an Accused, Suspect, Detaineee, Witness or other Person who has engaged Counsel for the purposes of his legal representation before the Tribunal.

"Counsel"   any person who has satisfied the Registrar that he is admitted to the practice of law in a State, or is a University professor of law, and

                    (a) has filed his or her power of attorney with the Registrar; or

                    (b) has been assigned under the Rules to a Suspect, Accused, Detainee, Witness or other Person.

                    Any reference to Counsel includes a reference to any co-counsel jointly and to each of them severally.

"Directive"   the directive entitled "Directive on Assignment of Defence Counsel". This is Directive No. 1/94 (UN Doc IT/73/REV.4) as amended.

"Rules"   means the Rules of Procedure and Evidence of the Tribunal adopted on 11 February 1994, as amended.

"Statute"	the Statute of the Tribunal adopted by Security Council resolution 827 of 25 May, 1993.

"Tribunal"	the International Tribunal for the Prosecution of Persons Responsible for Serious Violations of International Humanitarian Law Committed in the Territory of the Former Yugoslavia since 1991, established by Security Council resolution 827 of 25 May, 1993.

(2) In the event of any inconsistency between this Code and the Directive, the terms and provisions of the Directive prevail.

(3) Any term not defined in this Code has the same meaning given to it by the Statute or by the Rules.

(4) While Counsel is bound by this Code, it is not, and should not be read as if it were, a complete or detailed code of conduct for Counsel. Other standards and requirements may be imposed on the conduct of Counsel by virtue of the Tribunal's inherent jurisdiction and the code of conduct of any national body to which Counsel belongs.

(5) This Code must be read and applied so as to most effectively attain the objects and uphold the values expressed in the Preamble.

(6) General provisions of this Code should not be read or applied in a restrictive way by reason of any particular or illustrative provisions.

(7) The singular includes the plural and vice versa.

Article 2.

Entry into Force

This Code enters into force on 12 June 1997.

Article 3.

General Purpose and Application

(1) The general purpose of this Code is to provide for standards of conduct on the part of Counsel which are appropriate in the interests of the fair and proper administration of justice.

(2) This Code applies to Counsel as defined in Article 1(1) of this Code.

GENERAL OBLIGATIONS OF COUNSEL TO CLIENTS

Article 4.

Scope and Termination of Representation

(1) Counsel must advise and represent their Client until the Client duly terminates that Counsel's position, or the Counsel is otherwise withdrawn with the consent of the Tribunal.

(2) When representing a Client, Counsel must:

(a) abide by a Client's decisions concerning the objectives of representation if not inconsistent with Counsel's ethical duties; and

(b) consult with the Client about the means by which those objectives are to be pursued.

(3) Counsel must not advise or assist a Client to engage in conduct which Counsel knows is in breach of the Statute, the Rules or this Code and, where Counsel has been assigned to the Client, the Directive.

Article 5.

Competence and Independence

In providing representation to a Client, Counsel must:

(a) act with competence, skill, care, honesty and loyalty;

(b) exercise independent professional judgement and render open and honest advice;

(c) never be influenced by improper or patently dishonest behaviour on the part of a Client;

(d) preserve their own integrity and that of the legal profession as a whole;

(e) never permit their independence, integrity and standards to be compromised by external pressures.

Article 6.

Diligence

Counsel must represent a Client diligently in order to protect the Client's best interests. Unless the representation is terminated, Counsel must carry through to conclusion all matters undertaken for a Client within the scope of his legal representation.

Article 7.

Communication

Counsel must keep a Client informed about the status of a matter before the Tribunal in which the Client is an interested party and must promptly comply with all reasonable requests for information.

Article 8.

Confidentiality

(1) Whether or not the relation of Counsel and client continues, Counsel must preserve the confidentiality of his client's affairs and, subject to sub-article (2), must not reveal to any other person, other than to any assistants who need to know it for the performance of their duties, information which has been entrusted to him in confidence or use such information to his client's detriment or to his own or another client's advantage.

(2) Notwithstanding sub-article (1), and subject to Article 19 ("Conflicts"), Counsel may reveal information which has been entrusted to him in confidence in any one of the following circumstances:

(a) when the Client has been fully consulted and knowingly consents; or

(b) when the client has voluntarily disclosed the content of the communication to a third party, and that third party then gives evidence of that disclosure; or

(c) when essential to establish a defence to a criminal or disciplinary charge or civil claim formally instituted against Counsel; or

(d) to prevent an act which Counsel reasonably believes:

    (i) is, or may be, criminal within the territory in which it may occur or under the Statute or the Rules; and

    (ii) may result in death or substantial bodily harm to any person unless the information is disclosed.

(3) For the purposes of this Article, Counsel includes employees or associates of Counsel and all others whose services are used by Counsel.

Article 9.

Conflict of Interest

(1) Counsel owes a duty of loyalty to his or her Client. Counsel must at all times act in the best interests of the Client and must put those interests before their own interests or those of any other person.

(2) In the course of representing a Client, Counsel must exercise all care to ensure that no conflict of interest arises.

(3) Without limiting the generality of sub-articles (1) and (2), Counsel must not represent a Client with respect to a matter if:

(a) such representation will be or is likely to be adversely affected by representation of another Client;

(b) representation of another Client will be or is likely to be adversely affected by such representation;

(c) the Counsel's professional judgement on behalf of the Client will be, or may reasonably be expected to be, adversely affected by:

    (i) the Counsel's responsibilities to, or interests in, a third party; or

    (ii) the Counsel's own financial, business, property or personal interests; or

    (iii) the matter is the same or substantially related to another matter in which Counsel had formerly represented another client ("the former client"), and the interests of the Client are materially adverse to the interests of the former client, unless the former client consents after consultation.

(4) Counsel must not accept compensation for representing a Client from a source other than that Client or, if assigned by the Tribunal, from a source other than the Tribunal, unless:

(a) that Client consents after consultation; and

(b) there is no interference thereby with the Counsel's independence of professional judgement nor with the Client-Counsel relationship.

(5) Where a conflict of interest does arise, Counsel must-

(a) promptly and fully inform each potentially affected Client of the nature and extent of the conflict; and

(b) either:

(i) take all steps necessary to remove the conflict; or

(ii) obtain the full and informed consent of all potentially affected Clients to continue the representation, so long as Counsel is able to fulfil all other obligations under this Code.

Article 10.

Client under a Disability

When a Client's ability to make adequately considered decisions in connection with their representation is impaired because of minority, mental disability or any other reason, Counsel must:

(a) inform the Judge or Chamber of the Tribunal hearing the matter, if any, of the disability;

(b) take such steps as are necessary to ensure the adequate legal representation of that Client; and

(c) as far as reasonably possible maintain a normal Counsel-Client relationship with the Client.

Article 11.

Accounting for time

Counsel should account in good faith for the time spent working on a case and maintain and preserve detailed records of time spent.

CONDUCT BEFORE THE TRIBUNAL

Article 12.

Rules of the Tribunal

(1) Counsel must at all times comply with the Rules and such rulings as to conduct and procedure as may be applied by the Tribunal in its proceedings. Counsel must at all times have due regard to the fair conduct of proceedings.

(2) Counsel must not, unless permitted by the Rules or this Code or the Judge or Chamber hearing the matter:

(a) make contact with a Judge or Chamber of the Tribunal without first or concurrently informing counsel acting for any other party to the proceedings;

(b) submit exhibits, notes or documents to the Judge without communicating them within first or concurrently to counsel acting for any other party to the proceedings.

Article 13.

Candour Toward the Tribunal

(1) Counsel is personally responsible for the conduct and presentation of their Client's case, and must exercise personal judgement upon the substance and purpose of

statements made and questions asked.

(2) Counsel must not knowingly:

>(a) make an incorrect statement of material fact to the Tribunal; or

>(b) offer evidence which the Counsel knows to be incorrect.

(3) Despite sub-article (2)(a), Counsel will not have made an incorrect statement to another party to the proceedings or to the Tribunal simply by failing to correct an error on any matter stated to Counsel or to the Tribunal during proceedings.

(4) Counsel must take all necessary steps to correct an incorrect statement made by Counsel in proceedings before the Tribunal as soon as possible after Counsel becomes aware that the statement was incorrect.

Article 14.

Integrity of Evidence

Counsel must at all times maintain the integrity of evidence, whether in written oral or any other form, which is or may be submitted to the Tribunal.

Article 15.

Impartiality of the Tribunal

(1) Counsel must take all necessary steps to ensure that their actions do not bring proceedings before the Tribunal into disrepute.

(2) Counsel must not seek to influence a Judge or other official of the Tribunal by means prohibited by the Statute, the Rules or this Code.

Article 16.

Counsel as witness

Counsel must not act as advocate in a trial in which the Counsel is likely to be a necessary witness except where the testimony relates to an uncontested issue or where substantial hardship would be caused to the Client if that Counsel does not so act.

DUTY OF COUNSEL TO OTHERS

Article 17.

Fairness and Courtesy to Opposing Party and Counsel

(1) Counsel must recognise all other Counsel appearing or acting in relation to proceedings before the Tribunal as professional colleagues and must act fairly, honestly and courteously towards them and their Clients.

(2) Counsel must not communicate with the Client of another Counsel except through or with the permission of that Client's Counsel.

Article 18.

Dealing with Unrepresented Persons

(1) If, on behalf of a Client, Counsel is dealing with a person who is not represented by counsel, Counsel:

>(a) must not give advice to this unrepresented person if the interests of the person are, or have a reasonable possibility of being, in conflict with the interests of the Counsel's Client; but

(b) may advise the unrepresented person to secure legal representation.

(2) Counsel must inform the unrepresented person of the role Counsel plays in the matter, the person's right to counsel under the Rules, and the nature of legal representation in general.

This information must be given whether or not a conflict exists or may exist with the interests of Counsel's Client.

MAINTENANCE OF THE INTEGRITY OF THE PROFESSION

Article 19.

Conflicts

If there is any inconsistency between this Code and any other code which Counsel is bound to honour, the terms of this Code prevail in respect of Counsel's conduct before the Tribunal.

Article 20.

Misconduct

It is professional misconduct for Counsel, *inter alia,* to:

(a) violate or attempt to violate this Code or to knowingly assist or induce another person to do so, or to do so through the acts of another person;

(b) commit a criminal act which reflects adversely on Counsel's honesty, trustworthiness or fitness as Counsel;

(c) engage in conduct involving dishonesty, fraud, deceit or misrepresentation;

(d) engage in conduct which is prejudicial to the proper administration of justice before the Tribunal; or

(e) attempt to influence an officer of the Tribunal in an improper manner.

Article 21.

Reporting Misconduct

(1) If:

(a) Counsel knows that another Counsel has breached this Code or has otherwise engaged in professional misconduct; and

(b) that violation or conduct raises a substantial question as to the other Counsel's honesty, trustworthiness or fitness as Counsel

Counsel may inform the Judge or Chamber of the Tribunal before which Counsel is appearing.

Article 22.

Enforcement

Counsel must abide by and voluntarily submit to any enforcement and disciplinary procedures as may be established by the Tribunal in accordance with the Rules.

Article 23.

Amendment

This Code may be amended by the Registrar, after consultation with the Judges.

INDEX